NORTHUMBRIA

HISTORY AND IDENTITY

547-2000

Edited by

ROBERT COLLS

Phillimore

First published 2007
This paperback edition published 2019

The History Press
The Mill, Brimscombe Port
Stroud, Gloucestershire, GL5 2QG
© The Contributors, 2007, 2019

British Library Cataloguing in Publication Data.
A catalogue record for this book is available from the British
Library.

ISBN 978-0-75097-9043-1

Printed and bound by CPI Group (UK) Ltd

NORTHUMBRIA
HISTORY AND IDENTITY
547-2000

Benedictine monastery of Lindisfarne

Contents

Acknowledgements

Glasgow University Library, Department of Special Collections
The Master and Fellows of University College, Oxford
British Library, St Cuthbert in bishop's robes
Yale Center for British Art, Paul Mellon Collection
Northumberland Collections Service, Northumberland Record Office
Durham University Library
Beamish Photographic Library
Bodleian Library, Oxford
Manchester Art Gallery, J.M.W. Turner, Dunstanburgh Castle
The National Trust
Tate, London 2007, J.M.W. Turner, Norham Castle: Sunrise
Newcastle Central Library Local Studies Collection.
National Portrait Gallery
Charles Phythian-Adams would like to thank Mr Kenneth Smith for adapting the accompanying map from a national series drawn by him to the author's specification (to accompany the general volume mentioned in fn. 3) from funding generously provided by the Leverhulme Trust. He also gratefully acknowledges the helpful advice given by Rob Colls and Roey Sweet.

The Editor

ROBERT COLLS was born in South Shields and was Professor of English History at the University of Leicester before moving to De Montfort University in 2012. His last book was *George Orwell English Rebel* (OUP 2013), and his next book will be T*his Sporting Life: England 1760-1960* (2020).

List of Contributors

(Dates and information for this edition have been updated where possible.)

Mike Barke is Reader in Human Geography at Northumbria University.

John A Burnett was a research fellow at the University of Northumbria.

Robert Colls is Professor of Cultural History at De Montfort University, Leicester.

Nick Everett is Lecturer in English and American Literature at the University of Leicester.

Brian 'Bill' Griffiths was coordinator of the 'Wor Language' dialect project at the University of Northumbria. He was also a poet, a pianist, a publisher, a biker and a pamphleteer – but always mainly a poet. He died in 2007.

Andrew King is Lecturer in History at the University of Southampton.

Robert Lee was Lecturer in Modern British History at the University of Teesside. In a short career, the *Times Higher* described him as 'a historian who transformed the study of the English rural poor' with three brilliant books that came one after the other: *Unquiet Country* (2005), *Rural Society* (2006) and *The Church of England and the Durham Coalfield* (2007). He died in 2010.

Donald M MacRaild is Professor of History at the University of Roehampton.

Judith Murphy is a lecturer in history, culture and music at the University of Northumbria.

Alan Myers retired in 1986 to work as a freelance translator. As well as a passionate Northumbrian scholar, according to The Guardian he 'was one of the most acclaimed translators of Russian into English of his generation' and his work included Pushkin, Dostoevsky and Brodsky. He died in 2010.

Diana Newton is Reader in Early Modern British History at the University of Teesside.

Charles Phythian-Adams is Professor Emeritus of English Local History at the University of Leicester.

A.J. Pollard is Professor Emeritus of History at the University of Teesside.

Brian Roberts is Professor Emeritus of Geography at Durham University.

David Rollason is Professor of History at Durham University.

Joanna Story is Professor of Early Medieval History at the University of Leicester.

Rosemary Sweet is Professor of Urban History at the University of Leicester.

Paul Usherwood was Senior Lecturer in Art History at Northumbria University.

Natasha Vall is Professor of Urban and Cultural History at the University of Teesside.

Keith Wrightson is Professor of History at Yale University.

Introduction

When was Northumbria?

ROBERT COLLS

Northumbria was one of a number of European kingdoms that came into being after the dissolution of the Roman Empire in the fifth century. The name 'Northumbrians' first appears in 731, in Latin, in Bede's *Ecclesiastical History of the English People*.

Northumbria's boundaries were blurred and its heartlands could be surprisingly vulnerable, but at its greatest extent the kingdom ran from the lower reaches of the Humber estuary in the south, to the three corners of Cumbria, Strathclyde, and the Firth of Forth to the north. Bede names Ida as the founder of the 'royal lineage of the Northumbrians' in 547. In practice, Ida probably ruled over only 'Bernicia', northernmost of the two provinces which were unified in the course of the seventh century to make the kingdom. The southern province of 'Deira', with its capital at York, took in roughly what is called Yorkshire today. Bernicia, with its capital at Bamburgh, grew out of the old fortified Romano-British zone along Hadrian's Wall to take in roughly what are Northumberland, Tyne and Wear and County Durham. Neither of the two province names is English.

Northumbria was essentially an *Anglian*, or an English state, which is to say, it was made by Germanic invaders who first had to defeat, or degrade, or otherwise subjugate, the indigenous British. Very few Britons appear in Bede's writings. As he says, 'The British oppose the English through their inbred hatred and the … Catholic Church by their incorrect Easter and their evil customs, yet being opposed by the power of God and men alike, they cannot obtain what they want in either respect.' Caedmon, the first English Christian poet, has a British name. He declaims the song from God because, as a servant of the lowest class, he could not have learned it from men.

The first great king of Northumbria was the Bernician, Aethelfrith (reign 594-616), with his palace at Yeavering, who waged campaigns in all directions – in Strathclyde in 603, in Deira in 604, and at Chester in 615. He was followed by Edwin (reign 616-33), who married the Christian princess Ethelberga of Kent in

625, and was converted by her emissary Paulinus. After defeating the West Saxons in 626, Edwin was baptised at York in 627. He died at the hands of Penda of Mercia and Cadwallon, King of Gwynedd, at Hatfield, near Doncaster, six years later. After a period of internal strife, the Northumbrian crown was taken up by Oswald who, having set his cross and standard, defeated the Mercian army at Heavenfield, near Hexham, in 634. On this day Oswald avenged Edwin by killing Cadwallon. Yet Oswald had been no friend of Edwin. As sons of Aethelfrith, he and his brothers had had to spend time in exile from Edwin's Northumbria when they had come under the influence of St Columba's community on the island of Iona (f.565). Ionan monastic Christianity established itself in Northumbria during the reigns of Oswald (634-42) and Oswy (642-70).

Bede says Oswald was the maker of Northumbria as 'one people' and in matters of state, from the seventh century, there is evidence of itinerant courts, legal coinage, written documents, and tribute and taxation based on the household ('hid'). Not all Northumbrians shared the same degrees of freedom. Lowest was the 'ceorl'. The economy was mainly agricultural, and the settlements were scattered, with little surplus product. Roman roads, or at any rate Roman routes, prevailed.

Kings came and went but it is noticeable that the kingdom went on. There seems to have been some kind of aristocratic council, or formal hierarchy, which was able to command political consensus and influence kingship. If consensus was the mark of the aristocracy, continuity was the prerogative of the church – initially fragile and uncertain under Edwin, but resurgently Celtic, and embedded, under Oswald and Oswy. Even so, it was in Northumbria, at Whitby in 664, that the English church made the epic decision to be Roman rather than Celtic. The two traditions managed to make something new between them nevertheless, and a golden age of Northumbrian churchmanship was the result.

In or around 635 Aidan of Iona had founded the island monastery of Lindisfarne, just offshore from the royal capital of Bamburgh. Aidan was the first great missionary bishop of Northumbria. He died in 651, the same year that Cuthbert entered the monastery at Melrose, aged 16. Later, Cuthbert was sent to re-invigorate the Lindisfarne community in the manner of Aidan. Cuthbert accepted the decision of the Synod of Whitby but the simple asceticism of his personal ministry, and its devotion to the natural and animal world, was part of his continued devotion to a Celtic tradition. He was consecrated Archbishop, at York in 685, and died two years later on Lindisfarne, great saint of the Northumbrian *folc*. In honour of his 'elevation' (digging up) in 698, the Lindisfarne Gospels were written by Bishop Eadfrith.

The Northumbrian church grew rich, but not because its saints were pious. Aristocrats donated large sums of land and money in order to use the church as a perpetual corporation that would secure their hereditary rights. Many of the charges levelled against the church for corruption, therefore, were based on the actions of aristocrats whose clerical positions did not make them change either their secular appetites or political ambitions. Wilfrid (634-709) was the key Northumbrian churchman of these years. The man who had secured the momentous Whitby decision to turn to Rome was not going to flinch from the little local difficulty of making his church rich.

Northumbria's 'Golden Age', then, was Christian and cultural rather than political or military. Some cultural works but no important buildings survive. Most important are the manuscripts: the Lindisfarne Gospels (Lindisfarne, early eighth century), the Durham Gospels (Lindisfarne, early eighth century), and the Codex Amiatinus (Jarrow/Monkwearmouth, before 716), products of the most brilliant scriptoria of the western church. Just as golden were the scholarly works of Bede and Alcuin. Alcuin (735-804) was taught at York cathedral school by Egbert, pupil of Bede. Later, he became head of Charlemagne's palace school. Under him, the Abbey of St Martin at Tours became the main seat of European learning. Bede (672-735) was educated by Abbot Benedict Biscop at Monkwearmouth and Jarrow. His *Ecclesiastical History* was the first history of the English people, a people he made spiritually coherent by arguing for God's purpose through an English church. The work, it has to be said, was also a powerful piece of propaganda for Northumbria. It is dedicated to King Ceolwuf.

Bede argued that the period of his life, and for a generation before it, had seen favourable times. After his death, following a phase of aggression in the 740s, Northumbrians worked towards an agreement with the Picts. In the south they built a system of defensive earthworks against the Mercians. But in 793 the first Viking raids were recorded. Vikings came at Northumbria from the sea. 'Never before has such terror appeared,' wrote Alcuin to King Ethelred: 'It is now about 350 years that we and our fathers have dwelt in this most beautiful country and never before has such a terrible thing befallen … lo now the church of St Cuthbert is stained with the blood of the priests of God.'

In 866 the pattern of attack changed. This time Healfdene's Great Danish Army crossed the sea, wintered in East Anglia, and then moved north, taking the York heartland in the spring of 867 and defeating the Northumbrian army the following March. This was no mere raiding party. By 875 it had moved north again and imposed itself, temporarily, in the second Northumbrian heartland of the Tyne-Wall zone. The kingdom was now beginning to heave three ways: south of the Tees to the Danes, north of the Tees to the Bernicians, and west of the Pennines to the Cumbrians, connected to the kingdom of Strathclyde. It was in this uncomfortable position of Scots to the north and Norse to the south that a truncated Northumbria looked to Alfred's Christian English Wessex in the early years of the 10th century. Eric Bloodaxe, King of York, has sometimes been seen as the last king of Northumbria but, in truth, Northumbria had been in a condition of terminal fragmentation for nearly a century before Bloodaxe's assassination on Stainmore moor in 954.

In 875, in the midst of the Danish invasion, Bishop Eardorf and the Cuthbertian community on Lindisfarne had packed up their relics and treasures to begin seven years of wandering on the mainland before settling their bones, and his, at Chester-le-Street in 882. In 995 the cult of St Cuthbert – or the *Haliwerfolc*, or 'Saint's People' as they were called – was on the move again. This time they found their resting place at Durham, high above a bend in the river. In 1093 the foundation stone of the Cathedral was laid here, on the site of Cuthbert's relics, and there they stay, last living expression of the old kingdom of Northumbria.

When was Northumbria? As far as we can tell, Northumbria was between Aethelfrith and the coming of the Danish army – let us say, between 594 and 875, by which time the kingdom had ceased to exist as a single, coherent province. The intention behind this book is to examine the history and identity of the kingdom, and then to write about the history and identity of what happened next.

As we have seen, Northumbria may have been English but it was not England. Before the rise of 'England', Northumbria was just itself – north-east of nowhere in particular. As England rose from the south, however, and the other kingdoms, including Northumbria, passed away, the question moves from *when* was Northumbria to *how* did the territory that it occupied come to see itself, and understand itself, in ways that matched its history, its contemporary practical purposes, and its new and growing relationship with England? In other words, what happened to the identity of Northumbria once Northumbria was no more?

In all honesty, before 1066 it is difficult to say much about identities of any sort. Northumbria was a great kingdom, and it lasted nearly three hundred years, but its borders were porous and its loyalties are difficult to ascertain. Military as well as ethnic alignments pulled to various centres of power and one should never assume that the gravitational pull was always to an English south. For Northumbrians, the pull was just as likely to be Danish, or Scottish. As for London, under the Romans it had been provincial capital of *Britannia Superior*, so called because it was nearer to Rome. York had been the provincial capital of *Britannia Inferior*. After Rome, and the breaking of the kingdoms that followed her, the centripetal tendencies of London re-emerged with the Normans. Yet, centralist though the Norman state was, we must remember that like all feudal dynasties it built its sovereignties piecemeal, through systems of lordship and kingship rather than through any sense of manifest destiny. London was base camp, therefore, for a tensile Norman power that was most stretched in the north.

Northumberland and Durham were slow and resentful members of the Norman state. They suffered 11th-century invasions both ways, from the north and the south, and neither appeared in William's Domesday Book (1086). Northumberland remained an earldom outside the Crown until 1157, and Durham remained a palatinate, with special episcopal powers, in title at least, until 1836. New Castle – called *Pons Aelii* under the Romans – was begun in 1090 after yet another punitive expedition from the south, this time after the murder of Walcher, first Norman bishop, in 1081. The whole area harboured wayward loyalties to the London Crown until Henry III made absolute his claim to the earldom in 1242.

Even then, the first people to be identified as distinctive 'northerners' were barons with substantial connections to the Scottish aristocracy. In 1276 they did homage to Alexander II of Scotland. In 1296 a significant number sided with the Scots against Edward I. It was in such a context that the Percies, future earls of Northumberland, came to the region in the late 13th century as Lords of the Marches and Edward's henchmen on both sides of the border. Percy power waxed and waxed on the uncertainties of a ragged frontier. The Tudors continued to war with the Scots but in northern England their writ did not always run. There were rebellions in 1536 ('Pilgrimage of Grace') and 1569 ('Rebellion of the North') that engulfed the greater region. Border security stiffened with the Union of Crowns of England and Scotland in 1603 and the pacifications that followed. In the 1680s, however, and in the Jacobite rebellions of 1715 and 1745, the Northumbrian gentry were less than united in their loyalty to London. The corporation of Newcastle, whose loyalty was not in doubt and who kept their toasts Hanoverian and their gates shut, remained suspicious of the county until well into the 18th century. Victorian school textbooks talked of the events of 1688-9 – a Protestant succession and a Bill of Rights – as the key to political stability for all English counties *other* than Northumberland. Macaulay's *History of England* stated that 'a large part of the country north of the Trent was, down to the 18th century, in a state of barbarism'. It was only in the period beginning after the Jacobite defeat at Culloden in 1746 that historians could use the same phrases of 'law and order', and 'trade and commerce', for north-eastern England that they routinely used for the rest of the country. Given the timing of Welsh (1536) and Scottish (1707) incorporations into the central state, it is clear that north-east England was incorporated into a *British* polity rather than into an English one and that its historic identity and relationship with England more resembles theirs than it does England's.

The North East region is distinctive and different because it thinks it is. The territory has changed little for over a thousand years and the region continues to take a particular view of its history. Identity in this sense is an historical event, or a series of historical events, to do with a region's sense of relationship to its place and its past. Some peoples never experience this relationship, or live to forget it. North East England, on the other hand, as one of our authors makes clear, has long been seen as 'truly historical ground'. It is our hope that it remains so.

I would like to thank the contributors for agreeing to join me with this book. In writing chapters of great distinction and originality, they made my job easy. All but one directly address questions of history and identity. Mike Barke's chapter lays the foundations of identity in the modern period. I would also like to thank the librarians and archivists who helped, and those who waived or reduced fees when we explained our ideas and intentions. Thanks as well to Simon Thraves and Noel Osborne at Phillimore, who, just like last time, allowed me to get on with it. Special thanks go to my friends from the North, particularly the Laygate Lane alumni Jim Blance, John Gray and Albyn Snowden. I've enjoyed the *craic* for a very long time.

Finally and most importantly, I thank my wife Rosie for her true intellectual friendship. She has had to live with Northumbria more than anyone born in Wessex has a right to expect.

Robert Colls
Leicester
October 2007

Christian Kingdom

1

Northumbria: A Failed European Kingdom

DAVID ROLLASON

The kingdom of Northumbria first appears in historical writing in Bede's *Ecclesiastical History of the English People*, which has a reference to a king called Ida who, Bede states, began to rule in 547 and 'from whom the Northumbrian royal family trace their origin'.[1] More detailed information only begins to emerge in Bede's work with a king called Æthelfrith (592/3-616), after whose time Bede gives a reasonably coherent account of the kings of Northumbria.[2] Until the 630s, however, Northumbria consisted of two kingdoms, that of Deira, south of the Tees and north of the Humber, and Bernicia, north of the river Tees. According to Bede, these two kingdoms were united by King Oswald (634-42), although there was still at least a sub-king of Deira in the 650s when King Oswine of Deira was murdered by his Bernician colleague Oswiu in 651, and a king called Œthelwald who ruled Deira from then until 655.[3] As if this was a relatively recent state of affairs in his time, it may be significant that Bede felt the need to give what appears a tautologous definition of 'Northumbrians' as 'the nation inhabiting the district north of the Humber'.[4]

The period of Northumbria's political and military apogee seems to have been in the later seventh century through the eighth century, and this was followed by a period of political turbulence in the ninth, although we have far less historical evidence for this so that the degree of turbulence is hard to decide upon. In 866-7, at any rate, a major Viking invasion led by Ivar and Halfdan (Healfdene) captured the city of York, and resulted in the deaths of the two simultaneously reigning Northumbrian kings Ælle and Osberht, and effectively brought an end to the original kingdom of Northumbria. From then until 954, York was the centre of what historians usually

---

1 Colgrave, B. and Mynors, R.A.B. (eds), *Bede's Ecclesiastical History of the English People* (revised ed. Oxford Medieval Texts; Oxford, 1991), bk 5, ch. 23. What follows is a summary of Rollason, D., *Northumbria 500-1100: Creation and Destruction of a Kingdom* (Cambridge, 2003). References to sources and other works have nevertheless been given where appropriate.
2 Colgrave and Mynors (eds), *Bede's Ecclesiastical History*, bk 1 ch. 34, bk 2 ch. 2.
3 *Ibid.*, bk 3 chs 6, 23.
4 For example, *Ibid.*, bk. 2 ch. 5.

call the Viking kingdom of York, the last king of which, Eric Bloodaxe, was expelled and killed in 954 and his kingdom absorbed – in at least a loose way – into the nascent kingdom of England being created by the line of the former kings of Wessex. Meanwhile, the northern parts of the kingdom of Northumbria constituted the earldom of Bamburgh, centred on the fortress of that name, which was also in due course absorbed into the kingdom of England, and the region of Lothian to the north of the Tweed which ultimately became part of the kingdom of Scotland.[5]

Northumbria was thus a failed European kingdom, but it may nevertheless have been a serious political unit in its time so that the reasons for its failure are of considerable interest. A brief tour of its frontiers in Bede's time emphasises its size and importance.[6]

On the south, the frontier was the River Humber itself, west of which historians have generally been influenced by a poem inserted into the *Anglo-Saxon Chronicle* for 942 which, in describing the liberation of Mercia from Viking dominance by King Edmund of England, gives the northern frontier of Mercia (and so by inference the southern frontier of Northumbria) as 'Dore, Whitwell Gap and Humber river'. That Dore (Derbyshire), just to the south-west of Sheffield, was indeed on the Northumbrian frontier is confirmed by another annal, that for 829, according to which King Ecgberht of Wessex led an army 'to Dore against the Northumbrians; and they offered him submission and concord'.[7] Such meetings were often held on frontiers. Westwards again, the *Anglo-Saxon Chronicle's* annal for 922 notes that Manchester was 'in Northumbria', and it seems possible that the river Ribble formed the south-west frontier since in the Middle Ages it was the border between the see of York (for Northumbria) and that of Lichfield (for Mercia).[8]

That Northumbria extended on the west right to the coast of the Irish Sea is probable in view of the foregoing, but it is in large measure confirmed by evidence relating to Dacre, a church near Ullswater (Cumberland), where there is ecclesiastical sculpture dated to the eighth or early ninth century, and archaeological excavations have recovered what may be the remains of an early ecclesiastical site, presumably a monastery. Bede was in contact with it, for he knew the names of two successive abbots and was able to relate a miracle-story from it in some detail. This involved the cure of a young man's diseased eye by some of St Cuthbert's hair which had been cut off when his coffin had been opened in 698 at Lindisfarne (Northumberland) and the body found un-decayed. The monks of Lindisfarne had taken the hair 'to give as relics to their friends', amongst whom were evidently numbered the monks of Dacre. In addition, the early eighth-century *Lives* of St Cuthbert of Lindisfarne record him as having been in friendship with a hermit called Herbert, whose hermitage was on Derwentwater. In view of his English name,

---

5 For detail and full references, see Rollason, *Northumbria*.
6 For a fuller summary, see *Ibid.*, ch. 2. For more detail, see Blair, P.H., 'The Northumbrians and their Southern Frontier', *Archaeologia Aeliana*, 36 (1948), pp.98-126; Blair, P.H., 'The Bernicians and their Northern Frontier', in *Studies in Early British History* (ed. N.K. Chadwick, Cambridge, 1954), pp.137-72. See also Higham, N.J., 'Northumbria's Southern Frontier: A Review', *Early Medieval Europe*, 14, no. 4 (2006), pp.391-417.
7 Plummer, C. (ed.), *Two of the Saxon Chronicles Parallel with Supplementary Extracts from the Others* (2 vols; Oxford, 1892-9), s.a. 827 (recte 829).
8 *Ibid.*, s.a.

this man was probably Northumbrian and his presence on the lake in Cumberland points to Northumbrian control of that western area.[9] The occurrence of ecclesiastical sculpture in Northumbrian style even further west at Irton and Heversham is further confirmation,[10] as is Bede's statement that Edwin controlled the Isle of Man, which is hard to envisage if his kingdom had not extended to the Irish Sea coast.[11] Certainly Cuthbert was closely involved with Carlisle, where he was staying with the queen of the Northumbrians in 685 when news of her husband's defeat at the hands of the Picts became known.[12]

Moving further north-west, it seems certain that Northumbria embraced Galloway, the south-west part of contemporary Scotland, for Bede refers to Whithorn, an episcopal church near the western extremity of the Galloway peninsula, as 'belonging to the kingdom (*provincia*) of the Bernicians', and having a bishop with the English (probably Northumbrian) name of Pehthelm.[13] Also in Galloway was the early monastery of Hoddom (Dumfriesshire), from which ecclesiastical sculpture in notably Northumbrian style is now in the Museum of Scotland in Edinburgh;[14] and the great sculptured cross of Ruthwell, the decoration of which resembles sculpture from Bede's monastery at Jarrow (County Durham) in eastern Northumbria, and which has inscribed on it an early version of the English poem *The Dream of the Rood*.[15] There seems no doubt that Northumbrian cultural influence and ecclesiastical power was paramount in Galloway, and it is therefore reasonably certain that this area was in a real sense part of the kingdom of Northumbria.

The area between Galloway and the Firth of Clyde was not part of Northumbria, but constituted the kingdom of Strathclyde, which endured as a political entity until

1 *Irton Cross, Cumberland (Department of Archaeology, University of Durham, photographer T. Middlemass)*

9   Rollason, *Northumbria*, pp.28-9; Colgrave, B. (ed), *Two Lives of St Cuthbert: A Life by an Anonymous Monk of Lindisfarne and Bede's Prose Life* (Cambridge, 1940), pp.248-51 (ch. 28).

10   Bailey, R.N. and Cramp, R.J., *Corpus of Anglo-Saxon Stone Sculpture II: Cumberland, Westmorland and Lancashire North-of-the-Sands* (Oxford and New York, 1988), s.n.

11   Colgrave and Mynors (eds), *Bede's Ecclesiastical History*, bk 2 ch. 9.

12   Colgrave (ed), *Two Lives of St Cuthbert: A Life by an Anonymous Monk of Lindisfarne and Bede's Prose Life*, Bede's vita, ch. 27.

13   Colgrave and Mynors (eds), *Bede's Ecclesiastical History*, bk 3 ch. 4, bk 5 ch. 23; Hill, P., *Whithorn and St Ninian: The Excavation of a Monastic Town 1984-91* (Stroud, 1997).

14   Romilly Allen, J. and Anderson, J., *The Early Christian Monuments of Scotland* (2 vols; Balgavies, 1993), II, 439; Lowe, C.E., 'Hoddom', *Current Archaeology*, 135 (1995), pp.88-92.

15   See, for example, Cassidy, B., *The Ruthwell Cross: Papers from the Colloquium Sponsored by the Index of Christian Art Princeton University 8 December 1989* (Princeton, 1992).

2 *Ruthwell Cross, Dumfriesshire (detail)*

the early 11th century when it became part of the kingdom of Scotland. Strathclyde was a kingdom of the Britons, that is, the people who had dominated Britain at an earlier period, and whose kingdoms subsisted in Wales and south-west Britain.[16] Eastwards, however, the Northumbrian frontier was certainly on the Firth of Forth where, Bede tells us, the Northumbrian Trumwine was bishop of the church of Abercorn (Linlithgowshire), just to the east of Queensferry on the southern shores of the Firth. This church, Bede noted, was 'close to the firth which divides the lands of the English from those of the Picts'.[17] Moreover, there is sculpture in Northumbrian style from Abercorn itself, and also a very fine cross in a style often compared with that of the Lindisfarne Gospels from Aberlady (Haddingtonshire) to the east of Edinburgh.[18] Tynninghame, a little further south-east along the coast, was the site of a Northumbrian church and the hermitage of the eighth-century Northumbrian saint Balthere.[19] The circumstances in which Northumbrian power extended to the Firth of Forth are obscure, but historians have – perhaps optimistically – interpreted a laconic two words in the *Annals of Ulster* for 638, which read *obsessio Etin* (siege of *Etin*), as recording a Northumbrian conquest of *Etin,* identified with Edinburgh.[20]

This tour emphasises, therefore, that the kingdom of Northumbria embraced a substantial area, not far short of that of a much more enduring kingdom, that of the Franks, ruled in the late eighth and early ninth centuries by the great Frankish emperor Charlemagne.[21] In view of this, the after-life of the name Northumbria emphasises the scale of the kingdom's failure. In the late 20th century it was possible for the now defunct Northumbrian Tourist Board to use it with reference just to the counties of Northumberland and Durham; and in the Middle Ages its meaning was equally confined, if not more so. The *comes Northymbrie* (earl of Northumbria) in the late 11th century controlled only the land north of the Tyne and south of the Tweed, although at some periods he had at least notional control over the lands of the Bishop

16 Kirby, D.P., 'Strathclyde and Cumbria: A Survey of Historical Development to 1092', *Transactions of the Cumberland and Westmorland Antiquarian Society,* n.s. 62 (1962), pp.77-94; Duncan, A.A.M., *Scotland: The Making of the Kingdom* (Edinburgh, 1975).

17 Colgrave and Mynors (eds), *Bede's Ecclesiastical History*, bk 4 ch. 26.

18 Romilly Allen and Anderson, *The Early Christian Monuments of Scotland*, II, pp.418-20, 428.

19 Rollason, *Northumbria*, pp.28 n.34.

20 MacAirt, S. and MacNiocaill, G. (eds), *The Annals of Ulster (to A.D. 1131): Part I: Text and Translation* (Dublin, 1983), 121. See, for example, Kirby, D.P., 'The Kingdom of the Northumbrians and the Destruction of the Votadini', *Transactions of the East Lothian Ant. and Field Naturalists' Society,* 14 (1974), pp.1-13.

21 See, for example, Bullough, D.A., *The Age of Charlemagne* (London, 1973).

of Durham between the rivers Tyne and Tees.[22] The name of his earldom, which was a reminiscence of the so much more extensive kingdom of Northumbria, was perpetuated in the name of a much smaller area, the pre-1974 county of Northumberland, that is the land between the rivers Tyne and Tweed. The name of that county means 'the land north of the Humber', as Bede had once explained in the context of the name of the kingdom. But the county, its southern boundary many miles north of the Humber, is a tiny relict of an extensive kingdom which had ceased to exist.

Partly because of its failure we suffer from a lack of evidence as to what that kingdom's governmental capabilities were. Although we have the vivid if somewhat anecdotal accounts of Bede and the early saints' lives, such as those of Cuthbert, as well as the annalistic record in the *Northern Annals*, compared with the evidence surviving from the south of England we have virtually nothing in the way of law-codes or written documents (charters).[23] Nevertheless, we can perhaps glimpse a seriously powerful kingdom.

We have fragments of evidence, for example, of what appears to have been a hierarchy of government officials, beginning at the highest level with figures whom we see in the *Ecclesiastical History*, as well as in Stephen's early eighth-century *Life of Wilfrid*, who are referred to as 'sub-kings' (*subreguli*) or 'princes' (*principes*). Thus, when the late seventh-century King Ecgfrith was attacked by the Picts, 'he quickly mustered a troop of cavalry and putting his trust in God, like Judas Maccabeus, set off with Beornhaeth, his trusty sub-king (*audaci subregulo*)'.[24] Below this level we catch glimpses of senior officials called patricians (*patricii*), four of whom are referred to in the *Northern Annals*, who may perhaps have corresponded to the 'mayors of the palace' in the Frankish kingdom before the mid-eighth century.[25] Below them again we see prefects (*prefecti*). In Stephen's *Life of Wilfrid*, a prefect appears as responsible for the *urbs* of Dunbar and another for that of the unidentified site of *Inbroninis*, both of which were evidently suitable places for the king to imprison an important man such as Wilfrid, the influential Northumbrian churchman and Bishop of York. The prefect of Dunbar clearly possessed resources sufficient to do the job properly, for the king ordered him to keep Wilfrid 'bound hands and feet with fetters', which the prefect duly ordered blacksmiths to make. At *Inbroninis*, Wilfrid was kept 'under guard in hidden dungeons' under the supervision of the prefect, who is also described as a count (*comes*).[26]

Like their great Frankish contemporaries on the Continent, the kings of Northumbria were itinerant, moving from place to place in their kingdom, probably as a symbolic and also a real means of exercising and demonstrating their power, as well as a means of visiting and exploiting their landed estates.[27] Bede gives the following account of the itinerary of King Edwin:

---

22 See, for example, Lomas, R.A., *North-East England in the Middle Ages* (1992).
23 Rollason, *Northumbria*, pp.11-16.
24 Colgrave, B. (ed.), *The Life of Bishop Wilfrid by Eddius Stephanus* (Cambridge, 1927), ch. 19.
25 Thacker, A.T., 'Some Terms for Noblemen in Anglo-Saxon England c.600-900', in *Anglo-Saxon Studies in Archaeology and History* (ed. D. Brown, *British Archaeological Reports, British Series 92*; Oxford, 1981), pp.201-36.
26 Colgrave (ed.), *Life of Wilfrid*, chs. 36-8.
27 Brühl, C.-R., *Fodrum, Gistum, Servitium Regis: Studien zu den Wirtschaftlichen Grundlagen des Königtums im Frankenreich und in den Fränkischen Nachfolgestaaten Deutschland, Frankreich und Italien vom 6. bis zur Mitte des 14. Jahrhunderts* (2 vols; Cologne, 1968).

So great was his majesty in his realm that not only were banners carried before him in battle, but even in time of peace, as he rode about among his cities (*civitates*), estates (*villas*) and *provincias* with his thegns (*ministris*), he always used to be preceded by a standard bearer. Further, when he walked anywhere along the roads, there used to be carried before him the type of standard which the Romans call a *tufa* and the English call a *thuf.*[28]

The reference to different types of royal centres, to thegns and to the ritual aspect of the carrying of standards, suggests that this itinerary was an element in the exercise of serious, kingly power.

Moreover, it seems clear that this power was underpinned by many 'royal vills' (*villae regales*), such as Yeavering (Northumberland), and the unnamed vill where King Edwin was staying when he held a council to discuss the merits of adopting Christianity, as well as the unidentified royal vills at which Bishop Aidan of Lindisfarne is said to have preached. That such royal vills were surrounded by lesser settlements is suggested by Bede's account of the people flocking to hear Paulinus's preaching at Yeavering 'from every village and district' (*de cunctis viculis ac locis*).[29] The use of the diminutive (*viculi*) suggests that these villages were dependent on the royal vill of Yeavering. Yeavering, constructed in the early seventh century, was an impressive palace, even if built of timber, with a complex of halls, a substantial enclosure, an amphitheatre and a ritual building, possibly a temple converted into a church. In addition, it was not the only one in possession of the Northumbrian kings for nearby Milfield (Maelmin), which Bede tells us succeeded it as the royal centre in that part of Northumbria, seems to have been built in a similar way.[30] In the south of Northumbria, York was evidently a centre to rival its continental equivalents such as Charlemagne's great palace at Aachen in modern Germany. Indeed, the following contemporary description of the late eighth-century church, the Alma Sophia in York, has led one scholar to suggest that it may have been the model for the palace church at Aachen:[31]

This lofty building, supported by strong columns, themselves bolstering curving arches, gleams inside with fine inlaid ceilings and windows. It shines in its beauty, surrounded by many a chapel with its many galleries in its various quarters, and thirty altars decorated with different finery.[32]

That there may have been royal rituals there like those at Aachen is suggested by the 796 entry in the *Northern Annals* which describes King Eardwulf of Northumbria as having

---

28   Colgrave and Mynors (eds), *Bede's Ecclesiastical History*, bk 2 ch. 16.
29   *Ibid.*, bk 2 ch. 14, 13, bk 3 ch. 17.
30   Hope-Taylor, B., *Yeavering: An Anglo-British Centre of Early Northumbria* (London, 1977); Alcock, L., *Bede, Eddius and the Forts of the North Britons* (Jarrow Lecture, Jarrow, 1989).
31   Norton, C., 'The Anglo-Saxon Cathedral at York and the Topography of the Anglian City', *Journal of the British Archaeological Association*, 151 (1998), pp.1-42.
32   Godman, P. (ed.), *Alcuin: the Bishops, Kings, and Saints of York* (Oxford, 1982), lines 1509-14.

been 'raised to the insignia of the kingdom (*regni infulis est sublimatus*), and consecrated (*consecratus*) in York in the church of St Peter at the altar of the blessed Apostle Paul'.[33]

Despite their failure to survive, it seems probable that the kingdom did use written documents – as in other kingdoms, the contribution of the Christian church. In his *Life of Wilfrid*, Stephen describes the dedication of the church at Ripon as follows:

> Then the holy bishop Wilfrid stood in front of the altar, and, turning to the people, in the presence of the kings, read out in a clear voice the names of the lands which the kings had previously given him for the good of their souls, with the consent and signature of the bishops and all the princes (*principes*).[34]

This unquestionably refers to the existence of a charter with a witness-list, and there is a similar reference to charters in a letter which Bede wrote to Bishop Ecgberht of York.[35] The fact that Bede gives precise figures for the assessment in hides of the islands of Anglesey and Man, which King Edwin conquered, suggests that the kings maintained written records of land assessments.[36]

As for the kingdom's capability to mint coins, the evidence is much slighter. No Northumbrian king is known to have minted coins before Aldfrith (686-705), who issued silver pennies of quite high value, but these may have been more for prestige than for practical use. After his death, no further coins are known to have been minted until the silver pennies of Eadberht (737/8-58), from whose reign onwards there was a more or less continuous Northumbrian coinage. This declined steeply in precious metal content in the ninth century, however, resulting in the so-called *stycas*, which were effectively bronze coins but nevertheless produced in considerable quantities and possibly indicating substantial trading activity.[37]

On the face of it, it seems easy to attribute the failure of this apparently great kingdom to Viking raids and invasions. A series of sporadic raids afflicted the monasteries of Lindisfarne in 793 and Jarrow in 794, although it is not clear how destructive these were.[38] In 865, however, the so-called Great Army under Halfdan and Ivar landed in East Anglia, then moved north in 866 and in a complicated series of attacks seized York, killing the native Northumbrian kings and establishing a sort of Viking kingship, at least from the later years of the ninth century (Halfdan is stated to have ruled as king from 875 to 877), which lasted until the death of the last king, Eric Bloodaxe, in 954.[39] It is doubtful, however, whether the creation of this kingdom constituted the destruction of Northumbria in a real sense or whether it simply marked the emergence of a smaller successor state very similar in character. Viking kings ruled from York, which had been an important centre for the kings

---

33 Arnold, T. (ed.), *Symeonis Monachi Opera Omnia* (2 vols; Rolls Series 75; London, 1882-5), II, pp.57-8.
34 Colgrave (ed.), *Life of Wilfrid*, ch. 17.
35 Plummer, C. (ed.), *Venerabilis Baedae Opera Historica* (2 vols; Oxford, 1896), I, p.415.
36 Colgrave and Mynors (eds), *Bede's Ecclesiastical History*, bk 2 ch. 9.
37 North, J.J., *English Hammered Coinage, Volume I, Early Anglo-Saxon to Henry III, c.600-1272* (3rd edn; London, 1994).
38 Plummer (ed.), *Two Chronicles Parallel*, s.a.
39 Rollason, D. and Gore, D., *Sources for York History before 1100* (Archaeology of York, York, 1998), pp.63-9.

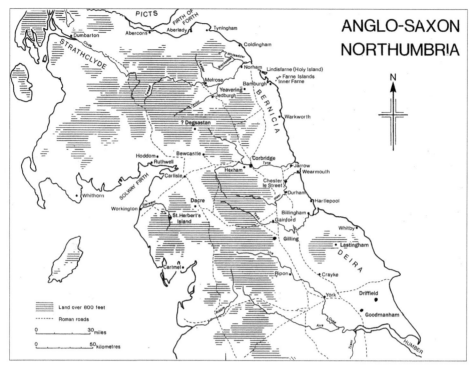

3 *Anglo-Saxon Northumbria*

of Northumbria, and, like them, they were closely associated with the archbishops, their coins even having on them the name of St Peter, to whom York Minster was dedicated. Moreover, the development of York under the Vikings was not especially Scandinavian in character, as can be seen in the styles of ecclesiastical sculpture as well as in remains of buildings, including the church of St Mary Bishophill Junior, and in what we can deduce of the governmental organisation.[40]

To the north of the Viking kingdom of York, there seems to have been another successor state in the shape of the earldom of Bamburgh. That this was very Northumbrian in character is suggested by the paucity of Viking place-names north of the river Tees, as well as by the fact that the earls ruled from Bamburgh, an ancient Northumbrian royal seat.[41] They might even have been scions of the Northumbrian royal family and the first of them, Eardwulf (*c*.890-912), was indeed called 'king of the north Saxons' by the contemporary *Annals of Ulster*.[42] At the end of the tenth century, Earl Uhtred (d.1016) patronised the religious Community of St Cuthbert, which had moved in the late ninth century from Lindisfarne and was established by 883 at Chester-le-Street on the river Wear between the rivers Tyne and Tees, and at Durham, also on the Wear, from 995. According to the Durham monk

40 Rollason, D., 'Anglo-Scandinavian York: The Evidence of Historical Sources', in *Anglo-Scandinavian York*, ed. R.A. Hall (York, 2004), pp.305-24, and this volume *passim*.

41 Rollason, *Northumbria*, pp.244-9.

42 MacAirt and MacNiocaill (eds), *Annals of Ulster*, 361. Note that the editors render the name *Etulbb* in the original as *Ethelwald*.

Symeon, writing in the early 12th century, he helped with the establishment of the Community at Durham.[43] There it developed as a community which, both before and after the Norman Conquest, had interests focused on the past of the kingdom of Northumbria, as is evident in its historical writings, in its claim to be successor of the church of Lindisfarne, and in the backward-looking style of ecclesiastical sculpture which it patronised, notably the decoration on the grave-cover now in the Monks' Dormitory at Durham Cathedral.[44]

In the western part of the former kingdom, the kings who emerged in the tenth century are described by our sources as 'kings of the Cumbrians'. These kings first appear with Owain, who was probably the ruler defeated along with others by King Æthelstan at the Battle of Brunanburh in 937; they continue with Dunmail (Donald), expelled in 945 by King Edmund of England who blinded his sons, and with Malcolm (d.997), who was also known as 'king of the Britons of the North'. It appears then that these kings began to rule the North West at least as early as the early tenth century and, to judge from sources for the somewhat later history of the region, their southern frontier was as far south as the monument known as the Rey Cross (or Rere Cross) on Stainmore (County Durham) on the line of the modern A66 road from Scotch Corner to Brough. They may have been, as some scholars believe, kings of Strathclyde who had conquered western Northumbria, or they may have been indigenous kings ruling what was another successor state of the kingdom of Northumbria in Cumbria.[45]

From a cultural and religious point of view, Cumbria as well as the area of the Viking kingdom of York continued in much the same way as the old kingdom of Northumbria had done. The dense distribution of ecclesiastical sculpture points to rapid assimilation of the incoming Vikings to the Christian culture of Northumbria.[46] Moreover, there are striking examples of the juxtaposition of pagan Viking and Christian images as if to emphasise the process of assimilation. There are possible examples of this at Lowther and Kirkby Stephen (Westmorland), although we cannot always be sure that we are seeing actual pagan images as opposed to images common to a Christian artistic tradition. In the famous and elaborate cross at Gosforth in Cumberland, however, there is no doubt. The sculptured scenes combine a representation of the Crucifixion of Christ with scenes from the end of the gods – the *Ragnarok* – in Scandinavian mythology. The church of Gosforth also preserves a sculptured stone, the so-called Thor's Fishing Stone, which in representing the god Thor fishing for the World Serpent is a definite allusion to Scandinavian paganism and was also, like the cross, presumably an attempt

---

43 Rollason, D. (ed.), *Symeon of Durham, Libellus de Exordio atque Procursu istius hoc est Dunelmensis Ecclesie* (Oxford Medieval Texts; Oxford, 2000), pp.148-9.

44 *Ibid.*, pp.lxxvii-xci; Rollason, D., 'Symeon of Durham and the Community of Durham in the Eleventh Century', in *England in the Eleventh Century: Proceedings of the 1990 Harlaxton Symposium* (ed. C. Hicks Stamford, 1992), pp.183-98; Cramp, R.J., 'The Artistic Influence of Lindisfarne within Northumbria', in *St Cuthbert, his Cult and his Community to AD 1200* (ed. G. Bonner, D. Rollason, and C. Stancliffe, Woodbridge, 1989), pp.213-228.

45 Kirby, 'Strathclyde and Cumbria'; Phythian-Adams, C., *The Land of the Cumbrians: A Study in British Provincial Origins, AD 400-1120* (London, 1996), pp.110-22.

46 Bailey, R.N., *Viking Age Sculpture in Northern England* (London, 1980), *passim*.

at assimilation and acculturation. Other representations of pagan mythology on ecclesiastical sculpture are less detailed than those at Gosforth, but it seems likely that they are to do with similar themes of conversion and integration.[47]

If the Viking raids resulted in a continuation of the kingdom of Northumbria in a similar but fragmented form, the destruction of these as political entities was the next stage. It can best be understood in terms of the 'heartlands' of the former kingdom of Northumbria, that is those areas where the kings were most powerful and most active and which were the centres of gravity of the kingdom. The distribution of churches, royal sites and other evidence suggests that they were located, for the former kingdom of Deira, in the Vale of York, Ryedale, the Yorkshire Wolds and surrounding areas; and for the former kingdom of Bernicia, in the hinterland of Lindisfarne and Bamburgh, and in the coastal area north to the Firth of Forth, and in part of pre-1974 County Durham from the river Wear north to the river Tyne. For what became the area of Cumbria, the former kingdom of Northumbria's heartland may have lain around the city of Carlisle.[48]

The Deiran heartland came under repeated military pressure from the kings of Wessex, who later became kings of England. They defeated the rulers of the Viking kingdom of York at the Battle of Tettenhall in 910, and in 927 King Æthelstan expelled the Viking king of York, Guthfrith, and ruled there until his death in 939, when Viking kings were re-established. Subsequent years saw a series of military attacks from the southern kings, including a campaign led by Eadred in 948 when he 'ravaged all Northumbria because they had accepted Eric Bloodaxe as their king'. His ravaging included the church of Ripon (Yorkshire), from which he seems to have removed the relics of the great Northumbrian bishop St Wilfrid, sending them to Canterbury, perhaps as a symbol of southern political dominance over Northumbria.[49]

A little later, probably in the late tenth or early 11th century, the Bernician heartland in the hinterland of Lindisfarne and Bamburgh was split by what historians know as the 'cession of Lothian'. The accounts of the written sources are various, but this area between the river Tweed and the Firth of Forth is stated to have been ceded to the Scots by King Edgar of England (957-75), on the initiative of Earl Oslac of York and Earl Eadwulf Evil Child of Bamburgh; or by Earl Eadwulf Cudel of Bamburgh, after the siege of Durham by the Scots in 1006; or as a result of the Scottish victory at Carham on the river Tweed in 1018. Whatever the truth of this, the beginnings of the creation of the Scottish border on the River Tweed in this period bisected the ancient Bernician heartland. In the west, the creation of Carlisle as a Norman fortress by King William Rufus in 1092 and the absorption of the kingdom of Strathclyde into the kingdom of Scotland earlier in the 11th century began the process of the creation of the south-western length of the Scottish border. This, too, effectively bisected the ancient heartland of north-west Northumbria around Carlisle.[50]

---

47 *Ibid.*, pp.101-43.
48 Rollason, *Northumbria*, pp.45-52.
49 Rollason, *Northumbria*, pp.265-7; Plummer (ed.), *Two Chronicles Parallel* (D) s.a. 948.
50 Meehan, B., 'The Siege of Durham, the Battle of Carham and the Cession of Lothian', *Scottish Historical Review*, 55 (1976), pp.1-19; G.W.S. Barrow, 'The Anglo-Scottish Border', *Northern History*, 1 (1966), pp.21-42; Summerson, H., *Medieval Carlisle: the City and the Borders from the Late Eleventh to the Mid-Sixteenth Century* (2 vols; Cumberland and Westmorland Antiquarian and Archaeological Society, Extra Series, Kendal, 1993); Duncan, *Scotland: The Making of the Kingdom*.

In these ways, the destruction of the kingdom of Northumbria went beyond its division into successor states. In shattering the heartlands of the ancient kingdom and in absorbing its remains into two separate kingdoms with a boundary which arguably had little respect for previous historical realities, little was left beyond reminiscence in the name of the earldom of Northumbria and then the county of Northumberland with which we began.

The medieval historians of the north, however, were intent on revivifying the Northumbrian past, at least in writing. The Community of St Cuthbert was a particular focus for such revivification, with the composition in the earlier 11th century of the text known as the *History of St Cuthbert*, which took the Community's traditions back to the ancient kingdom and the church of Lindisfarne. After the Norman Conquest and the reform of the Community as the Benedictine Durham Cathedral Priory in 1083, Symeon of Durham and others systematically collected materials, and Symeon produced both his *Tract on the Origins and Progress of this the Church of Durham*, and his *History of the Kings*, tracing Northumbrian history through the inclusion of sets of annals, including the so-called *Northern Annals* from eighth-century York.[51]

This interest was driven partly by practical considerations. Durham Cathedral Priory, of which Symeon was a precentor, claimed wide estates in Durham and Northumberland (especially the territories known as Norhamshire and Islandshire, that is 'North Durham') on the basis that it was the successor to the church of Lindisfarne and therefore entitled to the former lands of that church.[52] The history of the early kingdom of Northumbria in which Lindisfarne had been founded and its lands acquired was therefore of crucial importance, and Symeon's task was no less than to create a 'memory' of those times in a monastic community which was, in fact, a new foundation. But there were other motives too, including a desire on the part of the monks and their bishops, who were continental churchmen as a result of the Norman Conquest, to associate themselves and their church with the saints and sanctity of the age of Bede; for example, at the completion of the east end of the great new cathedral of Durham in 1104, the relics of St Cuthbert of Lindisfarne were translated into it and his shrine from then on became the focal point of the Cathedral. The past of the kingdom of Northumbria, its churches and its saints, was thus a matter of current importance, and Durham took a particular lead in promoting and developing it at least in the 11th and 12th centuries.[53] Then as now, the past was too important not to be manipulated. Then as now, a retrospection, almost a nostalgia, was created around the past for purposes of the present which bore little relation to what the kingdom of Northumbria had really been.

---

51 Johnson South, T. (ed.), *Historia de Sancto Cuthberto: A History of Saint Cuthbert and a Record of his Patrimony* (Anglo-Saxon Texts; Woodbridge, 2002); Rollason (ed.), *Symeon, Libellus de Exordio*.
52 Craster, E., 'The Patrimony of St Cuthbert', *English Historical Review*, 69 (1954), pp.177-199.
53 Rollason, 'Symeon and the Community of Durham; Rollason, D., *Saints and Relics in Anglo-Saxon England* (Oxford, 1989), pp.225-6, 235-6.

2

'Between the brine and the high ground': The Roots of Northumbria

BRIAN K. ROBERTS

Introduction

> *Between the brine and the high ground and the fresh stream water,*
> *Men will quake before Cunedda, the violent one.*
>
> *In Caer Weir and Caer Lywelyth fighting will shake the* civitates –
> *An encompassing tide of fire from across the sea ...*
> *His honour was maintained a hundred times before death came to our [stout] door post.*
> *The men of Bernicia were led in battle.*

These words provide a dramatic image of the troubled times between the collapse of Roman control and the appearance of stable Anglo-Saxon kingdoms under strong rulers. They are taken from verse once chanted in a British royal hall in praise of Cunedda, described as the '[stout] door post' of his kingdom, Bernicia.[1] Northumbria grew from intricate political alliances created by charismatic leaders, both British and Anglo-Saxon, who were able to define primitive states from the remains of the *civitates* or Roman local administrations. They had war bands to assist them, for they offered booty as reward. What follows develops four threads of argument that interlace like the patterns on a great Northumbrian stone cross. A first thread comprises a brief review of nature's contribution to the regional personality, while a second considers some archaeological evidences, assessing the contexts in which these survive and what they may mean. This leads to ruminations upon the interaction between natural contrasts in landscape and culturally assessed features such as the roads and route ways. A third

---

1 John T. Koch, *The Goddodin of Aneirin* (Cardiff, 1997), pp.xxxvi-xxxvii; translated from north British (a form of early Welsh), perhaps of the earlier fifth century. *Caer Weir* is either Durham or, more probably, Chester-le-Street, while *Caer Lywelyth* is likely to be Carlisle.

thread takes the discussion to the region's post-glacial woodlands and the region-wide patterns of clearances that provided focal zones for the development of early states. The distribution of burials falling between the fifth and the eighth centuries and place-name survivals derived from Old English, the language of the Anglo-Saxons, provide a means of exploring these ideas. A final thread focuses upon the distribution of Anglo-Saxon stone sculptures throughout the north and all four threads are drawn together in a brief conclusion looking at the roots of Northumbria. Above all, time and space, questions of chronology and distribution, provide a matrix in which to explore the past.

From Nature's Hand

The foundations of northern England are established by varied country rocks: the oldest and hardest appear as high land in the Lake District and the Cheviots and these old rocks run eastwards and downwards to form the underlying basement of the whole northern region. Around these two upland masses and over this basement lie undulating swatches of superimposed sedimentary rocks, comprising great thicknesses of sandstones, shale, mudstones, limestones and clays. From these raw materials uplift and erosion have etched arcuate scarp and vale topography (Fig. 1 – the superimposed outlines will be discussed later): upstanding scarps appear where the rock is hard, with vales where the country rocks are softer. Effectively the whole of northern England once comprised a vast uplifted and tilted block, highest in the west and north, where the upper younger sedimentaries have actually been worn away to expose basement rocks in the Cheviots and Lake District. Sedimentary rocks are seen clearly where limestones and sandstones appear in the tilted blocks of the northern and central Pennines and the North York Moors, all dipping in a broadly south-easterly direction. The sedimentary beds eventually slide between the slate-grey waters of the North Sea. The intrusion of molten magma into this sedimentary series – the Whin Sill – creates local diversity, notably in Teesdale, where it outcrops in the steeper northwards-facing valley sides; in southern Northumberland, where the central section of the Hadrian's Wall follows an outcrop; and finally in the seacoast at Bamburgh, Dunstanburgh and in the Farne Islands. Some of the sedimentary rocks originated in vast deltas, where great swamp-forests grew, forests that were episodically overwhelmed by further influxes of sand and mud. These events, some 250 million years ago, were to have a profound effect on the eventual cultural and economic history of the North East when finally the fossil forests were eagerly exploited as coal.

The main rivers of the region flow from west to east, originally developing on the upper surface of the uplifted block and consequently flowing both downslope and eastwards to the lower basin of the proto-Rhine, now the North Sea. Only in the Eden, occupying a trench where a great splinter slipped downwards, preserving some overlying old sedimentaries, and in the Lune and Ribble systems, do the river flows

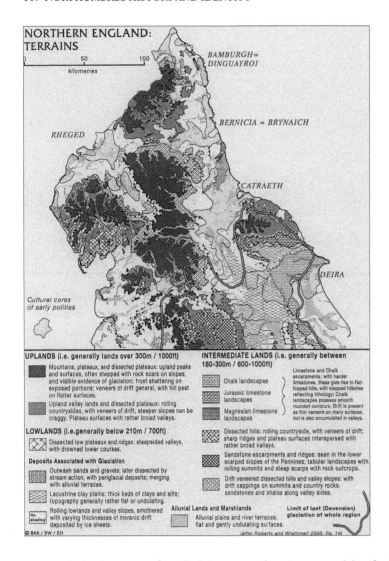

4 *Map: Northern England, Terrains*

differ because of underlying complexities caused by faulting. 'Consequent' or west to east flows are to be seen in the Tees, the smaller rivers of Northumberland, the South Tyne and the upper Wear, followed by the Swale, Ure, Nidd, Wharfe and Aire – *all* the latter draining to the Humber. Drainage developing 'subsequent' to the west to east lines and etching away softer rocks broadly at right-angles to the consequent flows created broad vales, isolating and defining the many upstanding escarpments. So it was that the subsequent drainage system of the Vale of York, developing in softer rocks, beheaded the rivers from the Pennines to take them all to the North Sea via the Humber.[2] Furthermore, in geologically recent times, all landscapes were altered by glaciation. In the uplands the ice masses caused severe erosion, grinding rock surfaces into smooth profiles whose gently stepped shapes echo the harder and softer bands beneath. Unsorted deposits, often called boulder clays, were plastered over the lowlands,

---

2   Andrew Goudie, *The Landforms of England and Wales* (Oxford, 1990), pp.1-34, fig. 1.3, pp.122-8.

where the ice-flows slackened. When this ice finally melted, a slow and discontinuous process, completed about twelve thousand years ago, vast quantities of water flowed, temporary lakes formed and river systems were redeveloped and sometimes redirected. All slopes and valley lands were smothered by redeposited sludgy materials and finally, in the lower areas, gravels, sands and clays accumulated, the result of sorting and deposition by meltwaters. Thus the Wear, once a south-bank tributary of the Tyne and flowing in what is now the Team valley, was redirected to cut through the escarpment of the Magnesian Limestone. In the Vale of York a series of slightly higher morainic ridges that developed at the snout of the glacier when forward motion ceased were separated by zones with lakes, some of which may have survived as late as 994 when the Scots plundered as far south as 'the lakes of Deira'.[3] The appearance of temporary lakes and the constant downwash of fine materials led to the appearance of clays in the alluvial basins and in the lower portions towards the Humber.

Why need any of this matter to the historian? Figure 4, of the terrains of northern England, is not a geology map, nor a relief map nor a soil map, but is a summative and much simplified interpretation of the characteristics of the land surface that can be easily seen and sensed by human beings. It is one way of glimpsing the 'whole' and a generalised template against which to assess the greater on-ground details of local regions and even units as small as an individual township or parish. On a bigger scale it is possible to think of the siting of the Roman wall and the lines of Roman roads, of the evident routeways through the hill masses, of the presence of well-drained plains suitable for agriculture, of hill pastures for the hunt and the grazing of domestic stock, and marshlands for the taking of fish and fowl. Sea and land, tidal ranges and river floods, altitude, latitude and local climate have all helped to define other fundamental limits. Sometimes these are starkly visible, as in the effect of increasing altitude, while others are only seen in the success or failure of a crop. Thus we are told that when spring-sown barley failed in his Farne Island retreat, St Cuthbert (c.634 to 687) sowed again 'long after the proper time for sowing it, and when there seemed no hope of any harvest', yet it miraculously yielded an abundant crop. We may exclude miracles, but such simple experiments must have been commonplace.[4] Not visible in the generalised framework, we have vast local variations in soil, that natural substance with which the farmer wrestles most intimately. In fact, farmers manufacture agricultural soils. They take the raw mineral materials left by the ice and meltwaters, remove the natural vegetation and expose the wholly natural soils developed since the ice retreated. Then they clear stones and tree stumps, direct their ploughing to assist drainage and create a tilth, plough further to kill weeds – natural plants growing where they are not wanted – continue to stone-pick, and where possible manure and rotate their arable crops. Good husbandry – an evocative word – involves keeping soils in good heart, 'warmed' and nurtured. Soils are the real groundwork of all prosperity and the recently glaciated and often stone-filled soils and marshy hollows of

3   Richard Fletcher, *Bloodfeud* (London, 2002), p.73; Anthony Long et al., *The Swale-Ure Washlands: Landscape History and Human Impacts* (Environmental Research Centre, University of Durham 2004)
4   Bertram Colgrave, *Two Lives of St Cuthbert* (Cambridge, 1985), pp.5-8 and 221.

the north initially presented farmers with greater difficulties for husbandry than those lands beyond the last ice fronts, where a far longer time than a mere twelve thousand years had elapsed since active glaciation and deglaciation.

Archaeological Evidences and Routes

Archaeological evidences, the sum total of all recoveries of remains, are much mapped and much discussed, but what do they really tell us? The distorting effect of an 'active archaeological society' is certain, but ultimately terrain conditions affect site discovery. By using air photography it took many decades for sites beneath arable to be recovered in quantity, and it is important to appreciate that what we now have represents no more than a fortuitously generated sample. Each square kilometre would need flying many times, in varied soil moisture conditions, in varied lights and with varied crops and growth stages to reveal all the sites present. In the uplands, however, the interplay of experience and fieldwork has multiplied sites greatly.[5] In more subtle ways, foothills and upland shoulders that carry pastures, or locations adjacent to lowland farmsteads or villages where old grass pasture is sustained, are situations in which slight earthworks reflecting two thousand and more years of cultural activity can litter each and every field, visible to the trained eye even though they photograph badly. On the other hand, archaeological survivals also reflect all subsequent land usages; the preparation of arable land described earlier, coupled with flows of soil materials into bottomlands, represent site attrition and site burial. In the former only the basal layers and ditches cutting the subsoil survive, while in the latter archaeological features are buried so deeply as to be undetectable at the surface. It is on hill-pastures and former commons where upstanding site survival is most evident, a distribution that has little if any relationship to the original overall intensity of occupation. All this affects the distribution maps we create.

Figure 5, the distribution of steadings and compounds of Iron-Age and Romano-British date, is often used as a distribution map of rural settlement in the Romano-British period.[6] It records a series of sites, farmsteads and hamlets, whose curvilinear or rectangular shapes, coupled with limited excavation, suggest that they fall in a time-span embracing the later Iron Age, the Roman period and even indeed the post-Roman centuries. The arrow, in western County Durham, in the middle of the map, is the location where a series of compounds are known in Upper Weardale, and neatly illustrates the power of a single discovery to affect perception of a pattern. Nevertheless, such sites are thin on the ground in Durham, but increase in density to both the north and the south of the county, conceivably implying a march zone between two tribal territories, probably those of the later Iron-Age Brigantes and the Votadini.[7]

5   George Jobey, 'Homesteads and settlements of the frontier area', in Charles Thomas (ed.), *Rural Settlement in Roman Britain* (Council for British Archaeology, London, Research Report 7, 1966), pp.1-14.

6   Nick Higham, *The Northern Counties to AD 1000* (London, 1986), fig. 5.1; Richard Hingley, *Rural Settlement in Roman Britain* (London, 1989), fig.10.

7   The Yorkshire distribution is complicated: one component, shown by the cross symbols, is 'conservative' in character (Margaret Faull, 'Roman and Saxon settlement patterns in Yorkshire: a computer-generated analysis', *Landscape History*, vol. 5, 1983, 21-40 and fig. 3). The other components, delimited by the fine stippled line, encapsulates no less than three sets of more detailed investigation published by Robin A. Butlin and Nick Staley (eds) in *Historical Atlas of North Yorkshire* (Otley, 2003), fig. 4.4; see also figs 3.7, 4.1 and 4.2.

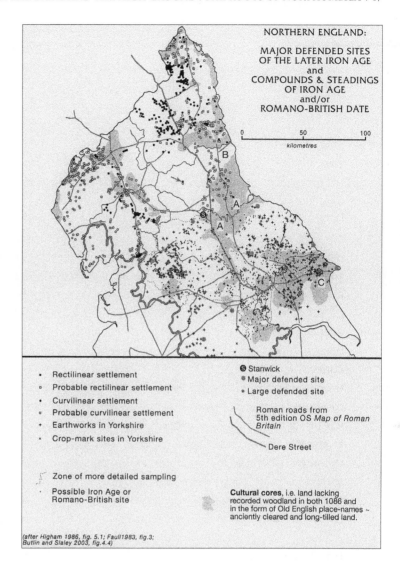

5 *Map: Major Defended Sites*

What does this distribution mean? What does it tell us about the North East in this period? The pattern of site recovery largely relates to post-Roman land-usage: sites survive on grazing areas, and are worn away in arable zones. Thus, we may suspect that in the farmlands of slopes around the Skerne and the Tees Valley, between Gainford and Stockton in County Durham (zone A), prime quality lands, many sites have been eroded away and buried, for this was an area formerly containing large concentrations of medieval villages and their arable fields although many of these are now depopulated.[8] In zone B, where no Romano-British sites appear, the territory once known as *Werhale*, includes lands given to the twin monasteries of Jarrow and Monkwearmouth. There are strong indications that, although eventually settled, this was once part of a tract of heath and woodland thrusting eastwards from the

---

8 Brian Roberts and Stuart Wrathmell, *Region and Place: a study of English rural settlement* (English Heritage, 2002), figs 1.1, 1.5 and 5.1.

Pennine foothills proper, reaching the sea between these monasteries (Fig. 6). The fact that numerous steadings do appear further to the west of zone B suggests the occurrence of post-Roman recession to the south of the Tyne, and we should not forget that site recovery is hindered here by 18th- and 19th-century industrialisation. In zone C, the Yorkshire Wolds and surrounding countryside, sites mass in large numbers. The area is recognised to have been the tribal territory of the Parisii in the Iron Age, the focus of intense Roman settlement, and in post-Roman and Anglo-Saxon times the heart of what became the kingdom of Deira.[9] The more intensive the inquiry, the more sites appear. A fine study of the Wolds by Cathy Stoertz shows that this zone is incredibly rich in material, while Dominic Powelsland's recoveries at West Heslerton, at the northern edges of Stoertz's study area, hint at the existence of hitherto unimagined quantities of material. This occurs at the scarp foot of the chalk, where it edges the Vale of Pickering, where downwash accretes materials making its varied soils a preferred settlement zone and where named medieval nucleated settlements are still concentrated.[10] Nevertheless, the more we look the more we can see that the lowlands, areas eventually dominated by nucleated villages and hamlets with their associated open, common townfields, were thickly occupied in the later prehistoric and Roman period. Work on pollen diagrams does, however, hint at great complexity of local patterns of clearance and woodland survival.[11]

We must note that some of the sites mapped in Figure 6, notably the curvilinear ones, could possibly be pre-Roman, for it was the Romans who brought straight-line regularity to northern landscapes. If so, then let us put ourselves in the position of a group of Roman military officers, with an engineer corps equivalent, moving into the area at the behest of the Emperor. The aim is to gain tribute, and if there is resistance, spoil and slaves, followed by tribute. This is not the place to document any of this in detail – the policies and treaties, the occupations and retreats – but the military advances must have been contingent upon two key factors: first the definition of a route, and second the existence of centres of population. 'Where is Cartimandua's *oppidum*?' may have been a useful question for Petillius Cerialis, the Governor of Britain in the early 70s, to ask, although such basic questions become less meaningful as time passes and intelligence and contacts reveal the situation.[12] If we turn to the Roman roads of the north, the legionary headquarters Chester and York form a baseline, and from Chester a road drives northwards via the Lune Gorge, over the inclement heights of

9   Faull, 'Roman and Anglo-Saxon settlement'; Helen Geake and Jonathan Kenny (eds), *Early Deira: archaeological studies of the East Riding in the fourth to ninth centuries AD* (Oxford, 2000).

10   Dominic Powelsland, 'West Heslerton Settlement Mobility: a case of static development', in Helen Geak and Jonathan Kenny (eds), *Early Deira*, 19-26; Catherine Stoertz, *Ancient Landscapes of the Yorkshire Wolds* (Royal Commission on the Historical Monuments of England, 1997).

11   Kevin Greene, *The Archaeology of the Roman Economy* (London, 1986), fig. 53, based on a synthesis by Peter Clark; Jacqueline P. Huntley, 'Environmental archaeology: Mesolithic to Roman Period', in Catherine Brooks, Robin Daniels and Anthony Harding (eds), *Past Present and Future: the archaeology of Northern England* (Architectural and Archaeological Society of Durham and Northumberland, Research Report 5, 2002), figs. 8.4, 8.5 and 8.6; the most recent broad synopsis of the environmental material is by Jim Innes in D. Huddart and N.F. Glasser (eds), *Quaternary of Northern England* (Geological Conservation Review Series, Joint Nature Conservation Committee, Peterborough, 2002), pp.356-65.

12   Sheppard Frere, *Britannia* (London, 1991), pp.83-5, fig 3.

Shap Fell, to the Eden valley and eventually Carlisle near the western end of Hadrian's Wall. Initially this was a gateway for thrusts further north, but eventually it became a centre for local government. Local populations – the Carvetii, living in the Eden Valley and on the Solway Plain – became part of the province and tribute payers.[13] On the other side of the Pennines, the great road from York eventually known as the Dere Street took a route north to Aldborough, thence to Catterick and the important Tees crossing at Piercebridge, where a substantial Roman bridge has been discovered. Then it passed north-westwards to the Wear Valley at Binchester and thence via Lanchester and Ebchester to Corbridge, a key Tyne crossing and bridging point, to cross the Cheviot mass at High Rochester on its way to Newstead in the Tweed valley.[14] Why, we may ask, were these routes selected by the army?

It can be no accident that the eastern trunk route passed through what became the market town of the Brigantes at Aldborough in Yorkshire – *Isurium Brigantum* – and, further north, passed no more than a mile and a half from what may have been a northern *oppidum*, or lowland fortress, of the same tribe at Stanwick Park. The establishment of the precise route probably followed the military advance, but was placed along the western side of the Vale of York, avoiding the Swale Ure washlands and crossing the west to east drainage lines well upstream, where flows were more episodic and speedy and fording points more frequent. To the west of the Pennines, the Manchester, Ribchester, Tebay Gorge and Eden Valley route steers a careful course avoiding the coast and the lower courses of the rivers, passing through the valleys and lower foothills to head towards the more populated zones of the Eden Valley and Solway Plain. But the routes had a political significance. Without going into the technicalities of either land survey or intelligence gathering, the Roman army knew where they were going on the east side of the Pennines, taking account of both potential client kingdoms and hostile territories with their important population concentrations.[15]

The Brigantian *oppidum* postulated at Stanwick was probably deliberately located between upland pastures and a well-populated zone further east.[16] The uplands gave extensive grazing lands for the cattle herds of the local aristocrats and their tenant farmers, and also provided routes across which the young bloods of other tribes to the west and north came to steal cattle and women. This made defences necessary, not least because there were also raids outwards, to prey on other tribes. The Tees Valley farmers would have produced cereals, cattle and dairy produce to keep themselves and the aristocratic warriors alive. The evidence that the middle Tees was then a well-populated zone in the later Iron-Age and Romano-British period is not conclusive, for steadings and compounds do not appear in great numbers. Nevertheless, Old English place-names and later taxation records suggest that in the Anglo-Saxon

---

13 Nick Higham and Barri Jones, *The Carvetii* (Stroud, 1985).
14 Barri Jones and David Mattingley, *An Atlas of Roman Britain* (London, 1990), map 4:31
15 Jones and Mattingly, *Atlas*, maps 4:32 and 5:23.
16 Butlin and Staley, *Atlas*, figs 3.6, 3.7 and 4.1.

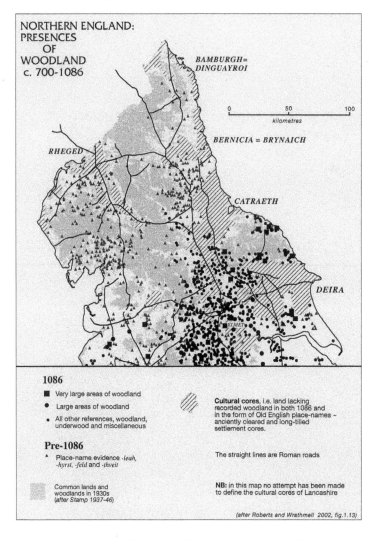

NORTHERN ENGLAND:
PRESENCES
OF
WOODLAND
c. 700-1086

BAMBURGH=
DINGUAYROI

0   50   100
kilometres

BERNICIA = BRYNAICH

RHEGED

CATRAETH

DEIRA

ELMET

1086

■ Very large areas of woodland

● Large areas of woodland

• All other references, woodland,
  underwood and miscellaneous

▨ **Cultural cores**, i.e. land lacking
  recorded woodland in both 1086 and
  in the form of Old English place-names ~
  anciently cleared and long-tilled
  settlement cores.

Pre-1086

▲ Place-name evidence -leah,
  -hyrst, -feld and -thveit

The straight lines are Roman roads

Common lands and
woodlands in 1930s
(after Stamp 1937-46)

NB: in this map no attempt has been made
to define the cultural cores of Lancashire

(after Roberts and Wrathmell 2002, fig.1.13)

6   *Map: Presences of Woodland*

and medieval period this was a populated and prosperous zone.[17] In Durham the Dere Street passes to the west of the concentration of steadings and conceivably precedes their development. The low numbers of curvilinear – probably Iron-Age – steadings in County Durham and southern Northumberland, in sharp contrast to the Solway Plain, imply colonisation in Roman times, when rectangular farmsteads were established. At one peat bog, Hallowell Moss, just to the west of Durham and at the southern edge of a wedge of waste (see below and Figure 3) in northern and western County Durham, the main period of extensive woodland clearance began at or soon after the time of Roman advance.[18] Once established, the Roman roads became route ways of continuing importance, which is why local Anglo-Saxon

17   Robin Glasscock, 'England in 1334', in H.C. Darby (ed.), *A New Historical Geography of England* (Cambridge, 1973), fig. 35; David Hill, *An Atlas of Anglo-Saxon England* (Oxford, 1981), fig. 25, a map of place-names recorded in 1086, indicating the settlements present in the later Anglo-Saxon period.
18   Alison Donaldson and Judith Turner, 'A pollen diagram from Hallowell Moss near Durham City', *Journal of Biogeography* 4, 1977, pp.25-33.

communities named the eastern route the Dere Street, the road leading *from* the north towards the territory of the *Deirans*, based on the lands in eastern Yorkshire.[19] This perspective is important when discussing Figure 6, a map of early woodlands in the region.

In summary, while the Roman army engineers responded to the constraints and possibilities latent in topography, there are signs that they initially sought 'all weather' routes, not too high and not too low, and fine-tuned these to carry the army to key strategic locations with native British population concentrations and fortifications. These military roads eventually created a potential for inter-regional contact and economic development that were to have long-lasting effects. Other subsidiary north to south roads developed on both sides of the Pennines, with cross-Pennine links and seaward routes to the coasts and harbours. The Gough map of about 1360 confirms the sustained pre-eminence of the two primary Roman 'army advance' routes on each side of the Pennines, although on the eastern side it portrays no routes north of Richmond and the Roman route to the north west through the Stainmore gap.[20]

Thus far, this view of the north of England has been land-based, but the sea was always, and still remains, a 'salt-road' of key social and economic importance. Traders, war parties, pirates, emissaries, refugees and fishermen all used this highway, although in early times it would be unwise to differentiate too strongly between these categories of seafarer. Nevertheless, at root there were fishermen, knowledgeable of local conditions and who we will, following Chaucer, call *shipmen*, men whose knowledge transcended the purely local and reached towards a wider view of the world. We should never underrate their skills. The traditional coble – inshore fishing boat – of the north-east coast has a sweeping prow and flat bottom but a flat stern, sloping beneath the boat, so that it could be reversed and easily beached on steeply shelving shingle shores.[21] Coastal vessels and coastal trade were part of the region's lifeblood, while the great coastal towers eventually erected by the Roman authorities along the Yorkshire coast – for who else could have afforded them? – were not merely against occasional seafarers.[22] You cannot raid for cattle in a boat, and moveable goods and slaves must have been the objects of any waterborne raids from the North Sea. One of the peculiarities of the Hadrian's Wall frontier is the fact that the Roman road along it, now called the Stanegate, stops at Corbridge and does not continue to Wallsend. Was the Tyne used for riverboats? This is speculation: the general depth of the river in Roman times was a critical factor, although if there were more valley side woodlands in the Roman period than today the general flow could have been more regular and catastrophic floods fewer than in historical times. In AD 209-11 the fort at South Shields was turned into a major defended stores base, with most of the interior buildings replaced by

19 Nick Higham, *The Kingdom of Northumbria* (Stroud, 1993), fig. p.122.
20 Catherine Delano-Smith and Roger Kain, *English Maps: a history* (The British Library, 1999), pp.46-7.
21 Peter Frank, *Yorkshire Fisherfolk* (Chichester, 2002), p.56, and chap. 4 *passim*.
22 Frere, *Britannia*, p.365.

granary-storehouses. At a later stage the appearance of a Roman army unit of 'Tigris Lightermen', 'manning light, shallow draught boats', could be an indicator of the use of this river for inland transport. [23] We should not forget that development of the coal trade after 1550 occurred in a lower river that was not systematically dredged until 1855. These points all bring us gently to the fact that the Tyne, below the confluence of the South and the North Tyne, was a considerable river, dangerous, chancy, destructive of bridges, tidal beyond Newburn, and a barrier between the lands to the north and those to the south.[24]

Woodland, Open Pastures and Settled Land

Figure 6, showing the presence of woodland between about 700 and 1086, is taken from a widely published map and the methods of construction and the assumptions involved have been discussed elsewhere.[25] Using the record of Domesday Book and the evidence of place-names, it builds an impression of the distribution of northern woodland. The inclusion of common wastes from 20th-century sources amplifies the picture, and the general reliability of the distribution it presents has been tested. Here, in County Durham, a reconstruction of the common wastes in about 1600, linked with the evidence of several hundred farms created from the unenclosed wastes between 1150 and 1350, has shown that the broader view is indeed trustworthy.[26] Included within Figure 6 is what is effectively a 'doodle' outlining lowland areas where the evidence implies that woodland was largely absent. Let us be wholly clear about this: the 'wooded' and 'open areas' in the map are *relatively* wooded and *relatively* open. Thus the shaded areas of Figure 6 define lands largely cleared and surrounded, indeed defined, by the presence of wooded zones and open pasture zones. This does not exclude the survival of some woodland within the 'open' zones. It is likely, albeit with many qualifications, that in the broad 'cleared land-open pasture-wood pasture' contrasts we are seeing the lineaments of a pattern that, both nationally and locally, goes back to the Roman period and perhaps even earlier.[27]

National mapping of settlement suggests that an important boundary between cleared and cultivated open-field countrysides and a more broken, fragmented type of countryside normal in Northumberland appears to shadow the scarp of the Magnesian Limestone where it cuts across County Durham. Before enclosure, between 1450

---

23 J. Collingwood Bruce, *Handbook to the Roman Wall* (13th edn, Newcastle upon Tyne, 1978), p.48; Greene, *Roman Economy*, fig. 11.

24 David Archer, *Land of Singing Waters* (Spredden Press, 1992), 112-13; see also Roberts, B.K. and Wrathmell, S., *An Atlas of Rural Settlement in England* (English Heritage, 2000), pp.34-7.

25 Roberts and Wrathmell, *Region and Place*, pp.27-31.

26 Brian Roberts, Helen Dunsford and Simon Harris, 'Framing Medieval Landscapes: Region and Place in County Durham', in Christian Liddy and Richard Britnell (eds), *North-East England in the Later Middle Ages* (Woodbridge, 2005), pp.221-37.

27 A corollary of these arguments is that the 'positive' mapping of woodland and wastes also creates a 'negative' distribution, and these 'unmapped' zones are in fact the populated areas where arable land has long been more abundant and populations greater. This assumption underlies the use of Fig. 6 in this study.

and 1850, the landscapes of the inner Midlands, the Vale of York and south-east Durham, termed 'champion countrysides', were wholly dominated by villages and their great tracts of open common arable fields. In contrast, to the north and west – including north-west Durham and all Northumberland – villages and hamlets supported by townfields were set amid countrysides retaining far larger amounts of rough pasture, used as common waste.[28] In County Durham, the wedge of former waste and woodland marked 'A' in Figure 5 appears to have been a borderland important on both a national and a local scale. This leads towards speculation about three frontiers: first, the boundary between Brigantian territory and Votadinian territory in the Iron Age, second the location of Hadrian's Wall, perhaps dividing the two, and third, the division between Bernicia and Deira. The discussion to follow draws together synoptic views of evidence from many disciplines, from many chronological periods and of many types, and it is contended that this information, presented through distribution maps, is indeed a powerful analytical tool. In circumstances in which there can be few uncontested answers, long time perspectives are useful. It was a short imaginative leap that took the author from Figure 6 to the territories identified as land cleared before AD 700, and then to see these 'cultural cores' as indications of the presence of known early polities, primitive kingdoms, in the post-Roman and earlier Anglo-Saxon periods.

The Yorkshire Wolds, the escarpments further west and north, and the Vale of Pickering lie at the heart of the kingdom of Deira. The distinctive character of this polity is attested by the area's long history of prehistoric settlement. It was substantively cleared in the Neolithic period, was the land of the Parisii in the Iron Age, and became a territory well supplied with local roads and focusing on the Malton-Norton area in the Roman period. The territory must always have had strong links with the Roman regional capital at *Eburacum*, York, and a tendency to expand control westwards into the Vale of York. Eventually documented as an Anglo-Saxon kingdom with its own royal house, Deira was one of the foundation stones of what became Northumbria, the 'land beyond the Humber'.[29] Far to the north lay Tweed, Till and Glen valleys, and coastal lands, here termed Bamburgh/*Dinguaryoi*, using the British name that was succeeded by the Old English *Bebbanburg* ('Bebba's fortress'). This territory was more fragmented, the product of local terrains where less fertile sandstone ridges intermixed with small areas of lowland with better agricultural potential. Bernicia – whose initial focus may have been located at, and east of, the confluence of the North Tyne and South Tyne and the eastern end of Hadrian's Wall – poses many questions. The name means 'land of the mountain passes' and is singularly appropriate for this tract, with the Tyne Gap leading westwards into Cumbria.[30] The recognition of *Catraeth* adopts an insight by Nick Higham that between Deira and Bernicia there lay a third entity, a territory once in the hands of Urien of Rheged. Finally, further south, south-west

---

28 Roberts and Wrathmell, *Region and Place*, fig. 5.1.
29 Higham, *Northern Counties*, figs 4.3, 6.2 and 6.3.
30 Kenneth Jackson, *Language and History in Early Britain* (Dublin, 2000), pp.701-5.

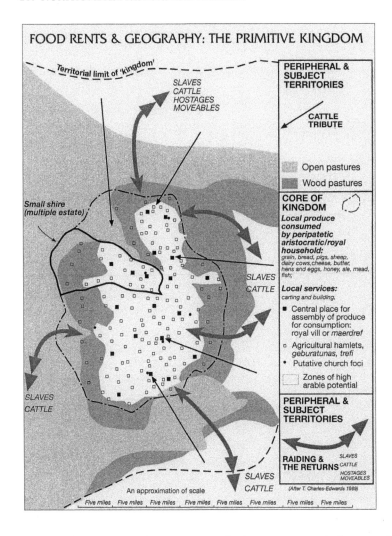

7 *Food Rents and Geography*

of York, was the territory of Elmet, set amid the woodlands around Leeds.[31] The picture is one of small tracts of better land, cultivated, populated, named and ruled: local polities sandwiched between the sea to the east, and, to the west, temperate savannas with open lands, scrub, and some blocks of woodland, together forming a 'sea' of pasture from which cattle raiders and slavers could appear. This picture may be compared with the Anglo-Scottish borders during the 15th and 16th centuries, where the reivers only have 'romance' when seen from distance.[32] Of course, these wastes also formed grazings as well as route ways, with shieling sites, summering grounds for cattle, and areas reserved for aristocratic hunting.

Can we explore the interior of these primitive kingdoms? Figure 7 creates a generalised picture. A central area of good agricultural land is well settled, with a scat-

---

31 Koch, *The Goddoddin*, xxvi-xxx, cites evidence showing Urien as a 'battle-victorious and cattle-rich sovereign', ruler of the 'men of Catraeth'. His study contains long analyses of the ancient text called *The Goddoddin* and concludes that *Catraeth* was indeed Catterick in North Yorkshire (xiii ff.). Urien was killed in 572-9 (xv). For a discussion of Elmet see Higham, *The Kingdom of Northumbria*, pp.84-5.
32 George MacDonald Fraser, *The Steel Bonnets* (London, 1995), pp.1-9.

ter of steadings and small hamlets. These are shown by the small open squares, and while in Old English these would be termed *geburatunas*, i.e. 'the settlements of the farmers', in Wales these were called *trefi*, a term sometimes appearing in Cumberland because the native pre-Anglo-Saxon population of the whole north were British, or Celtic, in character.[33] These farmers rendered produce to local rulers, the 'king', his family and chief retainers, and when Christianity appeared gifts of land were made to any churchmen the king supported. The black squares show more important settlements. These were places – royal vills – that the ruler visited regularly and where agricultural produce was collected for consumption. Loose conglomerations of hamlets were grouped into what historians call small shires, traces of which survived long into the medieval period, appearing in the records as Islandshire, Bedlingtonshire, Hexhamshire, Aucklandshire, Heighingtonshire, Burghshire, Allertonshire, Riponshire, Howdenshire and the like, each comprising one or more central localities with a lordly hall and a scatter of supporting dependencies. It is possible, indeed likely, that these 'shires', 'multiple estates' or 'extensive lordships' emerged in the period after Roman control when the money economy collapsed, but their roots may indeed be even older. In addition to renders of food and drink, the farmers also owed carting and building services. It is likely that each of the cultural cores seen in Figure 5 comprised a number of such small shires and from this base successful rulers raided neighbours and sought to draw from them tribute in the form of cattle, other produce and slaves. In this way the larger kingdoms, Deira, Catraeth and Bernicia, were established, until eventually the larger polities themselves contended for regional supremacy.[34] At first we can picture these primitive polities as surrounded by woodlands and open pastures forming border or frontier zones, but as population numbers increased, more and more of the grazing lands and wastes were colonised and permanently settled.

In Figure 8, to a base map of the cultural cores, two distributions have been added: first, the locations of burials and finds for three periods, the fifth and sixth centuries, the seventh century and finally those of the eighth century, using informative and stimulating maps created by Sam Lucy; secondly, the distribution of those Old English – Anglo-Saxon – habitation names considered the oldest.[35] The pre-eminent importance of Deira is clear: this is where immigrant Germanic people established themselves most thoroughly, an area where the rulers of long-established British populations, at first protected by Hadrian's Wall and the coastal defences, eventually invited in Germanic warriors as mercenaries. There is less evidence for the situation in Catraeth, but we must remember that the Roman villas appear at Chapel House Farm, Well, Castle Dykes, Piercebridge, Quarry Farm, with an outlier

33 Steven Basset (ed.), *The Origins of Anglo-Saxon Kingdoms* (London, 1989), chap. 2 by Thomas Charles-Edwards, 'Early medieval kingships in the British Isles'; Geoffrey Barrow, *The Kingdom of the Scots* (London, 1973), pp.7-68; Glanville R.J. Jones, 'The multiple estate as a model framework for tracing early stages in the evolution of rural settlement', in F. Dussart (ed.), *L'Habitat et les Paysages Ruraux d'Europe* (Les Congres et Colloques de l'Universite de Liege, vol. 58, 1971), pp.251-64.
34 Higham, *The Kingdom of Northumbria*, chap. 4.
35 Sam Lucy, 'Changing burial rites in Northumbria AD 500-750', in Jane Hawkes and Susan Mills, *Northumbria's Golden Age* (Stroud, 1999), pp.12-43,

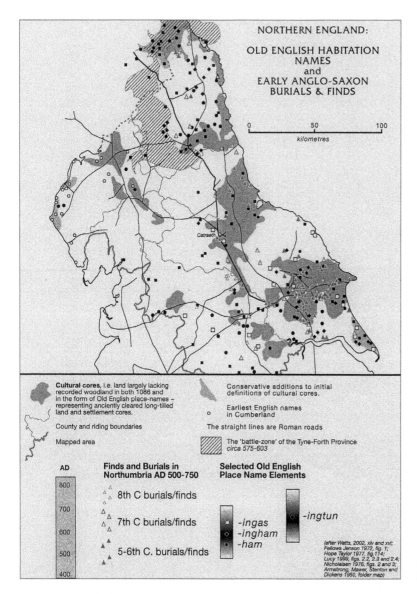

NORTHERN ENGLAND:

OLD ENGLISH HABITATION
NAMES
and
EARLY ANGLO-SAXON
BURIALS & FINDS

0   50   100
kilometres

Cultural cores, i.e. land largely lacking recorded woodland in both 1086 and in the form of Old English place-names – representing anciently cleared long-tilled land and settlement cores.

County and riding boundaries

Mapped area

Conservative additions to initial definitions of cultural cores.

Earliest English names in Cumberland

The straight lines are Roman roads

The 'battle-zone' of the Tyne-Forth Province circa 575-603

AD — **Finds and Burials in Northumbria AD 500-750**

8th C burials/finds

7th C burials/finds

5-6th C. burials/finds

Selected Old English Place Name Elements

-ingas
-ingham
-ham

-ingtun

(after Watts, 2002, xlv and xvi; Fellows Jenson 1972, fig. 1; Hope Taylor 1977, fig.114; Lucy 1999, figs. 2.2, 2.3 and 2.4; Nicholaisen 1976, figs. 2 and 3; Armstrong, Mawer, Stenton and Dickens 1950, folder map)

8 *Map: Old English Habitation Names*

at Middleham in Wensleydale, implying that this territory was also prosperous at that time. A Roman centre lay at Catterick (*Cateractonium*) and, while lacking the concentration found in Deira, a scatter of fifth- to sixth-century material implies an early Anglo-Saxon presence, perhaps employed as war bands and settled in the peripheries of the territory, along its north-east coast, as well as at the royal centre. We must remember that in both British and Anglo-Saxon societies the primary loyalties were to the chieftain and his dynasty, the family and the tribe. Violence between such groups probably exceeded that between Britons and Anglo-Saxons, accounting for kaleidoscopic patterns of alliances.[36] At first Germanic warriors

---

36 Koch, *The Goddoddin*, pp.xviii-xxi, xxx-xlii.

fought those they were paid to fight, and only later did intermarriage with local women and the rise of powerful Germanic chieftains with their own agendas initiate a process of Anglo-Saxonising the territory, perhaps by attracting further immigrant warriors and their dependants.

In Figure 8 the place name elements -*ingas* and -*ingham*, as in Easingwold, Edlingham, Billingham and Wolsingham, identify territories, estates or settlements linked to a named group or an individual, as indeed do names in -*ington*, for example Darlington, although this common construction may be of a slightly later date. Names containing -*ham*, as in Middleham, perhaps meaning a homestead, hamlet or village, may in fact pre-date names in -*ingas* and –*ingham*, and certainly in Figure 8 -*ham* names, along with -*ingas* names are seen to concentrate within or very near the cores of anciently cleared land.[37] There are unfathomable subtleties here, but what these names suggest is expansion outwards from the initial areas influenced by Germanic peoples, indicated by the fifth- and sixth-century burials. The contrast between the unity of Deira and the broken pattern of Northumberland is striking, the former suggesting perhaps more concentrated immigration by Germanic folk into a territory with a rich heartland, while the latter implies a more fragmented and less coherent pattern of Germanic land taking.[38] Nevertheless, in these patterns we glimpse something of the substance of the post-Roman polities, incipient states, and their piecemeal transition into early Germanic kingdoms such as Bernicia and Deira. Intricate warfare, blood feuds and alliances that welded these proto-kingdoms into Northumbria are not to be recounted here.[39] In addition, Figure 8 gives a realistic view of the expansion of such early polities outwards from their heartlands into the open and wooded pastures of the surrounding wastes. With such expansion it was inevitable that political conflicts and competition amongst rulers took place. Land and territory, warfare and plunder, tribute and renders were what generated the wealth that supported aristocratic lifestyles of the Northumbrian nobility.

In summary, we can envisage a series of long-settled cores, seminal zones, where husbanded soils could support significant local populations and the aristocracies who fed off the farmers. That these territories have not been finally and definitively defined is not in doubt. Nor were the territories ever completely stable, for they often broke up and reconstituted themselves. Only with the development of feudal tenures and the great estates associated with feudal landholding after the Norman Conquest of the later 11th century did the northern land systems lock into a recognisable historic pattern.[40]

---

37   Kenneth Cameron, *English Place Names* (London 1996), pp.66-72, 141-54; W.F.H. Nicholaisen, *Scottish Place-names* (London, 1976), figs 2 and 3; A.M. Armstrong, A. Mawer, F.M. Stenton and Bruce Dickens, *The Place-Names of Cumberland* (English Place-Name Society, 3 vols, 1950).

38   Undoubtedly, the whole northern series of Old English names now needs the sort of reassessment that Gillian Fellows-Jensen has undertaken for Scandinavian names (Gillian Fellows-Jensen, *Scandinavian Settlement Names in Yorkshire* (Copenhagen, 1972). More of the possible chronology of names could then be rigorously explored.

39   While place-name scholars do not systematically map them, the place of Old English topographic names – possibly in fact some the earliest in the sequence – is worth exploring. In Durham a proportion of names, such as Gainford, Coniscliffe, Egglescliffe, Aycliffe and Kellow, were once the centres of small shire estates.

40   Sydney Middlebrook, *Newcastle upon Tyne: Its Growth and Achievement* (Wakefield, 1968), fig. facing 35.

Early Polities and Peripheralities: a Short Case Study

Into this context came Christianity. At first this was Celtic, Irish in character, but after AD 627 the area came increasingly under the influence of York and its brand of Roman Christianity.[41] There can be no doubt that in Durham and Northumberland the earliest Anglo-Saxon stone sculptures, many bearing the burden of association with monastic foundations, are set on the edges of the embryonic states.[42] On one side lay the coast and the sea while on the other lay great 'seas' of waste, open rough land and some woodland. The importance of the seacoast in the location of Jarrow and Monkwearmouth has long been noted, while Lindisfarne, Hartlepool and Whitby all show the same land/sea liminality, as do Coldingham in Berwickshire and *Tyninghame* further north in East Lothian.[43] All these sites had access to some agricultural land (although certainly not of the best) and to the produce taken from the sea and, not least, to relatively easy and rapid travel along east coast seaways. There can be no better example of this than Whitby, difficult of access by land, particularly in winter, but selected as the location of a church meeting or synod in the year AD 664. A second set of sites, identified by stone crosses and grave markers and some early stone churches, are found inland, at or just beyond what may be thought of as a 'cultural shoreline' between the great wastes and the cultivated and more populated core regions. Sites such as Hexham, Corbridge, Gateshead, Gainford, Gilling, Ripon, Lastingham and Hackness confirm this pattern of liminality between relatively well populated and almost unpopulated zones. It is hard to believe on the basis of the surviving seventh-century churches that Escomb and Staindrop were not also monastic sites, but they were never documented as such, while place-names such as Ebchester and Romaldkirk hint at other foundations. Of course, many of these sites had deeper roots in British or Irish Christian foundations.[44]

We can see this process from surviving documentation: between c.654 to 656 Oedelwald, King of Deira, granted to Cedd, Bishop of the East Saxons, land to endow a monastery at Lastingham; between c.658 to 661 Alhfrith, sub-king of Deira, granted land to Wilfred at Ripon to found a monastery. At a later stage, between 830 and 845, Ecred, Bishop of Lindisfarne, granted Gainford to the church of St Cuthbert with its land in south Durham between the Dere Street and the hills to the west, land already in his possession. In about 883 Guthfrith, King of Northumbria, granted the great wedge of land in north-west Durham between the Tyne and the Wear and from 'the Dere Street to the sea', a grant inclusive of properties in *Werehale* that were formerly held by the monasteries at Jarrow and Monkwearmouth but by that date destroyed

41 Higham, *The Kingdom of Northumbria*, pp.119-39.

42 Rosemary Cramp, *County Durham and Northumberland* (Corpus of Anglo-Saxon Stone Sculpture, British Academy, 2 parts, 1984), figs 1,2 and 3; Richard Bailey and Rosemary Cramp, *Cumberland and Westmorland* (*ibid.*, 1988), figs 1,2 and 3; James Lang, *York and Eastern Yorkshire* (*ibid.*, 1991), figs 1, 3 and 4; James Lang, *Northern Yorkshire* (*ibid.*, 2001), figs 4 and 5.

43 The first element in Lindisfarne is the old name of North Lincolnshire, *Lindis*, and the second is *faran* (meaning 'travellers'). Eilert Ekwall, *The Concise Oxford Dictionary of English Place-Names* (Oxford, 1960), pp.298-9.

44 Higham, *The Kingdom of Northumbria*, pp.119-23, 149-66.

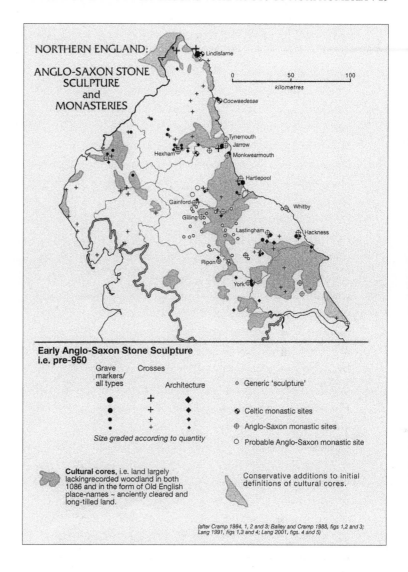

9 *Map: Anglo-Saxon Sculpture and Monasteries*

by Viking raiding.[45] Sometimes these grants are described in terms of 10, 40 or 50 *familiae*, 'families', either implying that peasants were already settled on the land or that the land had the potential to support that number. The correlation between these grants and their peripherality to older farmed cores suggests that reclamation and colonisation was taking place.

Of Land, People and Time

It is inevitable that the century and a half before AD 600 is a deeply shadowed time, with local leaders and their war bands vying for power that was often short-lived.

---

45 Hart, C.R., *The Early Charters of Northern England and the North Midlands* (Leicester, 1975), pp.131ff.

The shadows the maps represent allow us a glimpse of territorial patterns in what was essentially a borderland or marcher zone. To the north, and focused north of the Tweed, were the descendants of the Iron-Age Votadini, known as the Goddoddin by the mid-fifth century. To the south, in eastern Yorkshire, lay Deira, early settled by Germanic people, but established within the territory of the Iron-Age Parisii and whatever Roman-British polity succeeded them. Bernicia's British name was probably attached to the southern province of the Votadini between the Tweed and the Tyne, while, because of deficiencies in the record, *Catraeth,* as a territory and not merely a place, appears only in verse in praise of Urien of Rheged, a ruler whose effective base lay to the west in the Eden and Lyvennet valleys.[46] A great battle seems to have taken place at Catterick, the place, in *c.*570, when a confederacy of British warriors from Goddoddin to the far north, was heavily defeated by war bands termed 'Deirans'. The role of one British king, Urien, is critical. I see him as a British ruler who had extended his control over Catraeth. He was in confederacy with the Deirans and so operating with war bands of mixed British and Anglo-Saxon stock. In a magisterial review of the documentary evidence for the building of Northumbria, David Dumville[47] pointed to possible temporal way marks for any analysis: kingship in Deira is attested only from the 560s, although is likely to have been of greater antiquity, while Ida, the founder of the Anglo-Saxon ruling Bernician dynasty, centred at Bamburgh, traditionally took control in 547. Some Germanic settlement appeared in Deira by the middle of the fifth century, approximately within a decade or so of AD 450, and in Bernicia by about 500. None of these dates are beyond doubt, while an even less certain reference implies that Deira was separated from Bernicia – presumably the result of the conquest of Deira by Germanic rulers – again in the middle decades of the fifth century.[48]

Traditionally, Bamburgh and Bernicia were joined together by Ida, initiating the formation of a larger proto-Northumbrian kingdom.[49] However, Aethelfrith (592-616) was, it is said, the first Bernician king to rule Deira, probably in the decade 605-16, and Bede – who, it must be admitted, was notably 'anti-British' in his sentiments – notes that Aethelfrith 'conquered more territories from the Britons, either making them tributary or driving the inhabitants clear out, and planting English in their places'.[50] Important questions arise about the place of Catraeth within the pattern of early states. Warfare and expansion from a Bernician heartland north of the Tyne, implied in Figure 8, must inevitably have also involved thrusts southwards into and through the territory of Catraeth. It seems likely that Urien's death between 572-9 while besieging Theoderic of Bernicia (upon Lindisfarne) opened more fully the door for Bernician expansion southwards towards Deira.[51] Indeed, we can suggest

---

46 Koch, *The Goddoddin,* xv, xxvi-xxx, xxxiii, xl and xli; Thomas Owen Clancy (ed.), *The Triumph Tree* (Edinburgh, 1998), pp.79-90, notably p.87.
47 David Dumville, 'The Origins of Northumberland', in Steven Bassett, *Anglo-Saxon Kingdoms,* pp.213-22.
48 Higham, *The Kingdom of Northumbria,* p.78, fig. A.
49 Brian Hope-Taylor, *Yeavering: an Anglo-British centre of early Northumbria* (Her Majesty's Stationery Office, 1977) pp.285, 297.
50 Hope Taylor, *Yeavering,* p.285.
51 Koch, *The Goddoddin,* pp.xl-xlii.

that Aethelfrith's major conquests could only occur if Catraeth's rich and diverse agricultural lands had already been absorbed by him, perhaps between about AD 592 and 603. This expansion southwards of an Anglo-Saxon ruler based north of the Tyne would inevitably bring him into contact, if not conflict, with the Deirans who had been expanding westwards and northwards in the Vale of York. Whatever the detail, Aethelfrith's success ensured that the peoples living north of the Humber, both British and Anglo-Saxon, were drawn together into one kingdom and that their war bands were then able to create wider conquests, achieving victory over a British army at Chester in c.615. Political intrigue and warfare, both within the region and between Northumbria and its neighbours, continued to be a formative factor alongside the growth of the Anglo-Saxon church, once Roman Christianity was firmly established in AD 664 at the Synod of Whitby.[52] Included within Figure 8 are those sites where the Old English element *burh*, meaning 'a fortification', must have emerged from this troubled time, often, it will be noted, generally set peripheral to the polity cores, often with a relationship to both Roman roads and/or sea routes. Nevertheless, we must assume throughout, in spite of warfare, state building and the expansion of church power, that there was a steady increase in the numbers of farmers winning from the land the food needed to support all the ruling classes, kings, warriors, administrators, churchmen – and women – in their conspicuous consumption. At the level of the farmers there must have been sustained and relatively peaceful interaction between Britons and Anglo-Saxons, often no doubt with sex as the lubricant.

There is an essential convergence in the conclusions drawn from analysis of the maps created for this study. All of the four threads defined at the outset intertwine around the nature of the land. Links are present not in any crude deterministic sense but in the fact that the nature of the land provides the practical setting within which, and with which, successive societies established a *modus vivendi*, elements of continuity being always present. Land with a good agricultural potential and sustained husbandry provided essential economic support for all. Grain, cattle and people – farmers – were the foundation of all wealth, and regional differences that were the gift of nature have bound together all developments through time. The 'cleared land-open pasture-wood pasture' contrasts that underlie Northumbrian cultural geography and landscapes undoubtedly take root in prehistory. The contrasts they represent are a linking theme, not only through the time span of this discussion, but right into the period of industrial development in the 18th and 19th centuries, when, for instance, early coal pits, mining villages and waggon ways were often sited with reference to the waste lands surviving or recently enclosed. The location of a group of early monastic foundations, perhaps often with British precursors, in inland locations near the agricultural frontiers of the seventh century is surely an indicator of one role they were expected to play. In practical terms, the cultural cores containing royal estates, with monastic and other church foundations set at their edges, formed

---

52 Higham, *The Kingdom of Northumbria*, pp.76-83, 112, 113-24 and 132-9.

bases from which physical and cultural colonisation led to the eventual creation of the unified kingdom of Northumbria. The patterns that appeared remain part of the regional heritage, persisting in the Old English place-names that still frame our present lives, as indeed do 'the brine', 'the high ground' and 'the fresh stream' waters of the great rivers of Cunedda's praise poem, which may in fact come to us from a period as early as the fifth century AD.[53]

---

53 Koch, *The Goddoddin*, pp.xli.

3

'The Start of Everything Wonderful': The Old English Poetry of Northumbria

BILL GRIFFITHS

The North East of what was to become England was relatively tardily settled by 'Angles', in comparison with the 'Saxons' in the south of the country. Immigrants ventured to Kent and along the Thames and the Wash by the mid-fifth century AD, but Ida's foothold on Lindisfarne is traditionally dated to 547. Despite this, Northumbria was soon to rival Kent in its enthusiasm for Christianity and was first of all the Anglo-Saxon regions (kingdoms, if you prefer) to develop a culture of creativity that still has the power to impress.

This leap into prominence seems the result of adverse rather than favourable conditions. Northumbria was crucially divided in its allegiance between the two focuses of Bernicia (typified by the royal palace at Yeavering and the monasteries of Lindisfarne, Hexham and Jarrow) and Deira (typified by the churches of Ripon and York), leading to dynastic rivalry and occasionally overt hostility. This Christianity had its own tensions, resulting from the conflicting missionary influences of the Roman tradition from Kent, and the Celtic tradition from Ireland. Their subtly different emphases were resolved at the Synod of Whitby (664) in favour of the Roman Church; and Cuthbert, raised in the Celtic form of the faith, but accepting the transfer to Rome, became a symbol of the dual culture of the time: he was both hermit in the Celtic manner and bishop after the approved Roman model. That Bede was commissioned to write the definitive life of this saint is no coincidence: Cuthbert, with his humility, wisdom and empowerment, was the believable personification of northern Christianity, bringing to unity its rich roots in diverse traditions. It is both out of and because of this potentially unstable context that the flowering of Northumbrian arts took place.

Our appreciation of the culture of Anglian Northumbria today depends primarily on the beauty of the illuminated manuscripts, secondarily the surviving churches and monumental crosses – solid exhibits which we can all admire; but just as enduring (and more influential) has proved its 'intangible heritage' – the Latin works of Bede and his contemporaries, and – as damaged and enigmatic as any physical artefact – the poetic texts in Old English. The vernacular poetry is difficult to access because of the disquietingly 'alien' look and vocabulary of Old English and, to complicate the situation, only a handful of poetic texts can be ascribed to Northumbria with any certainty. This situation derives partly from the homogeneity of OE verse composition (in style, metre, diction, vocabulary), and partly from a general lack of indication of authorship or date for surviving poems. Yet the Northumbria of 650-750 can reasonably claim a high place as the initiator of Anglo-Saxon literary endeavour at a time when vernacular literature was slow to develop on mainland Europe.[1]

Caedmon's Hymn *and the techniques of OE poetry*

Caedmon's Hymn is one poem whose northern origin is clear – it is established when it was written and where and by whom. But it is only a short verse, that takes its place beside *Bede's Death Song* and the solitary 'Leiden' riddle as securely Northumbrian.[2] A short form of *The Dream of the Rood* is similarly attested by its place on the Ruthwell Cross (Dumfriesshire), though its relationship to the long form of the poem in the *Vercelli Book* manuscript remains problematic. A brief poetic couplet on the Franks Casket is Northumbrian by virtue of the artefact it adorns. Beyond that, claims remain unproven,[3] and the truly impressive *Beowulf* – of admired length and quality alike – continues to be an academic orphan. Its date of composition has been assessed at anything from the seventh century (because of its affinity with the main Sutton Hoo burial) to the early 11th century (the latest date for the sole manuscript). It is not our obtuseness, or lack of endeavour, that causes this uncertainty: the Anglo-Saxon poet seldom or never aimed at personal acclaim. His (or her) work was designed to fit into a tradition that was communal, anonymous and conformable.

The techniques of Old English verse are sufficiently conventional – static, one might almost say – to make dating by internal metrical evidence well-nigh impossible. The line definition depends on alliterative pattern (a sort of 'forward rhyme', suitable to linking words in languages where the stress falls on the first main or 'tonic' syllable of a word), and this is a structure common to other Germanic poetries (e.g. Old Saxon, Old Norse), not an invention of the Anglo-Saxons. Nonetheless, there is good reason

---

1   Missionaries to the continent, like Willibrord (658-731) to Frisia and Boniface (d.754) to Saxony, surely carried Anglo-Saxon cultural influence far afield. Christian vernacular poetry like the Old Saxon *Heliand c.*830 and OHG *Muspili c.*870 could well owe their inspiration to OE poetry.

2   A.H. Smith (ed.), *Three Northumbrian Poems* (Exeter University Press, 1978). An able recent edition is Daniel Paul O'Donnell, *Cædmon's Hymn: A Multi-media Study, Edition and Archive* (Woodbridge, 2005).

3   Various candidates have been put forward for inclusion in the Northumbrian 'canon', e.g. the OE poem *Andreas* (see A.S. Cook, 'The OE *Andreas* and Bishop Acca of Hexham', *Trans. of the Connecticut Academy of Arts & Sciences*, vol. 26 (1924), pp.245-332). In my *North-East Dialect: the texts* (Centre for Northern Studies, 2nd edn., 2002) I propose the *OE Rune Poem*. Such inclusions are unproven, but it is important to remember that cultural life in Northumbria by no means ceased with the Viking invasion.

for placing Caedmon at the head of the OE verse tradition. Or at least at the head of that tradition of verse we might call 'high poetry'.

In this style of verse, a 'classical' alliterative line is used with typically four stresses: one or two alliterations in the first half of the line link to an obligatory alliteration on the third stress. *Caedmon's Hymn* is the earliest example we have of this technique in OE, though we may assume some centuries of oral poetry preceding it. It is a modest enough composition, but it probably was then, and certainly is now, an icon of some significance – historically, culturally and metrically. The story from Bede's *Ecclesiastical History* is well enough known. The cowherd Caedmon is ashamed of his own lack of performance skill, but finds he is imbued with the power of composition after a dream in which a certain figure ('*quidam per somnium*', Bede bk 4 ch.24) commands him to produce song. Bede (whose caution may be as much a matter of avoiding controversy and doctrinal incorrectness as love of accuracy and respect for history) refuses to commit himself as to what kind of being this dream-visitor was. To ascribe the power to God, or even an angel, might seem inappropriate in the case of a cultural accessory like poetry. Miracles in Bede tend to be used like stars of approval: Cuthbert and Oswald receive many, the awkward Wilfrid is graded much lower. The inclusion of a miracle or a dream-vision in Bede's text is therefore a judicious, almost a political, act. But he also knew well enough the value of a good story, and was content to include the apparent miracle of Caedmon as part of his appendix to the life of St Hild, and to her credit.

This enables us to date Caedmon's experience to between 657 (the foundation of Whitby Abbey where Caedmon served) and 680 (the date of Hild's death). Thus we have the name of the poet as well as a location and a date – something pretty well unique in OE literature. However, Bede only gave a Latin version of the 'hymn', and it is to Anglo-Saxon scribes who restored the Old English as annotations to his Latin that we owe the text. There is no reason to doubt the authenticity of their contribution, and the earliest versions containing the OE 'Hymn' (the Moore and Leningrad manuscripts of Bede) date from within a decade or so of the composition of the *Ecclesiastical History* (completed 731). And this is it:

> Nu scilun *h*erga[n] *h*efen-ricæs uard,
> *Now we-should praise / heaven-kingdom's Guardian,*
>
> *m*etudæs *m*ehti and his *m*od-githanc,
> *Maker's might / and his mind-thankfulness (=mercifulness),*
>
> *u*erc *u*uldur-fadur sue he *u*undra gihuæs,
> *work of-glory-father / as he (of) wonders each,*
>
> *e*ci dryctin, *o*r astelidæ.
> *eternal Lord, / the-start established.*

He ærist scop *a*ldu barnum
He first formed / (for) men's sons

*h*efen to *h*rofæ, *h*alig sceppend.
heaven (=the sky) as roof, / holy Creator.

Tha *m*iddangard *m*oncynnes uard,
Then middle-earth / mankind's Guardian,

*e*ci dryctin, *æ*fter tiadæ
eternal Lord, afterwards ordained

*f*irum *f*oldu, *f*rea allmehtig.
for-people the-ground, / Lord almighty.

(Italicised letters in the OE bear the alliteration.)

In assessing this verse, an initial reaction might reasonably be puzzlement, even disappointment. It is both rather simple and yet convoluted, a condensed but obscure retelling of the story of the Creation; the style may seem rather laboured and reiterative. The adherence to a regular metrical structure partly accounts for this: redundancy of material is a product of the obligation to construct alliterative lines. (Formulas like 'ece drihten' are in effect useful ways of building an alliterative line: nearly every line above contains such formulae.) Other typical features are the use of compound nouns and a subordination of word order to alliterative need (possible in a fully inflected language like OE). Probably such techniques were already a feature of OE verse; it is Caedmon that is attributed with the first attempt to use the resources of vernacular verse in England for a Christian purpose. Bede further says that Caedmon went on to compose other songs or poems on religious themes, but whether he had any hand in the OE poems on biblical themes that have come down to us (Exodus and Genesis, for example) is – on balance – unlikely. They are generally of extended narrative form, whereas *Caedmon's Hymn* is more like a praise song in honour of God.[4] Along with the two other early verses from Northumbria in OE, it is evidence for the composition of short religious poems in the vernacular by the mid- to late-seventh century, arguably on the model of Latin piety; and with an indefinable debt to Irish vernacular composition,[5] yet an innovation sufficiently significant to add a special lustre to the cultural achievement we acknowledge as the 'Golden Age' of

4   Disquietingly similar to the *Caedmon's Hymn* is the opening of the *Lay of Grimnir* in the *Elder Edda*, traditional Old Norse texts set down *c.*1200: 'From Ymir's flesh the world was shaped / from his blood the salt sea / from his eyelashes the High Ones made middle-earth for men, / and from his brain the ugly-tempered clouds….' This may be a matter of common Germanic formulae; no Norse or even local pagan influence on seventh-century Northumbrian culture is expected, though the reverse is always possible.
5   The dependence on Irish literature is difficult to assess: Irish and Welsh vernacular poetry rhymes, and is more akin to the Latin hymn tradition, quite apart from the inevitable problems of dating and according priority; yet the Celtic respect for the vernacular could itself have served as an important model. For a useful overview of artefacts see Lloyd & Jennifer Laing, *Art of the Celts* (London, 1995), ch.5.

Northumbria. (Some self-promotion at that time must be reckoned with: while Bede is far from disparaging about the achievements of Christianity in Canterbury and elsewhere in England, his *Ecclesiastical History* establishes the status of Bernicia on the very eve of York becoming an archbishopric.)

The influence of Caedmon and other early Northumbrian poetry is considerably greater than might appear from a first scan of such short verses. Its priority in this new field of cultural endeavour led to the peculiarities of Northumbrian (or at least Anglian) grammar and vocabulary being adopted as proper to all verse composition in later Anglo-Saxon England – and to the confirmation of a particular poetic language that was still honoured by West Saxon scribes writing copies (and composing verse) in the 10th and 11th centuries. This consistency of tradition adds much to the problem of dating and localising any OE verse composition; yet in a sense it means that all OE verse is Northumbrian verse.

The Franks Casket

A brighter, more approachable fragment of OE verse is included in runes as part of the decoration of the whalebone box known as the Franks Casket, a Northumbrian artefact of the early eighth century. The wonderful carving exhibits both pictures and text: the scenes are equally religious and secular e.g. the Adoration of the Magi and the legend of Weland the Smith. The OE verse couplet celebrates the unwitting donor – the whale itself:

> Fisc flodu ahof on fergenberig
> warþ gasric grorn þær he on greut giswom
>
> (this-fish the-tide raised/stranded onto mountain-mound/shore;
> was ocean-beast mournful when he on the-grit/beach swam/ended-up.)

followed by the words 'hronæs ban' (whales bone) as though in solution to the riddle.

The form of expression is idiomatic and alliterative, but the choice of subject is neither humorous nor naïve; rather it celebrates the material that gave scope to the craftmanship, bringing our attention to the skill of the carving in an indirect and modest but entirely appropriate way. In two short lines it presents a vivid image, as graphic in a sense as the carved figures themselves, and likely to appeal to us today in a way *Caedmon's Hymn* cannot, for it deals with the tangible, directly and intimately.

ᚠᛁᛋᚳ·ᚠᛚᛟᛞᚢ·ᚪᚻᛟᚠ·ᛟᚾ·ᚠᛖᚱᚷᛖᚾᛒᛖᚱ

ᚦᚠᚱᚦ·ᚷᚪᛋᚱᛁ·ᚷᚱᛟᚱᚾ·ᚦᚪᚱ·ᚻᛖ·ᛟᚾ·ᚷᚱᛖᚢᛏ·ᚷᛁᚦᛟᛗ

10 *Franks Casket runes*

This does not mean it was a different tradition in Anglo-Saxon terms: the reality of the world (its science, if you prefer) was in every aspect subtended by God; the monsters of the deep, the fates of men, the operation of moon and tides were equally natural, explicable, significant in terms of the deity.

Nor does the use of runes for the inscription set the couplet apart. Runes were a version of the Latin alphabet adapted to carving on wood (and subsequently other solid materials), a separate tradition from that of ink on parchment, but a practical and not a pagan alternative. Whenever a stick is split or a plank smoothed, vertical strokes at right angles to the grain will show, and diagonal strokes likewise, but not horizontal cuts in the same direction as the grain. And that factor seems adequate to explain the form of the runic alphabet.[6] It is associated in Anglo-Saxon times with public inscriptions (on monuments, coins) and the secular world (jewels, rings and similar craftworks), and might be expected to be more easily recognisable in the non-monastic sphere than the true Roman alphabet. (In fact, several useful runes e.g. 'thorn', the form for 'th', later common as the 'y' of 'ye olde teashoppe', were adopted into use in writing manuscripts also.) Runes were no more (and no less) magical than any other alphabet.

The Ruthwell Cross

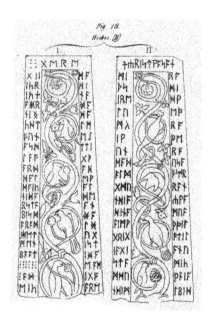

11 *J.M. Kemble's presentation in* Archeologia *vol.28 (1840) of Hickes' late 17th-century engraving of the runic panels on the Ruthwell Cross.*

On a higher dramatic plane is that section of the poem known as 'The Dream of the Rood' which survives on the Ruthwell Cross of the early to mid-eighth century. On the margins of two faces of the stone cross are inscribed four strips of runic lettering comprising a short passage as though spoken in the first person by the Cross of the Crucifixion. The inscription is now rather eroded – it was broken and buried by zealous Puritans in the 17th century, to be excavated and rehabilitated in the early 19th – but despite some damage and loss, the text (in runes) is at least partly recoverable. Also in doubt is its relationship to the longer poem dubbed *The Dream of the Rood*, found in the late 10th-century Vercelli Book,[7] in which an extended speech by the Cross, narrating the story of the Passion and the iconic significance of the Cross, is set as a 'dream vision', framed by an introduction and conclusion as spoken in the person of the dreamer.

This first person technique used (by the Cross itself) in both poems is typical of the Latin riddle

---

6 cf. P. Hunter Blair, *Northumbria in the Days of Bede* (London, 1976), p.158.
7 Vercelli Biblioteca Capitolare CXVII in Italy, where it was deposited or left stranded by Anglo-Saxon pilgrims.

format: such a riddle on the Cross by Tatwine (eighth-century)[8] is actually alluded to in the Vercelli *Dream*, but it cannot be asserted that the Ruthwell version has any similar direct dependence. Might it be a complete short poem or group of poems in its own right – comparable to other brief compositions attested in Northumbria – even composed especially for the Ruthwell monument? We can best explore this possibility by relaying a translation of the text on the cross (restored words, after the Vercelli version, are given in brackets):

1.
+ Stripped himself God almighty / when he purposed to ascend the gallows,
Brave before (all people)…

2.
I (raised up) the powerful King, Heaven's Lord: bow down I dared not.
People derided us both together. / I …

3.
+ Christ was on the cross.
Yet the keen ones / from afar came,
Noble people to the solitary one. / I witnessed all that …

4.
All pitted with arrows.
They laid him down, tortured of limbs. / They positioned themselves (at either end of his body.) …

Above represents the four vertical strips of runes, the bottom portion of which is lost in each case; to go further is tricky, as there are major differences between these lines and the corresponding material in the Vercelli version. Yet this is all the evidence we have. The four strips occupy two faces of the monument, and the initial + sign suggests that the poem is to be divided into two not four parts: Christ ascending and suffering on the Cross; and the Descent from the Cross. The whole is given a merciless impact by being narrated by the Cross in the first person.

But is it really a unified (albeit two-part) composition, potentially complete in itself? The snag here is the opening of fragment 3: it has impact, but it is only a half-line, without any resolution of the alliteration. This could suggest a pre-existing text that has been condensed to fit and make best use of the space available.

The text, or something like it, was clearly well known, as it is paralleled by the inscription on the 'Brussels Cross', a reliquary of *c*.1000:

---

8   The name *Beowulf* ('Bee-wolf') is generally taken to refer to a bear. The Brothers Grimm in their *Deutsches Woerterbuch* have an entry for *Bienenwolf*, which refers to a (later) German animal fable in which the name equals 'woodpecker'.

Rod is min nama. Geo ic ricne cyning
Cross is my name. Once I (the) powerful king

bær byfigendes, blode bestemed
Bore-aloft, trembling (was) with-blood drenched.

The fullest version, lines 39 to 65 in the Vercelli Book, *Dream of the Rood*, reads as follows:

Then the young man stripped himself, who was Almighty God;
bold, determined, he mounted the degrading gallows
brave in the face of the crowd, when he intended to free mankind.
I trembled as the man embraced me, but I dared not bow to the ground
or fall to the face of the earth: I had to stay firm in place.
As the rood I was reared up, I raised the Mighty King on high,
the very Lord of the Heavens, bow low I dared not!
They drove sombre nails into me: the signs of it are still visible,
open wounds of hate; but I dared not harm them any.
They derided us both as a pair: I was all with the blood hot-washed
that poured from his side as he surrendered his spirit.
There upon the hill I endured great hardship: I saw the Lord of Hosts
vilely racked. Then darkness wrapped
with its shadows the Saviour's body;
clouds obscured the day-shine
leaving it lightless under the sky. Lamenting his death,
all creation wept, for Christ on the cross.
Then eager helpers came from afar
to this prince's aid. I beheld it all.
I was with much sorrow troubled, yet I submitted to their hands,
humble in my courage. There they took hold of Almighty God,
lifted him down from the awful punishment. For then the soldiers had abandoned me,
left me standing splashed with blood, all pitted from sharp points.
They took him cramped of limb and stood them by the corpse's head.
There they gazed at the Lord of Heaven, as he rested himself a little while,
weary from the great ordeal ...

The several versions certainly attest the wide popularity of the image of the Cross (from Constantine's time onwards) and rather tell against a single line of descent of a fixed text. It may in the end be meaningless to debate whether the Vercelli *Dream* is an extension of the Ruthwell text, or the Ruthwell text an extract from a poem like the longer Vercelli. Opinion generally favours the unity (and therefore, in a sense, the 'priority') of the Vercelli version,[9] yet there is a terseness in the Ruthwell text that

---

9   For text of the riddle and much useful information on the OE poem see Jane Roberts, 'Some relationships between the Dream of the Rood and the Cross at Ruthwell', *Studies in Medieval English Language & Literature* (Tokyo), vol.15 (2000), pp.1-25.

ill accords with the verbose and rather sophisticated composition that is the Vercelli Book version. The latter is a more accomplished, extensive literary achievement; but the Ruthwell text has an energy that gains from its very brevity. In the longer Vercelli *Dream*, the Ruthwell 'episode' is arguably the most stark and effective part.

Beowulf?

The heyday of Northumbrian power was surprisingly brief: in Hunter Blair's view the fall of York in 867 'may be taken to mark the final destruction of the Northumbian kingdom'.[10]

The pitiable fate of Northumbria in the Viking period (793 on) hardly needs retelling. Anglo-Saxon monasteries, with their wooden outbuildings (probable) thatch or heather roofs, and so-vulnerable investment in manuscripts, were not easily defensible. Much of their heritage was combustible, and a torch would have been as feared a Viking weapon as a sword. Some gold and silver was likely to be accumulated in such religious centres, but their real wealth lay in landed estates. Vikings, brutal but not stupid, soon realised the potential here: if they knocked out or at least disabled the monastic organisation, then considerable land was freed for them to pick up and claim as their own. The associated change from raiding to settling may have been a long-term strategy as much as an afterthought or some pacification of Viking society. Yielding them land had a sort of mutual advantage: if the Church was content to share, there was no reason prelate and pagan could not co-exist and stability be re-established.

Monastic communities could and did survive the Viking challenge, if in an impoverished form: the story of the Community of St Cuthbert and its wanderings is one of the great English Church legends, and provides not only evidence of the practical power of saints like Cuthbert and Oswald, and the endurance in faith of their monks, but equally illustrates the common need of Christian and Viking to come to some sort of accommodation. A symbol of this could be the very name 'Durham' (*Deora holm*, 'the peninsula of wild animals'), combining what are taken to be Old English and Old Norse elements.

But the route to Durham lay through Chester-le-Street. Here the Community of St Cuthbert made its base from the 880s to the 990s, and it was during this period that Athelstan, King of the West Saxons, came to do honour to St Cuthbert, and restore to the Community some measure of its estranged lands (AD 934). The occasion was marked by the presentation of a copy of Bede's *Life of Cuthbert* – the original manuscript survives, remarkably, as Christ's College Cambridge MS 183. 'None of his predecessors on the throne loved the church of St Cuthbert as he did; none beautified it with gifts so numerous and so regal,' as Symeon of Durham put it. How did the Community acknowledge these substantial favours?

---

10   Hunter Blair, *op.cit.*, p.223.

It is quite likely that some of the OE poems we consider as 'secular' were monastic compositions, for who else had the time to practise the 'high' poetic tradition? When poems seem to 'quote' each other, is this a sign of oral tradition or awareness of written sources (or recollection of memorised written sources)? And is this the key to the great problem of dating OE verse – that its technical consistency derives from an ever-present manuscript corpus as a reference source?

We can justify the composition of secular verse in a monastic context if examples were written as presentations to lay patrons who earned respect by making great gifts to the Church. *The Battle of Maldon* – apparently a battle poem with a purely secular frame of reference – may arguably have been the monastic riposte to a grant of land and the gift of a tapestry from Byrthnoth's widow. That would at least account for the puzzling role that is accorded Byrthnoth as hero of the poem: he is a layman and capable of making mistakes; but he is a Christian and thus his noble death is given a martyristic colouring inside a 'heroic' poem.

Lay patrons would naturally expect some return for their donations to the Church. Benefit for their souls thereafter, certainly; a preservation of their memory in the local church calendar; some of that enduring 'dom' or reputation and renown that Beowulf rated so highly. But a tangible in-the-hand acknowledgement would surely be politic. The Church could hardly give a precious object in return – that would be to reverse the process of donation; but a poem – a sample of the intellectual achievement that the Church stood for (in one sense) – would be just the kind of the return that a lay patron might be expected to appreciate.

That the Community of St Cuthbert thought highly of Athelstan there can be no doubt. An inscription in his honour was added to the *Liber Vitae* – the book listing 'saved' souls (the members and patrons of the monastic community), a record of all those thought worthy to enter Heaven and a manuscript so important that the Community carried it with them throughout their wanderings. The grants that Athelstan bestowed on them included much land in eastern County Durham that arguably gave them the status and orientation to arrange a home in due course on the peninsula of Durham itself.

It is doubtless chance that the name 'Beowulf' (in the form 'Biuulf' or 'Biwulf') is included in this same *Liber Vitae* of Durham. It is part of a standard list, not emphasised in any way, and refers back to a monk of the pre-Viking period. Yet it is strange that this is the only recorded use of the name in England outside the poem. If the monk 'Beowulf' and the poem *Beowulf* have no other connection, this reference in the *Liber Vitae* is at least evidence that the unusual name was current in Northumbria.[11]

The poem is a celebration of a hero of superhuman dimension ('epic' as the narration of the adventures of a quasi-divine being through the medium of direct speech?). A member of a poorly documented tribe, the Geats, Beowulf arrives in Denmark to

---

11   For opinions on the unity of the Vercelli *Dream*, and its 'several distinct poetic experiences or strategies which give insight into the idea of the cross', see Carol Pasternak, 'Stylistic disjunction in The Dream of the Rood', *Anglo-Saxon England* vol.13 (1984), pp.167-86 (quotation from p.170).

help the worthy but ineffective King Hrothgar by ridding him of two monsters. Later in the poem, Beowulf tackles a dragon that threatens his home community back in Sweden – but himself dies in the act of victory.

Convincing arguments have been made for the composition of the poem by one author,[12] but that does not necessarily mean it was composed all in one go. Its quality of writing (the ability to use appropriate and effective words or invented compounds to construct alliterative verse) argues for painstaking composition over a long period. The episode with the dragon is so detached (in space, in time and in mood) from the glorious exploits of the younger Beowulf, that it almost seems a reaction to what has gone before. Has the poet regretted indulgence in the heroic ethos, and sought to make amends in a more balanced and cautionary conclusion? That the poem begins and ends with a funeral scene is no guarantee that it was thought out, as a whole, in advance: the scene of Scyld's boat funeral that opens the poem may well have been included to do honour to the pagan ancestors mentioned there, a lineage that was common to the kings of Wessex and Denmark, and to slip in an advance mention of the name 'Beowulf' in that honourable context.

The marvels of the Sutton Hoo find in Suffolk gave impetus to attributing an early date to the composition of Beowulf; but it should be remembered that boat funerals are also found in the Viking period.[13] The unusual aspects of Scyld's funeral suggest an antiquarian re-creation rather than contemporary record: a sense of ancient ambience for those who would not be well aware of the detail, and shedding a sort of historical verisimilitude on the legendary material that follows. Paradoxically, the whole poem is set in a consciously Christian mode: its well-known depiction of a 'haunted mere' echoes the apocryphal *Visio Pauli*. The dragon (I have argued) is of a Romano-Greek, non-Germanic type,[14] and not therefore a pagan oral composition, but a product of the established Christian epoch in England (from the eighth century on).

The further arguments that place the composition of *Beowulf* in the post-Viking period are detailed elsewhere;[15] the figure of Scyld as a common ancestor to both the Danish and West Saxon royal houses may be a gambit of conciliation, for it appears no earlier than the mid-ninth-century portion of the *Anglo-Saxon Chronicle*, and could be an Alfredian intervention.[16] The poem's attitude to the Danes is respectful, but

---

12   On the unity of language of *Beowulf*, see Janet Bately, 'Linguistic evidence as a guide to authorship…', in *Learning and literature in Anglo-Saxon England* (ed. M. Lapidge and H. Gneuss, 1985).

13   Boat funerals are not necessarily early in date. Viking examples of the late ninth century have been found at Ballodoole on the Isle of Man and recently in Yorkshire (per *The Guardian* 17 Feb 2004). That at Sandy in the Orkneys is dated to 875 x 950.

14   The flying, fire-breathing dragon of *Beowulf* seems to derive from Eastern (Roman, Byzantine) sources. See my *Meet the Dragon: An introduction to Beowulf's Adversary* (Loughborough, 1996).

15   For the likelihood of a post-Viking date for *Beowulf*, see Roberta Frank, 'The Beowulf poet's sense of history', in *The wisdom of poetry* (ed. L.D. Benson and S. Wenzel, Kalamazoo, 1982). She sums up: 'An Old English poem about northern heathens and northern heroes, opening with the mythical figure of Scyld from whom the ruling houses of both Denmark and England were descended, fits nicely with the efforts of Alfred and his successors to promote an Anglo-Danish brotherhood.' (p.60).

16   On the probability that the West-Saxon regnal genealogy found in the Anglo-Saxon Chronicle at 855 was an Alfredian insertion, see Alfred P. Smyth, *King Alfred the Great* (Oxford, 1995), p.467. The names Finn, Sceaf, Heremod, Geat, Beaw in the list all have parallels in the Beowulf poem. John Niles, in *A Beowulf handbook* (ed. R.E. Bjork and John D. Niles, Exeter, 1997, p.25) notes his own earlier (1993) contention that the extended West Saxon genealogies were composed after the Viking invasions and therefore may contain a blend of Anglo-Saxon and Scandinavian traditions. Against composition in honour of Alfred himself, we may note the menseful way in which Beowulf acts as regent for the deceased king's young sons (lines 2370-8).

An. DCCXCIII. Ðeþ pæþon þeðe · roþe-becna cumene oþeþ Noþðan-hẏmbþa lanð. ꝗ þ þolc eaþmlice bþeʒ-ðon þ pæþon oþmete liʒþæþcaþ. anð þoðenaþ. anð ʒeþeopene pæþon þẏþene ðþacan on þam lẏþte þleoʒenðe. Ðam · tacnum þona þẏliʒðe mẏcel hunʒeþ. anð litel æþteþ þam. þæþ ilcan ʒeaþeþ. on VI. iðuþ Ianuaþ . eaþmlice hæþenþa manna heþʒunʒ aðiliʒoðe Goðeþ cẏþi-can in Linðiþþaþena-éé þuþh hþeaþlac · ꝗ man-þleht .

A.D. 793. This year came dread-ful fore-warnings over the land of the Northumbrians, terrifying the people most woefully : these were immense sheets of light rushing through the air, and whirlwinds, and fiery dragons flying across the firmament. These tremendous tokens were soon followed by a great famine; and not long after, on the sixth day before the ides of January in the same year, the harrowing inroads of heathen men made lamentable havoc in the church of God in Holy-island, by rapine and slaughter.

12 *The annal for AD 793 in Ingram's 1823 edition of the* Anglo-Saxon Chronicle

they are the ones who need help from Beowulf, so their status is ambiguous i.e. unlike their dominance in the north in the ninth century. The whole context of outside help arriving to sort out local problems is redolent of the period of West Saxon reconquest of the north, a story in which Athelstan plays a major role. In Symeon of Durham's assessment, 'he everywhere overcame the numerous enemies by whom he was assailed from every quarter; he either slew them, or reduced them to subjection, or drove them out of the limits of Britain.' As to place of composition, an Anglian poet is likely given the skill and inventiveness with which the features of the Anglian poetic technique are handled. There are apparent allusions to the poem in a charter[17] quite possibly issued by Athelstan in 931 (which refers to Ham in Wiltshire, not far from Malmesbury; Athelstan favoured and was buried at Malmesbury Abbey). This could be some slender evidence for a transmission of the poem from north to south in Athelstan's reign. By this view, the poem *Beowulf* could be a tribute to that king: a celebration of the marriage of his daughter to King Sihtric of York in 926; or a record of his victories in the north in 927 and 937; or an acknowledgement of his generosity to the Community of St Cuthbert at Chester-le-Street in 934, concluding with an oblique elegy on his death in 939? As a sort of allegory, the earlier parts of the poem might represent the concern of the Anglians and settled Danish-Viking elements about the rise of Irish-Viking York;

17 That the charter uses *Beow(a)* rather than *Beowulf* may only attest the scribe's knowledge of the regnal list; the charter also includes a *Grendles Mere* and other possible literary references. Michael Lapidge in '*Beowulf*, Aldhelm, the *Liber Monstrorum* and Wessex', *Studi Medievali* 3rd ser., 23 (1982), notes of the occurrence of *Grendel* features in charters, 'they nearly all occur in an area of West Mercia and Wessex whose geographical centre is Malmesbury.' (p.179). However, Grendel need not be a southern concept: Raine's word list in BL MS Egerton 2868 includes the entry: 'grindle-stane – a grind-stone: 'one grindle stone' Knaresborough 5 Car I.'

the conclusion, however, is taken out of the Danish/politic/heroic context into a more neutral frame[18] which elaborates the misery of death, even within a justified and heroic life, and predicts problems to come.

Durham

But that is (I apologise) all speculation.

Let us return to the real Northumbria and the fortunes of the Community of St Cuthbert after it reached Durham (Durham City as we now know it). A rather straightforward poem in praise of Durham (compare the Latin genre, the *encomium urbis*) is recorded in two manuscripts of around 1200. A post-Conquest date of composition is apparent from the references to many relics held in the Cathedral – the remains of Bede did not arrive in Durham until the mid-11th century, for example. A likely context for its composition is the translation of the body of Cuthbert to its new resting-place in the Norman cathedral in 1104, a late date for an Anglo-Saxon poem, and especially for one written in tolerably good Old English diction and metre. The assumption is that it was composed to celebrate that special event; but the poem also rehearses the many beauties of the peninsula and the church in a general way that would appeal to pilgrims visiting the shrine of St Cuthbert – who might well enquire if they could pay for a copy to take away with them, please?

It opens with a pleasant picture of the Durham peninsula:

> Is ðeos burch breome geond Breotenrice,
> *Is this city famous throughout Britain,*
>
> steppa gestaðolad, stanas ymbutan
> *steeply based, stones around (it)*
>
> wundrum gewaexen. Weor ymbeorna[ð],
> *finely formed. The-Wear round-it-runs,*
>
> ea yðum strong, and ðerinne wunað
> *(with) river's currents strong, and therein live*
>
> feola fisca kinn on floda gemonge;
> *many of-fishes types in the-current among;*
>
> and ðær gewexen is wudafæstern mycel'
> *and there well-grown is forest-sector great;*

---

18 The removal of the scene from Denmark to Sweden in the poem might reflect the wish to associate English Danes with Athelstan's triumphs, but not his death?

wuniað in ðem wycum, wilda deor monige,
exist in the area wild animals many,

in deopa dalum deora ungerim…
in deep dales, of-animals a-countless-number…

There follow lists of the famous people whose relics are held in the cathedral. Cuthbert is prominent here, but even so only receives mentions in lines 10 and 16-17. Jane Roberts recently pointed out that the phrase 'breome bocere' of Bede, in the poem, is also found in Aldred's postscript to the *Lindisfarne Gospel* gloss of the mid-10th century.[19] The copying of this 'unusual phrase' – one with all the alliterative features appropriate to verse – suggests that the later poet knew of Aldred's work unless both drew on some earlier version of the *Durham Poem* (a possibility that would help explain the 'good' Old English of a late 11th-century composition).

The poem is not outstanding – from a literary standpoint – but forms an interesting boundary to this short tour of Northumbrian poetry. 'Northumbria' by then was a historical concept, surviving only in the shire-system as Northumberland; the Anglo-Saxons themselves had used the form *Northanhymbre* or *Northhymbre* – the people who lived northwards from the Humber; the Latin abstraction seems to be a later refinement.

Conclusion

The 'Caedmon initiative' (if we may so term it) comprises a relatively small body of OE verse in comparison with the whole corpus of OE literature. Apart from a tantalising reference to Bede composing an OE translation of St John's Gospel as his health finally failed,[20] there is little evidence for Northumbrian composition in OE prose. That they undertook to write in OE verse might be seen as the best way 'to convey the fundamental beliefs of Christianity to pagan people who could not read',[21] but it is doubtful if the Anglo-Saxon slave class, or even the average freeman, would gain much pleasure or enlightenment from the sometimes tortuous expressions of OE piety in verse. Rather, the composition and audience may alike have been monastic, the 'ad utilitatem ecclesiae' of his work on St John,[22] though that Church context in itself covers a whole technology of thought with relevance to the aims, strategies and reward system in a much wider political context.

The original aspirations may have been limited, yet in a sense it can be doubted if the flowering of OE prose in Alfred's reign would have come about without the

---

19   On the dating of *Durham*, I gratefully acknowledge the use of material from Jane Roberts' paper on Aldred, read at a conference at Manchester University, July 2003. She suggests in the paper that parts of Aldred's own inscription in the *Lindisfarne Gospels* form standard OE verse lines – a welcome addition to the Northumbrian corpus.

20   Bede, *Historia Ecclesiastica* (ed. C. Plummer, Oxford, 1896), vol.1, p.clxii.

21   Hunter Blair, *op.cit.*, p.121.

22   'for the use of the Church', Bede (ed. Plummer), vol.1, p.clxii.

example of Northumbria. That Alfred and his associates turned to Old English for lack of knowledge of Latin amongst readers of the time was one motive; but the *Preface* to the *Pastoral Care* suggests that he is writing with a modest return to the 'golden' standards of former times in mind, and asserts that in his day learning was relatively better maintained in the north (despite Viking dominance) than the south.[23] An OE version of Bede's *Ecclesiastical History* was probably the first of the mid- and late 10th-century translations that we have come to associate with the age of Alfred. And when, a century and more later, Ælfric embarked on alliterative lives of saints in Old English, his first attempt is believed to be a version of the life of St Cuthbert, and his inspiration to use alliterative techniques in a quasi-prose framework might well have been Bede's (Latin) verse life of Cuthbert.[24]

Certainly the train of 'high' OE verse composition flows uninterrupted from Northumbria through Mercia to Wessex – a process that led to many admirable poetic compositions like the *OE Exodus*, the *Phoenix*, and the lyrics *The Seafarer* and *The Wanderer*, uncertain though their place of composition must remain. This long tradition has been obscured by the rise of rhyme: from the 13th to the early 20th centuries, English verse composition has been dominated by Latinate rhyme, but its best writers have always been aware of the value of details of word sound, and Old English verse texts have been widely available and appreciated since the 1830s to reinforce this aspect of English poetry. An unimaginable sector of our literary history and resources would be absent if Caedmon had not turned over in his sleep and noticed.

---

23   The 'very few' learned men this side of the Humber as against the 'not many' beyond the Humber; the *Preface* to the *Pastoral Care* goes on to laud the glory of the Church in former generations.

24   See introduction of Malcolm Godden's edition of *Ælfric's Catholic Homilies: The second series* (EETS, sup.ser.5, 1979); Ælfric's homily on Cuthbert may have been intended to coincide with the foundation of Durham Cathedral in 995.

4

Bede, St Cuthbert and the Northumbrian Folc

JO STORY

Introduction

Anglo-Saxon Northumbria is a place known to many through the lives of two men and one book: Bede – the Jarrow scholar and monk (d.735); St Cuthbert – monk, hermit and bishop (d.689); and the Lindisfarne Gospels, made in honour of St Cuthbert in the early eighth century. The Gospel Book is the masterpiece, the *opus Dei*, of one creative hand, and it has come to symbolise the cultural genius of Northumbria in its 'Golden Age' in the later seventh and eighth centuries. Today it is probably the most instantly recognisable artefact from all of Anglo-Saxon England.[1] St Cuthbert also has a reputation that far transcends the achievements of his short episcopacy at Lindisfarne from 685-7. He is, in many ways, the region's first folk-hero because his greatness is testified by the witness of ordinary people in the kingdom – the Northumbrian *folc* – although it was recorded and disseminated by a community of clerics, first at Lindisfarne, then (after Viking predation) at Chester-le-Street, and finally, from 995, at Durham where his body still rests.[2]

In recent years both the saint and his Gospel Book have become iconic symbols of the regional identity of North East England. It is no surprise that those who seek such unifying symbols should find them in St Cuthbert since this role was attributed to him by his earliest Anglo-Saxon biographers. To them, he symbolised the unified Northumbrian Church by bringing together the most admirable traits of the Irish Church (in which he had been trained) with the orthodox practices of Rome. The miracles credited to St Cuthbert after his death were proof of divine approval.

It is largely thanks to Bede, however, that we know anything very much about the land in which Lindisfarne's Gospel Book and saint belong. Bede both defined

---

1 Brown, M.P., *The Lindisfarne Gospels: society, spirituality and the scribe* (London, 2003).
2 Bonner, G., Stancliffe, C. and Rollason, D.W., *St Cuthbert: his cult and community to AD 1200* (Woodbridge, 1989).

Northumbria's Golden Age and was a product of it. It is through his writing, especially his *Ecclesiastical History of the English People*, that we can come close to understanding both the ties that bound Northumbrian society in the seventh and eighth centuries, and the tensions that it was under. Through Bede, we know that seventh-century Northumbria was ruled by kings who came from two dynasties which had their power bases in the two constituent parts of the kingdom: Deira in the south, centred on York, and Bernicia in the north, with its capital at Bamburgh. The Deiran ruler Edwin (d.633) was the first to convert to Roman-style Christianity under the influence of his southern Anglo-Saxon overlords. He was also considered to have been a Bretwalda ('wide-ruler') over regions and peoples beyond Northumbria. But it was under the Bernician kings descended from the line of Æthelfrith (d.616), such as Oswald (d.642), Oswiu (d.670) and Ecgfrith (d.685), that Northumbrian power reached its zenith, and under them that Irish churchmen began to evangelise the northern parts of the kingdom.

With the conversion to Christianity came the attendant tools of literacy and an administrative hierarchy based on complementary networks of bishoprics and monasteries.[3] The consolidation of this system in Northumbria was one of Bede's prime concerns not least because, in his opinion, the rate of conversion was outstripping the ability of the Church to minister to its converts. Furthermore, by the 730s, the pious desires of the nobility to found monasteries, combined with the increasing importance attached to written records (charters) of such donations, was beginning to have a significant impact on the way in which land was controlled and on the king's ability to retain loyal followers. Bede worried that Northumbrian noblemen were acquiring charters recording the donation of land for the foundation of a monastery under false pretences: the land donated was given 'in perpetuity' to the Church, and was thus alienated from the king's patronage for ever.[4] This threatened to restrict the king's ability to reward younger followers and to consolidate land in the hands of noblemen who continued to live in and control the monasteries that they had founded. Lacking patronage and promises of land for service at home, young Northumbrian *thegns* were seeking lords outside the kingdom. Bede feared that the growth of 'false monasteries' in Northumbria and the draining away of Northumbrian youth to 'foreign' lords was weakening the military and spiritual condition of the kingdom and leaving it dangerously exposed to pagan raiders.

These anxieties of Bede show that, barely a century after the arrival of the first missionaries in Anglo-Saxon York, the systems for controlling the Northumbrian state and church had become inextricably entwined, and that the ecclesiastical and political élite came from the same families. Bede's historical writing and his letters to fellow Northumbrian clergy give considerable insights into the lives of these people at the top of Northumbrian society. The lives of those who were the subjects of the kings, and the

---

3 Blair, J., *The Church in Anglo-Saxon society* (Oxford, 2005).

4 Bede, *Letter to Bishop Ecgberht of York*, dated 5 November 734 (ed. C. Plummer, *Venerabilis Baedae opera historica*, 2 vols, Oxford, 1896), i, pp.405-23; trans. L. Sherley-Price, *Bede. Ecclesiastical History of the English People* (Harmondsworth, 1990), pp.337-51; D. Whitelock (trans.), *English historical documents* 1 (London, 1979), no. 185 (hereafter *EHD* 1), no. 170.

parishioners of the bishops, are addressed less often. Nevertheless, in Bede's accounts of battles, councils, political alliances and miraculous wonders, many incidental references and anecdotes cast an oblique light on the life and death of ordinary Northumbrians in the seventh and early eighth centuries. This is the subject of our chapter.

Bede and the Northumbrian Folc

In the spring of 764 Abbot Cuthbert of Wearmouth and Jarrow wrote a letter to Lull, an Englishman who was bishop of Mainz in Germany. Abbot Cuthbert explained that he was trying hard to fulfil Lull's commission for copies of a number of the works of Bede.[5] But progress had been slow, he said, because the recent Northumbrian winter had been 'horrible' and the monastery had been beset by 'cold, ice and widespread storms of wind and rain, so that the hand of the scribe has been prevented from producing a great number of books'. Lull had requested copies of Bede's prose and verse *Life of St Cuthbert*, but it is likely that he also knew Bede's *Ecclesiastical History of the English People* since, in other letters, he seems to have derived the list of the books he wanted from the bibliography that Bede had added to his autobiographical note in the last chapter of that work.[6] By 764 Bede had been dead for nearly thirty years and Abbot Cuthbert's correspondence with Lull is one of many pieces of evidence which shows that Bede's reputation as a scholar and teacher had spread quickly beyond the borders of his own country. By the mid-eighth century, copies of his many works were circulating abroad, especially in the eastern regions of Francia and in Germany which had been colonised by Anglo-Saxon missionaries eager to spread their Christian faith among those continental peoples they considered to be their distant kin.[7]

We tend now to think of Bede as an historian whose presentation of his homeland's recent past provides us with the framework for understanding the entire period and also – since he was the first to apply *Anno Domini* dates systematically – with critical tools to do so. During his lifetime, however, Bede was known rather more for his exegetical works on the Scriptures and for his writings on natural science. But, first and foremost, Bede was a devout Christian whose special monastic vocation and 'chief delight, has always been in study, teaching and writing'.[8] As a teacher he was able to make things known to his students at Jarrow; as a writer he was able to share

---

5 Abbot Cuthbert, *Letter to Lull* (ed. M. Tangle, *Die Briefe des heiligen Bonifatius und Lullus*, Monumenta Germaniae Historica, Epistolae Selectae 1, Hanover, 1921, no. 116); *EHD* 1. On Lull see, most recently, J.T. Palmer, 'The "vigorous rule" of Bishop Lull: between Bonifatian mission and Carolingian church control', *Early Medieval Europe* 13 (2005), pp.249-76.

6 Bishop Lull, *Letter to Abbot Cuthbert* (where he requests Bede's works *On the building of the Temple*, *On the Song of Songs* and his epigrams in heroic and elegiac metre) and Abbot Cuthbert's reply, *Letter to Bishop Lull* (ed. Tangle, *Die Briefe*, nos 126 and 127). See also Bishop Lull, *Letter to Æthelbert, archbishop of York* (requesting the four books on Samuel, three on Ezra and Nehemiah, four books on the Gospel of St Mark) (ed. Tangle, *Die Briefe*, no. 12); *EHD* 1, no. 188. Bede's autobiography and autobibliography is found in the *Historia Ecclesiastica* V. 24 (hereafter *HE*, cited by book and chapter number) (ed. and trans. B. Colgrave and R.A.B. Mynors, *Bede's Ecclesiastical History of the English People*, Oxford, 1968, pp.566-71).

7 McKitterick, R., *Anglo-Saxon missionaries in Germany*, Eighth Brixworth Lecture 1990, Vaughan Paper 36 (1991), reprinted in her *Frankish kingdoms and culture in the early middle ages* (Aldershot, 1995), ch. 1; D.W. Rollason, *Bede and Germany*, Jarrow Lecture 2001; on the Frankish transmission of the *DTR* see J. Story, 'The Frankish Annals of Lindisfarne and Kent', *Anglo-Saxon England* 34 (2005), pp.59-109.

8 Bede, *HE* V.24 (ed. and trans. Colgrave and Mynors, *Bede's Ecclesiastical History*, pp.566-7).

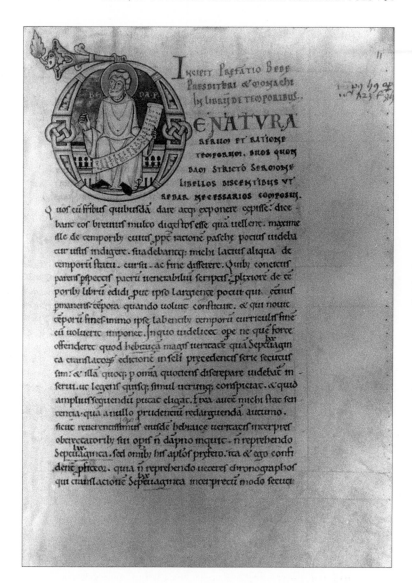

13 *Image of Bede, Folio 35r of ms. Hunter 85, Glasgow University Library*

his learning with students far removed from him in time as well as space. It was one of the hall-marks of Bede's vocation, however, that he never forgot the pastoral needs of ordinary men and women – the English-speaking Christians of Northumbria who knew no Latin and whose contact with the established Church can have been little more than sporadic.[9] About six months before his death, Bede had chastised Ecgberht, Bishop of York, about the inadequacy of pastoral care received by ordinary Northumbrians. The diocese of York, which covered most of Northumbria, was too big and the number of Christians too great for a single bishop to visit annually; part of the solution, he argued, was for more priests to be trained so that every Northumbrian village could more often hear a preacher and receive the sacraments and grace of

---

9   Thacker, A., 'Monks, preaching and pastoral care in early Anglo-Saxon England', in *Pastoral Care before the Parish*, ed. J. Blair and R. Sharpe (Leicester, London and New York, 1992), pp.137-70.

baptism.[10] Bede told Bishop Ecgberht that the Lord's Prayer and the Apostles' Creed must be memorised by everyone, laity and clergy alike. To this end, he had often provided priests with English translations of both texts so that the fundamentals of the faith could be taught, recited accurately and understood by all – even 'the unlearned, that is, those who know only their own language'.

Very little of Bede's vernacular writing has survived. We have only a short five-line 'Death Song' attributed to him by Cuthbert (the later abbot and correspondent of Lull), who had noted it down as he waited beside Bede's deathbed.[11] Abbot Cuthbert recalled that Bede was familiar with 'our poetry' and this comment, combined with his interest in the story of the herdsman-poet Cædmon at Whitby, suggests that Bede may have had considerable involvement in vernacular learning.[12] Furthermore, Abbot Cuthbert said that, as he lay dying, Bede had begun a translation of the Latin Gospel of St John into Old English, along with a response to a work by the seventh-century Visigothic scholar, Isidore of Seville, called, 'The Wonders of Nature'.[13] These two projects aptly encapsulate the two major aspects of Bede's work – to illuminate the marvels of the Word of God, and the world that was God's creation: 'I cannot have my pupils learning what is not true, and loosing their labour on this after I am gone.'[14]

Bede is fundamental to the story of Northumbria not only because his ideas and writings were distributed widely in the eighth century (as Abbot Cuthbert's and Bishop Lull's letters and numerous early manuscripts of his works show) but also because those writings remained influential and were recognised in the centuries following his death as works of a 'doctor of the church' and the 'father of English history'.[15] It is Bede's analysis of the development of the English Church in his *Ecclesiastical History of the English People* that has provided the basic framework for understanding the political structures and cultural dynamics of (what archaeologists often call) the 'middle Saxon' centuries, *c*.AD 600-800. For sure, other contemporary texts amplify Bede's narrative and provide important information where his account is wanting, and archaeological evidence comprehensively challenges his neat mid-eighth-century views of the earliest phases of the Anglo-Saxon influence on Britain in the fifth and sixth centuries. Even so, it is primarily through Bede's writing that we get not only the big picture, but the detail, of Anglo-Saxon life before the eighth century. Through his

---

10   Bede, *Letter to Bishop Ecgberht of York* (above, note 4).

11   Bede died on 25 May 735, see Abbot Cuthbert, *Letter to Cuthwine on the death of Bede*, ed. and trans. Colgrave and Mynors, *Bede*, 579-87; trans. Sherley-Price, *Bede*, pp.357-60. The earliest version of Cuthbert's letter is in a ninth-century manuscript from St Gallen. The later, English, copies of the letter preserve a West Saxon version of the poem, while those that were copied on the Continent have the original Northumbrian dialect of the Death Song. Not all the manuscripts attribute the composition of the poem to Bede. On the textual variants of the letter, see E. van K. Dobbie, 'Caedmon's Hymn and Bede's Death-Song (New York, 1937) and N.R. Ker, 'The Hague Manuscript of the *Epistola Cuthberti de obitu Bedae* with Bede's Song', *Medium Aevum* 8 (1939), pp.40-4.

12   On Cædmon, see Bede, *Historia Ecclesiastica*, IV.24; also, Bill Griffiths, 'Old English Poetry of Northumbria' in the present volume.

13   Isidore of Seville, *Liber Rotarum* or *De natura rerum*. An eighth-century Latin copy of the Gospel of St John made at Wearmouth-Jarrow was recovered from the tomb of St Cuthbert in 1104; Webster, L. and Backhouse, J., *The Making of England. Anglo-Saxon Art and Culture AD 600-900* (London, 1991), no. 86.

14   Brown, G.H., *Bede the Educator*, Jarrow Lecture 1996.

15   Bede was made 'doctor ecclesiae' in 1899, and 'sanctus' in 1935; Campbell, J., 'Bede (673/4-735)', *Oxford Dictionary of National Biography* (2004).

anecdotes and analogies we gain access to the daily lives and experiences of individual ordinary Anglo-Saxons. For example, he records the Old English names of the months that were used before the English became Christian and reflected the agrarian phases of the year. He said that the month of May had been called *Thrimilchi* because then the cows could be milked three times daily because of the richness of the grass; August was *Weodmonath* because of the profusion of weeds that grew; November was the *Blodmonath* because that was when cattle were slaughtered and consecrated to the pagan gods.[16] Bede's Anglo-Saxons are not only the 'big men' – the bishops, kings and saints of Golden Age Northumbria – but also include, if we read carefully, some of those who were part of the *folc*, the 'common people' of Anglo-Saxon Northumbria.

In Old English, the mother-tongue of Bede and his compatriots, the word *folc* was used in contemporary vernacular sources only in the singular – as a collective noun meaning 'a people', a group who defined themselves or who were defined by others as belonging together by virtue of their shared ethnicity and/or identity. *Folc* – and its Latin equivalent, *gens* – commonly used to be translated as 'tribe' or 'nation'. Disliking its racial overtones and pejorative connotations of primitivism, post-colonial scholars tend now to avoid the term 'tribe' since, in common parlance, it is loaded with a reductive sense of the primitive and the overly homogeneous – terms certainly inappropriate in an early medieval context where definitions of political identity and ethnicity (be they genetic or cultural) were porous and layered. The word 'nation' (Latin: *natio*) is also problematic in an early medieval context because of its 19th- and 20th-century associations with the concept of a 'nation-state' and attendant connotations that nations are coterminous with their territory, or ancestral homelands, bounded by fixed borders.[17] In Anglo-Saxon England a *natio*, *gens* or *folc* did not necessarily live within fixed borders, and then (as now) what it meant to be a 'Northumbrian', a 'Mercian' or a 'West Saxon' depended only in part on geography.[18] Other factors such as language, dialect, kinship and stories of a shared past were just as important.

Nevertheless, the Old English word *folc* was also used adjectivally to describe an object, a concept, a person, or a land belonging to, or being held in common by, 'the people'. So we find *folcland* for land that was held in common and could not be alienated in perpetuity by written charter; *folcriht* for 'common law' or 'public right'; *folccu* for the 'folk's cow', a cow that belongs to the herd; *folccwen*, 'the people's princess'; or *folctalu* for 'folktale' in the sense of a common story, or genealogy, or shared line of descent. The adjective *folcisc* meant 'popular', 'commonplace' or 'vulgar'.

---

16   Bede, *De Temporum Ratione Liber* (hereafter *DTR*), ch. 15 (ed. C.W. Jones, *Bedae opera de temporibus*, Cambridge MA, 1943, reprinted in *Beda Venerabilis opera didascalica*, Corpus Christianorum Series Latina 123B, Turnhout, 1977, 329-32); trans. F. Wallis, *Bede: The Reckoning of Time*, Translated texts for historians 29 (Liverpool, 1995), pp.53-4.

17   On the significance of the recovery of the languages and history of the early middle ages to 19th- and 20th-century nationalist political thought and action, see Geary, P.J., *The myth of nations: the medieval origins of Europe* (Princeton and Oxford, 2002).

18   In Anglo-Saxon England, the word *folc* could be used geographically when naming a people in relation to their neighbours or a physical landmark; thus, in East Anglia, the 'north folk' were so called in relation to the 'south folk'. On the borders of Northumbria, see Hunter Blair, P., 'The Northumbrians and their southern frontier', *Archaeologia Aeliana*, 4th series 26 (1948), 98-126 and 'The Bernicians and their northern frontier', in *Celt and Saxon: studies in the early British border*, ed. N.K. Chadwick (Cambridge, 1963), pp.63-118, reprinted as chapters 4 and 8 in his *Anglo-Saxon Northumbria*, ed. M. Lapidge and P. Hunter Blair (Aldershot, 1984). Also, Rollason, D., *Northumbria 500-1100: creation and destruction of a kingdom* (Cambridge, 2003), pp.20-53.

In none of these cases were there connotations of class prejudice; the *folc* is 'ordinary', 'everyday' and 'everyone'. OE *'folc'* is not a pejorative term implying low status.

Time and Place

Bede's *Ecclesiastical History of the English People* was his most extended piece of historical writing and is that which has had the most enduring impact. It was completed in 731 and told the story of the establishment of the Church and the consolidation of Christianity among the English in Britain. It was modelled on another, earlier *Ecclesiastical History* written in Greek by Eusebius of Caesarea. Bede knew Eusebius' *History* through Rufinus' late fourth-century Latin epitome, and he learned there the history of the Christian Church from its beginnings until the victory of the Roman emperor Constantine over his rival Licinius in 324, after which the legality of Christianity was consolidated within the Roman Empire. Bede's *Ecclesiastical History* was, therefore, a bold and ambitious work, evolving from a lifetime's study of the work of God as manifested in the Scriptures and by the natural world. For Bede, recent history continued the record of the human past as told in the Bible and was as much a reflection of God's creation and activity on Earth as the ebb and flow of the tides.

The *Ecclesiastical History* was one of the books that King Alfred considered 'necessary for all men to know'. He ordered it to be translated into Old English in the late ninth century.[19] But before Alfred's time it was not the *Ecclesiastical History* but another of Bede's books – called by its Latin title, *De Temporum Ratione* (*DTR*) or 'On the Reckoning of Time' – which was the most popular of his works, to judge by the number of surviving copies made in England and Francia in the eighth and ninth centuries.[20] Eighty-four copies of the *DTR* made between *c*.750 and *c*.900 survive (from a total of 245 medieval copies). The *DTR* was a textbook on *computus* – the methods of calculating time – and, as such, was an essential precursor to the sophisticated chronology of the *Ecclesiastical History* (not least in its novel use of the *Anno Domini* dating in the Easter Tables that prefigured the main text). Bede wrote the *DTR* in response to a long-running and heated debate over the proper calculation of the dating of Easter, and the clear, comprehensive solution he proposed ensured the popularity of the book and the diffusion of his calculating system. By the end of the eighth century clerics and scholars all over Europe measured according to Bede's method not just the recurring annual cycle of the feasts of the Christian calendar, but also the linear time by which the Age of Christ and the biblical epochs before it could link the past to the present and the present to the future.

The *DTR* was popular because in it Bede described problems, explained answers and provided the means to calculate solutions in ways that his Jarrow pupils and

---

19   Alfred, *Prose preface to Gregory's* Pastoral Care; S. Keynes and M. Lapidge, trans. *Alfred the Great: Asser's* Life of King Alfred *and other contemporary sources* (Harmondsworth, 1983), pp.28-33 and 124-6; Miller, T. (ed.), *The Old English version of Bede's Ecclesiastical History of the English people*, 4 vols. Early English Text Society, original series 95-6 and 110-11 (London, 1890-8); D. Whitelock, 'The Old English Bede', *Proceedings of the British Academy* 48 (1962), pp.67-103.

20   Jones (ed.) *Beda Venerabilis*, 263-544; trans. Wallis, *Bede: Reckoning*, 3-249. See also W. Stevens, *Bede's Scientific Achievement*, Jarrow Lecture 1985.

others like them could easily comprehend. In the *DTR* we see Bede at his educational best, explaining abstract theories about the science of God's creation to his pupils in Northumbria in terms of their everyday environment. For example, in Chapter 32 Bede seeks to explain why the same calendar days differ in length in different parts of the world. This happens, he says, because the world is round, like an orb set in the middle of the universe; the Earth 'is not merely circular like a shield or spread out like a wheel, but resembles more a ball, being equally round in all directions'.[21] This means that in wintertime the rays of the sun traversing the southern sky are 'blocked by the bulge of the Earth' which causes the sun to rise later and set earlier for 'those of us placed towards the north' than for those who live further south. Bede knew that the length of the day and night at the summer and winter solstices varied from place to place depending on latitude. He compared his own observations of the length of the night at the winter solstice in northern England with data collected from other parts of the world as gleaned from the works of the Roman author, Pliny, and others. From this he knew that his own location was far to the north of a world that must have been spherical in shape.[22] Experienced long-distance travellers who were familiar with the annual cycle of the Christian calendar may have noticed that, even within Britain, the set hours of particular services and feast days occurred at different phases of the day in different places, depending on latitude. But few of Bede's pupils in Jarrow were likely to have travelled far and were unlikely to have observed this phenomenon directly, let alone to have thought about why it occurs. So Bede described a phenomenon that was theoretical for most of his audience and furnished it with an explanation that is stranger still. Yet he helped his students to grasp these abstract notions by providing tangible, familiar, childhood analogies – comparing the Earth with a ball and contrasting the sphere of a ball with the disc of a shield.

He went on to explain that the ball-like shape of the Earth means that it is divided into five different zones, only two of which were temperate and habitable by men. The central zone around the waist of the world is hot and cannot be crossed, on either side are temperate zones which are habitable (but men could live only in the north since they could not cross the arid central zone), and beyond that at both poles are cold zones where no man can live. He advised his students to visualise this model by imagining a scene that would have been familiar to them all:

> Indeed, an illustration of these zones – which is quite easy to grasp – is furnished by people who, in the icy cold of winter, warm themselves at an oblong hearth. Like the middle zone [of the world], the fire itself, as well as whatever is near to it, cannot be touched because of the heat, while things placed at some distance from the flames on either side grow stiff with the ambient cold. But those that are between the two are tempered and appropriately positioned to be warmed, whether they who construct this

---

21   Pliny, *Historia Naturalis* 2.64.160. Bede, *DTR*, ch. 32 (ed. Jones, *Beda Venerabilis*, 380-1); trans. Wallis, *Bede: Reckoning*, pp.91-3.
22   Bede, *DTR*, ch. 30-3 and *HE* I.1 (ed. Jones, *Beda Venerabilis*, pp.371-86); trans. Wallis, *Bede: Reckoning*, pp.86-96. Stevens, *Bede's scientific achievement*, pp.8-9.

hearth for themselves for light and warmth under the sky in the dark of a cold night care to stand on one side of the fire or the other.[23]

Bede described other experiments that his students could do to satisfy themselves of the truth of a complex, abstract idea. Explaining why it is that the moon can sometimes appear higher in the sky than the sun, even though it is closer to the Earth, he advises his students to go at night time into 'a very large hall, or better, a church, immense in its length, breadth and height, and ablaze with countless lamps burning in honour of a martyr's feast day'. Look there, he says, for:

> ... two very large lamps of marvellous workmanship, hanging by chains from the ceiling, but the one which is nearer to you when you enter is also closer to the floor. However, the hall is so vast, and the height of those distant lamps so great that with your night vision you can make out the light and rays of flame more than you can the vessel itself which contains the fire. Now, indeed, as you start to advance towards the lamps, looking straight at them, and beyond towards the ceiling or opposite walls, and the lamp which is nearer appears higher to you ... [24]

The tall, narrow church of Jarrow would have served well for an experiment such as this, and it is entirely possible that Bede had his own church in mind when he explained it. He talks here about complex metaphysical science, but his explanation takes us out of the pages of the book and into the physical reality of the world in which he lived. We can imagine, perhaps, the monks of Jarrow singing the processional chants as they walked into their church on a winter night, where, because it was the feast of a saint, the large hanging lamps had been lit. It is not hard to imagine Bede among the processors, fixing his eyes on the light of the lamps as he walked into the church, and his mind wandering from the words of the hymns to the perplexing problems of the movement of the heavenly bodies.

We know a lot about the physical environment in which Bede spent most of his life; archaeological investigation has amplified what Bede and others recorded about the community at Wearmouth and Jarrow after its foundation in 674.[25] We can be sure that, in comparison even with the royal palaces of the day, Wearmouth and Jarrow were marvellous and exotic places. For a start, the churches were built of stone whereas timber was the building material of choice for most secular buildings. The stone of the churches was quarried from old Roman structures nearby and, Bede says, the community's founding abbot, Benedict Biscop, had had to bring masons and

---

23   Bede, *DTR*, ch. 34 (ed. Jones, *Beda Venerabilis*, 390-1); trans. Wallis, *Bede: Reckoning*, pp.99, 318.

24   Bede, *DTR*, ch. 26 (ed. Jones, *Beda Venerabilis*, 361); trans. Wallis, *Bede: Reckoning*, pp.78, 304-5. Hunter Blair, P., *The World of Bede*, p.271, and Colgrave, B., *Bede and his Times*, Jarrow Lecture 1958, 16.

25   Wearmouth was founded in 674, Jarrow in 681. Bede, *Historia abbatum*, ch. 4, 7 (ed. C. Plummer, *Venerabilis Bedae opera historica*, 2 vols, Oxford, 1896, i, 364-87 and 370); trans. J.F. Webb and D.H. Farmer, *The Age of Bede* (Harmondsworth, 1988), pp.185-210 at 188-90. See also the earlier, anonymous, *Vita Ceolfridi*, ch. 7, 11-12 (ed. Plummer, *Venerabilis Bedae*, pp.388-404 at 390-2); trans. D. S. Boutflower, *The Life of Ceolfrid, Abbot of the Monastery at Wearmouth and Jarrow* (Sunderland and London, 1912), pp.60-3. On the Anglo-Saxon archaeology, architecture and sculpture of Wearmouth-Jarrow, see Cramp, R., *Wearmouth and Jarrow Monastic Sites*, 1 (Swindon, 2005); Taylor, H.M. and Taylor, J., *Anglo-Saxon Architecture*, 2 vols (Cambridge, 1965), i, pp.338-49, 432-46; Cramp, R., *Corpus of Anglo-Saxon Stone Sculpture* 1, Northumberland (Oxford, 1984), no. 206-40.

glaziers from Francia to oversee the building work since such skills were unknown to the Northumbrians.[26] This is not to suppose that Anglo-Saxon timber buildings were unsophisticated in comparison; timber-built halls were imposing buildings which could be as much as 20-25m in length, making use of vast amounts of timber and complex construction techniques to display ostentatious wealth and access to scarce skills and resources.[27] But stone was chosen for the new churches at Wearmouth-Jarrow for symbolic as well as pragmatic reasons; worked stone was readily available nearby and, in reusing the materials of the old Roman Wall, stone churches symbolised the solidity of the Christian faith and its Roman origins.

Physically, therefore, the churches that were the focus of the monastery's daily devotions called to mind not just Imperial Rome of the classical past, but also Christian Rome of the present day. This connection was made even more explicit in the fixtures and fittings of the buildings, and in the daily rituals of the community. Bede tells us that Benedict Biscop had brought from his six trips to Francia and Rome many objects to adorn his churches: relics of the apostles and martyrs; liturgical vestments and sacred vessels; panel paintings that contrasted stories from Old and New Testaments with scenes from the Book of Revelation as well as images of the Virgin and apostles; and a great many books that formed the core of the library that was to make Bede's Jarrow so extraordinarily influential.[28] Biscop, with the help of Pope Agatho, had even persuaded John, the arch-cantor of the basilica of St Peter in Rome, to return with him to Northumbria. John taught the Wearmouth-Jarrow community to sing the liturgy in the same way as was done every day at the shrine of St Peter; Biscop thus rejected the multiplicity of hybrid liturgical practices that he had encountered in his journeys through Francia and secured for his own community the 'purest' liturgy that he knew.[29] The sights and sounds of Biscop's Jarrow, thus, were those of mid-seventh-century Rome.

Despite the international origins of his monastery, and quite unlike its well-travelled founding abbots, we have very little evidence that Bede ever went far beyond Jarrow. He had been born in 673 on one of the monastery's estates and had entered the community aged seven. In his letter to Bishop Ecgberht of York, written in the autumn of 734, he tells of his journey to 'your monastery for the sake of study', but we do not know whether that monastery was in York or elsewhere. Similarly, there are hints in Bede's correspondence with the monks of Lindisfarne that he may have

---

26   Bede, *Historia abbatum*, ch. 5 (ed. Plummer, *Venerabilis Bedae*, 368); trans. Webb and Farmer, *Age of Bede*, p.189.

27   For example, among excavated seventh-century timber buildings, A4 at Yeavering (Northumberland) was 25.3m (83ft) long and Building C12 at Cowdery's Down (Hampshire) was 22.1m (72.5ft) long; B. Hope Taylor, *Yeavering: an Anglo-British centre of early Northumbria* (London, 1977), 58-62; Millett, M. and James, S., 'Excavations at Cowdery's Down Basingstoke, Hampshire, 1978-81', *The Archaeological Journal* 140 (1983), pp.151-279 at 215-17. For comparative plans see also James, S., Marshall, A. and Millett, M., 'An early medieval building tradition', *The Archaeological Journal* 141 (1984), pp.182-215.

28   Bede, *Historia abbatum*, ch. 5-6, 9 and 15 (ed. Plummer, *Venerabilis Bedae*, pp.368-70, 373 and 379-80); trans. Webb and Farmer, *Age of Bede*, pp.189-91, 194 and 200-1. Laistner, M.L.W., 'The Library of the Venerable Bede', in *Bede: his life, times and writings. Essays in commemoration of the twelfth centenary of his death* (ed. A. Hamilton Thompson, Oxford, 1935), pp.237-66. See also Parkes, M.B., *The Scriptorium of Wearmouth-Jarrow*, (Jarrow Lecture 1982); Lapidge, M., 'Surviving booklists from Anglo-Saxon England', in *Learning and literature in Anglo-Saxon England. Studies presented to Peter Clemoes* (ed. M. Lapidge and H. Gneuss, Cambridge, 1985), pp.33-89.

29   Bede, *Historia abbatum*, ch. 6 (ed. Plummer, *Venerabilis Bedae*, 368-70); trans. Webb and Farmer, *Age of Bede*, pp.190-1. Bede, *HE* IV.18 (ed. and trans. Colgrave and Mynors, *Bede*, pp.388-91).

known the island from first-hand experience, but the evidence is ambiguous. The world mainly came to Bede through the pages of books and through messengers sent out to gather the information that he needed. This makes his achievements all the more remarkable, since he was evidently able to extrapolate from local observation of natural phenomena to holistic, global models as recorded by contemporary correspondents or ancient observers. Although his personal experience was geographically limited, his mind was unhindered by the physical constraints of his own monastic environment.

A good example of Bede's ability to extrapolate from his local Northumbrian environment into a wider principle lies in his innovative discussion of the phenomenon of tides.[30] Tidal activity was not much discussed by classical scholars such as Pliny since tides are insignificant in the Mediterranean. It was only in the sixth and seventh centuries that observations of the much greater tidal ranges on the Atlantic coasts of Gaul and Ireland were recorded and scholarly discourses about their cause began to circulate. Bede's observations of the tides along the coast of north-east England allowed him to clarify a theory that had correlated the daily timing of the tides with the daily appearance of the moon, and to extrapolate from that a new idea about the phasing of the tides with the 'drag', that is, the gravitational pull, of the moon. For the first time, also, he noted that there were local variations in the regular pattern of the tides along a coastline, sometimes between places that were quite close together, which demanded intimate local knowledge (now called the 'rule of port'):

> But we who live at various places along the coastline of the British sea know that where the tide begins to run in one place it will start to ebb at another at the same time. Hence it appears to some that the wave, while retreating from one place, is coming back somewhere else; then leaving behind the territory where it was, it swiftly seeks again the region where it first began … those who live to the north of me on the same coastline usually receive and give back each tide sooner than I do, and those to the south, much later.[31]

Wesley Stevens has argued that to make these observations Bede must have enlisted the help of many monastic communities on the coasts of Britain, most obviously at Lindisfarne where there must have been local, detailed, empirical knowledge.[32] Twice daily, with the ebb and flow of the tides, the island of Lindisfarne was connected to the mainland in a rhythm that was analogous to the dual function of the community that lived there: Lindisfarne was simultaneously an island-monastery, devoted to prayer and cut off from the secular world, and, at the same time, a mainland-bishopric which had duties to provide pastoral care in the outside world and to act as adviser to kings and nobility.[33]

---

30   Stevens, *Bede's Scientific Achievement*, pp.10-18; Wallis, *Bede: Reckoning*, pp.307-12.
31   Bede, *DTR*, ch. 29 (ed. Jones, *Beda Venerabilis*, 370); trans. Wallis, *Bede: Reckoning*, pp.82-5.
32   Stevens, *Bede's Scientific Achievement*, pp.13-15. See also Bede's prose *Vita S. Cuthberti*, ch. 17 (hereafter *VCB*) (ed. and trans. B. Colgrave, *Two Lives of St Cuthbert: a Life by an anonymous monk of Lindisfarne and Bede's Prose Life*, Cambridge, 1940, pp.214-17), and Webb and Farmer, *Age of Bede*, pp.65-6.
33   *VCB* ch. 16 (trans. Colgrave, *Two Lives*, pp.207-9), and Webb and Farmer, *Age of Bede*, 63; *HE* II.3 (ed. and trans. Colgrave and Mynors, *Bede*, pp.142-5).

Men and Women

Unlike Bede's monastery at Wearmouth-Jarrow that had been founded by men trained in Francia and Rome, the monastery at Lindisfarne had been established in 635 by Irish monks under the patronage of King Oswald (634-42) who had converted to Christianity when exiled in Ireland. After the Synod of Whitby in 664, the community on Lindisfarne began the process of converting to the liturgical practices of Rome, but according to Bede the transformation was neither rapid nor smooth. The Irish bishop of Lindisfarne, Colman, and his supporters, had returned to Ireland after their defeat at the Synod, but for years afterwards arguments persisted within the remainder of the Lindisfarne community about their manner of living. The man chosen to 'teach the true rule of monastic life … and to illustrate it by his own perfect example' was St Cuthbert, prior of the monastery from the early 670s, bishop of the see from 685-7 and hailed as a saint eleven years after his death when his coffin was opened and the body was found to be whole and undecayed.

Bede says that under St Cuthbert's rule, chapter meetings at the monastery were fractious and that he dealt with these arguments by 'walking out, calm and unruffled'.[34] The real power of St Cuthbert's mission to Lindisfarne, however, was in the *posthumous* promotion of his achievement and reputation. St Cuthbert's successors at Lindisfarne, aided by Bede, succeeded in creating a cult focused on his bodily relics and the memories of his deeds that proved to be an extremely powerful centrifugal force which ultimately transcended the place with which his life and works were associated, becoming a symbol for the region as a whole.

St Cuthbert's reputation was secured for posterity by the *Lives* (Latin: *Vitae*) that were composed about him within a generation of his death. These early *Vitae* were compilations of the memories of men and women who had encountered the saint personally, and every subsequent medieval account of St Cuthbert was based on them. St Cuthbert's earliest biographers often recorded the names of these informers as well as their stories, thereby giving the accounts an air of authenticity as well as personal colour. St Cuthbert's story is thus another means by which we can get close to the *folc*, since his early biographers illustrated his piety with stories and anecdotes of a simple lifestyle mixed with a taste for the company of the neighbourhood poor over the Northumbrian élite.

The process by which the cult of St Cuthbert was created in the forty or so years after his death is well known; Michelle Brown has argued that the Lindisfarne Gospels, made 'for God and for St Cuthbert and – jointly – for all the saints whose relics are in the island', should be seen as a product of Eadfrith's Lindisfarne episcopacy (698-721) and as part of the same process of cult-creation as the commissioning of three hagiographic accounts of the saint's *Life*.[35] Bede's role in this process was crucial. At

---

34 *VCB* ch. 16 (trans. Colgrave, *Two Lives*, pp.210-11), and Webb and Farmer, *Age of Bede*, p.64.
35 Brown, *The Lindisfarne Gospels*, esp. pp.102-4. Previous arguments about the date of the Gospels had assumed that they were made before Eadfrith became bishop: see, for example, Lowe, E.A. (ed.), *Codices Latini Antiquiores*, 11 vols and supplement (Oxford,

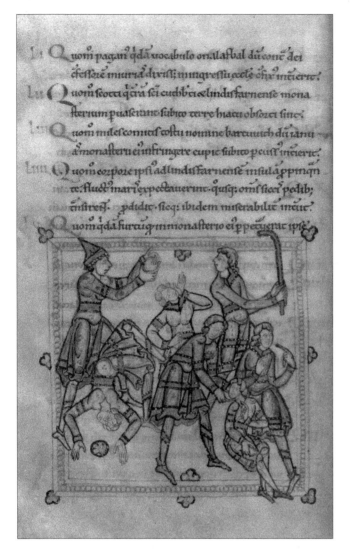

14 *Cuthbert's young friends playing, Bede's Life of St Cuthbert, Univ ms. 165 page 8, Bodleian Library, Oxford*

the request of Bishop Eadfrith he wrote two of the three early *Vitae* of Cuthbert, one in verse composed *c*.705 and another, prose, version *c*.720. He also wove the narrative of the saint's deeds and miracles into his *Ecclesiastical History* that he finished in 731.[36] The structure of these accounts conforms to the formulae of traditional hagiography; St Cuthbert's childhood, his monastic vocation, illness, death and miracles parallel those of other early Christian saints, such as St Anthony of Egypt, for example. Nevertheless, St Cuthbert's *Vitae* also reflected a strong sense of time and place, and

1934-71), ii, no. 187; Kendrick, T.D., Brown, T.J., Bruce-Mitford, R.S.L. (eds), *Evangeliorum Quattuor Codex Lindisfarnensis*, 2 vols (Olten and Lausanne, 1956-60). Brown's redating of the Gospels has a major impact on the dating of other manuscripts and objects from the Northumbrian 'Golden Age' which are usually dated in relationship to it. On St Cuthbert's cult, see Bonner, G., Stancliffe, C. and Rollason, D., *St Cuthbert: his cult and community to AD 1200* (Woodbridge, 1989); Kirby, D.P., 'The genesis of a cult: Cuthbert of Farne and ecclesiastical politics in Northumbria in the late seventh and early eighth centuries', *Journal of Ecclesiastical History* 46 (1995), pp.383-97.

36 The *VCB* is edited and translated in Colgrave, *Two Lives*, pp.141-307. Bede's verse or metrical *Vita S. Cuthberti* (hereafter *VCM*) is in W. Jaager (ed.), *Bedas metrische Vita sancti Cuthberti* (Leipzig, 1935).

recorded many carefully observed anecdotes about the Northumbrian people among whom Cuthbert ministered.

Bede's verse and prose *Vitae* of St Cuthbert were closely modelled on an earlier version written by an anonymous author some time between 699 and 705, which is recognised as one of the earliest English examples of the hagiographic genre.[37] It is remarkable also for its author's evident familiarity with the Northumbrian landscape and with the people local to Lindisfarne whose lives intersected with St Cuthbert as witnesses to his miracles. Most of the the Anonymous' stories are about events that took place at Lindisfarne or close to it, and were told to the author by local informants who were often neither noble nor monastic – the Lindisfarne *folc*. He makes it clear that he was himself a monk at Lindisfarne, referring to Cuthbert as 'our bishop' and Lindisfarne as 'our monastery'. The opening chapter of the *Life* shows that he wrote it at the behest of Bishop Eadfrith and that his primary audience was the Lindisfarne community itself. The formulaic hagiographic motifs which the Anonymous used in his account demonstrate that he was widely read and knew of a Christian world beyond north-east Anglo-Saxon England, but the focus of the Anonymous' *Life of St Cuthbert* is very much Lindisfarne itself. St Cuthbert's relevance was universal, but in the Anonymous' hands the theatre of action was local.

This contrasts with Bede's versions. Bede's verse *Life of St Cuthbert*, it has been argued, was written initially as a contemplative text to be read alongside the Anonymous' prose account. Bede says that he wrote it for 'John' who was to undertake a pilgrimage to Rome, to furnish him with memories of home, although there are indications that he revised the poem *c.*720, around the same time that he composed the longer, prose work.[38] Some have argued that he added little of substance to the Anonymous' account, and that his prose style was verbose in comparison to the simple elegance of the earlier *Life*.[39] However, Bede made significant changes to the story, adding some details and omitting others. These reveal much about the changing audience and function of St Cuthbert's cult in the second and third decades of the eighth century, as well as Bede's political agenda, and served to widen the appeal of St Cuthbert's cult to a bigger potential audience both within Northumbria and beyond it. In Bede's hands, and in contrast to the Anonymous' interpretation, St Cuthbert became a saint for *all* Northumbrians, representing the unity of the Northumbrian church. As represented by the Anonymous, Cuthbert was a holy man whose life and deeds were focused on Lindisfarne. In this context, therefore, St Cuthbert's *Life*, as

---

37 The *Vita S. Cuthberti Auctore Anonymo* (hereafter *VCA*) bk. iii 1, *hanc insulam nostram que dicitur Lindisfarnae* (ed. and trans. Colgrave, *Two Lives*, 59-139). All the extant copies of the *VCA* were written on the Continent, revealing the popularity of Cuthbert's cult abroad from at least the early ninth century (the date of the earliest of these). However, copies must have survived in England, since several English copies of the *VCB* are glossed with names of witnesses to Cuthbert's miracles that are known only through the *VCA*. See Bullough, D., 'A neglected early ninth-century manuscript of the Lindisfarne *Vita S. Cuthberti*', *Anglo-Saxon England* 27 (1998), pp.105-37.

38 On Bede's *VCM*, see Lapidge, M., *Bede the Poet*, Jarrow Lecture 1993 (1994) and *idem*, 'Bede's metrical Vita S. Cuthberti', in *St Cuthbert*, ed. Bonner et al., pp.77-93, both reprinted in his *Anglo-Latin Literature, 600-899* (London, 1996), pp.313-38 and 339-55, and *idem*, 'Prologomena to an edition of Bede's metrical "Vita Sancti Cuthberti"', *Filologia mediolatina* 2 (1995), pp.127-63.

39 Colgrave, *Two Lives*, 15. The *VCA* itself conforms to early hagiographic formulae.

refashioned by Bede, provided an antidote to the resurgent reputation of St Wilfrid, whose long period as bishop in Northumbria (664-709) had been turbulent and divisive, and whose cult was being promoted actively through a recently composed *Vita* by his disciple, Stephanus.[40]

Bede's *Vitae S. Cuthberti* also prefigured the narrative thrust of the *Ecclesiastical History*. There, Bede's primary objective was to trace the roots of Christianity and the establishment of the Church among the English; St Cuthbert's role in that process, as presented by Bede, was one of unifier and consolidator. Even though he was bishop for barely two years, the combination of St Cuthbert's Irish training and his apparent willingness to conform to Roman traditions after the Whitby decision marked him out as an aspirational figure for the Northumbrian church as a whole. Even though Bede's account of St Cuthbert's time as prior and bishop of Lindisfarne suggests that his ideas and leadership did not go unchallenged, it was through his 'perfect example' that he was able to overcome these differences both in life and, even more comprehensively, through a series of posthumous miracles that reinforced the rightness of his actions to those of his followers left behind: 'For I know that, although I seemed contemptible to some while I lived, yet, after my death, you will see what I was and how my teaching is not to be despised.'[41]

Both Bede and the Anonymous were careful to provide the names of individuals who were eye-witnesses to the events of St Cuthbert's life, so as to make unassailable the authenticity of their accounts. Bede said in the preface to his prose *Vita*:

> I have written nothing about the saint without first subjecting the facts to the most thorough scrutiny and have passed on nothing to be transcribed for general reading that has not been obtained by rigorous examination of trustworthy witnesses … with the help of those who had actually known him. I occasionally mention some of their names in the body of the book so that you can see for yourselves exactly what the sources are.

However, Bede's selection of St Cuthbert's miracles, and the witnesses to them, was subtly different from those used by the Anonymous. These differences reflect in part his access to alternative sources but also his authorial intentions. Bede's motivation in retelling the *Life of St Cuthbert* was to widen his subject's appeal beyond the narrow confines of the Lindisfarne community. Bede did not abandon the image of St Cuthbert as a man whose sanctity was linked closely to the environment and the *folc*. But his *Life* also lifted St Cuthbert's reputation from that of local healer to that of bishop and saint: 'many came', Bede reminded his readers, 'not only from the region of Lindisfarne, but also from the furthest parts of Britain'.[42]

---

40   The exact extent and base of St Wilfrid's see varied considerably over the course of his long episcopacy, which was interrupted several times by periods of forced exile. Stephanus, *Vita Wilfridi*; B. Colgrave (ed.), *Eddius Stephanus, Life of Bishop Wilfrid* (Cambridge, 1927); W. Goffart, *Narrators of Barbarian History* (Princeton, 1988), pp.235-328.

41   *VCB* 39 (ed. and trans. Colgrave, *Two Lives*, pp.282-5).

42   *VCB* 22 (ed. and trans. Colgrave, *Two Lives*, pp.228-31).

To this end, in his prose version of the *Life*, Bede dropped the names of many of the local people who had been linked by the Anonymous with St Cuthbert's life on Lindisfarne, and chose instead to add new miracle stories told to him by people associated with his own monastery at Wearmouth-Jarrow. Some of the stories, and the names of the men who retold them, had been unknown to the Anonymous. For example, he added the story of St Cuthbert's acceptance into the monastery of Melrose by Prior Boisil, the details of which had been told to him by Sigfrith, 'a veteran servant and priest of God' now living at Jarrow but who had been at Melrose at the time of St Cuthbert's entry there.[43] Similarly, Ingwald, an aged and blind priest at Wearmouth, had told Bede a story that he had heard directly from Cuthbert about the miraculous provision of food for himself and his horse on a journey in early winter.[44] Interestingly, although the Anonymous also knew this story, he had recorded the name of the place where it had happened, but not the name of his source. Another Jarrow priest, this time un-named in Bede's *Vita*, had told him of St Cuthbert's posthumous cure of the hermit Felgild's facial deformities.[45]

Two further stories known to Bede but not to the Anonymous were told about the communities of holy men and women whose monastery was based on the south bank of the Tyne, near the mouth of the river (perhaps at the Roman fort at South Shields) and thus not far from Bede's home at Jarrow.[46] The first of these was reported to Bede by a Jarrow monk, who had heard it from a 'simple peasant, incapable of telling a lie'; the peasant had witnessed the efficacious effect of St Cuthbert's prayers as he saved a group of monks being swept out to sea on rafts that were bringing timber to the monastery.[47] A second miracle occurred at the same monastery after it had been taken over by a community of nuns led by Abbess Verca, and was told to Bede by a monk who had lived at Wearmouth for some time and was eventually buried there. This brother was one of two who drank from the same cup as St Cuthbert, and tasted wine instead of water.[48] A marginal gloss in two late manuscripts of Bede's *Vita* names the monk as Fridumund, suggesting the persistence of a local tradition at Wearmouth-Jarrow about this Christ-like miracle.

Bede interpolated several stories into his narrative that had been told to him by men linked with Wearmouth-Jarrow. He also chose to emphasise the stories recalled by bishops, abbots and abbesses whose rank or reputation was recognised throughout Northumbria and beyond; in doing so, he linked memories of St Cuthbert with men of power rather than with the peasantry. For example, Bede five times referred by name to Eata, abbot of Melrose then bishop of Lindisfarne, whereas the Anonymous had named him only once.

---

43   *VCB* 6 (ed. and trans. Colgrave, *Two Lives*, pp.172-5).

44   *VCB* 5; *VCA* i.6 (ed. and trans. Colgrave, *Two Lives*, pp.70-1 and 168-71). The miracle happened near *Kuncacester*, on the banks of the river Wear (i.e. later Chester-le-Street).

45   *VCB* 46 (ed. and trans. Colgrave, *Two Lives*, pp.300-7).

46   The site of this monastery is not known for sure, but the Roman fort at South Shields (Arbeia) is a possible location since objects of eighth-century date, including a gilded cruciform mount and a stylus, have been found there; Colgrave, *Two Lives*, pp.342-3 and 353; Bidwell, P., 'Arbeia and Segedumum', *Current Archaeology* 200 (2005), pp.408-11 (suggesting that Arbeia may have become the site of a royal palace).

47   *VCB* 3 (ed. and trans. Colgrave, *Two Lives*, pp.160-5).

48   *VCB* 35 (ed. and trans. Colgrave, *Two Lives*, pp.266 n.12 and 353).

The Benedictine Monastery of LINDISFARNE Founded by St Aidan in the reign of St Oswald: the seat of the diocese of Bernicia AD 635-875: restored as a cell to Durham 1082

15 *Benedictine monastery of Lindisfarne*

The Anonymous reported an occasion when Abbess Aebbe of Coldingham had sent for St Cuthbert, but it was Bede who stressed that Aebbe was a woman of impeccable royal association, 'honoured among all for her piety as well as for her noble birth, as she was born of the same mother as King Oswiu'.[49] Oswiu's daughter, Abbess Aelflaed of Whitby, and Bishop Trumwine were sources for both Bede and the Anonymous, but Bede stressed that he had heard Aelflaed's accounts directly from the mouth of Abbot Herefrid of Lindisfarne who had had them from the princess herself. A Whitby-centred source probably also accounts for Trumwine's recollections of St Cuthbert; he had been a bishop in Pictland, based in Abercorn, but had been forced to flee south after the defeat of the Northumbrian army by the Picts at the Battle of Nechtansmere in 685 and had spent his remaining years in the royal monastery at Whitby.[50]

Bede did retain several stories told first by the Anonymous that were connected with the local men and women of Lindisfarne, but he omitted the names of those

---

49   *Soror uterina regis Osuiu*, ie they had the same mother, Acha (wife of King Aethelfrith), but not necessarily the same father. Compare the *VCB* 10 with *VCA* ii.3 (ed. and trans. Colgrave, *Two Lives*, pp.78-83 and 188-91).

50   *HE* IV.26 (ed. and trans. Colgrave and Mynors, *Bede's Ecclesiastical History*, pp.426-31.).

whose relevance was merely parochial and emphasised others whose reputation and status held greater weight in the world beyond. For example, he omitted the name of a Lindisfarne priest called Elias who, with Bishop Trumwine, had been the Anonymous' source for a story about St Cuthbert's childhood; Bede attributed the story entirely to 'the most holy bishop'.[51] He also supplied the name of Baldhelm as the source of one of the unattributed miracle stories told by the Anonymous. Baldhelm had been a servant of one of King Ecgfrith's bodyguards and had been cured of a 'foul disease' by St Cuthbert to become eventually a priest at Lindisfarne and was still alive when Bede wrote his prose *Vita S. Cuthberti* and had told Bede his story himself.[52] Another priest at Lindisfarne, called Cynimund, 'still alive and renowned far and wide for his great holiness and age', was the primary source for a story told only by Bede about some disobedient monks from Lindisfarne who had visited St Cuthbert at his hermitage on Farne. They had ignored his instruction to cook and eat a goose that was hanging on the wall of his cell before returning home; as a consequence, the monks (Cynimund among them) were marooned by stormy weather for seven days until they remembered St Cuthbert's instructions and boiled the goose.[53] Both Bede and the Anonymous told the story of the servant Walhstod, who had suffered from a stomach complaint for a long time and was cured of it by the dying Cuthbert. But Bede interpolated this story into the much longer, apparently verbatim, account of St Cuthbert's last days as told to him by Herefrith, a 'sincerely devout priest and present abbot of Lindisfarne'. Herefrith had commented on drafts of Bede's prose Vita S. Cuthberti during visits to Jarrow and was evidently one of Bede's most respected informers, providing him with details for several stories, including what purports to be a verbatim account of St Cuthbert's death.[54] The point of Wahlstod's story shifts between the accounts given in the two Lives, away from the Anonymous' focus on Walhstod as the humble recipient of a miraculous cure, to proof of St Cuthbert's healing powers as reported to Bede by Abbot Herefrith, the official spokesman of the Lindisfarne community.

Bede's concentration on Abbot Herefrith's testimony replaced the Anonymous' reliance on the witness of a humble Lindisfarne priest called Tydi. Four stories were attributed to Tydi in the Anonymous' account, all of which were retained by Bede but without once naming Tydi as the source.[55] Bede also dropped the name of Plecgils, a priest from Melrose, when retelling the fable of the otters that came out of the sea to warm St Cuthbert's feet; this has the effect of refocusing the story on the testimony of the more illustrious Abbess Aebbe of Coldingham.[56] The Anonymous also told a story about a 'certain woman called Coenswith, who is still alive, a nun and a widow, who had brought [Cuthbert] up from his eighth year until manhood ... he called her

51 *VCA* i.3 (where Trumwine is called Tumma) and *VCB* chs. 1, 24 (ed. and trans. Colgrave, *Two Lives*, pp.64-7, 154-9, 234-9).
52 *VCB* 25 and *VCA* iv.7 (ed. and trans. Colgrave, *Two Lives*, pp.120-3 and 238-41).
53 *VCB* 36 (ed. and trans. Colgrave, *Two Lives*, pp.266-71).
54 *VCB* preface and chapters 8, 23, 37, 38 (ed. and trans. Colgrave, *Two Lives*, pp.142-7, 180-5, 230-5, 270-83).
55 *VCA* ii.4; ii.5; iv.6; iv.15 (ed. and trans. Colgrave, *Two Lives*, pp.82-7, 118-21, 132-5).
56 *VCA* ii.3 and *VCB* 10 (ed. and trans. Colgrave, *Two Lives*, pp.78-83, 188-91).

mother, and often visited her' in a village called *Hringuaham*.[57] Bede re-told the story but omitted Coenswith's name (and that of her village), calling her simply 'a woman devoted to God' who St Cuthbert visited often because she was 'given to good deeds and had brought him up from his earliest years'.[58] By cutting out the local details Bede's version sharpened the focus onto St Cuthbert himself. Interestingly, a similar sort of editorial intervention is apparent in a group of late copies of the Anonymous' *Life* made on the continent which seem to have derived from a 12th-century exemplar made in Trier; these copies omitted the personal and place-names of the Lindisfarne *Life*, presumably because the editor of the exemplar thought them distracting or irrelevant to his continental audience.[59] That these omissions are often the same as Bede's may suggest that the 12th-century Trier editor of the Anonymous' text knew Bede's version of the *Life* as well.

In the *Vita S. Cuthberti*, Bede pointedly used Abbot Herefrith's eye-witness testimony of St Cuthbert's deathbed speech to underscore the saint's adherence to the orthodox practices of the Church in the face of current and forthcoming adversity: 'Strive to learn and to observe most diligently the catholic statutes of the fathers, and practise with zeal those rules of regular discipline which the divine mercy has deigned to give you through my ministry'. 'But have no communion', Herefrith's report continued,

> with those who depart from the unity of the catholic peace, either in not celebrating Easter at the proper time or in evil living. And you are to know and remember that if necessity compels you to choose between one of two evils, I would much rather that you should take my bones from the tomb, carry them with you and departing from this place dwell wherever God may ordain, than that in any way you should consent to iniquity and put your necks under the yoke of schismatics.[60]

Bede did not explore the implications of St Cuthbert's prediction in his *Vita S. Cuthberti*, saying simply that, in the year after his death, 'so great a blast of trial beat upon that church [of Lindisfarne] that many of the brethren chose to depart from the place rather than be in the midst of such dangers'. We have to go to the *Ecclesiastical History*, where Bede says in unemotive language that during this period the Lindisfarne bishopric was administered by the Romanist cleric, St Wilfrid.[61] In the troubled times of the early eighth century, Bede and others were able to revive St Cuthbert as a figure whose humanity, piety and calm conviction in the face of opposition both within his own community and outside it, could be used to inspire concord where before there had been difference. This blurring of the lines of distinction between the Irish and Roman practices that had characterised the earliest decades of Christianity in

---

57   *VCA* ii.7 (ed. and trans. Colgrave, *Two Lives*, pp.88-91).
58   *VCB* 14 (ed. and trans. Colgrave, *Two Lives*, pp.200-3). Lapidge, 'Bede's Metrical Vita S. Cuthberti', 351-2.
59   Ed. and trans. Colgrave, *Two Lives*, pp.15, 43.
60   *Ibid.*
61   *HE* IV.29 (ed. and trans. Colgrave and Mynors, *Bede's Ecclesiastical History*, pp.438-43).

Anglo-Saxon Northumbria was a theme matched in Bede's *Ecclesiastical History* by the blurring of the borders between the two Northumbrian sub-kingdoms of Bernicia and Deira. In Bede's hands, the unification of the kingdom of Northumbria itself was a parallel process to the consolidation of a unified Northumbrian church.

Bede and the Anonymous author of St Cuthbert's *Life* both used the testimony of named individuals to sharpen the veracity of the miraculous events associated with St Cuthbert in life and after his death. The Anonymous favoured the stories of men and women local to Lindisfarne where St Cuthbert had spent the last part of his life, thereby harnessing the locality of the island to the legacy of his memory and corporeal remains. Bede's version broadened the saint's appeal by incorporating the memories of people based elsewhere whose name and rank ensured the credibility of their testimony in circles far beyond Lindisfarne. But both authors used the testimony of those poor Northumbrians among whom St Cuthbert ministered: Hadwald the shepherd who tended Abbess Aelflaed's flocks and who was killed falling from a tree; the shepherds whose summer huts provided a refuge for St Cuthbert and his horse in a winter storm; the villagers who fought the fire burning the thatch of a house in the eastern part of the village of *Hringuaham*; the peasants who lived in the villages that were far away on steep and rugged mountains where St Cuthbert went to preach for two or three weeks at a time. These are the seventh- and eighth-century *rustici*, *populi* or *vulgi* whose experiences of life, death and landscape are otherwise so inaccessible. The intersection of their lives with that of St Cuthbert preserves a few fleeting impressions of the ways of life of the *folc* of Anglo-Saxon Northumbria.

Border and Coalfield

5

'Northumbria' in the Later Middle Ages

A. C. KING AND A. J. POLLARD

Where, and what, and when was 'Northumbria'? Was it the Anglo-Saxon kingdom at its widest extent from the Forth to the Humber, or was it just Northumberland and Durham? The Surtees Society, when it was founded in 1834, set out to publish works from the widest regional territory:

> Manuscripts illustrative of the intellectual, the moral, the religious, and the social condition of those parts of England and Scotland, included on the east between the Humber and the Firth of Forth, and on the west between the Mersey and the Clyde, a region which constituted the Ancient Kingdom of Northumberland.

Yet, in spite of such a great territory, most of the early members of the Society were 'naturally' drawn from the counties of Durham and Northumberland.[1] And this is how Anthony Emery saw it in his history of the great houses of late medieval England. He took it for granted that 'Northumbria (Northumberland and County Durham)' had a unity provided by geography and history and in this view he is certainly in good company.[2] 'Northumbria' today is used as an alternative for the more prosaic 'North East', for its romantic associations to attract tourists, for commercial branding, or to impart cultural significance. Northumbria might have shrivelled in its borders between the seventh and 21st centuries, but *the idea* of it still survives.

So, where and what was 'Northumbria' between the outbreak of the Anglo-Scottish Wars and the Reformation? Between 1296 and 1540 was there anything identifiable on the ground as a Northumbrian rump? Was there any idea of a Northumbria retained in the minds of those who lived through those three centuries?

---

1 Hamilton Thompson, A., *The Surtees Society, 1834-1934* (Surtees Society, 150, 1939), p.2.
2 Emery, A., *Greater Medieval Houses of England and Wales, 1300-1500: Volume1, Northern England* (Cambridge, 1996), p.9.

I

The process by which Northumbria retreated over the early medieval period from west of the Pennines, north of the Tweed and south of the Tees was complex and extended. The collapse of the Anglo-Saxon kingdom in the face of Viking invasions and the formation of successor 'states' in the early 10th century led ultimately to a permanent political division at the Tees. There was Viking intrusion north of the river, but it was a Viking king of York who first recognised the land between Tees and Tyne as a separate patrimony of St Cuthbert. The Tees remained the northernmost limit of the expansion of Wessex in the 10th century, leaving the lands to the north to the Community of St Cuthbert and the shadowy earldom of Northumberland, an ill-defined march contested with the kingdom of the Scots. In the 11th century it was also the initial northern limit of the Anglo-Norman kingdom and the reason for its exclusion from the Domesday Survey of 1086. Some early Anglo-Norman texts refer not to *Northumbria* but to *Norteisa*.[3] A similar process of contraction took place to the west where a kingdom of Cumbria emerged, which was ultimately, if not from the beginning, an extension of the Scottish kingdom of Strathclyde. The Pennine ridge thus emerged as the boundary it has remained ever since.[4]

The definition of the Tweed as the northern boundary took longer to emerge. In the 12th century it was still not certain whether Northumbria would be the southernmost part of Scotland rather than the northernmost part of England: it remained an extensive march contested between the two kingdoms. And so, in April 1139, King Stephen's precarious position forced him to concede the earldom of Northumbria (*comitatum Northumbrie*) to Henry, son and heir of David I of Scotland, with authority between Tyne and Tweed[5] – this despite the Scottish defeat at the Battle of the Standard, near Northallerton in Yorkshire, in the previous August. And David tried to extend his influence to the Tees, supporting the attempts of his chancellor, William Cumin, to intrude himself into the bishopric of Durham. Writing at the end of the 12th century, the Yorkshire chronicler William of Newburgh described the parlous state of England during Stephen's reign, adding, 'But the northern region, which had fallen under the power of David, King of Scots, as far as the river Tees, remained peaceful through that king's diligence.'[6] However, the peaceful accession of a resurgent Henry II, coupled with the succession to the Scottish throne of the 12-year-old Malcolm IV, ensured that Northumbria was returned to English rule. Then, some sixty years later in October 1215,

3   Barlow, G.W.S., *Feudal Britain* (London, 1967), p.18; Aird, W.M., *St Cuthbert and the Normans: the Church of Durham, 1071-1153* (Woodbridge, 1991), pp.71-98, 185.

4   Rollason, David, *Northumbria, 500-1100: Creation and Destruction of a Kingdom* (Cambridge, 2003), pp.244-55; Phythian-Adams, Charles, *The Land of the Cumbrians: a Study in British Provincial Origins, AD 400-1120* (Aldershot, 1996), pp.77-8, 110-22.

5   Richard of Hexham, 'De gestis regis Stephani', in *Chronicles of the Reigns of Stephen, Henry II and Richard I*, ed. Richard Howlett, Rolls Series 82 (4 vols, 1884-9), iii, p.177.

6   William of Newburgh, *The History of English Affairs. Book 1*, ed. P.G. Walsh and M.J. Kennedy (Warminster, 1988), p.98 (our translation); Stringer, K.J., 'State-Building in Twelfth-Century Britain: David I, King of Scots, and Northern England', in J.C. Appleby and P. Dalton (eds), *Government, Religion and Society in Northern England, 1000-1700* (Stroud, 1997), pp.40-62 and the references therein.

during their rebellion against King John, the barons of Northumberland solemnly invested Alexander II of Scotland with the county of Northumberland – albeit probably on the condition that Alexander held it as a fief of the English Crown. They were led by Eustace de Vesci and Robert de Ros, lords of Alnwick and Wark on Tweed respectively, both of whom also held Scottish lands, and both of whom were married to illegitimate daughters of William the Lion, King of Scotland (1165-1214). The barons of Yorkshire followed suit in the following January; but Durham, under Bishop Richard Marsh, John's chancellor, largely remained loyal to King John, and indeed de Vesci was killed while besieging Barnard Castle.[7]

The principal landholders were subjects of the kings of both England and of Scotland, most famously Bruces and Balliols. During the long peace of the 13th century, as Keith Stringer has shown, the legal divide between the kingdoms of England and Scotland roughly along the Tweed did not mean social or economic separation. A perennial and immediate problem was how to resolve disputes and deal with cases involving subjects of different kings. Before the outbreak of war in 1296 a system of local law was adopted with its own codification, whereby six Scots and six English would adjudicate according to the custom of the March. The 'Law of the March' was in effect devolved by the two kings. Thus there existed a sophisticated local system which brought together communities on either side of the border.[8] The north-eastern extremity of the kingdom of England and south-eastern part of the kingdom of Scotland formed in the 13th century an extensive, settled and peaceful march.

Within that march the lower Tweed valley was a flourishing centre. Berwick was one of Scotland's most prosperous ports, drawing on a hinterland in both England and Scotland. Tenurial arrangements and agricultural practice were the same on both sides. A significant tract of land on both sides of the river near the mouth of the Tweed (North Durham in England and Coldingham in Scotland) was held by the Bishop of Durham and Durham Cathedral Priory respectively. North Durham, comprising Islandshire and Norhamshire, had been acquired by the bishopric in its early days, when it was based on Lindisfarne; Coldingham had been granted to the priory by the king of Scots in the first decade of the 12th century. The inhabitants of the lower Tweed valley thus shared an affiliation with St Cuthbert. Just as it had been one of the principal focal points of the Anglo-Saxon kingdom of Northumbria, so for almost two hundred years, between 1100 and 1300, the lower Tweed valley was an economic, social and cultural zone that happened to be divided by an international boundary.[9]

It was the 300-year Anglo-Scottish war, a specific historical phenomenon, which determined that the boundary would become a border, and that the lower Tweed

---

7   Holt, J.C., *The Northerners. A Study in the Reign of King John* (2nd edn, Oxford, 1993), pp.131-3, 138.

8   Stringer, K.J., 'Identities in Thirteenth-Century England: Frontier Society in the Far North', in Claus Bjørn, Alexander Grant and Keith J. Stringer (eds), *Social and Political Identities in Western History* (Copenhagen, 1994), 28-66; Neville, C.J., *Violence, Custom and Law: the Anglo-Scottish Border Lands in the Later Middle Ages* (Edinburgh, 1998), pp.1-14.

9   Lomas, R.A., 'St Cuthbert and the Border, c.1080-c.1300', in R.H. Britnell and C.J. Liddy (eds), *North-eastern England in the Later Middle Ages* (Woodbridge, 2005), pp.13-28.

would cease to be a local focus and become a frontier. Not until the war with Scotland, and in particular Edward I's insistence (in contrast to his father) that all Scots had to accept his overlordship, and by implication the laws of England, that the curtain finally descended on ancient Northumbria and divided it as irrevocably from its northern territories as it had been earlier separated from its southern. Even then the outcome was not certain. For two decades after the English victory at Neville's Cross in 1346, southern Scotland was in English hands, only slowly wrested back by the Scots after 1369. Roxburgh remained an English outpost until 1460, Berwick still is. A survey of 1415 listed Roxburgh and Berwick amongst the castles within the county of Northumberland.[10] There was even some revival of cross-border landholding during this time, albeit on a minor scale. In February 1347, John de Strivelyn – himself a Scot who had adhered to the English and settled in Northumberland – was granted various Scottish lands forfeited to Edward III by their recalcitrant Scottish lords. And in *c.*1354 the Northumbrian John de Coupland, the captor of David II at Neville's Cross, acquired lands in Roxburghshire while serving as keeper of Roxburgh (although he disposed of them just four years later). From the other side of the border, Sir Edward de Letham, a Berwickshire knight in the English allegiance, was rewarded with the wardship of Etal Castle in Northumberland during the long minority of John Manners. He was also part of a consortium of prominent Northumbrian knights who acquired the wardship of Thomas de Heton, heir to extensive estates around Chillingham.[11]

Similarly, the Percys were exceedingly reluctant to abandon their claim to Jedburgh, and Durham Cathedral Priory refused to give up on Coldingham until the late 15th century. The shifting allegiances of the Scottish earls of March were symptomatic of this; they were, after all, the lineal descendants of the 'house of Bamburgh', the last Anglian earls of Northumbria. In 1296 Patrick Dunbar, earl of March, faced something of a dilemma as he held the Northumbrian barony of Beanley as well as his Scottish estates. He sided with Edward I and died in the English allegiance in 1308; but in the aftermath of the battle of Bannockburn (1314) his son went over to the Scots, though he briefly adhered to the English-supported regime of Edward Balliol, in 1333-5. His successor, George (his great-nephew), was instrumental in the restoration of Coldingham to Durham when it was confiscated by the Scots in 1379; he defected to the English in 1400, and fought for the Percys at Homildon Hill in 1402 and Shrewsbury in 1403, before making his peace with the Scots in 1409. As if to symbolise his status as a representative of an older cross-border tradition harking back to ancient Northumbria, he was before his death admitted to the confraternity of St Cuthbert at Durham.[12]

10   Cadwallader Bates, 'The Border Holds of Northumberland', *Archaeologia Aeliana*, 2nd ser., xiv (1891), pp.13-15.
11   Rotuli Scotiæ, ed. D. Macpherson (2 vols, Record Commission, 1814-19), i, p.689; 'MSS of the Duke of Roxburghe', Historical Manuscripts Commission, Fourteenth Report, Appendix, iii (1894), p.8; Calendar of Patent Rolls 1354-8, p.283; Calendar of Patent Rolls 1367-70, p.119; Calendar of Fine Rolls 1356-68, p.235; Goodman, Anthony, 'The Anglo-Scottish Marches in the Fifteenth Century: A Frontier Society?', in Mason, Roger A. (ed.), *Scotland and England, 1286-1815* (Edinburgh, 1986), p.20; Macdonald, A.J., *Border Bloodshed: Scotland and England at War, 1369-1403* (East Linton, 2000).
12   Cockayne, G.E. et al. (ed.), *The Complete Peerage*, rev. and ed. V. Gibbs (12 vols, London, 1910-59), iv, pp.507-9; Macdonald, A.J., 'Kings of the Wild Frontier? The earls of Dunbar or march, c.1070-1435', in Steve Boardman and Alasdair Ross (eds), *The Exercise of Power in Medieval Scotland, c1200 -1500* (Dublin, 2003), pp.139-58.

Writing towards the end of the 14th century, Thomas Burton commented in his chronicle of Meaux Abbey in Holderness that in 1346 the ambition of the King of Scots, David II, had been to annex England north of the Humber to Scotland, and thus in effect restore Northumbria to Scotland.[13] David II's subsequent defeat at Neville's Cross (1346) was inflicted by troops recruited from throughout the north, the area of the old Anglo-Saxon kingdom, and the battle was fought within view of Durham Cathedral. On another occasion, the forces of 'Northumbria' were unable to act with such impressive unity, for John de Fordham, Bishop of Durham, notoriously failed to turn up with the Durham contingent at Otterburn in 1388, for which one contemporary chronicler held him partially responsible for the English defeat.[14] From time to time thereafter levies from the northern counties were summoned to defend the border, often with success, such as the notable English victory at Homildon Hill, 1402.[15] In 1463 the Earl of Warwick even called upon the York clergy to resist the Scots. On this and other occasions Durham contingents were raised as well, taking with them the famous banner of St Cuthbert, successfully recovering Berwick in 1482, for instance.[16]

The heritage of ancient 'Northumbria', which Scots and English sometimes shared and sometimes contested, was slow to fade. Nevertheless, the exigencies of war between the two kingdoms served to undermine it by sharpening national distinctions and hardening the border that divided them. The day-to-day defence of north-east England was organised around the 'English Marches against Scotland', under Wardens of the March appointed by the Crown. The Marches incorporated the three border counties of Northumberland, Westmorland and Cumberland. Perhaps by virtue of its status as a county palatine, constitutionally independent of the Crown, the bishopric of Durham south of the Tyne/Derwent was not included, for all that bishops of Durham themselves sometimes served as March Wardens. On the other hand, the bishopric's enclaves of Norhamshire, Islandshire and Bedlingtonshire in Northumberland *were* subject to the warden's authority, their franchise notwithstanding. North of the Tyne/Derwent, Northumberland gained a separate jurisdiction of its own, as the East March (periodically split into the East and Middle Marches). It was the forces of the East March alone who won the English victory at Homildon Hill.[17] South of the Tyne, Durham was far less directly touched by the wars. It suffered invasion by the Scots on several occasions between 1311 and 1322, again in 1346, in 1388 and finally in 1461; but otherwise Scottish raiding was largely confined to beyond the Tyne.

Consequently, the burden of policing the eastern frontier fell substantially on the shoulders of the men of Northumberland. As a result political society there became more militarised than in Durham; while a successful military career led to advancement in the

---

13 *Chronica monasteride Melsa a fundatione as annum 1396*, ed. E.A. Bond (RS 43: 3 vols, London, 1866-8), iii, p.60.

14 *The Westminster Chronicle, 1381-1394*, ed. L.C. Hector and Barbara F. Harvey (Oxford, 1982), pp.347-51; Dobson, R.B., 'The Church of Durham and the Scottish Borders, 1378-88' in A.E. Goodman and J.A. Tuck (eds), *War and Border Societies in the Middle Ages* (London, 1992), pp.124-54.

15 Macdonald, Alastair J., *Border Bloodshed: Scotland, England and France at War, 1369-1403* (East Linton, 2000), p.155.

16 Pollard, *North-Eastern England*, pp.16, 227, 237-9.

17 Storey, R.L., 'The Wardens of the Marches of England towards Scotland, 1377-1489', *English Historical Review*, 72 (1957), pp.593-615.

royal government of the county, the same was less true of the palatine administration. There were few cases in Durham of upward mobility following success on the battlefield to match John de Coupland, the Lilleburns, the Hetons, the Manners or the Ogles in Northumberland. The Grays of Heton, who owed their all but hereditary hold on the bishops' castle at Norham to their martial prowess, are an exception which proves the rule – for Norham, an enclave of the bishopric within Northumberland, was on the Anglo-Scottish border, overlooking a crossing of the Tweed. In so far as the men of Durham did become engaged in the routine defence of the border, by the 15th century it tended to be in the West March under the 1st Earl of Westmorland and his successors. Thus, Sir William Claxton of Claxton and Horden was retained in 1403 to serve the 1st Earl of Westmorland in the garrison of Carlisle.[18]

Whether on the East or West March, military service for the men of Durham was more distant. It may be that this reality was marked in stone by the pattern of newly built castles which ostentatiously dotted the landscape of Northumberland, a fashion which had less impact on Durham and points further south. Many of the Northumberland gentry chose to mark the enhanced status and wealth which military service had brought (and, perhaps, to protect that wealth from marauding Scots) by building elaborate tower houses or fashionable courtyard castles, such as the Feltons at Edlingham, the Herons at Ford, the Manners at Etal, the Hetons at Chillingham and the Ogles at Bothal. Fewer such residences were built by the Durham gentry in the late Middle Ages. The pattern reveals that they had more in common with their Yorkshire neighbours, such as Rokeby at Mortham, or Conyers at South Cowton. Mortham, possibly built by Sir Thomas Rokeby from the profits of service to the Crown in the reign of Edward III, is a fine example of a march-style castle, sited well away from the March itself. While the architectural style reflects a common northern, late medieval fashion, some of it designed for increased comfort, the greater concentration of such castles close to the border perhaps indicates a greater perceived military need.[19]

II

By 1400 the English counties of Durham and Northumberland were in reality all that was left of Northumbria, the rump of the ancient kingdom. They had become the constituent parts of an *English* Northumbria defended against the Scots. These two counties were in fact – and this is too little appreciated – but one royal county: Northumberland, or, in Latin, *comitatus Northumbrie*, stretching from the Tees to the Tweed. The medieval county emerged out of the earldom of Northumberland, following the deposition of Earl Robert de Mowbray in 1095. Durham was, technically, the largest and most significant of several liberties within that earldom.[20]

18   Barker, B.A., 'The Claxtons: a North-Eastern Gentry Family in the Fourteenth and Fifteenth Centuries' (University of Teesside PhD thesis, 2004), p.148.
19   Emery, *Greater Houses*, I, pp.25-9, 54-5, 65-7, 91-5, 285-6, 380-3, 398.
20   The others were Norhamshire, Islandshire and Bedlington (all part of the liberty of Durham); Tynemouth (a dependency of the Benedictine Abbey of St Albans); Hexham (held by the Archbishops of York); Tynedale; and Redesdale.

16 *Edlingham Castle*

This is made explicit in disputes from time to time over the precise limits of the Palatinate, especially in the vexed matter as to whether the lordship of Barnard Castle lay within its bounds. The late medieval lords, the Beauchamps until 1449, owed their title to royal grant after the confiscation from the Balliols, not to the bishop. Thereafter they were careful to maintain this legal nicety. Thus in 1400, shortly before his death, Thomas Beauchamp, Earl of Warwick, conveyed to his son and heir, Richard, the lordship which, the conveyance specified, lay within the wapentake of Sadbergh, which is in the body of the county of Northumberland.[21] Other instances arose, not only in respect of Barnard Castle but also Hart, in the possession of the Cliffords. Always the legal point at issue was whether the property lay in the county palatine, in which case superior lordship lay with the bishop, or within the county of Northumberland, in which case it lay with the king.

At one point, the constitutional nicety of one county might have been given a new reality – albeit as an accidental by-product of Richard I's insatiable demand for money. This occurred when the wapentake of Sadberge and the earldom of Northumbria were sold to Bishop Hugh du Puiset of Durham in 1189, making him lord of all the land between Tees and Tweed.[22] While Sadberge became permanently annexed to the bishopric, nothing came of this short-lived re-unification of the earldom and the Palatinate. The idea that there was technically but one county may offer the explanation as to why there was no parliamentary representation for Durham until the 17th century; it was subsumed in that of Northumberland. In so far as Durham could enjoy a voice in Parliament, it was through its bishop, the prior of the priory and their proctors, or, presumably, friends who sat for Northumberland, another county, or an amenable

---

21   National Archives, E40/658. We owe this reference to Melanie Devine.
22   Scammell, G.V., *Hugh du Puiset Bishop of Durham* (Cambridge, 1956), pp.49-50.

borough. Looked at from the narrow point of view of royal administration, therefore, there is no problem: Durham was part of the county of Northumberland (*comitatus Northumbrie*), just as its earl was the earl of Northumbria (*comes Northumbrie*), or sometimes earl of the Northumbrians *(comes Northumbrorum)*.

The diocesan boundary marched with the county boundary of Northumberland. Here was another unifying administrative feature; spiritual as distinct from secular. Just as there were significant jurisdictional enclaves within the county of Northumberland, so also there were ecclesiastical enclaves within the diocese; Hexham was attached to the diocese of York, Tynemouth Priory to St Albans Abbey. The priory of Durham enjoyed special privileges as well as extensive estates, enabling it to exercise a considerable degree of independence north of the Tyne as well as between Tyne and Tees. There were three archdeaconries, Northumberland, Durham and the Priory, in parishes appropriated to it throughout the diocese. The archdeaconry and consistory courts heard cases concerning clerical rights, the discipline of the clergy, church attendance, sexual misconduct, marital litigation, defamation and probate.[23] There were thus two coterminous jurisdictional and administrative bodies, county and diocese, touching on every aspect of people's lives. The inhabitants might have been faced by a bewildering array of overlapping jurisdictions and administrations, but the civil and ecclesiastical enclaves of external corporations apart, they all lay within the boundaries of the county/diocese of Northumberland/Durham.

The overlapping jurisdictions of the county/diocese of Northumberland/Durham found some expression – albeit in violent opposition to the royal administration – in the 1317 plot against Louis de Beaumont, a Frenchman provided to the bishopric by the request of Edward II, at the instigation of Queen Isabella. While travelling to Durham for his consecration, Beaumont was kidnapped by the Northumbrian knight Sir Gilbert de Middleton, who, for good measure, also robbed the two cardinals travelling in his company. Excommunicated for his sins, and beyond hope of rehabilitation, Middleton then laid claim to the title of 'Duke of Northumbria' (*ducem Northumbrie*) – at least according to the well-informed *Historia Aurea*.[24] Whether or not the pretended title was intended to signify just Northumberland, the plot encompassed the bishopric as well. Beaumont was ambushed near Rushyford in Durham, then hauled off to imprisonment in Mitford Castle, near Morpeth, along with his brother Henry. Middleton's main co-conspirators, John de Eure and Walter de Selby, both held lands in the bishopric and in Northumberland. And when Middleton resorted to banditry, his range extended south of the Tyne, for he extorted at least 450 marks protection money from 'the community of the bishopric of Durham'.[25]

---

23   Lomas, R.A., *North-East England in the Middle Ages* (Edinburgh, 1992), pp.92-103; Storey, R.L., *Thomas Langley and the Bishopric of Durham, 1406-1437* (London, 1961), pp.164-91; Harvey, Margaret, 'Church Discipline in Late Medieval Durham', in Britnell and Liddy, *North-East England*, pp.119-26.
24   Lambeth Palace MS. 12, f. 226.
25   Durham Cathedral Muniments, MC 4049, 5053; printed in A.E. Middleton, *Sir Gilbert de Middleton* (Newcastle upon Tyne, 1918), pp.47-8, along with the author's rather lame attempt to absolve his forebear from the charge of levying blackmail.

17 *Alnwick Castle photographed in 1889*

Yet the plot had its roots in Northumberland. Beaumont's brother Henry was an unpopular court favourite who had recruited a number of knights from the county into his retinue. His sister, Isabella, was the widow of John de Vesci, Lord of Alnwick; her custody of Bamburgh Castle, granted to her by Edward I, had been a matter of controversy, and the Ordinances of 1311 had called for her removal. Clearly, it was feared that Louis' instalment in the bishopric would enhance Henry and Isabella's standing north of the Tyne.[26]

Occasionally, the men of the North East could act together to further their interests, as when 'the people of the county of Northumberland and of the bishopric of Durham' sent a petition to the Crown, probably in 1341. They complained that robbers and malefactors indicted by the county's coroners were hiding out in the bishopric (and *vice versa*), and called for records to be kept so that the coroners in one jurisdiction would know who had been indicted in the other.[27] However, the very nature of this petition points to the jurisdictional chasm that separated county and bishopric – for all the fact that the bishopric was theoretically part of the county. That the Crown had to be requested to arrange for such co-operation serves to highlight the absence of such co-operation at a routine level. Durham and Northumberland were in practice treated by the Crown as entirely separate political communities, and tended to act as such.

As the 1317 plot reveals, the principal families of North East England held land

---

26 King, Andy, 'Bandits, Robbers and *Schavaldours*: War and Disorder in Northumberland in the Reign of Edward II', *Thirteenth-Century England IX*, ed. Michael Prestwich, R.H. Britnell and Robin Frame (Woodbridge, 2003), pp.125-8.
27 *Northumberland Petitions. Ancient Petitions Relating to Northumberland*, ed. C.M. Fraser, Surtees Society clxxvi (1966), pp.125-6.

both sides of the Tyne. While Percy interests were concentrated north of the river, and Neville interests to the south, the Eures and the Lumleys, for example, straddled both. There were also less important families who held lands north and south of the Tyne, such as the Claxtons, the Surtees and the Selbys. Generally, however, the gentry tended to be one or the other; few held office in both the bishopric and in Northumberland. Sir Thomas Gray, author of the *Scalacronica*,[28] served the bishops of Durham not only as constable and sheriff of Norham, but also as a justice in the bishop's court at Durham. However, he was far more prominent north of the Tyne, being the first named on the 1346 petition from the community of the knights and sergeants of Northumberland.[29] Similarly, the Feltons played a leading role in the royal administration of Northumberland; and although they also owned lands within the Palatinate they played no part in its administration. Conversely, the Lumleys held property in Northumberland, of the Percys, but confined their attentions entirely to the Palatinate. The Eures, whose principal seat was at Witton le Wear, were active in both counties, and in Yorkshire. The most successful member of the family, Sir Ralph, was sheriff of and MP for Northumberland several times, but his principal commitment was to the Palatinate, being lay steward under successive bishops from 1391 until his death in 1422.[30]

These men identified with separate communities. This was made explicit in the negotiations undertaken separately in the early 14th century to buy off the Scots.[31] In August 1312, for instance, four 'envoys' appointed by the people of the community of the bishopric between Tyne and Tees agreed a ten-month truce at a cost of 450 marks.[32] Both Durham and Northumberland were accustomed to act independently as self-proclaimed communities, whether petitioning to the Crown or coming to terms with the Scots. Just how separate they became is revealed more than two centuries later in 1523 when the Earl of Westmorland was briefly acting as the vice warden (to the Duke of Richmond) of the East and Middle March. He petitioned the Crown that he be granted a convenient place in Northumberland 'to lie upon', and that he be given authority to retain 'Northumbrians' in his service and appoint all officers of the Crown in the county. It was necessary, he explained, because 'I am a stranger in that country having neither kinfolk nor allies there, nor no lands there at this day, whereby I might entertain them and have their assistance'.[33] The Earl of Westmorland, whose principal seats lay at Brancepeth and Raby in the bishopric, without land, kith or kin

---

28   The *Scalacronica* relates the history of Britain from the Creation to its author's present day, ending at 1363. It was the first historical work known to have been written by a member of the English lay nobility since the Norman Conquest. See *Sir Thomas Gray's Scalacronica, 1272-1363*, ed. Andy King, Surtees Society ccix (2005).
29   National Archives, C 49/7/20; King, Andy, 'Scaling the Ladder; the Rise and Rise of the Grays of Heton, *c.*1296-*c.*1415', in Britnell and Liddy, *North-East England*, pp.59-60.
30   Roskell, J.S. et al., *The History of Parliament: The House of Commons, 1386-1421* (Stroud, 1992, 4 vols), iii, pp.38-43.
31   Scammell, J., 'Robert I and the North of England', *HER* 73 (1958), pp.385-403; McNamee, C., *The wars of the Bruces: Scotland, England and Ireland, 1306-1328* (East Linton, 1997), pp.129-40.
32   *Registrum palatinum Dunelmense*, ed. T.D. Hardy, i (RS, 1873), 204-5. We owe this reference to Matt Holford.
33   BL, Caligula B.VI, fos 510-11. We are grateful to Claire Etty for drawing our attention to this evidence. The earl's situation was temporary for at the time the Neville estate in southern Northumberland, at Biwell, was in the hands of the dowager countess. Of course, he may have been making an excuse to be relieved of his post; if that is so, the reasons he chose to advance are revealing.

there, was a foreigner in Northumberland. When the King did not grant his request, Westmorland resigned.

The armorial decorations that adorned the residences of the local lords also reflected this separation between Northumberland and Durham. On his voguish new gatehouse at Bothal Castle, Northumberland, licensed in 1343, Robert Bertram chose to display the arms of Northumberland neighbours such as John de Coupland, William Felton, Roger de Horsley, John de Ogle and Robert Delaval, in the illustrious company of Edward III and the Black Prince, and the local luminaries Henry Percy and William, Lord Greystoke. The only Durham arms displayed are those of the Conyers (though the Yorkshire Scargills also appear). On his brand new castle at Lumley in the Palatinate, licensed in 1389, Ralph Lumley displayed the arms of Richard II, Henry Percy, Earl of Northumberland, Ralph, Lord Neville, William, Lord Hilton, and Sir Thomas Gray of Heton. Of these, only Percy and Gray held lands in Northumberland (though Lumley did himself), and Gray had strong Durham connections.[34] The social horizons of both Bertram and Lumley seem to have been restricted by the Tyne.

And then there is Newcastle. What role was it beginning to play as a focal point? It was, as is well established, the principal port on the east coast between Berwick and Hull. It rose rapidly in prosperity in the 12th and 13th centuries, exporting wool, cloths, lead and above all coal, and importing a range of goods, luxury as well as basic, including spices, wine, grain, tiles, timber and iron. It had its own mint and was the advance supply base for Scottish operations.[35] Newcastle was also the head customs port for the north-east coast with member ports stretching from Berwick to Whitby. By the 14th century it had successfully suppressed rival ports such as Yarm and Hartlepool, turning them into subsidiaries. While its flourishing trade, especially in coal, with east coast ports to Grimsby and points south is well documented for the early 16th century, nothing is recorded of its role as an entrepot more locally. One suspects that there was a flourishing trade up and down the coasts of Northumberland and Durham in goods transhipped into light vessels at Newcastle.[36] The evidence of Durham Priory's purchases of provisions towards the end of the Middle Ages suggests that Newcastle emerged as the commercial centre for its region. The priory employed an extensive network of agents to purchase its supplies. During the 15th century they became more localised and focused on Newcastle.[37] It is likely that other significant institutional and corporate purchasers, such as the households of the earls of Northumberland, the bishops of Durham and other religious houses within an equivalent distance, also purchased from Newcastle merchants. The city was the

34   Hunter Blair, C.H., 'The Armorials of Northumberland', *Archaeologia Aeliana*, 3rd ser., vi (1910), pp.178-81, and pl. iii, vi; Cadwallader Bates, 'Border Holds of Northumberland', pp.288-91. Note that as these armorials have long since lost all trace of their tinctures, there is some dispute over their identification.

35   Kermode, Jennifer, 'Northern Towns', *Cambridge Urban History, vol. 1, 600-1540*, ed. D. M. Pallisser (Cambridge, 2000), pp.669-71; Fraser, *Chamberlain's Accounts*, xviii; Threlfall Holmes, 'The Import Merchants of Newcastle upon Tyne, 1464-1520: some evidence from Durham Cathedral Priory', *Northern History*, xl: 1 (2003), pp.71-87; Wade, J.F., 'The Overseas Trade of Newcastle upon Tyne in the late Middle Ages', *Northern History*, 30 (1994), pp.31-48.

36   Kowaleski, M., 'Port towns: England and Wales 1300-1540', *CUH*, 472 -6; Fraser, M., *The Accounts of the Chamberlains of Newcastle upon Tyne, 1508-1511* (Society of Antiquaries, Newcastle, record series 3, 1987), pp.xviii-xxi.

37   Threlfall Holmes, 'Import Merchants', *passim*.

commercial focus for both northern Durham and southern Northumberland.

A sure sign of Newcastle's commercial dominance is the manner in which the city's position was contested, especially by North Shields and Gateshead, both of whom clearly feared, and were ultimately unable to prevent, the establishment of a Novocastrian hegemony on the Tyne. The Abbey of Tynemouth especially resented the claim of Newcastle to a monopoly of all trade in and out of the Tyne. From the end of the 13th century until the early 16th century its town of North Shields fought a long running battle for a share until having to concede a Newcastle monopoly in 1530. Gateshead, and its lord the bishop of Durham, particularly resented Newcastle's claim to control the southern end of the Tyne bridge, determined in the bishop's favour in 1416. But the bishop also had to resist the claim of Newcastle boatmen to carry all the coal on the Tyne, even from the south bank. In the 16th century Newcastle finally secured full control of the river, but only after generations of struggle.[38]

In the 14th century the town retained close social and political links with the county that lay to its north, political links which were hardly typical of the relationships of large towns at the time.[39] Until 1400, sessions of Northumberland's county court were customarily held at the royal castle which had given the town its name, and was in the charge of the sheriff. The Northumbrian gentry formed many marriage alliances with Newcastle burgesses, and *vice versa*. There was also some overlapping of personnel between the formally separate administrations. Hugh de Sadlingstones was elected to represent Northumberland in both the Parliaments of 1339, and that of April 1343. In April 1341 he was elected to represent the burgesses of Newcastle. When Alan del Strother was appointed sheriff of Northumberland in November 1356, an elder brother, William, was serving as mayor of Newcastle, having married into the town's oligarchy. A separate political community, with its own administration and parliamentary representation, the borough eventually acquired its own sheriff, in 1400, and was thereby also removed from the jurisdiction of Northumberland.[40]

In the 15th century social aspirations and political links extended southwards as well. An analysis of the 26 men known to have served as Newcastle's MPs between 1386 and 1421, most of whom were prominent merchants and holders of civic office, reveals a significant number, over half, buying property in the neighbouring countryside, not only in Northumberland but also in Durham.[41] The most spectacularly successful was Roger Thornton (d.1430), who built up a substantial estate in both counties and on its basis married his son into the peerage, and established a new gentry dynasty. Others married into the ranks of the landed gentry. Social mobility worked the other way, too; sons of county families, such as William Middleton, William Redmarshall,

---

38 Craster, H.E., *A History of Northumberland, viii: Tynemouth* (1907), pp.285-93; Welford, R., *A History of Newcastle and Gateshead in the Fourteenth and Fifteenth Centuries* (Newcastle, 1884), pp.201, 222, 257-9; Manders, F.W.D., *A History of Gateshead* (Gateshead, 1973), pp.7-9; Storey, *Thomas Langley*, p.54; Roskell, *History of Parliament*, i, p.546.

39 Tuck, Anthony, 'The Percies and the Community of Northumberland in the Later Fourteenth Century', *War and Border Societies in the Middle Ages*, ed. Anthony Tuck and Anthony Goodman (London, 1992), 183; Lomas, *North-East England*, pp.166-8.

40 *Early Deeds Relating to Newcastle upon Tyne*, ed. A.M. Oliver, Surtees Society cxxxvii (1924), pp.215-16; Roskell, *History of Parliament*, iii, pp.317-19. The rising fortunes of the Strother family are outlined in Lomas, *North-East England*, pp.69-70.

41 Roskell, *History of Parliament*, i, p.548.

John Strother and Robert Swinburne invested in Newcastle or served the borough in an administrative capacity and prospered. Sampson Hardyng (d.1427), who sat in Parliament 11 times (six times for Newcastle and five for Northumberland between 1382 and 1421), was equally at home in both town and country, acting frequently as a trustee for both burgesses and gentry, holding royal office in borough and county and owning property in both. His son William (1395-1460), of Newcastle gent. and Northumberland esq., continued in the family tradition. John Booth, Member of Parliament six times between 1411 and 1423, seems to have made his career in the service of the 2nd Earl of Northumberland, on the strength of which he acquired an estate at Holingside, County Durham.[42] And then there were the lawyers such as Robert Whelpington, whose clients included the borough of Newcastle, individual Newcastle burgesses and county gentry, and later Robert Rodes, nine times Member of Parliament between 1427 and 1442. Rodes (1400-74), the son a Newcastle lawyer, built up a spectacularly successful practice, being steward of John, Duke of Bedford's estates in Northumberland and for many decades steward of Durham Priory.[43]

By the end of the Middle Ages Newcastle lay at the centre of an extensive commercial and political network. During the later Middle Ages the town emerged as the focal point of the county and the bishopric, but it was still in important respects a town in Northumberland, rather than, as yet, the centre of a new Northumbria. Indeed there is little to suggest that its emerging pre-eminence extended beyond the Coquet or into the Tees lowlands. In so far as Newcastle did establish itself as the dominant town, it was the dominance of a 'core' close to the Tyne, leaving north Northumberland and south Durham as 'peripheries'.[44]

III

What did the idea of 'Northumbria' mean to the people who inhabited the north-east corner of England, or to those who lived south of the Tees? What was the 'Northumbria' they imagined?

As David Rollason has shown, many of the institutions of late medieval north-eastern England retained features which derived ultimately from the Anglo-Saxon kingdom: the liberty of St Cuthbert; the regal powers of the Bishop of Durham as the head of that community; and the right of sanctuary, which was defined as early as the ninth and tenth centuries.[45] More broadly, the very character of the Palatinate as an ecclesiastical liberty may itself have derived from the sacerdotal nature of Northumbrian kingship which was so closely linked to the cult of St Cuthbert. And one corporation, the Priory of Durham, the custodian of the body of St Cuthbert,

---

42 *Ibid*, ii, p.293 (Booth); iii, pp.288-90 (Hardyng); iv, pp.596-8 (Thornton); Wedgwood, J.C., *History of Parliament: Biographies of the Members of the Commons House, 1439-1509* (London, 1936), p.423 (Hardyng).

43 Roskell, *History of Parliament*, iv, pp.826-7; Wedgwood, *History of Parliament*, p.722.

44 But see Miranda Threlfall-Holmes, *Monks and Markets: Durham Cathedral Priory 1460-1520* (Oxford, 2005), p.226, who concludes that the evidence 'reveals the north-east to have had a vigorous independent mercantile culture', independent, that is, from London.

45 Rollason, *Northumbria*, p.286.

dedicated itself to the preservation of that spiritual and historical link with ancient Northumbria. In 1083 the church at Durham was purged. Its secular canons were expelled and a new, austere Benedictine community was established. The new monks, recruited from Monkwearmouth and Jarrow, had a pressing need to demonstrate that they were the true successors to St Cuthbert's community at Lindisfarne, and thus they assiduously promoted his cult, with spectacular success.[46]

Linked to this is the notion of the people living within the county palatine of Durham, and by extension the land they occupied, being under St Cuthbert's special protection. The concept of the 'Haliwerfolk', the people of the saint, had continuing resonance in the later Middle Ages. It was to them that King John granted a charter of liberties in 1208. In 1433, when a faction challenged Langley's palatine authority in the name of Goddes Kirk and Saint Cuthbert of Duresme, the notion of the Haliwerfolk was still germane.[47] It is not surprising therefore that whenever the people of the saint were threatened by the Scots in the later Middle Ages his banner was ceremonially carried on the field of battle, more usually than not with the desired effect. This protection extended, of course, to the Northumberland enclaves and throughout the diocese.

The monastic community did its best to promote its saint, encouraging visitors (and a valuable income stream) to his shrine. It maintained a long historical tradition celebrating his life and their existence, where necessary embellishing the relationship between him, themselves and his people. And it kept alive, in the *Liber Vitae*, the book of remembrance used since the ninth century, the awareness of how the saint continued to work, in answer to the monks' prayers, for the good of the souls of the departed named therein. Sustaining the memory of St Cuthbert as a continually living presence was a significant element in the creation of a special identity and a shared history for the people of the saint. But who precisely these people of the saint were is harder to pin down. In many ways they went beyond the confines of Durham and its diocese. The charters by successive Scottish kings bestowing Coldingham on the monastery in the early 12th century, which may or may not have been forged by the monks, reveal, as Dick Lomas points out, that the monastic community maintained the belief that St Cuthbert's patrimony, and thus his people, extended into south-east Scotland. Many of those listed in the *Liber Vitae* for special prayers came from well beyond the two counties of Northumberland and Durham.[48] Nevertheless, Durham was the focal point, and it was to Durham that Cuthbert's pilgrims came.

That there was something substantial to the attachment to St Cuthbert as a specific focus of identity is indicated also by the fact that it was contested. This is made apparent by the determination of the Minster establishment at York to deny it or, rather, to assert their superiority over it. This is demonstrated in the metrical history available to all visitors to the Minster as a kind of cathedral guide which claimed the cultural leadership of the whole of northern England and south-west Scotland.

46   *Ibid*, pp.287-90.
47   Aird, *St Cuthbert and the Normans*, p.5; Storey, *Thomas Langley*, pp.125-6.
48   Rollason, Linda, 'The Late Medieval Non-Monastic Entries in the Durham *Liber Vitae*', in D.Rollason et al., '*The Durham Liber Vitae and its Context* (Woodbridge, 2004), pp.127-37; Lomas, 'St Cuthbert and the Border, c.1080-c.1300', Britnell and Liddy, *North East England*, pp.23-4.

18 *Holy Island photographed in 1893*

It is also revealed in the cycle of windows created for its eastern arm in the early 15th century. Here, it has been argued, the Minster re-emphasised its position as the mother church of the northern provinces and reminded viewers of its historic role as the ecclesiastical head of ancient Northumbria, in which St Cuthbert is but one tributary saint. The claim to superiority was periodically put into practice in the assertion by the Archbishop to administer the diocese of Durham during a vacancy, a claim vigorously countered, if usually in vain, by the Cathedral Priory of Durham in the superior name of St Cuthbert.[49] Perhaps we see here, many centuries later, the inheritance of the Anglo-Saxon kingdom of Northumbria still being contested in an ecclesiastical arena.

From the late ninth century, and especially after their move to the peninsula on the Wear in 995, the monks at Durham had represented themselves as the true successors of the kings of Northumbria. The justification for the reform of the monastery at the end of the 10th century was to restore it to the condition of its golden age. When Symeon of Durham came to write the official history of the church in the first

49   Holford, M.L., 'Locality, Culture and Identity in late medieval Yorkshire, c.1270-c.1540' (unpublished University of York DPhil thesis, 2001, 120-36); Norton, Christopher, 'Sacred Space and Sacred History; the Glazing of the Eastern Arm of York Minster', *Proceedings of the Conference of the International Viturarum Medii Aevi* (Nurnberg, 2004), pp.4-7, 13; for one incident in the long-running dispute over archidiaconal jurisdiction see Storey, R.L., 'The North of England', in S.B. Chrimes and others (eds), *Fifteenth-Century England, 1399-1509* (Manchester, 1972), pp.140-1.

decade of the 11th century he emphasised its continuity not only with St Cuthbert but also with the glorious king of Northumbria, St Oswald. His later history of the kings of Northumbria further emphasised the place of the community of St Cuthbert at the heart of the Anglo-Saxon kingdom. The history which was thus created, and sustained throughout the monastery's existence and extended by later authors, maintained a powerful foundation myth which positioned the priory not only as the keeper of the flame of St Cuthbert, but also as the custodian of Northumbrian identity.[50] As the line was drawn more firmly between Scotland and England, and as English national identity was forged in the course of the later centuries, this became defined as exclusively English.

Northumbria and its glorious past, albeit increasingly its glorious *English* past, were well known to late medieval chroniclers beyond the cloisters at Durham. Bede's *Ecclesiastical History of the English People* was still widely read in late medieval England; and Bede almost invariably referred to the Anglian kingdom of Northumbria as 'the province of the Northumbrians' (*provincia Nordanhymbrorum*).[51] The usual terms used by late medieval historians writing in Latin to describe ancient Northumbria were 'the land of the Northumbrians' (*terram Northumbrorum*) or 'the kingdom of the Northumbrians' (*regnum Northumbrorum*). Thus, writing in the mid-14th century, Ranulph Higden, author of the enormously influential *Polychronicon*, related how 'the kingdom of the Northumbrians began under Ida son of Eoppa ... and he ruled in Bernicia'. Indeed, in the description of England which prefaced this work, Higden distinguished between 'Northumberland proper' (*Northumberlond propie*), from Tyne to Tweed, and the 'Northumbrian region' (*plaga Northimbrana*) which had once stretched from Humber to Tweed. It may have been an awareness of Northumbria's past which led some chroniclers to refer to the area covered by the old kingdom in their present day in the same terms. Writing during Edward II's reign, one chronicler referred to Gilbert de Middleton's robbery of the cardinals, perpetrated near Rushyford, south of Durham, as taking place in 'the land of the Northumbrians' (*terram Northamhimbrorum*). Others writing in Latin used the term *Northumbria* in the same sense: describing a Scottish raid in 1315, the chronicler John of Trokelowe claimed they had devastated 'the whole of Northumbria and the Western parts, from Carlisle to York'.[52] The term 'Northumbrian' was sometimes even used as a synonym for 'Northern Englishman'. For instance, the northern rebels against John

50   Rollason, *Northumbria*, pp.244-8; Piper, A.J., 'Dr Thomas Swalwell, Monk of Durham, Archivist and Bibliophile (d.1539)', in J.P. Carley and G.C.G. Tite (eds), *Books and Collectors, 1200-1700* (1997), pp.71-100; *idem*, 'The Historical Interests of the Monks of Durham', in D.W. Rollason (ed.), *Simeon of Durham: Historian of Durham and the North* (1998), pp.310-32.

51   *Bede's Ecclesiastical History of the English People*, ed. Bertram Colgrave and R.A.B. Mynors (Oxford, 1969), *passim*. No fewer than 18 copies of the *Ecclesiastical History* were made in England in the 14th century alone; Davis, R.H.C., 'Bede After Bede', *Studies in Medieval History Presented to R. Allen Brown*, ed. C. Harper-Bill, C.J. Holdsworth and J.L. Nelson (Woodbridge, 1989), pp.104-5. Naturally, Durham Cathedral Priory possessed a fine copy (which is still in the Cathedral library – MS B.ii.35).

52   *Polychronicon Ranulphi Higden monachi Cestrensis*, ed. C. Babington and J.R. Lumby, Rolls Series xli (9 vols, 1865-86), v, p.342; *Vita Edwardi Secundi*, ed. Noel Denholm-Young (London, 1957), pp.82-3; *Johannis de Trokelowe et Henrici de Blaneforde chronica et annales*, ed. H.T. Riley, Rolls Series xxviii (1866), p.91.

had been identified by contemporaries as a distinct faction, usually referred to as the 'Northerners' (*Aquilonares* or *Norenses*); and the chronicler Ralph de Coggeshall used the terms *Northanhumbrenses* and *Norenses* interchangeably.[53]

There was generally little consistency in late medieval applications of the idea of Northumbria. Writing at St Albans at the turn of the 15th century, Thomas Walsingham refers several times in his works to the *Northumbrenses*, *Northumbria* or, once, to the *provincia Northumbrorum* ('the province of the Northumbrians'), generally in relation to the Scottish wars. Sometimes, he is clearly referring to the county of Northumberland or its inhabitants, as when he describes the Scots invading 'Northumbria on the East March'. Elsewhere, however, his meaning is ambiguous; and, on one occasion, he explicitly uses 'Northumbrian' to mean simply 'Northerner', referring to 'all those of the North, that is, all the Northumbrians' (*cunctorum borealium, id est Northamhumbrensium*).[54] Generally, however, by the 14th century, Latin works used *Northumbria* in a contemporary sense to refer to the county of Northumberland, north of the Tyne/Derwent. This was, for instance, clearly what was meant in an early 14th-century York chronicle, in Latin, when it related that 'Northumbria, Gilsland, Cumberland, Allerdale and Copeland' bought a truce from Robert Bruce in 1312. Similarly, John of Tynemouth's *Historia Aurea* (written in the mid-14th century) describes a Scottish raid in the aftermath of Bannockburn which devastated 'Northumbria and the bishopric of Durham', a formula implying that his conception of present-day 'Northumbria' definitely excluded Durham.[55] This usage was common even within the boundaries of the ancient kingdom, as when, writing in the 1430s, John Wessington, Prior of Durham, ascribed the collapse of his priory's revenues partially to the loss of income from churches due to 'the war between the kingdoms, and mainly from Northumbria, where many of the said churches are situated'.[56]

Those who wrote in either French or English in the 14th century used 'Northumberland' indiscriminately to refer to both the ancient kingdom and to the present county. Thus the *Brut* names the fifth of the seven Saxon kingdoms as 'Northumberland'. The *Scalacronica*, written (in French) by the Northumbrian Sir Thomas Gray, devotes an entire chapter to the fifth realm 'Northumbreland, from the Trent to the Firth'. Geoffrey Chaucer mentioned 'Alla, kyng of al Northumbrelond' in one of his *Canterbury Tales*.[57] Most explicit is the Cornishman John Trevisa's English translation of Higden's *Polychronicon*. Translating Higden's passage quoted above,

---

53 *Radulphi de Coggeshall chronicon Anglicanum*, ed. Joseph Stevenson, Rolls Series xlvi (1875), pp.167, 170, 178, 183; Holt, *The Northerners*, pp.8-9.

54 *The St Albans Chronicle. The Chronica maiora of Thomas Walsingham. Vol. I, 1376-1394*, ed. and trans. John Taylor, Wendy R. Childs and Leslie Watkiss (Oxford, 2003), *passim*, quotes at pp.952, 720 (our translations).

55 *Chronicle of St Mary's York*, ed. H.H.E Craster and M.E. Thornton, Surtees Society cxlviii (1934), 53-4; London, Lambeth Palace, MS 12, f. 225v.

56 *Historiæ Dunelmensis scriptores tres*, ed. James Raine, Surtees Society ix (1839), app. p.ccl. As a historian of the Priory, Wessington would have been well aware of Northumbria's former status.

57 British Library, Cotton MS Cleopatra D.iii f. 109v (for the Anglo-Norman French text of the *Brut*); *The Brut*, ed. Friedrich W.D. Brie, Early English Text Society, 1st ser., 131, 136 (2 vols, 1906, 1908), i, p.95 (for the Middle English translation); Corpus Christi College, Cambridge, MS 133, ff. 104v.-108r. (the *Scalacronica*); 'The Man of Law's Tale', l. 578, *The Riverside Chaucer*, ed. Larry D. Benson (3rd edn, Oxford, 1987), p.95 (see also the reference to 'Northumberlond', l. 508, p.94).

19 *St Cuthbert in bishop's robes*

Trevisa wrote of 'þe kyngdom of Norþumberlond under oon Ida, þe sonne of Eoppa ... and Ida regnede ... in Brenicia'; and he added an aside of his own that 'Brenicia is þe northside of Northumberlond, and streccheþ to þe Scottische see'.[58] Translating the description of England, he wrote of 'Norþhumberlond' from Tyne to Tweed, and also 'Norþhumberlond, þat was somtyme from Humber anon to Twede'.[59]

By the later 15th and early 16th centuries the use of the word to describe only the modern county north of the Tyne had become established. John Warkworth, writing in the 1470s, described how the Lancastrians in the early years of Edward IV's reign 'hade kepte certeyne castelles in Northumberlond', referring to his home county. Writing of the same events at approximately the same time, the London citizen William Gregory referred ambiguously to the Lancastrians as landing in 'North Homberlonde'. He makes it clear later in his narrative, however, that he had the modern county in mind since he tells the reader that Edward IV went to Durham while Ralph Percy 'returned

58 *Polychronicon*, v, 343.
59 *Polychronicon*, ii, 89, v, 343.

again into Northumberlond'. And in 1523, as we have seen, the Earl of Westmorland referred to the county in which he claimed to be a stranger as Northumberland, and its inhabitants, as has since become conventional, as Northumbrians.[60]

When it comes to the educated laymen of late medieval Northumberland, the idea of a contemporary Northumbria has little resonance. The 1st Earl of Northumberland, known for his learning, possibly had ancient Northumbria in mind in 1405 when he formed his wildly ambitious conspiracy to partition England with Owain Glyndwr and Edmund Mortimer. Even so, the scheme belonged to the realms of fantasy, and had no basis whatsoever in political reality.[61] Two other sons of the county, Sir Thomas Gray and John Hardyng, two of England's earliest lay historians, both included much about the Anglian kingdom in their chronicles. Whether this actually did anything to foster a sense of Northumbrian identity in their minds is, however, debatable. Sir Thomas Gray saw himself and his neighbours in the far north of the county as men of the march and not men of either Northumbria or Northumberland.[62] John Hardyng, writing a century or so later, focused not on the marches, but on 'the north'. He is at pains in his verse history to demonstrate that his 'northerners' are good fighting men, as are Gray's marchers. He draws a clear distinction between the north and the south, but where, in his mind, the line lay is harder to detect. He concentrates on the eastern borders, on the Percys, with whom his career began, and on Northumberland, the land of his birth. His lack of interest in the Nevilles leads to a lack of interest not only in the West March, but also in the Palatinate. Thus when he assured Edward IV at the beginning of his reign that the Percys had the 'hertes of the people by north', one can be reasonably certain that he had the far North East in mind.[63] Between the marcher and the northerner, in the pages of the writings of these hardened warriors, Northumbria seems to disappear.

How ordinary men and women viewed all this we can only speculate. Their thoughts have not survived. We can glimpse them in manorial, judicial and ecclesiastical records, especially those that lived in the more intensely populated south-east Durham lowlands. And we can discern there a significant contrast between those who lived by the sea, and those who lived in the arable lowlands or up in the remote pastoral dales and highland districts of the north-western parts, especially of Northumberland. One might assume, nevertheless, that all their horizons were narrower than those of the monks of Durham or gentry of both counties. If Northumbria meant anything to them it is likely to have been in a form mediated orally through traditions familiar to their betters. In so far as the inhabitants of the county palatine of Durham were themselves 'people of the Saint', we may suppose that identification with St Cuthbert

---

60   *A Chronicle of the first thirteen years of the reign of King Edward IV*, ed. J.O. Halliwell (Camden Soc., 1839), p.2; 'William Gregory's Chronicle of London', in *The Historical Collections of a Citizen of London*, ed. J. Gairdner (Camden Soc., 1876).

61   A copy of the conspirators' agreement is printed by Henry Ellis, *Original Letters Illustrative of English History*, 2nd series, i (London, 1827), pp.27-8. The 12 northern and midlands counties specifically allocated to the earl included Northumbria and Westmorland, but neither Durham nor Cumberland. Perhaps he considered the latter two to be part of 'Northumbria'?

62   King, A.C., 'Englishmen, Scots and Marchers: National and Local Identities in Thomas Gray's *Scalacronica*', *Northern History* 36 (2000), pp.223-4, 228.

63   Macdonald, A.J., 'John Hardyng, Northumbrian Identity and the Scots', in Britnell and Liddy, *North-Eastern England*, pp.29-42.

in the here-and-now was more immediate than any association that the saint himself carried with a long-lost Anglo-Saxon kingdom. And likewise, those living closer to the Scottish border, more aware of threats and opportunities offered by war, might have shared more immediately some of the attitudes expressed by Gray and Hardyng, rather than a memory of an ancient kingdom uniting them with their northern neighbours. One cannot suppose that 'Northumbria' was a notion any more sharply etched in the minds of ploughmen, laundresses, carpenters, alewives and highland thieves than in the minds of great ladies, lawyers, merchants, monks and gentry.

IV

Does this add up to a late-medieval 'Northumbria'? Territorially, the land between Tees and Tweed, being the rump of the Anglo-Saxon kingdom, enjoyed a superficial unity defined by the shared boundaries of the county of Northumberland and the diocese of Durham. However, internal differences were greater than any apparent unity. To a significant degree Northumberland and Durham were separate entities. Although by the end of the Middle Ages Newcastle was beginning to assert the dominance of a 'primate' town, emerging, as it were, between the two, it did not as yet promise to become the focal point of a new 'Northumbria' in the imagination of its inhabitants and outside observers. Ancient Northumbria had disappeared; the modern Northumbria had not yet been invented. Yet, if ancient Northumbria no longer existed, it was still remembered in some quarters, its memory kept alive by the monks of Durham and other chroniclers. It was remembered now as being exclusively English. When it was not confused with the truncated county of Northumberland north of the Tyne and Derwent, it was usually remembered as being vaguely north and east of the Humber. Already, however, the linguistic confusion between Latin and English was leading to its being identified more narrowly with the county of Northumberland. Even so, the shadowy awareness of a spectral Northumbria served to sustain the memory beyond the Middle Ages. By the time it was reworked in the late 19th century it was associated with romanticised, late medieval borders and borderers, located in time not just with the age of Bede but additionally with the era of the Anglo-Scottish wars. Thus the experience of the later Middle Ages helped to reshape the very idea of Northumbria itself in the modern historical imagination. Northumbria was already on the way to becoming the brand name for an English region.

6

'Dolefull dumpes': Northumberland and the Borders, 1580-1625

DIANA NEWTON

Sometime early in 1597 Shakespeare's *King Henry IV, part I* was first performed.[1] In it the rebellion against the king by his one-time allies, including Henry Percy, Earl of Northumberland, was re-enacted. Their two sons resolved the situation, when Harry 'Hotspur' Percy was killed on the battlefield by Prince Hal. On one level, *Henry IV* reflected contemporary concerns and perceptions about the north, whose perfidious inhabitants posed an abiding threat to legitimate authority. On another level, this was a generic north which, from a southern perspective at least, was rather vaguely and imprecisely defined as 'the remnant northward lying off from Trent'.[2] Notwithstanding the pejorative 'remnant', Shakespeare's northern territories were inexactly conceived, while his (southern) audiences were unlikely to be much exercised by their exact location or composition. At its southernmost limits, this 'north' did correspond, almost, to the ancient kingdom of Northumbria, albeit marked out as a fluctuating zone rather than a linear boundary.[3] But it was at its northern extremities that the ancient kingdom was most clearly defined, especially in the popular imagination. Northumbria, together with the Anglo-Scottish border, exercised a powerful effect on both inhabitants and commentators alike.

In 1975, the Watts made plain the significance of the Anglo-Scottish border: the first chapter of their book about Northumberland was entirely concerned with 'The Northumberland border and border institutions in 1586'.[4] Years of Anglo-Scottish

---

1 It was entered on the Stationers' Register in February 1598. See *King Henry IV, part I*, ed. David Scott Kaston, for Arden Shakespeare (London, 2002), p.76.

2 In Act III, these were among the parts of the kingdom that Hotspur expected to be given on defeat of the king.

3 For the process of defining and redefining Northumbria see Rollason, David, *Northumbria, 500-1100. Creation and destruction of a kingdom* (Cambridge, 2003).

4 Watts, S. J. with Watts, Susan J., *From border to middle shire. Northumberland, 1596-1625* (Leicester, 1975), chapter 1. This was similar to the preoccupations of a history of the north-western counties, written two hundred years before, which declared that those counties' history was so connected with border laws and service that 'some account thereof seems to be necessary'. Subsequently, 134 pages were devoted to the subject. See Joseph Nicolson and Richard Burn, *The history and antiquities of the counties of Westmorland and Cumberland* (London, 1777).

wars had resulted in the development of a distinct body of law and government which survived into the late 16th and early 17th centuries. Government and administration was dependent on march wardens, whose principal obligation was to keep their wardenry, or march, prepared against incursions from the Scots by maintaining fortifications and ensuring their tenants were sufficiently armed. Wardens also presided over their own courts, which enforced those march laws peculiar to the borders, 'rendering unique sentences of redress, reparation and compensation'.[5] This was in addition to the commissioners of the peace – sheriffs, lords lieutenant and other officials – who, in common with their counterparts in the rest of the kingdom, conducted local government in Northumberland. It meant that there was an unusual degree of authority in the hands of the wardens. At the same time, the area inevitably was more militarised than elsewhere in the kingdom.

The enduring potency of the ancient kingdom was given expression in the preface to the first of 15 volumes that comprised *A history of Northumberland*, begun at the end of the 19th century. In electing to make Bamburghshire its first subject, 'it was felt that there could be no more appropriate beginning for the work than a volume concerned with the ancient Northumbrian capital'.[6] According to Robert Colls, the 'regional intelligentsia' of the late 19th century had rediscovered Northumbria as a 'region' to accommodate 'born-again Geordies', who were searching for a more finely drawn identity than 'Englishness'.[7] As part of the drive, 'New Northumbrians' such as Edmund Bogg appropriated its distant history: in particular, the martial fame of its heroic race. But, how were these virile Victorian border heroes regarded in the popular imagination of their own day? And how did contemporaries, not least the central authorities in London, regard Northumberland's frontier society in general? How accurate were such impressions; especially the extent of its militarisation? And what was the impact of the extirpation of the borders, in 1603, when it was thought that the area would be transformed from a troublesome international frontier to a peaceful heartland? Above all, how great was the gulf between the perception and reality of this half-remembered kingdom?

Popular Memories

From at least the late Middle Ages, the people of Northumberland had 'prided themselves on being different from other English folk, projecting their menfolk as a warrior elite' – most notably in ballads that venerated their chivalrous heroism on the borders. [8] Ballads, originally sung by minstrels in the houses of the nobility and

---

5   For the evolution of border customs and legal practices, see Cynthia J. Neville, *Violence, custom and law: the Anglo-Scottish border lands in the later middle ages* (Edinburgh, 1998), *passim*. For an overview of the situation, see *From border to middle shire*, chapter 1.

6   *A history of Northumberland, issued under the direction of the Northumberland County History Committee* (Newcastle, 1893-1940), i, p.vi.

7   Colls, Robert, 'Born-again Geordies', in Robert Colls and Bill Lancaster (eds), *Geordies. Roots of regionalism* (Edinburgh, 1992), pp.3-4.

8   Goodman, Anthony, 'Border warfare and Hexhamshire in the later Middle Ages', *Hexham Historian*, xiii (2003), pp.50-1.

gentry, were made increasingly available in printed form to become a part of a wider popular culture. In 1624 Abraham Holland commented on the ubiquity of Chevy Chase as part of a wider appetite for 'penny sheets'.

> … North-Villages, where every line
> Of Plumpton Parke is held a work divine.
> If 'o're the Chymney they some Ballad have
> Of Chevy-Chase …[9]

Few of the border ballads were preserved in their 16th-century renditions, however. Those that were so preserved (known as 'Child A') were seriously distorted in later 18th-century editions (known as 'Child B').[10] For example, the language employed by the two versions of the clash between Percy and Douglas – which had excited Sir Philip Sidney's admiration – was markedly different.[11] 'Child A' was rousing and animated: Douglas saluted Percy as 'the manfullyste man yet art thowe / that ever I conqueryd in filde fightynge', and Percy, after Douglas's death, lamented that 'Wo is me for the[e]! / To haue savyde thyy lyffe, I wolde haue partyde with my / landes for years thre[e]'. 'Child B', on the other hand, by the 18th century had degenerated into a work akin to doggerel verse; to be delivered in a manner that was sing-song rather than lyrical. Hence, Douglas glibly recited to Percy, 'Thou art the most courageous knight / that ever I did see', while Percy flatly intoned 'Erle Douglas, for thy life, / I wold I had lost my land'. The contrast between the stirring version of events as related in the 16th-century version and the lack-lustre and banal version as related in the 18th is striking. The heroism of a Widdrington ancestor, with his dogged bravery touched by tragedy conveyed by the narrator of the earlier version, was completely transformed:

> For Wetharryngton my harte was wo
> that euer slayne shulde be;
> For when both his leggis wear hewyne in to,
> yet he knyled and fought on hys kny.

The same elegy became ludicrous in the later version, which recounted

> For Witherington needs must I wayle
> as one in dolefull dumpes,
> For when his leggs were smitten of,
> he fought upon his stumpes.

By transposing heroic deeds into comedic burlesque, any sense of pride in the Widdrington family and their countrymen was eliminated. While the humdrum

---

9   Watt, Tessa, *Cheap print and popular piety, 1550-1640* (Cambridge, 1991), pp.3, 39.
10   According to F.J. Child in his edition of *The English and Scottish popular ballads*, first published in 1882-98.
11   See in *English and Scottish popular ballads*, eds Helen Child Sargent and George Lyman Kittredge (Boston and New York, 1904).

20 *This image of Fourstones, from 1838, depicts Northumberland as the 'wild, romantic, untamed place' envisaged by the Newcastle intellectual élite of the 19th century (reproduced by permission of Northumberland Collections Service)*

verse that replaced the Northumbrian mode of speech, which 'shews the antiquity of their blood', also served to dilute the distinctiveness of border culture.[12]

Ballads that celebrated the gallant exploits of the nobility were not the only expressions of life on the borders. There were also 'riding ballads', which concentrated on the feuds and frays of those slightly lower down the social scale. Very few of these survive, largely because they were not part of the repertoire of minstrels later distorted through print. Instead, the 'riding ballads' preserved the value systems of the 'riding surnames' and reflected the often violent, impoverished and superstitious conditions that prevailed in the north-eastern uplands at the end of the 16th century. One example, 'The fray o' Hautwessell', concerned Sir Robert Carey, in his capacity as warden of the middle march, repulsing a raid on Haltwistle by the Liddesdale Armstrongs.[13] These poor man's ballads defined another cultural identity on the borders, which endured longer. Because they were transmitted orally to a more restricted audience than that which celebrated the heroics of the Percys and their followers, they were not diluted or perverted through wider dissemination.[14] The 'riding ballads' represented an exceptionally potent sense of local identity grounded in its own particular customs and practices.

---

12   Fox, Adam, *Oral and literate culture in England 1500-1700* (Oxford, 2001), p.5. In 1603 it was claimed that the inhabitants of Northumberland's articulation of 'the Saxon language' was 'more incorrupteth then the south'. See State Papers [SP] 14/7/83. The antiquaries of the 'long eighteenth century' continued to salute the area's Saxon past, which is traced by Rosemary Sweet in this volume.

13   Richardson, M.A., *The local historian's table book* (Newcastle, 1842), ii, pp.310-12.

14   In the 18th century, the Ettrick Shepherd's mother famously censured Sir Walter Scott, who printed much of the border balladry, thus: 'They were made for singin' and not for readin', but ye hae broken the charm now, an' they'll never be sung mair.' See Reed, James, *The border ballads* (London, 1973), p.11. The Ettrick Shepherd, apparently, was James Hogg.

Contemporary Estimations of Northumbrian Identity

The territorial north may have been an ill-defined part of the kingdom in the wider imagination but its people had a very clear identity. They had long been marked by their bellicosity – a reputation appropriated by outside observers to explain that ostensibly pan-northern rebellion of 1536, the Pilgrimage of Grace.[15] In his systematic and comprehensive description of the counties of England, published in Latin in 1586 and in English in 1610, the antiquary William Camden concluded that this warlike disposition was peculiar to the inhabitants of Northumberland. He contended that it was the landscape and situation of the county which had formed its temperament. The land was 'for the most part rough', which 'seemed to harden the inhabitants, whom the Scots their neighbours also made more fierce and hardy';[16] characteristics that were simultaneously embodied by Shakespeare in his Hotspur. But the perceived disposition of Northumberland was more complex than that. Conclusions about its belligerence were being drawn at almost exactly the same time that central government was castigating those same parts of the kingdom for being insufficiently militarised. Since at least 1580, the decline in standards of border service had been a cause for reproach. That year, the Lord President of the Council of the North, the Earl of Huntingdon, had sent a very negative account of the state of the borders that concentrated on the 'decay of service' there. The chief reason was the long period of peace with Scotland which meant that many landlords had 'utterlie forgotton the necessitie of kepinge able men and furniture'. Francis Walsingham, the Queen's Secretary of State, reached a similar verdict four years later.[17] Given that the border counties of Northumberland and Cumberland, as well as Durham and Westmorland, enjoyed many attractive financial rewards in return for defending the realm,[18] it could be argued that the central authorities had cause for concern.

Notwithstanding the fact that there had not been an official Scottish enemy since 1551, the unofficial Scottish enemy in the guise of desperate marauders and thieves was regularly exhibited as evidence of Northumberland's idiosyncrasy. Report after report was sent up to central government, lamenting the state of the 'country' as a result of Scottish raids. At the same time, it was also claimed that Northumberland had a particularly lawless population who were virtually ungovernable. In particular, the recently abolished liberties of Tynedale and Redesdale had long been in thrall to the 'riding surnames', who operated a kind of protection racket that was organised around kin-groups and extended across the length of the Anglo-Scottish

---

15   For a further discussion see Holford, Matthew, 'Being northern in later medieval England: cultural identity and political change', paper read at the Regions and Regionalism in History International Colloquium, AHRB centre for NEEHI, 9-12 September 2004.

16   Camden, William, *Britain, or a chorographicall account of the most flourishing kingdomes, England, Scotland, and Ireland*, trans. Philemon Holland (London, 1610), p.799.

17   SP 59/20/194, 59/20/198, 59/23/82, 59/23/90.

18   They had been exempted from paying parliamentary subsidies throughout Elizabeth's reign, nor were they subject to contributing to privy seal loans.

border.[19] Also known as 'reivers' or 'clansmen', in respect of wealth and influence they were often barely distinguishable from the governing elites. But they were part of a configuration that was described as 'notorious robbers … and murderers … [who] lorded it with impunity'.[20] A very lengthy appraisal 'concerning the abused government and afflicted state of Northumberland', sent to the Queen in 1597, ran to five very closely written pages.[21] It was a woeful portrayal of a wretched and beleaguered part of England, which catalogued shortcomings in every aspect of life. Church and religion were inadequately provided for; there was minimal education at all levels; local justice was discharged irregularly and unsatisfactorily; the conduct of trade was not properly regulated; felons were inappropriately bailed; fines were not levied; sheriffs, wardens and their deputies were defrauding the Crown of its dues, while the recent commission appointed to inquire into conditions in the middle march was composed of the worst offenders in that respect; the custodians of castles were not resident in them; Scots held tenements in England; days of truce were not held; and the English warden was openly colluding with his Scottish counterpart to the detriment of the county as a whole. The anonymous reporter claimed that the responsibility for this dismal state of affairs lay with the Justices of the Peace, who 'appeare not at their quarter sessions in any due order, and often kepe non at quarter days'. William Camden's findings reinforced this verdict on Northumberland. He arranged the counties of England according to the peoples who had first inhabited them. Whereas the 'bishopric of Durham', together with Yorkshire, Lancashire, Westmorland and Cumberland, was found to have been inhabited by the 'Brigantes', Northumberland was alone in having been peopled by the 'Ottadini', a particularly perfidious race.[22] Thus was established its ethnic distinctiveness; confirmed by its peculiarly unruly and seditious population.

Yet, the evidence does not bear out this negative impression of Northumberland, especially the calumny regarding the inadequate performance of the county's Justices of the Peace: for Quarter Sessions were held regularly and were as well attended as elsewhere in the kingdom.[23] Nor does Northumberland emerge as less law-abiding. Notwithstanding the obvious difficulties in reconstructing patterns of crime from incomplete records, certain broad conclusions can be drawn. A comparison of presentments and indictments before Quarter Sessions in Northumberland and Worcestershire reveals a broadly similar rate of petty crime.[24] And even the incidence

---

19   For a discussion of these in Northumberland, see Watts, *From border to middle shire*, pp.25-30, and for Cumberland see Spence, R.T., 'The pacification of the Cumberland borders, 1593-1628', *Northern History*, xiii (1977).
20   Calendar of letters and papers relating to the affairs of the borders of England and Scotland, ed. Joseph Bain, Edinburgh, 1894-6, ii, nos 652 and 763; Robson, Ralph, *The English highland clans* (Edinburgh, 1989), p.204.
21   SP 59/36/223.
22   Camden, *Britain*, 796.
23   There is a single volume, entitled the *Vetera Indictamenta*, which contains copies, in an early modern hand, of original indictments and presentments, for both general gaol deliveries and general sessions of the peace in Northumberland, which also records attendance lists. Northumberland Record Office [NRO] (Morpeth), QS1. The gap between 1618 and 1627 is filled by material covering public office in the Delaval family papers, NRO (Gosforth), 1DE7/51-98.
24   NRO (Morpeth), QS1; J.W. Willis Bund (ed.), *Calendar of the quarter sessions papers, 1591-1643* (Worcester, 1900), *passim*.

of murder was not markedly worse in Northumberland. Between 1597 and 1604 there were 18 murders in Northumberland: in the same period there were 12 in Hertfordshire, but 26 in Sussex.[25] Significantly, all of the murders recorded in Northumberland up to 1597 were committed by 'riding surnames': thereafter, they were responsible for only one of the subsequent 18 murders perpetrated up to 1604. By then, the families were in decline and their deadly activities were almost over.[26] Northumberland may have been a border county, but that did not predispose it to being any less well-behaved than the rest of the kingdom. Instead, it seems that the gentlemen of Northumberland had decided it was in their best interests, in order to continue the favourable financial relations they enjoyed with central government, to promulgate a perception of acute crisis in the area.[27] By exaggerating the lawless nature of Northumberland, they could also justify any shortcomings in their performance as county officers.

The geographical area that was most subject to censure from central government for its lawlessness did not correspond neatly to the county of Northumberland. This censured area was quite specifically the middle march, and especially the upland parts of Redesdale and Tynedale, extending into County Durham along Weardale and Teesdale. A shared culpability was with Bewcastle and Gilsland in the west marches. This demarcation was recognised in a letter written in August 1595 by the Bishop, Assize Judges and Lord Eure, complaining about the dismal conditions in the north-eastern reaches of the realm. They identified two distinct sub-regions. One corresponded with the bishopric, or, more substantively, with lowland Durham and Northumberland. This was a Northumberland that was not defined principally by its proximity to the borders, but accorded more with the law abiding and 'civilised' parts. The other comprised the highland, or western parts, in the turbulent uplands where most of the frontier was located. Blame for the stinging criticisms in the appraisal of 1597 could only be apportioned to these parts. Certainly, it is true that there was adequate provision of schools and cure of souls in the lowland parts of both Durham and Northumberland,[28] and it is equally true that the location of the 'riding surnames' activities, who operated in Redesdale and Tynedale, as well as in Bewcastle and Gilsland in Cumberland, and across the border in Teviotdale and Liddesdale in Scotland, were clearly geographically conceived regions. Rather than racial factors giving rise to banditry, it seemed to be the physical landscape, which extended beyond any administrative boundaries, that was to blame.[29] And so it continued.

25   NRO (Morpeth), QS1; J.S. Cockburn (ed.), *Calendar of assize records. Hertfordshire indictments, Elizabeth I* (London, 1975), 130-65; *idem, Calendar of assize records. Hertfordshire indictments, James I* (London, 1975), 18; *idem, Calendar of assize records. Sussex indictments, Elizabeth I* (London, 1975), pp.333-422; *idem, Calendar of assize records. Sussex indictments, James I* (London, 1975), pp.3-5.

26   NRO (Morpeth), QS1.

27   According to Anthony Goodman, in a private communication, the border shires' exemption from subsidy in the 14th and 15th centuries, and numerous further petitions for relief, show that borderers were well versed in talking up their poverty and defencelessness.

28   Newton, Diana, *North-east England: governance, culture and identity, 1569-1625* (Woodbridge, forthcoming), chapter 5.

29   See, for instance, Roberts, Brian K., *Landscapes of settlement, prehistory to the present* (London, 1996), p.58, fig.3.8: Landscapes and territories. Both the physical regions and the types of landscape bisect the north-eastern parts of England, north to south, and extend into the north-western parts.

A proclamation issued in 1617, 'for the better and more peaceable government of the middle shires of Northumberland, Cumberland and Westmorland',[30] reiterated that all writs should run in Hexhamshire, North and South Tynedale and Redesdale (as well as Bewcastle), notwithstanding any pretended claims of liberty or franchise they might assert. Although the border marches were three distinct administrative sectors, in contemporaries' eyes they shared many characteristics, especially insofar as they conformed to southern prejudices.

The Governance of Northumberland

Throughout the 16th century the Tudors had endeavoured to impose greater administrative centralisation, religious uniformity and cultural homogeneity on the kingdom. Parliament had devised new local arrangements to integrate England and Wales, while liberties and franchises were abolished. Underlying these initiatives was a resolute attempt to impose a general 'English civility' upon the whole kingdom.[31] Steve Ellis has argued that the dynasty's ambitions ultimately were doomed to failure in the marcher societies of the borderlands, especially in Northumberland: a failure which Tudor officials attributed to the fact that its inhabitants were not really 'civil Englishmen' at all.[32] Government attitudes were clear: they condemned the border region as inferior to the rest of England.

> As it was at the firste, in all other uncivill places, Soe can it not now be expected, that those people can yet for some few yeares (notwithstanding what good mean soever) be reduced to like civill obedience, as the other partes of this kingdome are, that have ever lived in subiection to lawe & Justice, for (being even from their cradells bredd and brought upp in theft, spoyle and bloode), they are by use and custome, become thereunto even naturallie inclined, havinge (as is too well knowne, and the late Judges of that Northern circuite can well reporte, what good proofe & testimonie thereof was given them) never almoste tasted of anie lawe civell or devine …[33]

At the same time, King James VI of Scotland was encouraging his nobility to adopt the kind of behaviour that was more suited to a Christian and civil society and to abandon their 'barbarous feidis', as an 'exampill to the far Hielandis and Bourdouris,

---

30   *Stuart royal proclamations*, ed. James F. Larkin and Paul L. Hughes (Oxford, 1973), 374-81. This enlarged a law made in 1495.

31   For a discussion of 'civility' in early modern England, see Bryson, Anna, *From courtesy to civility, Changing codes of conduct in early modern England* (Oxford, 1998), especially chapter 2; Peter Burke, Brian Harrison and Paul Slack's 'Preface' to their (eds), *Civil histories. Essays presented to Sir Keith Thomas* (Oxford, 2000); John Gillingham, 'From *civilitas* to civility: codes of manners in medieval and early modern England', *TRHS*, 6th ser. xii (2002), pp.271-2. For its relevance in the north-eastern parts of the kingdom see, Newton, *North-east England*, chapter 5.

32   Ellis, Steven G., 'Civilizing Northumberland: representations of Englishness in the Tudor state', *Journal of Historical Sociology*, xii (1999).

33   SP 14/5/43. For the theme of civility in official discourse, see Brown, Keith M., *Bloodfeud in Scotland, 1573-1625: Violence, justice and politics in early modern society* (Edinburgh, 1986) and Goodman, Anthony, 'Religion and warfare in the Anglo-Scottish marches' in Robert Bartlett and Angus MacKay (eds), *Medieval frontier societies* (Oxford, 1989).

21 *The city of Durham was perceived by George Andrews and R.W. Billings, in 1845, as ordered and stately (Gibby Negatives 61)*

quhair sic forme of unquheit is usit'.[34] On either side of the Anglo-Scottish border, it would seem, official discourse stressed the incivility of those living there.

Ultimately, the imposition of highly centralised administrative structures – successful in the south and eastern parts of the kingdom – led to serious and continuous tensions between central government and local political communities on the borderlands.[35] The far north-eastern reaches of England, in particular, were subject to such stresses and strains, as central government sought to impose its will. The composition of the commissions that were regularly empanelled to look into deficiencies in those parts increasingly excluded natives of Durham as well as Northumberland. This carried with it an inherent contradiction. On the one hand the north-eastern reaches were being criticised for turbulence; on the other hand, the

---

34 Brown, *Bloodfeud in Scotland*, pp.192, 200.
35 Morrill, John, 'The British problem, *c*1534-1707', in John Morrill and Brendan Bradshaw (eds), *The British problem, c1534-1707, state formation and the Atlantic archipelago* (Basingstoke, 1996), 6; Ellis, Steven G., 'Tudor state formation and the shaping of the British Isles', in Ellis and Sarah Barber (eds), *Conquest and union, fashioning a British state, 1485-1725* (London, 1995), pp.62, 44.

natural governors were regarded as ineffectual and unfit to determine local affairs. If any of the gentlemen of Northumberland had consulted Tacitus, available in a newly translated edition, they would have discovered a less attractive aspect of the 'civility' that was being imposed. His account of Britain's conquest by the Romans related the fate of the native British who, 'under the thumb of the Romans "by little and little they proceeded to those … vices" which "the ignorant termed civilitie" but which were in truth nothing more than "a point of their bondage"'.[36] The experiences of the Northumberland gentry in the mid-1590s, as they were ousted from positions of responsibility in the government of their county, were similar to those of their ancient ancestors and exemplify as well the way in which the central authorities regarded this particular part of the kingdom as overly independent, with a character distinctive from elsewhere in England. By imposing a metropolitan civility, Northumberland's sense of separateness and autonomy might thereby be suppressed. In Westminster's determination to exert greater control over the north was tacit acknowledgement that independent action had to be stifled.

The big opportunity came in 1595. After years of appearing to do very little in response to the regular bulletins of murder and mayhem, central government responded particularly resolutely to what appeared to be just a couple more letters reporting the parlous state of the far north. That August, Toby Matthew, Bishop of Durham, together with Judges Beaumont and Drewe, in Durham for the Assizes, and Ralph, Lord Eure, wrote to Lord President Huntingdon. Their purpose was to express their concerns about what they saw as the deplorable state of Durham and Northumberland. They reported that both English and Scottish outlaws 'conspired together to make this Busshoprick of Duresme an open spoile and prey to the utter impoverishing and undoing of the poorer sorte, and to the Endangering of such persons of the better sorte'.[37] Five days later Eure wrote, as 'one principall subiecte in this land yt concerneth', to the Queen's principal minister, Lord Treasurer Burghley.[38] Adopting a rather more sensational tone, he acquainted him of the 'distress, calamity, pyttifull complaints, which the cryes of wydowes and fatherless children, even to the skyes in this bushopricke of Durham, by the great theifte, intolerable sufferance of Northumberland, and the weaknes or rather dastardie (if I may so tearme yt) of the inhabitants there'. He went on to tell of an area where the normal processes of law had broken down. He pleaded with Burghley to provide some 'speedie redresse' for the consolation of the 'comfortless and distressed people' of the bishopric who were suffering at the hands of those from Northumberland's highlands. In the event, the 'speedy redresse' turned out to be Eure himself, who was nominated by Burghley to replace Sir John Forster, who had been warden of the middle march for 35 years. Eure's response to this honour was to declare immediately that he was 'terrified greatlye to

---

36 *Fower bookes of the histories of Cornelius Tacitus*, trans. Henry Savile (Oxford, 1591), p.250, cited in Quentin Skinner, *Visions of politics, volume II, Renaissance virtues* (Cambridge, 2002), 306. And see Rosemary Sweet in this volume for how the conquest of Britain by the Romans continued to be regarded as a 'problematic episode' by the antiquarians.
37 SP 59/30/117.
38 SP 59/30/131.

undertake so great a charge knowing myne infinite wants', and to beg for a house that would be 'safe and fitting' for him as he endeavoured to 'reforme thes abuses in the inland gentlemen if they have combined with the outlawes'.[39] Although he distinguished between the highland and the lowland parts, he seemed to regard the whole of Northumberland with some trepidation: even the prospect of living within sight of the uplands, in Hexham.

The Privy Council informed Forster that they had appointed a commission to 'inquire and examine in what state the wardenry shalbe left by you'. It received the full co-operation of a significant proportion of the Northumberland gentry, who had crossed swords (figuratively, at least) with Forster at some point in his long career as warden. They confirmed the conclusions reached by the commission in a report of their own, which a third account, from Huntingdon's secretary, John Ferne, corroborated.[40] The picture presented by the commission was truly wretched. Established religion was suffering for want of preachers, there being 'scant three ... to be found in the whole country', so that the superior 'number and diligence of the Semyn[aries] with more liberty resorting thither, being driven from oth[er] places of both the realmes' were having little difficulty in finding willing converts to Roman Catholicism. Common law was undermined by the warden 'using [another] coorse of Justice' in his own best interests. Marcher justice was rendered ineffective by '[the unlawfull complots and combynacons of the] Englishe with the Scottes', while the Treaty of Berwick – concluded in 1560 between England and Scotland – was perverted by the Scots with what appeared to be Forster's compliance. The commissioners claimed that there had been 200 murders since 1567-8 and, of two thousand furnished horsemen certified two years before, only one hundred could be accounted for. It concluded that this 'contagion' or 'Gangrene thus noysomely molest[ing the foot of the kingdome]' affected the part of the bishopric 'next aioning to Northumberland, along parte of the Rivers of Tease, weare and darwent', where there were instances of assaults on houses more than seventy miles from the border. From the Scottish border to the river Tees, the shared experience of the upland parts of north-eastern England was one of alarm and consternation. And, as might have been expected, while the gentlemen of Northumberland drew special attention to the tortures inflicted by the Scots on the English, Ferne's conclusion, that the cause of the mischief lay with the degree of Anglo-Scottish 'convenues and conferences', predictably, was very similar to those of the commission:

> The wardens and opposite officers, being ever chosen of borderers bred and inhabiting there, they do contynewally cherishe their favourites and strengthen themselves by the worst disposed.

---

39 SP 59/30/162.
40 *Acts of the Privy Council of England, 1595-6*, ed. J.R. Dasent and others (London, 1890-1964), pp.45-6; BL MS Cotton Caligula D, ii, fos 230ff; Historical Manuscripts Commission, *Marquis of Salisbury manuscripts* (London, 1883-1926), v, pp.476-7, 493-4.

The vexed question of whether it was preferable to rely on officers with local knowledge, and concomitant partialities and prejudices, or on potentially neutral, but less well-informed, 'outsiders' had long exercised the Crown. The distinction between public responsibility and private interest was demonstrated by the 'monotonous regularity' with which the assize judges were required to address the problem of separating public 'bees' from private 'drones'.[41] It was a predicament common to the whole kingdom and central government adopted one position after another over how to tackle it. On the borders, Burghley and Huntingdon's inclination towards appointing wardens from outside the ranks of the Northumberland gentry, in 1595, was a departure from the conclusion drawn earlier in Elizabeth's reign that 'the estate of Northumberland so standeth at this presente that none can occupie the office of the warden, but suche one as is naturallie planted in the countrye'.[42]

Within a year of his arrival in Northumberland, in 1596, it became abundantly clear that Eure was proving to be quite unequal to the task of governing the middle march. He was attracting precisely the same criticisms as had Forster before him, and another commission was soon appointed, prompted by 'complaint on either side of both the wardens and the deputies'. Not the least of Eure's faults had been his failure to cultivate appropriate allies. The consensus in favour of Eure in opposition to Forster soon collapsed and Eure found himself at loggerheads with a significant proportion of the Northumberland gentry, including the powerful and influential Widdringtons. The upshot was that Henry Widdrington and certain other Northumberland gentlemen withdrew themselves from the middle march, declaring themselves unable to live under the warden's rule. That their departure had serious repercussions for the government of the borders was appreciated by the Queen and her Principal Secretary, Sir Robert Cecil, if not by Eure himself. When the Widdringtons, Selbys and others accompanied the Earl of Essex on his voyage to the Azores it was time for central government to take a hand. With the Queen receiving 'howerly complaint of the Borders devastation', Cecil relayed her insistence that they return 'for she in no sort likes that they should leave the frontiers soe weakened'.[43] This was a clear instruction that policing the international frontier with Scotland was the business of the local gentry.

Of far more significance than Westminster's centralising ambitions, was the growing threat of war with Ireland, late in 1594. It was by no means clear that the King of Scotland would not ally himself with the Irish rebels, making the borders the frontline against an enemy state. In such times it was felt that the security of the realm could not be left solely to the gentlemen of Northumberland. It was unfortunate that Eure proved to be such a disaster, driving away experienced governors of the borders, and leaving the area dangerously exposed. He resigned early in 1598 to be replaced by another outsider, Sir Robert Carey. It was probably no coincidence that

---

41   Cockburn, J.S., *A history of English assizes, 1558-1714* (Cambridge, 1972), p.161; Hindle, *The state and social change in Early Modern England, 1550 - 1640* (Basingstoke 2000), pp.21-3.
42   SP 59/1/50.
43   SP 12/264/61.

it was during central government's attempt to govern the middle march through an outside agent that *Henry IV, part I* was first performed. For Percy's rebellion was set against a background of northern resentment at the Crown's intervention in its affairs. More worrying was the temporary alliance that had been forged by Percy and Douglas against Henry IV, which had potential parallels in the late 1590s when Scotland might have joined forces with the Irish. These treacherous tendencies had long antecedents. According to the classical authorities upon whom Camden relied, Northumberland's original people, the 'Ottadini', were noted for having 'called in the Caledonians to assist them and take arms with them' against the 'Britans'. Ancient precedents were utilised to reflect current concerns, as the unpredictable and unreliable border continued to perplex the central authorities.

The Impact of the Union of the Crowns on Northumberland

Northumberland's peculiarity as a border county, and its concomitant financial privileges, were negated by the Union of the Crowns in March 1603. At a stroke, the border between the two sovereign states of England and Scotland was set to vanish. King James made plain his perception of the changed status of the borders in one of his final charges to the Scottish Privy Council before he left for England on 5 April. He declared that 'the pairt of baith the cuntreyis quhilk of lait wes callit the "Mairches" and "Bordouris" and now be the happie unioun is the verie hart of the cuntrey'.[44] In May, he predicted, rather optimistically, that 'the Inhabitants thereof [would be] reduced to perfect obedience'.[45] At the very end of 1607, the Bishop of Durham wrote enthusiastically to Salisbury that measures taken in the area meant, 'I doubt not but *it will in short time* civilize us to be as orderly and obedient as any other part of the kingdom'.[46] Once the north-eastern parts were tamed, they might also be deemed prosperous enough to contribute to the levies which the rest of the country was subject to. The fiscal immunity of Durham was already being relaxed in the 1590s. Collectors for privy seal loans had been nominated for that county in 1590 and again in 1598. It was thus expedient for the Northumberland gentry to continue labouring their deleterious condition and reiterating their deliberately manufactured accounts of distress. When they claimed, with regret, that they were unable to contribute to the privy seal loan, issued to the new King in 1604, they said it was because conditions in their part of the kingdom had not improved since his accession. The principal reason for this continued state of affairs, they explained, was 'that Justice hath not his dewe course here, as in other Cyvill partes of this Realme'.[47] They ended their letter

---

44 *The register of the privy council of Scotland*, ed. David Masson (Edinburgh, 1877-98), vi, p.560.
45 *The political works of James I* (reprinted from the edition of 1616), ed. Charles Howard McIlwain (New York, 1965), p.292.
46 HMC, *Salisbury*, xix, p.377 (my italics).
47 SP 14/9A/230.

by predicting that 'when yt shall please god to better our estates, wee will be readye to offer and yeald unto his matie, the uttermost of our powers'.

In the short term these arguments seem to have prevailed. None of these men's names appeared on the registers of receipt for the 1604 loan and they were not subject to the Subsidy of 1606.[48] However, by January 1609 it was considered that their estate had indeed been bettered, for Sir Ralph Delaval, the sheriff, was instructed to draw up a list of freeholders with a view to contributing to a forthcoming loan. In March he had to order the bailiffs of Glendale, Morpeth and Castle wards to distrain the lands of persons who still owed money to the Crown.[49] Significantly, he had not required the bailiffs of either Coquetdale or Tynedale wards to engage in a similar pursuit. It must be assumed that there were no freeholders of sufficient substance in the two western wards to have been assessed for contributing to the loan; thus confirming the disparity between the upland and lowland parts of the county. In 1611, a list of persons and sums fit for a loan to the King included names from Northumberland (as well as Westmorland and Cumberland) and Newcastle. Three years later, when the Privy Council appealed to the counties and towns for money and plate to compensate for that lost in the recent 'addled' Parliament, both counties Durham and Northumberland were approached, and Durham, Newcastle and Berwick were included amongst the prospective cities, towns and boroughs. The Bishop of Durham, and then the Dean, were invited to make a voluntary gift to the King, should he be required to engage in an 'auxilarie warre' to recover the Palatinate, in 1620. And, two years after that, the sheriffs, Justices of the Peace, mayors, and other officers of the counties and towns of the two counties were asked for the names of those willing to make a voluntary contribution, for the same purpose.[50] For financial reasons, at least, the negative reputation of the north-eastern confines of the country had been well and truly extinguished, and by 1625 the whole area was considered a fully functioning part of the realm.

Paradoxically, the eradication of the borders appeared to make little impact on the natives of Northumberland. Throughout most of the first three sessions of the 1604 Parliament their Members of Parliament displayed a marked lack of interest. It has been argued that while, in theory, border statutes established a strict iron curtain between Carlisle and Berwick, the reality was very different. For much of the time, long before 1603, the borders were more apparent than real and only recognised by the native borderers when it suited them.[51] If the identity of the borders was illusory (when it was an undeniable political presence) before 1603, the consequences of its dissolution thereafter were correspondingly inconsequential.

---

48   E 401/2584-5; 3 Jac I, c26, *Statutes of the realm*, ed. A. Luders and others (London, 1810-18), iv, ii, 1124-5.

49   NRO (Gosforth) 1DE7/18 and 1DE7/20-22.

50   1 Elizabeth, 21, xxvii; *APC, 1590-1*, 187; *APC, 1597-8*, 558-9; SP14/67/45; *APC, 1613-14*, 491-6; *APC, 1619-21*, 291-3; *APC, 1621-3*, 176-8.

51   Galloway, Bruce, *The union of England and Scotland, 1603-1608* (Edinburgh, 1986), p.65; Meikle, Maureen, *A British frontier? Lairds and gentlemen in the eastern borders, 1540-1603* (East Lothian, 2004), especially chapter 8.

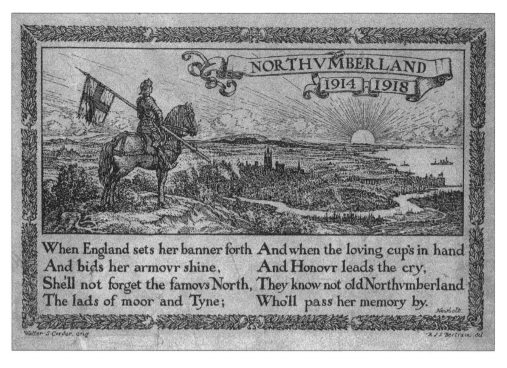

When England sets her banner forth And when the loving cup's in hand
And bids her armovr shine,   And Honovr leads the cry,
She'll not forget the famovs North, They know not old Northvmberland
The lads of moor and Tyne;   Who'll pass her memory by.

22   *Warrior Border Country, as seen in 1918, illustration by Walter Corder and verse by Sir Henry Newbolt*

Newcastle: the Cultural Capital of Northumbria?

Meanwhile, Newcastle was forging another identity of its own. It had long been an important trading and commercial centre, but the enormous upsurge in coal-mining, in the 1580s, meant that it became an alternative means of occupation for those from the upland region of Northumberland's borderlands. It also meant that the concomitant increase in migrant workers, not just from the former liberties but also from further afield, brought problems associated with rapid population movement. This potentially unruly and miscreant immigrant workforce was juxtaposed against the cultural sophistication of those belonging to Newcastle's upper echelons. Hugh Trevor-Roper was convinced that it was the 'merchant-freemen' of Newcastle 'who, in a barbarous country, among illiterate and boorish squireens, constituted a single element of civilisation'.[52]

The town continued to influence its environs into the early modern period and beyond. North Sea networks established as a result of Newcastle's trading interests meant that its culture was increasingly exposed to external influences. Newcastle's account books have abundant evidence of payments to itinerant poets, players and other entertainers right up to the outbreak of the Civil War in 1642. These groups were reinforced by the regular arrival of travelling players, a phenomenon which reached its zenith at the

---

52   Trevor-Roper, 'The bishopric of Durham and the capitalist reformation', *Durham University Journal*, ns vii, 2 (1946), p.47.

end of the 16th and beginning of the 17th centuries.[53] With its links to the capital and the continent, Newcastle was a receptor and a conduit for the full range of cultural impulses. It was also a centre of sociability. Gentlemen of Northumberland had town houses there.[54] When the process of 'the re-making of the North East', according to Keith Wrightson in this volume, took shape, this Newcastle-focused identity was to subsume, though never entirely erase, the earlier sub-regional identities.

Memories of the borders continued to resonate. In 1595, the courtly soldier Sir Philip Sidney had written enthusiastically about 'the olde song of *Percy* and *Duglas*', which saluted Henry ('Hotspur') Percy's martial prowess against the Scots.[55] Sidney's 'soul-stirring words' were later taken up by the Novocastrian intellectual élite in the 19th century, as part of their evocation of Northumbria's distant past.[56] They firmly rejected the 'dolefull dumpes' in which the Widdrington ancestor had found himself. Instead, as Robert Colls shows in this volume, they concentrated on the exhilarating milieu occupied by its celebrated medieval heroes. Theirs was a wild, romantic, untamed place – peopled by independently minded survivors – which had endured up to the beginning of modern times. Almost the last border experience was from Sir Robert Carey. After an unproductive time spent at court, he had greeted his appointment to the deputy wardenship of the west march, in 1593, with relish. 'I took myself to the country,' he wrote in his memoirs, 'where I lived with great comfort: for we had a stirring world, and few days passed over my head but I was on horseback, either to prevent mischief, or to take malefactors.'[57] This was what the 'New Northumbrians' wanted to hear.

---

53   Professional actors periodically touring the country can be traced back to the 15th century, but from 1559 the practice was closely regulated, and persisted long after permanent purpose-built theatres were erected in the capital. See Keenan, Siobhan, *Travelling players in Shakespeare's England* (Basingstoke, 2002), pp.2-3, 13-14 and *passim*. Gurr, Andrew, *The Shakespearean playing companies* (Oxford, 1996), p.36. For payments see Tyne and Wear Record Office, Chamberlains' account books, TW 543/18*ff* and printed in *Records of early English drama: Newcastle upon Tyne*, ed. J.J. Anderson (Toronto and Manchester, 1982).

54   See King, Rebecca, 'Aspects of sociability in the North East of England, 1600-1750', PhD thesis, Durham University, 2001; William Gray's *Chorographia or a survey of Newcastle upon Tyne: 1649* (pr. Newcastle, 1818).

55   Sidney, Sir Philip, 'An apologie for Poetrie', in *Elizabethan critical essays*, ed. G. Gregory Smith (Oxford, 1904), i, p.178.

56   In particular was The Society of Antiquaries of Newcastle upon Tyne, founded in 1813, which continues to pride itself on being the oldest provincial antiquarian society in the country. It was Edmund Bogg who so acclaimed Sidney's importance.

57   *The memoirs of Robert Carey*, ed. F.H. Mares (Oxford, 1972), pp.22-3.

7

'Truly historical ground':
Antiquarianism in the North

ROSEMARY SWEET

On 23 September 1691, William Nicolson, Archdeacon of Carlisle, wrote to his fellow antiquary, Ralph Thoresby in Yorkshire: 'I have some prospect of retrieving part of the (almost) lost history of that ancient kingdom [Northumbria]; with the discovery of the manners, government, language, &c of the people, more fully than the most of our antiquaries have hitherto done.' [1]

No history of Northumbria as such was forthcoming, but by the early 19th century there was a substantial corpus of works which covered the history and topography of the northern counties, and through these publications we may detect the presence of distinct regional and cultural identities. [2] These were not neatly coterminous – they could conflict – but cumulatively they contributed to the expression of a remarkably strong sense of historical difference and a regional consciousness that differentiated the north from the rest of England, and was equally conscious of close links with the lowlands of Scotland: a region which might, without too much distortion, be referred to as Northumbria. In fact, Nicolson generally referred to the kingdom of Northumberland, rather than Northumbria, reflecting a semantic confusion that was widespread at the time. His own conception of the kingdom comprised the counties of York, Durham, Northumberland, Cumberland and Westmorland, with parts of Lancashire. [3] Whilst Northumberland was generally taken to refer to the county, and Northumbria to the Saxon kingdom, there was little consistency in the

---

1 Hunter, J. (ed.), *Letters of Eminent Men, Addressed to Ralph Thoresby, FRS, now First Published from the Originals*, 2 vols (London, 1832), i, p.116.
2 Nicolson was deflected into an ecclesiastical career and eventually became Bishop of Derry. His collections are held in the Bodleian Library, Oxford. He did, however, undertake the revisions for Northumberland and Yorkshire for Edmund Gibson's 1695 edition of William Camden's *Britannia*. For this, and his subsequent career, see James, F.G., *North Country Bishop: A Biography of William Nicolson* (1956).
3 Bodleian MS Top. Gen. c. 27 (2), fol. 14.

long 18th century in distinguishing between the names of the kingdom and the county. Nicolson, and his 18th- and 19th-century successors, all used the terms interchangeably. The Saxon kingdom was seen as an extended version of the later county – or the county a reduced version of the former kingdom. Thus, over a century later, in the *Beauties of England and Wales* John Britton described how, in the period between the fall of Rome and the Norman Conquest, 'Northumberland was abridged of its extent by degrees'.[4]

Most of these antiquaries who laboured upon the antiquities of Northumbria were also topographers, and as such were alert to the modern landscape and economy of coal-mining and farming. The narrative construction of the historical region, therefore, mirrored the emergence of an economic region based on the coalfield. A number of historians, most notably Keith Wrightson, have suggested how the development of the coal industry and the early stages of industrialisation contributed towards the emergence of a north-eastern regional identity during this period. Whilst this may have subconsciously influenced antiquaries and topographers to conceive of their work in a broader framework and to look beyond the county boundaries, the modern emergence of a northern industrial region had its counterpart in a sense of northern historical distinctiveness. This was formalised in the early 19th century with the establishment of the Society of Antiquaries of Newcastle upon Tyne (1813) and the Surtees Society (1834), both of which were instituted to promote the study of the history and antiquities of the northern region, rather than simply a single county – in contrast to many of the other local antiquarian and topographical societies of the 19th century.[5] The founding statement of the Surtees Society announced its agenda to be

…the Publication of inedited Manuscripts, illustrative of the intellectual, the moral, the religious, and the social condition of those parts of England and Scotland, included on the East between the Humber and the Firth of Forth, and on the West between the Mersey and the Clyde, a region which constituted the Ancient Kingdom of Northumberland.[6]

There are four distinct areas in which we may observe the development of an antiquarian or historical regional identity. The first, in point of chronology if not significance, was the study of the Roman antiquities with which the north was so richly endowed. For most antiquaries and historians in the 18th century, the Roman era represented the point at which history could be said to begin, and antiquaries had the advantage of working with textual sources and a ready supply of antiquities which were more or less open to explanation. Despite the contemporary vogue for druidical antiquities, exemplified by antiquaries such as William Stukeley, interest

---

4   Hodgson, J. and Laird, F.C., *The Beauties of England and Wales*, 18 vols (1813), xii, p.9.
5   Levine, P., *The Amateur and the Professional: Antiquarians, Historians and Archaeologists in Victorian England, 1838-1886* (Cambridge, 1986), pp.31-69; Piggott, S., 'The origins of the English County Archaeological Societies', in *idem, Ruins in a Landscape. Essays in Antiquarianism* (Edinburgh, 1976), pp.171–95; the purport of the institution of the Antiquarian Society of Newcastle upon Tyne was declared to be 'Inquiry into Antiquities in general, but especially into those of the North of England, and of the Counties of Northumberland, Cumberland and Durham, in particular', *Archaeologia Aeliana*, 1 (1822), p.vii..
6   Hamilton Thompson, A., 'The Surtees Society, 1834-1934', *Surtees Society*, 150 (1935), p.2.

23 *Emblem of the 20th Legion*

amongst northern antiquaries in the ancient Britons was relatively weak. Rather, the description of the Roman Wall and the ancillary camps, roads and fortifications proved a richly productive seam. The period of Roman occupation offered a straightforward conceptual framework for the investigation and interpretation of the region's history. In addition, the element of fieldwork which this involved necessitated close attention to landscape, which in turn heightened awareness of the north as a distinct topographical region.

The second phase of historical regional identity follows chronologically from the Romans and was based upon the study of the ecclesiastical history of the North East. It found its centre not in the Roman wall but in the city of Durham. It was concerned with the legacy of Bede's *Ecclesiastical History*, the legend of St Cuthbert, and the history of the bishopric, all of which was intimately bound up with the history of the Northumbrian kingdom which succeeded the Roman province. Bede's history was the key text, the more so because, by comparison with the highly visible remains of Roman occupation, the Anglo-Saxons had left relatively few marks upon the landscape and little in the way of material culture. Nevertheless, because of the close historical ties and continuity between the Northumbrian kingdom and the bishopric of Durham, 'Northumbria' had a clearer profile and left a stronger historical legacy in the 18th-century imagination than did any of the other kingdoms of the Saxon heptarchy.

In the later 18th century the Saxon legacy came to be seen in a more positive light, as a sense of English national identity traceable to its Anglo-Saxon roots assumed greater literary prominence. Attempts to trace Northumbrian words and customs to Saxon (what we would call Old English) origins and, more broadly, to rediscover the Northumbrian roots of contemporary Northumberland gained ground: a development which constitutes my third area of investigation and which we might consider under 'literary and linguistic' antiquarianism. Scholars had long been aware that the dialect of Northumbria was closely related to Old English but the late 18th-century appreciation that Englishness derived from the Anglo-Saxons allowed northern antiquaries to make claims for the local dialect and culture as a more purely English variant, uncorrupted by the taints of foreign influence. It also drew upon the work of Scottish antiquaries, such as John Pinkerton, who tried to assert an alternative and superior 'northern' or 'gothic' culture, with affinities to Scandinavia, Germany and the north of England, against what they saw as the Gaelicisation of Scottish culture. This interest in dialect, manners and customs posited a cultural unity to the North as a loosely defined Northumbrian region that encompassed Durham, Northumberland, lowland Scotland and even Yorkshire, and could be traced back to a Saxon past.

The fourth context for historical regional identity is constituted by the long-standing importance of genealogy and family history. Pride in ancestry, heraldry and genealogy were hardly new phenomena in the 18th century, but the assiduity and thoroughness with which the subject was researched – and by those who did not necessarily have a personal connection to the families in question – showed a marked increase. Collectively these family histories embodied the history of the region; the historic patterns of family networks and alliances, property ownership and office-holding were all traced out within the northern counties. The history of the leading landowners was intimately bound up with the events that had shaped the region: there were those who claimed to trace their lineage back to the Saxon kingdom, to have arrived with William the Conqueror or to have played a leading role in the long history of border warfare. The high degree of local autonomy and power exercised by the great magnate families such as the Percys was reflected in the way that local history was so intimately connected with family history.[7]

Roman Antiquities

Any historical endeavour will be shaped by the sources available to it. For all antiquaries, wherever they were based, the period of the Roman invasions and occupation was comparatively well documented by the Romans themselves, particularly in comparison with the periods immediately preceding and following it. Roman antiquities were more accessible, more abundant, more easily legible than those of the Saxons, Danes, or even Normans who had replaced them, and were more readily assimilated into a historical framework. Many shared the opinion of Samuel Johnson that 'all that is really *known* of the ancient state of Britain is contained in a few pages'. Prior to the period of Roman occupation there was simply no history to be told.[8] Availability of sources aside, however, the study of domestic antiquities in the North, or anywhere else, cannot be fully understood except in relation to the fascination with Roman antiquities which had captivated the learned élite of Europe since the Renaissance. English gentlemen were educated to believe that the Roman

7   The distinctive pattern of landownership in Northumberland and Durham, with the concentration of large amounts of land in the hands of a few magnates as opposed to the more dispersed patterns of Cumberland and Westmorland, enhanced this tendency. See Phythian-Adams in this volume.

8   Boswell, J. (ed.), *Life of Johnson,* 2 vols (London, 1949), ii, p.238.

republic and its empire represented the peak of human achievement and civilisation. Part of the appeal of Roman antiquities was that they brought to mind the very precepts and qualities for which the Romans were admired. In the words of John Wallis, historian of Northumberland, 'They bring before us, as in perspective, *Roman* wisedom, *Roman* piety, *Roman* loyalty, *Roman* gratitude, *Roman* generosity and hospitality, *Roman* courage and magnanimity.'[9] Roman antiquities were also more legible: any educated gentleman could expect to be able to read a Roman inscription and locate it within a history of republican and imperial Rome with which he was familiar from his boyhood education. Saxon runes posed far more of a challenge, and were inelegant, indecipherable and uninteresting. The power of classical Rome over the 18th-century mind was further accentuated by the vogue for travel. The Grand Tour was largely the preserve of the wealthiest members of the landed élite, but the numerous volumes dedicated to describing the antiquities to be found in Italy, and the widespread market for prints of classical architecture and sculpture, ensured that there was an extensive reading public already convinced of the inherent value of studying Roman antiquities. It was, then, an act of patriotism and economic virtue, as many self-righteous antiquaries proclaimed, to study the remains left by the Romans in Britain, rather than travel abroad, with all the concomitant risks of physical and moral corruption.[10]

The antiquaries of the northern regions of Britain were becoming increasingly conscious that the area had enjoyed a relationship with the Romans very different from that of the more easily pacified southern regions, and that it was particularly rich in Roman military antiquities. A series of publications, including Robert Smith's essay on the Roman Wall published in the revised edition of Camden's *Britannia* in 1722, Alexander Gordon's *Itinerarium septentrionale* (1726), John Horsley's *Britannia romana* (1732) and William Stukeley's *Itinerarium boreale*, published posthumously in 1776 but based upon a tour made in 1725, all drew attention to the undiscovered – and unappreciated – richness of Roman antiquities in the north of England and Scotland. Stukeley waxed lyrical on the quantity of Roman antiquities to be found in the north: the Romans, he said, were never idle, setting up military pillars, making and repairing public roads, building altars, carving inscriptions and minting coins. There was no need to travel to Italy: imperial Rome, he claimed, could scarce exceed the prodigious quantities of ruins and memorials, the glorious show of towns, cities, castles and temples to be found on the south side of the wall.[11] It should be noted that Stukeley never actually visited Italy.

The conquest of Britain by the Romans had always been a problematic episode for historians and antiquaries. Whilst on the one hand it was believed that the Romans had been responsible for introducing civilisation, arts, architecture and ultimately the first preaching of Christianity, on the other hand they had also comprehensively

---

9   Wallis, J., *The Natural History and Antiquities of Northumberland: and of so Much of the County of Durham as Lies Between the Rivers Tyne and Tweed; Commonly Called, North Bishoprick*, 2 vols (1769), i, p.ix.
10   Sweet, R., *Antiquaries: the Discovery of the Past in Eighteenth-Century Britain* (2004), p.36.
11   Stukeley, W., *Itinerarium curiosum*, 2nd edition (1776), p.67.

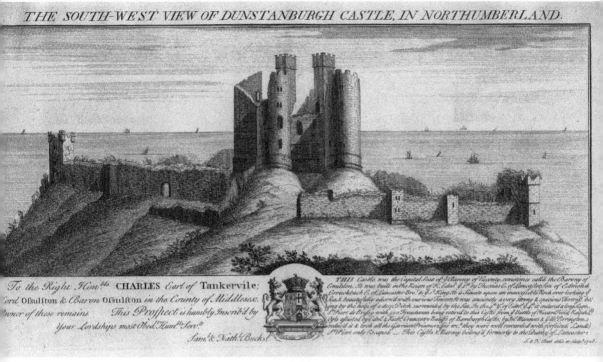

24 *South-west view of Dunstanburgh Castle, by Samuel and Nathaniel Buck, 1728*

conquered the indigenous native Britons.[12] Moreover, with the arts of civilisation, they had brought the seeds of luxury and dissipation, and had thereby been responsible for leaving the British inhabitants vulnerable to the marauding attacks of Saxon pirates. The northern regions, however, had taken much longer to succumb, and it was only with difficulty that Roman authority was established and maintained. Whilst archaeologists today might view the Roman Wall more as a channel of communication or border crossing, for 18th-century antiquaries it was unequivocally a structure of military defence, erected in order to mark the limits of Roman authority and to keep out those who threatened to disrupt the *pax romana* from the north. The wall was in fact an indication of the uneasy hold that the all-powerful Romans had exercised in this northernmost outpost of their empire. It established a theme of equivocal authority exercised by a superior southern power, set against the defiant defence of liberties on the part of the Brigantes. Their manly independence was contrasted with the effete passivity of the south. The original inhabitants were, according to Stukeley, a 'bold and hardy people … strong and hardy in body, fierce in manners'.[13] All these themes would be rehearsed again and again in the historical interpretation of subsequent periods of Northumbria's history. This narrative also established the northern region as one particularly rich in the military antiquities of Roman occupation. 'In *Britain*,'

---

12 Thoresby, R., *Ducatus Leodiensis* (1715), pp.vii-ix.
13 Stukeley, *Itinerarium curiosum*, p.55.

25 *George Allan esquire and William Hutchinson esquire*

wrote John Wallis, author of *The Natural History and Antiquities of Northumberland* (1769), 'no part had their company more or longer than *Northumberland*. Here they had their cities, their castles, and their towns.'[14]

In the course of the 18th century antiquaries gradually unpicked the logic behind the wall: the relationship of the camps and milecastles; the sophistication with which it was conceived; the means of communication. It was no longer just a heap of old stones but a highly complex structure through which a minority occupying force could keep an entire region under control. By the time that the Hanoverian government was considering the construction of a military road along the path of the former Roman road, the whole complex of road, wall, ditch and rampart had become a much more familiar entity and had acquired a rich meaning as a symbol for the history of the northern regions. It denoted the bravery and independence of the native peoples. They 'were esteemed the bravest race of Britons, and consisted of those heroes who would not submit to the invaders as they advanced in conquest, but with a true patriotic virtue strove to retain their native liberty'.[15] It evoked the perpetual instability of the border area (not just in the Roman era, but under the Saxons, the Normans), the tenuous hold of central authority through the medieval and early modern periods, and the recurrent conflicts which continued through the 17th and the 18th centuries. In the years after 1707, and again after the final defeat of the Jacobite threat in 1746, the wall acquired an added resonance as its ruins highlighted the redundancy of such structures under the *pax Hanoveriensis*. It became one of the defining landmarks of the north.

Thus the Roman Wall became a noted feature of the tourist itinerary. Antiquaries and travellers traversed its length and it became the subject of publications aimed at the popular travelling market, such as John Warburton's *Vallum Romanum* published in 1756, or William Hutton's *Roman Wall* of 1802. As antiquarian tours became increasingly affordable and fashionable for the polite travellers of 18th-century Britain, the wall became more widely celebrated as an object of curiosity and admiration. Its length and scale – the very basis of its fame and reputation – ensured that it could not be assigned to a single county. It dominated the volumes on both Northumberland

14 Wallis, *Natural History and Antiquities of Northumberland*, p.v.

15 Hutchinson, W., *The History and Antiquities of the County Palatine of Durham*, 3 vols (Newcastle, 1785-94), i, p.ii. Histories aimed at a more popular readership, such as John Baillie's *Impartial History of the Town and County of the Town of Newcastle upon Tyne and its Vicinity* (Newcastle, 1801), pp.11-13, chose to elaborate upon this theme: the Romans had conquered only through superiority of arms; in courage and resolution they were inferior.

and Cumberland in the popular series *The Beauties of England and Wales*. Antiquaries, topographers and traveller writers had to produce maps which transcended county boundaries and discuss the construction of the wall as something which cut across the north as a whole. For the first half of the century attention had been focused upon the western end of the wall around Carlisle. The main road north from London, however, passed through Newcastle, not Carlisle, and for most people travelling from the south, the starting point for an investigation of the wall began at the eastern end, on Tyneside. There were few who, like William Hutton, walked from end to end in both directions.[16] Thus, as the volume of traffic going north steadily increased in the years following the suppression of the Jacobite rebellion, the focus of inquiry shifted eastwards from Carlisle towards Newcastle. Investigations of the wall extended out from Northumberland and subsequent passage into another county did not necessarily provoke notice. John Wallis described it as 'the glory, the pride of Northumberland'.[17] It was as if the kingdom of Northumbria was reabsorbing the counties of Cumberland and Westmorland.

Among the works most commonly cited by visitors to the north of England were those by William Hutchinson.[18] Hutchinson was not particularly highly regarded by his peers as an antiquary, but he was prolific, and in terms of the somewhat confined world of antiquarian publishing, relatively successful. Hutchinson professed himself an antiquary, but is better seen as one who sought to realise the commercial value of the reading public's interest in national history and domestic antiquities. Both his *View of Northumberland* and *The history of Cumberland* derived much of their content and structure from a description of the Roman Wall, the various stations and camps along the route, complete with cross sections and reconstructions. But whilst Hutchinson was willing to allow that the Romans had brought the arts of civilisation to Britain and introduced order, he argued that their contribution to the history of the British people, and in particular the people of Northumberland, was easily over-rated. In Hutchinson's narrative the Roman influence was largely negative and compared badly with the defeated Brigantes, who fought bravely under an elected chieftain (anticipating the freeborn qualities of the English constitution)[19] alongside the Saxons who eventually displaced them and were heir to many of the virtues which Hutchinson had first projected onto the Ancient Britons.[20] Those in closest contact to the Romans, he argued, became enervated, dissipated, servile and submissive – in need of a bracing dose of Saxon masculine aggression, independence and virtue.

---

16 Hutton's journey is described in his *The History of the Roman Wall, which Crosses the Island of Great Britain, from the German Ocean to the Irish Sea. Describing its Antient state and its Appearance in the Year 1801* (London, 1802).

17 Wallis, *Natural History and Antiquities of Northumberland*, i, p.vii.

18 An outline of Hutchinson's biography and publications is given by Hodgson, J.C., 'William Hutchinson, FSA, the historian of three northern counties', *Archaeologia Aeliana*, 3rd ser., xiii (1916), pp.166-83.

19 The Britons 'were esteemed the bravest race of Britons, and consisted of those heroes who would not submit to the invaders as they advanced in conquest, but with a true patriotic virtue strove to retain their native liberty'. Hutchinson, *Durham*, i, p.2.

20 Rather than presenting the Saxons as the first of a series of piratical, pagan invaders, Hutchinson emphasised how they had originally come to Britain at the invitation of the Brigantes, who were struggling to withstand the incursions of the hostile Picts. The parallels with the Hanoverian Succession were obvious and the implications there for anyone to draw out. Hutchinson, *View of Northumberland*, i, p.vi.

The Saxon Era and Christian Conversion

Hutchinson's personal enthusiasm lay with the Saxon era and it was here that his conception of the kingdom of Northumbria began to assume some kind of authority. Many historians and antiquaries on the other hand were reluctant to engage with the Saxon period: the paucity of records, the uncertainty of the times, the constant feuds and fighting rendered it uncertain and unsatisfying, and they passed over it as quickly as possible, noting only the division into shires under Alfred, the introduction of trial by jury, and the liberties of the constitution. However, by the end of the 18th century there was an increasingly nationalist strain in historical literature which was much more sympathetic to the history of the Anglo-Saxons than had been the case in the Augustan era.[21] But apologists for the Saxons still had to struggle to overturn well-established prejudices, shared even by those of a Whiggish outlook, who viewed the Saxons as primitive barbarians.

Many antiquaries passed rapidly over the Saxon period, looking forward to the Norman Conquest and the compilation of Domesday Book, which at last provided some documentary evidence from which to work – particularly pertinent for a landholding élite, the prime consumers of county histories. Domesday Book represented crucial information about patterns of land tenure in the 11th century. The northern counties, however, were not covered. The Saxons and Danes, true to the 'northern traditions' of hardiness, military valour and the defence of liberty, had rebelled against the Norman invaders. 'The stout Northumbrians' who, in the words of one north Yorkshire historian, 'zealously opposed' the rule of William the Conqueror were forced to rebel in defence of their freedom.[22] In the Harrying of the North all was laid waste and lawlessness prevailed, so that the Domesday commissioners dared not enter the territory; in such a way the reticence of Domesday Book on the north of England was explained. But it was a major gap for northern antiquaries. A transcript of the relevant section of Domesday Book and an accompanying essay had become a staple element of any county history by the end of the century and established the county framework around which the remainder of the study might be conducted.[23] Northern antiquaries did not have that option, but they did have far richer sources for the preceding period in Bede's *Ecclesiastical History* and later monastic chroniclers such as Simeon of Durham. Bede's history, nominally of England, was heavily biased towards the Northumbrian kingdom where Christianity had first become securely established in England. Conveniently enough, the area excluded by Domesday Book was essentially that of the 'patrimony of St Cuthbert' and the Northumbrian church

---

21   Sweet, *Antiquaries*, 189-229 ; Newman, G., *The Rise of English Nationalism: a Cultural History, 1740-1830* (1987), pp.109-118.

22   Graves, J., *The History and Antiquities of Cleveland in the North Riding of the County of York* (Carlisle, 1808), p.16.

23   Sweet, *Antiquaries*, 235-6. The Bolden Boke did, of course, offer much information of a similar nature to that of Domesday Book and was much used by George Allan, for example, in his collections towards a history of Darlington (see Durham Chapter Library MS Allan 15). Its coverage of the missing counties, however, was not complete, and it lacked the iconic significance of Domesday Book.

which had nurtured the flowering of Anglo-Saxon spirituality. But the towering importance of Bede's history for the historical identity of the north of England was not simply a consequence of the dearth of other sources. The roots of early Christianity in England had encouraged the Saxonists of late 17th-century Oxford, such as George Hickes, William Elstob and Edward Thwaites, as well as William Nicolson, to pursue their researches in Old English.[24] All these men grew up in the north of England. In studying the early Saxon church they were at the same time engaging in acts of local piety, ensuring recognition for the role of the Northumbrian kingdom in the larger narrative of the country's conversion to Christianity. Implicit, too, in the work of these antiquaries was a hostility to Rome – not the Rome of military imperialism to which Hutchinson objected, but the similarly corrupt and effeminising Rome of the Pope and Roman Catholicism. The revival of scholarly interest in the Northumbrian kingdom, therefore, drew as much on 18th-century national pride as local chauvinism.

Hutchinson's account of Northumberland was prefaced with a history of the Northumbrian kingdom which allowed him to expatiate on the virtues of the Saxons, the progenitors of the English race, and more particularly the people from whom the modern inhabitants of Northumberland could unequivocally be said to trace their descent. He deliberately set out to challenge the generally unflattering account of the Saxons found in most histories of Britain. David Hume, author of one of the most widely read histories published in the 18th century, had described the government of Northumbria as in a state of 'universal anarchy' until its subjection to Egbert of Wessex.[25] For the historian of England, tracing the emergence of the modern 18th-century state, there was little value in romanticising the history of a minor kingdom for which even the names of the various kings could not be established with any certainty. The kingdom of Northumbria had to pass away before the unified English state could come into existence. In deliberate contrast to this orthodoxy, Hutchinson was unrelentingly positive in his attitude towards the Saxon period, both for its importance as what another antiquary called the 'seedbed' of our national history, and as the basis for claiming a regional distinctiveness for Northumberland and its vicinity. The Saxons were heroic, whilst the Britons, corrupted by Roman influence, who had requested Saxon assistance against the barbarian Picts, were guilty of the grossest ingratitude.[26] When the Saxons asserted control, he argued, they could not be accused of a breach of faith; it was the only reasonable response to secure their own relationship with the fickle and unstable Britons. He concluded this apologia with a rousing tribute to the legacy of the Anglo-Saxon constitution:

24 George Hickes was born in the parish of Kirby Wiske, near Thirsk, Yorkshire; William Elstob was born in Newcastle; William Nicolson was born in Great Orton, Cumberland; Edward Thwaites was born at Crosby Ravensworth, Westmorland. According to Richard Gough, *British Topography*, 2 vols (London, 1780), ii, p.56, Elstob was also collecting materials on the history of the northern counties and was preparing a history of his native town.

25 Hume, D., *The History of England, from the Invasion of Julius Caesar to the Revolution in 1688*, 8 vols (1778), p.70.

26 Hutchinson, *Durham*, i, p.ix. Britons in close contact with the Romans were lulled into passiveness and submission, but 'as these practices could contaminate only such as had an intimate intercourse with the Romans, a detestation of bondage, and the innate love of liberty broke out in many places at a distance from the Roman garrisons, and secret cabals were held unnoticed by the incautious legions'.

Authors, in the warmth of accusations, neglect the consideration of the advantages we finally derived form the Saxons; no less than THE MAXIMS OF OUR COMMON LAW, AND THE ORIGINAL PRINCIPLES OF OUR INESTIMABLE CONSTITUTION. If we inherit anything from the Britons, it consists of their *ferocity, instability,* and *ingratitude.* Without the Saxon arms, this island, like the regions of the east, would have been over-run and desolated by a banditti, worse than Tartars, and become a den of thieves, pirates and robbers.[27]

Hutchinson's sentiments were echoed by other authors such as John Baillie, in whose *History of Newcastle* the city's moot hall was traced back to its Saxon origins and described as the place 'from which the glorious palladium of British freedom, trial by jury, took its origins'.[28] In this version of Anglo-Saxon history, the Northumbrian rulers – early converts to Christianity – compared very favourably with the evil and treacherous rulers of the kingdoms to the south. Hutchinson's admiration for the Saxons, however, was limited to the kingdom of Northumbria and did not extend to the country as a whole. Indeed the unification of the kingdoms under the overlordship of Egbert in 826, conventionally seen as a key moment in the emergence of the English polity, was referred to as 'subjection' rather than unification.[29]

Similarly, the Danes were barely countenanced. Their contribution to the history of Northumberland was, he avowed, negligible, and they had made no lasting impact upon the people, their manners and customs, or their language. The Danelaw did not become the object of antiquarian research until the 19th century, and even then the focus was almost exclusively upon Yorkshire. 'To trace all the ravages those Barbarians committed,' wrote Hutchinson, 'would lead to descriptions tedious and painful.'[30] Danish Kings such as Cnut fleetingly appeared in the narrative, with no allusions made to their territorial power or to their subjugation of the Saxons. It was not just Hutchinson who downplayed the impact of the Danes in Northumberland. Neither Henry Bourne nor John Brand gave them any quarter in their histories of Newcastle; John Wallis simply abandoned the attempt to identify any Danish monuments, and the Danes were barely mentioned in John Britton's early 19th-century synthesis in the serial publication, *The Beauties of England and Wales*. In Yorkshire and Cumberland, by contrast, Danish influence was presented as unequivocal. The cultural and administrative distinctions that were consequent upon Danish settlement helped to ensure that 18th-century antiquaries primarily conceived Northumbria as comprised of Durham and Northumberland.[31] Hutchinson considered the influence of the

---

27   Hutchinson, *View of Northumberland*, i, p.vi.
28   Baillie, *History of Newcastle*, p.196.
29   Hutchinson, *View of Northumberland*, i, p.xxvi. Sharon Turner's history of the Anglo-Saxons, first published in 1799, offered a much less positive assessment of the Northumbrian contribution to Anglo-Saxon history, emphasising the murderous violence and instability of the kingdom: 'of the Anglo-Saxon governments the kingdom of Northumbria had always been the most perturbed'. Turner, S., *The History of the Anglo Saxons*, 2 vols (London, 1799), i, p.224.
30   Hutchinson, *View of Northumberland*, i, pp.1-2.
31   Drake, W., 'A letter to the Secretary, on the origin of the English language', and *idem*, 'Some further remarks on the origin of the English language', *Archaeologia*, 5 (1779), pp.306-17, 379-89. Drake's articles explored the Danish influences upon the Yorkshire dialect.

Danes when he came to describe what he called the 'Bewcastle obelisk', whose Saxon carvings were assumed at the time to be Danish runic inscriptions. The Danes, he reminded his readers, had brought with them pagan customs and had practised 'hocus pocus tricks' in those areas where they were most numerous and least disturbed – such as Cumberland. The current superstition of the borderers around Bewcastle, he suggested, showed that even in the late 18th century they were not 'utter strangers to the black arts of their ancestors'.[32]

Over the course of his literary career, Hutchinson effectively covered the entire area of the ancient kingdom of Northumbria, bar the southern regions of what had been Deira, stretching down into Yorkshire. The success of this effort to revive the contours of the Anglo-Saxon kingdom was, however, always limited. Despite the lists of the names of the kings of Bernicia and Deira which he drew up, there was little he could do to relate his historical vision of the Anglo-Saxon kingdom to the topography and landscape that he saw around him. Few antiquaries in the 18th century had the skill to distinguish Saxon burial mounds or Saxon camps. The Saxons had left fewer coins than their Roman predecessors and they had been far less assiduous in marking their presence in the landscape with roads or fortifications. When it came to describing the landscape and physical remains of the past in the Northumbrian countryside, Hutchinson found few monuments to remind him of the Northumbrian kingdom. The only specimens of what were thought to be Saxon antiquities were to be found in the remains of Saxon churches; but even these were rare survivals – the Danish raids, it was believed, had destroyed all trace of the original Saxon foundations at Lindisfarne, Hartlepool or Whitby.[33] Hutchinson was no expert in matters of architectural history, a discipline which was only just beginning to emerge, but by the time he was writing there were sufficient publications available from which he could lift the appropriate descriptions of what was assumed to be Saxon, pre-Conquest architecture. At Hexham he highlighted the rounded Saxon arches and the disproportionately heavy pillars – an error of taste, he said, that was to be found in most Saxon churches. Five years later, however, when he came to describe the remains of the monasteries at Jarrow and Wearmouth in *Durham*, he had acquired rather more proficiency in appreciating what antiquaries persisted in calling Saxon architecture, noting the varieties of carved ornament and the solidity of construction.[34]

The most obvious reminder of the Saxon Northumbrian kingdom was, in fact, the spiritual and administrative structure of the modern diocese of Durham. It is significant that the full title of John Wallis's history of Northumberland included 'so much of the county of Durham as lies between the Rivers Tyne and Tweed; commonly called, North Bishoprick'. The territorial boundaries of the bishopric

---

32 Hutchinson, W., *The History of the County of Cumberland*, 2 vols (Carlisle, 1794), i, p.85.
33 Hutchinson, *View of Northumberland*, ii, p.142; Sharp, C., *A History of Hartlepool* (Stockton, 1816), pp.7-8; Charlton, L., *The History of Whitby and of Whitby Abbey* (London, 1779), pp.40-1; Young, G., *A History of Whitby, and Streoneshalh Abbey*, 2 vols (Whitby, 1817), i, pp.45-8.
34 Hutchinson, *View of Northumberland*, i, 99; *Durham*, ii, pp.474-5.

26 *Durham Cathedral (by Thomas Girtin, 1799)*

of Durham were, of course, of greater extent than the county of Durham itself. The archdeaconry of Northumberland extended over the entire county, and there were also the peculiars of Norham and Bedlington in Yorkshire, reminders of the earlier more extensive sway that had been exercised from Lindisfarne. As such, the bishopric of Durham, the heir to the original patrimony of St Cuthbert, was a constant commemoration of the kingdom of Northumbria. The local pride that was felt in the history of the Cathedral and the lineal descent that could be traced through its history and bishops back to the original mission of Aidan, meant that Northumbria maintained an imaginative presence in the 18th century that none of the other kingdoms of the Saxon heptarchy enjoyed. Sir Cuthbert Sharp, one of the founder members of the Surtees Society, made Durham the nerve centre of the Northumbrian kingdom. As a native, he asserted that the region encompassed by the present county of Durham formed the source of Saxon Northumbria's opulence and strength, and emphasised that the episcopal see of Durham was first established at Lindisfarne by Aidan.[35] Although Mercia might have been more richly endowed with Saxon charters (which contemporary antiquaries such as Owen Manning were beginning to elucidate), there were few narratives around which to construct a history of that kingdom. The career of the Mercian king, Penda, universally reviled by the 18th-century antiquaries as an evil pagan responsible for the defeat of the saintly Oswald, simply confirmed the prejudices of 18th-century readers against

---

35 Sharp, *Hartlepool*, p.9.

the Saxon period. Even Wessex, the power base of Alfred, remained ill-defined and under-conceptualised, seldom featuring in the antiquarian literature of the time. Alfred's fame was dependent upon his posthumous reputation as King of England and patron of learning, rather than his actual career as king of Wessex.

Nor was it just Durham that proudly claimed its place in the history of early Christianity. Other communities, such as Hartlepool or Cleveland and Whitby, traced back their earliest settlement to Saxon monastic communities, taking as much pride in their Saxon origins as other towns took in a Roman foundation. Newcastle was one town that could boast Roman origins: it was identified as Pons Aelii, the second station of the wall from the eastern end. Unlike many towns, however, it could also claim a distinctive history, even in the obscurity of the early Middle Ages, as Monkchester, refuge for monks when the area was prey to foreign invaders.[36] Crucially for the conception of the North East as a centre of early Christianity, Durham could not claim to be the only religious centre of importance. Henry Bourne explained the importance of Newcastle – or Monkchester– in the early Middle Ages:

> When now it is considered that the Business of Religion went on so Briskly throughout the whole Kingdom of the Northumbers; it is rational to suppose that this Place, as it was not only convenient for the monastical Life as to Retirement, but also a Security to it too (being at that Time a garrison'd Fort) was certainly as early inhabited by the Monks as the abovementioned Time; and besides if we consider the Veneration it is mention'd with by many Historians for the severe and rigid Lives of it's [sic] Monks; how it was the most eminent Place in the North, for the monastical Life, so very famous on that account, as to change it's [sic] former Name to that of Monkchester: There can scarce be allowed it a later Time to arrive at such a Pitch of Eminency and Glory.[37]

Some antiquaries, such as John Britton, who compiled the section on Northumberland for the *Beauties of England and Wales*, were sceptical about this idea of a monastic centre. But Britton, we should note, was a southerner from Wiltshire. John Brand, however, Newcastle born and bred, was thoroughly convinced. The second volume of his *History of Newcastle* was praised by reviewers for its account of the expanding coal trade and Newcastle's place in the industrial economy of the North East. But Brand also provided an exercise in demonstrating Newcastle's place in the golden age of the Northumbrian kingdom. 'The Saxons … held it in the greatest esteem, and during the heptarchy made it the chief seat of the king of the Northumbers, who adorned it with so great a number of monasteries that from this it obtained the name of Monk-Chester.'[38]

The bishopric and palatinate of Durham had long been an anomaly within the administrative history of the north. Durham's local pride lay in the fact of its peculiar jurisdiction, awarded because of the highly vulnerable foundations to royal authority

36 Bourne, H., *History of Newcastle upon Tyne* (1736), pp.5-6; Brand, J., *History and Antiquities of the Town and County of the Town of Newcastle upon Tyne*, 2 vols (1789), i, pp.202-3; Hodgson, J., *The Picture of Newcastle upon Tyne* (Newcastle, 1807), p.2.
37 Bourne, *History of Newcastle*, p.9.
38 Brand, *History of Newcastle*, ii, p.383.

in the area and the Crown's need to bring alongside the educated clergy, the wealth and influence of the church. By the 18th century Durham had lost much of its former administrative autonomy, but it retained legal privileges as a palatinate, which was the basis upon which a sense of regional difference and identity could be constructed. For those antiquaries who sought to trace back the historical antecedents of the bishopric, the conversion of the Saxon kings of Northumbria to Christianity was the pivotal point for the region's history. It was the arrival of Aidan's mission from Iona, at the invitation of King Oswald, that marked the point at which the Christian history of the region could be said to begin, and as such it took precedence over the Roman occupation. True to this spirit, in the 19th century Robert Surtees began his history of Durham with a general account of the Saxon kingdom and divided up the rest of the narrative bishop by bishop.[39] The sites of Bede's *Ecclesiastical History*, the churches of Aidan, Wilfrid, Cuthbert and the other luminaries of Saxon Christianity, were all deeply honoured in memory. As we have seen, few places could boast of any structural continuity with the buildings erected by the early missionaries, but the legends associated with them, and their place in the narrative by which England was converted to Christianity, were carefully recorded in topographical works.[40] For these ecclesiastical antiquaries the landscape of Northumberland was not one of Roman occupation so much as one of Christian conversion.

As a legal and ecclesiastical centre, Durham was full of lawyers and clerics. Many interested themselves in the legal antiquities of the Palatinate. Recurrent challenges to the authority of the bishop had generated a rich corpus of material and a tradition of legal antiquarianism, often running in families, which was concerned with defending the rights and privileges of the bishopric. In the 18th century the practical necessity of amassing and making copies of such information was less pressing than had been the case in the 17th century, when Oliver Cromwell had tried to abolish the Palatinate, but disputes over property were increasing in volume as enclosure and the expansion of mining greatly increased the value of the land held by the bishop.[41] This antiquarian research produced a volume of material that is hard to match in any other urban or ecclesiastical centre. In the 17th century important collections of documents pertaining to the property, rights and privileges of the diocese had been built up by two families of ecclesiastical lawyers in particular, the Mickletons and Spearmans. Much of the Spearman collection was originally drawn up by John Spearman at the instigation of William Nicolson, who had requested a summary account of the ancient state of the county palatine for his own projected history.[42] John Spearman had been under-sheriff of the county of Durham and deputy registrar of the Court of Chancery, and was therefore not only imbued with what his son described as

---

39 Surtees, R., *The History and Antiquities of the County Palatine of Durham*, 4 vols (1816-40), i, pp.i-xiv.
40 See for example, Charlton, *Whitby*; Hutchinson, *View of Northumberland*; Sharp, *Hartlepool*; Thoresby, *Ducatus Leodiesis*; Wallis, *Natural History and Antiquities of Northumberland*.
41 See in particular the Spearman and Mickleton collections in Durham Chapter Library and in Durham University Library.
42 Spearman, G., *An Enquiry into the Ancient and Present State of the County Palatine of Durham* (Durham, 1729), introduction. See also Gough, *British Topography*, i, pp.329-39.

'great skill and judgment in his profession and unbiased affection for Church and Government' but also with considerable expertise in the documents of the Palatinate's legal, administrative and ecclesiastical history.[43] In the 18th century Spearman junior carried on his father's research, but turned it against the bishop in a critique of episcopal estate management and political influence. There were others who, without sharing the same immediate professional interest in these records, similarly occupied themselves in making notes, taking transcriptions and creating indexes. They copied charters, compiled lists of bishops and other officeholders, and drew up tables of fees, property rentals and the endowments of vicarages.[44] Documents were passed from antiquary to antiquary around Durham and Northumberland, anticipating the constituency from which the Newcastle Society of Antiquaries and the Surtees Society would draw their membership in the next century. Material relating to contemporary events was also amassed – election ephemera and poll books, newspaper cuttings or taxation records – all of which pertained exclusively to Northumberland, Durham and occasionally to Yorkshire.[45] Very little of this antiquarian endeavour was ever published, although almost every antiquarian and topographical publication during the period acknowledged the assistance of Christopher Hunter, George Allan and others like them.[46] This kind of activity – collecting rather than writing for the public – driven partly by an urge to collect and to possess, was also informed by a strong belief in the importance of the preservation of property and local privilege.

It was also an exercise in commemoration: for it is important not to underestimate the extent to which antiquarianism was driven by this impulse to honour the dead and to keep their example alive before the living. It should be of little surprise, therefore, to find that many of the antiquarian collections made in Durham concerned the life of St Cuthbert and the history of his shrine. The lawyers and clerics of the 17th and 18th centuries were essentially continuing a tradition that had begun with monastic chroniclers such as Simeon of Durham; a genealogy of influence which the 17th-century antiquary Robert Hegg made clear in the preface to his 'Life of St Cuthbert' where he listed in succession all the authorities who had written on St Cuthbert before him.[47] Hegg's essay had originally been planned as an account of the 'Antiquities' of Durham Cathedral, but the life of St Cuthbert and the subsequent fate of the shrine took precedence. Hegg readily admitted that it was far from being a history of the church, but it was barely even the inventory of antiquities that he claimed. The antiquaries of the 18th and early 19th centuries went some way to making good that deficiency. The records of the bishopric of Durham continued to provide a focal point

43 *Durham Philobiblon*, vol. 1, pt 6 (1951), pp.40-5 outlines the main groupings of the Mickleton and Spearman collections.
44 We might note in particular the contributions of the physician Christopher Hunter, the clergymen Thomas Randall and John Mann, and George Allan, a lawyer based at Darlington.
45 The collections of George Allan and John Mann are particularly rich in this respect.
46 George Allan got as far as publishing proposals for a history of Durham. He had made extensive collections for a history of Darlington and had begun printing his history of hospitals of the region *Collectanea ad statum civilem et ecclesiasticum comitatus dunelmensis spectantia, ex variis codicibus tam manuscriptis, quam impressis sine ordine congesta* on his privately owned press (Durham Chapter Library MS 26).
47 Hegg, R., *The Legend of St Cuthbert, with the Antiquities of the Church of Durham* (1663). George Allan published another edition of this text in 1777.

for antiquarian inquiry and by the 19th century antiquarian curiosity in the history of the bishopric gained further impetus from the High Church interest in ecclesiastical history and the early Church. Sir Cuthbert Sharp was always of the view that the Surtees Society, of which he was a founding member, should restrict itself to the publication only of such records as were related to the bishopric of Durham.[48] Sharp's vision was agreed to be too narrow in scope but, nevertheless, the initial publications were almost all concerned with the history of the bishopric and its period of Anglo-Saxon glory.

Popular Antiquities

Initially, the Oxford Saxonists of the late 17th century had studied Saxon – or Old English as it would now be termed – as a means to an end, but in the process they had become aware that the local dialect of the North East was closer to the original Saxon than modern English, and unlike the dialect of Yorkshire, had been less influenced by the Danish settlers.[49] As interest in the origins of English language and culture strengthened, so too did interest in the vernacular traditions of the North East. Those who read Thomas Percy's *Reliques of English Poetry* (1765) with such enthusiasm may have been caught up in a general vogue for primitive simplicity, but Percy himself, as an antiquary and chaplain to the Duke of Northumberland, was also fascinated by these pieces as historical artefacts and the productions of a 'gothic' (in this context, Saxon) tradition.[50] Percy's correspondence with the Scottish antiquary George Paton reveals his parallel interest in the Scots dialect, as manifested in the collections of poetry published by David Herd and Sir David Lindsay, and the historical links between Northumbria and lowland Scotland that were evident in the linguistic connections.[51] Another of Paton's correspondents was Joseph Ritson of Stockton on Tees, who also made collections of verse and poetry from Durham, Northumberland, Yorkshire and Caledonia.[52] Like Percy he was intrigued by the relationship between Old English and Scots,[53] but he was fiercely critical of Percy's editorial methods and the way in which he had given a false polish to a popular art form.[54] In 1824 John Brockett

---

48 Hamilton Thompson, 'The Surtees Society', p.13.
49 There is a considerable literature on the 'Oxford Saxonists', but for an overview see Douglas, D.C., *English Scholars 1660-1730* (2nd revised edn, Rochester, N.Y., 1951), pp.52-97; Fairer, D., 'Anglo-Saxon Studies', in Mitchell, L.G. and Sutherland, L. (eds), *The Eighteenth Century*, in Ashton, T.H. (ed.), *The History of the University of Oxford*, 8 vols (Oxford, 1986), v, pp.807-28.
50 Groom, N., *The Making of Percy's Reliques* (Oxford, 1999).
51 British Library Add MS 32,332.
52 Ritson, J. (ed.), *The Bishopric Garland: or, Durham Minstrel. Being a choice collection of excellent songs, relating to the above county* (Stockton, 1784); *idem, The Northumberland Garland; or, Newcastle Nightingale: a Matchless Collection of Famous Songs* (Newcastle, 1793). These were published together with *The Yorkshire Garland: A curious Collection of old and new Songs* and *The North Country Chorister* in one compilation as *Northern Garlands* (London, 1810). His collections of Scottish verse, with an attack on John Pinkerton (whose *Select Scottish Ballads* Ritson had demonstrated to be forgeries) was planned for publication as *The Caledonian Muse: a Chronological Selection of Scottish Poetry* (1785) but was destroyed by fire at the printing house. The text alone was published in 1821.
53 National Library of Scotland Adv MS 29.5.8, fol. 170, 8 Jan 1782, Joseph Ritson to George Paton. On Ritson see Bronson, B. H., *Joseph Ritson: Scholar at Arms* (Chicago, 1938) and Butler, M., 'Popular Antiquarianism', in McCalman, I. (ed.), *An Oxford Companion to the Romantic Age: British Culture, 1776-1832* (Oxford, 1999), pp.328-38.
54 Ritson, Joseph, *Observations on the Three First Volumes of the History of English Poetry* (1782). Ritson's principal target was Thomas Warton, but he regarded Bishop Percy as Warton's partner in crime.

issued proposals for a *Glossary of North Country Words in Use*, reminding his potential subscribers that there were many words and phrases preserved in Northumberland that had fallen into disuse elsewhere, many of which could be found in Shakespeare, Beaumont, Fletcher and Johnson. The Northumbrian dialect, he implied, preserved a purer form of English.[55] Such was the success of the publication, a second edition was in preparation in 1825. Similarly, the Surtees Society highlighted the need for further studies of the Saxon language – the very foundation of the English tongue, as it was termed – commencing with an edition of the Saxon interlineations of the Latin Ritual of Alcfrid, King of Northumberland (686-705). There was also an increasing awareness of how an understanding of Old English and local dialect could in itself be a source of historical knowledge where other evidence was lacking: 'much curious matter in philology', argued John Hodgson, 'might be gleaned from well selected lists of vulgar words, and the names of farmhouses, glens, brooks and especially fields.'[56] The Saxons may not have left their mark on the physical landscape, but as Anthony Hedley pointed out to the Society of Antiquaries of Newcastle upon Tyne, even had there been no other historical record, their 'lasting, general and deep rooted possession of the island' would have been evident from place-names alone.[57]

With an interest in dialect and language went an interest in popular customs. The Newcastle antiquary, Henry Bourne, was one of the first to publish on this subject, with his *Antiquitates Vulgares* (1725). Although his evidence was entirely derived from the Newcastle area in which he lived and worked, he gave little attention to the value of the customs as expressive of local traditions or as historical survivors of former periods and rather concentrated on their religious value or superstitious weakness. Bourne's heir – to both the history of Newcastle and his treatment of popular customs – was John Brand, whose *Popular Antiquities* was published in 1777. Brand was addressing a reading public which was already accustomed to the idea that 'manners and customs' were illustrative of the particular and distinctive characteristics of the society with which they were associated. His work – considerably expanded by Sir Henry Ellis in the 19th century – is generally regarded as one of the formative works in the development of folklore studies, laying the foundations upon which the romantics of the 19th century would develop their understanding of local and national culture. Brand drew heavily upon his own observations and those of other antiquaries who were active in the region – including Shaw's history of Morayshire and Pennant's northern tours. In the shorter term Brand's study stimulated interest in the particular customs of the North East, and William Hutchinson, ever ready to reap the fruits of other people's scholarship, included a supplement on North Country customs to his *View of Northumberland* in 1781. The Northumbrian antiquaries were not alone in making local customs and manners the

---

55   Durham Chapter Library Raine MS 36: *Preparing for Publication, price 7s 6d A Glossary of North Country Words in Use. From an Original Manuscript in the Library of John George Lambton Esq MP, edited by John Trotter Brockett.*

56   Hodgson, John, 'On the Study of Antiquities', *Archaeologia Aeliana*, i (1822), p.xviii.

57   Hedley, A., 'An essay towards ascertaining the etymology of the names of places in the county of Northumberland', *Archaeologia Aeliana*, i (1822), pp.242-62.

object of their observation, but the historic remoteness of the region, it was argued, had preserved 'lingering traces' of ancient and better times that had been lost in other areas more open to external influences.[58] By the early 19th century the cumulative effect of these publications was to build up an image of the North East as a region of primitive simplicity: 'truly historical ground'[59] – an image which was perhaps the more cherished as the rapid social and economic changes of the coal fields produced a society which many found deeply threatening.

Family History

Sharp's nostalgia for 'ancient and better times' was also manifest in his copious collections of genealogical and family history. Nor was he alone, because such material dominated the collections of other antiquaries such as Christopher Hunter, George Allan, James Raine, Robert Surtees and John Hodgson. Hodgson – himself no scion of the landed élite (his father was a mason and he was a clergyman and a schoolteacher) – was emphatic about the need to preserve family memorials as

an inspiration to virtue and prudence, and because, as he candidly allowed, such family records were the only accounts surviving of certain periods of history.[60] They were a 'treasure house' for almost every kind of history and the 'healthiest food' with which the spirit of patriotism could be nourished.[61] The useful task of the antiquary, therefore, was to preserve the pedigrees of the past as the foundation for society of the future. This did not mean that he had an unlimited appetite for flattering the pride of minor landed families. His appeals for information upon the history of Northumberland, he noted with some dismay, far from being productive of material, had simply generated flurries of requests for further information on obscure points of family history:

27 *The Rev. John Hodgson (1779-1845).
Clergyman, antiquarian, campaigner for safety in
mines, and author of* History of Northumberland
(1820-40).

---

58 Sharp, *Hartlepool*, p.151: 'The manners and customs observed at Hartlepool, doubtless, at one period prevailed more or less over the whole of the adjacent country, and the above reasons will sufficiently account for their preservation here, at a time when general (would it could be said advantageously) innovation is every where making such rapid progress.'
59 Hutchinson, *View of Northumberland*, i, pp.2-3.
60 On Hodgson see Fraser, C.M., 'John Hodgson: County Historian', *Archaeologia Aeliana*, 5th ser., xxiv (1996), pp.171-85.
61 Hodgson, J., 'Ancient charters respecting monastical and lay property in Cumberland and other counties in the North of England from originals in the possession of William John Charlton of Hesleyside Esq', *Archaeologia Aeliana*, ii (1830), p.382.

will you be kind enough to give me all the information you can about our family, *at your earliest convenience?* We think we spring from them ----s, who were once owners of ---- Castle. We have the same arms; but I am sorry to say we know nothing beyond my grandfather. The -----s say they are related to us, but we do not spell our names in the same way.[62]

Family history of this kind was not confined to the north; rather it was the bedrock of antiquarian activity throughout the country (hardly surprising since the landed gentry constituted the principal market for such publications).[63] Northern antiquaries, however, were particularly conscious of the importance of family history and genealogy. In a region where the control of central government had been weak historically, matters of defence and law and order had effectively been placed in the hands of the great families such as the Percys and the Nevilles. This power then filtered down through their kinsmen to the lesser families. The events in which the leading families had been caught up – the revolt against William the Conqueror; the wars against Scotland; the Pilgrimage of Grace or the rebellion of the Northern earls in 1569 – were all events that had involved the north as a region. It was through the exploits of these families that the distinctive history of the region could be told. The preservation of their genealogies and their pedigrees, the recording of their exploits and their family histories, was, in effect, the history of Northumbria. William Gray had made his point in the first antiquarian/topographical publication of the North East, *Chorographia* of 1649:

> The Nobility and Gentry of the North, are of great antiquity, and can produce more ancient Families than any other part of England....The Noblemen and Gentry of the North hath been alwayes imployed in their native countrey, in the warres of Kings of England, against the Scots; all of them holding their land in Knights service, to attend the warres in their own persons, with horse and speare, as the manner of fighting was in those dayes.[64]

The focus on families and pedigrees helped to break down the county boundaries and to revive the idea of a Northumbrian kingdom. Family histories defied the simple county boundaries: the network of kinship and the complexities of property holding spread across the north – through Durham, Northumberland, and into Cumbria and Westmorland. The landholdings of major families such as the Percys, Dacres and Nevilles spread throughout the north and down into Yorkshire. Lionel Charlton's *History of Whitby*, published in 1779, boasted at least five members of the Percy family on the subscription list. While Charlton was clearly fortunate in having secured the interest of fellow antiquary Thomas Percy, the family chaplain, in his

---

62   Raine, J. (ed.), *Memoirs of John Hodgson*, 2 vols (1857), i, p.269.
63   Sweet, *Antiquaries*, pp.36-44.
64   Grey, W., *Chorographia: or A Survey of Newcastle upon Tine* (Newcastle, 1649), p.41; see also Ridpath, G., *The Border History of England and Scotland, Deduced from the Earliest Times to the Union of the Two Crowns* (1776), p.iv. Ridpath dedicated the history to the Duke of Northumberland on the basis that the annals were 'in some measures a regular history of the Percy family'.

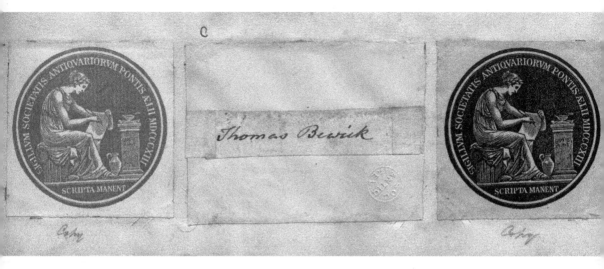

28   *Two woodcut seals of Newcastle Society of Antiquaries, by Thomas Bewick (1753-1828)*

publication, he was able also to exploit the Percy family's pride in its own ancestry. In the 12th and 13th centuries members of the Percy family had been important benefactors to the Abbey and had even numbered amongst the priors. Hutchinson's volumes frequently cross referenced each other in trying to untangle family histories and family connections. The Featherstonehaughs of Kirkoswald, he reminded the readers of his history of *Cumberland*, were descended from the family of Featherstone Castle in Northumberland, and an engraving of the castle could be found in his *View of Northumberland.*[65]

Places were defined by their association with a particular family even more frequently than they were defined by the presence of Roman antiquities or early Christian associations. This much is self-evident in any of the county histories or topographical tours of the period. Time and again the author would omit any architectural description or antiquarian observation in favour of giving a condensed version of the family history. Churches were described in terms of epitaphs, inscriptions and sepulchral monuments. The castles, peel towers and fortified manor houses that marked the landscape of the border regions were the occasion for recounting that family's role in the history of border conflict and for reflecting upon the present peace and prosperity that rendered such structures redundant. Ancient buildings represented continuity, and in particular the continuity of the families who had built them. Ruined castles and fortifications symbolised not so much the passing of a landed élite, but its modern re-invention as improving landowners and the redundancy of such structures in a time of peace and stability. Hutchinson's account of the Percy family comprised both a lengthy narrative of border warfare refracted through the history of the Percy family, but also a fulsome tribute to their modern role as paternalistic, improving landowners,

---

65   Hutchinson, *Cumberland*, i, p.207.

generous in their philanthropy and affable in their condescension. Hutchinson had derived much of the topographical material on the modern state of Northumberland from another topographer, Thomas Pennant, but this was one instance in which he composed his own material. Where Pennant presented a picture of an aristocracy that had lost its traditional feudal dignity in the pursuit of commercial profit and superficial elegance, Hutchinson insisted that they still retained their grandeur – only without the grim association with cruelty and oppression which 18th-century opinion held to be inseparable from the feudal order. On the contrary, hospitality was dispensed from the generous hands of the Duke and Duchess, who maintained a benign regime of propriety and economy.[66]

Conclusion

The antiquarian literature of the 'long' 18th century can be shown to have evinced a strong sense of a distinctive northern regional identity, which writers used as an organising principle for their research, and attempted to capitalise upon in appealing to a primarily regional readership. But the people who wrote and read most of the works discussed here would have only represented a small minority of the population. One must be doubtful, therefore, of the extent to which it is possible to argue that the 'Northumbrian' region existed in the minds of any but an élite readership. Recovering a sense of the historical consciousness of those below the literate élite is hugely problematic; yet studies of ephemeral literature – chap books, ballads and proverbs – produced at the conjunction of oral and literate cultures have been suggestive of a strong sense of historical traditions, bounded by locality, as contributions to this volume show.[67] Ballads such as 'Chevy Chase' or Sir Walter Scott's *Border Ballads* (1802) may have been admired by the London *literati*, but they also fired the imagination of local readers such as Thomas Bewick, who relished the local connection and identified with the Border traditions they celebrated.[68] A closer investigation of the popular literature produced by publishers such as Thomas Saint may tell us more about how far the antiquarian concerns outlined here would have resonated with a less erudite audience. In the 19th century, however, as Robert Colls' chapter in this volume shows, the production and consumption of history books reached a broader readership, and these patterns of thinking about a Northumbrian past provided the framework for 'popular' representations. It is on antiquarian traditions that the modern imagining of a 'New' Northumbria was constructed.

---

66   Pennant, T., *A Tour in Scotland in 1769* (London, 1774), p.22; Hutchinson, *View of Northumberland*, ii, pp.195-6.
67   Fox, A., *Oral and Literate Culture in England 1500-1700* (Oxford, 2001) and the essays in Fox, A. and Woolf, D.R. (eds), *The Spoken Word: Oral Culture in Britain, 1500-1850* (Manchester, 2002) and Woolf, D.R., *The Social Circulation of the Past: English Historical Culture, 1500-1730* (Oxford, 2003).
68   Bewick, T., *A Memoir* (London, 1862), 10, quoted in Reed, J., *The Border Ballads* (London, 1973), p.13.

8

Elements of Identity: The re-making of the North East, 1500-1760

KEITH WRIGHTSON

When William Camden published his *Britannia* in 1586, he guided his readers through the counties of northern England in the following order: Yorkshire; Richmondshire; Lancashire; the 'Bishoprick of Durham'; Westmorland; Cumberland; and then via 'the Picts Wall' to Northumberland. In later editions of his great chorographical survey, and in the English translation published in 1610, the itinerary was slightly modified, moving from Richmondshire to Durham, then to Lancashire, before proceeding through the north western counties and along the wall to Northumberland. John Speed, in the 'chorographicall part' of his *Theatre of the Empire of Great Britain* (1611), provided another variant, passing from Yorkshire to Durham, then through Westmorland, Cumberland and Northumberland. Whatever the route taken, however, all of these authors separated Northumberland and Durham.[1] This simple fact serves as a reminder that in the late 16th and early 17th centuries, the notion of a north-east region comprising the counties of Durham and Northumberland scarcely existed. As Adrian Green has recently observed, 'regions do not appear to have been the primary spatial units of geographical identity' in this period: 'the English county was always a more meaningful geographical unit'.[2] Northumberland and Durham were certainly seen as part of a larger 'north'. But they were *distinct*

---

1   Camden, W., *Britannia, sive Florentissimorum regnorum Angliae, Scotiae, Hiberniae, et insularum adiacentium ex intima antiquitate chorographica descriptio* (London, 1586). There were five subsequent Latin editions, culminating in that of 1607, which was translated by Philemon Holland as *Britain, or A chorographical description of the most flourishing kingdoms, England, Scotland and Ireland* (London, 1610). Speed, J., *The Theatre of the Empire of Great Britaine* (London, 1611). The 1607 edition of Camden, and the subsequent translation were illustrated with the county maps of Christopher Saxton. These were originally drawn in 1574-8 and were subsequently issued as an atlas. The 1590 edition also places Westmorland and Cumberland *between* Durham and Northumberland: Saxton, C., *Atlas of the counties of England and Wales* (London, 1590).

2   Green, A., 'Houses in north-eastern England: regionality and the British beyond, c.1600-1750', in S. Lawrence (ed.), *Archaeologies of the British. Explorations of identity in Great Britain and its colonies 1600-1945* (London, 2003), pp.59, 60-1. cf Charles Phythian-Adams' description of the county as 'the most relevant *named* entity above the level of the township to which the individual could feel some real sense of belonging': Phythian-Adams, C., 'Introduction: an Agenda for English Local History', in C. Phythian-Adams (ed.), *Societies, Cultures and Kinship, 1580-1850. Cultural Provinces and English Local History* (Leicester, 1993), p.19.

parts of that vaguely defined entity. They were not perceived by the chorographers and cartographers who pioneered the Elizabethan 'discovery of England' as specially conjoined, as somehow belonging together as a natural regional unit.[3]

We might say, then, that there is nothing primordial about the north-east region as we currently understand it. Insofar as it has acquired a distinctive identity, it is an historical creation, and perhaps a relatively recent one at that. Indeed, it has been argued forcefully that we should not expect to find it before *c.*1800: that it is essentially a creation of 19th-century industrial society.[4] Clearly there is much to be said for such a view. Yet perhaps it goes too far. Regional identities, like other forms of social identity are 'neither remorselessly permanent nor frivolously malleable'. They are modified and reinterpreted over time 'as external events and internal realignments … encourage new understandings of collective traditions'.[5] They change. But they do not emerge from a void. There has to be something to be worked on, and it is the making and remaking of those deeper 'collective traditions', the constituent elements of identity and the forces that shape and reshape them, that concern us here.

Charles Phythian-Adams, in trying to define an 'intermediate plane of reference' for English local and regional historians – one lying between the local community and the national society – starts with geography. By examining watersheds and river systems, he divides England into 14 regional zones or 'cultural provinces', some derived from river basins, some being 'littoral zones' formed by 'groups of broadly parallel or slightly convergent rivers' with a shared watershed and coastal outlet. In his view Northumberland and Durham constitute such a littoral zone, shaped by the Tweed, Tyne and Tees, and edged with 'overlap' or 'transitional' areas in the Tees Valley, Stainmore, and the Tweed lowlands.[6]

As Phythian-Adams recognises, however, geography can only be a starting point. If his 'geographically identifiable' zones are to become 'culturally meaningful', something more is required. Their significance lies primarily in their potential as

---

3 The term 'Northumbria' was used by Saxton, but to him it was simply the Latinate name for Northumberland. Durham, for him, as for most of his contemporaries, was 'the Bishoprick' – 'Dunelmensis Episcopatus (qui comitatus est palatinus)'. This was a misleading practice, since the Bishop's ecclesiastical jurisdiction included Northumberland, and the Palatinate of Durham included northern Northumberland (Norhamshire and Islandshire) and the liberty of Craik in North Yorkshire. The term 'bishoprick' was nevertheless used by most contemporaries to describe Durham between Tyne and Tees. Antiquarian scholars were perfectly aware of the former 'Kingdom of Northumbrians'. Speed, for example, listed it among the many early kingdoms and principalities which were now component parts of the 'The British Empire' and included a short history of its kings. However, he rightly regarded it as having included all of the northern counties, and mistakenly believed that Bernicia, its north-eastern heartland, extended only from Lowland Scotland to the Tyne, rather than to the Tees: Speed, *Theatre*, B1 verso, and pp.302-5. For the phrase 'discovery of England', see Hoskins, W.G., 'The Rediscovery of England', in *Provincial England. Essays in Social and Economic History* (London, 1965), pp.209ff.
4 Pollard, A.J., *North-eastern England during the Wars of the Roses. Lay Society, War, and Politics 1450-1500* (Oxford, 1990), p.10. The 'evolution of the region' during the era of high industrialisation is the central theme of McCord, N., *North East England. The Region's Development 1760-1960* (London, 1979). McCord defines the region (p.13) as including 'the two old counties of Durham and Northumberland, together with the city and county of Newcastle-upon-Tyne, while the border town of Berwick and part of North Yorkshire are annexed as essential parts of the region during the period considered'.
5 The phrases quoted are from Jenkins, R., *Social Identity* (London, 1996), 62, and Smith, A.D., *Nationalism. Theory, Ideology, History* (Cambridge, 2001), p.20.
6 Phythian-Adams, 'Introduction: an Agenda', pp.9-10, 14, 16, and Figure 1.2 (p.xvii). It can also be said to be implied in the first county maps of Saxton and Speed, which include hills and river systems and also show 'overlaps' between Northumberland, Durham, Cumbria and North Yorkshire in the form of tributary streams and settlements just over the county borders which were deemed significant enough to include in individual county maps: Saxton, *Atlas* and Speed, *Theatre, passim.*

'influential matrices for the creation of human territories'. Such zones, he argues, have a certain 'directional logic' and a 'shared susceptibility' to outside sources of cultural influence. Each offers an 'underlying axis of activity' through which it can develop as 'a meaningful context for its inhabitants'.[7] Such development, where it occurs, would presumably require the emergence of patterns of interaction linking people and institutions more closely within a given geographical area, while at the same time establishing boundaries indicated by reduced levels of such involvement.[8] One might envisage it in terms of magnetic fields, exerting influence on flows of goods and people; felt more powerfully here, less so there.

For such an emergent entity to acquire larger cultural meaning, however, the concrete realities of economic, social and institutional linkage would also need to be complemented by a less tangible sense of similarity and difference. Regional self-consciousness cannot simply be assumed. It involves both a sense of identification with the region as a whole, and a perception of its place in relation to larger entities. It emerges, to borrow Richard Jenkins' formulation of the dialectic of social identity, from 'an ongoing, and in practice simultaneous, synthesis of (internal) self-definition, and the (external) definitions of oneself offered by others' – especially powerful others, for there is a politics to all this.[9]

That processes of this kind were very much part of the Industrial Revolution era in Britain is beyond question. Pat Hudson, for example, has described the emergence of the industrial West Riding of Yorkshire as 'an internally integrated yet outward-looking whole'.[10] And no doubt Britain's regional structures and identities as they currently stand are to a very large extent a product of the last two centuries. In the case of north-east England, however, I think things go rather deeper. The argument of this essay is that the emergence of the North East as a coherent regional entity, with a distinctive regional identity, was a phenomenon of the period roughly 1560 to 1760. That emergence was of course very much to do with industrial and commercial development. Edward Hughes perhaps exaggerated when he wrote of this region that 'the Industrial Revolution occurred here much earlier … than anywhere else', and that 'already by 1750 the predominant industrial and social character of the North East was set as in a mould', but he was right in spirit.[11] At the same time, however, the emergence of the North East involved more than its precocious industrial development. It required also the waning of other, older, alignments and patterns of relations, and the dissolution, or reconfiguration, of alternative sources of identity. The new North East was constructed on, and partly out of, the rubble of an older North, and in tracing the overall process of supercession, it is with that older North that we must begin.

---

7   Phythian-Adams, 'Introduction: an Agenda', pp.9, 10, 12.

8   cf. Michael Mann's conception of societies as networks of social interaction with boundaries marked by 'a certain level of interaction cleavage': Mann, M., *The Sources of Social Power, Vol. I: A History of power from the beginning to AD 1760* (Cambridge, 1986), pp.13-14.

9   Jenkins, *Social Identity*, p.20.

10   Hudson, P., 'Capital and credit in the West Riding wool textile industry *c.*1750-1850', in P. Hudson (ed.), *Regions and Industries. A perspective on the industrial revolution in Britain* (Cambridge, 1989), p.71.

11   Hughes, E., *North Country Life in the Eighteenth Century. The North East, 1700-1750* (Oxford, 1952), pp.xiv, 407.

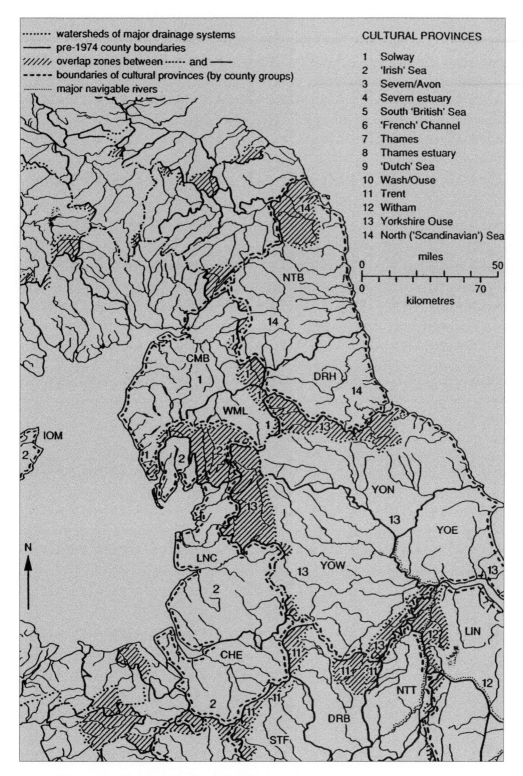

29 *Northern Cultural Provinces (from Phythian-Adams ed.,* Societies, Cultures and Kinship, 1580-1850. Cultural Provinces and English Local History, *Leicester University Press, 1993)*

The old North

Phythian-Adams' north-eastern littoral zone is certainly geographically identifiable. It provided a matrix in the sense of an environment for development. In the late 15th century and for much of the 16th century, however, it would be harder to claim that it represented a single, dominant axis of activity for its inhabitants. For, in many respects, it appears less an integrated whole than a mosaic of localised societies, fragmented jurisdictions and sectional loyalties that drew the people of its constituent communities into a variety of configurations. To this extent it was in a sense polycentric or multi-focal.

This is evident if we consider the local economy. At the turn of the 16th century the area remained overwhelmingly rural. Contemporaries stressed the unpropitious nature of the climate for agriculture, 'the air sharp and very piercing', the land 'exposed to extremity of weathers', with 'the most part of it being rough, and in every place hard to be manured save only towards the sea'.[12] In 'this accursed country whence the sun is so removed', population was sparse by general English standards, and concentrated in two distinct areas – south-east Northumberland and the lower Tyne valley on the one hand, and south-east Durham and the lower Tees valley on the other.[13] Settlement had contracted during the demographic slump of the later Middle Ages, concentrating population into these more favourably endowed areas and accentuating the distinctiveness of the region's agricultural zones and their contrasting patterns of settlement and spatial organisation.[14] The eastern lowlands were distinguished by nucleated village settlements practising open-field agriculture. This was the principal area of arable cultivation, producing crops of oats, rye, barley, peas and beans, though even here farming inventories reveal that most households' wealth lay primarily in the modest herds and flocks that were grazed on the extensive township commons.[15] In the uplands of the west, beyond an intermediate zone in which the pastoral emphasis loomed still larger, the landscape was dominated by open commons and wasteland, segmented by the dales. Beyond Rothbury, Bellingham, Hexham, Wolsingham and Staindrop settlement was in tiny hamlets or isolated farmsteads. Small crops of oats, bigg and rye were won in the valley bottoms for domestic use, but agriculture was overwhelmingly dominated by cattle raising.[16]

12 Speed, *Theatre*, p.83, 89. cf. Smailes, A.E., *North England* (London and Edinburgh, 1960), pp.52-3.

13 Watts, S.J. and Susan J., *From Border to Middle Shire. Northumberland, 1586-1625* (Leicester, 1975) pp.39, 40-1; Hodgson, R.I., 'Demographic Trends in County Durham, 1560-1801', University of Manchester School of Geography Research Papers, No. 5 (1978), pp.11-14.

14 Pollard, *North East England*, pp.56-7. For the late medieval contraction of the cultivated area, see also Dunsford, H.M. and Harris, S.J., 'Colonization of the wasteland in County Durham, 1100-1400', *Economic History Review*, 2nd Series, LVI (2003).

15 Hodgson, R.I., 'The progress of enclosure in County Durham, 1550-1870', in H.S.A. Fox and R.A. Butlin (eds.), *Change in the Countryside: Essays in Rural England* (London, 1978), pp.84-5; P.W. Brassley, 'The Agricultural Economy of Northumberland and Durham in the period 1640-1750' (unpub. University of Oxford B.Litt. thesis, 1974), 5; Watts and Watts, *Border to Middle Shire*, 44-5. For case studies of particular communities, see Levine, D. and Wrightson, K., *The Making of an Industrial Society. Whickham, 1560-1765* (Oxford, 1991), pp.87-9; Reid, D.S., *The Durham Crown Lordships in the sixteenth and seventeenth centuries and the aftermath*, Durham County Local History Society (1990), p.133.

16 Hodgson, 'Progress of enclosure', 84-5; Brassley, 'Agricultural Economy', 3-4; Watts and Watts, *Border to Middle Shire*, pp.41-3. For a vivid reconstruction of the pastoral economy of the northern uplands in general, see Winchester, A.J.L., *The Harvest of the Hills. Rural Life in Northern England and the Scottish Borders, 1400-1700* (Edinburgh, 2000).

Each of these contrasting agricultural 'countries', as contemporaries termed them, could be further subdivided into districts focused on particular market towns: Northumberland had at least eight of these in the early 16th century, and Durham seven (with Yarm providing an eighth on its southern border). In a rural economy still primarily oriented towards household subsistence, it was within these localised districts of exchange that most of the inhabitants of Northumberland and Durham probably conducted most of their affairs. A few towns exerted a broader influence: Durham City as the seat of the bishopric; Berwick and Darlington as the principal markets of north Northumberland and south Durham respectively, and of course Newcastle-upon-Tyne and Gateshead. Yet it would be difficult to claim that Northumberland and Durham yet contained a *single* urban focal point. As the largest city in the North East, Newcastle drove a trade in imported luxury goods, such as wine and spices, and exported hides, fish, and the poor quality short-staple wool of the region. It was also well known as a supplier of millstones, lead, and above all the coal won from pits close to the city. Yet in the late 15th and early 16th centuries coal and lead shipments were at a very low ebb. Nor was the demographic situation conducive to a high level of commercial production focused on the city. The principal north-eastern commodity traded over long distances was probably livestock, and in this trade the flow was in a different direction – south to the cattle and horse fairs of Darlington and Northallerton. As a provincial centre, Newcastle was certainly important, but historians of the period stress that it was still no match for York, the true capital of the old north. Indeed, it has been plausibly argued that the relative prosperity of south-east Durham and the Tees basin, together with the continuing dominance of York, pulled the economic centre of gravity of much of the North East southwards towards the Tees.[17]

If Northumberland and Durham lacked clear definition as a coherent economic region, the area was even less unified in administrative and political terms. To be sure, both counties were included in one embracing jurisdiction in the form of the bishopric of Durham, extending from the Scottish border to the Tees and from the coast to the high Pennines. Nevertheless, prior to the Reformation neither the ecclesiastical peculiar of Hexham nor the monastic houses which exercised considerable ecclesiastical patronage in the North East were subject to the bishop's authority. Nor was the diocese itself necessarily regarded as a natural unit. In 1553, at the height of the Reformation, it was temporarily dissolved and there were plans to divide it into two separate dioceses of Newcastle and Durham.[18] In terms of secular jurisdictions the area was a complex and confusing mosaic. Before the Act of Resumption of 1536, the territories subject to the Palatinate of Durham, the liberties of Tynedale and Redesdale,

---

17   Everitt, A., 'The Marketing of Agricultural Produce', in J. Thirsk (ed.), *The Agricultural History of England and Wales, Vol. IV, 1500-1640* (Cambridge, 1967), pp.468, 590; Kermode, J., 'Northern Towns', in D.M. Palliser (ed.), *The Cambridge Urban History of Britain, Vol. I, 600-1540*, pp.661, 669-70, 678-9; Pollard, *North East England*, pp.4, 39-43, 75-77.

18   Loades, D., 'Introduction'; Kealing, S., 'The Dissolution of the Monasteries in the Border Country', 37; Loades, D., 'The Dissolution of the Diocese of Durham, 1553-4', *passim* – all in D. Marcombe (ed.), *The Last Principality: Politics, Religion and Society in the Bishopric of Durham, 1494-1660* (Nottingham, 1987).

30 *Newcastle upon Tyne, seen from the south bank, 1783, History and Antiquities of the Town and County of the town of Newcastle upon Tyne (Yale Center for British Art)*

and the regality of Hexhamshire meant that in roughly half of Northumberland and Durham the king's writ did not run. Thereafter, the jurisdiction of the palatinate courts continued to be exercised (albeit now in the king's name) in County Durham, in Norhamshire and Islandshire in north Northumberland and in Howdenshire in north Yorkshire, but excluded the rest of the region. In contrast, Northumberland and Newcastle enjoyed parliamentary representation while County Durham did not. The border jurisdictions of the wardens of the east and middle marches added further complexity to the administrative and judicial map, and after 1560 both counties also became subject to the authority of the Council of the North, seated at York.[19]

Given such a situation, the county, let alone the region, was scarcely the most salient of geographical identities in north-east England. Political power lay not so much with county magistrates as with the great men of the area who were able to combine authority delegated by the Crown with a pre-existing position as the leaders of local society – in effect its 'natural rulers'. As elsewhere in England, this meant in practice the great landowners. One of these, the bishop, was usually a reliable crown servant. The position of the earls of Northumberland and Westmorland, the Percies and the Nevilles, however, was more ambiguous. Each of these lords of exceptionally large landed estates headed a personal 'affinity' of retainers, clients and tenants, which served as 'a markedly cohesive and integrating factor' within their respective spheres

19   Ellis, S.G., *Tudor Frontiers and Noble Power. The Making of the British State* (Oxford, 1995), pp.34-5; Loades, 'Introduction', in Marcombe (ed.), *Last Principality*, p.2; Lapsley, G.T., *The County Palatine of Durham. A Study in Constitutional History, Harvard Historical Studies VIII* (New York and London, 1900), p.196.

of influence, but which tended also to segment the region into personalised power blocs. Royal administration in north-east England was for the most part 'conducted through the mediation and according to the interests' of these magnates, and their combination of sources of authority meant that often enough, as contemporaries frequently recognised, 'the magnates, not the crown, tended to be the focus of local loyalties'. (Among the quasi-autonomous 'surname' groups of the border marches, with their recognised surname leaders, even that was highly contingent.) Such particularistic loyalties further obscured the identity of the North East as a region. This was in part because they provided rival foci of authority – the Percies holding sway in Northumberland and the Nevilles in southern County Durham. It was also because in both cases their lands and affinities of retainers extended well beyond the boundaries of the two counties, most notably into Cumberland and North Yorkshire. They were part of the political structure of a larger north.[20]

All this considered, the notion of the North East as a coherent regional entity in the early 16th century seems seriously compromised. If the area possessed a common denominator as a region, that lay perhaps in the fact that both Northumberland and Durham were part of the hinterland of the Scottish border. In a sense the border was the great determinant of the area's social and political complexion. It explains the great estates and jurisdictional liberties granted in the North East; the toleration of exceptional concentrations of magnate power; the peculiarly generous tenancies granted to the peasantry in return for the obligation to serve, when called, in 'defensible array'; the bizarre anomaly of the plundering 'surname' clans and the perennial insecurity that still inhibited the economic development of parts of the region. Yet even these things were not peculiar to Northumberland and Durham. They were shared with Cumberland and Westmorland.[21] Perhaps the north-eastern counties at this point in time are best thought of as part of a larger border zone – a geographically distinct part, and one with its own peculiar institutions, but for the most part lacking a distinctive collective identity economically, administratively, politically, or in the consciousness of its inhabitants. Little wonder that the early cartographers and chorographers felt no need to place them together.

A critical Threshold of Change

In suggesting that the North East was 're-made' in the period c.1560-1760, I do not mean to imply that these older characteristics of the North were wholly wiped away. What was most significant, however, was that some features of the old North were certainly erased, while almost simultaneously other elements in the economy and

---

20 James, M.E., *Family, Lineage and Civil Society. A Study of Society, Politics and Mentality in the Durham Region, 1500-1640* (Oxford, 1974), pp.27-35, quoting p.35; Ellis, *Tudor Frontiers*, p.41; Pollard, *North East England*, pp.12-13, 123ff., 141, 401-2, quoting pp.401-2.

21 Pollard, *North East England*, 14ff., p.144; Ellis, *Tudor Frontiers*, 41; Watts and Watts, *Border to Middle Shire*, 44; Reid, *Crown Lordships*, pp.37, 43, 61-2; Drury, J.L., 'More stout than wise: tenant right in Weardale in the Tudor period', in Marcombe (ed.), *Last Principality*; Hughes, *North Country Life*, Appendix B.

society of Durham and Northumberland acquired greater prominence and centrality and the capacity to redefine the area. In that process the later decades of the 16th century and the early decades of the 17th century can be said to have constituted what Anthony Giddens calls a 'critical threshold of change': a period in which 'a set of relatively rapid changes may generate a long-term momentum of development'.[22]

It was in those decades, I would argue, that a combination of political and economic change set Northumberland and Durham on converging courses, and initiated the creation of a distinctive regional entity. That would take two centuries and more to work out fully. Essentially, however, it involved a gradual transformation of the ways in which the economy and society of the region functioned spatially: changes in its 'fields of force' and 'directional logic', in the structures of economic and social power, in the most salient flows of goods and people, which cumulatively strengthened and tightened its internal linkages and redrew its boundaries. This re-articulation of political, economic and social networks created an immanent regional identity in the form of both greater internal connectedness and a shared relationship to the larger national society and its metropolitan core. That immanent identity crystallised with the development of a distinctive social structure, changes in the self-perception of its component classes, and the dialogues that were initiated between their own self-definition and their growing awareness of how they were perceived by others. In all this I would emphasise that for the most part the nascent north-east region was created from within, in the activity and responses to changing circumstances of the people of the area – *all* the people, for this is very much a story of the agency of every element in north-eastern society: the gentry and aristocracy; commercial and industrial entrepreneurs; the professional clerisy; farmers; labouring people. Nevertheless, that agency was always exercised in circumstances which were strongly influenced by more extensive forces, and on occasion external interventions played a vital role.

The old North never wholly died. Parts of it, however, were amputated, and perhaps the most important such surgical intervention was the destruction of quasi-autonomous magnate power in the North East. Tudor monarchs had no objection to aristocrats as such. They preferred to rule through them. But they disliked over-mighty and obstreperous men.[23] The great magnates of Northumberland and Durham proved to be both, and in consequence their power and position as semi-independent foci of loyalty was destroyed. From the time of Cardinal Wolsey onwards the spheres of influence of both the Nevilles and the Percies were gradually weakened by the building up of alternative affinities of gentlemen directly linked to crown service and of undivided loyalty. With the crisis of the Reformation, and the religious dissidence of the Catholic northern earls, the reduction of their authority became the more

---

22   Giddens, A., *The Constitution of Society: Outline of the Theory of Structuration* (Cambridge, 1984), p.246. His full definition of such a 'critical threshold' period is one in which 'a set of relatively rapid changes may generate a long-term momentum of development, that development being possible only if certain key institutional transformations are accomplished initially'.
23   For the relationships between the Crown and the aristocracy under the Tudors see, e.g., Williams, P., *The Tudor Regime* (Oxford, 1979), ch. 13, and Bernard, G.W., *The Power of the Early Tudor Nobility: a study of the Fourth and Fifth Earls of Shrewsbury* (Sussex, 1985).

imperative. It is a long and chequered story; but the final debacle was decisive. The rising of the northern earls in 1569 – which drew most of its support from south Durham and north Yorkshire – demonstrated both their weakened capacity to raise their clients and tenantry in rebellion and their continued status as a potential threat. The Nevilles were utterly destroyed, their lands passing to the Crown. The Percy heir recovered his estates, but was required thereafter to reside in Sussex, and by the 1580s, 'the Percy interest in Northumberland consisted of little more than estate agents and bailiffs'.[24] Meanwhile, the gradual recasting of the structures of power in the North East was also furthered by the Act of Resumption of 1536, which ended the jurisdictional independence of the great franchises of the area (including the Palatinate of Durham), and by the Royal Supremacy over the Church. The king's writ now ran in Durham rather than the bishop's. The great monasteries were dissolved and their lands and patronage redistributed. Redesdale and Hexhamshire were incorporated into Northumberland (the former in 1542, the latter in 1572).[25]

All this was for the most part episodic and contingent, rather than the product of planned, deliberative action, but the cumulative outcome was momentous. After 1569, the aristocratic affinities which had been a source of both cohesion and segmentation in north-eastern society were gone, and the linkages established by such aristocratic power blocs to adjacent counties were severed. This change, together with the abolition of the region's great liberties, made possible the greater salience of the counties as units of government and spheres of gentry administrative and political activity. Durham was now governed by the bishop in concert with leading gentry families closely aligned to the Crown. Northumberland was contested by rival aspirants for local office vying for court favour. Politically and administratively the counties of the North East were 'normalizing'.[26] Perhaps also the enforcement of the Reformation may have given greater prominence to the diocese of Durham as a unifying institution, though this possibility remains speculative. In sum, the jurisdictional mosaic of north-eastern society was simplified; recast into two county units and one diocesan unit – still complex and distinctive, to be sure, but less dispersed than formerly.

Finally, in 1603, the Union of the Crowns of Scotland and England in the person of James VI and I ended the border – not as a legal reality (that awaited the Union of 1707), but as a practical problem and as a standing threat. Undoubtedly 1603 was only a marker in a longer process of re-orientation that began with the Scottish Reformation, and continued after 1603 with the gradual pacification of the border zone. King James certainly flattered himself when he declared in 1607 that the 'Middle Shires' of his imagined Kingdom of Great Britain were already 'planted and peopled

---

24 James, M., *Society, Politics and Culture. Studies in Early Modern England* (Cambridge, 1986), chs 2, 3, 7; James, *Family, Lineage and Civil Society*, ch. 2; Watts and Watts, *Border to Middle Shire*, pp.55ff (quoting p.58); Marcombe, D., 'A Rude and Heady People: the local community and the Rebellion of the Northern Earls', in Marcombe (ed.), *Last Principality*; K.J. Kesselring, '"A Cold Pye for the Papistes": Constructing and Containing the Northern Rising of 1569', *Journal of British Studies*, p.43 (2004).

25 Lapsley, *County Palatine of Durham*, pp.196-8; Ellis, *Tudor Frontiers*, 35; Kealing, 'Dissolution of the Monasteries' and Loades 'Dissolution of the Diocese', both in Marcombe (ed.), *Last Principality, passim*.

26 James, *Family, Lineage and Civil Society*, pp.51, 150-60; Watts and Watts, *Border to Middle Shire*, chs 5, 9.

with Civilitie and riches' and a place of 'ease and happy quitenesse'.[27] Nevertheless, 1603 marked symbolically the end of the dominant grand fact of the socio-political structure of north-eastern England. It was no longer a bulwark against an actively hostile neighbour; an insecure frontier zone.[28] And the effective abrogation of the border arguably transformed its basic orientation. Northumberland and Durham no longer faced north, as it were, in concert with their neighbours and led by their great men. They were freed to look inwards, perhaps even to reinvent themselves.

'The benefit of coales'

These changes mattered. They went a long way towards accommodating Durham and Northumberland to the emerging norms of Tudor and Stuart government. However, they would not in themselves have created a north-eastern region. They were perhaps necessary, but not sufficient, causes of the process I am trying to describe. The sufficient cause was *coal* – or rather the combination of the urgent fuel needs of the rapidly growing cities of south-east England (especially London) and the capacity of the North East to supply those needs from accessible seams located close to water transportation.

William Gray, in his *Chorographia* (1649), waxed poetic on the coal trade. He believed that 'our most provident and glorious Creator hath so furnished all countries with severall commodities, that amongst all nations there might be sociable conversation and mutuall commerce'. In 'these northern parts' (a significant phrase) the principal such commodity was coal: 'Most of the people that liveth in these parts, lives by the benefit of coales.' He also noted that this 'trade of coale began not past fourscore yeares since': that is, around 1570.[29]

Essentially he was right. The coal trade was of course of medieval origins, but in the mid-16th century only around 15,000 tons was being shipped annually from the Tyne to London. By the late 1580s, as London demand grew, shipments reached around 50,000 tons a year (most of it from the most accessible seams close to the river in Winlaton, Whickham and Gateshead). In the early 17th century, with the full exploitation of the Grand Lease of the collieries in Whickham and Gateshead (extorted from the bishop of Durham by Queen Elizabeth and subsequently transferred to a consortium of Newcastle merchants), they reached 150,000 tons a year. Around 1650, with further colliery development both north and south of the river, the Tyne was shipping some 300,000 tons annually to London and probably a further 200,000 tons to other provincial English ports. By then a second major area of coal production was developing on the Wear around Harraton, Herrington, Lumley, and Chester-le-Street, exporting through Sunderland. This activity expanded

---

27   Watts and Watts, *Border to Middle Shire*, pp.19-30 and ch. 7; Braddick, M.J., *State Formation in Early Modern England, c.1550-1700* (Cambridge, 2000), pp.376-8.
28   That role was certainly to be temporarily revived in the Bishops' Wars, the Civil Wars and then in the Jacobite risings of the 18th century. My point is simply that it was no longer a permanent fact of political life.
29   Gray, W., *Chorographia, or a Survey of Newcastle upon Tyne* (Newcastle, 1649), pp.84-90.

in the later 17th century, and by 1700 the combined 'sea-sale' of the Tyne and Wear was around 700,000 tons a year. From the turn of the 18th century, the widespread adoption of transportation on wooden waggonways made possible the exploitation of the 'western collieries' extending inland to Pontop, and further development took place both to the north of the Tyne and on the Wear. By 1750, the total sea-sale of the North East was close to one million tons a year, with probably over 950,000 tons more being consumed locally.[30]

It is worth pausing briefly to take stock of this extraordinary set of developments. First, by 1750, the North East was producing a grand total of close to two million tons of coal annually. E.A. Wrigley calculates that the heat provided by burning one ton of coal is equivalent to that attainable from the dry wood yielded by an acre of woodland. In terms of energy production, then, the miners, coal owners and merchants of the North East had provided England with the equivalent of two million acres of woodland per year.[31] The impact on the national economy of this wealth of cheap fuel was extraordinary.

The industry that achieved all this was also extraordinary, especially as compared with other coalfields of the time. The collieries of the North East were exceptional in scale: one 20-acre area in Benwell colliery, for example, saw some 40 pits sunk, worked and abandoned in the years 1616-36 alone.[32] As industrial undertakings they were also exceptional in their nature. 'Well before the eighteenth century,' writes John Hatcher,

> The greater collieries possessed many of the characteristics commonly used to distinguish the classic new industrial enterprises of the industrial revolution from their predecessors. Production was concentrated on a single site, or a cluster of proximate sites; substantial amounts of capital were sunk into fixed assets; and they were operated by sizeable, specialist, full-time workforces.[33]

The north-east coalfield, which by the mid-18th century stretched north to south from Blyth to Lanchester, Witton Gilbert and Hetton-le-Hole, and westwards along the rivers to Belsay, Ovingham and Medomsley, was 'the most advanced coalfield in the world'.[34] Its miners worked deeper. Elaborate systems of drainage, ventilation and transportation had been pioneered and developed. Production, once seasonal, was usually continuous. Productivity was high, even by the standards of the 19th century. Innovative management structures and accounting procedures had evolved to keep

30   Nef, J.U., *The Rise of the British Coal Industry*, 2 vols (London, 1932), I, pp.24-42; Hatcher, J., *The History of the British Coal Industry, Vol. 1. Before 1700* (Oxford, 1993), pp.41, 45, 70-96; Flinn, M.W. and Stoker, D., *The History of the British Coal Industry, Vol. 2. 1700-1830 The Industrial Revolution* (Oxford, 1984), pp.20-3, 26, 35. The figures quoted are those provided by Hatcher and Flinn. For an account of the growth of the Tyneside industry focused on the parish of Whickham, see Levine and Wrightson, *Making of an Industrial Society*, ch. 1.

31   Wrigley, E.A., *Continuity, chance and change. The character of the industrial revolution in England* (Cambridge, 1988), pp.54-5.

32   Nef, *Rise of the British Coal Industry*, i, 370. For the scale of the Whickham collieries, see Levine and Wrightson, *Making of an Industrial Society*, pp.68, 78-80.

33   Hatcher, *Coal Industry*, p.282.

34   Hatcher, *Coal Industry*, p.187.

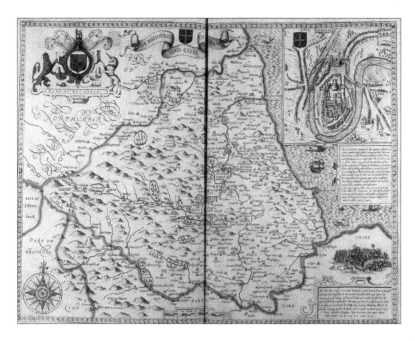

31 *Speed's map of the Bishoprick and Citie of Durham, 1611. See also front endpaper. (Yale Center)*

the enterprise going and well monitored, and to facilitate planning. All this had been achieved by partnerships of landowners and merchants, working with an emerging middle-management structure of overmen, staithmen, fitters and viewers, and a growing army of specialist pitmen, waggonmen, and keelmen ('many thousand' of them, as Gray averred). Having little in the way of an established industrial tradition to build on, they created one, pragmatically, step by step. They took great risks, both financial and physical, competed ferociously in what became known as a 'fighting trade', and collectively (if not always individually) they triumphed.[35]

Finally, we must consider the implications of the fact that if the north-east ports shipped a million tons of coal in 1750, almost as much again was consumed locally: mostly the 'small coal' deemed unfit for export to southern consumers. This had long been the case, and it is indicative of the extent to which other industries were emerging, especially along the Tyne, to take advantage of the region's cheap fuel. Salt production by boiling brine was one of the first. There were allegedly 20 salt pans at South Shields in the 1570s, and certainly over 170 working at North and South Shields in 1716 – 'the largest concentration of salt works in Britain'. Iron had been produced on the Derwent since at least the mid-16th century, but the region's significance in the production of metalwares of all kinds was massively enhanced when Ambrose Crowley moved first to Sunderland, and then after 1691 to Winlaton and Swalwell, creating an exceptionally integrated industrial complex which by 1720 was 'the largest iron manufactory in Europe'. It employed around a thousand workers known

---

35   Hatcher, *Coal Industry*, pp.250-6, 282, 305, 345-6; Lewis, M.J.T., *Early wooden railways* (London, 1970), pp.91-5 and ch. 8; Pollard, *The Genesis of Modern Management. A Study of the Industrial Revolution in Great Britain* (London, 1965), pp.61-9. For case studies illustrating all these characteristics, see Levine and Wrightson, *Making of an Industrial Society*, ch. 1; Clavering, E. and Rounding, A., 'Early Tyneside Industrialism. The lower Derwent and Blaydon Burn Valleys', *Archaeologia Aeliana*, Fifth Series, XXIII (1995).

locally as 'Crowley's Crew'. Then there was glass (11 glassworks by 1696) and the manufacture of coarse earthernware, and the myriad of activities involved in servicing and supplying the collieries and the collier fleets (e.g. the production of candles, rope, sails, leather-wares, and ship-building and repair). Nor was ancillary industrial activity wholly confined to the lower Tyne and Wear. From the late 16th century, the moribund leadmining industry of the North Pennines underwent marked revival and expansion. Lead roads from South Tynedale, Allendale, Blanchland, Alston Moor, Stanhope and even Middleton-in-Teesdale, wound their way down to the Derwent/Tyne confluence, where the ore was smelted and exported.[36]

The point of all this will be obvious. By the early 18th century, by a process of gradual agglomeration, an industrial zone had emerged between the rivers Blyth, Wear, and Derwent, with outliers stretching up into the North Pennines. It was based upon coal, but was already surprisingly diverse. It lay across adjacent areas of Northumberland and Durham like a thick belt, clinching the two counties together. It transformed the economic nature of the North East, making it one of the first areas of Britain to be 'rendered geographically distinctive by industrial activity'.[37] And by doing so it created new fields of force in the region; a centrally located regional core of economic power and an 'axis of activity' that had consequences for areas well beyond the immediate confines of its increasingly bizarre industrial landscape.

New Felds of Force

One such consequence was demographic. There is much that remains obscure about the demographic history of the North East in this period (especially in the case of Northumberland). What we do know, however, tells a fairly clear story.

As we have seen, in the mid-16th century the North East had been fairly thinly peopled by English standards. In the following century, as elsewhere in England, the populations grew – rising by some 70 per cent in County Durham, which was more or less the national norm. The really striking feature of demographic expansion in the North East, however, was the fact that the population of the emergent industrial belt rose much faster than that. Along the Tyne from Ryton to South Shields population growth was dramatic, and the same was true of the industrialising Wear valley. Nor did this growth stabilise in the later 17th century, as in most of England. It continued, especially in the Wear valley and the western colliery district of Tanfield and Lanchester parish. In sum, overall population increase in the North East was heavily concentrated into an increasingly densely peopled central zone. Elsewhere in Northumberland and Durham the growth in local populations was modest. The demographic weight of

---

36 For an excellent overview of the industries along the Tyne, see Ellis, J., 'The "Black Indies": Economic Development of Newcastle, *c.*1700-1840', in R. Colls and B. Lancaster (eds), *Newcastle upon Tyne. A Modern History* (Chichester, 2001), pp.6-10, quoting p.7; Flinn, M.W., *Men of Iron. The Crowleys in the Early Iron Industry* (Edinburgh, 1962), *passim*, quoting p.74; Clavering and Rounding, 'Early Tyneside Industrialism', pp.253ff; Knight, M.S.P., 'Litigants and Litigation in the Seventeenth-Century Palatinate of Durham' (unpub. PhD thesis, University of Cambridge, 1990), pp.423-4.

37 Smailes, *North England*, p.5.

the whole region was shifting decisively to the industrial parishes of Tyneside and northern County Durham.[38]

To take some specific examples: in Whickham, the epicentre of coal production on the Tyne, the population quadrupled between 1563 and 1666, rising from 93 to at least 367 households. It had doubled again by 1736 when it was reported to have 700 resident families. In Chester-le-Street, on the Wear, the number of households rose by 160 per cent between 1563 and 1674, and doubled again between 1674 and 1736. The rural south Durham parish of Sedgefield, in contrast, saw population increase of only 30 per cent between 1563 and 1674, and then stabilisation until 1736. Upland Stanhope actually witnessed a 25 per cent decline in households from 1563-1674, though numbers picked up again by around 60 per cent between 1674 and 1736.[39]

These varying experiences provide a clue to what was going on. The precipitous population growth of the industrial parishes must certainly have owed something to natural increase. But some of them also had very high mortality rates, partly as a result of mining accidents, mostly because their denser populations rendered them particularly susceptible to the spread of infectious disease. Their extraordinary growth was clearly the result principally of migration. This is well attested by the fact that in the baptismal registers of Whickham almost three-fifths of the surnames recorded in the period 1603-28 were new as compared with the period 1571-1602, while at Chester-le-Street manorial tenants expressed anxiety about the influx of 'incoming poor', 'inmates', 'undersettlers' and 'forainers' occasioned by the coal workings. Most of these migrants (on surname evidence) probably came from within the region, from places like Sedgefield and Stanhope, or from rural Northumberland. The coal workers of Whickham at the turn of the 17th century, for example, included men known to have originated in Birtley, Pelton, Eighton, Gainford and Hartlepool, as well as nearby Blaydon and Newcastle. Perhaps many such migrants to the industrial heartland had learned their skills as pitmen in the small 'land-sale' collieries that dotted the North East. But some came from even further afield. It is well known that in the early 18th century many Tyneside keelmen were of Scottish origin, but there was already a substantial Scottish minority in the area by the 1630s. Later Ambrose Crowley would bring in Walloons from the southern Netherlands to teach locally hired workers to make nails.[40]

At the heart of this emergent demographic core area were the towns of the lower Tyne and Wear, which grew with the surging trade in coal, salt, metal-wares, and other commodities.[41] The population of Newcastle itself grew five-fold between the

---

38 Hodgson, 'Demographic Trends', *passim*; Brassley, 'Agricultural Economy', pp.15, 17, 22-8; Kirby, D.A., 'Population Density and Land Values in County Durham during the Mid-Seventeenth Century', *Transactions of the Institute of British Geographers*, 57 (1972), pp.89-91.

39 Levine and Wrightson, *Making of an Industrial Society*, pp.155, 172-6, 206; C. Issa, 'Obligation and Choice: Aspects of Family and Kinship in Seventeenth-Century County Durham' (unpub. PhD thesis, University of St Andrews, 1987), pp.44-5, 66, 85.

40 Levine and Wrightson, *Making of an Industrial Society*, pp.179-80, 185-7, 207-9; Lasker, G.W. and Roberts, D.F., 'Secular Trends in Relationship as Estimated by Surnames: A Study of a Tyneside Parish', *Annals of Human Biology*, 9 (1982), p.301; Issa, 'Obligation and Choice', pp.56-7, 60; Durham County Record Office [Henceforward DRO], Q/S OB 7, pp.113-15.

41 The coastal trade in coal alone 'grew at an average annual compounded rate of 2.3 per cent between 1564 and 1685'. By the 1610s it employed 27.8 per cent of England's total merchant shipping tonnage, almost equalling the tonnages employed in fisheries and in foreign trade. By the 1660s it employed a staggering 43.9 per cent of English merchant tonnage, eclipsing that employed in fishing and foreign trade. In 1702, even after the massive growth in English overseas trade in the late 17th century, the coastal coal trade still accounted for 29.2 per cent of English tonnage: Hatcher, *British Coal Industry*, pp.8, 471 (Table 13.1).

1540s and the 1740s (from around six thousand to thirty thousand inhabitants). Sunderland expanded with the Wear coal trade, especially in the later 17th century, and by 1712 was petitioning for a new church to cater for a population 'of late years much increased'. At South Shields they contented themselves with requesting an extension to the graveyard in 1637, 'the number of the inhabitants much increasing and the said place groweinge verie populous by reason of the new buildings of salt workes'. The North East was developing a 'compact, highly articulated urban system' centred on Newcastle – 'the Metropolis of these Counties', as Samuel Hammond put it in 1659 – but incorporating also Gateshead, North and South Shields, and of course Sunderland. Even beyond those places, the network of industrial villages closely connected to them could be seen as dispersed suburbs.[42]

The effects of these developments, however, extended far deeper into Northumberland and Durham. The coalfield needed to be supplied, its dense population of industrial workers needed to be fed, and the historians of agrarian change in this period are agreed that it was response to these opportunities that was the principal factor in transforming the rural economy of the region.

It was not entirely so. The 16th and early 17th centuries witnessed price inflation as well as population growth. In such a context, northern landlords (like their fellows elsewhere) had strong incentives to improve their estate incomes: by edging up entry fines and annual rents; by converting inflexible customary tenures into leaseholds; by encouraging the 'engrossing' of small tenancies into larger, more profitable, commercial holdings, and by enclosing open fields and commons to create individually managed farms. Already in the late 16th century there were sharp complaints of the consequences of such initiatives, from tenants, from religious moralists and from those concerned about the region's military potential.[43] Thereafter the decline of border insecurity and the revision, or outright abolition, of the 'tenant right' associated with border defence, certainly made it easier for landlords to push through such policies. Perhaps much would have changed anyway. What is beyond doubt is that the commercial opportunities afforded by the development of the coalfield provided a powerful additional incentive and markedly accelerated the process.

Whatever the combination of motives and causes, the 17th century brought massive change on the land. In most parts of the region customary tenures were in headlong decline and leasehold tenure was in the ascendant. Rents rose. Five-fold increases in

---

42   Tuck, R., 'Civil Conflict in School and Town, 1500-1700', in B. Mains and A. Tuck (eds), *Royal Grammar School, Newcastle-upon-Tyne: A History of the School in its Community* (Stocksfield, 1986), pp.2, 37; Ellis, J., 'Urban Conflict and Popular Violence: The Guildhall Riots of 1740 in Newcastle-upon-Tyne', *International Review of Social History*, 25 (1980), p.334; Hughes, *North Country Life*, pp.12-13; Knight, 'Litigants and Litigation', p.413; Walton, J.K., 'Area Surveys 1540-1840: (e) North', in P. Clark (ed.), *The Cambridge Urban History of Britain, Vol. II, 1540-1840* (Cambridge, 2000), p.128; Hammond, S., *God's Judgement upon Drunkards, Swearers and Sabbath-Breakers* (London, 1659), 'To the Justices of Peace in the Nation, Especially these Northerne Parts'.

43   For the general context, see Wrightson, K., *Earthly Necessities. Economic Lives in Early Modern Britain* (New Haven and London, 2000), chs 5-8. For the North East specifically, see James, *Family, Lineage and Civil Society*, pp.75-7; Watts and Watts, *Border to Middle Shire*, pp.47-9; Drury, 'More stout than wise', *passim*; Reid, *Durham Crown Lordships*, pp.137-40; Creighton, H.M., 'The Northumbrian Border', *Archaeological Journal*, XLII (1885), pp.75-6; *Calendar of State Papers Domestic, 1595-7*, pp.347-8; Reid, D.S. (ed.), *A Durham Presentment of 1593, illustrating the Decay and Renewal of Durham Agriculture in the late Sixteenth Century*, Durham County Local History Society (1979).

estate rentals were not unusual in Northumberland in the early 17th century, and the experience of Durham was similar (though the Crown, the Bishop and the Dean and Chapter of Durham lagged behind lay landlords). Consolidation of holdings into larger farms was evident in both the lowland and upland zones, and though small tenancies remained numerous in some areas, the proportion of the land held in such units was substantially reduced. Most visibly of all, enclosure steadily advanced across the lowland areas of the region: the Tees basin; the east Durham plateau; the southern Wear lowlands; the coastal plain of Northumberland; the coalfield itself. This was usually accomplished by agreement between landlords and their more substantial tenants, though on occasion it was strongly resisted. As with the other developments listed, enclosure was not unique to the North East, but it was unusually complete. Most of lowland Northumberland was enclosed by 1700. Of lowland Durham it was said in 1726 that 'nine parts in ten are already enclosed and consequently improved in value and rents to a degree almost incredible'.[44]

Most of these enclosures were of former town fields (the uplands remained mostly open until after 1750), and on many of the newly enclosed farms variants of 'alternating husbandry' were practised, including from the early 18th century the sowing of clover and 'improved' grasses. The overall effect was to accentuate emphatically the existing pastoral emphasis of agriculture in Northumberland and Durham.[45] Given the soils and climate of the North East, it is hardly surprising that no serious effort was made to meet the bread corn needs of the urban-industrial zone. As Gray said of Newcastle in 1649, the four northern counties together were 'not able to serve this town with corne, not three months in the yeare'. Such needs were better met by imports from East Anglia, notably from King's Lynn (a major coal-receiving port), supplemented in years of bad harvest with grain from the Baltic.[46] What the farmers of Durham and Northumberland supplied was dairy produce, meat, draught animals, fodder, hides and tallow. They were now specialised producers for the highly specialised market provided by the region's urban-industrial core, and the process by which they became so transformed both the landscape in which they farmed and the geographical orientation of much of their activity.

The flows of goods and people that linked the villages and market towns of Durham and Northumberland to the urban-industrial zone, however, were not uni-directional. They were reciprocal, and indeed circulating. Newcastle importers supplied bread corn to a grain-poor region, as we have seen: 'an Aegypt to all the shires of the north

---

44   Watts and Watts, *Border to Middle Shire*, pp.47-8, 71-2, and ch. 8; Reid, *Durham Crown Lordships*, pp.42-3, 46-8, 137ff.; Brassley, P., 'Northumberland and Durham', in J. Thirsk (ed.), *The Agrarian History of England and Wales, Vol. V.1 Regional Farming Systems* (Cambridge, 1984), pp.47-51; Winchester, *Harvest of the Hills*, pp.16-17; Horton, P.H., 'The Administrative, Social and Economic Structure of the Durham Bishopric Estates, 1500-1640' (unpub. MLitt. thesis, University of Durham, 1975), p.213; Hodgson, 'Progress of enclosure', pp.86-92.

45   Brassley, 'Northumberland and Durham', pp.51ff.; Hodgson, 'Progress of enclosure', pp.93-5; Hughes, *North Country Life*, p.143.

46   Gray, *Chorographia*, p.91; Thirsk, J. and Cooper, J.P. (eds), *Seventeenth-Century Economic Documents* (Oxford, 1972), p.343. This dependence on imported food could leave the area dangerously exposed to shortages in years of bad harvest: see e.g. Levine and Wrightson, *Making of an Industrial Society*, pp.197-200, 382-3.

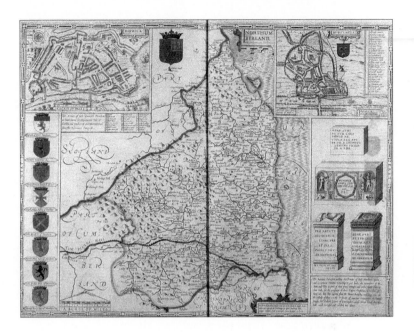

32 *Speed's map of Northumberland, 1611. See also back endpaper. (Yale Center)*

... All quarters of the country come', as Gray put it.[47] But there was much more to it than that. In 1635 Sir William Brereton noted of Newcastle's busy markets that 'much provision comes out of Northumberland'. He also observed that, 'This towne unto this countrye, serves in stead of London: by meanes whereof the countrye is supplyed with money.' A century later Henry Bourne agreed: 'It is the Money arising from the Coal Trade that almost entirely Circulates in this great Town and adjacent Country,' and fifty years after that Joseph Grainger, surveying the region's agriculture, saw the same. The coal industry employed many thousands, thus 'causing an immense circulation of money in the adjacent towns, to the great encouragement of trade, agriculture and population, *not only there, but at a distance also*'.[48]

So it did. The wealth generated by the North East's industrial heartland knit the area together. And the coastal trade further connected it to Britain's vibrant and expanding commercial networks. It is significant that, of the non-residents engaged in commercial litigation in Newcastle's Sheriff's Court in 1659 (mostly over trade debts), one third came from the urbanised Tyne valley strip from Swalwell to Shields, many others came from the small towns of Northumberland and Durham (especially coastal towns), and a substantial minority were based in the port towns of southern England, from Boston in Lincolnshire to Rye in Sussex. It is also instructive that in 1733, 'Surgeon Forster's Pectoral Elixir', a concoction produced in Durham and alleged to give 'wonderful relief' from asthma, coughs, and catarrhs, was available from stockists in Newcastle, Berwick, Morpeth, Hexham, Alnwick, North and South

---

47 Gray, *Chorographia*, p.91.
48 'The Journal of Sir William Brereton, 1635', in Hodgson, J.C. (ed.), *North Country Diaries*, Surtees Society, CXXIV (1915), pp.16, 19; Bourne, H., *History of Newcastle upon Tyne* (Newcastle, 1736), p.158; Grainger, J., *General View of the Agriculture of the County of Durham* (London, 1794), p.11 (my italics).

Shields, Sunderland, Hartlepool, Barnard Castle, Stockton, Wolsingham, Darlington, 'Chapel in Weardale', and Bishop Auckland (as well as in Richmond, Alston, and a few other places in north Yorkshire and Cumberland).[49]

By then, the commercial connectedness of the North East (both internally and externally) was striking, and it impacted markedly on the material culture of the area. Inventories of domestic goods provide striking evidence of how new standards of comfort and convenience were being achieved in the north-east region. This is evident in the inventories of Whickham and Chester-le-Street from at least the turn of the 17th century. More broadly, Lorna Weatherill's comparative study of changing consumption patterns from 1675-1725 reveals that, after London and Kent, it was Durham and Northumberland – and in particular the gentry, urban professional, and commercial people of the region – that entered earliest and most fully upon the possession of the 'new goods' of the age: clocks, china dishes, knives and forks, utensils for hot drinks and so on. In this, their experience was in very marked contrast to that of Cumberland and Westmorland, their neighbours in the 'old' North. Adrian Green has also shown how, from around 1600, in the North East, prosperous families of gentry and middling status rebuilt their houses in currently fashionable national styles, and by doing so were 'able to define themselves in relation to their immediate community and in relation to wider social affiliations'.[50]

It is no accident that, as Defoe tells us, Newcastle in the 1720s had 'the largest and longest key for landing and lading goods that is to be seen in England', or that in 1706 a Lancashire parson's wife consulted her Newcastle cousin when she wanted to learn 'the best way of making coffee'. Industrial development provided the money, and the city at the heart of that process had become what John Brand called the 'great Northern Emporium of Commerce'. The north-east region was fusing together under the pressure of the two great forces of industry and commerce.[51]

Social Identities

Economic specialisation and internal trade created the North East as a distinctive regional entity: an immanent identity had emerged. The re-making of the North East, however, also involved two further developments: the emergence of a distinctive social structure, and the creation of a sense of collective regional identity, or at least of the assumption that the inhabitants of Northumberland and Durham enjoyed a special relationship, both in their own eyes and those of others. These developments were intimately related.

49 Muldrew, C., *The Economy of Obligation. The Culture of Credit and Social Relations in Early Modern England* (Basingstoke and London, 1998), p.213. For Surgeon Forster's elixir, see the advertisement in *The Newcastle Courant*, No. 403, 13 January 1732/3.
50 Levine and Wrightson, *Making of an Industrial Society*, pp.89-92, 101-4, 147, 212, 231-41; Issa, 'Obligation and Choice', p.51; Weatherill, L., *Consumer Behaviour and Material Culture in Britain, 1660-1760* (London and New York, 1988), pp.43, 51-2, 74 and *passim;* Green, 'Houses in North East England', pp.66-9.
51 Defoe, D., *A Tour Through the Whole Island of Great Britain*, Everyman edition, 2 vols (London, 1962), ii, p.250; Pennell, S., 'The Material Culture of Food in Early Modern England, *c.*1650-1750' (unpub. DPhil thesis, University of Oxford, 1997), p.123; Brand, J., *Observations on Popular Antiquities: Including the whole of Mr Bourne's Antiquitates Vulgares* (Newcastle, 1777), p.346.

By the turn of the 18th century, the social order in north-east England had at least two distinctive features: first, an unusually well integrated composite élite of landed gentry, wealthy merchants and substantial professional people; and, secondly, an exceptionally large and geographically concentrated industrial workforce.

From the late 16th century onwards, a symbiosis of land, trade, and industry had been vital in forming partnerships and in raising the capital necessary to expand the coal trade on both Tyne and Wear. Over time, the sheer intensity of such involvement created 'a gentry whose strength was based on a fusion of mercantile and mining wealth with land'.[52] Some of its members, like Sir Ralph Cole or William Cotesworth, had risen from relatively humble origins to great wealth through the coal trade and crowned their success by acquiring land. Others came from ancient gentry families which had become heavily engaged in industrial enterprise, like the Lambtons, Lumleys and Delavals. There were merchant dynasts who became landowners (the Ridleys, the Liddells), and landowners who chose to enter trade (the Claverings, the Bowes). There was much rivalry and conflict amongst them, to be sure, but they could also hold together politically in the interests of the trade, or as members of cartels, and they were commonly allied by marriage and kinship.[53]

The North East's gentry were not only deeply involved in trade and industry; by the early 18th century they were also increasingly urbanised. The wealthiest of them spent part of the year in London, but by 1700 the North East itself was developing a sophisticated urban social season, centred on Newcastle and Durham and revolving around the race meetings, assemblies, assize balls, plays, concerts, clubs and societies patronised by the members of an emergent 'polite society'. The visiting lawyer Joseph Taylor described attending a genteel entertainment in the Bigg Market in 1705, at which he became so enamoured of three local beauties that he later hired musicians to serenade them as Violetta, Astraea, and Enamoretta. On such occasions the gentry intermingled with the mercantile and professional élite of the city – and they did so on less salubrious occasions also, as at the cock-fights organised (again in the Bigg Market) between 'the Gentlemen of *Bishoprick* and the Gentlemen of *Newcastle*', or 'the Gentlemen of *Newcastle* and the Gentlemen of *Northumberland* '.[54] By a process of mutual acculturation the North East's gentry became acutely commercial in their

---

52   Reid, *Durham Crown Lordships*, 7. cf. Hatcher, *British Coal Industry*, pp.253-4, and the detailed examples in Clavering and Rounding, 'Early Tyneside Industrialism'.

53   Reid, *Durham Crown Lordships*, pp.8-9, 53-4, 96; Brassley, 'Northumberland and Durham', pp.43-4; James, *Family, Lineage and Civil Society*, pp.68-71. For their rivalries and cooperation, see e.g. Levine and Wrightson, *Making of an Industrial Society*, pp.44-49, 59-76. The most illuminating study of the competitive business environment of the period, and of attempts to stabilise it, is Ellis, J., *A Study of the Business Fortunes of William Cotesworth, c.1668-1726* (New York, 1981).

54   Green, A.G., 'Houses and Households in County Durham and Newcastle, *c.*1570-1730' (unpub. PhD thesis, University of Durham, 2000), pp.269ff. For a vivid account of the emergent world of polite sociability, see King, R.F., 'Aspects of Sociability in the North East of England, 1600-1750' (unpub. PhD thesis, University of Durham, 2001), esp. chs 3-5, and for aspects of its subsequent development, Green, A., "'A Clumsey Countrey Girl": The Material and Print Culture of Betty Bowes', and Berry, H., 'Creating Polite Space: The Organisation and Social Function of the Newcastle Assembly Rooms', both in H. Berry and J. Gregory, *Creating and Consuming Culture in North-East England, 1660-1830* (Aldershot, 2004). For Joseph Taylor, see Cowan, W. (ed.), *A Journey to Edenborough in Scotland* (Edinburgh, 1903), p.90. Cockfights advertised in *Newcastle Courant* No. 403, 13 January, and No. 406, 3 February 1732/3.

attitudes and values, while the commercial élite of the area became increasingly genteel. 'Every gentleman … from the highest to the lowest, is as solicitous in the pursuit of gain as a tradesman,' sneered Elizabeth Montagu. Here, John Brand proudly countered, 'the Names of *Merchant* and *Gentleman* are synonymous Terms'.[55] Together they constituted a composite élite, united in their devotion to the interests of their industries and trade.

If the élite of the North East could be said to have been in part the creators and in part the creation of the coal trade, much the same could also be said of the region's industrial workers. In the absence of any fundamental change in the arduous techniques of winning and transporting coal prior to the introduction of the waggonways, they inevitably grew in numbers as the output of the industry expanded (and when the waggonways came, they introduced a whole new sector). If the Newcastle coal-owners were right in claiming that 5,800 men were employed in winning and transporting coal on Tyneside in 1637/8, then that figure would need to be multiplied at least four-fold to account for the output of both the Tyne and the Wear in 1750.[56] And that was for the coal industry alone.

The industrial workforce was *large*. It was also *geographically concentrated*, and it was *mobile*, not only in the sense that the urban-industrial zone attracted migrants, but also because the dynamics of the industry involved much movement across the coal field from colliery to colliery.[57] Some of its additional characteristics deserve emphasis. Hewers and sinkers, the most skilled colliery workers, were very well paid by the standards of most labouring people of the day, as were many colliery craftsmen and the most experienced Crowley smiths. Those who were less well paid had at least the advantage of regular work (a relatively unusual thing at this time). They remained vulnerable to industrial accidents, to periodic work stoppages occasioned by bad weather, flooding, wars, or trade disputes, and like all labouring people they could be swiftly reduced to poverty by sickness, injury, or simply advancing age. By the standards of their day, however, they were well off.[58] They were also much denigrated for their rough ways. In 1659 the preacher Samuel Hammond anticipated George Whitefield's characterisation of colliers when he observed, 'methinks I am amongst the Indians', and in 1705 the salters of Shields were described as 'very brutish, and seem to have no Notion of Religion or decency'. (Salters and keelmen caused scandal by habitually working on the Sabbath.[59]) Yet they appear to have known their own worth, to have developed an independent, not to say truculent, spirit, and to have had strong solidarities. 'Wee presume to inform your worships what our demands is, which we hope is Reasonable and Legall,' begins one keelmen's petition of 1677. In

---

55   Montagu quoted in Ellis, 'Black Indies', p.12; Brand, *Observations on Popular Antiquities*, p.346.
56   Nef, *Rise of the British Coal Industry*, ii, pp.137-8.
57   Levine and Wrightson, *Making of an Industrial Society*, pp.53, 165-72, 191-2, 230.
58   Hatcher, *British Coal Industry*, pp.381-2 and ch. 11; Levine and Wrightson, *Making of an Industrial Society*, ch. 3, sections 3, 5.
59   Hammond, *God's Judgement*, 93; Cowan (ed.), *Journey to Edenborough*, 88; DRO Q/S OB 5, p.217, Q/S OB 8, p.58.

1701, 'Crowley's Crew' ran several bailiffs out of Winlaton for attempting to distrain some of their workmates for debt, 'so that none of [them] dare come within ye said town'. And as is well known, both the keelmen and increasingly the pitmen were very well organised amongst themselves, a fact attested by their frequent involvement in small-scale stoppages, and capacity to launch occasional large-scale strikes.[60]

How far the workforce of the Tyne and Wear can be said to have developed a distinctive *regional* identity by the 18th century is a difficult question. They were certainly aware of their specific occupational identities, and referred to themselves proudly as Keelmen, Pitmen, Waggonmen, 'Crowley's Crew', 'Wear Water Men' and 'Tyne Water Men'. But such specific solidarities need not preclude a larger sense of identity. They had come to the urban-industrial zone from all over the region and many must have retained connections elsewhere. They were inducted into distinctive industrial cultures of skill and solidarity, but they also retained many of the beliefs and habits of the older culture from which they came (as recorded by Bourne and Brand, the regional pioneers of the study of 'popular antiquities'). They were members of a distinctive regional speech community, which was both inclusive (to them) and exclusive (to outsiders). 'They speak very broad,' observed William Stukeley, 'so that ... one can scarce understand the common people, but are apt to fancy oneself in a foreign country.' They lived close to one another, interacted and intermarried. And they were capable also of acting in concert. In 1662 miners from both Tyne *and* Wear are said to have petitioned the king for redress of their grievances. In the strike of 1731, 'Tyne Water Men' and 'Wear Water Men' consulted with one another and acted in concert to destroy the enlarged coal-corves to which they objected. The 1740 grain riots in Newcastle involved common action by Heaton pitmen, keelmen, waggonmen, 'Crowley's Crew' and the Newcastle poor to bring down food prices. In 1765 the entire coalfield was brought to a halt by carefully synchronised common action, and the pitmen of both counties put their case jointly to the public in newspaper advertisements, and to their employers in negotiations.[61] By then they were certainly aware of a regional industrial identity, and they had a very sharp tactical sense of the place of their industry in the national economy.

If we turn again to the landed, commercial and professional élites of the region, the case is even clearer. Of course they were keenly aware of their status as the leading inhabitants of separate counties and particular towns (which they frequently had a hand in governing). But they were also intermeshed economically and socially, as we have seen, and from time to time they also acted together politically – not

---

60   Tyne and Wear Archives, Keelmen's Papers, 394/1; DRO Q/S OB 8, p.20. For industrial relations, organisation, stoppages and strikes, see Fewster, J.M., 'The Keelmen of Tyneside in the Eighteenth Century, Part I', *Durham University Journal*, New series, 19 (1957), and Levine and Wrightson, *Making of an Industrial Society*, ch. 4, sections 5-7.

61   Levine and Wrightson, *Making of an Industrial Society*, pp.368, 383, 390-1, 402, and (for the events of 1731 and 1765) ch. 5, section 7; Brand, *Observations on Popular Antiquities, passim*; Fox, Adam, *Oral and Literate Culture in England, 1500-1700* (Oxford, 2000), pp.69, 72-3, 75, 82; Stukeley, W., *Itinerarium Curiosum*, 2nd edition, 2 vols (London, 1776), II, p.65; Webb, S., *The Story of the Durham Miners* (London, 1921), p.2; Ellis, J., 'Urban Conflict and Popular Violence', *passim*.

only in lobbying on behalf of the coal trade, but also, for example, in agitating for parliamentary representation for County Durham.[62]

No doubt the coal trade also had a central role in the development of a sense of common interest among these people. Yet there are signs also of a more elaborate awareness of the region as a meaningful social area. These were highly literate participants in the burgeoning print culture of the age, and consideration of some of the things they read is revealing. In the early 18th century Newcastle produced many newspapers with a wide circulation throughout the northern counties, and from them one can glean a sense of the 'imagined community' that they addressed, and helped to create. This is not so much a matter of the news stories – which usually concerned national or international affairs and were often lifted from London papers – but of the advertisements that were carried. In the eight issues of the *Newcastle Courant* from January to March 1733, for example, there were advertisements of farms for lease or sale in 19 Durham locations (from Chester-le-Street to near Darlington), 14 Northumberland locations (as far north as Rock), and four places in Cleveland and Richmondshire, two areas of north Yorkshire which clearly maintained a close relationship with their northern neighbours. In addition houses were advertised for sale in Sunderland, Gateshead, Durham, Whickham and Stockton; teachers based in Bishop Auckland and Houghton-le-Spring advertised their services; and horse races were announced in Sedgefield, Wylam and Wideopen.[63]

Equally interesting are the local histories and chorographies produced in the area from William Gray's *Chorographia* (1649) to Hutchinson's *County Durham* (1785-94). All of them stressed the significance and achievements of the coal industry for the whole 'country' (i.e. the region centred on Newcastle). More generally, however, they were concerned to remind their readers of a deeper regional past, and to encourage them to incorporate it into their sense of themselves. Gray gave brief accounts of 'the kingdome of the Northumbers', the noble families of Northumberland and Durham, the border wars and the blood feuds of the 'surnames'. Hutchinson's subject was County Durham, but he included a long account of the kingdom of Northumbria as prolegomenon to the foundation of Durham, and much regional medieval history. As significant as the contents of these volumes, however, were the lists of those who had subscribed to their publication. In the histories of Newcastle by Bourne (1736) and Brand (1789), these subscribers' lists are virtually a roll call of the polite society not only of Newcastle, but also of Durham and Northumberland: aldermen; landed gentlemen; leading clergymen; lawyers. There were outliers, too. Bourne had five London subscribers, mostly with readily identifiable northern names. Brand netted thirteen London-based

---

62   The Durham gentry and Newcastle merchants co-operated to agitate for parliamentary representation for County Durham from 1610 onwards: Foster, A.F., 'The struggle for Parliamentary Representation for Durham, *c.*1600-1641', in Marcombe (ed.), *Last Principality*, pp.180ff.

63   On the Newcastle press, see Wilson, K., *The sense of the people. Politics, culture and imperialism in England, 1715-1785* (Cambridge, 1995), pp.324-5; *Newcastle Courant*, Nos. 403-410, 13 January-10 March 1732/3. Green, 'Houses and Households', ch. 7 traces the emergence of a regional property market advertising in the Newcastle papers, and suggests (p.193) that it extended from the Scottish border to a segment of the North Riding of Yorkshire (Richmondshire and the Yarm/Northallerton area) which had become oriented towards the North East rather than southwards to York.

subscribers and also a certain Mr George Carr of St Petersburg.[64] In sum, among the educated élite of the North East there was demand for, or at least a sense of obligation to support, the recovery of the regional past – an enterprise conducive to the further elaboration of an identity that was shared, if not quite common.

Region and Metropolis

No doubt the north-east region meant different things to different people. For some it was simply the matrix of their immediate lived experience; their effective social area. For others, the readers of the antiquarian clerisy, it was a more defined entity, containing layers of time. The common ground was coal. If a 'collective cultural identity' had emerged in the North East by the mid-18th century it derived ultimately from the changes wrought in the preceding century by the growth of the coal trade. Coal was a very powerful symbol around which to build a sense of belonging. It was also the dominant element in the perception of the region from outside. The rise of the coal trade made people conscious of Newcastle, Sunderland and the north-eastern counties in a wholly new way. Already in 1611 John Speed, though dealing with Durham and Northumberland separately, had noted the importance of coal in both cases – he saw that connection at least. And coal was the litany of later visitors. 'This country all about is full of this coale ... Upon a high hill two mile from Newcastle I could see all about the country, which was full of coale pitts.' (Celia Fiennes); 'We had the pleasure to see the fires by the Cole pits, which are everywhere round Newcastle, burning all night.' (Joseph Taylor); Daniel Defoe's sense of wonder is almost palpable in his description of the scene as he rode from Chester-le-Street to Newcastle in 1724:

> When in this country we see the prodigious heaps, I may say mountains of coals which are dug up at every pitt, and how many of these pitts there are, we are filled with ... wonder to consider where the people live that can consume them.[65]

He knew the answer: the urban South East and above all London. No one was fitter than this sharp observer of the webs of commerce to express the complementarity of the North East and the metropolis. But he was not alone. To the inhabitants of southern England the North East meant Newcastle and Sunderland, and those places in turn meant coal. As visitors they both admired and were shocked by the industry. As consumers they read anxiously in their newspapers of any industrial trouble that might threaten their supply.[66]

---

64 Gray, *Chorographia*, pp.27, 98-109; Hutchinson, W., *The History and Antiquities of the County Palatine of Durham*, 3 vols (Newcastle 1785-94), Vol. I; Bourne, H., *History of Newcastle upon Tyne or, the Ancient and Present State of that Town* (Newcastle, 1736); Brand, J., *The History and Antiquities of the Town and County of Newcastle-upon-Tyne*, 2 vols (London, 1789).

65 Speed, *Theatre*, pp.83, 89; Morris, C. (ed.), *The Illustrated Journeys of Celia Fiennes, 1685-c.1712* (London and Exeter, 1982), p.176; Cowan (ed.), *Journey to Edenborough*, p.88; Defoe, *Tour*, ii, p.250.

66 The 1731 troubles were reported in *Ipswich Journal*, 6 February 1731, and the *Gloucester Journal*, 9 February 1731. The 1765 stoppage was very widely reported, especially in the London press: see Levine and Wrightson, *Making of an Industrial Society*, pp.409-25.

That symbiotic relationship between the North East and the metropolis was one of the most important creative relationships in the economic and social history of Britain, and indeed of the industrialised world. It created wealth and power, new social formations, and new identities. Fuel from the North East made the prodigious growth of London possible. London's demands, and perceptions, helped re-make the North East as one of the 'archetypes of large-scale, capitalist and geographically concentrated industrial organization'.[67]

By 1760 much of this had already been accomplished. To be sure, it was not the North East of Stephenson and Armstrong: steam, steel and engineering were still mostly in the future. It was not the North East of the 20th century, struggling to reconcile its inherited pride with a gnawing sense of vulnerability to decline. They did not yet even call it the North East: it was 'these counties'; 'this country'; 'these northern parts'. But it was *a* North East; a distinctive regional society with an established sense of its own special identity, and the essential foundation for everything that was to come.

---

67   Dietz, B., 'The North-East Coal Trade, 1550-1750: Measures, Markets, and the Metropolis', *Northern History*, 22 (1986), pp.288-9; Smailes, *North England*, p.6.

9

The New Northumbrians

ROBERT COLLS

'Correct your maps: Newcastle is Peru'
> (Tony Harrison, after John Cleveland)

Is the North East English?

In the North East of England in the second half of the 19th century a cultural movement appeared that sought to identify the region as an historic nation. The seventh- and eighth-century Anglian kingdom of Northumbria was its underlying inspiration, though medieval and early modern histories were woven in as well, and the counties of Northumberland and Durham were its homeland, though the city of Newcastle upon Tyne was its centre of operations. I have called the men and women of this movement 'New Northumbrians' and it is the aim of this chapter to sketch their feelings and ideas. For the most part they were local notables rather than full-time men of letters or politicians, and there was no headquarters, though the Newcastle Literary and Philosophic Society might be said to have served as a forum. Above all, even though most New Northumbrians were clear-cut modernists, they were historicists too, and the historic significance of the region was never far from their thinking. Their mission was to affirm the modern world by re-charging it with historic meaning. Being a New Northumbrian, therefore, was about living in a rapidly changing present but at the same time drawing one's being from a rich and meaningful past. In other words, the New Northumbrians promulgated a doctrine of enchantment that gave them enchantment. In this period many English regions defined themselves in terms of how English they were but in certain key ways the New Northumbrians defined themselves in terms of how English they were *not* – of a European kingdom that had existed before 'England' began; of a history that had stayed at the edge; of a modern, northern, civilisation that was a democratic

33 *Sir James Radcliffe, 3rd Earl of Derwentwater (1689-1716) by George Vertue after Sir Godfrey Kneller. A Jacobite executed for treason, his estates were sequestrated and conferred upon Greenwich Hospital.*

alternative to what was being promulgated in the south. If in 1914 we were to have stopped a New Northumbrian in Grey Street and asked him 'Is the North East English?', his answer would have been 'yes', but he would have surely qualified it with remarks about the irony of being northern and being English at the same time. At the very least, he would have asked us to remember our history.

New Northumbrians found a way to vent their frustration with English history. Because United Kingdom Unionism made it difficult for them to express their northern-ness politically,[1] like the Scots and the Welsh and most of the Irish, they had no alternative but to express themselves in the guise of an alternative but cultured, and historic, people. Up to 1914, this gave them a much lower profile than, say, Irish republicans who had crossed the line from Unionism to Nationalism, but put them on a par with Welsh, or Scottish, or Irish home rulers who did not cross that line. As a cultural movement, the New Northumbrians were much looser and more inclusive than they would have been had they been a political organisation, but, like their Welsh and Scottish counterparts, what politics they did have tended to be Liberal edging into Radical. As to the beginnings of the movement, if one really insisted on a time and place, I would suggest the mural paintings at Wallington Hall commissioned by Sir Walter Trevelyan of William Bell Scott in 1856.[2] As to membership, of three things we can be sure. First, there was no 'membership' as such; this was a network of influence, not a club. Second, though we can speculate about New Northumbrian beginnings from the mid-1850s, as a modern intelligentsia with regional interests those beginnings go back to Enlightenment traditions covered elsewhere in this volume.[3] Finally, it has to be said that all kinds of northerners could be New Northumbrians except nearly all of them. Women were a minority and, of the men, they had to have the time, the money, the education, and the contacts.[4]

Consider for a moment the officers of Newcastle Literary and Philosophical Society in 1874.[5] All were drawn to a popular northern ideology but, equally, all saw themselves

---

1 Although the 'Home Rule All Round' slogan did give some northern Liberals ideas on English devolution: Fawcett, C.B., *Provinces of England* (London, 1919 (1960)), p.19.

2 William Bell Scott (1811-90), b. Edinburgh, educ. Edinburgh High School, Royal Academy 1842, Master, Newcastle School of Design 1843-64, friend of Rossetti and Swinburne. *Scenes from Northumbrian History* are Building the Roman Wall; St Cuthbert; Descent of the Danes; Venerable Bede; Spur in the Dish; Bernard Gilpin; Grace Darling; Iron and Coal.

3 Roey Sweet's chapter lays the foundations of mine. See also Jenny Uglow's account of 18th-century club and intellectual traditions – 'a small informal bunch who … nudge their whole society and culture over the threshold of the modern': *The Lunar Men* (London, 2002).

4 There were some outstanding women painters, including Laura Knight and Isa Thompson, but they felt isolated: Laura Newton with A.B. Gerdts, *Cullercoats* (Bristol, 2003), p.18.

5 81st *Annual Report*, 1874.

as 'gentlemen' with time for scholarship. President was Sir William George Armstrong, Newcastle's leading industrialist. Armstrong had been a member since 1836, had given his first lecture in 1844 and would give his last in 1895. The Society's magnificent library and lecture room were his gift.[6] Along with the vice presidents Edward Charlton (doctor and local historian) and John Clayton (town clerk and antiquarian), and committee men Thomas Hodgkin (banker and historian) and John Wigham Richardson (shipbuilder and collector), Armstrong was a wealthy man whose commitment to the region went way beyond owning large portions of it. He was a grand patron and, among the grandees, we can include Algernon, 4th Duke of Northumberland (archaeologist), Sir Walter Trevelyan of Wallington Hall (archaeologist and naturalist), Joseph Cowen of Stella (politician and newspaper proprietor), the bankers Howard Pease and Robert Spence, and the landowners and developers Ralph Carr Ellison and John Hodgson Hinde.[7] The Society wanted to popularise its ideas (it extended its membership in 1856 and 1889) but that

34 *Thomas Hodgkin (1831-1913). New Northumbrian, Quaker banker and scholar. Tenant of Bamburgh Castle 1894-99, and Barmoor Castle 1899-1913.*

did not mean relinquishing its power of patronage. Men such as these were used to lording it but even when lordship was not to their taste, as with the Cowens, whose patronage over such vital civic bodies as the Tyne Improvement Commission, or the Free Library, gave them enormous power to make their views known, and heeded.

Secretary to the Lit & Phil in 1874 was Robert Spence Watson, of Gateshead, solicitor, company director, and the country's leading lay Liberal. No man in the Society knew as much, cared more, or lectured as long. As chairman of the Newcastle Public Library book committee, he had a lot of say in what the region read. In his famous 1898 Lit & Phil lectures Watson described himself as 'a devoted Northumbrian with an intense ... belief in the Northumbria of old and the Northumberland of today'.[8] Vice president John Collingwood Bruce (schoolmaster and scholar), and committee man James Clephan (newspaper editor) we might put in Watson's camp as second-order New Northumbrians – not immensely rich, or landed, but hard-working activists who were knowledgeable, and known for it. W.E. Adams, Cowen's editor at the *Chronicle* for many years, was hugely influential, and lawyers and company secretaries were prominent in this rank too, including Richard Welford (Steamship Owners' Association), and William Weaver Tomlinson (North Eastern Railway). Richard Oliver Heslop, steel merchant, led the revival of interest in dialect speech,

---

6   108th *Annual Report*, 1901.
7   The County Durham grandees Robert Surtees, of Mainforth Hall (1779-1834), and Sir Cuthbert Sharp, of Sunderland and the Hartlepools (1781-1849), were important precursors of the New Northumbrians.
8   *Lectures delivered to the Literary & Philosophical Society on Northumbrian History, Literature and Art* (Newcastle, 1898), p.26.

35 *Robert Spence Watson (1837-1911). New Northumbrian, solicitor. His many civic roles included honorary secretary of Newcastle Literary and Philosophical Society 1862-92 and president of the National Liberal Federation 1890-1902.*

and Thomas Wilson, another company secretary though of an earlier generation, was regarded as an authority.[9]

Finally, among the officers of 1874 there was committee member T.P. Barkas, bookseller and gallery owner – representative of a third group of New Northumbrians who had an interest in selling things to do with northern identity. A market in regional products was emerging.[10] Increasingly we have to account for New Northumbrians who weren't born there, or who didn't live there, but who still made money by their enthusiasm for the place.[11] Out of an early 19th-century local tradition that included the bookselling and publishing Bells, Eneas MacKenzie, and Emerson Charnley, this third group included men such as David Dippie Dixon, Robert White, and the Allan brothers who, towards the end of the century, along with Spence Watson and Cowen, successfully marketed the music hall entertainer Joe Wilson (1841-75) as a true Northumbrian balladeer. Wilson had sold his copyright to the Allans and they, in turn, turned his songs and drolleries into commodities.[12] In this category, painters and engravers, along with architects, deserve a section to themselves, and the great Newcastle engraver Thomas Bewick must be mentioned, though he was in a league of his own. Architects are particularly important, especially the leading architect of modern Newcastle, John Dobson, and his tutor David Stephenson. Ralph Hedley was the most popular painter of our period, and a committed New Northumbrian, but there were plenty of other painters of landscapes and seascapes as well, including, earlier, the Richardsons and John Wilson Carmichael, and later, the Cullercoats colony led by Henry Hetherington Emmerson which for a time included the brilliant American Winslow Homer. Finally, there were curates Hodgson and Raine following in the 18th-century tradition of the antiquarian reverends Bourne and Wallis. In 1866 William Henderson thanked no fewer than 12 clergymen for their help in the making of his *Notes on the Folk Lore of the Northern Counties*.[13]

From the 1860s up to 1914 the Newcastle Lit & Phil was the major forum for New Northumbrian thinking. Originally founded in 1793 as a 'conversation club', it made serious attempts to widen its membership in the second half of the 19th century. Members met to give papers, lead excursions, join excavations and generally

9   Thomas Wilson (1773-1858) had started work in the pits at eight years old. His long dialect poem the 'Pitman's Pay' (1843) became a prime authority for later dictionaries and glossaries.
10   The first mass market was in printed texts and images: Anderson, Patricia, *The Printed Image and the Transformation of Popular Culture 1790-1860* (Oxford, 1991).
11   Other New Northumbrians who were not born there included W.S. Gibson (Fulham 1814), Thomas Hodgkin (Tottenham 1831), Richard Welford (Upper Holloway 1836), Ralph Hedley (Richmond, Yorks 1850) and W.W. Tomlinson (Driffield 1858).
12   *Newcastle Daily Chronicle*, 29 October 1890.
13   First published in 1866; this edition London 1879.

use the Society like a club or common room or university library. This serves to remind us that the New Northumbrians had their antecedents and that there were other societies to consider. The region had a natural history, too; plants and rocks and animals had their place. Overlapping institutions included the Society of Antiquaries (1813), the Typographical Society (1817), the Natural History Society (1829), the Surtees Society (1834), the Tyneside Naturalists' Field Club (1846), the Archaeological Society of Durham and Northumberland (1861), the Bewick Club (1883), the Hancock Museum (1884), the Laing Art Gallery (1904) and, most important of all, the chummy but profoundly political pages of Joseph Cowen's *Newcastle Weekly Chronicle*.[14]

Cowen was the Liberal member for Newcastle, and the friend and accomplice of Mazzini, Kossuth, Herzen, Bakunin, Garibaldi and others. An ardent nationalist and supporter of Irish home rule, insofar as New Northumbrianism had a political direction, it tended Cowen's way.[15] The radical newspapermen Annand, Clephan and Adams worked for him, and Ralph Hedley's painting career owed something to the *Chronicle* too, but the Gateshead solicitor Spence Watson was as far to the left as Cowen (though he was a Gladstonian, which Cowen was not) while up at Wallington Hall Sir Walter Trevelyan played the strange part of the non-drinking, non-sporting, non-Tory, squire.[16]

Whatever their exact position on the political spectrum, these men were committed to something deeper and wider. It was no hardship that the Lit & Phil had banned the discussion of politics for at heart these men were nationalists, and reached out beyond party.

Survivals in Culture

In 1871 Edward Tylor's immensely influential *Primitive Culture* posited the 'science of ethnography' as the 'study of the laws of human thought and action'. Tylor organised what he saw as universal cultural practices into various 'species'. These species ranged from elementary physical objects such as agricultural implements, to practical activities such as cooking, to things of the mind such as customs and beliefs. Those species which continued to be practised in advanced societies, without understanding, usually by the poor and uneducated, Tylor labelled 'survivals in culture'. His main contention was that survivals could be traced back to primitive cultures where they retained their context and meaning. Tylor, therefore, advocated ethnography as a sort of cultural time-travel whereby experts could penetrate the lost meanings of their day.[17] What they learned

---

14 Cowen took full ownership from 1859. The *Chronicle* also published the *Monthly Chronicle of North Country Lore and Legend* from 1887 to 1891.

15 The Conservative influence was less marked; Tory New Northumbrians included Carr Ellison, Hodgson Hinde and Cadwallader Bates.

16 From 1868 the region was dominated by the Liberals, holding 21 out of 23 seats in 1880. In 1886 there were serious fallings out over Irish Home Rule – with Cowen retiring hurt, the Spence Watson camp moving to the Gladstonian left, and the Armstrong camp to the Unionist right.

17 Archaeology also was organised on ethnographic principles from General Pitt Rivers onwards: Bradley, R., 'Archaeology, Evolution and the Public Good', *Archaeological Journal*, 140, 1983, pp.4-7.

36 *R.O. Heslop (1842-1916). New Northumbrian, iron merchant to the shipbuilding industry. Dialectician.*

might be trivial, to do with cooking or, say, the origin of a superstition. Or it might be profound, to do with what it was to be human, over very long periods, from one generation to the next.[18]

At first, Tylor had been concerned to compare across cultural practices. But in a century where nation-states were striving to turn inchoate peoples into historic nations, his theory appeared to offer a way of explaining what that might mean.[19] All one had to do was find some aboriginal peoples, and apply the method. Moreover, by stressing what was actually practised and believed over what was merely recorded or written down, usually by outsiders, Tylor's method appeared to go straight to the heart of who the people were. That they could not explain themselves – 'frequently rude, irrational and senseless' according to the President of the Folklore Society – allowed the ethnographically advanced to speak on their behalf.[20] So, George Sturt, for example, wrote about a wheelwright who did not think, but just 'felt it, in his bones', while, according to Albert Mansbridge, certain Oxford dons 'yearned to be in contact with the fundamental facts of life' through contact with people like Sturt's wheelwright. From D.H. Lawrence's 'blood' instinct, to Freud's 'unconscious', to all European schools of peasant painting, and folk music, and folk lore, to Lenin's theory of revolution – survivals in culture encouraged sympathetic intellectuals to take the place of poor people, and do their thinking for them.[21]

Yet intellectuals did not have everything their own way, even in their own estimation. They knew themselves to be more rational and better educated than the poor, but they did not claim all the virtues. When soldiering was required, for instance, they recognised that those with less to lose had more to give.[22] Only the poor could give their lives so cheaply. Only the unlettered could build an archive by word of mouth. Only those on the unchanging edge could know that it was, in fact, the unchanging

18   Gomme, G.L., *Ethnology in Folklore* (London 1892), p.6. The Folklore Society was founded in 1878, and provided a steady stream of researchers. On the antiquarian background to folk study in Britain, and the long wait for a 'British Grimm' to lend method to the collecting, see Dorson, R.M., *The British Folklorists* (London, 1968), p.88.

19   Antiquarians including Sir Walter Scott and the Stockton collector Joseph Ritson, as well as Bourne (fn. 42) and Brand (fn. 23) had been aware of endangered customs since the 18th century: Sweet, Rosemary, *Antiquaries* (London, 2004), pp.335-41. For a strong northern example just before Tylor's theory, see Henderson's *Folk-Lore of the Northern Counties*, p.viii.

20   This is not to say that all those who spoke on their behalf spoke against. Many spoke in favour. George Bourne saw the English village as a survival place but also as the stronghold of the labourer and his culture. Francis Heath defended the old English 'peasant' from those who were out to destroy him: Bourne, G., *Change in the Village* (London, 1912 (1966)), pp.4-5; Heath, F., *Peasant Life in the West of England* (1872. London 1883) pp.344-45.

21   Sturt, G., *The Wheelwright's Shop* (Cambridge, 1923 (1980)), p.20; Mansbridge, A., *An Adventure in Working-Class Education* (London, 1920), p.xx; Lenin, V.I., 'What Is To Be Done', in *Selected Works* (Moscow, 1902 (1967)), vol. i, p.163. Ralph Vaughan Williams said 'song is the beginning of music': *National Music* (London, 1959 (1934)), p.31.

22   They had more 'courage, honesty, [and] generosity': Tylor, E., *Primitive Culture* (New York, 1903 (1871)), p.29.

centre.[23] Survivals in culture provided special openings for peripheral peoples. It was through these openings that the New Northumbrians walked to find their land.

Historic Land

Pride of place was Redesdale, near Otterburn, 15 miles south of the Scottish border and a long way from anywhere else. It was here that the traditions of the 16th century moss troopers were said to have lingered longest: 'The Scots ... hath made the inhabitants of Northumberland fierce and hardy ... being a most warre-like nation.'[24] Here, too, the dialect was said to be purest.[25] Indeed, dialect started the 1860s being seen as a drag on the morals of the poor, but ended the decade regarded as a national treasure.[26] In 1871 Tylor had thought it indicated 'more or less connexion of ancestral race' but soon the claim was being made that dialect speakers had saved the English language by preserving its Old Norse origins.[27] Far from slandering the national tongue, it was the poor what spoke it best.[28]

Special interest was shown in 'burring', that throaty slurring of the 'r' sound found across much of Northumberland. In 1890 the celebrated philologist Alexander Ellis thought it had no value as a survival in culture. Two years later, Richard Heslop argued that it had. The great Dr Murray of Oxford had told him of a popular tradition which dated burring with Harry Hotspur.[29] Had not Shakespeare given Hotspur the 'shibboleth' of the burr upon his tongue?[30] At this point philology left off and wishful thinking blew in. Readers were told that the Northumbrian poor took in Hotspur's burr with their mother's milk.[31]

But there was a paradox. Those who had retained the oral tradition were said not to understand it; while those who claimed to understand it did so by reading and writing. In fact, New Northumbrians celebrated the authenticity of the oral tradition almost entirely in print. Those who did the writing, therefore, had to claim their authority by pretending, *somehow in the work*, not to be writers at all.[32]

---

23 Squire, C., *The Mythology of the British Islands* (London, 1910), p.5. This was one of 35 volumes in the same series beginning with Matthew Arnold's *The Study of Celtic Literature* (London, 1867).

24 Gray, William, *Chorographia* (Newcastle, 1813 (1649)), p.37. William Brown, 'head of a great number of thieves or moss troopers', was hanged at Newcastle as late as 1743: John Brand, *The History and Antiquities of the Town and County of Newcastle upon Tyne* (London, 1789), ii, pp.523-4.

25 Gomme, *Ethnology*, p.185.

26 State of Popular Education in England, *Parliamentary Papers*, 1861, xxi, pt ii, pp.339-42. Other reclaimed survival practices included superstition and well-worship: Andrews, W. (ed.), *Bygone Durham* (London, 1898), p.241; Hall, Rev. G. R., *Notes on Modern Survivals of Ancient Well-Worship in North Tynedale* (Newcastle, 1878), p.14.

27 Tylor, *Primitive Culture*, p.49.

28 Wright, E.M., *Rustic Speech and Folk-Lore* (Oxford, 1913), pp.xix-xx.

29 Heslop, R. Oliver, *Northumberland Words. A Glossary of words used in the County of Northumberland and on Tyneside* (London, English Dialect Society, 1892), pp.i, xii, xxii-xxiv; Ellis, A.J., *English Dialects. Their Sounds and Homes* (English Dialect Society, 1890), pp.2, 125.

30 Defoe referred to the 'shibboleth' as 'a difficulty in pronouncing the letter "r"': Defoe, Daniel, *A Tour Through The Whole Island of Great Britain* (Harmondsworth, 1978 (1724-6)), p.538. See Shakespeare's description of Hotspur 'speaking thick', *Henry IV, part II*, act ii, scene 3. For the Percy dynasty and other British warrior heroes: Gibson, W.S., *An Historical Memoir of Northumberland* (Newcastle, 1862); and Ebbutt, M.I., *Hero-Myths and Legends of the British Race* (London, 1912).

31 Gibson, *op. cit.*, p.103. The case was still being made 60 years later: Thomson, H., *Highways and Byways in Northumbria* (London, 1921), p.200.

32 For painters trying to paint like writers trying to write, that is, naively: Newton, *Cullercoats*, p.23.

It is impossible to overestimate the influence of Sir Walter Scott in this. He told his readers that the Earl of Northumberland was 'a formidable name to Scotland' and, by fixing the true time and spirit of The Border, Scott taught the whole country how to feel and write Northumbrian.[33] His *Minstrelsy of the Scottish Border* (1802-03) opened up the area as a literary place based upon oral traditions, and the epic works that followed, particularly *Marmion* (1808) and *Rob Roy* (1818), secured a bridgehead for the region into the national culture.[34]

> And now the vessel skirts the strand
> Of mountainous Northumberland;
> Towns, towers, and halls, successive rise,
> And catch the nuns' delighted eyes...
> And Warkworth, proud of Percy's name;
> And next, they cross'd themselves, to hear
> The whitening breakers sound so near,
> Where, boiling through the rocks, they roar,
> On Dunstanborough's caverned shore.
> (*Marmion*, Canto second)

Early on in his researches, the historian of County Durham, Robert Surtees, had made friends with Scott. Their correspondence was never less than warm. Scott told Surtees in 1806 that he would 'treasure' his advice. Surtees told Scott in 1807 that 'every trace' of Scotland was dear to his mind.[35] Sir Walter showed the Durham man how to see his county as a land resembling Scotland – as in *Rokeby* –'Where Tees in tumult leaves his source / Thundering o'er Caldron and High Force'. Surtees, on the other hand, faked a border ballad that he passed off onto the Scotsman as genuine.[36]

On Surtees' death in 1834 a Society was founded in his name devoted to the histories of England and Scotland in the territory of the old greater Northumbria. No less a devotee of Scott was James Raine, historian of 'North Durham'. As he said, there was a turning point in his work whence 'came Sir Walter Scott'. Raine acknowledged Sir Walter's almost single-handed popularisation of a tradition of northern-ness and wagered that Durham antiquarians would 'not be disappointed [if] they look for instances of chivalry and romance ... when the very pen of chivalry and romance ... was engaged in their delineation'.[37] Of other New Northumbrians, by their own testimony, Scott was Walter White's constant guide, Robert White's first inspiration, Cuthbert Sharp's greatest mentor, Howard Pease's 'kindred spirit', and W.W. Tomlinson's tutor in all arts of the imagination. Spence Watson said Sir Walter was 'as much a Northumbrian' as

---

33 Scott, Walter, *The Minstrelsy of the Scottish Border* (Edinburgh, 1861 (1802)), vol. i, pt i, p.121.
34 Ruddick, W., 'Sir Walter Scott's Northumberland', in J.H. Alexander and D. Hewitt (eds), *Scott and His Influence* (Aberdeen, 1983), pp.20-30.
35 Surtees, Robert, *History and Antiquities of the County Palatine of Durham* (London, 1840) vol. iv, memoir by George Taylor, pp.18-30.
36 'Death of Featherstonhaugh', in Scott, *Minstrelsy*, vol. i, pt ii, pp.86-9, and *Marmion: a tale of Flodden Field* (Edinburgh, 1815 (1808)), pp.399-403. W.M. Egglestone, *Stanhope and its Neighbourhood* (Stanhope, 1882), p.3; Taylor, *op. cit.*, p.16.
37 Raine, Rev. J., *History and Antiquities of North Durham* (London, 1852), p.iii.

Caedmon had been, and Algernon, 4th Duke, added a high tower to his castle simply on the great man's say so.[38]

Scott's imitators were numerous, and by mid-century they had showed the region how to historicise itself.[39] Before that mid-century tipping-point, historicism had been a minority interest in the region. Cobbett had visited in 1832 and wasted not a word on its history.[40] Two years later Surtees was unsparing in his stylistic criticisms of his predecessor, Hutchinson, as Hutchinson, in turn, had made no bones about his inability to write historical works interesting enough to make some money. He told John Bell the printer that in the hands of a 'laborious penman' such as he, 'Honour and Profit have wings'.[41] In 1846 and 1854 the topographical and historicist painters M.A. and G.B. Richardson had been forced to leave for Australia because they too could not find a market for their works, though they would find fame later when the new city was ready to be compared with the old.[42] Similarly failing to find recognition, the antiquarian John Hodgson published his histories from the 1820s to the 1840s but could not find enough patrons. John Collingwood Bruce, on the other hand, publishing from the 1850s and using Hodgson to the point of plagiarism, became the most renowned local historian of his day.[43] Through him, rather than through the more worthy Hodgson, Hadrian's Wall became the second most written-about antiquity in Britain.[44] Cowen's *Weekly Chronicle* tapped into this market in the 1870s, and in 1887 *The Monthly Chronicle of North Country Lore and Legend* was launched,

> To collect and preserve the great wealth of history and tradition, legend and story, poetry and song, dialect and folk lore, which abounds in the ancient kingdom of Northumbria ... no district is richer ... no district, it is thought, will have a stronger desire than our own to see those characters and incidents ...[45]

The region was becoming more interested in its past, and more interesting in itself.

---

38 *Monthly Chronicle North Country Lore and Legend*, vol. v, Sept 1891; White, W., *Northumberland and the Border* (London, 1859), p.315; Welford, R., *Men of Mark Twixt Tyne and Tweed* (Newcastle, 1894) vol. iii; Sharp – *Records of Society of Antiquaries of Newcastle 1813-1913* (Newcastle, 1913); Pease – *Archaeologia Aeliana*, 4th ser, vol. v (1928); Tomlinson - *Archaeologia Aeliana*, 3rd, xiv (1917); Watson - *Lectures, op cit.*

39 See the publications of M.A. Richardson of Newcastle, published in Charnley, Emerson: *Tracts, Poetical, Legendary, Biographical etc. relating to the Counties of Northumberland and Durham* (Newcastle, 1844).

40 Though he lays into the ancient privileges of Newcastle Corporation, he doesn't tarry in Bede's Jarrow: Cobbett, William, *Cobbett's Tour in Scotland; and in the four northern counties* (London, 1832), p.35.

41 Hutchinson, William, *The History of the County of Cumberland* (Wakefield, 1974 (1794-7)), p.xxi.

42 See for instance their *Proposals for publishing by Subscription The History and Antiquities of Newcastle and Gateshead* (1840), Central Library L942.82. They expected to earn a living out of antiquarianism but not many did. The Typographical Society, for instance, usually published fewer than twenty copies at a time.

43 Raine, Rev. J., *A Memoir of the Rev. John Hodgson*, vol. ii (London, 1858), pp.309-10, 391-2, 400-3. Gibson criticised poor Hodgson for the 'chaotic ... state in which these important materials of history are printed in these unattractive volumes': Gibson, *Historical Memoir*, p.122. Surtees acknowledged that Hutchinson (*History of Durham*, 2 vols, 1785, vol. iii, 1794) had suffered from (an un-gentlemanly) lack of time and money: *History and Antiquities of the County Palatine of Durham* (1816), vol. i, p.8. Nineteenth-century historians drew heavily on 18th-century antiquarians who had their own sense of survivals in culture: especially Bourne, H., *The History of Newcastle upon Tyne: or, the Ancient and Present State of that Town* (Newcastle, 1736); Wallis, J., *Natural History and Antiquities of Northumberland*, and Brand, John, *History and Antiquities* and *Observations on the Popular Antiquities of Great Britain* (London, 1849 (1777)).

44 First was Stonehenge.

45 *Monthly Chronicle*, i, 1887, p.1.

Written Region

In writing about the region there were four major conventions. Each shared in the paradox of writing about an illiterate people who were deemed to understand more than the writer. All were influential in shaping the way history and natural history came to be written in 19th- and 20th-century Britain, and persist today both in their own right and in documentary film making. Examples are legion.

First convention was *travelling*. Many New Northumbrians took the first-person stance of the traveller, usually a walker, and here Wordsworth was the guide, not Scott.[46] Bogg came up from Leeds, Bradley from Rye. White asked, 'Who is for a holiday between the Tyne and the Tweed?' and travelled up from Middlesex.[47] Travelling had two uses. First, it opened up the writing to a national market – Bradley said he wrote for the 'South Saxon traveller', Runciman called on London stockbrokers to hurry north[48] – and second it allowed readers to join in the travelling. It did not matter whether the writer had actually travelled or not. What mattered was the convention that he had. That way, all readers saw what the writer saw, or said he saw, preferably in the way he said he saw it – usually chanced upon, sudden, as if snatched from experience. Although this was the age of rambling and hiking, so insistent was the geographical description that these books were clearly intended more for the fireside than for the fellside. Secure in his Tyneside terrace ('Tyneholme'? 'Cheviot Villa'? 'Simonside'?), the armchair-hiker read his way across hundreds miles without as much as a blister.

Commercial directories were written expressly for travellers. They grew in size and scope as the century progressed, and usually came with a heavy historical digest and special emphasis on topography and buildings. Although driven by ends far removed from the Society of Antiquaries, Messrs Bulmer & Co., and Kelly & Co. and all the other commercial directory publishers can still be regarded as fellow travellers in the making of a New Northumbria.

Second convention in writing about the region was *fancy*. Writers went forth in search of rejuvenation: 'before you stretches a long vista of anticipation', 'as if a sceptre was placed in your hand'.[49] The main exercise of the day was to personify the place; to fancy past and present as a single consciousness. Tomlinson declared that antiquarians 'must re-visualise ... what is dead'. Hodgkin told his little band of Holy Island (Lindisfarne) pilgrims that 'we must, in imagination, clear away ... reconstruct'.[50] Maps took walkers on, but fancy structured the experience once they got there. Solitude was the key, for history had to be taken in reveries. When, as occasionally happened, the writer's

---

46   See his *Guide to the Lakes* (1822, and many editions): Ian Ousby, *The Englishman's England. Taste, Travel and the Rise of Tourism* (Cambridge, 1990), p.183.

47   White, *Northumberland*, p.1; Bogg, E., *Two Thousand Miles of Wandering in the Border Country, Lakeland, and Ribblesdale* (Leeds, 1898), p.1; Bradley, A.G., *The Romance of Northumberland* (London, 1908), *Preface*. John Wallis had begun the literary travelling convention in 1769 with 'Three Journeys' through the antiquities of Northumberland. His approach predated Scott and the romantic style: Wallis, *Natural History and Antiquities*, vol. ii.

48   Bradley, *op. cit.*, p.1, p.v; Runciman, J., *The Romance of the Coast* (London, 1883), p.299.

49   White, *Northumberland*, p.3.

50   *Archaeologia Aeliana*, 3rd ser., xiv, 1917, pp.136-41; *Archaeologia Aeliana, Centenary*, 1913, p.80.

transport of delight was dented by a charabanc of trippers looking for lunch, he could at least take comfort that their choice of rural byway was as good as his.[51] Angling was particularly good for solitude. Charles Kingsley pronounced it the 'sport of sports' for overworked businessmen. The Northumberland Angling Club was founded in 1881 but when it lost its waters it still carried on as a club, eating suppers and singing songs in the dialect.[52]

Third, although the movement in general can be seen as modernist, there was an *anti-modern* strain in New Northumbrian writing. Writers did not embrace urban-industrial society even though they understood only too well that it was usually their own. White's 'heart rejoice[d] at the sight of the hills' but sank at the sight of the people (this view would change). Their towns besmirched them, their dialect was 'slovenly' (this view would also change). Bates' history did not know how to conceive what happened after 1746, while on the Tyne Bradley said he had 'no concern here with these smokey scenes' and invited readers to head for Alnwick instead. In the Durham coalfield, 'with history for our companion', Gibson invited his initiates to turn away from 'the busy paths of commerce'.[53]

Fourth convention was the point of view of *the outsider* who finds her way inside. Iris Wedgwood's Dorking friends thought she was going to a foreign place and reminded her to mention the cornfields, if there were any. Survivals in culture, in their human form at least, were harder to get to know than landscapes. Bradley warned his readers that the Northumbrian peasant 'will never speak or even nod to you of his own accord'. ('Taciturnity is a mere Border trait, inherited from times when every alien face might indicate a foe.'[54]) The traveller in search of locals had to be continually on the look out, snooping round, trying to worm his way in.[55] Caught in a reverie, he was the consummate insider. Spotted by a native, he was a stranger. Taking the cinder road from Scotswood to Blaydon, the Yorkshire picture framer Edmund Bogg

> at intervals … encounter[ed] groups of miners and furnacemen
> lounging at the cross road ends, inns or upon the bridges,
> smoking 'the pipe of peace' themselves but doing their best
> to disturb the peace of strangers by staring them out of
> countenance as they approach and indulging in ill-timed
> personal observations and jokes regarding their appearance.[56]

These writers – on the move, sedentary, critical, fanciful, sensitive, watchful – created the conditions for a new northern identity. They hoped to spread the word. Bates resolved to use the 'evidence which has accumulated during the last half-century' in

---

51   They weren't always so vulgar. William Woodruff recalled a 'sharabang' of Lancashire weavers in the 1920s spellbound by 'the great silence of the moors': *The Road to Nab End* (London, 2003), p.115.
52   Bradley, *Romance of Northumberland*, p.14; Lowerson, J., *Sport and the English Middle Classes* (Manchester, 1993), p.43.
53   White, *Northumberland*, pp.1, 56, 60, 77, 80, 83; Bradley, *op. cit.*, pp.2, 9; Gibson, W.S., *Descriptive and Historical Notices of Some Remarkable Northumbrian Castles, Churches and Antiquities* (Newcastle, 1868), p.91.
54   Wedgwood, Iris, *Northumberland and Durham* (London, 1932), p.184; Bradley, *op. cit.*, p.81.
55   White, *Northumberland*, p.77.
56   Bogg, *Two Thousand Miles*, p.68.

order to produce 'a Guide to Northumbrian history that the Quaysider from Newcastle can carry on his bicycle'.[57] He wanted to make history continuous with present practical life – the connection that distinguishes all dead peoples from living ones.

In 1898 the Newcastle Literary and Philosophical Society sponsored a series of lectures on 'Northumbrian History, Literature and Art'. The Society had been closely linked with the Cambridge University Extension movement since 1879. During the 1880s class numbers had soared to between 200 and 350. By telling his packed audience what Northumbria had been, in Spence Watson's eyes he was effectively telling them what she actually was: 'cradle of religion', 'saviour of England', 'epitome of the world'. Here was the difference between survivalists, poking among the ruins of dead civilisations, and New Northumbrians, who saw in those civilisations the living folk.[58] The folk ideal, indeed, denied conscious construction and took in everyone and everything over long durations of iteration and reiteration, imitation and replication. In a nation as old as the English, in a region as authentically in touch with its past as Northumberland and Durham, it was written that folk traits could not be mere survivals. On the contrary, they were true to life. In the Lit & Phil lectures, Northumbrians were identified as a living race of Angles, Celts and Norse – a people with fighting in their veins.[59] In its shape, jutting into the North Sea, the land mass was conceived as strutting upon the map, 'defiant game cock fragment of the world'.[60] As for their dialect, it was 'a well of Northern English undefiled'. Harry Haldane's *Newcastle Folk Speech* was selling in Central Station for sixpence. He thought that the Tynesider should not be

> accused of corrupting his native language; on the contrary, he is the transmitter of good old English, and he gets out of the depths of his throat, and well round his mouth, the most carefully preserved gutturals and vowel sounds of the old Danish and Saxon fore-elders.[61]

Instead of scattered survivals, therefore, how the region looked and sounded were natural and persistent qualities, to be witnessed every day in the gait and *craic* of the people.[62] Durham schoolchildren were told that even now they were Cuthbert's *halywerfolc*. Sunderland schoolchildren were advised that even now Bede was a fellow citizen.[63] William Bell Scott's murals painted living Northumbrians into the faces of historic ones, and H.H. Emmerson's 'Bereaved' (1888) painted friends into the faces

---

57   Cadwallader Bates, *The History of Northumberland* (London, 1895), pp.ii-iii. See Readman, P., 'The place of the past in English culture 1890-1914, *Past and Present*, 186 (2005).

58   Hodgkin, T. et al, *Lectures, delivered to the Literary and Philosophical Society, Newcastle-upon-Tyne, on Northumbrian History, Literature and Art* (Newcastle, 1898), pp.2, 27, 193, 196.

59   Gibson, *Historical Memoir*, p.30; Haselhurst, S.R., *Northumberland* (Cambridge, 1913), p.64.

60   Terry, J.F., *Northumberland. Yesterday and Today* (Newcastle, 1913), p.10. See also Bradley, *Romance of Northumberland*, p.7.

61   Palmer, W.J., *The Tyne and its Tributaries* (London, 1882), p.256. 'Harry Haldane' was R.O. Heslop.

62   Music received different treatment, but New Northumbrians were just as interested just as early: Bruce, J.C., *Northumbrian Minstrelsy* (Newcastle, 1882), and Doubleday, Thomas, *Letter to His Grace the Duke of Northumberland on the Ancient Northumbrian Music* (London, 1857). See chapters by Jude Murphy and Natasha Vall in this volume.

63   A memorial was erected in 1903 together with a wave of verification that Bede belonged as much to Sunderland as to Jarrow: John Robinson, *National Memorial to the Venerable Bede* (Sunderland, 1903); *Sunderland Daily Post*, 26 May 1903.

of fisherfolk and he himself into the portrait of 'Johnnie Armstrong's Farewell' (1886) according to Scott's *Minstrelsy* version of the old moss trooper legend.[64]

In the dialect, a late-century resurgence of song, story, and music hall bore witness to its strength. Heslop visited South Shields and portrayed pit talk as a survival in culture. He believed, indeed, that it had been possible to visit the pitmen and 'pass abruptly' from the modern age into the historic.[65] In truth, here was a language in full spate among a people noted for their fertility.[66] If Shields' large modern collieries and thousands of red-lipped Geordie pitmen were survivals in culture, then we have to admit that they were more than surviving. Nor did they need to be told that they talked different. They too understood the difference between how they spoke and 'standard English' and were not inclined to change it. In any case, dialect was selling lots of books, newspapers, and entertainments to speakers and non-speakers alike. Only this time, and just for a change, it was the middle classes who were being invited to share the workers' English and not the other way.[67] There was plenty of workers' English to share. Joseph Wright's *English Dialect Dictionary* (1896-1905) contained 100,000 words, including 1,300 for a fool.[68]

As a flourishing commercial activity in Newcastle, dialect literature can be traced from at least the beginning of the 19th century. A strong strain of caricature prevailed. Heroes were often colliers or sailors, and sometimes quayside beauties, all projecting a place of substance and spirit. The phonetics was always more a performance than a transcription. Appearing at the Theatre Royal, Sunderland, in November 1844, Mr Topliff's 'London Merry Night' included a fair batch of local songs including Border Ballads, *Hey awa maw Bonny Bairn*, and an air 'harmonised from the Melodies of the Tyne and Wear' called *Maids get up and bake your pies*. *Bob Cranky*, the pitman on a spree, was a subject of many songs: the prototype for music hall stars to come, Cranky was re-invented so many times throughout the century that he came to stand for 'Geordies' in general.[69] The most popular song denoting 'Geordies' to themselves and to others, George Ridley's *The Blaydon Races*, first sung for a workers' benefit night in 1862, came straight out of the Cranky tradition. The singing of songs was very clearly associated with expressions of local and national identity and music halls and concert rooms represented the modern region just as powerfully as the Lit & Phil. Joe Wilson the singer was just as famous as Sir William Armstrong the industrialist.[70] It wasn't just New Northumbrians who visited Warkworth Castle. Geordies went there, too. As Ned Corvan made clear,

---

64   Eden, F.S., *School History of the County Palatine of Durham* (Oxford, 1909), p.256; Mitchell, W.C., *History of Sunderland* (Sunderland, 1919), ch. xv; *Scenes from Northumbrian History*; Newton, *Cullercoats*, plate 14; *Monthly Chronicle*, ii, 1888, p.218.

65   Heslop, *Northumberland Words*, pp.xii, 256; presidential address, Small Pipes Society, *Transactions*, i, 1894.

66   Simon Szreter, *Fertility, class and gender in Britain 1860-1940* (Cambridge, 2000), ch. 7 fig. 7.i.

67   'The older writers wrote for their own amusement ... now Tyneside songs are generally launched into popularity from the stage of the concert hall': *Allan's Illustrated edition of Tyneside Songs and Readings* (Newcastle, 1891 (1872)), *Introduction*.

68   Wright, *Rustic Speech*, ch. 2.

69   *Handbill*, Monday 4 November 1844, NCL, Wilson Collection, vol, x; Colls, *The Collier's Rant - Song and culture in the industrial village* (London, 1977), chs. 2, 5.

70   *Newcastle Daily Journal*, 20 February 1875. For the knowingness, and seriousness, of song, see the Northern Political Union dinner toasts and speeches in honour of Thomas Atwood, in 1832. They include to 'The People, the true source of legitimate power' – *Rule Britannia*; 'Corporation Reform' – *Canny Newcastle*; 'The Chairman' – *Because he was a bonny lad*: in Welford, *Men of Mark*, p.154.

Sum folks may jaw 'boot a fine breeze,
Praise Warkwith's shores and hikey seas;
Praise steam-boat trips an' caller air,
Or spend a day devoid o' care.
They may tell o' wondrous things they see,
Sic as cassells, an' rooins, an' lots o' space;
'Boot monks an' mermaids deein' queer feats
An' rabbits dancin' polkas on the Coquet at neets

But lads aw've got a different tyel
For aw wonce had a trip doon there me-sel.[71]

Dialect, therefore, marked a primary line of identity. It entered professional engineering in a published glossary in 1849. It became the subject of academic research in 1872. *The Newcastle Weekly Chronicle* started a weekly glossary, subjecting it 'to the scrutiny of innumerable readers', in 1887.[72] Joseph Skipsey, a former pitman who wrote dialect poetry, took up the post of curator of Shakespeare's birthplace at Stratford in 1889.[73]

A people with their own language were entitled to their own homeland. Survivalists had been energetic in identifying special places, but in a region on the move it wasn't long before what applied in a general way to special places applied, in a particular way, to all places. The coach parties and railway ramblers, the Sunday cyclists and amateur naturalists, the full-time travellers and part-time romantics, all made their way out west into the Pennines, or north into the Cheviots, or east by train straight to the coast.[74] Getting away was easy. The inland carriage of coal and other minerals to the three great industrial rivers and, later, the region's huge lead in the production and distribution of electricity, gave it the first and probably the most intensive transport system in the world. On arrival, there were bottles to swig, sandwiches to eat, cameras to click. Few realised that the pictures they took were but popular versions of Tylorian ethnography: of the old and wise, carrying the oral tradition; of the young and innocent, eager to listen; of cottage and costume, and implements, mowing the hay, reaping the harvest, curing the herring. Fishing villages were well worth a visit. Cullercoats was handy for Newcastle and attracted painters as well as photographers. Its fisher folk brought 'a reassuring sense that the degeneration of the race is not proceeding in wholesale fashion'.[75] Facing the sea border of a nation that was increasingly defining itself as

---

71   Corvan, Ned, 'Warkworth Feast', in *Corvan's Song Book* (Newcastle n.d.) – 'Sung with great applause by him at all the Music Halls and Promenades in the North of England'.

72   Heslop, *Northumberland Words*, p.xxvi. Joseph Cowen was described by Heslop as 'an effective public speaker, notwithstanding his local accent', and in Lawson, W., *Lawson's Tyneside Celebrities. Sketches of the Lives and Labours of Famous Men of the North* (Newcastle, 1873), p.13. Cowen had been expensively educated. It is possible his accent had been deliberately retained, or acquired: Kelly, J., *Biographical Dictionary of Modern British Radicals 1830-70* (Brighton, 1984), vol. ii, pp.159-64.

73   There was some confusion whether he was curator or caretaker but either way he didn't enjoy it. Spence Watson was one of his referees: *Newcastle Leader*, 5 September 1903.

74   Frederick A. Wills ('Vagabond' of the *Evening Chronicle* and 'Wayfarer' of the *North Mail*) synthesised all these rhetorics and practices: *The Rambles of a Vagabond* (Newcastle, 1936).

75   Ellis, *English Dialects*, p.2; for the revival of dialect see Wilson, Joe, *Tyneside Songs and Drolleries* (East Ardsley, 1970 (1890)); Colls, *Collier's Rant*, pp.38-50; Vicinus, M., *The Industrial Muse* (London, 1974), pp.185-237; Joyce, Patrick, *Visions of the People* (Cambridge, 1991), ch. 8; Pahlsson, C., *The Northumbrian Burr. A Sociolinguistic Study* (Lund, 1972), p.25; Heslop, *Northumberland Words*, p.256; Terry, *Northumberland*, p.10.

an 'island race', the main theme of the paintings – heroic rescue from the sea – showed a community forming and re-forming itself in adversity.[76] Little wonder that Grace Darling's exploits on the night of 7 September 1838, performed as they were in the deepest and most Northumbrian of places, made her into a New Northumbrian heroine.[77] Her monument was erected in Bamburgh in 1844 but restored in 1885 and 1895. When Edward Charlton wrote in the same vein about another 'intelligent, handsome and strongly-built race', this time on the Border, he celebrated tens of thousands who bore the name Charlton, Milburn, Robson or Dodd, or who knew others who did.[78] No wonder Baden-Powell was drawn to the region as a country 'teeming with romance'. The first Boy Scouts' camp pitched up at Humshaugh in 1908. The boys roamed about looking for King Arthur. As for the look of the land, some writers complained that Northumberland did not look English because its skies were too grey or because it had no patchwork enclosures 'on fortuitous and artistic lines'. No matter: Bates rejected English history by proclaiming Northumberland's to be a 'drum and trumpet history' instead, and the more rugged the terrain and brilliant the rain and shine, the more excitable the writing and striking the difference.[79] Beneath sleeting skies, people leaned into their homeland.[80]

37   *Grace Darling (1815-1842) by Henry Perlee Parker (1838). New Northumbrian heroine and daughter of the keeper of the Longstone lighthouse on the Farne Islands. Grace's skill and bravery helped her father save nine persons from the wreck of the SS* Forfarshire *on 7 September 1838.*

Nothing historicises a land more than its architecture. Sir Walter Scott's Northumberland and Durham was full of castles and keeps. In the 1820s, Lord Durham and Matthew Russell had turned to the neo-gothic to restore their castles at Lambton and Brancepeth. Later, Alnwick became the primary site of New Northumbrian mythology. 'Alnwick! I never heard the old song of Percy and Douglas that I found not my heart moved than with a trumpet.' This castle had also

76   Newton, *Cullercoats*, fig. 43, plate 11. Painters exhibiting at the Royal Academy summer exhibition in these years preferred to paint coastal and other extreme landscapes: Howard, Peter, 'Painters' preferred places', *Journal of Historical Geography* (1985), 11, 2, pp.145-6.

77   She and her father, keeper of the Longstone light in the Farne, rowed through a stormy night to save nine survivors. She was 23 years old and died from consumption four years later. See Hope, Eva, *Grace Darling. Heroine of the Farne Islands* (London, 1873), and *Monthly Chronicle*, 1888, p.265.

78   Charlton, E., *Memorials of North Tynedale and its Four Surnames* (Newcastle, 1871), p.101. This had not been the view thirty years before. Rev. Gilley, Vicar of Norham, on the 'Border peasantry': Report on the Sanitary Condition of the Labouring Population by Edwin Chadwick, House of Lords, *Parliamentary Papers*, 1842, xxvi, p.22.

79   Bradley, *Romance of Northumberland*, p.2; Girouard, M., *The Return to Camelot. Chivalry and the English Gentleman* (London, 1981), p.256; Bogg, *Two Thousand Miles*, p.68. Bates' declaration (*Northumberland*, p. iii) was a straight rejection of J.R. Green's famous declaration that his English history was not a drum and trumpet history: *Short History of the English People* (London, 1888).

80   Bogg, *op. cit.*, p.2; Haselhurst's biography of the Tyne, *Northumberland*, pp.73-5; Terry, *Northumberland*, p.114; Wedgwood, *Northumberland and Durham*, p.70.

38 *Cadwallader Bates (1853-1902). New Northumbrian, landowner and owner of Heddon Colliery and Brick company. Educated Eton and Cambridge. Proprietor of Langley Castle.*

suffered from some 18th-century neo-gothic but, as Gibson remarked in 1862, it was now 'the fashion to respect and preserve historical monuments' and the 4th Duke followed accordingly.[81] Ford Castle was restored by the Marchioness of Waterford in 1865; Stanhope Castle by Mrs Pease and the Ecclesiastical Commissioners in 1875; Newcastle keep and gatehouse by the Society of Antiquaries in 1848 and 1883; Dilston Castle by Lord Allendale in 1874; Lindisfarne Castle by Lutyens for Edward Hudson in 1901; Cartington Castle by Lord Armstrong in 1889, and Bamburgh Castle six years later when Thomas Hodgkin moved out, and his landlord moved in – Hodgkin moving to Barmoor Castle, at Beal. Langley Castle was restored by the latter-day Jacobite, Cadwallader Bates, in the 1890s. Nothing gave this Old Etonian coal owner more pleasure, we are told, 'than to pass an evening with his fellow members discussing some hoary theme within the old castle'. Lord Lambton was memorialised in 1848 with a classical temple on Penshaw hill – high on the north Durham skyline. John Bowes, yet another coal owner, memorialised his wife and art collection in a French chateau by Pellechet, at Barnard Castle, 1871-85. Howard Pease lived in 'Otterburn Towers', where he built a round tower and 'felt himself a part of the history of the place'. Charles Mitchell lived in 'Jesmond Towers', in Newcastle's northern suburbs, where he too felt safe from raiders. Newcastle, famous for its classicist renaissance in the 1830s, started building furiously in all historicist styles from the 1860s. The more styles the better, in fact, because only a plurality of styles conveyed the passage of time which is what historicism is. While the municipality was straining to build monumentally, the churches medievally, and the mining engineers exquisitely, in French, next to Central Station, Lord Armstrong dropped his own little bit of Northumbria into a city which could not have its park, Jesmond Dene, without its tower, its ruins, its 'glen', its 'grotto', and 'dingles'.[82]

Homelands must have capitals. Newcastle gained city cathedral status in 1882. This was achieved not without opposition. Survivals in culture vied with the metropolis for the honour. Among them was Alnwick, home of the Percys; Bamburgh, ancient

81   On the Lambton and Brancepeth restorations: Girouard, *Return to Camelot*, pp.69-72; on Alnwick, Gibson, *Historical Memoir*, p.78, and Bogg, *Two Thousand Miles*, pp.107-8. William Wordsworth's 1833 paean for Lowther Castle began 'Lowther!'
82   Allsopp, B. and Clark, V., *Historic Architecture of Northumberland* (Newcastle, 1970), pp.33-40; Terry, *Northumberland*, p.51; Kelly's, *op cit.*, p.18; *Archaeologia Aeliana*, 4th ser., vol. v, 1928, p.114; *Newcastle Weekly Chronicle*, 3 May 1902. The Society of Antiquaries had regarded the Castle 'with longing eyes' since its inception in a pub long room in 1813: *Records of the Society 1813-1913* (Newcastle, 1913), p.3.

stronghold of the kings of Bernicia; and Lindisfarne, island hermitage of St Cuthbert. In the end, Newcastle's businessmen stumped up £60,000 for a bishop and instead of putting the capital in the sea, the see was put in the capital.[83]

Modern Region

In a time of great change, it was reassuring to bring past and present together.[84] At Jarrow, Gibson saw Palmer's vast iron shipyards, but he also saw Eigfrid's Saxon fleet.[85] Upstream at Elswick, Terry saw in every battle cruiser a serpent ship, in every riveter a son of Odin.[86] The main thing was to keep up the historic reverie and still see the possibilities of modern life. But when modern life was deemed incorrigible, smoke and fire made it historic again. Thus, Bell in Middlesbrough saw 'turrets and pinnacles', not chimneys and kilns; Palmer saw 'towers and battlements', not chemical works; and Tomlinson, under 'certain conditions' in 'these fire-wasted landscapes', saw 'a sombre grandeur'. And as for the men who worked there in fustian and moleskin, they were cropped into 'shadowy' and 'unearthly' figures.[87]

Industrialists were harder to reclaim for the present. Early in the century they had been portrayed as social wreckers.[88] By the middle of the century, however, it was clear they were here to stay and had to be saved from their earlier reputation. Saved first by Thomas Carlyle and his friends, who turned them into 'captains of industry', northern industrialists returned to favour in the 1860s.[89] While the 'Southron' remained full of that 'benevolent enthusiasm' which 'bespeaks the open richness of his fruitful land', it was deemed that the north demanded more strength and method from its sons. For many New Northumbrians therefore (not a few of them businessmen) the best kind of northerner was a businessman.[90] In this sense, William George Armstrong was the movement's real and symbolic leader.[91]

Armstrong bestrode the modern region. A self-made manufacturer of guns and warships, bridges and cranes, as well as Newcastle's greatest benefactor, he employed

83 Jagger, P.L., 'The Formation of the Diocese of Newcastle,' in W.S.F. Pickering (ed.), *A Social History of the Diocese of Newcastle* (Stocksfield, 1981), pp.24-39, 44-6; and Smith, J., 'The Making of a Diocese 1851-82', in Robert Colls and Bill Lancaster (eds), *Newcastle upon Tyne. A modern history* (Chichester, 2001).

84 Terry, *op. cit., Introduction*; Clark, T.T., *Ralph Gardner and The Tyne* (North Shields, 1881), p.5.

85 Gibson, *Historical Memoir*, pp.110-11.

86 Terry, *Northumberland*, p.106. See Kipling, Rudyard, 'Big Steamers', *Twenty Poems* (London, 1930).

87 Lady Bell, *At The Works. A study of a manufacturing town* (Newton Abbot, 1969 (1907)), p.12; Palmer, *The Tyne*, p.x; Tomlinson, W.W., *Comprehensive Guide to the County of Northumberland* (London, 1889), p.38; Bogg, *Two Thousand Miles*, pp.49, 54.

88 From *Blackwood's Magazine*'s mockery of political economy in the 1820s, to Tennyson's poetry in the 1850s, to Arnold's criticism of provincial middle-class 'Hebraism' in the 1860s, the business classes were seen as inimical to national solidarity: *Blackwood's Magazine*, 18 (1825), pp.20-31; Arnold, Matthew, *Culture and Anarchy* (Cambridge, 1979 (1869)) – 'the Nonconformist is not in contact with the main current of national life', p.14. Compare this with Samuel Smiles' celebratory 'manual of provincial, bourgeois culture': Harrison, R., 'Afterword' to S. Smiles, *Self Help* (London, 1968 (1859)), p.262.

89 Thomas Carlyle and Charles Kingsley were the major translators of commerce into gentlemanliness. Smiles' concluding chapter was called 'Character: The True Gentleman'. For a modest celebration of the businessman as the region's defining figure: Lawson, *Tyneside Celebrities*, p.13.

90 Lawson, *op. cit.*, pp.8, 17. John Ruskin's *Modern Painters* (1843-) identified character with landscape: Garrigan, K.O., *Ruskin on Architecture* (Wisconsin, 1973), p.113.

91 William George Armstrong, Baron Armstrong of Cragside (1810-1900), gunmaker, inventor and designer: educ. Bishop Auckland grammar school, partner in Newcastle law firm 1833, secretary Newcastle & Gateshead Water Co. 1844, manager Elswick Engineering 1847, knight and CB 1859.

over 20,000 men at the Elswick works in a vast international engineering company. At Cragside, near Rothbury, his newly minted motto 'Strong in Arms' reflected his Liddesdale ancestry, but the house enjoyed the most up-to-date electrics and hydraulics. Perched on a bluff, the 16th-century style of architecture reflected the region's most historic era, but the gardens – 1,700 acres, seven million trees, 31 miles of walks, three lakes – were landscaped using the most modern machinery.[92] He changed the balance and topography of Newcastle. He built Cragside out of a 'silent glen'.[93] He restored Bamburgh at a cost of one million pounds.[94] When he died in 1900 he was unquestionably the richest man in the region.[95]

But you could call William George Armstrong almost anything but a capitalist. This son of a corn merchant was a 'chief', a 'leader', a 'knight', a 'baron', a 'commander',

> an hydraulic engineer, an artillerist, a shipbuilder ...
> a general worker in the applied sciences ...
> a philanthropist and public benefactor ...
> a Fellow of the Royal Society ... [his] name
> stands out as a Mount Blanc or a Matterhorn.[96]

Sir William Armstrong could not be described as a man who made a great deal of money employing other men to make guns, any more than Sir Joseph Cowen could be described as a man who made a great deal of money out of bricks.[97] In an age of re-enchantment, the achievements of men such as these could not be best described in the language of political economy. While industrialisation had resulted in great development it had also brought great trauma in the process. And because result without process is magic, to see the great industrialists as magicians was to exculpate them from the process, and celebrate them only for the result. Thus the property developer Richard Grainger had brought 'a magic transformation' to Newcastle, the shipbuilder Charles Mark Palmer had waved his 'magic wand' over Jarrow, the steelmaker Isaac Lowthian Bell had waved his over Middlesbrough, and Armstrong, 'the wizard', had waved his over Elswick, then Cragside, then Jesmond. In the magical arts, historians counted for just as much as capitalists. By creating 'a grand connecting-link between the long-buried past and the ever-living present', 'as

---

92   The National Trust, *Cragside* (London, 1984); Dixon, D.D., *Upper Coquetdale, Northumberland. Its history, traditions, folklore and scenery* (Newcastle, 1913), pp.432-4. 'The term "crag", so common in the county, fittingly recalls the normal scenery': Haselhurst, *Northumberland*, p.4.
93   *Newcastle Weekly Chronicle*, 23 August 1884.
94   Terry, *Northumberland*, p.113; Dixon, *op. cit.*
95   He left £1.399m in his will. McCord, N., *North East England* (London, 1979), pp.133-8; McClelland, K., 'Some aspects of work and the reformation of class 1850-80', in Patrick Joyce (ed.), *The Historical Meanings of Work* (Cambridge, 1987), pp.181-3; Benwell Community Project, *The Making of a Ruling Class* (Newcastle, 1978), p.113, p.117.
96   Christie, Rev. J., *Northumberland. Its history, its features, and its people* (Newcastle, 1893), p.142.
97   Modern knighthoods could do much for a man. A Northumbrian hierarchy for 1905 started with a triumvirate of Duke, Bishop and Sheriff and ended with vets. As a solicitor by training, Armstrong would have ranked in the sixth cohort; as an engineer by inclination he would have ranked in the tenth; but as a man with a knighthood he ranked in the third: Pike, W.T. (ed.), *Northumberland. At the Opening of the Twentieth Century* (Brighton, 1905). Members of Parliament were ranked in the second cohort, in strict alphabetical order except for Messrs Burt and Fenwick, miners' members for Morpeth and Wansbeck, who came last. With 31 years' service in Parliament, Thomas Burt was by far the senior MP, but found himself at the back of the queue.

if by the wand of some old magician', the historian John Collingwood Bruce had given 'character to a town and to an epoch'.[98]

Some places were so modern they were reckoned to have no past worth saving. Lady Bell's Middlesbrough, for instance, stood 'on no historic foundation', and there had been a time when ultra moderns had wanted to turn Newcastle's very origins, its Norman keep, into a railway signal box.[99] But New Northumbrians saw the identity of the modern as ineradicably historicist, and could not contemplate one without the other. To Heslop, the soul of the old dalesmen lived on in the miners. To Gibson, the swords of moss troopers had been turned into iron ships. To Christie, Armstrong's field guns stood with Roman javelins and Hotspur's spear.[100] In 1878 they resisted the demolition of Carliol Tower for a library, just as in the 1830s they would

39 *Cragside, Rothbury, photographed in 1885. Lord Armstrong's private New Northumbria.*

have resisted the demolition of the keep for a signal box. At the 1887 Tyneside Industrial Exhibition, alongside the glittering guns and the heavy machinery stood massive models of the old Tyne Bridge and keep. The modern region had been re-enchanted because its identity had been rendered continuous, and layered. More than two million people attended the industrial exhibition in a fortnight and they certainly hadn't all gone to carp about the evils of industry.[101]

For over fifty years people had written in praise of north-east industry, and no man represented it more in the world than the region's favourite son, George Stephenson.[102] Everywhere one looked there were industries and conurbations fed by railways. From 1851 to 1911, Northumberland and Durham, with Glamorgan, were the fastest growing counties. In less than sixty years, the population of Newcastle had increased threefold to well over a quarter of a million. Civic chiefs stood astonished

98   For Grainger – Hodgkin, *Lectures*, p.214; for Palmer and Bell – Lawson, *Tyneside Celebrities*, p.266, p.366; for Armstrong – T. Bulmer & Co., *History and Directory of Newcastle upon Tyne* (Newcastle, 1887), p.84, Terry, *op. cit.*, p.110; for Bruce – Lawson, *op. cit.*, p.285, *Newcastle Journal*, 8 April 1892. See also Aaron Watson, *The Magazine of Art*, vi, 1883, p.114.
99   Bell, *At The* Works, p.12; Terry, *Northumberland*, p.87.
100   Heslop, *Northumberland Words*, p.xvi; Gibson, *Historical Memoir*, p.xi; Christie, *Northumberland*, p.12.
101   Bulmer, *History and Directory*, p.106.
102   Colls, Robert, 'Remembering George Stephenson', in Colls and Lancaster (eds), *Newcastle*. Stephenson died in 1848 but was not historicised until 1862 with a statue, near Central Station; in 1875, at the jubilee of the Stockton-Darlington line; and in 1881, on the centenary of his birth.

at the speed and scale of the changes. Every borough saw itself as a microcosm of progress and there was no shortage of businessmen who now regarded themselves, not always without reason, as heroic innovating entrepreneurs. In 1906 Swan Hunter and Wigham Richardson launched the *Mauretania* at the Neptune Yard, Wallsend. Equipped with Parsons' 70,000 horsepower steam turbines, from 1907 to 1929 she was the Blue Riband Atlantic liner, biggest and fastest in the world. She was also the *Integral*, Zamyatin's science fiction ship in his ultra modernist fantasy *We*.[103] In marine engineering, in coal, in civil engineering, in iron and steel, in chemicals, in electricity, in retail, north-east industry led the way. 'We might sweep round the whole circuit and meet similar metamorphoses in every line of radiation.'[104] A new social order was in the offing and New Northumbrians believed the old world would have to step in to redress the balance of the new.[105]

Labour Region

The other strand of modern opinion was rather different and lay in the labour movement. For every job lost in agriculture, the 19th century had brought eight better-paid jobs in coal.[106] Skilled workers were unlikely to regret the passing of recent times when wages had been low and associations unlawful, or of a distant past when serfdom had shackled labour to the land.[107] Two of the greatest modern trade unions were strongest in the North East: the Miners' Federation, described in 1897 as the 'best organised of the eight great divisions into which we classified the trade union forces'; and the United Society of Boilermakers and Iron Shipbuilders, of the metal unions 'incomparably the strongest' at a time when the United Kingdom built 80 per cent of world shipping and Sunderland built a quarter of that.[108] The trade unions, co-operative societies, clubs and institutes, football and cricket, cycling and rambling clubs, friendly societies, building societies, permanent relief funds, aged miners' homes schemes and Methodists, were all self-consciously modern movements. Their confidence in the future was strong because they all looked back to the bad old days as the time before they existed. The Pittington Amicable Cooperative Society, for instance, was proud

---

103   Myers, Alan, 'Zamyatin in Newcastle', *Slavonic and East European Review*, 68 (1990).

104   Scott, J. (ed.), *The Ecclesiastical, Political and Civic Chiefs of Newcastle-upon-Tyne* (Newcastle, 1901), p.14; Middlebrook, S., *Newcastle-upon-Tyne. Its Growth and Achievement* (Wakefield, 1968), p.258.

105   Robert Spence Watson (1837-1911) was their exemplary figure. An arch progressive in the present and a sturdy conservative when it came to the past, only his populism surpassed them both: Hon. Sec. Newcastle Lit & Phil 1862-93, founder and president Armstrong College later King's College and the University of Newcastle upon Tyne, president National Liberal Federation 1890-1902, umpire in over 100 trade disputes from 1864. Left £35,000 in his will.

106   Hunt, E.H., 'Industrialisation and Regional Inequality: Wages in Britain, 1760-1914', *Journal of Economic History*, xlvi (December 1986), p.956.

107   Key legislation liberating trade unions was in 1871, 1875 and 1906. See Fox, A., *History and Heritage. The Social Origins of the British Industrial Relations System* (London, 1986).

108   Webb, S. and B., *Industrial Democracy* (London, 1919 (1897)) pp.430, 433. Northumberland and Durham miners' unions stayed out of the MFGB (f. 1888) until 1908. Their reluctance was more to do with their comparative strength than weakness: Garside, W.R., *The Durham Miners 1919-60* (London, 1971), pp.24-5. The Webbs had estimated Northumberland and Durham as the most highly unionised counties in Britain for 1892. Hunt reckoned that over half those counties' adult males were organised. Webb, S. and B., *The History of Trade Unionism, 1660-1920* (London, 1920 (1894)), pp.741-3; Hunt, 'Regional Wage Variations', p.332.

of its rising membership, its sales, profits, dividends, reserves and proportion of share capital – a business relationship all the more impressive because it had not been exploitative.[109] In 1907 the Durham miners' leader, John Wilson, recalled the pitmen's 'Bond', and saw in it a tyrannical contract of hire only recently defeated by trade unionists like him.[110] The German, Duckershoff, observed that nowadays 'wages, and indeed everything concerning the workmen, are regulated by the Union'.[111] His fellow countryman, Baernreither, believed that British trade unions prefigured the future.[112] The Durham Miners' Association dated the regeneration of the coalfield from the time when it was formed, in the 1860s; the Cooperative retail societies dated it from when they started to open stores, in the 1850s; the Primitive Methodists dated it from when they first began to sustain growing congregations, in the 1820s.[113] All three movements published their jubilee histories and abstracts of progress.[114] At the Durham Miners' Gala (founded 1871) every banner proclaimed the modern achievements of the most productive coalfield in Britain. Alongside Biblical allegories and symbols of mutuality

40 *John Collingwood Bruce (1805-92). New Northumbrian, schoolmaster and scholar of the Roman Wall: 'high, influential and conspicuous' in the life of Newcastle (Rev. Richard Leitch, funeral oration, Newcastle Daily Journal, 8 April 1892).*

– very appropriate for a movement led by Methodists – came banner pictures of new colliery headgear, new miners' halls, new miners' homes, new red-brick terraces, new rest homes, new headquarters and new men in lounge suits who ran it all from modern offices.[115] This was a time when it was easy for Durham miners to think the future was modern, and that it lay with them.

109 Ross, A.B., *Jubilee History of Pittington Amicable Industrial Society Ltd., 1874-1924* (1924), p.76.

110 The breakthrough came in the 1860s with the formation of owners' and workers' organisations, and the 1872 decision of the owners to negotiate exclusively with their counterparts: Church, R., Hall, A. and Kanefsky, J., *History of the British Coal Industry*, vol. iii, *1830-1913* (Oxford, 1986), pp.652-58.

111 A German Coal Miner (Ernst Duckershoff), *How the English Workman Lives* (London, 1899), p.20.

112 Wilson, J., *A History of the Durham Miners' Association* (Durham, 1907), p.275; Baernreither, J.M., *English Associations of Working Men* (London, 1889), p.xiii. David Cannadine's study of the historiography of the Industrial Revolution neglects progressive Liberal and Labour opinion during the first phase c.1880-1920. If he had taken note of their optimism and modernism, his conclusions would have been different. Cannadine also concentrates too heavily on opinion in London and Oxbridge. He misses the regional dimension. The new Englishness could find little that was culturally conducive in the industrial north. Some of these criticisms also apply to Wiener's much flawed thesis, which fails to take account of the looking forward behind the apparent looking backward, or indeed of any intelligentsia, such as the New Northumbrians who were active in trying to make past and present continuous: Cannadine, D., 'The Present and the Past in the English Industrial Revolution 1880-1980', *Past and Present*, 103 (May 1984), pp.134, 167; Wiener, M.J., *English Culture and the Decline of the Industrial Spirit 1850-1980* (Cambridge, 1982), pp.41-80.

113 Methodists saw themselves, and were seen, as modern movements breaking up traditional mores: Dawson, Rev. J., *Peter Mackenzie. His Life and Labours* (London, 1896), p.51; Parkinson, George, *True Stories of Durham Pit Life* (London, 1912), p.10.

114 Wilson listed the blows for modern freedoms since 1869: the abolition of the miners' bond, the inception of checkweighmen, conciliation and arbitration boards, more 'mental activity', more 'sobriety, education and association', the diminution of accidents, improved housing, and 'the moral acceptance that working men have a right to franchise' (p.344).

115 Moyes, W.A., *The Banner Book* (Newcastle, 1974).

But the New Northumbrians were moderns as well. Consider Joseph Cowen. No provincial newspapers were more modern than his, and no force was more influential than they.[116] The *Chronicle* offices sat at the heart of modern Newcastle – near the Stephenson monument, across from the Institute of Mining Engineers, down from Central Station.[117] A strong supporter of Labour, the miners especially, Cowen dressed and talked (something) like a pitman in his Sunday best. His New Northumbria was both progressive and historicist: the 1891 'gathering' of 470 corresponding contributors to the *Monthly Chronicle* met in the keep before moving on to the *Chronicle* offices to see how a modern newspaper was mass produced. They referred to themselves as 'a movement', and an 'intellectual brotherhood', and remarked upon the warmth of exchanges regardless of party. Speakers were received 'with a storm of applause', and for the first time in the record women appear to have been present in number.[118] This was the nearest the New Northumbrians got to a political rally. But for them – unlike the labour organisations who hardly tried – reconciling past and present wasn't easy. They were a union of sentiment rather than ideas, or interests, and had had to make their peace with modernity not by embracing it but by cropping it, or romanticising it, or avoiding it, or by trying to arrange it so that all who lived in it lived in a sort of smoothed out present.[119]

But whichever way they made their peace with the past, even with the help of Cowen's army of talented journalists and contributors, there were some limits to the historical imagination.

For a start, there were some minor disillusions with the land itself. Some saw Redesdale near Otterburn as hallowed ground, but in 1889 Tomlinson had to admit he saw nothing but a 'monotonous stretch of dreary moorland'.[120] Alnwick, too, had been trumpeted as a prime site of pilgrimage, but the town wasn't as old as it looked and Warkworth, not Alnwick, had been the principal home of the Percys. As for the modern earls of Northumberland, they were only very distant relatives of the old heroes. Alnwick's tall column in honour of one of them says it was raised by a grateful tenantry to a noble duke, but it was not. The tenants were too hostile, or poor, and the duke finished the column himself.[121]

More seriously, for a discourse which placed so much emphasis on the land, New Northumbrians were apt to forget that so few owned any.[122] They were apt to forget, too, that for a discourse which set such store by racial health, their towns were among

---

116   If Armstrong was the leader, and Spence Watson the exemplar, Cowen's newspapers were power houses of the movement: Joseph Cowen (1829-1900), 'The Blaydon Brick', b. Blaydon, educ. private and Edinburgh University, Chartist and Nationalist, inherits his father's coal and firebrick business, newspaper proprietor 1859, MP for Newcastle 1873-86. Left £500,000 in his will.
117   Gosman, F., *A Day in Newcastle: A Guide* (Newcastle, 1878).
118   *Newcastle Weekly Chronicle*, 23, 30 May 1891.
119   Although women were not prominent in the movement, at any rate in its higher echelons, note the training of upper-class young women in mental control and reverie: diaries of Henrietta Trotter and Lady Cecilia Ridley, Durham County Record Office D/X/277/I and Northumberland County Record Office ZRI/32/6.
120   Tomlinson, *Comprehensive Guide*, p.296.
121   Bradley, *Northumberland*, p.15. In 1865 the *Newcastle Journal* could describe the deceased Algernon, Duke of Northumberland, as 'the greatest of all the Percys': Thompson, F.M.L., *English Landed Society in the Nineteenth Century* (London, 1963), p.81. On the column, White, *Northumberland*, p.167, but see Tomlinson, *op. cit.*, p.373, for more of the grateful tenantry.
122   Thompson, *op. cit.*, pp.114-15, 117.

the most diseased places in England.[123] Getting close to the workers was the hardest part. The most favoured workers (the least changed and most survived) were those seen as closest to nature: fishermen, peasant-types, shepherds, and so on.[124] But there were so few. In 1911, for instance, in the whole of the two counties the census recorded 1,607 fishermen and 1,266 shepherds. There were no 'peasant' categories and, even if we offset the lack of peasants by counting in agricultural labourers, they were hardly representative either: Northumberland had more dressmakers, County Durham had more boilermakers.[125] Shepherds were portrayed as the Border élite, most of them voted Liberal and it is sheer joy to find that Coquetdale's best collie was called 'Gled' in honour of the Prime Minister. And yet, County Durham had more ticket collectors and Northumberland more commercial travellers.[126] What horror to find that County Durham had more female local government officers than fishermen.

The big battalions of miners were a special case that no one could ignore. Nor could anyone deny their intimacy with nature and, as the largest single occupational group with a reputation for solidarity and organisation, they were a prize for any movement which wanted to confirm its authenticity and modernity at the same time.[127] So powerfully did the miners speak for themselves, however, it was not easy to speak on their behalf. In this light, not surprisingly perhaps, the leading New Northumbrian wrote a biography of the most eloquent coal miner.[128] What is more, miners were at the forefront of industrial conflict. It was difficult to conscript them into New Northumbrian ranks when any day they might be in conflict with a New Northumbrian coal owner.[129] In other words, if you wanted the miners in your movement, the most strenuous feats of imaginative reconstruction were called for. By emphasising their closeness to nature, their ancient arts, their clannishness, their fighting qualities, their pit talk, what could be interpreted as the survival value of their 'peculiar traits and habits', and even their ethnicity, it was possible to look into the coalfield and see a folk rather than a proletariat.[130] This approach could lead to some very strange writing indeed. Boyle, for example, began his discourse on mining

---

123   Dewsnup, E.R., *The Housing Problem in England* (Manchester, 1907) pp.49-50, 70; Hadfield, J., *Health in the Industrial North-East 1919-39* (Withernsea, nd) p.35; Goodfellow, D.M., *Tyneside. The Social Facts* (Newcastle, 1942), pp.25, 28-9, 32.

124   Bradley, *Romance of Northumberland*, p.62; Tomlinson, W.W., *Historical Notes on Cullercoats, Whitley and Monkseaton* (London, 1893), pp.93-5, 132; Christie, *Northumberland*, pp.55-6; Lang, A., *Custom and Myth* (London, 1885), p.18; Bradley, p.62.

125   *Census of England and Wales 1911*, x, Occupations and Industries, 1 (HMSO, 1914), pp.168-72, 238-42.

126   Dixon, *Upper Coquetdale*, pp.59-64; Christie described shepherds as 'the aristocrats of labour in the highlands of Northumberland': *Northumberland*, p.96.

127   In 1914 there were 239,000 coalminers recorded for Northumberland, Durham and Cumberland: Mitchell, B.R. and Deane, P., *Abstract of British Historical Statistics* (Cambridge, 1962), p.119. Even so, when one breaks down the gross figures, in 1911 Northumberland had more female domestic servants (27,367) than coal-face workers (23,652).

128   Spence Watson, Robert, *Joseph Skipsey: his life and work* (London, 1909). Watson found a second working-class hero in Thomas Dixon, of 57 Nile Street, Sunderland, cork cutter and correspondent of John Ruskin in the latter's *Time and Tide, by Weare and Tyne* (1867): see Corder, Percy, *Life of Robert Spence Watson* (London, 1914). Ruskin's letters were sent to newspapers, none of them north-eastern: Cook, E.T. and Wedderburn, A., *Works of John Ruskin* (London, 1908), xvii, pp.313-466.

129   Cadwallader Bates' history is absurdly misinformed on industrial relations: see his summary of the miners, *History*, pp.275-6.

130   Fynes, R., *Miners of Northumberland and Durham* (East Ardsley, 1971 (1873)), p.v. Observers had long seen pit communities as culturally apart and ethnically distinct. That they were 'a race apart' was an observation not diminished by government inspectors and modern social investigators. From within the industry, pitmen were said to be 'bred' to it. Cobbett foolishly thought that 'Here is the most surprising thing in the world: thousands of men and thousands of horses lived continuously underground: children born there ...': Colls, Robert, *The Pitmen of the Northern Coalfield* (Manchester, 1987), pp.11-16; Whellan, William, *History, Topography and Directory of Northumberland* (London, 1855), pp.133-6; Cobbett, *Tour*, p.38.

41 *Gathering of New Northumbrians, 1891: local correspondents to the* Monthly Chronicle of North Country Lore and Legend *(vol. 5, 1891)*

life in County Durham in 1892 with a modern section on the miners, followed by some local lore and legend, followed by a sketch of contemporary Chester le Street, followed by the curious tale of 'The Brag of Picktree'.[131] This was Folk Marxism in the making.

The simple truth was that the modern North East was a labour region, and the New Northumbrians found that hard to accept. Working-class associations in the two counties represented their members alright, but along with the rest of the British labour movement they were progressive and federal in their thinking, with a politics based on trade, not identity. After the General Strike of 1926, it was clear

---

131 Boyle, J.R., *The County of Durham* (London, 1892), pp.99-131.

that class issues would determine the region's future. New Northumbrian ways of seeing went on, of course, well into the 1930s and beyond, but without their earlier sense of mission.[132]

Nevertheless, up to 1926 the New Northumbrians were a movement broad and flexible enough to stand for the cultural region, untrammelled by the actual interests and feelings of those they claimed to represent. Eighteenth-century antiquarians had talked loosely of Northumberland and Durham, Cumbria and lowland Scotland as a distinct area, a kingdom even. New Northumbrians made that early European kingdom their template, laid other histories over it, and took their place alongside a lot of other modern rhetorics that were actively seeking to change how people thought and felt about themselves – in new civic and county identities for instance, or in schools and colleges and youth movements, or in the army, or through sport or architecture, subjects scarcely dealt with here but vital all the same.[133] Further research into all these themes will pay rich rewards.[134]

What is more, the New Northumbrians succeeded in annexing the modern identity of north-east England not only because they had in their ranks the talent and resources of men like Armstrong, Watson, and Cowen, but also because their brand of identity politics was beginning to dominate the national agenda. After three generations of industrialisation and globalisation, a new English nationalism was beginning to show.[135] The English were being told that regardless of the modern world they were *essentially* a peasant folk who lived in country villages, or they were seafarers who had launched the empire in the billowing days of Good Queen Bess. And now that a few Oxford dons[136] had declared the Industrial Revolution to be a national calamity, national identity was taking up residence again in the south where a reformed public-school system, a rebuilt imperial capital, a global money market and a rekindled love of the countryside were all finding new life. The middle classes were learning to love their suburban Home County homes. At the height of their *northern* industrial powers, therefore, the English, the most urban people in the world, were being told that their true spirit had its being in college cloisters and south country lanes.[137]

---

132   For the pivotal significance of the General Strike in British politics see McKibbin, Ross, *Classes and Cultures. England 1918-1951* (Oxford, 1998), p.58. For an example of how the New Northumbrian conventions went on into the 1930s, see Fairfax, J., 'Moors and Fells', in H.J. Massingham (ed.), *The English Countryside* (London, 1939).

133   'All buildings carry meaning, and all may convey a message': Whyte, William, *Oxford Jackson. Architecture, Education, Status and Style 1835-1924* (Oxford, 2006), pp.24-5. See Usherwood, P., Beach, J., Morris, C., *Public Sculpture of North East England* (Liverpool, 2000).

134   And has done so in the work of Kota Ito, 'The making of community identity in Newcastle upon Tyne 1850-2000' (unpublished PhD, University of Leicester, 2007).

135   There were growing English identity crises, with rural depopulation, urban poverty and overcrowding, mass immigration, Irish nationalism, and suffragette feminism. Abroad, threats stemmed largely from imperial and commercial rivalries, particularly the war in South Africa: Colls, Robert and Dodd, Philip (eds), *Englishness. Politics and Culture 1880-1920* (London, 1986), and Kumar, Krishan, *The Making of English National Identity* (Cambridge, 2003).

136   Notably Arnold Toynbee and friends: *Lectures on the Industrial Revolution* (London, 1906 (1884)).

137   This argument was first established by Colls and Dodd in 1986 and taken further by Kumar in 2003. For debates over how much further, see Kumar, Smith, Reynolds and Colls in *Nations and Nationalism*, 13, 2 (April 2007). Rubinstein traced the southward tilt of the middle classes and Wiener tried to connect the culture of southern élites to declining economic performance: Rubinstein, W.D., 'Education and the Social Origins of British Elites 1880-1970', *Past and Present*, 112 (August 1986); Wiener, *Decline of the Industrial Spirit*, p.42. For southern geographical bias in the representation of English culture and landscape: Gammon, V., 'Folk Song Collecting in Sussex and Surrey 1843-1914', *History Workshop*, 10, Autumn 1980, pp.67-8; Howkins,

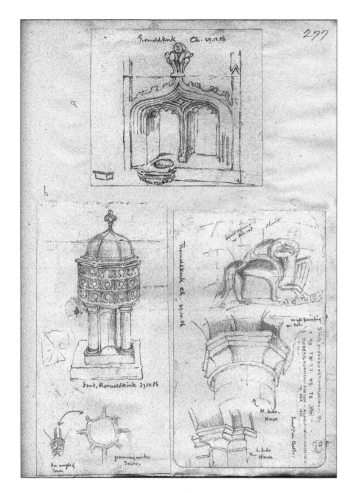

42   *The sketch book of Robert Blair, Romaldkirk Church, County Durham, 27 April 1886.*

If Englishness lived in the south, what place for the north of England? Far away from the metropolis and the great defining forces of English political life, with no national institutions, no fashionable schools, no glamorous military bases, and no royal palaces or estates – the North East was at the wrong end of the map. With no downland, no thatched cottages, no county cricket, no literary icons and precious few college cloisters or drawling gentlemen in them – it looked wrong and it talked wrong. The Bowes family of County Durham may have been about to produce a future queen, but when they did it was Elizabeth Bowes-Lyon's Scottish-baronial, not her northern-industrial, ancestry that was invoked.

But north-east England was a heartland of the Industrial Revolution. It had the oldest and the best organized working class. Its most famous sons were known all over the world as England's greatest industrial revolutionaries. If dirty cities, growing trade unions, and clanking steam engines were a threat to Englishness, there were

---

A., 'The Discovery of Rural England', in Colls and Dodd, *Englishness*, p.64. For a more complicated view of the bias: Matless, D., *Landscape and Englishness* (London, 1998), pp.16-18.

plenty up north. This is not to say that the New Northumbrians were anti-English. On the contrary, they were pro-English, but only in their own way. By establishing their own distinctive people and place they shifted the balance of national history: Cuthbert over Augustine, Durham over Canterbury, Northumbria over Wessex, Norse over French, or Latin, balladry over poesy, moorland over downland, iron and coal over college and cloister.[138] In politics, up to 1914, New Northumbrians were nearer the Scots and Welsh than the southern English. New Northumbrians did for the North what Kenneth Morgan's Welsh national revivalists did for Wales: they brought a 'new depth' to the business of being Northern, and they made history 'a living element in the daily experience of the … people'.[139] In culture, the movement had to wait for over fifty years before its credo was distilled into a single work of art – Basil Bunting's *Briggflatts*.[140]

New Northumbrians, then, were English people who found other ways of being English. To be born in this place, to speak, or to be able to speak this dialect, to look like this, to work

43 *Jimmy Durham (1885-1910), 2nd Battalion Durham Light Infantry, found in 1886 on the battlefield in Egypt and raised by the regiment.*

like this, to share this fate, was to be a Northumbrian. But the most important gift was the imagination, for that controlled all the others. In 1913 Jean Terry rehearsed her drum and trumpet history where Border heroes fell in bloody encounters for noble ends. According to her, men died but the *geist* went on.[141] One year later, tens of thousands of men would roll up for Empire, for Britain, for England, for county, for Northumbrian homeland, race, language and history, all in their ethnic regiments – the Northumberland Fusiliers, the Durham Light Infantry, the Tyneside Scottish, the Tyneside Irish – never to return. Nothing, they were told, could be more natural.

---

138   But see Dave Russell's claim that the myths and memories of the ancient kingdom 'have never been able to generate' an alternative to (southern) versions of Englishness: *Looking North. Northern England and the National Imagination* (Manchester, 2004), p.274.

139   Morgan, K. O., *Rebirth of a Nation. Wales 1880-1980* (Oxford, 1981), p.90.

140   Bunting was abroad for most of the inter- and immediate post-war years and missed the break with historicism. He came back to a region that, in his own eyes at least, remained New Northumbrian. About the only thing Basil Bunting and Cadwallader Bates ever could have shared was interest in the life of Eric Bloodaxe, murdered 954, last king of an independent Northumbria (or so they reckoned). See David Rollason and Nick Everett's chapter in this volume.

141   Terry, *Northumberland*, p.184.

10

The Irish and Scots on Tyneside

JOHN A. BURNETT AND DONALD M. MACRAILD

Jack Lawson recalled Boldon Colliery at the turn of the century as 'a typical example of the way in which the county of Durham had become a sort of social melting pot owing to the rapid development of the coalfield during the nineteenth century'. On the streets you could hear all the dialects: Lancashire, Cumbrian and Yorkshire; Staffordshire, Cornish, and Welsh; and Scots and Irish. 'It was a polyglot population, and the Durham dialect, so marked among the children, did not hold unrivalled sway among the elders.'[1] What Lawson said of Boldon could be said of the region as a whole.

This chapter tells two stories of migration. The Scots merged into the host society more readily and from an earlier point, offering a cultural distinctiveness that was embraced rather than rejected. This was not so with the Irish. For them, religion and politics attracted hostility and rejection, though not as much as in some other regions.

Early Arrival, Settlement and Distribution

The Act of Union in 1707 strengthened the economic and commercial bonds between England and Scotland. Scottish labour was a significant presence on the wharves of the Tyne and Scots were involved in the riotous activity that shook Newcastle's quayside in 1740.[2] In this period, the connection between the region and Scotland was not merely reflected in migratory interactions, important though these were. Proximity and place also shaped politics in the north. In 1745, as the Jacobite army of Prince Charles moved south and occupied Edinburgh, the people of Newcastle – the next major population centre if the army chose to march south

---

1 Lawson, Jack, *A Man's Life* (London, 1949), p. 37.
2 Ellis, J., 'Urban conflict and popular violence: the Guildhall riots of 1740 in Newcastle upon Tyne', *International Review of Social History*, 25 (1980).

down the east coast – were panicked not by their Scots inhabitants, but by their Scottish neighbours. The walls were strengthened, a militia was raised and clergymen united to 'preach loyal sermons on the dangers of popery'. But locals, showing a wariness of alienating the large number of poor resident Scots involved in the coal trade, 'differentiated "savage Highlanders" from the more civilised Lowland Scots'.[3] The Jacobite episode yielded a unified response in Newcastle, but Scots remained ethnically distinctive. The Newcastle-Scots dissenters, who signed a petition in 1772 for exemption from the 39 Articles of the Church of England, were criticised for bringing with them 'the Prejudices of their Education and that invincible attachment to the Peculiarities of their own Country which so strongly marks the character of the North Britain [sic]'. As Wilson has shown, Scots Protestants 'had few entrees into the political nation except through a rabid anti-Catholicism and [expressions of] loyalty'.[4] As the disloyalty of the Stuarts passed into memory, so likelihood of Scottish integration grew.

For the Irish, Catholicism remained *the* one definition of their difference well beyond the 19th century. Catholicism marked out much of the Irish community as different. In the 18th century persons of that faith began to register in social reportage concerning the poor of towns such as Newcastle.[5] Whilst Catholics were noticed, and though they sometimes faced violence and exclusion, the region did not develop the sort of sectarian culture associated with, for example, Lancashire in this period. Nor did the Irish in the North East evoke the depth of loathing they found in the West of Scotland. A sign of this relative calm is revealed by the knowledge that the region did not even merit a visit in 1834 from Sir George Cornewall Lewis, who investigated the poor Irish of Scotland and England in connection with Poor Law investigations at that time.[6] By 1851, however, as new pits opened and as new industry developed on both banks of the Tyne, the North East became one of the four most important regions for Irish migration.

While most of the Irish on Tyneside were Catholics, a significant minority was Protestant.[7] Indeed, the Protestant cohort goes some way to explain the early and important Orange presence in the North East. The Orange Order, founded in 1795 in Ulster, was imported into England and Scotland by soldiers returning from the suppression of the Irish Rising of 1798. In the North East, the Order offered a meeting place for Scots and Irish migrants alike. In 1835 the region had eight lodges: two in Newcastle, and one each in Durham, Sunderland, Wallsend, North Shields, Morpeth and Darlington.[8] Printed records note the names of lodges in various towns, and one of the earliest Orange songbooks from this period was published on Tyneside

3   Wilson, K., *The Sense of the People: Politics, Culture and Imperialism in England, 1715-1785* (Cambridge, 1995), pp.333-4.
4   *Ibid*, pp.369-70.
5   *Report of Newcastle-upon-Tyne Catholic Defence Association* (1827) in S. Doherty, 'English and Irish Catholics in Northumberland, *c*.1745-1860' (PhD, Queen's University of Belfast, 1987), pp.63-4.
6   PP (8936) XXXIV: *A Report into the Condition of the Irish Poor in Great Britain, 1834* (1836).
7   See MacRaild, D.M., *Faith, Fraternity and Fighting: Orangeism and Irish Migration in the north of England, c.1850-1920* (Liverpool, 2005), chs 1-2.
8   *Select Committee Report on Orange Institutions in Great Britain and the Colonies* (1835), appendix 19, pp.141-4.

around 1817.[9] No clue was given as to membership.[10] Certainly, Rainton and Murton remained important pockets of Orangeism until the early 1880s. During the mid-19th century, the Orange press made regular mentions of a vigorous North East scene, mostly focusing on the frequent meetings and dinners at local hostelries. In 1852 there was a gathering of Orangemen at the *Wheatsheaf Inn*, Gateshead; in 1854 an un-named lodge (no. 1211) met in Heworth at the *Royal Standard*; and in the same year Newcastle members gathered to celebrate both the foiling of the Gunpowder Plot (1605) and the legacy of William of Orange.[11]

The high proportion of Ulstermen among the Irish partly explains such ultra Protestant celebrations. Belfast, Newry and Londonderry had historic connections with the Isle of Man (an important staging post), Barrow, Whitehaven, Workington and Maryport. The assistant overseer of the poor for Newcastle demonstrated that contemporaries were aware of these patterns when he told a parliamentary enquiry in the 1850s that '[t]he Irish mostly land at Whitehaven'; they then 'so far as I have learned make their way directly to Newcastle'.[12] Middlesbrough, Sunderland and the towns of Tyneside were also major settlement points; and most towns in between had distinct Irish-born populations at mid-century, though these proportions were generally not as high as in the core areas of Lancashire, Yorkshire and western Scotland.

Consolidation, Growth and the 'Condition of England'

During the 1840s, the people of north-east England rallied to the distress calls emanating from two famine-torn worlds: Ireland, and the Highlands and Islands of Scotland. Various charity balls and other fundraising events were held with assorted local dignitaries in attendance. Despite the massive differences in scale, the north of Scotland initially was afforded pre-eminence. There was more first-hand reporting of the situation in the Highlands and greater press coverage for charitable events on Tyneside.[13] Irish fundraising came later and was smaller in scale, supplemented by collections at local works, or under the auspices of the fledging Roman Catholic community.[14]

The Catholic Irish met a contradictory response from the host population. Sometimes the mood was positive; at other times it was not. For example, the drama of the St Patrick's Day parade of 1846 was appreciated as a contribution to the culture of a city which enjoyed a reputation for street sociability:[15]

9   *Loyal Orangemen's Song Book: Being a collection of the most approved songs now in use by that Institution* (North Shields, 1815?).
10   Local remembrances some years later associated the new waves of Orangemen with the blackleg labour introduced by Lord Londonderry from his Irish estates in 1844. The point was made very forcibly by a Sunderland lawyer, W.W. Robson, as he defended Irish Catholics in Jarrow against charges laid before them for attacking an Orange procession in the town in 1879. *Jarrow Guardian*, 25 July 1879.
11   *Orange and Protestant Banner*, February 1852; October, November 1854.
12   *Poor Law Reports*, Parliamentary Papers, 1854-55, xiii, p. 31.
13   The *Gateshead Observer* carried a series of reports on the Scottish famine: 2, 9, 16 January 1847.
14   *Ibid.*, 9 January, 17 April 1847.
15   Lancaster, Bill, 'Sociability and the city', in R. Colls and B. Lancaster (eds), *Newcastle-upon-Tyne: A Modern History* (Chichester, 2001), pp.319-40.

On St Patrick's day (Tuesday), the members walked in procession through the streets of Newcastle and Gateshead, with music and banners. The number was about two hundred; and they presented a brilliant spectacle, arrayed in their peculiar dresses and decorations, of which green formed the predominant colour.'[16]

The *Observer* also carried a report entitled 'Catholic Lectures' which noted that, during the past two weeks, the Rev. W.A. Grant of St Cuthbert's College, Ushaw, had been delivering a series of 'instructive lectures' in Newcastle which examined the 'solemn services and ceremonies' used by the Catholic Church.[17] The report ended by claiming that the heightened attention given by the audience 'must convince the reverend gentleman of the great interest they experienced in the various subjects which he so plainly and so eloquently brought before them'.[18]

The newspaper set a more foreboding tone in a piece on a speech given at a dinner held for seamen under the auspices of a local Protestant organisation, the South Shields Loyal Standard Association. It was reported that the Rev. Mr Griffiths, curate of St Hilda's church, instructed his audience to set a 'good example' when they visited other parts of the world. This was important not just in 'heathen lands', he said, but 'shores where the people were sunk in Roman Catholic idolatry and superstition'. He inviting his audience to show, by their actions, 'the superiority of Protestantism over Romanism', and the dinner concluded with songs including 'The Genius of Albion'. This particular melody, 'breathing defiance to France' and 'smelling of brimstone and saltpetre', was punctuated with choruses from 'God Save the Queen', 'Hearts of Oak' and 'Rule Britannia'.[19]

Such an attitude was clearly a contributory factor to the violence that sprung up in the region during the 1840s. An incident at Felling offers an interesting example of the way the press sought to manage a potentially explosive incident in such a manner as to moderate behaviour.[20] On 13 June 1846, the *Gateshead Observer* reported how 'three to four hundred Irishmen' had made 'an unprecedented attack on their English fellow-workmen' at the Lee & Allen chemical works. The English workers retaliated, leaving a number of Irishmen severely wounded. The report concluded in dismissive fashion: 'Meanwhile we will not enter into the causes of the conflict.'[21] There was a critical backlash and the newspaper apologised, adding that it was happy to report that the workmen at the chemical works were now 'on the most friendly terms'.[22] The charm offensive continued with a lengthy and detailed description of the 'extensive' chemical works of Messrs Lee & Co. and the firm's excellent labour relations.[23] The reporters praised the 'order and harmony with which

---

16 *Gateshead Observer*, 21 March 1846.
17 *Ibid.*
18 *Ibid.*
19 *Ibid*, 24 January 1846.
20 Kearney, Tony, *Painted Red: A Social History of Consett 1840-1990* (Consett, 1990), 4-5; *Newcastle Journal*, 16 August 1848.
21 *Gateshead Observer*, 13 June 1846.
22 *Ibid.*
23 *Ibid.*, 27 June 1846.

the two races mingle and labour together, with no observable distinction amongst them, save the differing stamp which Nature has imprinted upon the face of Celt and Saxon', concluding that: 'There is, we believe, none but the kindliest feeling between the sons of the sister-countries.' The key point about the potential for social harmony among workers would be spelled out a decade later. In an explanation of the sectarian division of labour that characterised the dirty and unhealthy chemical industry of the Tyne, the same newspaper commented:

> A hard-working fellow is Pat, and shirks no labour, however severe or however dirty. An Englishman or a Scotchman may not be very fastidious, and yet there are jobs in our chemical or other works which neither John or Sandy likes to put his hand to.[24]

The famine exacerbated already growing fears about the 'Condition of England'. Tyneside was not untypical in making the Irish scapegoats for a deeper social malaise. As elsewhere, ratepayers in Newcastle, Sunderland and other major towns of the region began to complain that the Irish were costing them dear in poor rates.[25] If conditions were already poor, so the logic seemed to say, the Irish made them worse:

> The great influx of Irish during the last few months has caused all the lodging houses to be overflowing. In rooms of very small dimensions and very imperfect ventilation, sixteen or twenty persons sleep at night … In Manningham's Entry, Sandgate, in a wretched garret, fifteen feet by ten feet (the average height not six feet) … lay a poor woman called Bridget Carroll, with her four children all ill of fever, in a most abandoned state, for being unable to keep themselves, their neighbours, for fear of contagion, had refused them any aid.[26]

While the Irish poor suffered miserable conditions in large centres, like Newcastle, they also had to contend with poor environs in smaller places, in market towns such as Morpeth, where ordinary Irishmen, including Michael Connolly, lived in a small dwelling with no fewer than 17 boarders.[27]

Any pity that may have been shown to a starving Ireland did not diminish the anger directed against the insurrectionary activity of the Young Irelanders in 1848.[28] In a press item headed 'England for the English', Irish migrants were reminded of the sleeping giant in their midst:

> Our friend Pat should not have all the fun to himself. His cry of 'Ireland for the Irish' should be met by the cry of 'England for the English'. He is eternally grumbling because Englishmen hold office in Ireland. Well, then, let Englishmen retort the growl, and try

---

24   *Ibid.*, 19 July 1856.
25   *Newcastle Journal*, 1 May 1847. A point regularly made elsewhere, see Neal, F., *Black 47* (Basingstoke, 1997), *passim*.
26   *Newcastle Journal*, 19 June 1847.
27   See Doherty, 'English and Irish Catholics', 189ff. Also Rawlinson, R., *Report to the General Board of Health … Borough of Morpeth and the Village of Bedlington* (London, 1849).
28   Saville, J., *1848: the British State and the Chartist Movement* (Cambridge, 1988), *passim*.

to get rid of their Irish rulers. Why should the Duke of Wellington, an Irishman, be Commander-in-Chief of the Army? And Mr. Fergus O'Connor, another Irishman, be Commander-in-Chief of the Chartists? There is Mr. McGrath too, whose name smells woundily of Ireland:- he is Chairman of the National Convention. And is not Mrs. Bray, a Limerick lady, the nurse of our youngest Princess? Pat 'rules the Court, the Camp, the Commons'. And yet the Celtic rogue is continually complaining that the Saxon has all his own way![29]

Political tensions in Ireland presented problems enough, but in 1850 Protestants organised petitions and large open-air meetings to protest at the restoration of the Catholic hierarchy in England and what they saw as the 'Papal Aggression' of the Vatican's naming of 14 new cardinals, of whom only four were Italian and one was Dr Nicholas Wiseman, the new Archbishop of Westminster. In May 1851 the self-styled Newcastle 'No Popery' lecturer, 'Ranter Dick', was met with violent opposition from the Sandgate Irish – captured in a local song, the 'Horrid War i' Sandgeyt'.[30]

The mid-century period bore witness to a regular flow of such incidents.[31] Consett, the 'Yukon' of the north, was divided along ethnic lines, with adjoining communities in Consett (largely Protestant) and Blackhill (largely Catholic) fostering serious disturbances from the 1840s. None was of significant scale until 'The Battle of the Blue Heaps' of April 1858 in which armed mobs numbering up to 2,000 men were only dispersed by the arrival of a 200-strong contingent of the Nottingham Militia.[32]

In 1858 more violence erupted in Sunderland. At first the mayor thought his town had been the site of Orange-Green violence of the type seen at Felling two years before.[33] The Sunderland riot of 27 September 1858 apparently occurred because an Irish publican, Michael Digney, lost his alcohol licence.[34] The fact that a rival beerseller, Michael Norton, was allowed to continue with his trade incensed Digney. He and his friends went round to Norton's pub in Robinson's Lane and attacked him. A fight soon became a riot and the resulting magistrates' session was a carnival of walking wounded, which the press captured with a mocking, racialised tone:

As complainant after complainant came into this court, and the unmistakable Milesian phiz popped up in the witness box, the display of adhesive plaster was seen to be most abundantly spread over each luckless skull ... [but] the breadth of the plaster did

---

29   *Gateshead Observer*, 22 April 1848.

30   See Cooter, 'Irish in County Durham and Newcastle', 112-15. Also Scott, Caroline L., 'A comparative re-examination of Anglo-Irish relations in nineteenth-century Manchester, Liverpool and Newcastle-upon-Tyne' (unpublished PhD, University of Durham, 1998), p. 104 and ch. 3 more generally.

31   Opposing views on the relative ease of Irish integration into the North East are provided by Cooter, R.J., 'The Irish in County Durham and Newcastle', and Neal, F., 'English-Irish conflict in the North East of England', in J.C. Belchem and P. Buckland (eds), *The Irish in British Labour History*, conference proceedings in Irish Studies, 1 (Liverpool, 1992), pp.59-85.

32   Kearney, 'Painted Red', pp.2-8.

33   For a fuller discussion of the context and meaning of this violence, see MacRaild, D.M., '"Abandon Hibernicisation": Priests, Ribbonmen and an Irish Street Fight in the North East of England in 1858', *Historical Research*, 76, 194 (Nov. 2003), pp.557-71.

34   *Sunderland Herald*, 24 September, 1 October 1858.

not exactly correspond—a broadly hinted insinuation that Pat trusted more to the number of square inches in the plaster than to the strength of his case on its own unadorned merits.[35]

Two weeks later the mayor received new intelligence about the riot and was anxious to discover whether it had been the result of divisions between Orangemen and Ribbonmen. The Ribbon Society, an anti-Orange organisation first formed by Catholics in Ireland in 1819,[36] was a shadowy, clandestine organisation which, until this point, had made little or no impact on Tyneside or Wearside. The events at Sunderland turned out not to be Orange-versus-Green affairs but the result of power struggles within the local Ribbon Society.[37] The bishop immediately sent his right-hand man to investigate the matters. At about the same time, the Vatican itself was being warned of such activities among the Irish in the North East.[38]

Forging Cultures

The Scots attracted much less attention. Lacking the Irishman's badge of religious difference, many were better off, too, from artisans and skilled workers to doctors and industrialists. Scots clerics were much more likely to be Protestant, often Presbyterian. Skilled Scottish workers were in such demand in the local shipyards in the 1850s that labels such as 'Little Aberdeen' or 'Scottish Colony' were ascribed to the residential clusters they formed. Scotsmen – capitalists and workers alike – were behind the launch of Hebburn's shipbuilding tradition. And across the water the situation was similar. At Howdon, Clelland's yard was opened by a Scot and relied heavily upon Scottish and Irish labour.

From the 1860s, there was a noticeable Scottish dimension to the North East's renascent Orange tradition. One prominent Scotsman who made regular appearances on the Orange platform was the Rev. Thompson, of the Caledonian Church, Newcastle. As he addressed dinners and soirées, Thompson's colleagues included men with names such as Reid, Buchanan, Douglass, Robertson and M'Pherson. The latter, a resident of Newcastle, demonstrated his ethnic allegiances and his literary pretensions by reciting 'a piece of poetry of his own composition, referring to the events of 1688'.[39]

As the century progressed, the terms 'Scotch' or 'Caledonian', which had been used to describe some of the churches in the region, were slowly abandoned:

Proximity to Scotland does not suffice to explain how religious life and methods in Northumberland have been to so large an extent moulded by Presbyterian influences. Presbyterianism was no recent upstart there and no mere intruder from the North. Its

35 *Ibid.*, 1 October 1858.
36 See Belchem, J.C., *Merseypride: Essays in Liverpool Exceptionalism* (Liverpool, 2000), pp.67-100.
37 MacRaild, 'Abandon Hibernicisation', p. 565.
38 Fr Frederick Bethum, a Catholic missionary in Gateshead, divulged to the Vatican that many Irish Catholics in the Tyneside area were members of secret societies. *Vatican Archives*, Scritture Originali Nelle Congrgazioni, Vol. 13 (1852-4), p. 295, cited by Neal, 'English-Irish conflict', pp.65, 82 n.25.
39 *Orange and Protestant Banner*, May 1865.

venerable career and associations, however chequered, give it a right to be considered a native plant, indigenous to this soil; and those who mingle with the Northumbrian Presbyterians are soon made aware how quickly they resent the idea of their own Presbyterianism being in any sense 'Scotch', either of recent importation or of foreign development.[40]

Others were more willing to acknowledge the Scottish connection. A cursory glance at the local and regional press demonstrates the influence of Scotsmen in the Presbyterian church and the few existing records of the region's Scottish societies point to a largely middle-class membership.

It was, however, a robust and developing regional economy that lured and retained most migrants. The Irish were well placed to take advantage of new opportunities, and in places such as Bedlington, Bishop Auckland, Shotley Bridge and Consett, mining, iron-making and, later, steelmaking occupied increasing numbers. At Tow Law Irish migrants were able to obtain work as miners, reflecting a shortage of native labour and an easier seam-type. But not without opposition. Indeed, in the coal districts workers and owners generally shared a degree of hostility to all long-distance migrants, though some employers sought out experienced miners, such as the Cornish.[41] The Irish were sought after for trades where work was a daily act of endurance. Thus they found a firm foothold in the red-hot conditions of the gas industry. Men such as the 'staunch Roman Catholic' manager of one Durham coking works demonstrated the migrant's networking skills by giving jobs to fellow Irish co-religionists whilst sending his men, who were being paid to shovel coal and tend furnaces, up to the Catholic church or youth club to mend gates or seal boilers.[42] In this way, work, nationality and religion came together.

The Scots had been less numerous than the Irish during the famine period, but this began to change from the 1860s. By the end of the century they were generally twice as numerous as the Irish-born (Table 3). The Irish generally lived more along the riverside or in densely populated poor areas elsewhere. Occupational matters brought these groups together, but ethnic geographies kept them apart.[43]

A strong communal presence was partly shaped by geographically well-defined living quarters. It was also shaped, in the Irish case, by their utter dominance of the Roman Catholic churches and schools. By the later 19th century there were more than 60 Catholic churches and missions in County Durham and Newcastle, most of them with schools. The priesthood of the North East was more English than Irish and undoubtedly served to dampen down nationalist ardour, though the linking of 'faith' and 'nation' remained an important emotional attachment.[44]

---

40 Drysdale, Rev. A.H., *History of the Presbyterians in England: Their Rise, Decline and Revival* (London, 1889), p. 567.
41 And the unions sometimes paid to send them home, which tells another story about the struggles of pit workers which cannot be gone into here. For migrant miners, see Church, R., *The History of the British Coal Industry*, vol. 3: *1830-1914: Victorian Pre-eminence* (Oxford, 1986), pp.219-24; for the North East context of such labour-relations issues see Colls, R., *Pitmen of the Great Northern Coalfield: Work, Culture and Protest, 1790-1850* (Manchester, 1987).
42 Hudson, Mark, *Coming Back Brockens* (London, 1995), p. 85.
43 Barke, M., 'The people of Newcastle', in Colls and Lancaster (eds), *Newcastle upon Tyne: A Modern History*, figs 7.10 and 7.11, p.161, and the discussion around there.
44 Cooter, R.J., 'The Irish in County Durham and Newcastle, c.1840-1880' (MA, Durham University, 1972), 62-107 (figures from App I, pp.271-2).

In 1872 Hugh Heinrick, 'special correspondent' for the Dublin-based *Nation* newspaper, made a whirlwind tour of England reporting back on Irish activity in an effort to assess and tap potential votes for the Home Rule movement. Included in his analysis was a colourful depiction of the lives of the Irish. Although Irish workers remained over-represented in the heavy and dirty aspects of most trades, Heinrick noted strong suggestions of social improvement. He noticed in Newcastle greater signs of social and economic achievement – the emergence of a genuine Irish middle class for instance – that might only be bettered in Liverpool, Glasgow or Manchester. Throughout the area that Heinrick called the 'Vale of Tyne' he estimated there were some 83,000 Irish.[45] A similar survey was conducted twenty years later by the Liverpool-Irish nationalist organiser, John Denvir. Drawing on eye-witness accounts and extensive first-hand experience of travelling and campaigning, Denvir felt the Irish in Newcastle had 'attained to good social and public positions' – men such as Bernard McAnulty, the businessman, nationalist and councillor, was one of the 'foremost citizens of the place'. Yet, as late as 1890, the Irish continued to dominate the most disagreeable sectors, such as Tyneside's chemical industry. In Sunderland and Newcastle, where many had begun to break into craft trades, most were still working on the waterfront, usually as labourers, but also in shipbuilding. Others were found to be working in fitting works and engine shops, iron-works, blast-furnaces, or in the pits. Denvir was quite sure the Irish had also begun to break into coal-face hewing, an elite occupation.[46] Both men noted an obvious political culture among these Irish and a clear cultural sense too, shaped by their affinity for sport, culture and religion.

In a booklet of Geordie Ridley's songs produced in 1863, the 'Gateshead Poet and Vocalist' was described as the 'most successful delineator … of local, Irish, Comic and Sentimental Songs'.[47] There was clearly a market for Irish culture of this sort, as was reflected in the melodies adopted from popular Irish airs such as 'Pat of Mullingar' for Ridley's 'Joey Jones'. Indeed it has been claimed that this appropriated air 'is lent a characteristically Irish bravado and self-praise by the Irish tune'.[48] Similarly, The Keel Row – 'undisputedly a Tyneside song' – had 'a slight Scottish influence' due in part to the contribution of Scots to the occupation of keelman.[49]

Scots migrants were also particularly involved in physical pursuits, such as association football. Scottish professionals were brought into the leagues of northern England to a raise the standards of play.[50] On a less lofty level, different local and regional football leagues carried numerous teams with clear Scots markers, such as 'Tyne Dock Caledonians', 'Jarrow Caledonians', 'Hebburn Black Watch', 'Cramlington Black Watch', 'Monkseaton Celtic' and 'Monkseaton Rangers'. 'Shankhouse Blackwatch'

45   'Letter XV', H. Heinrick, *A Survey of the Irish in England (1872)* (London, 1990), edited with an introduction by A. O'Day.
46   Denvir, J., *The Irish in Britain from the Earliest Times to the Fall of Parnell* (London, 1892), pp.442, 443, 444.
47   Harker, D., *Geordie Ridley: 'Gateshead Poet and Vocalist'* (Newcastle, 1973), p. 9.
48   *Ibid*, p. 13.
49   Simpson, D.A., *Hadrian's Vale and Geordieland: The people, history and folklore of the River Tyne and Roman Wall Country* (Durham, 1991), p. 37.
50   See Garnham, N. and Jackson, A., 'Who invested in Victorian football clubs? The evidence from Newcastle-upon-Tyne', *Soccer and Society*, vol. 4, no. 1 (2003), pp.57-70.

(of Shankhouse, population 1,000) was one of the great teams of the 1880s and '90s. Between 1884 and 1895 they won the Northumberland Football Association Senior Challenge Cup six times, and in 1887 reached the fifth round of the FA Cup before losing 0-4 to Aston Villa at St James' Park. While Scottish names may have been chosen simply on a whim or because of fashion and popularity, their location often corresponded with other ethnic markers such as Presbyterian churches, Burns clubs, and the like.

In a fundraising concert for Hebburn Argyle FC held in the Artillery Drill Hall in Hebburn, in December 1891, a large audience was present which 'showed that the club must have earned a very great measure of public favour'.[51] The programme was varied but included 'some of the best songs of England, Scotland, and Ireland, and one or two of those also which have found favour in our own neighbourhood'. The chairman for the evening, Dr Tonar, addressed the audience during the interval. He praised the members of the club and called for other clubs to be formed.[52] He believed that football was a 'manly game', requiring 'manly exercise'. Hebburn Argyle, moreover, he felt were deserving of great honours because they 'belonged to the place'.[53]

At a workhouse Christmas concert in Hebburn reported in January 1909[54] the entertainment was supplied by a number of people and included songs such as 'Dear Little Shamrock' and 'Auld Scotch Song'. The report noted how 'Mr John Foy gave several humorous Irish and local ditties. Mr Peter Taylor scored with his imitations of [Harry] Lauder, in "Foo the Noo", "Scotch Bluebell" and "Early Rising".'[55] Perhaps a more intriguing item of news was listed immediately below the Christmas concert report, communicating a 'successful social' that was held in the St Andrew's Institute 'in connection with St. Aloysius' Institute'.[56] These institutions relate to the main Presbyterian and Roman Catholic churches in the shipbuilding district of Hebburn. Although there was intermittent ethnic and religious tension in these areas, the dominant characteristic was one of co-existence based on shared circumstances.

Thus, in November 1891, a local newspaper reported that the Walker branch of the [Irish] National League hosted a concert in the Mechanics' Hall, held in order to raise funds for 'Irish evicted tenants'. The evening's proceedings consisted mainly of songs that, 'as might be expected, were of a National character'.[57] The same edition of the paper also informed readers that the Burns' Club, 'a thoroughly Scotch Institution', would be holding a celebration of 'good old St Andrew' in the same venue the following week. In addition to this, 'a grand Scotch night' had been arranged by those who ran the weekly concerts in St Kilda's. The proceedings were described in typical fashion: 'All the music and songs will be Scotch, and the latest Scotch minister who has just come to this town – Rev. Wm. Angus, of the Congregational Church – gives

---

51 *Jarrow Express and Tyneside Advertiser*, 4 December 1891.
52 *Ibid.*
53 *Ibid.*
54 *Wallsend Herald*, 1 January 1909.
55 *Ibid.*
56 *Ibid.*
57 *Jarrow Express and Tyneside Advertiser*, 27 November 1891.

the address. Other Scotch features could be named, but these will suffice. I need not say that the hall will be crammed that night.'[58]

The local Orange Order, with its Irish, Scots and English members, experienced a remarkable transformation in fortunes between 1880 and 1900. There was a dramatic downturn in support in east Durham, which had once been a stronghold among Irish workers on Londonderry lands. But the west Durham movement, focused on Consett, remained stronger for much longer, finally closing in the 1970s. Much earlier than that, in the 1880s, there was a striking disappearance of the five-strong lodge network in the south Northumberland pit-villages of New Hartley, Seaton Delaval, Backworth, Holywell and Dudley.[59] At about the same time, the shipbuilding towns of the north bank of the Tyne assumed leadership. In the 1870s, Wallsend became home to many Scots and Irish shipyard workers and these men instituted Loyal Orange Lodge 395 'Inniskillen True Blues'. North Shields, Walker and Howdon also developed lodges at about the same time.[60]

The press coverage of the Orange Order in the North East was thin by comparison to the interest shown in Cumberland and Lancashire. Moreover, the political culture of Tyneside was such that Irish nationalists were given approving press reportage at every turn. There was some justification for this in terms of numbers: when a parade of the Ancient Order of Hibernians (AOH) turned out at Wallsend in 1912, at a time when Home Rule politics was high on the agenda, 500 marchers from nine towns showed up. The concern of the AOH, however, was essentially religious, and a priest from St Columba's church, Fr Toner, played upon the schools' question. This Irish Catholic turnout compares to the mere hundred Orangemen who, in the previous month, had marched the Sunday before the 'Glorious Twelfth' in Hebburn.[61] And sometimes the strength of local Irish Catholic elements translated into hard political currency, not least at election time. A Home Rule candidate stood at least once in a North East constituency: Alderman J. O'Hanlon ran at Jarrow in 1907. His candidature, though not a success, split the Liberal vote and aided Pete Curran's victory for Labour. O'Hanlon's nationalist poll compared favourably with the situation in the Lancashire town of Barrow-in-Furness, where, in 1894, a Home Ruler recorded an abject 15 votes.[62] O'Hanlon was not some out-of-place crank; he had enough credibility later on to become Mayor of Wallsend.[63] Tyneside was a regular stopping-off place on the nationalist lecture circuit. Most of the big names found time to receive the generally approving reception offered by Tyneside's large crowds and strong Liberal press.[64]

The Unionists – among whom there were Scots and Irish together – were not without their own political attractions. The dramatic Carsonite campaign against the third Home

58   *Ibid.*
59   *Blyth Weekly News and Northumberland Advertiser*, 31 May 1879, 25 December 1880.
60   No. 43 [North Shields] account book (expenditure), 1877-1910.
61   *Wallsend Herald and Advertiser*, 12 July 1912.
62   *Barrow and District Year Book, 1908* (Barrow, 1908), p. 83.
63   He was mayor of the town from 1913-14: Richardson, W., *History of the Parish of Wallsend* (Newcastle, 1923), p. 398.
64   See, for examples, *Jarrow Guardian*, 22 March 1912.

Rule bill, between 1912 and 1914, provided political theatre in the lives of his followers.[65] The provincial press certainly took a keen interest in Carson's movements, reporting his punishing schedule of speaking engagements on almost a daily basis.[66] The great Orange hero merited numerous fulsome mentions in the minutes of the lodges, particular at the time of his visit to the North East in the autumn of 1913, when he addressed an anti-Home Rule meeting in Durham's Wharton Park.[67] Orangemen also involved themselves in a torchlit procession in Wallsend, and a huge indoor meeting at the town's rink.

The mass meeting that followed in the evening was one of the biggest events ever seen in Wallsend. The local Olympia skating rink – which was described as 'possibly one of the largest buildings of its kind in the province' – could hold 15,000 persons, and it was crammed full.[68] More than 500 stewards had been taken on to marshal the crowds, at one point using semaphore.[69] The hall was decked out in patriotic style as 'Union Jacks fell from every girder'.[70] Bonar Law and Carson entertained the crowd for more than two hours. Bonar Law promised that in resisting a Home Rule measure that was not first tested against the Ulster electorate, Carson's support would enjoy the wholehearted endorsement of the entire Unionist party.[71] The grand procession after the meeting was the local Unionists' way of welcoming and thanking Carson and Bonar Law for their efforts.

War and Depression

After the war Irish political issues reached a new intensity, but they quickly dissipated after partition (1922). The various Scottish organisations seemed to be willing to support campaigns that had a cultural nationalist dimension, such as the Scots language movement, but the regular members shied away from sponsoring overtly political causes, or even from debating contentious issues. Scots speakers confidently asserted the view that political union with England was a partnership with mutual benefits. Indeed, speakers regularly claimed that Scots had played a disproportionate role in making Britain the first industrial nation and that they had a special aptitude for Empire-building.[72] Moreover, Scots in the North East of England were not only comfortable with a dual sense of national identity; they were also very proud of where they lived. The Irish also faced pressures of hybridity, but lacked the replenishments through new migration which sustained Scots communities (see Table 4).

---

65 See Jackson, D.M. and MacRaild, D.M., 'The Conserving Crowd: mass Unionist demonstrations in Liverpool and Tyneside, 1912-13', Boyce, D.G. and O'Day, A. (eds), *The Home Rule Crisis* (Palgrave, 2005).
66 See, for example, *Newcastle Evening Chronicle*, 18 September 1913.
67 *Ibid.*
68 *Shields Daily News*, 20 September 1913; *Newcastle Daily Chronicle*, 30 October 1913.
69 *Newcastle Daily Chronicle*, 30 October 1913.
70 *Evening Mail*, 29 October 1913.
71 *Daily Chronicle*, 30 October 1913.
72 Finlay, R.J., *A Partnership for Good? Scottish politics and the Union since 1880* (Edinburgh, 1997); Forsyth, D.S., 'Empire and Union: Imperialism and National Identity in Nineteenth Century Scotland', *Scottish Geographical Magazine*, vol. 113, No. 1 (1997), pp.6-12.

The impression from the press is of a Scottish migrant community which effortlessly participated in organisations that drew members from the wider community.[73] Whilst fraternal greetings were exchanged with other Scottish organisations in the region, and invitations to attend concerts, lectures or bowling tournaments were graciously accepted, there were also determined voices demanding members uphold 'local' pride. Part of this stemmed from perennial concerns regarding the financial health of the individual club, but there were clear expressions of identifying with the local district or town and not appearing 'too Scotch'.[74] The high point of the Scots calendar – Burns Night – would see a ritualistic outpouring of affection for the bard and the homeland, but also praise for the Scots contribution to the North East from local dignitaries.[75] Scottish organisations were conduits for integration in other ways, such as sponsoring literary competitions in local schools, sending representatives to Armistice Day, or making regular and substantial donations to local charities and good causes.[76] In the Scottish case, a strong desire to contribute to the local community *and* the retention of a strong sense of ethnic identity were not mutually exclusive.

What made this process of integration easier for the Scots was an apparent affection for, and from, their northern neighbours. Certainly there were sometimes criticisms from Englishmen of the excessive boasting at events like Burns dinners, but most seemed to dismiss these comments as humorous hyperbole rather than deliberate arrogance. The fact that these events were patronised by prominent Tynesiders undoubtedly helped, but there were other ways in which Scottish culture was received favourably. Citations of Scots, or some crude approximation of the 'mither tongue', sometimes would be used to describe Scottish related items of news and – occasionally – these would be blended with the regional dialect.[77] Articles on prospective holiday destinations would invariably feature Scotland, with glowing recommendations. The treatment of newsworthy items from north of the border did include those designed to play up the comical stereotype of the dour, parsimonious and God-fearing Scot, but there were many that indicated an admiration for shared values and attributes born out of similar industrial landscapes. Other aspects of Scottishness were also included but they tended to be more romanticised, as with items relating to the Highlands, or vainglorious, as with a series on the British army that focused on Scottish regiments.[78] This appreciation of Scottish, and indeed Irish, culture would strengthen over the course of the 20th century.

The First World War was a watershed with respect to this sense of cohesion. In addition to the fact that newspapers regularly included humorous sketches and cartoons involving 'Geordie', 'Paddy' and 'Jock', the war years were instructive for the manner in which both Scots and Irish communities were embraced by the regional press as constituting

---

73 *Jarrow Express and Tyneside Advertiser*, 6 February 1891.
74 Durham County Record Office (DCRO), Darlington Burns Association, D/XD/82/2, minute for 8 November 1907.
75 *Darlington & Stockton Times*, 1 February 1913.
76 Particular sensitivity was evident in the Newcastle club's abandoning plans for a Burns statue and making substantial donations to local causes. See *Glasgow Herald*, 21 January 1935.
77 *Jarrow Express and Tyneside Advertiser*, 23 December 1892, 29 July 1892.
78 *Ibid*, 16 December 1892, 25 March 1892.

part of the 'local' sacrifice for the war effort.[79] Enthusiasm for both the Tyneside Scottish and the Tyneside Irish Brigades was certainly evident in the recruitment of volunteers. Indeed, the local Burns clubs and, more importantly, the bagpipe bands, were a powerful means of encouraging men to enlist – and not just for Scots:[80]

> The renown of Scottish fighting men, and the picturesqueness of Scottish garb and customs, rather than a desire to pose as genuine Highlanders, was the stimulus among the independent Tynesiders. They were as proud of being headed by pipes and drums and entitled Scottish as they were proud of being of the Northumberland Fusiliers – the celebrated Fighting Fifth – and being of a Division that was largely composed of Tynesiders like themselves.[81]

Although Scottish men were an important part of this fighting force, the esteem of Scottish regiments, allied to the colour of the music and the uniform, meant that the attempt to keep the Tyneside Scottish for men of Scottish blood or affiliation was abandoned. But there was also a desire that the uniform of the Tyneside Scottish should reflect both the traditions of Scotland and Tyneside. Therefore, the tartan was of a 'modest black and white check' and the cap badge of a 'rather more pronounced Scottish as well as Tyneside character'.[82]

44 *Caricature of Sir Harry Lauder published in* The Whitley Bay Guardian, *5 August 1922, for his visit to the region.*

Worth considering is the alacrity with which this brigade was able to furnish itself with a pipe band. Brigadier General Trevor Ternan, commanding officer and author of a regimental history, commended the generosity of those 'friends' who had supplied both the uniforms and the instruments.[83] Whether these donors were members of the Scottish community in the North East is difficult to ascertain, but certainly the Sunderland and the Darlington Burns Clubs were able to establish pipe bands through a combination of general fundraising and contributions from clubs and individual members.[84] Both bands were popular in the recruitment drives for both the Tyneside Scottish and, in the words of Ternan, 'our old friends and rivals the Tyneside Irish Brigade'.[85]

The positive media treatment of the Tyneside Irish demonstrates the way in which the Great War unified those of different ethnic backgrounds. In the aftermath of the Easter Rising of 1916, the *Newcastle Weekly Chronicle* played up the loyalty of the

---

79   *Newcastle Weekly Chronicle*, 8 January 1916.
80   Tyne & Wear Archive Service (TWAS), Sunderland Burns Club, SX 74/1/3.
81   Anon., *The Tyneside Scottish, 1914-18 (N.F.): Harder than Hammers* (nd, no publisher), pp.1-2. The motto 'Harder than Hammers' derived from the local sentiment that 'whilst a hammer might be broken the fighting spirit of the Tyneside Scot could not be'.
82   Ternan, Brig. Gen Trevor, *The Story of the Tyneside Scottish* (Newcastle, c.1919), p. 18.
83   *Ibid.*
84   Pipe bands were established by both the Darlington and Sunderland Burns Clubs within weeks of the proposals first being mentioned in 1907 and 1913 respectively. See TWAS, SX/ 74/1/3; DCRO, D/XD/82/2.
85   Ternan, 'Tyneside Scottish', p. 16.

A SCOTCH-IRISH COMEDY !

McFADDEN'S FLATS

Starring

CHARLIE   CHESTER

and

MURRAY   CONKLIN

Said McFADDEN :

" No porridge-eating daughter of a Scot will marry a McFadden while I have me health!"

Said McTAVISH :

" Awa' wi' ye' ! Keep that Irish spalpein o' yours away from ma bonnie dochter!"

The funniest Comedy combination the Screen has known for years.

45 *Advert for a 'Scotch-Irish comedy' to be held at the Scala Theatre in South Shields.*

'local' Irish men in the army in the face of German provocation. Regular reports of their bravery paved the way.[86] The brigade itself did not return until June 1919. On their arrival at Newcastle Central Station they were acclaimed by a large crowd and paraded through the streets by the pipes and drums of the Tyneside Scottish. Attendance at a civic reception hosted by the Lord Mayor of Newcastle was followed a few days later with the presentation of the Colours of the Brigade to the city's St Mary's Roman Catholic Cathedral.[87]

During the economic depressions of the inter-war period, the region and its people became associated with economic hardship. Whilst ethnic tension may have reduced as communities bonded through shared adversity, difficulties remained: 'The influx of Irish black-legs, ignorant, violent, improvident, drunken, priest-attended, had not been forgotten … It was a common saying that prosperity would not return to the north until every Scotchman went home, bearing two Irishmen on his back.'[88] There were also anxieties about the growing political influence of the Irish. By the later 1920s the Irish were coming to prominence in local Labour politics. The appearance of larger numbers of local councillors with Irish names, who were perceived to favour their own people, also encouraged criticism. There was rancour, for example, in the Blyth Labour Party, when one councillor, Mr Mordue, claimed some candidates for county council elections were opposed because they were Catholics.[89] In the same year, an unemployed woman in Blyth wrote to her local newspaper to put a different perspective: 'Mr Mordue would be better employed if he try and combat Roman Catholic intrigue in his party. Will he take a census of the Catholic Irishmen who are employed by the Blyth Corporation?'[90] While it is true that there was a strong Catholic presence in south Northumberland politics by this time, the ethnic aspect was rapidly diminishing. Mordue's critic was demonstrating the extent to which a formerly anti-Irish bias had transmuted into an anti-Catholic

---

86   See *Newcastle Weekly Chronicle*, 20 May 1916, 15 July 1916, 22 July 1916.
87   Sheen, J., *Tyneside Irish: A History of the Tyneside Irish Brigade Raised in the North East in World War One* (Newcastle, 1998), pp.175-9.
88   Welbourne, E,. *The Miners' Unions of Northumberland and Durham* (Cambridge, 1923), pp.199-200.
89   *Blyth News and Ashington Post*, 30 April 1931.
90   *Ibid*, 9 November 1931.

sectarianism.

Conclusion

When Consett steelworks was about to close, in 1980, the song 'No Surrender' by Irishman, Ron Kavana, and Durham-born Paul Winstanley, demonstrated another point about the Scots and Irish in the North East: [91]

> When the boots rang on the catwalk,
> In the foundry's fiery glare,
> The clanging heat and dusty reek
> Told us who we were.
> But who are we now that it's gone,
> And we're on the dole
> We're Consett men, proud and strong
> And you'll not damn our soul.

The folk tradition of the area is the result of the fusing together of different musical idioms. But this debt to Irish traditional music, as with the songs of Tommy Armstrong, or the influence of the Scottish 'bothy ballads', as in Jock Purdon's work, is sometimes overlooked.[92] Scots and Irish migrants have played an important role as carriers and, to a lesser extent, custodians of folk music. For example, there is some evidence to suggest that Scottish migrants were enthusiastic supporters of the Northumbrian bagpipe in addition to the more obvious shared musical heritage with the 'Half-long' or 'Border' bagpipe.[93] Collaborative enterprise in the making of instruments and in publishing musical scores requires further investigation but it was undoubtedly recognised that there was much to be gained from adapting melodies and tunes. The folk revival of the 1950s saw an explosion of musical creativity across different traditions.[94] As the editors of this collection of Northumbrian pipe tunes acknowledged, the musical repository of Scotland and Ireland provided particularly rich pickings.[95] Just as Highland bagpipe players purloined tunes from the fiddle, with the compass or range altered to suit, so too with the Northumbrian pipes.[96] In the 1960s and 1970s, enthusiasts of 'Northumbrian' culture were putting forward strident claims for the synchronicity of the music and place in language reminiscent of the 'Celtic Twilight' movement a century or so earlier.[97]

---

91 Kearney, 'Painted Red', p. 96.
92 Atkinson, Frank, *Life and Tradition in Northumberland and Durham* (London, 1977), pp.146-7.
93 See Fraser, A.D., *Some Reminiscences and the Bagpipe* (Edinburgh, 1907).
94 Charlton, F., Ross, C. and Wright, R., *The Northumbrian Pipers' Tune Book: A Collection of Tunes for the Northumbrian Smallpipes and other Folk Instruments* (Newcastle, 1970).
95 *Ibid.*
96 Donaldson, W., *The Highland Pipe and Scottish Society, 1750-1950* (East Linton, 2000), p. 355.
97 See the 'Foreword' by the Earl of Tankerville in *Northumbrian Pipers' Tune Book*.

11

Northumberland and Durham Settlements 1801-1911

MIKE BARKE

Modern geographical descriptions of the region have identified three component parts, with the industrialised areas of the rivers Tyne and Wear at the core, surrounded by the coalfield which, in turn, merges into a rural and mainly upland environment.[1] This chapter will explore the extent to which this geographical symmetry was reproduced in patterns of demographic change.

Asymmetric Growth

Between 1801 and 1911 the population of Northumberland and Durham grew from 478,223 to 2,066,753. Northumberland began the 19th century with the larger population (168,078), but County Durham (149,384 inhabitants in 1801) grew much more rapidly. In the first half of the 19th century Northumberland's population grew by 81 per cent and Durham's by 162 per cent. In the second half of the century Durham had a growth rate of 5.8 per cent per annum compared with Northumberland's 1.3 per cent.

Equally important was the changing geographical distribution of population and the structure of settlements. In 1821, 60 per cent of the North East's population lived in settlements of less than 2,000 people and there were no towns with a population of 50,000 or over. By 1911 over 40 per cent of the region's population were living in towns of 50,000 or more and Newcastle had a population of 250,000.[2] This urban growth was very much a feature of the later 19th century.[3] But any temptation to think of the 19th century in terms of progressive and continuous industrialisation and urbanisation should be avoided. Not only was the first part different from the

---

1 Rowe, D.J., 'The north-east', in Thompson, F.M.L. (ed.), *The Cambridge Social History of Britain 1750-1950, Volume 1, Regions and Communities* (Cambridge, 1990), pp.415-70.
2 McCord, N., 'Some aspects of change in the nineteenth-century North East', *Northern History*, vol. XXXI (1995), pp.241-66.
3 Ashington, with a population of only 1,002 in 1871, increased to nearly 25,000 by 1911.

later decades, but within each decade there were distinct fluctuations. Far from the simple picture of a rural periphery characterised by rural depopulation, a coalfield area showing spectacular and continuous growth, and urban areas showing rapid growth, 19th-century north-east England was much more varied in its population history, especially so in the ostensibly 'rural' areas.

Industrial economic enterprise was not the sole preserve of the core areas of the lower Tyne and Wear rivers and the coalfield. The exploitation of mineral reserves in Redesdale and upper North Tynedale led to substantial labour recruitment in a predominantly agricultural area and the construction of a completely new village at Ridsdale.[4] Although the parish of Corsenside showed a 54 per cent increase between 1801 and 1851, between 1841 and 1851 the population actually fell spectacularly from 1,108 to 579. As the census notes: 1841 – 'The increase of population (from 524 in 1831) is attributed to the prosperous state of the ironstone works.' 1851 – 'The stoppage of those works has caused half the population to leave the parish, and will account for the large number of uninhabited houses.' Similar fluctuations were found in many other areas. Bailey and Culley's agricultural report of 1805 noted that 'Hexham has long been famed for its manufacture of gloves, which employs about 300 hands. To establish manufactures of woollens, two or three essays have been lately made at Alnwick, Mitford, and Acklington; and a cotton mill has been lately erected at Nether Witton.'[5] A directory of 1822 drew attention to the local importance of collieries at Alnwick 'producing some of the best in England' (p.567), iron works at Bedlington, 'supposed to be the largest in the north of England', 'valuable lead mines at Coal-cleugh and Allenheads', and 'extensive bottle works' at Seaton Sluice.[6] A note by the Census Commissioner for Long Framlington [*sic*] parish in 1831 observed, 'The decrease of population is attributed to the reduced number of labourers employed in coal mines.' In many other parts of the rural periphery, the development of lime burning and quarrying created significant local employment opportunities.

The Demographic Transition: early to mid-19th century

The rapid population growth in Britain in the 18th and 19th centuries is usually attributed to a demographic transition from a pre-industrial to an industrialised regime, the former being associated with very high levels of fertility and mortality. But the precise mechanisms at work are a matter for considerable debate. The classic model posits a situation where the transition is initiated by a decline in mortality which is subsequently followed by a decline in fertility but the time lag between the two produces a period of very rapid population growth.[7] This view is supported by

4   Roberts, I.D., 'Iron making in Redesdale and North Tynedale in the nineteenth century: the problems of rural exploitation and diversification', *Northern History*, vol. XXXVI (2) (2000), pp.283-98.
5   Bailey, J. and Culley, G., *General View of the Agriculture of Northumberland, Cumberland and Westmoreland*, Facsimile third edition (Newcastle upon Tyne, 1972), p.176.
6   Pigot's *Directory* for Northumberland (1822).
7   Wrigley, E.A. and Schofield, R.S., *The Population History of England, 1541-1871; a Reconstruction* (London, 1981).

Lawton who argues that 'reduced mortality was a more significant agent of population change in the late eighteenth and early nineteenth centuries than fluctuations in birth rate.' (p.330).[8] However, elsewhere it has been claimed that the English experience after 1750 was slowly falling mortality and rather rapidly rising fertility.[9] In other words, the English demographic transition was due more to increasing fertility than to declining mortality. Which of these scenarios did the North East support? Prior to the institution of civil registration of births, deaths and marriages in 1837, the main source of equivalent data is the Anglican parish registers. Although much debate surrounds the accuracy and usefulness of these registers,[10] they remain the only reasonably comprehensive source.[11]

For Northumberland generally, and with the exception of Newcastle, several broad trends are discernible. In the early part of the 18th century there appears to have been some modest natural increase of population but, particularly in the 1780s, in accordance with national trends, the number of burials exceeds the number of baptisms.[12] In the first decade of the 19th century, however, the number of baptisms in relation to the number of burials increases almost everywhere, with the exceptions of Glendale and Coquetdale. In these two wards the difference between the numbers of baptisms and burials does not change very much right through to the 1820s.

The parish data for County Durham appear to show slightly different trends, especially in the early 18th century when the number of baptisms and burials appears to be broadly equivalent. But in the Durham wards, as in the Northumberland ones, it is in the first decade of the 19th century that the number of baptisms starts to diverge positively and significantly from the number of burials, although, in the two main urban areas of Sunderland and Durham City, burials remained at a high level through to the 1840s. In both counties, however, through the classic period of the demographic transition, the underlying trend remains relatively clear: baptisms change in a positive direction. What caused this positive change?

One of the most widely recognised features of English fertility was its relationship to 'nuptuality' (the prevalence of marriage). The relationship of fertility to marriage can be manifest in several ways, for example by the proportions actually marrying, or the age of marriage, or sexual behaviour within marriage. We can test the role of nuptiality itself and the extent to which it varied across the North East using the recorded number of marriages, and the baptism data as a surrogate for births. Table 1 shows these two measures for the period 1796-1825.

---

8 Lawton, R., 'Population and Society', in Dodgshon, R.A. and Butlin, R.A. (eds), *An Historical Geography of England and Wales* (London, 1978).

9 Hinde, A., *England's Population: A History Since the Domesday Survey* (London, 2003)

10 Wrigley and Schofield (1981), *op. cit.*, pp.15-16.

11 Despite the many problems of under recording, plus the strength of religious nonconformity in different areas, and the problems of non-recording of infants who died before they could be baptised, they remain the only comprehensive source from which information about fertility, mortality and nuptiality can be inferred.

12 Wrigley and Schofield (1981), *op. cit.*, pp.532-5.

Table 1 Crude Marriage Rates and Baptism Rates in Northumberland and Durham Wards, 1796-1825

Ward	Crude Marriage Rate (marriages per 1,000 population)			Baptism Rate (baptisms per 1,000 population)		
	1796-1805	1806-1815	1816-1825	1796-1805	1806-1815	1816-1825
Bamburgh	3.75	4.29	3.63	20.36	22.71	21.29
Castle	11.19	7.16	6.39	25.23	26.30	25.66
Coquetdale	6.30	5.30	4.37	16.70	18.07	17.45
Glendale	2.69	2.46	2.49	10.54	11.82	9.09
Morpeth	6.44	6.77	6.79	21.44	26.46	27.66
Tindale	6.42	6.47	6.04	22.53	23.63	23.93
Newcastle	12.78	13.37	13.77	27.87	34.17	36.71
Berwick	2.56	4.52	3.89	12.87	15.05	16.12
Chester	10.17	8.20	8.38	30.92	31.93	33.60
Darlington	7.36	8.66	7.75	31.62	32.49	32.18
Easington	11.01	8.94	8.43	26.83	29.95	30.33
Stockton	7.07	7.01	7.00	27.90	27.83	30.19
Norhamshire	1.54	1.93	2.00	7.80	8.68	9.55
Islandshire	1.14	2.58	3.34	8.82	10.16	12.59
Durham	13.29	9.43	7.43	33.09	35.71	28.18
Sunderland	10.18	9.04	10.59	33.57	38.51	35.77

It is clear that the rates of both marriages and baptisms varied quite considerably. The marriage rate is generally higher in the larger urban areas and in those wards where mining was a significant activity, and lower in the deep rural areas. The rate of baptisms (which is our measure of births) varied similarly. If there was a demographic transition in the late 18th and early 19th centuries in north-east England, it was not a transition that was uniform across the area. Nevertheless, the relationship between marriages and fertility appears to be close (for the three periods 1796-1805, 1806-15 and 1816-25 the correlation coefficients between crude marriage rates and baptism rates are +0.871, +0.909 and +0.925 respectively). We can be fairly sure that the proportions marrying, therefore, seem to have been a key explanatory variable in fertility patterns.

What seems to have been significant in influencing the marriage rate was the nature of the local economy. Of particular significance was the culture of male breadwinning in coalmining districts.[13] Men worked whilst women were expected to stay at home and raise children. This is the very scenario described in the remarks added to the parish returns for Washington in 1821:

> The Pitmen commonly marry at an early age; and in this Parish they have ... numerous families. It is an advantage to them to have families; because their Boys find work in the

---

13 Hunt, E.H., *Regional Wage Variations in Britain, 1850-1914* (Oxford, 1973), p.225.

Pits when they are very young; beginning to get work and wages from the age of seven or eight. The Earnings of the Pitmen far exceed those of Agricultural Labourers; whilst their Girls have the same advantage of field work as the others. But … the Pitmen … are liable to casualties which disable them at times. They form a very distinct race, inasmuch as they marry almost exclusively amongst themselves, and bring up their Sons to their own course of life. They also live very much together, keeping little society with other classes of people.

Table 2 Birth and death rates per 1,000 live population, 1841

Area	Mean Crude Birth Rate 1841-2	Mean Crude Death Rate 1840-2
Darlington, Stockton, Hartlepool, Easington	30.27	16.38
Auckland, Teesdale, Weardale	29.18	22.02
Durham, Lanchester	25.27	16.24
Houghton le Spring; Chester le Street	35.32	22.27
Sunderland	36.99	25.98
South Shields	48.07	34.00
Gateshead	33.11	25.07
Newcastle upon Tyne	32.28	26.90
Tynemouth	38.89	23.07
Castle Ward, Hexham	29.33	18.57
Haltwhistle, Bellingham, Glendale	29.81	14.56
Morpeth, Alnwick, Belford, Rothbury	28.05	22.06
Berwick upon Tweed	32.68	18.67

The preceding observations are speculative. From the 1840s it becomes possible to examine demographic trends with more precision (Table 2). Vital statistics started to be recorded following the Civil Registration Act in 1837.[14] However, it is widely recognised that in the early years civil registration – despite being compulsory – was often deficient and therefore any conclusions should still be treated with caution.[15]

Most striking is the remarkably high birth rate for South Shields, a town with 4,000 seamen, a further 2,400 workers in the docks and shipyards and 200 pubs and (apparently) 150 prostitutes.[16] Intriguingly, the other seaport town, of Tynemouth across the river, had the second highest crude birth rate, albeit nearly 10 percentage points behind South Shields. Birth rates were high across the whole of the region. Death rates varied more markedly, with the main urban areas showing the worst figures largely due to overcrowding and inadequate sanitary provision. In the Pipewellgate area of Gateshead in 1843 a population of over 2,000 was served by only three privies

14   Drake, M. (ed.), *Population Studies from Parish Registers* (Matlock, 1982), p.vi.
15   Wrigley, E. A. (ed.), *An Introduction to English Historical Demography* (London, 1966), pp.44-95.
16   Foster, J., *Class Struggle and the Industrial Revolution* (London, 1974), p.88.

or sanitary conveniences (these could include communal middens, ash closets and pail closets but not, at this time, water closets),[17] and in North Shields in 1850 there were only 130 privies for nearly 8,000 people.[18] In Newcastle two out of every ten babies did not survive their first year, but in rural Northumberland and the market towns the chances of survival were twice this. Although some rural areas, particularly in Northumberland, were relatively healthy, others were less so. Levine and Wrightson have argued that the external contact of the coal producing districts made many ostensibly 'rural' areas an extension of the demographic experience of urban England, with considerable vulnerability to epidemic disease and, in the case of males, mining accidents.[19] At Stanhope, the mean age at death in the years 1855-7 was 33.6 years.

In terms of the two conflicting interpretations of the demographic transition it appears that different parts of the North East support each one. In most areas there was indeed a rapid rise in fertility, stimulated by a high marriage rate. Other areas experienced more modest increases in fertility but relatively lower rates of mortality were sufficient to produce population growth.

Mobility: early to mid-19th century

The rector of Washington parish noted in his observations on the 1821 census that 'the families of pitmen emigrate to and fro'. He explained an apparent decrease in the number of marriages by 'a considerable change of inhabitants which took place in one quarter of the Parish by the laying off of an old Colliery. The younger pitmen who had belonged to it readily found work elsewhere.' This clearly suggests a very fluid situation with regard to mobility, and implies something rather different from the popular conception of a 'tight-knit' community. The relationship between capital and labour was governed by an annual contract of employment called the 'bond'.[20] On the expiry of the old bond miners were free to seek fresh employment. In the Tyneside collieries some 28 per cent of hewers left their place of work for a new one, whilst in the Wearside group 29 per cent left their former collieries. Turnover was especially high in the lower Tyne and mid-Wear pits. However, most of the moves appear to have taken place within well-defined circuits.[21]

It is now recognised that levels of mobility in pre-industrial society were considerably higher than previously thought,[22] and that in the North East the specific patterns of mobility associated with coal miners and their dependents added a further dimension to 'normal' mobility.[23] In the parishes of Newburn, Ovingham, Hexham and Haltwhistle

---

17   Rowe (1990), *op. cit.*, p.456.
18   Ranger, W., *Report to the General Board of Health on a preliminary inquiry into the sewage, drainage, and supply of water, and the sanitary condition of the inhabitants of the Borough of Tynemouth* (London, 1851), pp.29-42.
19   Levine, D. and Wrightson, K., *The Making of an Industrial Society: Whickham 1560-1765* (Oxford, 1991), p.200.
20   Sill, M. and Barke, M., 'Coal Miner Mobility: North East England in the early Nineteenth Century', *Journal of Regional and Local Studies*, vol. 7 (1) (1987), pp.35-54.
21   See Colls, R., *The pitmen of the Northern Coalfield* (Manchester, 1987), pp.120-5.
22   Clark, P. and Souden, D. (eds), *Migration and Society in Early Modern England* (London, 1987), p.213.
23   Millard, J., 'A new approach to marriage horizons', *Local Population Studies*, vol. 28 (1982), pp.10-31.

between 1830 and 1859, the number of extra-parochial grooms tended to increase over time and marriage 'horizons' (the distance between the parish of residence of the groom and the parish of residence of the bride) increased also, although in a somewhat irregular manner.[24] Interestingly, evidence from north-east England has been used to claim that the marriage registers significantly underestimate the amount of migration in the late 18th and early 19th centuries.[25] Mobility of labour has been identified as a key feature in population change in 17th-century south Durham, for example.[26] Work on migration into Darlington in the mid-18th century, based on settlement papers,[27] has demonstrated the probability that migration was responsible for between 50-75 per cent of the total population growth in the 1767-93 period and that, whilst the majority of this migration was relatively short range, some well-established migration paths existed, most notably down the Tees valley from Barnard Castle and vicinity – 'Darlington prospered by the decay of Barnard Castle's industries'.[28] Thus, even before what is considered to be the major period of industrialisation, strategically located towns such as Darlington were growing through inward migration.

As noted earlier, new opportunities for employment, with their consequent migration streams, were not limited to urban areas. Contemporary accounts noted the extent of agricultural improvement in the first half of the 19th century,[29] and Howkins reckons that large areas of Durham and Northumberland were not under the plough until the end of the 18th century, leading to widespread demand for new labour.[30]

Specific features of the organisation of labour in particular industries also served to promote mobility, most notably in coal mining and some aspects of agriculture. Due to the existence of an annual contract of employment, local circuits of mobility appear to have existed in some of the region's agricultural areas. This was most notable in north Northumberland,[31] where one estimate[32] suggested that four out of ten families would move each year: 'there is a real sadness in the sight of the annual migration of so large a proportion of our farm families' leading to

> roads from morning to evening thronged with carts piled with the furniture and bedding of a large portion of our population ...The people themselves consider the flitting a sorrowful time. They lose the companionship of those with whom they have worked ...

---

24 Davison, J.P., 'A Study of Marriage Horizons in the Tyne Valley, 1830-1859' (unpublished BA (Hons) Dissertation, Department of Environment, Newcastle Polytechnic, 1992.

25 Smith, A.T. and Pain, A.J., 'Estimates of historical migration in County Durham', *Annals of Human Biology*, vol. 16 (6) (1989), pp.543-7.

26 Kirby, D.A., 'Population density and land values in County Durham during the mid-seventeenth century', *Transactions, Institute of British Geographers*, vol. 57 (1972), pp.83-98.

27 Barke, M., 'Migration into Darlington in the mid-eighteenth century: some tentative observations', *Bulletin, Durham County Local History Society*, vol. 27 (1981), pp.16-28.

28 Bradshaw, F., 'Social and Economic History', in *Victoria County History of Durham*, Vol. II (Durham, 1907), p.244.

29 Colbeck, T.L., 'On the agriculture of Northumberland', *Journal of the Royal Agricultural Society*, vol. VIII (1847), pp.422-38.

30 Howkins, A., 'The English farm labourer in the nineteenth century: farm, family and community', in Short, B. (ed.), *The English Rural Community* (Cambridge, 1992), pp.85-104.

31 Long, J., *Conversations in Cold Rooms* (Woodbridge, 1999), p.82.

32 Neville, H.M., *A Corner in the North* (Newcastle upon Tyne, 1909), p.30.

46 *Labour mobility: 'Flitting Day' at Hay Farm, Ford. Male farm workers (hinds) and their families were normally employed on a one-year contract. On 12 May each year many would 'flit' elsewhere in search of a new contract.*

> Strangers take the place of those who have gone, and our Border folk are not good at making friends with new comers.[33]

> Among the hinds there are not many to be found who were born in the parish where they are at present employed … it is an evil of great magnitude that your agricultural population should be a moving population … they lose all the advantages which belong to a home, and the feelings of home.[34]

There was considerable exchange of population and labour from village to village and the movement of labour across the border from Scotland was an integral part of this circuit. The recruitment of Scottish agricultural labour was facilitated by the fact that in the principal border town of Berwick upon Tweed the hiring of farm servants took place earlier than it did in Scotland.[35]

Table 3 shows the aggregate birthplace pattern for both counties. About one quarter of Durham's population (including Chester Ward East Division, Islandshire and Norhamshire) were born outside the county and about one fifth of Northumberland's – but with the latter showing a slightly larger proportion of Scottish, Irish and longer distance migrants.

33 Neville, *op. cit.*, p.30.
34 Gilly, W.S., *The Peasantry of the Border: An Appeal on their Behalf* (Edinburgh, 1841), p.7.
35 Anon., 'On the hiring markets in the Counties of Northumberland, Berwick and Roxburgh', *Quarterly Journal Agriculture* (1834-5), pp.379-86.

Table 3 Birthplaces for Durham and Northumberland, 1841

	Co. Durham	Co. Northumberland
% born in County	75.5	80.1
% born in other Counties	20.1	12.3
% born in Scotland	2.2	4.8
% born in Ireland	1.7	2.1
% born elsewhere	0.5	0.7

Not surprisingly, relatively high proportions of migrants were found adjacent to the rivers Tyne and Wear in response to the employment opportunities created by early industrialisation.[36] Although over much of rural Northumberland the proportion of these longer distance migrants was generally low, short-range migration was frequent. The picture that emerges is not one of stable, unchanging pre-industrial communities. Rather, it is a picture of frequent movement of population in response to changing personal circumstances and the organisation of labour in various industries, as well as the simple fact of growth and decline of actual employment opportunities.

Demographic Variations: mid- to later 19th century

From the mid-19th century it becomes possible to examine demographic change with more precision. Table 4 shows these components of change in summary form.
The most obvious trends are rural depopulation and urbanisation but these trends were not consistently present across the region. Morpeth experienced growth with particular significance of net migration gain in both the 1850s (largely due to industrial growth at Bedlington) and the early 1900s (with exploitation of the concealed coalfield) but suffered migration loss in the 1870s and 1880s.[37] Newcastle and Sunderland experienced net migration loss in several decades, albeit cancelled out by natural gain, but also experienced some loss due to short-range suburbanisation within the city region.[38]

Differential migration also had important implications for the structure of households and the nature of local communities. For example, in Alwinton in 1851 only 12 per cent of households were of one or two persons, but by 1901 26 per cent were so constituted, a trend resulting from the lack of local employment for younger family members. In contrast, during the same period, the expanding suburb of Bensham (Gateshead) saw a substantial increase in the proportion of families with children under the age of 15 at a time when the proportion of children in local communities was generally falling.

---

36 Smailes, A.E., 'Early industrial settlement in north-east England', *The Advancement of Science*, vol. VI (24) (1950), pp.325-31.
37 Willis, I., 'Morpeth: A Northumbrian market town in the nineteenth century', in Faulkner, T.E. (ed.), *Northumbrian Panorama* (London, 1996).
38 Lawton, R., 'Population changes in England and Wales in the later nineteenth century: an analysis of trends by Registration Districts', *Transactions, Institute of British Geographers*, vol. 44 (1968), pp.55-74.

Table 4 Components of population change, Northumberland and Durham Registration Districts, 1851-1911

District	1851-61	1861-71	1871-81	1881-91	1891-1901	1901-1911
Darlington	A	C	B	B	A	A
Stockton	A	C	A	A	B	B
Sedgefield					B	C
Hartlepool		A	B	A	A	D
Auckland	C	A	B	B	B	B
Teesdale	B	B	B	B	D	B
Weardale	B	B	D	D	*D*	D
Lanchester				B	A	A
Durham	A	A	A	B	B	B
Easington	A	B	B	B	B	C
Houghton le Spring	B	A	A	B	B	A
Chester le Street	A	B	A	B	B	A
Sunderland	A	A	A	B	B	B
South Shields	A	C	A	A	A	B
Gateshead	A	C	A	A	A	B
Newcastle	C	A	B	A	A	B
Tynemouth	A	A	A	A	A	A
Castle Ward	B	B	A	A	C	C
Hexham	B	B	B	D	B	B
Haltwhistle	D	B	B	D	B	B
Bellingham	B	D	D	*D*	C	D
Morpeth	C	A	B	B	A	C
Alnwick	B	A	B	B	B	B
Belford	*D*	*D*	*D*	*D*	B	B
Berwick	*D*	*D*	*D*	*D*	*D*	*D*
Glendale	*D*	*D*	*D*	*D*	*D*	*D*
Rothbury	*D*	*D*	*D*	*D*	*D*	*D*

Key: ***italics*** = OVERALL population loss

A – natural gain>migration gain	**E** – migration loss>natural loss
B – natural gain>migration loss	**F** – natural loss>migration gain
C – migration gain>natural gain	**G** – natural loss>migration gain
D – migration loss>natural gain	**H** – migration gain>natural loss

Turning to the trends of natural population change within the region, Table 5 shows the change in crude birth rates through the latter part of the 19th century. In line with national trends the birth rate declined by the end of the century, particularly from the1870s.[39] But throughout most of the region, and especially in the mining districts and large towns, the birth rate remained higher than the national level (averaging 27.2 for 1901-10).[40] Nationally, one of the major factors identified earlier – the marriage rate – ceased to be the principal regulator of fertility.[41] It has been argued that the fertility decline in the later 19th century 'had relatively little to do with changes in nuptiality, but a great deal to do with changes in the behaviour of married women'.[42]

Table 5 Crude Birth Rates (births per 1000 resident population) in Northumberland and Durham Registration Districts, 1851-1911 (*)

District	1851	1861	1871	1881	1891	1901	1911
Darlington	32.43	37.06	39.84	35.21	29.04	28.82	26.33
Stockton	41.33	43.63	45.14	38.48	35.52	33.15	28.12
Sedgefield	-	-	-	-	-	36.71	32.29
Hartlepool	-	42.97	45.03	40.93	38.03	35.56	29.36
Auckland	41.99	47.01	45.08	38.31	38.42	35.43	32.75
Teesdale	31.93	34.50	31.78	29.34	27.83	26.43	24.21
Weardale	40.11	38.04	37.43	31.28	29.53	27.93	23.20
Lanchester	-	-	-	38.62	36.14	36.68	33.22
Durham	38.98	40.02	42.30	38.14	37.02	33.49	32.07
Easington	40.97	45.50	45.77	41.36	41.64	40.01	35.60
Houghton le Spring	37.33	41.84	43.94	45.40	41.36	39.59	36.29
Chester le Street	39.27	43.64	43.16	40.29	39.20	39.37	35.56
Sunderland	41.67	39.18	41.84	39.55	38.25	36.67	21.85
South Shields	40.21	40.71	44.44	39.55	37.69	36.06	30.84
Gateshead	42.23	41.40	43.06	40.75	37.51	37.71	32.46
Newcastle	35.05	38.21	40.06	37.17	35.84	33.64	27.66
Tynemouth	38.72	40.23	40.69	37.74	36.28	35.61	30.18
Castle Ward	31.08	32.92	33.39	31.51	22.02	30.74	25.03
Hexham	31.78	33.07	31.80	30.55	26.86	26.98	24.13
Haltwhistle	32.76	31.77	32.49	32.48	26.55	28.20	23.72
Bellingham	28.38	28.58	31.54	24.40	21.62	22.45	22.38
Morpeth	33.69	37.38	43.14	39.67	35.09	34.95	31.33
Alnwick	31.59	31.08	29.34	29.63	28.99	27.26	24.51
Belford	31.00	29.98	25.03	26.38	24.77	23.51	19.78
Berwick	33.97	32.09	29.16	29.98	26.33	24.88	24.22
Glendale	31.52	28.79	28.11	25.87	22.61	20.37	21.25
Rothbury	26.06	27.70	29.33	25.19	21.74	21.47	19.76

(*) The rates shown are actually the mean of the first three years of the decade

39   Woods, R.I., *The Demography of Victorian England and Wales* (Cambridge, 2000), p.48.
40   Hardy, A., *Health and Medicine in Britain since 1860* (Basingstoke, 2001), p.180.
41   Teitelbaum, M.S., *The British Fertility Decline: Demographic Transition in the Crucible of the Industrial Revolution* (Princeton, 1984), p.117.
42   Hinde (2003), *op. cit.*, p.226.

47 *'Fisher lassies' splitting herring at Seahouses under watchful supervision. In the 19th century many women workers, who split, gutted and packed the herring into barrels, followed the fishing at its various ports on Britain's east coast.*

If this was the case in the North East then we would expect the correlation between the marriage rate and the birth rate to become less significant towards the end of the century.

But it was not the case. At a time when, nationally, the relationship between marriage rates and birth rates was being severed, it still remained strong in the North East. One possible factor that may explain the unexpected lower relationship in mid-century could be fluctuations in the proportion of 'marriageable' partners, particularly in terms of age. But the relationship between the birth rate and the proportion of married women in the reproductive age group is close and, although the correlation shows a slight decline in 1891, it increases in 1911. The evidence therefore seems to suggest that, contrary to the national picture, in north-east England a strong relationship remained between marriage and child bearing.

This was especially so in the coal-mining areas.[43] Throughout the second half of the century, the lack of employment opportunities for women also encouraged heavy female out-migration and a shortage of eligible women. A strong pressure to marry young developed. This created a situation of high potential fertility which would be exacerbated by the fact that coal mining was one of the most dangerous occupations[44] and earnings were unstable.[45] A further factor was also important in explaining the lack of conformity

43 Woods, R.I. and Smith, C.W., 'The decline of marital fertility in the late nineteenth century: the case of England and Wales', *Population Studies*, vol. 37 (1983), pp.207-25.
44 Woods, R.I. (2000), *op.cit.*
45 Friedlander, D., 'Demographic patterns and socio-economic characteristics of the coal mining population in England and Wales in the nineteenth century', *Economic Development and Cultural Change*, vol. XXII (1973), 39-51; Haines, M.R., *Fertility and Occupation: Population Patterns in Industrialization* (New York, 1979).

with national trends. One of the explanations for fertility decline nationally has been the 'social diffusion' theory, where the idea of control of fertility is initiated in the urban middle-class population and is then diffused through the social hierarchy and from urban to rural areas.[46] In many north-east mining communities there simply was no middle class to have contact with and in many rural areas the situation was similar.[47]

Table 6 shows mortality rates for the region's Registration Districts in the latter part of the 19th century.

Table 6 Crude Death Rates (deaths per 1000 resident population) in Northumberland and Durham Registration Districts, 1851-1911 (*)

District	1851	1861	1871	1881	1891	1901	1911
Darlington	21.02	21.78	24.26	17.71	17.07	15.96	13.86
Stockton	20.76	23.31	23.60	21.51	21.71	16.16	15.56
Sedgefield	-	-	-	-	-	24.77	18.42
Hartlepool	-	23.22	25.07	21.00	18.29	16.88	16.04
Auckland	22.02	23.38	25.61	21.36	19.35	18.22	14.83
Teesdale	18.73	21.10	18.78	16.52	18.32	15.80	13.15
Weardale	17.89	22.19	20.62	17.65	18.09	16.14	13.09
Lanchester	-	-	-	18.01	18.85	17.33	14.25
Durham	20.80	20.36	25.55	21.41	20.69	18.66	16.31
Easington	18.25	21.26	24.96	22.61	21.89	19.92	15.66
Houghton le Spring	20.92	23.75	24.61	21.24	20.85	19.57	15.55
Chester le Street	21.86	20.28	24.11	20.72	19.76	19.06	15.32
Sunderland	25.24	21.50	27.55	23.47	23.06	20.76	17.43
South Shields	22.89	21.56	27.40	20.84	20.79	19.69	15.66
Gateshead	25.37	22.90	26.21	22.22	20.91	19.52	14.68
Newcastle	26.76	27.05	29.66	22.46	21.96	20.31	16.63
Tynemouth	22.25	24.83	24.25	20.02	20.29	19.13	14.44
Castle Ward	17.44	18.92	20.70	18.43	18.20	17.37	12.61
Hexham	17.85	19.81	18.28	18.12	17.98	16.50	12.94
Haltwhistle	16.93	18.63	17.03	17.50	16.65	15.25	13.98
Bellingham	15.21	19.44	16.53	15.34	19.29	14.25	13.91
Morpeth	19.53	22.27	24.49	19.69	21.03	19.50	15.78
Alnwick	16.84	20.22	19.29	17.45	19.26	15.14	12.83
Belford	16.98	17.68	16.08	14.20	14.29	14.95	12.48
Berwick	19.27	19.14	20.14	18.48	18.64	17.70	14.12
Glendale	14.17	15.57	12.63	15.15	15.95	14.90	12.76
Rothbury	13.37	18.28	14.69	15.06	18.08	17.08	12.34

(*) The rates shown here are actually the mean of three years, e.g. 1860, 1861 and 1862

---

46 Banks, J.A., *Prosperity and Parenthood: A Study of Family Planning among the Victorian Middle Classes* (London, 1954), *passim*.
47 See Szreter, S., *Fertility, Class and Gender in Britain, 1860-1940* (Cambridge, 1996) for further critical discussion of the 'social diffusion' hypothesis.

Table 7 Infant Mortality Rates (deaths of children under 1 year of age per 1000 live births) in Northumberland and Durham Registration Districts, 1851-1911 (*)

District	1851	1861	1871	1881	1891	1901	1911
Darlington	139	136	169	137	135	136	114
Stockton	157	150	179	151	161	160	125
Sedgefield	-	-	-	-	-	167	129
Hartlepool	-	155	179	153	148	136	127
Auckland	152	154	183	161	168	169	108
Teesdale	115	120	114	119	132	108	86
Weardale	132	121	133	120	144	130	82
Lanchester	-	-	-	147	160	167	136
Durham	171	142	178	159	164	174	144
Easington	151	147	178	162	166	144	157
Houghton le Spring	167	169	177	148	167	157	135
Chester le Street	148	136	176	161	165	153	154
Sunderland	170	146	178	166	169	136	141
South Shields	156	142	181	141	160	158	131
Gateshead	188	149	185	166	164	169	133
Newcastle	219	175	194	163	165	161	127
Tynemouth	152	142	168	149	153	170	132
Castle Ward	139	106	140	127	141	159	113
Hexham	119	126	104	117	127	141	106
Haltwhistle	100	93	91	106	115	106	105
Bellingham	41	102	88	85	107	109	80
Morpeth	126	155	144	123	157	176	147
Alnwick	108	84	115	97	122	126	94
Belford	89	89	95	90	95	92	119
Berwick	117	101	118	106	104	134	72
Glendale	69	70	65	113	92	113	67
Rothbury	76	88	93	85	90	115	67

(*) The rates shown here are actually the mean of three years, e.g. 1860, 1861 and 1862

Variation in mortality is rather less than the variation in birth rates and the trends are broadly similar across the region. However, death rates in many settlements remained above the national average, largely due to the risks to health involved in the nature of many occupations and the higher working-class and badly housed component of the total population. Mortality did decline significantly by the early 20th century, however, and the most widely recognised explanation for this relates to the conquest of infectious diseases.[48] But there remains considerable debate about whether this was primarily due to medical improvements, or environmental factors, or improvements in the standard of living and nutrition. In interpreting Newcastle's declining death rate,

---

48   McKeown, T., *The Modern Rise of Population* (London, 1976), pp.44-72.

48   *On the large farms of north Northumberland, as a condition of their employment, male agricultural workers (hinds) would normally also have to provide female workers (bondagers). The photograph shows a group of bondagers at Kirknewton.*

the case for the latter has been argued,[49] but compulsory vaccination against smallpox and the marked reduction in typhus after the 1870s also played an important part, as did the overall improvement in water supplies across the region.[50]

A widely recognised feature of national demographic change in the later 19th century is that, whilst overall mortality rates declined significantly, a matching decline in infant mortality did not take place until the very end of the century. Contrary to the national trend, in a number of places in Northumberland and Durham infant mortality continued at a high level up to and beyond 1911 and in some places actually got worse. This trend is usually asserted to be a particularly urban phenomenon and especially characteristic of large cities,[51] but Hexham, Morpeth, Alnwick and Berwick all showed their worst infant mortality rates in the early 1900s.

49   Barke, M., 'The people of Newcastle: a demographic history', in Colls, R. and Lancaster, W. (eds), *Newcastle upon Tyne: A Modern History* (Chichester, 2001), pp.133-66.

50   McCord, N. and Thompson, R., *The Northern Counties from AD 1000* (London, 1998); Rennison, R.W., *Water to Tyneside: A History of the Newcastle and Gateshead Water Company* (Newcastle, 1998).

51   Williams, N. and Mooney, G., 'Infant mortality in an "Age of Great Cities": London and the English provincial cities compared', *Continuity and Change*, vol. 9 (2) (1994), pp.185-212.

A major factor in this continuing high infant mortality was the susceptibility of very young children to diarrhoeal diseases,[52] producing a marked seasonality of infant deaths (especially in urban areas).[53] In north-east England there was indeed a seasonal pattern of infant mortality. In Newcastle, for example, between 1875 and 1911 some 39,983 children died in the first year of their life. Of these, 12,667 or 32 per cent died in the third quarter of the year between July and the end of September. In the combined rural registration districts of Haltwhistle, Bellingham, Belford, Glendale and Rothbury, of the 3,043 infant deaths over the same period, only 742 or 24.4 per cent were in the third quarter. The most frequently recorded cause of summer infant deaths was, of course, diarrhoea. In five sample years of 1875, 1889, 1890, 1900 and 1910, there were 628 deaths from diarrhoea in Newcastle but two thirds of these (412) took place between July and the end of September. Morgan has suggested that enteric diseases spread by flies breeding in horse manure caused high levels of infant mortality and the explosive growth in the number of horses in late 19th-century expanding towns was therefore responsible for continuing high infant mortality levels.[54] Although most pronounced in overcrowded urban areas, the spectre of summer deaths from diarrhoea was not solely limited to such locations. In the market towns of Morpeth and Hexham in the third quarter in the same years there were 251 deaths, or 51 per cent, from diarrhoea.

Mobility: mid- to later 19th century

Some familiar forms of mobility began to emerge. Although rural depopulation had been deplored for many years it had been uneven both in space and time, [55] but from mid-century there was a steady and consistent flow out of rural areas.[56] The local historian Dippie Dixon quoted a typical example of High Barton farm near Whittingham, where 'There are at the present time only two families, where, about the year 1830, there were seven families each supplying their quota of field workers'.[57]

However, the rapid growth of urban areas through migration can be over-estimated (Table 4). In Newcastle, in only three decades of the 19th century did migration gain exceed natural gain.[58] Within the larger towns a marked feature of mobility was the rapid turnover of population, especially in working-class districts, a 'churning' of population in search of marginal improvements in accommodation, wages, or access

---

52   Morgan, N., 'Infant mortality, flies and horses in later-nineteenth century towns: a case study of Preston', *Continuity and Change*, vol. 17 (1) (2002), pp.97-132.

53   Williams, N., 'Death in its season: Class, environment and the mortality of infants in nineteenth century Sheffield', *Social History of Medicine*, vol. 5 (1992), pp.71-94.

54   Morgan, N. (2002), *op. cit.*

55   Dixon, D.D., *Whittingham Vale* (Newcastle upon Tyne, 1895), pp.174-5; Christie, J., *Northumberland: Its History, Its Features and its People* (Carlisle, Newcastle and London, 1904).

56   Lawton, R., 'Rural depopulation in nineteenth century England', in Steel, R.W. and Lawton, R. (eds), *Liverpool Essays in Geography* (London, 1967), pp.227-56.

57   Dixon (1895), *op. cit.*, pp.174-5.

58   Barke, M. (2001), *op. cit.*, p.136.

to jobs.[59] The migration history within Newcastle of the Goodburn family, resident at 17 Percy Street at the 1891 census, was not untypical and may be traced from the unusually precise recording of the birthplaces of their children. The father, John Goodburn, employed as a brass finisher, had been born at 9 Percy Street in 1842. His wife Sarah gave birth to their first child at 3 Oakes Place. Their next three children were born at 3 Park Place and the youngest, aged nine at the time of the census, had been born at 19 Lisle Street. A more frequently recognised feature of mobility was the process of suburbanisation of the middle classes (Jesmond, Bensham) which set in train copycat moves: the middle classes followed the élite, and the lower middle class followed the middle class. Such developments introduced new daily rhythms within urban areas based on longer but regular journeys to work,[60] facilitated by developments in public transport.[61] This process led to the emergence of 'city regions' as recognisable elements in the spatial structure of the North East.[62]

The coal-mining industry produced its own patterns of mobility. Throughout the century these were modified in quite subtle and complex ways. At mid-century, in the relatively newly exploited sections of the coalfield, by far the most common source of labour was provided by short-range movement from other parts of the Durham coalfield.[63] For example, at Hetton, where John Buddle had demonstrated that 'hidden' coal seams continued under the Magnesian limestone, 53 per cent (339 individuals) of coal miners who were heads of households in 1851 had been born in County Durham, but of these 211 (62 per cent) originated in the old mid-Wear section of the coalfield immediately west of Hetton. The majority of remaining Durham-born miners had moved to Hetton from the lower Tyne, especially Jarrow and Hebburn where coal production had peaked earlier, followed by a decline after about 1820. A further 182 coal miners (28 per cent) had been born in Northumberland, the vast majority in the areas to the south east of the 'ninety fathom dyke', where mining had also peaked in the 1820s and 1830s in locations such as Benton, Longbenton and Wallsend.[64] Other small but significant sources of labour were the declining Pennine lead dales of the Alston area (24 miners), Swaledale and Reeth (29 miners). Elsewhere, more specific factors affected migration patterns. In the long-established mining area of West Rainton, for example, acquired by Lord Londonderry in the early 19th century, a significant minority of miners present in 1851 had been born

59 Barke, M., *Social Change in Benwell* (Newcastle upon Tyne, 1977); MacRaild, D.M. and Martin, D.E., *Labour in British Society, 1830-1914* (Basingstoke, 2000), p.66.

60 Barke, M., 'The middle class journey to work in Newcastle upon Tyne, 1850-1913', *Journal of Transport History*, Third Series, vol. 12 (2) (1991), pp.107-34.

61 Barke, M., 'The development of public transport in Newcastle upon Tyne and Tyneside, 1850-1914', *Journal of Regional and Local Studies*, vol. 12 (1) (1992), pp.29-52.

62 Barke, M., 'Newcastle/Tyneside 1890-1980', in Gordon, G. (ed.), *Regional Cities in the UK, 1890-1980* (London, 1986).

63 Smailes, A.E., 'Population changes in the colliery districts of Northumberland and Durham', *Geographical Journal*, vol. 91 (1938), pp.220-32.

64 Sill, M., 'Mid-nineteenth century labour mobility: the case of the coal-miners of Hetton-le-Hole, Co. Durham', *Local Population Studies*, vol. 22 (1979), pp.44-50.

in Ireland on Lord Londonderry's estates in County Down and had initially been brought to the village during the 1844 strike.[65]

Over the century, longer distance migration gained in importance.[66] At Willington, the number of coal miner heads of households born outside the North East increased from 225 in 1861 to 431 in 1881, with the mining areas of West Cumberland being especially important sources and, most interestingly, 23 from the Somerset coalfield.[67] For Wingate Colliery, Sill notes, 'the owners ... advanced £4 to each Cornish family in order to pay for the transport of themselves and their families to Durham', the money being repaid in instalments deducted subsequently from their wages.[68] Such processes affected the structure of settlements: 'As some of the Benton migrants [to Hetton] lived in neighbouring blocks of cottages ... something akin to an organised movement of mineworkers is suggested.'[69]

The recruitment of specialist labour over longer distances was not limited to coal mining. The developing iron-making centre of Consett attracted large numbers of Scots and Irish workers in the 1850s and 1860s.[70] Shipbuilding was an industry significantly affected by the trade cycle and this led to periodic flows of workers between north-east yards and the Clyde.[71] A feature of the shipbuilding industry was the high turnover of labour, especially the lesser skilled,[72] and the frequent disputes between labourers and the skilled workers who paid them.[73] But also at Crook, where Irish coke workers formed the largest single national group, a comparison of their names from the 1851 and 1861 censuses shows that of the 134 Irish-born at the former date only one was identifiably still residing there in 1861.[74] In the case of Armstrong's Elswick engineering works, even if the recruitment of labour was not direct there was certainly an overt attempt to secure local supplies of skilled labour through stimulating the provision of housing within the Elswick and Benwell areas.[75] Elsewhere, the direct provision of housing was used as an incentive. Palmer built dwellings and established a building society for his workers at Jarrow and Andrew Leslie similarly provided housing for some of his key workers at Hebburn. Although there is no direct evidence of conscious recruitment, it is perhaps significant that, of 43 households so housed in 1861, 25 heads had been born in Scotland.[76]

---

65 MacRaild, D.M. and Martin, D.E. (2000), *op.cit.*, p.96.

66 Sill, M., 'E.G. Ravenstein and coal miner migration: East Durham in the nineteenth century', *Durham County Local History Society Bulletin*, vol. 32 (1984), pp.2-23.

67 Ayre, P., 'Patterns of Migration into a South-West Durham Mining Community' (unpublished BA (Hons) Dissertation, Department of Environment, Newcastle Polytechnic, 1991).

68 Sill (1984), *op. cit.*, p.15.

69 Sill (1979), *op. cit.*, p.49.

70 MacRaild, D.M. and Martin, D.E. (2000), *op. cit.*, p.67.

71 MacRaild, D.M. and Martin, D.E. (2000), *op. cit.*, p.80.

72 Clarke, J.F., *Power on Land and Sea* (Newcastle upon Tyne, 1977), p.35.

73 McCord, N., *North East England* (London, 1979), pp.128-38.

74 McManus, M., 'From townland to township: the complex evolution of a dissipative famine Irish community in County Durham', *North East History*, vol. 35 (2004), pp.7-53.

75 Barke, M. (1977), *op. cit.*; Benwell Community Project, *The Making of a Ruling Class* (Newcastle upon Tyne, 1978).

76 Clarke, J.F., *Building Ships on the North east Coast, Part 1* (Whitley Bay, 1997), p.288.

Table 8 Selected settlements – population, sex, age, employment, birthplace and household size, 1851 and 1901.

Area	Popula-tion	Sex Ratio (males per 1000 females)	% aged under 15	% emp. in Agri-culture (&)	% local born (*)	House-holds of 1 or 2 per-sons	Mean House-hold size ($)
Rural Agricul-tural:							
Norham 1851	3315	937	39.8	50.8	47.0	16.0	5.13
Norham 1901	2149	883	31.6	46.3	36.6	23.7	4.31
Alwinton 1851	699	1003	34.5	52.3	43.3	12.0	5.27
Alwinton 1901	481	1100	31.2	52.0	32.6	25.7	4.62
Whittingham 1851	705	975	38.2	43.8	36.0	14.3	5.46
Whittingham 1901	439	942	30.5	35.9	26.2	19.4	4.18
Rural Fishing:							
Seahouses 1851	701	986	44.6	11.4	39.1	25.0	4.38
Seahouses 1901	685	991	34.3	2.9	62.3	19.3	4.71
Cullercoats 1851	694	881	39.0	2.9	76.8	23.6	4.34
Cullercoats 1901	1748	964	37.9	0.0	66.7	15.3	4.55
Mining/Quarry-ing:							
Crook 1851	936	1277	38.1	2.4	14.2	12.0	5.12
Crook 1901	1927	1054	36.4	0.3	51.4	15.7	4.75
Stanhope 1851	1158	1060	37.7	4.6	75.6	16.6	4.60
Stanhope 1901	1944	970	33.5	3.7	68.9	22.8	4.44
Easington 1851	918	1072	37.5	41.2	36.6	18.0	4.74
Easington 1901	1424	1257	34.2	8.3	10.0	17.6	5.19
Urban/Suburban:							
Hexham Priest-popple 1851	864	886	39.8	6.5	60.3	23.2	4.38
Hexham Priest-popple 1901	775	909	30.6	1.9	50.1	23.9	4.31
Bensham 1851	1276	769	32.4	2.7	48.2	12.8	4.71
Bensham 1901	2294	946	35.0	0.2	48.9	15.8	4.67
Pipewellgate 1851	926	1013	44.6	0.6	36.7	14.0	5.02
Pipewellgate 1901	953	1072	44.2	0.0	66.3	21.3	4.31
Jesmond 1851	1309	589	48.7	2.8	46.7	18.4	4.91
Jesmond 1901	1631	580	20.0	0.5	44.4	13.4	4.90

(&) calculated as a proportion of total economically active

(*) 'local born' is defined as born within parish of current residence

($) Households are defined following Anderson's methodology. See Anderson, M., 'Standard tabulation procedures for houses, households, and other groups of residents in the enumeration books of the censuses of 1851 to 1891', in Wrigley, E.A. (ed.), *Nineteenth Century Society* (Cambridge, 1972).

Social Character of Settlements, 1851 and 1901

Table 8 (opposite) shows a range of rural and urban areas with different socio-economic characteristics.

It is immediately apparent that north-east settlements differed markedly in their characteristics although there are also some surprising similarities between areas with very different economies. Mining communities showed the usual high proportion of males to females,[77] but so, too, did inner-city slum areas like Pipewellgate in Gateshead and remote rural areas like Alwinton. Trajectories of development within local areas were also reflected, as in the case of the two city suburbs of Jesmond and Bensham. The sex ratio of the former was heavily biased towards females, mainly because of the very high proportion of female servants residing within the area, and this was maintained to the end of the century. Bensham shared this feature for 1851 but the sex ratio had changed dramatically by 1901 reflecting the declining status of the suburb. Mean household size was particularly high in rural areas, especially in 1851, as it was in mining districts and Pipewellgate. By 1901 it had fallen everywhere, mainly reflecting the national trend towards smaller families and the reduction of living-in servants, although Cullercoats, Seahouses and Easington were exceptions.[78] In the case of Cullercoats, suburban middle-class growth provided accommodation for larger nuclear families. At both Seahouses and Easington new economic opportunities led to more lodgers, in the case of the former thanks to the opening of the new harbour in 1889, and in the latter because of the beginning of large-scale exploitation of the concealed coalfield.[79]

Households

Laslett maintained that the mean household size in England (including servants) changed little from the 16th century through to the end of the 19th century, remaining at a fairly constant 4.75 persons. In seven of the 12 sample settlements in 1851 the mean household size exceeded this figure (Table 8). More significantly, the majority of the population of each settlement lived in households of five or more people, even in places with very different economic bases. For example, in 1851, three-quarters of the population in both Crook and Norham lived in households of over five people. Moreover, as Armstrong has pointed out, 'the constancy of mean household size concealed a series of shifts in household composition', structural changes that detailed census data allow us to reconstruct.[80] Despite the unusual honesty of John Frost, of 34 Veatch's Buildings, Pipewellgate, who recorded himself co-residing with his 'mistress',

---

77   Friedlander, D. (1973), *op. cit.*
78   Wall, R., 'The household: demographic and economic change in England, 1650-1970', in Wall, R. (ed.) *Family Forms in Historic Europe* (Cambridge, 1983), p.496.
79   Moyes, W.A., *Mostly Mining* (Newcastle upon Tyne, 1969), pp.67-100.
80   Armstrong, W.A., 'A note on the household structure of mid-nineteenth century York in comparative perspective', in Laslett, P. and Wall, R. (eds), *Household and Family in Past Time* (Cambridge, 1972), p.214.

Annie Duffy, in their one room in 1901, it is widely recognised that, in England, the nuclear family was the normal form of domestic organisation from the 16th century onwards,[81] and that the local character of employment opportunities was the main feature regulating the incidence of marriage and, therefore, subsequent child bearing and rearing.[82] Richard Wall has traced the historical relationship between the trend of real wages and the headship rate (that is, the proportion of persons by age who headed their own households) in a series of English communities.[83] If the relationship is a close one it seems likely that more men in their 20s and 30s would marry and form their own households in those communities where incomes or prospective incomes were relatively high. Table 9 shows for each locality the proportion of males aged 21 to 30 who (a) were household heads and (b) had ever been married. The traditional interpretation would be that a higher marriage rate and earlier marriage implies relatively buoyant economic prospects. Table 9 confirms that place of residence had a massive impact on the propensity to marry.

Table 9 Headship rates and proportions ever married, males aged 21-30, 1851 and 1901

	1851		1901	
	Males 21-30 Heads of Households	Males 21-30 ever married	Males 21-30 Heads of Households	Males 21-30 ever married
Norham	·28.0	36.2	20.0	21.4
Alwinton	13.0	9.3	19.5	17.1
Whittingham	16.0	24.0	19.2	23.1
Seahouses	57.4	55.3	20.9	29.8
Cullercoats	44.1	50.8	47.1	51.0
Crook	41.0	50.4	29.6	36.5
Stanhope	41.3	46.8	27.6	30.7
Easington	31.3	45.8	30.4	34.5
Hexham	40.0	44.4	27.3	30.1
Bensham	80.9	92.1	38.0	39.6
Pipewellgate	51.6	66.1	60.3	66.2
Jesmond	34.7	38.9	20.7	25.0

In 1851 the extremes were represented by Alwinton, possibly the remotest part of Northumberland, where only 16 per cent of 21- to 30-year-olds were heads of their own household and, on the other hand, the rapidly expanding Gateshead suburb of Bensham, where no less than 81 per cent were household heads. Although by 1901 the range was reduced it still remained considerable. Of equal interest is the difference between the proportion who were heads and the proportion who were 'ever married'.

81   Laslett, P. and Wall, R. (eds), *Household and Family in Past Time* (Cambridge, 1972), *passim*.
82   Levine, D., *Family Formation in an Age of Nascent Capitalism* (New York, 1977), pp.45-87.
83   Wall, R., 'The household: demographic and economic change in England, 1650-1970', in Wall, R. (ed.), *Family Forms in Historic Europe* (Cambridge, 1983), pp.493-512.

In most cases the latter exceeded the former, indicating the inability to set up an independent household upon marriage. Whilst we can only speculate on the individual reasons for this, it was particularly pronounced in areas where housing supply was under severe pressure through rapid growth – Pipewellgate, Bensham, Easington and Crook. Such shortages imply that married couples and possibly their offspring were living with other households. But in Alwinton and Seahouses in 1851 more young men were independent heads of households than were actually married. Clearly, the nature of domestic life for young men of the same age varied quite remarkably across the North East.

Perhaps the most extreme case of the closeness of ties between the nature of work and the nature of the household concerned agricultural workers in

49 *Providence Place, Pipewellgate. Multi-occupied dwellings with outside stairs and shared facilities.*

north Northumberland, where family hiring was a common practice and the family remained the essential working unit up to the First World War. This was reinforced by the fact that regular workers were provided with accommodation (rather like pitmen): 'Throughout the greater part of this county, and especially upon the large farms, there are very few servants kept in the house.'[84] This explains the surprisingly low proportion of resident (farm) servants in Norham (Table 10). Male workers had also to provide a female worker, even if they were unmarried. The pressures to encourage marriage and, indeed, to ensure a regular supply of offspring into the workforce, are obvious. Households in Norham, in 1851, possessed the highest proportion of offspring, a feature that runs contrary to the assertion that 'industrial urban areas offered to children greater opportunities to continue to live with parents than had been available in domestically organised rural societies'.[85]

In terms of 19th-century household structure, previous studies[86] have noted the high proportion of households with resident kin, the high proportion of lodgers, the decline in the proportion of resident servants, increase in co-residence of parents and married children and increasing proportion of 'other kin' resident.[87] In accordance

84 Bailey, J. and Culley, G. (1972), *op. cit.*, p.164.
85 Anderson, M., *Approaches to the History of the Western Family, 1500-1914* (Basingstoke, 1980), p.26.
86 Anderson, M. (1972), *op. cit.*; Armstrong, W.A. (1972), *op. cit.*
87 Foster (1974), *op. cit.*

with these studies, the proportion of resident servants declined everywhere apart from Jesmond and, marginally, in Hexham Priestpopple (the latter largely because of an increase in the number of resident shop assistants who were classed as 'servants'). The proportion of lodgers varied considerably across north-east settlements in ways that are not necessarily explicable by rural-urban difference. Rather they reflected differences

Table 10 Structure of Households, 1851 and 1901
(Position in household as % of total population)

Area	Head of Household	Spouse	Offspring	Relatives	Resident Servants	Lodgers, Boarders, Visitors
Rural Agricultural:						
Norham 1851	19.4	13.7	52.2	7.7	5.0	1.9
Norham 1901	22.8	13.7	46.6	11.1	3.8	1.9
Alwinton 1851	18.5	10.9	39.0	11.5	13.3	6.7
Alwinton 1901	21.9	13.2	44.1	9.7	7.8	3.3
Whitingham 1851	18.0	12.4	47.7	10.2	8.8	2.9
Whittingham 1901	23.7	15.5	42.6	7.7	5.2	5.2
Rural Fishing:						
Seahouses 1851	23.0	15.4	50.6	7.3	2.1	1.6
Seahouses 1901	20.6	16.0	50.8	6.7	1.6	4.2
Cullercoats 1851	22.9	14.0	47.3	7.3	4.9	3.6
Cullercoats 1901	21.9	16.2	50.8	6.4	1.5	3.1
Mining/Quarrying:						
Crook 1851	19.7	15.9	39.9	5.7	3.7	15.0
Crook 1901	20.8	16.8	48.6	6.2	1.9	5.6
Stanhope 1851	21.6	13.3	44.1	8.6	5.0	7.4
Stanhope 1901	22.0	15.6	48.6	7.8	3.1	2.9
Easington 1851	19.8	13.9	42.5	9.1	6.8	8.0
Easington 1901	19.0	14.3	45.3	4.8	3.7	12.8
Urban/Suburban:						
Hexham Priest-popple 1851	22.1	14.3	44.5	7.9	3.1	7.6
Hexham Priest-popple 1901	23.2	14.3	44.2	5.8	3.7	8.6
Bensham 1851	20.5	15.5	41.3	7.3	9.9	5.5
Bensham 1901	21.1	16.6	51.9	5.6	1.6	3.2
Pipewellgate 1851	20.0	16.5	50.8	5.9	2.4	4.4
Pipewellgate 1901	22.6	16.9	52.1	6.2	0.3	2.0
Jesmond 1851	19.3	12.1	41.3	7.7	16.2	3.4
Jesmond 1901	18.1	13.7	40.0	7.1	16.9	4.2

in economic opportunity and variations in housing provision. In general, however, the proportion of lodgers declined although the very different settlements of Whittingham, Seahouses, Easington, Hexham Priestpopple and Jesmond all showed increases.

Different levels of accidents and mortality were associated with different forms of employment. For example, both Cullercoats and Seahouses in 1851 had a relatively

Table 11 Resident relatives (% of all kin, excluding siblings) by relationship to household head, 1851 and 1901

Area	Sons & Daughters in Law	Nephews & Nieces	Grandchildren	Other Relatives	All Relatives as % of total population
Rural Agricultural:					
Norham 1851	5.1	16.1	32.3	46.5	7.7
Norham 1901	3.4	13.1	31.6	51.9	11.1
Alwinton 1851	2.6	23.7	34.2	39.5	11.5
Alwinton 1901	4.2	17.0	29.8	48.9	9.7
Whittingham 1851	6.8	31.1	28.4	33.8	10.2
Whittingham 1901	0.0	23.5	20.6	55.9	7.7
Rural Fishing:					
Seahouses 1851	2.0	7.8	47.1	43.1	7.3
Seahouses 1901	4.3	15.2	39.1	41.3	6.7
Cullercoats 1851	2.0	27.4	33.3	37.2	7.3
Cullercoats 1901	10.0	18.0	37.8	34.2	6.4
Mining/Quarrying:					
Crook 1851	9.6	11.5	15.4	63.5	5.7
Crook 1901	6.7	16.8	26.9	49.6	6.2
Stanhope 1851	9.0	9.0	31.0	51.0	8.6
Stanhope 1901	12.8	14.2	28.4	44.6	7.8
Easington 1851	12.0	21.7	32.5	33.7	9.1
Easington 1901	4.3	18.8	27.5	49.3	4.8
Urban/Suburban:					
Hexham Priestpopple 1851	5.8	18.8	55.1	20.3	7.9
Hexham Priestpopple 1901	8.9	17.8	42.2	31.1	5.8
Bensham 1851	4.3	21.5	16.1	58.1	7.3
Bensham 1901	3.1	16.2	21.5	59.2	5.6
Pipewellgate 1851	5.6	16.7	46.3	31.5	5.9
Pipewellgate 1901	6.8	20.3	42.4	30.5	6.2
Jesmond 1851	2.0	23.0	24.0	51.0	7.7
Jesmond 1901	3.4	16.0	17.6	63.0	7.1

high proportion of children living with their mother only, the majority of whom were widows. However, this feature was not apparent to the same extent in mining communities, possibly because of the different age structures of the communities involved. For example, Crook in 1851, due to its very youthful overall age structure, had a relatively high probability of both parents being alive. As families grew older, the greater was the probability of one or both parents dying or leaving.

The final feature to examine concerns the presence within the household of relatives of various kinds. This is shown in Table 11. There were only small variations between the different settlements in the proportion of relatives resident and, perhaps more surprisingly, this changed little over the second fifty years of the century. Crook, Norham and Pipewellgate showed actual increases in the proportion of relatives resident, whilst all other areas showed marginal declines. However, the structure of this component of the sample households did vary quite remarkably. Contrary to the generally accepted view of the 19th century as a period of increased co-residence of parents and married children, the proportion of sons- and daughters-in-law did not constitute a particularly significant component of co-residing kin, although it did increase significantly in Cullercoats between 1851 and 1901.[88] Only in Stanhope did it persist as a significant proportion.

It is difficult to interpret these changes through the conventional view of co-residence with parents in the early years of marriage being a solution to the problems of affordability in forming one's own separate household immediately upon marriage, an issue likely to be reinforced in areas where housing was in generally short supply. Such a situation may be expected to be more likely in urban areas, especially in the poorer districts such as Pipewellgate, but this is clearly not the case. Rather more significant as resident kin were nephews and nieces. The decline of such 'extended' families is usually interpreted as being a product of urbanisation but Table 11 does not support this view as the proportion of resident nephews and nieces generally increased in the urban industrial areas over the 1851-1901 period. More significant was the proportion of children living with their grandparents. This was high in both rural and urban areas but especially so in areas of known high adult mortality rates. Finally, the highest category of all was 'other relatives', and although some authorities have noted this group as a growing aspect of household structure in urban industrial society,[89] in Table 11 there is, once again, no obvious rural-urban differentiation. It becomes tempting to 'disclaim any association of a particular household type with either urbanization or industrialization'.[90] Residential household complexity was a feature of Norham, Alwinton and Whittingham just as much as it was of Pipewellgate, Bensham and Jesmond.

88 Anderson, M. (1972), *op. cit.*; Wall, R. (1983), *op. cit.*
89 Anderson, M. (1972), *op. cit.*; Foster, J. (1974), *op. cit.*
90 Wall (1983), *op. cit.*, p.511.

50 *Bensham Road, Gateshead. Church, Bank and Tramway are all physical signifiers of lower-middle-class respectability.*

Conclusion

The counties of Northumberland and Durham experienced a demographic explosion in the course of the 19th century. The characteristics of this explosion may be summarised succinctly. Early on it was driven mainly by a high rate of natural increase which, in turn, was fuelled by a high marriage rate. Considerable short-distance migration produced pockets of youthful population with a high reproductive potential. In the latter part of the century, the birth rate remained high, especially by national standards, and unlike many other areas of England and Wales was still strongly linked to a continuingly high marriage rate. But longer distance migration became much more common in the later 19th century, with destinations focused on large towns. The death rate remained high by national levels, with especially high levels of infant mortality. At mid-century rural-urban differentials were very limited but as the century progressed they worsened in urban areas, especially in the case of infant mortality. Although the proportion of nuclear families increased, by 1901 it was still common for household structures in many areas to be much more complex than this. But the apparent unity bestowed upon the region by its geographical structure was not reflected in uniform patterns in these features of demographic change. Rural areas experienced different trajectories of development. Patterns in the coalfield were highly fluid. Urban areas grew at different times and at different rates. Household structures showed some surprising similarities between places with very different economic bases, for example in household size across agricultural and mining districts. When viewed on a national scale the North East demonstrated some distinctive features but within this dramatically changing region the demographic and social character of settlements varied almost equally dramatically.

12

Rebuilding the Diocese in the Industrial Age: The Church of England and the Durham Coalfield, 1810-1920

ROB LEE

I

About two-thirds of the way through the film *Billy Elliott*, our hero from the east Durham coalfield is in London, preparing for an audition at ballet school. In the changing-rooms, a middle-class lad attempts to make conversation.

'Where are you from?' he asks.

'I'm from County Durham.'

'Durham!' exclaims the middle-class lad. 'Isn't there an amazing cathedral there?'

'Dunno,' says our Billy. 'I've never been.'

The scene confirms the heavy implication of the film that late 20th-century working-class communities are essentially insular: Billy's Dad has already confessed that he is making his first trip to London. But there is more to it than this. The exchange between the two boys reveals that to middle-class, southern sensibilities, County Durham means Durham city, and Durham city means Durham Cathedral. For Billy Elliott, however, Durham means coal; it means the men who dig it, and the communities that live by it. Those other places, peopled by ecclesiastics and academics on the Wear peninsula, inhabit another world altogether.

It was not meant to be like this. For a succession of Durham bishops – Baring, Lightfoot, Westcott and Moule – the last decades of the 19th century, and the first of the 20th, represented an opportunity for outreach into the Durham coalfield. Their ambition was to revive the Church of England's fortunes in a region that was the country's principal area of coal production. Population increase and industrial development since the early 1800s had raced ahead while the Church was still struggling

51 *The Rev. W. Wilson and John Horsley (parish clerk), Joseph Bouet, c.1830. An image indicative of the domineering nature of the Church of England in the early 19th century.*

to pull its boots on. By the middle of the 19th century, it seemed clear that religious need was being catered for by Methodism and other Protestant nonconformist denominations, or by Roman Catholicism. Often, it was not being catered for at all.

Durham's Victorian missionaries were faced with a set of circumstances and problems that were peculiar to the diocese. First of all, the Church in Durham was laden with legend in a way that sustained a powerful connection with the earliest days of Christianity in the north of England. Secondly, the Durham diocese was phenomenally wealthy. And, thirdly, its administration was trapped in a medieval infrastructure that bore little relation to the rapidly changing landscape of population and industry. The object of this chapter is to assess the effectiveness of the diocesan mission, and to interpret the successes and failures of its work in the context posed by these unusual difficulties. What was the Church of England trying to achieve in Durham between 1860 and 1920? How did this differ from the preceding fifty years? Did the Church make any meaningful impression on the life of the coalfield? And how, in any case, might this be measured?

Durham's unique legacy wove an almost mystical aura around the cathedral on the hill. Here lie the remains of Cuthbert and Bede, so crucial to the development of Christianity in England. Here, too, was the seat of the prince bishops, who for centuries had governed their Palatinate with all the delegated authority of regional kings. By the early 19th century both these strands of tradition were feeling the wind of change – Cuthbert was exhumed in 1827 as part of an investigation that combined antiquarianism with high politics, and the last, lingering ceremonial powers of the prince bishop reverted to the Crown on the death of Bishop Van Mildert in 1837. Nevertheless, even in its most progressive moments, the diocese never seemed fully to conceal its dismay that a glorious past of saints and princes had somehow given way to a more prosaic world of Labour councillors and working men's clubs. At the same time, increasing political sophistication among the miners seemed to run against the paraphernalia of long-dead saints and bishops. 'Whether the bishop is acting legally or not we cannot say,' grumbled the *Newcastle Weekly Chronicle* about a burial dispute in 1873, 'but his lordship's predecessors are said to have enjoyed all manner of privileges, royalties, franchises and immunities by virtue of a *jura regalia* which King Canute conferred on the Church when once upon a time he paid a visit of pilgrimage to the shrine of St Cuthbert.'[1]

This resentment – that the Church enjoyed privileges that it had earned only in ancient times – naturally extended to its wealth. Criticism was not confined to Durham, but Durham did provide a particularly vivid example of just how rich and out of touch the Anglican Church was felt to have become. In 1832 the wealth of the Church, its sometimes shady origins and its scandalous misuse, had fallen under the critical scrutiny of a radical writer named John Wade.[2] Wade saw parallels between the over-privileged Church of England and the Church of Rome in the last days before the Reformation, and found much to confirm his thesis within the cloistered walls of Durham. Clerical incomes on a scale that made critics of the Church sit up and take notice were to be found in the Durham diocese at places like Stanhope, Bishopwearmouth and Houghton-le-Spring, where incumbents who were frequently pluralists enjoyed livings that were among the richest in the country.[3] The wealth of the diocese itself, built from the rents and royalties of landownership and mineral extraction, underwent a meteoric rise from the late 18th century. By 1831, the Bishop's annual income stood at almost £22,000, comfortably outstripping those of the Bishops of London and Chester, even though they had bigger and more populated dioceses to oversee. Including the value of the Dean and Chapter's holdings, the yearly corporate income of Durham Cathedral now stood at £28,000: over £10,000 more than that of Canterbury.[4] Wade's perception was that the Church contributed to a nexus of power and wealth that was preventing England from becoming a true meritocracy.

Whatever the fairness and accuracy of Wade's critique, it is clear that, even while he was writing it, the Durham diocese was rapidly being overtaken by events. At the core of the problem was population increase, generated by expansion in the coal industry. During a century that saw the country's population increase by 330 per cent, County Durham's increased by 780 per cent. The ecclesiastical infrastructure of the diocese, which had been designed to meet the needs of dispersed, often thinly populated settlements, simply could not cope with this demographic revolution. Its ancient parish churches at the heart of old rural communities now stood remote and empty, well away from the new centres of population. Many newly built mining townships went unvisited by their parish clergymen, whose rectories had been positioned to serve the medieval parish, and who now found themselves living in some half-forgotten backwater.

---

1 *Newcastle Weekly Chronicle*, 'Our Colliery Villages' series, 14 June 1873.
2 Wade, J. (ed.), *The Extraordinary Black Book: An Exposition of Abuses in Church and State* (London, 1832), pp.6-9 and *passim*.
3 Heesom, A., *The Founding of the University of Durham*, Durham Cathedral Lecture Series (1982), *passim* has much more on this. Heesom notes (p.13) that 'in 1832 44% of all the incumbents in the Archdeaconry of Durham were pluralists, while in the cathedral all the minor canons and ten of the twelve prebendaries were pluralists'. Parson's *Trade Directory* (1828), p.262 sets the value of the living of Houghton-le-Spring at £2,500 p.a., 'one of the richest rectories in England'.
4 *Ibid.*, 17; Maynard, W.B., 'The ecclesiastical administration of the Archdeaconry of Durham 1774-1856' (unpublished PhD, Durham University, 1973), p.18.

A succession of 19th-century bishops had done their best to address this problem, and had encouraged the building of new churches and the creation of new parishes wherever they could, but without the co-ordinated will of the Anglican establishment – landowners and patrons as well as the diocesan authorities – there was a limit to how much they could achieve. In 1858 a committee of the House of Lords, appointed to enquire into the state of religious provision in the mining districts, reported that the counties of Northumberland and Durham were less well provided with church accommodation than any other counties in England. The situation, the committee declared, was one of 'spiritual destitution'. Of course, this bore all the hallmarks of a distinctively Anglican view. There *was* religion in the coalfield: immigrant communities were bringing Catholicism, or the Methodism that was often espoused by a new generation of colliery managers and trade union leaders alike. Naturally, the Church of England was concerned to maintain its own denominational strength, and the unpalatable truth was that in some communities it would be arriving as little more than a minority, dissenting, sect.

The High Toryism of the Cathedral had long been at odds with the radically inclined city and county that surrounded it, but now the narrow, strangulated loop of the river beneath began to take on a symbolic new aspect. The lofty eminence that loomed above it had become isolated in so many ways: an island of tradition amid a sea of change; of wealth amid deprivation; of unearned income amid commercial drive. The Church in Durham seemed to have collapsed in upon itself, with an inner core that was centred on the Cathedral and neglected by the margins. This, in 1860, was the unpromising starting-point for Durham's internal diocesan mission.

II

A public meeting held in Newcastle in January 1860 marked the formal start of the Church of England's mission into the Durham coalfield. Here a commitment was made to 'provide clergy who shall minister among that portion of the population which cannot be fully reached by the existing parochial machinery, more especially among the Pitmen, Miners and Ironworkers in the outlying districts'.

In terms of transforming the 'existing parochial machinery', it cannot be denied that the results of this meeting were astonishing. An archdeaconry of 86 parishes in 1800 had become a diocese of 262 parishes by 1920. One hundred and thirty-two of these new parishes had been created since that 1860 meeting.[5] The work was seen straightforwardly as a matter of 'mission', often indistinguishable from the missionary work being undertaken in the colonies. 'A body of missionaries is absolutely necessary for the Pit districts', wrote the Rev. H. Ridley of Durham St Cuthbert, and, as William Scott of New Seaham put it, 'I believe a well organised Diocesan Home

---

5   The geographical area described in this chapter as 'the diocese of Durham' was, strictly speaking, only its southern archdeaconry before 1882. In that year the northern archdeaconry, roughly equating to the county of Northumberland, became the Diocese of Newcastle.

Mission providing faithful men to preach from parish to parish … would tend much to stir up the brethren and to commend our church and its ministers to the mining population where at present they are ignorant of and prejudiced against us.' When the Rev. Richard Hutt was appointed to the new living of Easington Lane in 1868, it was the fact that his previous job had been Principal of the Kaffir Training Institution in South Africa that marked him out as 'eminently qualified'.[6]

More generally, it seems to have dawned on the Church that missionary zeal in these hearts of darkness was best imparted by men who could establish a rapport with their working-class parishioners. This entailed a radical change in clergy recruitment. Table 1 is based on the baptism records of approximately 2,000 clergymen ordained in the Durham diocese between 1810 and 1920. It shows that in the early decades of the 19th century, clergymen whose fathers had been members of the aristocracy or gentry – or had themselves been clergymen – constituted 67 per cent of all Durham ordinands. By the early 20th century that proportion had tailed off to 29 per cent, while over the same period recruitment from the lower-middle and working classes had increased from 23 to 53 per cent. By 1920 over half of Durham's new clergymen came from lower-middle or working-class backgrounds.

Table 1 Percentage of clerical ordinands from different social backgrounds in the Durham diocese 1810-1920, analysed in three 20-year cohorts

Father's occupation type	% of ordinands in this social group, 1810 - 1830	% of ordinands in this social group 1855 - 1875	% of ordinands in this social group 1900 - 1920
clergyman	44.9	22.4	23.0
aristocracy; gentry	21.8	12.7	5.9
professional middle class	10.3	26.5	18.3
lower middle class	14.1	13.3	23.0
skilled working class	7.7	22.7	26.4
unskilled working class	1.2	2.6	3.4

SOURCE: Durham University Palace Green Library: Durham Diocesan Records, Ordination Papers 1810-1920.

What did this mean? It meant, in essence, that one of the central criticisms levelled at the diocese – that it had too many irrelevant, inefficient parishes that were being treated as the playthings of rich families – had begun to be addressed.

The antagonism expressed by Wade in his *Black Book* had been fuelled not simply by the wealth of the Church in Durham, but by the fact that much of this wealth was enjoyed by clergymen who hardly visited their parishes and who contributed nothing to the spiritual well-being of their congregations. These men were either straightforward non-residents, choosing to live somewhere more congenial, or were pluralists, whose time was spent looking after another parish. Between 1801 and 1820 the Bishop of Durham had granted no fewer than 243 licences for non-residency. Thirty-eight of

---

6   Durham County Record Office EP/EL SM 14/1 History of Lyons parish, 1869-1944.

these had been granted because of problems with the incumbent's health – although these could, of course, be relative. The Rev. J. Greville at Whickham, for instance, was suffering from a 'nervous complaint affecting his stomach & Head' which, his doctor felt, could only be alleviated by 'exercise on horseback ... cheerful company ... [and] passing the winter in Bath'.[7]

Sixty years on, clergymen were still being granted leave of absence from their parishes on grounds of ill-health, frequently brought on by their proximity to coal-mining activity. All three clergymen in South Shields' principal parishes were absent for this reason in the 1860s, while at Dalton-le-Dale the Rev. Udney Allen had found that his 'residence in a neighbourhood highly charged with carbonaceous matter had induced so much disturbance of the Functions of the Liver as to have induced secondary incipient disease of the lower intestine'.[8] Yet, during the same 60-year period, the two greatest causes of clerical non-residence had been removed: the fact that the vicar held another living and chose to live in his other parish, and the absence of an adequate parsonage house for him to live in. Between 1800 and 1850, 273 licences had been granted for these reasons; between 1850 and 1910, just ten. The Pluralities Act of 1838, imposing strict residency obligations upon beneficed clergymen, had brought about a revolution in the patterns of absenteeism.

III

By the late 19th century, then, a combination of Durham's own reform initiatives and national legislation meant that the landscape of Church of England parishes was beginning to look very different. Townships where clergymen had once been strangers were now often parishes in their own right; they had new churches and new, approachable vicars who lived 'over the shop' in convenient new rectories.

This, at least, was the theory, and it was a theory designed not only to answer the crisis of 'spiritual destitution' in the coalfield but also to meet the political threat posed by material destitution. Canon Body brought with him a bleak message to the opening of the Framwellgate Mission in Durham in 1887. 'They were,' he said,

> living on the brink of a volcano and ... unless they could convince these people ... that the rich *did* care about them, and that Christians *did* love them ... the end of such a state of society must be social chaos.[9]

The Church of England was uniquely well placed to act as a kind of social lubricant between rich and poor because, as the Rector of Gateshead acknowledged, the Church stretched its tentacles far and near, high and low into society's controlling institutions.[10]

---

7   Durham University Palace Green Library DDR/EA/CLN 2 John Clark, MD to Shute Barrington, 13 August 1803.
8   Durham University Palace Green Library DDR/EA/CLN 2 Edward Long (surgeon) to Bishop Charles Baring, 27 September 1873.
9   *Durham Chronicle,* 6 May 1887.
10   Davies, Rev. J., *The Working Man in Relation to the Church of England* (London, 1861), p.24.

Even before the reforms, some clergymen took their responsibilities very seriously indeed. Their incumbencies almost became defined by the regularity of their visits to the homes of parishioners. Not only was the Rev. Horatio Spurrier of Shildon regularly to be seen 'stooping to enter the meanest hovels', he demanded nothing less of his curates, too:

> I have always made it a duty and a joy to visit personally every House in the Parish … I have taken the streets in a certain order, & when all have been visited I have repeated the method … I expect my curates to follow the same plan … visiting at least 10 families on each of 4 days a week. I expect them to make notes of their work, & to show their books every Monday.[11]

Spurrier reported to his Bishop that he was received 'cordially' on all his visits, and sources not usually sympathetic to the Church of England were prepared to acknowledge that his brand of pastoral care really did achieve results. His parish was said to be characterised by cleanliness, good housing, an engaged and sympathetic vicar; all reasons why Shildon 'worked' as a community.[12]

But other clergymen in the 1860s thought they were making less headway. At Thornley, near Kelloe in the east of the county, the Rev. William Shute found only grinding poverty and a formidable lack of interest in any message brought by the Anglican Church. 'The condition of the poor,' he wrote, 'is generally speaking very bad indeed.' He found that little support was forthcoming from the colliery owners, 'and the colliery staff being mostly Dissenters, the pitmen are induced to attend chapel'.[13]

The truth was that many new coalfield communities were not well disposed toward Anglican clergymen, whatever their background. All too often incumbents found that simply by being 'the parson' they were automatically placed on the side of 'Them' rather than 'Us'. This was a sifting that miners seemed almost invariably to carry out, irrespective of the merits and beliefs of the individual clergymen in question. And, of course, there were plenty of clergymen who richly deserved their classification. At Whitburn, in 1844, the Rev. Thomas Baker – enjoying the tenure of a living worth £1,200 per year – antagonised his parishioners by campaigning vigorously against a repeal of the Corn Laws at a time when the families of striking miners in the district were almost on the point of starvation.[14] At Penshaw, the Rev. James Waters seemed majestically untroubled by the extent of his ignorance. The bishop's visitation of 1861 probed away at the social awareness of the diocesan clergy, but failed to elicit many insights from Mr Waters:

---

11 Durham University Palace Green Library AUC/4/1 Visitation Returns, 1861.
12 *Newcastle Weekly Chronicle*, 'Our Colliery Villages' series, 7 June 1873.
13 Durham University Palace Green Library AUC/4/1 Vistitation Returns 1861.
14 *Durham Chronicle*, 26 January 1844.

[*Q: How many people regularly attend your church?*]
A: I do not know.
[*Q: How many attend dissenting chapels in your parish?*]
A: I do not know. No good people, I fear.
[*Q: How many people in your parish neglect all worship?*]
A: I do not know. Too many infidels among them.
[*Q: What is the population of your parish, and how many of them are extremely poor?*]
A: I have not the slightest idea.[15]

At Hebburn St Cuthbert the first rector found the smoke and fumes of the industrial river valley so intolerable that he ordered his new rectory to be built high on a breezy hilltop, remote from church and parishioners alike and demonstrating a capacity to escape that was, of course, denied to the vast majority of his flock.[16] Here and elsewhere were signs that the end of absenteeism did not always herald an era of mutual respect. Newly resident clergymen moved into rectories that were designed in the style of country houses, with sweeping drives and cedar-shaded lawns, standing apart from the hurly-burly of the working community. To the miners of the colliery row – often hastily built, and insanitary – the contrast could scarcely have appeared greater, or more telling.

Even so, the fact that the Durham diocesan mission had begun to introduce a different class of clergymen into its new coalfield parishes was demonstrated less by the rectories themselves than by the size and nature of rectory households.[17] If there were two distinct types of clergymen, there were two distinct sets of circumstances in which they lived. There were households like that at Denton, where the Rev. William Apter and his wife Amelia could afford no servants at all to help with their five children; and Crook, where the Rev. John King and his wife Louise – the parents of seven children – could afford only one live-in domestic help. These were rectories that contrasted

52 *An unidentified clergyman wields a pick during the 1912 strike, possibly in Seaton Delaval, Northumberland*

15   Durham University Palace Green Library AUC/4/1 Visitation Returns 1861.
16   Durham County Record Office EP/Heb.SC 14/293.
17   Information on rectory households has been sourced from census returns, 1901.

53 *A group of young miners, from Cornsay Colliery*

sharply with those to be found at Sunderland St Michael (three children and five servants), Brancepeth (three children and five servants) and Stanhope (seven children and nine servants).

The census returns for 1901 indicate that the rectory at Brancepeth contained not a single Brancepeth-born resident. Thomas Archdale's household of nine at Tanfield, on the other hand, included five people that had been baptised in the parish. The vicarage at Dipton in 1901, serving the parish of Collierley, was similar in nature to that at Tanfield. Here lived the Rev. Richard Tuson, a Lancashire man, with his Collierley-born wife, his Dipton-born daughter, and his Collierley-born servant. Tanfield and Dipton rectories suggest the possibility that under certain circumstances the clergyman could 'go native'. In proletarian parishes like these the rectory was often subsumed into a complex maze of township streets and rows. Here clergymen lived alongside coalminers, married local women, and brought up children who were the neighbours and contemporaries of the children who might later become rectory servants. They occupied, quite simply, a different world from that of many 19th-century incumbents in the Durham diocese.

There are signs that proximity could foster a real bond of understanding between the clergyman and his working-class neighbours. Asked on their visitation returns in 1912 to say whether the recent wave of strikes in the coalfield had affected their relationships with the mining community, clergymen like Alexander Begg at Usworth responded that it had brought them closer together: 'Yes, it helped some of our people to see that the clergy did not stand aloof from them in comfortable isolation, and it brought us all more in touch with each other.' The vicar at Kirk Merrington had offered practical help in finding employment for his unemployed parishioners, while for Arthur Watts at Witton Gilbert, a thaw in social relations represented an opportunity for the Church's mission: 'The late coal strike brought us into close personal touch in relieving children and truly destitute cases, to the better knowledge of each other. A cordial feeling is left behind, and thus an open door.'[18]

But for many clergymen the 1912 strikes put up barriers rather than opened doors. 'I have noticed a growing spirit of independence and a desire to resist any sort of authority,' wrote one; 'the industrial unrest has weakened the sense of duty and responsibility of the people,' wrote another, 'there is a lack of grit and personal character.' For the Rev. W. D. Shepherd of Gateshead Venerable Bede, industrial unrest brought only 'class hatred', where 'clergy are looked upon as in league with masters and therefore suspected'.

'Class hatred', and the fact that it acted as a barrier to the Church's missionary work, may well have been high on the diocesan agenda when it embarked upon its strategy for placing working-class clergymen in working-class parishes. However, it does not necessarily follow that 'mission' was intended to be a two-way process. The secular side of the missionary's task was to teach and to reform and, if he could communicate effectively with his subjects, so much the better. But mutual understanding and engagement were no more than secondary considerations. Indeed, on those occasions where it came close to being achieved, the diocesan authorities tended to react with distaste, as we shall see.

IV

Often the very process of church-going seemed designed to remind the poor of their station in life: church seating arrangements, for instance, kept the well-to-do in the best seats near the pulpit and chancel and relegated the poor to free seats in galleries or out of sight at the west end. For some, church had become a place in which they were made to feel inadequate and ashamed. Writing in 1912, the Rev. Thomas Palmer at Bearpark noted 'a shyness of church owing to clothes',[19] and he was not alone. A number of early 20th-century clergymen found that people were not coming to church because they were embarrassed to be seen there. At Westoe, the Rev. H. Shaddick reported that many parishioners could only be persuaded to attend

---

18   Durham University Palace Green Library AUC 4/12 Visitation Returns 1912.
19   Durham University Palace Green Library AUC 4/12 Visitation Returns 1912.

'a "Lantern" service in a darkened church' when what they were wearing could not be seen.[20]

Table 2 shows clerical responses to the 1861 visitation question which asked, 'How many of the extremely poor do you have in your parish?' The answers indicate that the majority of clergymen acknowledged the presence of at least a little 'extreme poverty' in their midst, but that only three considered the problem to be really acute. As framed, the question seems to invite ill-defined and subjective replies – what, after all, was 'extreme poverty'? – but, by asking it, the diocesan authorities revealed a streak of social inquisitiveness that was a feature of their visitation enquiries. While 'poverty' would have been regarded as inevitable, a question about 'extreme poverty' was intended to seek out the much more dangerous condition of destitution, whose sufferers enjoyed neither the means nor the hope of surviving without parochial aid. The relative absence of destitution in the coalfield parishes was probably due to the fact that, compared with other working-class occupations, mining was by no means badly paid.

Table 2 Responses from sixty-nine incumbents of mining parishes to the question in their 1861 Visitation Return, 'how many of the extremely poor do you have in your parish?'

No Reply	'Many' extreme poor	'Some' extreme poor	'A Few' extreme poor	'No' extreme poor
17	3	17	21	11

SOURCE: Durham University Palace Green Library: AUC 4/1 1861 Visitation Returns.

Judging the extent of poverty in purely financial terms is, however, one-dimensional. There are other, more rounded measures, and they were beginning to attract varying degrees of attention from the working clergy and other contemporary observers.

The first of these was the issue of housing. Asked about housing conditions in 1912, Durham clergymen were fairly evenly divided in their opinions. Forty-five per cent thought conditions were good; 40 per cent thought conditions were bad. The causes of bad housing divided them still further. For some it was due to the rapacity of colliery owners; for others, the inefficiency of councils (sometimes held to be the same thing as many councils were dominated by colliery interests); for others yet it was the undesirable nature of the tenants that caused the problem.

Linked to the quality of housing was the issue of sanitation. Here, too, certain clergymen demonstrated a keen appreciation of what was going on. At Hamsteels, for instance, the Rev. Edward Rust observed that 'Cornsay Colliery is abnormally unhealthy owing to a radical defect in the original plan of the village. The houses are built in Terraces up the hillside, one above another, so that the drainage of one row comes down to the next instead of being built end on to the hill slope as they should be.'[21]

---

20   Durham University Palace Green Library AUC 4/14 Visitation Returns 1928.
21   Durham University Palace Green Library AUC 4/12 Visitation Returns 1912.

But for every Edward Rust there was a Blythe Hurst, seemingly incapable of seeing (or smelling) what was in front of his nose. Asked to contribute to the enquiry about poverty in 1861, Hurst had responded, with some complacency, 'I think we are all poor together.'[22] Eleven years later, while Hurst was still the incumbent, a newspaper reporter visited the township of Annfield Plain, whose westernmost houses lay just beyond the garden wall of Hurst's rectory:

> Here dwells and ministers the Rev. Blythe Hurst ... The pit-houses proper are merely navvies' huts ... They are of wood, and lined with lath and plaster. They are laid out in rows and surrounded by the Slough of Despond ... It is almost superfluous to say that there are no privies; but is necessary to add that there are no ash-pits, no drains, no sanitary arrangements of any sort. Whatever filth living beings deposit is tossed out anyhow, and gets trodden down and worked into the mire or dust, in which 'the days of happy childhood' are passed by pitmen's offspring. Here small-pox of the most loathsome type is raging; and when it is gone there will be something more malignant to take its place.[23]

Infant mortality rates offer a second means of measuring poverty. They are determined by calculating the number of children dying before their first birthday per thousand live births in the same year. County Durham had consistently high rates: 145 deaths per 1,000 in 1861 (8 per cent higher than the national median), and 105 deaths per 1,000 in 1921 (59.1 per cent higher than the national median).[24]

Three factors exacerbated the situation: the unhealthy environment of the mining and urban community; the higher rates of infant mortality always associated with migrant populations;[25] and the fact that County Durham, in common with other mining districts, had very high rates of fertility, with all that that implied for the physical and economic well-being of families.[26]

The effect upon the mining community can be seen when a comparison is made with Durham parishes where there was *no* mining (Table 3). Twenty-seven per cent of all burials in the churchyards of mining parishes between 1851 and 1860 were of children who died before the age of one. Fifty-four per cent were of children who died before the age of thirteen. Infant mortality rates – at least of those visible to Anglican registers – ran at 234.6 per 1,000 births. In each category the figures were significantly higher than those of non-mining parishes.

---

22   Durham University Palace Green Library AUC 4/1 Visitation Returns 1861.
23   *Newcastle Weekly Chronicle*, 14 December 1872.
24   Lee, C.H., 'Regional Inequalities in Infant Mortality in Britain 1861-1871: Patterns and Hypotheses', *Population Studies*, 45 (1991), pp.57-8.
25   Williamson, J.G., 'Urban disamenities, dark Satanic mills and the British standard of living debate', *Journal of Economic History*, 41 (1981), pp.75-83.
26   Millward, R. and Bell, F., 'Infant mortality in Victorian Britain, the mother as medium', *Economic History Review* LIV (2001), pp.699-733.

Table 3 Infant and child deaths in Co. Durham, compared between mining and non-mining communities 1851-1860

	Deaths of children aged 0-1 as % of all deaths recorded 1851-60	Deaths of children aged 0-12 as % of all deaths recorded 1851-60	'Anglican' Infant Mortality Rate per 1,000 baptisms 1851-60
Mining Communities	27.4	53.7	234.6
Non-mining communities	20.9	39.9	167.9

SOURCE: Burial and baptism registers of 21 County Durham parishes.

As they maintained their burial registers, parish clergymen were compiling invaluable documents of social record, and many clues to the life-styles and life-chances of their parishioners may be gleaned from them. In the agricultural village of Middleton St George, for instance, the vicar made regular entries recording the deaths of people aged seventy and over. This was a very different record from that of his colleague at Winlaton who was frequently reduced to entering the lives of babies in minutes rather than in months or years.[27]

But if clergymen were receiving any kind of social or demographic message from the burial entries, they seldom let on. At Kelloe the Rev. Rowland Webster reported to his bishop that he had no 'extreme poor' in his parish, despite burying 32 individuals during the preceding summer, not one of whom had been more than 14 years, and only three of whom had reached the age of six.[28] At Birtley, the Rev. Francis Bewsher thought the condition of the poor was 'good', even though 59 per cent of the funerals he had conducted in the preceding ten years had been for children aged less than 13 years.[29]

In mining parishes, of course, the Grim Reaper did not only swing his scythe at children. The conduct of mass funerals in the wake of pit disasters offered the clergyman a third potential touchstone with the lives of his parish poor. For a time, rectors whose parishes were visited by successions of disasters seemed to take on the guise of the 'recording angel' as they entered the toll in their burial registers: John Carr at Jarrow conducted 50 such funerals between 1828 and 1830.[30] Thomas Dixon at Washington conducted 61 funerals between 1828 and 1833.[31] W.A. Scott at Seaham conducted 190 funerals between 1871 and 1880.[32]

Death on this scale had a profound impact. The Seaham explosion in 1880, for instance, not only killed 164 miners, but also widowed 107 women and orphaned 241 children, most of whom now fell upon the mercy of public assistance.[33]

27 Middleton St George – Durham County Record Office EP/Mi SG 7. Winlaton – Durham County Record Office EP/Win 1/22.
28 Durham University Palace Green Library AUC 4/1 Visitation Returns 1861; Durham County Record Office EP/Ke 19, 20.
29 Durham University Palace Green Library AUC 4/1 Visitation Returns 1861.
30 Durham County Record Office EP/JA SP 1/45 Jarrow St Paul burial register 1813-41.
31 Durham County Record Office EP/Wa 1/30 Washington burial register 1813-37.
32 Durham County Record Office EP/NS 16 New Seaham burial register 1860-1900.
33 Durham County Record Office EP/NS 52 Seaham explosion Miners' Permanent Relief Fund.

As the recorder of deaths and the conductor of funerals, the vicar had first-hand, irrefutable evidence of the true cost of coal, and clergymen who raised their head above the parapet and drew the fire of angry coal owners were not unknown in the Durham coalfield. The Rev. John Hodgson's account of the Felling Colliery disaster in 1812 was a major source of irritation for the coal-owning Brandling family, and Hodgson over-reached himself further (in their eyes) by throwing his weight behind the development of Humphry Davy's safety lamp. Many decades later, the Rev. Arthur Watts of Witton Gilbert railed against the loss of life being caused by the coal owners' refusal to suspend the use of gunpowder in dusty mines, like the one that blew up at Easington in 1886.[34]

Undoubtedly, too, there were those being drawn closer to their parishioners as they watched the impact of pit disasters, and the tardy, inadequate responses of the pit owners. After the Seaham explosion in 1871, the Rev. W. A. Scott – who sometimes had a difficult relationship with the Londonderry family – was the first to form a relief fund for widows and orphans. Nine years later an even worse tragedy occurred in his parish. Scott almost broke down as he conducted the funeral service over a mass grave, and in a lengthy address he told the mourners that 'he never loved and admired them as he did that day'.[35]

More often, however, the response of the Church was a kind of agonised helplessness. 'To the mourners I do not venture to say much,' announced Bishop Moule after the Stanley disaster;[36] 'How can I attempt to console you?' asked Bishop Lightfoot after the explosion at Tudhoe in 1882.[37] At Washington in 1908, and again at Stanley in 1909, Bishop Moule waved a piece of card at those who had come to hear him speak. It was a bookmark, made by his mother. 'The back ... appeared to be a tangled confusion of meaningless threads running in all directions. Turned round, however, it spelt "God is love".'[38]

V

Many clergymen in the coalfield reached the conclusion that immigration worked to the detriment of mission. They did not hesitate to point out to their bishop that a 'here today, gone tomorrow' mentality was a breeding-ground for immorality and irresponsibility.[39] As the vicar of Kelloe pointed out, all these comings and goings meant that clergymen simply could not get to know (and thereby exercise any influence over) their parishioners: 'The great hindrance to ministerial usefulness here is the continual migration of the Pitmen and their families from one colliery parish to another.'[40]

---

34 Watts, Rev. A., letter to the *Durham Chronicle*, 10 December 1886.
35 *Durham County Advertiser*, 17 September 1880.
36 Durham County Record Office EP/Bea 14/3 Stanley Beamish parish magazines, 1906-10.
37 *Durham County Advertiser*, 21 April 1882.
38 Durham County Record Office EP/Wa 14/101 Washington parish magazine, March 1908. See also *Durham County Advertiser*, 19 February 1909.
39 See, for example, Thomas Dixon, South Shields St Hilda, Durham University Palace Green Library AUC 4/1 Visitation Returns, 1861.
40 Durham University Palace Green Library AUC 4/1 Visitation Returns, 1861, Rev. Rowland Webster, Kelloe.

Bishop Hensley Henson, writing in the 1920s, reflected on the social cost of this impermanence of church and community.[41] The modern diocese had been cut adrift from its history, Henson argued, and this was a mistake, for how else could the community defend itself against present secular threats? Henson chose Bede Day in 1927 to announce how the Venerable Bede's tradition of teaching – a torch now carried by the trainee teachers of Bede College – was an essential weapon in 'the battle between civilisation as we know it … and the new order of society which the Russian revolutionaries claim to have set up'.[42]

Henson was invoking Durham's great religious heritage – the heritage of Cuthbert and Bede – in order to imbue the diocese with a sense of identity that it all too evidently lacked. But the legacy of Durham's past – its enormous wealth; its vast, unwieldy parishes – had undoubtedly been a factor in its *failure* to establish an identity among the mobile, migrant masses that constituted the bulk of its population. A past that had acted as an *impediment* to identification was now being superceded by a different version: one that could act as identification's cornerstone.

Henson was by no means the first diocesan notable to have reached into the distant past for protection against the subversive threat *du jour*. In 1827, for instance, clerics of Durham Cathedral had gathered round as the huge grave-slab covering St Cuthbert's tomb was levered up from the floor. What they found there when they stepped forward with their lanterns and peered into the void beneath held far greater significance than the mere satisfaction of antiquarian curiosity. The exhumation of Cuthbert, supervised by the cathedral librarian James Raine, took place in the context of heightened tensions over Catholic Emancipation.[43] Raine was keen to prove that the body in the grave was that of Cuthbert, and that it had decomposed like any other human corpse. He could thus dismantle, at a stroke, two alternating Catholic beliefs: that the saint's body was incorruptible, and that it had been spirited away to a secret hiding place at the time of the Reformation. A scientific debunking of these theories would, Raine hoped, consolidate the view of Catholics as superstitious deceivers who were not to be trusted with any form of political office.

The national debate about Catholic Emancipation was underscored by a contemporary local crisis: the number of Irish-Catholic immigrants who were beginning to be attracted by County Durham's increasing industrial prosperity. Large-scale Irish Catholic immigration disrupted the Anglican mission in a number of ways. Firstly, there was the constitutional threat caused by a large influx of people who, some claimed, owed their principal allegiance to the Bishop of Rome rather than the British monarch. Secondly, a body of Catholic workers who were untouched by the restraining hand of Anglicanism seemed immune to its missionary message

---

41 Bishop Hensley Henson, Quadrennial Visitation of Durham Diocese (nd), cited in *When the Pit Closed: A Report on Ministry in former Mining Villages* (Bishop Auckland, 1982), 36.
42 *Durham Chronicle*, 3 June 1927.
43 Raine, Rev. J., *St Cuthbert, with an account of the state in which his remains were found* (Durham, 1828).

of obedience and deference. In 1861 the rector of Esh, Temple Chevallier, had warned of the social and political (as well as the religious) dangers posed by the rapid expansion in his parish of the Roman Catholic Ushaw College.[44] Twenty years later his successor, the Rev. Edmund Lee, must have felt that those warnings were about to come to fruition. When Henry Chaytor, the principal colliery owner at Esh, attempted to break the trade union by evicting its members and their families from colliery houses, it was the Catholic authorities who stepped in to help. Father Fortin, the local Catholic priest, earned himself a place in mining folklore by opening his schoolroom to the homeless women and children, while the governors of Ushaw College opened up their fields and allowed the striking miners to camp there.[45]

Catholics were warned against trade unionism by their Church,[46] but the events at Esh were echoed by other incidents in which Catholic clergy and Catholic congregations demonstrated

54 *Herbert Hensley Henson, Dean of Durham, 1912-18, Bishop of Durham, 1920-39*

a bond that few Anglican priests managed to emulate. It was Catholic priests who intervened in a conflict between English and Irish workers at Blackhill, for instance, and used their negotiating skills to act as *intermediaries* between communities and the law rather than as the *representatives* of the law that their Anglican counterparts so often resembled.[47]

As it emerged from the political shadows, the Catholic Church began to make a bold statement about its longevity and legitimacy in the North East: it revived the ancient diocese of Hexham; it adopted St Cuthbert as its diocesan patron; it built large and prominent churches and dedicated them to the saints of the ancient northern church.[48]

This was a stratagem that the Church of England would also come to adopt. The post-1880 period saw a sudden rash of Anglican Church dedications to figures such as Columba, Aidan and Oswald: figures from the very early, evangelising history of the northern church that had scarcely ever been claimed as patron saints before the

44   Durham University Palace Green Libray AUC 4/1 Visitation Returns, 1861.

45   Emery, N., *Mines and Marras* (Durham, 1991).

46   Treble, J.H., 'The attitude of the Roman Catholic church towards trade unionism in the north of England, 1833-1842', *Northern History*, 5 (1970), pp.3-113.

47   Neal, F., 'English-Irish Conflict in the north-east of England', in P. Buckland and J. Belchem (eds), *The Irish in British Labour History: Conference Proceedings in Irish Studies No. 1* (Liverpool, 1992), p.66.

48   Morris, M. and Gooch, L., *Down Your Aisles: The Diocese of Hexham and Newcastle 1850-2000* (Hartlepool, 2000) p.13.

late 19th century.[49] This coincided with a diocesan re-structuring that saw, in 1882, the creation of the Diocese of Newcastle and the separation of Northumberland's ecclesiastical administration from that of County Durham. The change meant that in its new, reduced form the Durham diocese had reverted to something that closely resembled the boundaries of the old Palatinate.

VI

That secular radicalism represented only a minority position in an era of overwhelmingly preponderant religious belief can scarcely be doubted. Trapped below ground and doomed to a lingering death after massive pit explosions, men at Hartley and at Seaham collieries had time to scratch last messages to loved ones before they died. 'Five o'clock, we have been praying to God,' wrote one; 'The Lord has been with us. We are all ready for heaven,' wrote another. And again: 'Bless the Lord we had had a jolly prayer meeting, every man ready for glory. Praise the Lord.'[50]

These messages, however, came from a religious tradition that was *not* Anglican. The problem for the Church of England in Durham lay in the fact that industrialisation (and, alongside it, Methodism) had completely outflanked the diocese's medieval parochial structure. After 1860 the Church made a monumental effort to claw back this lost ground; to reorganise itself and make its voice heard. But what cannot be ignored is a sense that the diocese's post-1860 mission was an attempt to re-invigorate a Church that the broader community had already decided it neither wanted nor needed.

By the early 20th century a cold blast of reality was blowing around the diocese, and clergymen like Alexander Begg at Usworth were prepared to acknowledge that the working classes had established for themselves an effective code of morality that now operated quite independently of the Church's teaching.[51] At Deaf Hill, the Rev. Stephen Davison had worked hard to turn young parishioners away from the anti-religious influence of the Independent Labour Party, but he recognised that he was probably fighting a losing battle. 'Social and industrial problems,' he wrote, 'will, I fear, be solved apart from Church influence.'[52]

The Church of England in Durham certainly worked hard to shed the kind of minimal engagement that the Rev. James Waters had once shown at Penshaw. Men who had 'not the slightest idea' about what was going on in their parishes had no place in the early 20th-century diocese. Indeed, the diocese was for a time *led* by a churchman who most certainly did know what was going on in the coalfield parishes and whose intervention in the 1892 strike earned him a lasting reputation for decency and fair play. However, Bishop Westcott refused the term Christian Socialist for himself, and preferred cooperation over the justice of the case.

---

49 Of 16 dedications to these saints in the diocese, only one pre-dates 1880.
50 McCutcheon, J.E., *Troubled Seams: The Story of a Pit and its People* (Durham, 1955), 127. For the Methodist penetration of the coalfield see Robert Colls, *The Pitmen of the Northern Coalfield* (Manchester, 1981), part II.
51 Durham University Palace Green Library AUC 4/13 Visitation Returns, 1924.
52 Durham University Palace Green Library AUC 4/12 Visitation Returns, 1912.

55 *The Church of England leads the way. Blackhall miners and their vicar leave Durham Cathedral after the Miners Gala Service, 1939*

Even so, there were clergymen who appear to have been radicalised by their experiences in mining communities – James Duncan at Dawdon; Harry Watts at Shildon; William Hodgson at Escomb – all of whom antagonised Bishop Henson by misdirecting their sympathies during the General Strike. 'I am convinced,' fumed Henson, 'that the least respected and least respectworthy clergymen in any diocese are those who thrust themselves into politics, generally as protagonists of Labour.'

Henson may have consoled himself that the socialist vision of Duncan, Watts and Hodgson seemed to owe more to an English past than to a Russian future. Duncan re-introduced elements of High Church ritual into services at Dawdon; Hodgson oversaw the restoration of Escomb's Saxon church; and Harry Watts marked Easter 1924 by putting on his own production of a medieval Mystery Play.[53] The strong appeal of an English past was a factor, too, in the increasingly regular invocation of Cuthbert and Bede and, as coal mines began to encroach upon the far banks of the river Wear, the Cathedral itself must have appeared more and more the enigmatic symbol of another – lost – world.

But this was scarcely the close, practical connection between church and community that the Durham mission had been designed to facilitate. In so many important ways, the community on the hill in the 1920s, under the staunchly anti-trade union leadership of Bishop Henson, seemed little closer to the people of its hinterland than it had in the 1820s under the unyieldingly traditionalist leadership of Bishop van Mildert. Henson may not have been burned in effigy like his predecessor, but he was a target for hostility at the Miners' Gala in 1925, where miners brandished placards saying, 'To Hell with Bishops and Deans' and where the equally anti-union, anti-socialist Dean Welldon narrowly avoided the fate of being thrown into the river by a hostile crowd.[54]

Bishop Henson '[did] not wish to give the impression that the Church has failed in the mining districts,'[55] but sixty years later the Church was *still* having to acknowledge the marginality of its position in community life. 'Attendances are low and clergy morale is often reduced by the low numbers,' wrote the Rev. Peter Hood, vicar of Esh and Hamsteels in 1982. Moreover, 'attendance at all worship seems to be mainly of the older generation', and in the affiliated groups 'there are Young Wives who are grandmothers and Mothers Union members who are nearly all great-grandmothers.'[56] It was a grim picture, recognisable to Billy Elliotts everywhere.

---

53   Durham County Record Office EP/Daw 6/2 PCC minutes 1919-30; EP/ES 17 Vestry Minutes, 1 June 1927; EP/Sh 52 PCC minutes, 29 January 1924.
54   Emery, N., *Banners of the Durham Coalfield* (Stroud, 1998), p.48
55   Bishop Hensley Henson, Quadrennial Visitation of Durham Diocese (nd), cited in *When the Pit Closed: A Report on Ministry in former Mining Villages* (Bishop Auckland, 1982), p.36.
56   *When the Pit Closed*, p.22.

Cultural Region

13

Myths of Northumberland: Art, Identity and Tourism

PAUL USHERWOOD

Northumberland as it appears in visual art of the last 200 years is largely a figment of the tourist imagination. In this it is no different from various other parts of Britain, for instance Norfolk as it appears in the work of the Norwich School in the first decades of the 19th century, or Cornwall in the work of the St Ives artists in the early and middle years of the 20th century.[1] Each has its own tourist myths. What is special about Northumberland, however, is the richness and potency of the myths. This chapter looks at three of these in turn: a myth of the place, first, as somewhere historic and diverting; second, as authentic and testing; and third, strange and enchanting.[2]

Historic and diverting Northumberland

> ... here is abundant business for an antiquary; every place shows you ruined castles, Roman altars, inscriptions, monuments of battles, of heroes killed and armies routed and the like ... (Daniel Defoe visiting Northumberland in 1725)

---

1   See Brown, David Blayney, 'Nationalising Norwich: the "school" in a wider context', in David Blayney Brown et al., *Romantic Landscape: the Norwich School of Painters* (London, 2000), pp.24-36.

2   I am using 'myth' here as Roland Barthes does when he describes a Basque-style house glimpsed in a Paris suburb as demanding to be seen as embodying the very essence of the Basque region in Spain: see 'Myth Today', *Mythologies* (London, 1972), pp.124-5. My particular way of categorising the different myths of Northumberland is based on the typology of various kinds of tourist experience in Eric Cohen's study of kibbutzim in Krausz, E. (ed.), *The Sociology of the Kibbutz; Studies of Israeli Society, volume 2* (London and New Brunswick, 1983), p.183.

56 *J.M.W. Turner,* Dunstanburgh Castle, *1828 (Manchester Art Gallery)*

The myth of Northumberland as quintessentially historic and diverting emerges with the type of tourist experience that offers temporary respite from normal routine. In the 18th century, when tourism in the county first flourished, this usually derived from trips to various must-see sights such as the battered ruin of Dunstanburgh Castle, Warkworth Hermitage (made famous by Thomas Percy's retelling of a medieval legend in his hugely popular *Reliques* of 1765), and Lindisfarne Priory with its associations with St Cuthbert. We know, for instance, from the sketchbook of the London water-colourist Thomas Girtin that the places the antiquarian tourist James Moore visited during a five day trip in August 1792 included Gateshead Monastery, Tynemouth Priory, Bothal Castle, Warkworth Castle, Bamburgh Castle, Lindisfarne Priory and Copeland Castle.

At first, the images produced by artists catering for this antiquarian taste tended to be stiff and lacking in atmosphere. Gradually, however, they became more detailed and more accurate.[3] They also became more concerned with natural scenery, or what

---

3   See, for instance, those made for Samuel and Nathaniel Buck's '*Castles, Monasteries, Palaces etc in England and Wales*' between 1720 and 1750.

at the time was called the 'picturesque'. Originally this term meant any tract of land that resembled, or could be perceived as, a picture, but soon it came to mean scenery that was wild, gnarled, rough and intricate. Thus the waterfall at Hareshaw Linn near Bellingham, with its 'impending trees giving infinite beauties to the landskip', was considered somewhere worth visiting and drawing. So also were the precipitous tree-covered hills overlooking the 'sequestered vale' at Nunsbrough near Dilston.[4]

'Picturesque' as a term, however, need not be confined to landscapes of this particular era. It can be used also, for instance, of the engraved illustrations and tail-pieces of Thomas Bewick. Admittedly, when these first appeared they were probably enjoyed more for their delightful, if sometimes astringent, comments on country life in general.[5] However, by the late 19th century, the period of the Bewick Club and various other self-conscious attempts to advocate Northumbrian culture, they were usually viewed through tourist eyes, and Bewick himself had come to be regarded as not simply a rural but quintessentially a Northumbrian artist; in Ruskin's phrase, as the 'strongest pine' on the Northumberland hillside.[6]

By the same score 'picturesque', meaning colourful and quaint, can be used of the paintings of the pitmen painters of the Ashington Group in the 1930s. Ostensibly these may seem to offer an almost documentary account of the artists' immediate everyday world: whippets, football, the daily life underground. In truth, however, they were also shaped by a tourist's outsider viewpoint in as much as they were influenced, certainly as regards choice of subject, by the teaching of the Royal College of Art-taught WEA tutor, Robert Lyon, and by Tom Harrisson, Humphrey Jennings and Julian Trevelyan of Mass Observation. And, indeed, one would hardly expect it to be otherwise. After all, generally speaking, amateur artists, which is what the Ashington Group were, seldom choose subjects from everyday life of their own accord, if only because, as the wife of one of them (Oliver Kilbourn) remarked, that is not what people have on their walls at home.[7]

Not all artists working in picturesque manner at the turn of the 19th century came to Northumberland in the company of antiquarian tourists. Some, like Edward Swinburne, the younger brother of Sir John Swinburne of Capheaton, were resident there already. A member of the gentry and therefore necessarily an amateur, Swinburne was taught to draw by a star of the metropolitan art world, J.M.W.Turner, and was competent enough to exhibit watercolours at the Newcastle exhibitions in the 1820s and provide images for engraved illustrations in antiquarian histories such as the

---

4   Hutchinson, W., *A View of Northumberland with an excursion to the Abbey at Mailross in Scotland* (Newcastle upon Tyne, 1778) vol. 1, pp.172 and 180.

5   This is not true of all his work: see, for example, the large engraving, *The Chillingham Bull* (1789).

6   See Quinn, Peter, '"Their strongest pine": Thomas Bewick and regional identity in the late Nineteenth Century', and Newton, Laura, 'The Bewick Club and the Cullercoats Connection', in David Gardner-Medwin, *Bewick Studies: Essays in Celebration of 250th Anniversary of the Birth of Thomas Bewick 1753-1828* (Newcastle upon Tyne, 2003), pp.111-49. It is worth adding that among the various references to regional culture that appeared on the streets of Newcastle in these years are a bust of Bewick at the site of his workshop in St Nicholas' Churchyard in 1902 and a statue of Bewick on Boots the Chemist's new premises at 45 Northumberland Street in 1912.

7   Feaver, William, *Pitmen Painters: the Ashington Group 1934-84* (London, 1988), p.22.

Rev. John Hodgson's *History of Northumberland* (1820-40).[8] Indeed, his work was held up as an example that even professional artists might seek to emulate; or so, at least, thought Teresa Cholmeley, a guest at Capheaton in 1805:

> I do so wish he [the London-based professional John Sell Cotman] could see Swinburne's *trees*, and was more acquainted wi[t]h Swinburne himself, whose taste and knowledge and experience are certainly all of the highest class, with the gentlest and most pleasing of manners. He has one glorious drawing of Girton's [*sic*] ... and a fine one of Varley's.[9]

As for professional artists, there were various ways in which they catered for the new antiquarian-picturesque taste. First, there was teaching. As we have already noted, Turner – Girtin's friend, contemporary and one-time fellow apprentice in London – did his share of teaching, although never, it has to be said, to the extent of making it his main source of income. Secondly, of course, there was production of work for the art market. Again, Turner is a good example of how this worked. He painted watercolours for print publishers to reproduce and sell as black-and-white engraved illustrations. He also, as he became more established, produced watercolours and oils for exhibiting under his own name at one or other of the growing number of public exhibitions, notably the Royal Academy summer exhibition in London.

Northumberland was seen as having much to offer artists and Turner was typical in being especially drawn to the county. Indeed, on one occasion on his way to Scotland it is recorded that he made public his feeling by, in typically eccentric fashion, standing up in the coach as it was crossing the Tweed and making a low bow to the ruins of Norham Castle. The specific reason he did this, he explained to his bemused travelling companions, was that several years before he had made a drawing or painting of Norham (this was probably *Norham Castle on the Tweed, Summer's morn*, Royal Academy, 1798) and, as the expression went, this had 'taken', with the result that ever after he always had more commissions than he could execute.[10]

One reason for the demand for views of medieval ruins at the end of the 18th century was that they seemed to suit the turbulent nature of the times. To political pessimists they suggested the passing of the old order, or the precarious nature of what had replaced it. To those of a more progressive bent they exemplified the kind of stern, heroic fortitude in the face of adversity that would be needed in future.[11]

However, there were other, more prosaic reasons as well. Around this time firms like Winsor and Newton and Reeve's began to sell water-colour paints in convenient small, hard cakes. Also, stage-coach travel was becoming faster, cheaper and more comfortable. In addition, Britain was frequently at war with France in these years, which

---

8 See Usherwood, Paul, *Art for Newcastle: Thomas Miles Richardson and the Newcastle Exhibitions, 1822-1843*, Tyne and Wear Museums, 1984, pp.81-3.

9 Letter, 7 August 1805, quoted in Gill Hedley, *The Picturesque Tour in Northumberland and Durham, c.1720-1830* (Laing Art Gallery, 1982), p.40.

10 Thornbury, Walter, *The Life and Correspondence of J.M.W. Turner* (London, 1877), p.139.

11 Bermingham, Ann, *Landscape and Ideology: the English Rustic Tradition 1740-1860* (London, 1987), p.70. See also Uvedale Price, *An Essay on the Picturesque, as Compared with the Sublime and the Beautiful* (London, 1796-8), Vol. 2, p.301.

meant that not only was there a patriotic interest in native scenery and antiquities, but also tourists who might otherwise have ventured onto mainland Europe for the time being had to content themselves with exploring their own islands.

Then, in the early years of the 19th century, another factor came into play: Walter Scott's poems and novels, several of which featured locations in the county: *The Minstrelsy of the Scottish Border* (1802-3), *Marmion: a Tale of Flodden Field* (1808), *Rokeby* (1813), *Guy Mannering* (1815) and *Rob Roy* (1817). These were hugely popular, so much so that, as Scott himself noted, the effect could sometimes be to put actual buildings and remains at risk.[12] A case in point was a Roman statue at Risingham. 'Between a miserable inn called Tom-pill and Otterbourne (that is supposing you to come from Hexham),' the writer remarked in a letter home,

on a small brook near a place called Wood[b]urne is the curious roman town or camp of Risingham. Near this stood the figure called Robin of Risingham, now not existing. It was mentioned in the notes to a certain poem called Rokeby and acquired such celebrity that the Boor on whose ground it stood, teased with the number of visitors, broke it to pieces. I wish the fragments were in his bladder with all my heart.[13]

Nor was the popularity of Scott's works merely a passing fad. It persisted well on into the 20th century. As late as 1914, for instance, one comes across the historian G.M. Trevelyan likening the sight of the traditional New Year foxhunt on the Cheviot hills to Diana Vernon's hunt on the mountainside above Biddlestone Hall in *Guy Mannering*.[14]

Not surprisingly, much art about Northumberland owes a debt to Scott. Certainly this is true of William Bell Scott's eight-canvas, Pre-Raphaelite-inspired 'History of the English Border' cycle at Wallington Hall (1856-61). It also applies to the little stone basin in a pseudo-Gothic niche in a wood on Flodden Hill known as Sybil's Well and inscribed with the words 'Drink weary pilgrim and stay / Rest by the well of Sibyl Grey' (1880s), as well as the large granite memorial marking the site of the Battle of Flodden outside the village of Branxton (1910).[15] Sybil's Well was inspired by a famous passage in *Marmion* in which the protagonist dies, with his lover, Clara, tenderly 'laving' his brow beside a stone basin inscribed with the words 'Drink, weary pilgrim, drink and pray, / For the kind soul of Sybil Grey'.

Inasmuch as these three works were produced for patrons who were actually resident in Northumberland, they might not seem to count as 'tourist art'. However, it should be noted that none of the people in question was a native Northumbrian; each of them moved to Northumberland relatively late in life. Sir Walter Trevelyan, who commissioned the Wallington cycle, settled there when he was 48 years old;

---

12   Some measure of the commercial success these works enjoyed can be gained from the fact that, even at a guinea-and-a-half 'splendid quarto', 2,000 copies of *Marmion* were sold in two months and 8,000 in three months. See Sutherland, John, *The Life of Walter Scott* (Oxford, 1995), p.126.

13   A letter, 1816, cited in Frank Whitehead and Philip Yarrow, 'Scott and Northumberland', *Archaeologia Aeliana* (1986), 5th series , vol. XIV, p.172.

14   Trevelyan, G.M., 'The Middle Marches', in *Clio, a muse and other essays, literary and pedestrian* (London, 1914), pp.160-1.

15   'History of the English Border' is what the cycle is called in the publicity for a series of photographs that the dealer Ernest Gambart published in 1861 at the time that he exhibited the paintings at his Piccadilly gallery.

57 *William Bell Scott,* Iron and Coal, *1861 (Wallington Hall, The National Trust)*

Lady Waterford erected Sybil's Well when she was 41; and Commander Francis Norman, the man chiefly responsible for setting up the public subscription for the Flodden Memorial, began to live in Berwick only after he had retired from the navy at the age of thirty.[16] A key motivation behind each of the three works I have

---

16 Sir Walter Trevelyan was influenced to commission the cycle, it seems, by his artistically inclined wife Pauline who, although (or because) she herself was not a Northumbrian, felt that Wallington rather than Nettlecombe, the Trevelyans' other mansion in Somerset, offered the scope she craved to express her individuality. See Surtees, Virginia (ed.), *Reflections of a Friendship: John Ruskin's Letters to Pauline Trevelyan, 1846-1966* (London, 1979), p.viii. For the Flodden memorial see Paul Usherwood et al, *Public Sculpture of North-East England* (Liverpool, 2000), pp.15-16. Commander Norman, it is worth noting, was also to the fore in the Victorian restoration of Berwick's Elizabethan fortifications and the erection of the town's Jubilee fountain in 1897.

mentioned, therefore, was probably the special need a newcomer sometimes feels to proclaim an attachment to, or a sense of affinity with, his or her adopted home;[17] hence, in the case of the Wallington cycle, the insistent use of local subject matter and of Trevelyan and his wife and friends as models for figures in several of the scenes.[18] And hence, in the case of all three, the similarity of the Northumberland that emerges to the Northumberland as it was presented in late 18th- and early 19th-century visitors' views of picturesque antiquities such as, say, Thomas Girtin's watercolour of Dunstanburgh (1797, Laing Art Gallery), or Turner's (1828, Manchester City Art Gallery), both showing the battered remains of the 14th-century castle as the backdrop to a scene of men salvaging cargo or wreckage after a tremendous storm.[19] That is to say, the myth of Northumberland that these three works help to project is of a place peculiarly ancient and steeped in violence. Indeed, this is even true of *Iron and Coal* (1861), the last and best known painting in the Wallington cycle. For although this work is usually discussed as a celebration of Tyneside's mid-19th-century technological and industrial achievements, when viewed *in situ* at Wallington it presents its protagonists – a group of workmen hammering away in Robert Stephenson's Newcastle locomotive works – as very much the modern-day counterparts of the various men-at-arms (Romans, Danes, Border Reivers) who appear elsewhere in the series.[20]

Nor is celebrating modern-day technology by referring to Northumberland's ancient and violent past something unique to *Iron and Coal*. It is also true, for instance, of Samuel Smiles' paean to Robert Stephenson's many-arched railway bridge over the Tweed in his *Lives of the Engineers* (1862). For although this is concerned with a feat of modern-day engineering, interestingly the author feels compelled to tell the reader that

> … no alarm spreads along the Border now … Chevy Chase and Otterburn are quiet sheep pastures. The only men at arms on the battlements of Alnwick castle are of stone. Bamburgh Castle has become an asylum for shipwrecked mariners, and the Norman Keep at Newcastle has been converted into a Museum of Antiquities.[21]

---

17   Their motives were therefore rather different, it should be noted, from those of the Lorrains at Kirharle, the Blacketts at Wallington or the Percys at Alnwick in the previous century when they commissioned the celebrated Northumbrian-born gardener Lancelot 'Capability' Brown to improve the appearance of their estates. What Brown gave patrons like these was a natural-seeming landscape, one that, as Peter Waddell, the hothouse gardener at Alnwick, wrote in 1782, was 'elegantly diversified by Hills and Dales, small Clumps and single Trees scattered on the Slopes and in the Vallies'; in other words, not obviously Claudian or classical but certainly not especially Northumbrian either. See Laing Art Gallery, *Capability Brown and the Northern Landscape* (Newcastle upon Tyne, 1983), p.22.

18   It is easy enough, for example, to spot the doleful, moustached Sir Walter Trevelyan as one of St Cuthbert's companions on the Farnes, or the black-haired, rosy-cheeked Lady Pauline among the idle Britons not getting on with Building of the Roman Wall in the first scene.

19   Interestingly, for either compositional or narrative reasons, Turner shows the southern elevation of the castle in the 1828 watercolour with the dramatic sweep of Embleton Bay, north of Dunstanburgh, in front of it rather than behind.

20   For the standard interpretation of the work, see Usherwood, Paul, 'William Bell Scott's *Iron and Coal*: northern readings', in Laing Art Gallery, *Pre-Raphaelites: painters and patrons* (Newcastle upon Tyne, 1984), pp.39-56.

21   Smiles, Samuel, *The Lives of the Engineers* (London, 1862), Vol. III, p.415.

58 *Flodden Memorial, 1910*

There are additional ways in which *Iron and Coal* resembles this particular passage of Smiles. It does so also by, as it were, blurring the boundary between the two geographic areas of Northumberland and the Borders with a caption underneath the painting which reads:

> In the NINETEENTH CENTURY, The Northumbrians show the World what can be done with Iron and Coal.[22]

What are the implications of merging Northumberland together with the Borders? In the first place, it associates Northumberland with the warfare and hostility between England and Scotland that for so long dominated the story of the Borders. Secondly, it casts Northumberland as somewhere that, like the Borders, can be viewed as a kind of oasis of aboriginal authenticity whose inhabitants, as Ruskin once said of the Border people, are 'a scarcely injured race, whose strength and virtue yet survive to represent the body and soul of England before her days of mechanical decrepitude and commercial dishonour'. In the case of the Borders, according to Ruskin, this was a consequence of the 'extreme sadness' of the area's history, a sadness that constantly surfaces in the famous ballads, the Borders being of course, as Ruskin again noted, 'a singing country – that which most naturally expresses its noble thoughts and passions in song'.[23]

Ruskin was not alone in seeing the area as inherently tragic. G.M. Trevelyan, the grandson of Sir Charles Trevelyan, Sir Walter's cousin and heir and, incidentally, the model for the most prominent of the hammering workmen in *Iron and Coal*, did so as well. In one of his essays the great historian makes the claim that the people of the Borders in Walter Scott's day were like the Greeks in Homer's time:

> cruel, coarse savages, slaying each other as beasts of the forest; and yet … also poets who could express in the grand style the inexorable fate of the individual man and woman, and infinite pity for all the cruel things which they none the less perpetually inflicted upon one another.[24]

---

22 This caption was added somewhat later by Lady Pauline Trevelyan. It is worth noting that Walter Scott's *Border Antiquities* (1814) also fuses Northumberland together with the Borders; the Borders are described as though they take in not only southern Northumberland but also much of County Durham. Indeed, so, too, do the present-day signs on the main roads north or west out of Newcastle which welcome motorists to 'Northumberland – England's Border Country'.

23 John Ruskin, letter on 'The Extension of Railways in the Lake District' (1876) in E.T. Cook and Alexander Wedderburn (eds), *The Works of John Ruskin* (London, 1908), vol. 34, p.141, and John Ruskin, *Fors Clavigera* letter 32 (August 1873) in Cook and Wedderburn, *The Works of John Ruskin* (1917), vol. 27, p.594.

24 Trevelyan, George Macaulay, 'The Middle Marches', in *Clio, a Muse and other essays literary and pedestrian* (London, 1914), p.173.

That it was possible for Borders people to be two such different things simultaneously might seem implausible. However, it should be remembered that the acts of bestial violence to which Trevelyan refers had occurred a very long time before and therefore seemed to be things which, as the 19th-century French writer Ernest Renan famously remarked of the savagery of Saint Bartholomew's Day, 'ought already to have been forgotten'.[25]

And this is probably the reason why in 1910, almost 400 years after the Battle of Flodden, Commander Norman and his friends were able to persuade themselves that the time was right to replace the simple wooden cross on Flodden Field with the large granite affair that stands there today. By 1910, it would have seemed, sufficient time had passed for there to be no longer any danger of fresh animosities being stirred up. Similarly, it was why a century earlier Walter Scott had thought it legitimate to take an interest in Northumberland's blood-thirsty past.

59 *Pauline Trevelyan decorations (Wallington Hall, The National Trust)*

> ... the recollection of [the two nations'] former hostility has much of interest and nothing of enmity. The evidences of its existence bear, at the same time, witness to the remoteness of its date; and he who traverses these peaceful glens and hills to find traces of strife, must necessarily refer his researches to a period of considerable antiquity.[26]

Nor, it is worth adding, would Scott or anyone else at the time have said the same about the Scottish Highlands. There, by contrast, in the early 19th century, the kind of hostility to which he refers would have seemed anything but remote. The last Jacobite rebellion had occurred only fifty years before and the clearances were even then in full swing. Hence the seemingly very different attitude that Sir Charles Trevelyan displayed towards the Scottish and Northumbrian poor in the mid-19th century. In his role as a Treasury official Trevelyan stuck rigidly to free-market principles when it came to organising relief for victims of the Highland Clearances in the late 1840s; a pound of meal and 'at least eight hours hard work', he asserted in a letter, was the best regime for what he called the 'moral disease' of destitution.[27] Yet at home at Wallington he was willing to help out William Bell Scott with his *Iron and Coal* at the end of the 1850s by playing the part of a proud member of the Northumbrian

---

25 *Qu'est-ce qu'une nation?* (1882), cited in Benedict Anderson, *Imagined Communities: Reflections on the Origins and Spread of Nationalism* (London, 1991), p.199.

26 Scott, Walter, *Border Antiquities of England and Scotland* (London and Edinburgh, 1814), p.iv.

27 In a letter from Trevelyan to the Celtic historian William Skene in 1848, quoted by Neal Ascherson in *Stone Voices: The Search for Scotland* (London, 2002), p.181.

labour aristocracy hammering away in Robert Stephenson's Newcastle locomotive works in the middle of the painting. Perhaps the explanation is that he saw the latter as his way of contributing to what in effect was the semi-private game of charades that members of the Trevelyans were playing when they appeared as figures in one or other of the paintings in the Wallington series. Indeed, he may have thought it peculiarly fitting that the designated heir to the Trevelyan estate and a figure associated with great reforms in the public sphere should appear in this particular painting with its Whiggish enthusiasm for progress of all kinds. In any case, it is possible that he saw this as not so much a way of honouring the Northumbrian working class as of visualising the power that he as a member of the gentry had over them: of, as it were, appropriating their otherness.[28] Nevertheless, whatever his reason, it would certainly have helped that by the end of the 1850s it was universally assumed that the turbulent phase of Northumberland's history, unlike that of the Scottish Highlands, was long since over.

Authentic and testing Northumberland

Not all art works depicting or sited in Northumberland in the last two centuries have presented the county as steeped in history. Some, by contrast, have catered for travellers seeking to enrich their lives through immersion in a more authentic way of life.

Many 18th- and 19th-century picturesque views, for instance, were produced by young ladies struggling (but never quite managing) to attain proficiency in sketching natural scenery. This was also true of the garlands of native wild flowers painted by Sir Walter Trevelyan's wife Lady Pauline and her aristocratic lady friends on the pilasters between each of the scenes in Bell Scott's Wallington cycle in the 1850s. These were executed very much under the guidance of, and indeed sometimes actually with the help of, Lady Pauline's mentor and occasional house-guest, John Ruskin.[29] And this was true as well of the much more ambitious series of Raphaelesque biblical scenes in tempera on the walls of the schoolroom at Ford (1862-83) by another of Ruskin's aristocratic protégés, Lady Waterford – the same Lady Waterford who commissioned Sybil's Well.[30]

However, it should be noted, while all of these works implied that Northumberland was a place where supposedly personal renewal was to be sought, the renewal in question was always in practice assumed to be only for the sensitive, cultivated

---

28 I am suggesting that this may have been a version of the 'colonial mimicry' that Homi K. Bhabha discusses in his essay 'Of mimicry and man' in *The Location of Culture* (London and New York, 1994), pp.85-92.

29 Buoyed up by the seeming success of the murals that Rossetti and friends painted at the Oxford Union, Ruskin played a key role in encouraging Lady Pauline to make the Wallington saloon a Pre-Raphaelite showcase and was sent Scott's plan to vet: Virginia Surtees (ed.), *Reflections of a Friendship: John Ruskin's Letters to Pauline Trevelyan, 1846-1966* (London, 1979), p.112. Much to Scott's disgust, Ruskin contributed a pilaster garland himself.

30 Ruskin's style of teaching aristocratic amateurs is nicely illustrated in a letter to Lady Waterford of April 1862, in which he first fawningly praises his pupil's rendering of the Sacrifice of Cain and Abel – 'especially as a lesson to children how to behave in church! Which I suppose it was meant for' – and then goes on to find her drawing of the serpent defective, advising her to 'Go to the British Museum some day, and look at the skull of the cobra!' Quoted in Michael Joicey, *Louisa Anne, Marchioness of Waterford* (Etal, 1991), p.19.

60 *James Turrell,* Kielder Skyspace, *2000*

few. Hence, for instance, the note of slight disdain in Walter Scott's response to an American visitor who had the temerity to confess that he found the great writer's native Border territory somewhat less exciting than his works had led him to expect. 'It may be pertinacity', Scott replied, but

> to my eye these grey hills and all this wild border country have beauties peculiar to themselves. I like the very nakedness of the land; it has something bold, and stern and solitary about it. When I have been for some time in the rich scenery about Edinburgh, which is like ornamental garden land, I begin to wish myself back again among my own honest grey hills; and if I did not see the heather at least once a year, I think I should die.[31]

Of course, by the end of the 20th century, with people flocking to the hills of Northumberland in ever greater numbers, it was becoming hard to find such nakedness and solitude – hard but still not entirely impossible: or so, at least, claimed Northumberland National Parks (established in 1956) when they publicised Kielder Water and Forest Park in the 1970s.

The idea of Kielder as a tourist-worthy, testing type of landscape first came into being in 1926 when the newly established Forestry Commission (a particular *bête noire*, incidentally, of G.M. Trevelyan's) began planting out the hills of this part of south-west Northumberland with vast blocks of quick-grow Douglas Fir and Norwegian Spruce. At the time there were few objections. However, it was a different story in the late 1960s when the Northumbrian Water Authority proposed adding a giant seven-mile-long reservoir. This, by contrast, sparked bitter and prolonged protests led by two local squires, Sir Rupert Spiers and Major F.J. Charlton, the 'dam-busters' as they were called, who claimed that the creation of the largest man-made lake in Europe would

---

31   Quoted in Howard Pease, *The Lord Wardens of the Marches of England and Scotland* (London, 1913), pp.4-5.

mean the loss of 3,000 acres and the destruction of 180 people's homes – the 'rape of a fair valley'.[32] However, significantly in terms of the myth of Northumberland we are discussing here, Northumbrian Water responded to these charges not by simply pointing out the practical benefits of a giant reservoir; they emphasised how rugged and 'natural-looking' the new facility would be.[33] For instance, Sir Frederick Gibberd, the London architect responsible for the landscaping, went out of his way to reassure the first planning inquiry that the newly constructed lake would, as he put it, be kept free of 'music, Coke and bikinis'.

Subsequently this tasteful, not to say stern, image of the new Kielder was reinforced by the installation of a number of pieces of public art. Usually these in themselves are not particularly challenging. Interestingly though, in terms of the way these works were sited – in remote areas and often with large distances between them – they made considerable demands on the viewer. Indeed, the most expensive and critically lauded of them, *Kielder Skyspace* (2000) by the American land artist James Turrell, was sited on a remote hill-top called Cat Cairn at the end of a long, bumpy, poorly signposted track. Only the intrepid and hardy, in the Walter Scott mould, are ever likely to find it.[34]

Strange and enchanting Northumberland

In addition to those artists who have approached Northumberland in either a diversionary or an experiential manner, there is, finally, a third group: those artists who have gone there, either literally or in their imaginations, in order to discover some kind of alternative lifestyle or consciousness that will change – in fundamental ways – not just their patrons' and audiences' lives, but their own as well. I am labelling such artists 'experimental tourists'.

Turner, I believe, was an experimental tourist, at least in the latter part of his career. For by then his fame and fortune were such that he was in a position to ignore audiences, critics and patrons' expectations as regards 'finish' in large-scale paintings. Admittedly, when it came to making his will he chose not to include unfinished large-scale works in his bequest to the nation.[35] Nevertheless, significantly, he persisted in leaving such paintings in a semi-abstract state which suggests that, even though he may not have seen such works with our post-American Abstract Expressionist eyes, he in some way recognised that they had certain distinctive visual qualities that were worth cherishing.

---

32 *Newcastle Evening Chronicle*, 2 April 1971 and 16 March 1972. There was also concern that it would destroy the nesting sites of a number of rare birds including goosanders, kingfishers and half the UK population of hen harriers (*Newcastle Evening Chronicle*, 3 March 1972).

33 The promised benefits included supplying industry on Teesside and at Consett with the water that it thought at the time it needed, and giving the 'typical Geordie' the means to have more than one bath a week: *Newcastle Evening Chronicle*, 10 February, 26 February, 16 March 1972.

34 *Kielder Skyspace* is a small, circular, half-buried chamber with a three-metre hole in the roof that allows visitors to look straight up at the sky and marvel at the surprising and ever-changing quality of natural light.

35 Gage, John, *Colour in Turner: poetry and truth* (London, 1969), p.8.

61   *J.M.W. Turner,* Norham Castle: Sunrise, *c.1845 (Tate)*

One of the most celebrated of these 'colour-beginnings' is *Norham Castle: sunrise* (Tate, *c.*1845).[36] As we have seen, Turner painted the ruined castle overlooking the Tweed on several occasions earlier in his career: in 1798, 1815 and 1817. However, this extraordinary late painting, often nowadays regarded as one of his greatest works, is different from earlier versions in that it is a large oil rather than a smallish watercolour and it is painted in the tentative manner of a preparatory sketch; it is nothing more in fact than a few feathery patches of blue, yellow and orange on a white ground. Thus while the earlier watercolours of Norham in their accumulation of telling details seem to make some kind of comment on the relative economic success of England and Scotland, or the benefits of the Act of Union of 1707, this appears much more apolitical and timeless – a meditation simply on the magical, transformative power of light. Even so, or because of this, it also seems to have something to say about the character of Northumberland as a county: namely, that Northumberland is, to borrow a phrase that Scott uses in *The Lay of the Last Minstrel* (1805), a place of 'inchantment'. And inasmuch as that is the case, it has something in common, surprising as it may seem, with the otherness of the dark, rainy stretch of land on the right-hand side, the 'barbarian' side, of William Bell Scott's *The Building*

---

36   Some scholars give this work a rather earlier date, for instance in *Turner 1775-1851* (Tate Gallery, 1974), p.173.

62 *William Bell Scott,* Building the Roman Wall, *1855 (Wallington Hall, The National Trust)*

of the Roman Wall (1857), the first in the series to which *Iron and Coal* belongs, at Wallington.[37] Indeed, it has something in common also with Northumberland as it appears in recent photographs by the London-based Belgian artist, Uta Kögelsberger. *Kielder 2002*, for instance, makes use of the giant spaceship-like concrete valve tower in the middle of the reservoir to create an eerie, arctic night-like effect. I say 'makes use of' because, as is the way with Kögelsberger's work, this image seems to use rather than depict something in the landscape as a way of evoking the kind of shifts of perception we all experience when, as the artist herself puts it, we find ourselves deprived of visual information by darkness and have to compensate imaginatively for what our eyes cannot see.[38]

Meanwhile, ten miles south of Kielder, just over the Cumbrian border, lies another landscape where artists have discovered the same kind of otherness: the bleak marsh and moorland of Spadeadam. Spadeadam was leased from the Forestry Commission in 1956 for the purpose of testing and developing Blue Streak, a medium-range missile which, it was hoped, would eventually replace Britain's ageing V bombers.[39] It was chosen because it was believed that the natural bedrock there could cope with the weight of the huge concrete test rigs and the enormous thrusts generated in firing trials. Also, significantly in the context of what I am discussing here, it seemed beyond the pale – a kind of no-man's land.[40] As a result, for a brief period in the late 1950s it became the scene of frantic activity, not unlike the landscape beside Hadrian's Wall in Roman times. First, six hundred construction workers arrived, and then hundreds of skilled technical staff from Hawker Siddeley

---

37 Michel Foucault's term 'Heterotopia' might apply here: a place outside civilisation, where hegemonic culture is at once contested and inverted. See Michel Foucault, 'Of Other Spaces', *Diacritics*, Spring 1986, vol.16, no.1, pp.22-7.

38 The Foreword to *Uta Kögelsberger* (Newcastle upon Tyne, 2004).

39 Interestingly, this part of the Irthing Valley was for a time in the late 1960s and early '70s considered as a possible site for Northumbria Water's giant reservoir (*Newcastle Evening Chronicle*, 29 October 1969). Kielder, however, was eventually chosen as the new 'Ullswater' because it could produce three times the amount of water.

40 Hancock, S.R., 'The Blue Streak Project' (unpublished typescript, 1997), p.24. The Isle of Wight, one of the other sites considered, did not have this advantage: see testimony of Fred and Maureen Nicol in the oral history archive compiled by Fiona Deal as part of Louise K. Wilson and John Kippin's exhibition, 'Blue Streak' at Tullie House, Carlisle, 4 October-16 November 2003.

63 *Uta Kögelsberger,* Kielder 2002

64 *Marcus Coates,* Finfolk, *2003 (photograph Mark Pinder)*

65 *John Fairnington and others,*
Cement Menagerie, *1962-81*

at Stevenage and Rolls Royce at Derby.[41] In 1960, however, the government changed its mind. It started developing Blue Streak as a civilian satellite-launcher rather than a military rocket.[42] And then, in 1973, in a further switch of policy, it moved the whole Blue Streak project to French Guyana and converted Spadeadam into an RAF electronic warfare training range. What one finds therefore today if one visits the site is both Blue Streak debris and a bizarre assortment of old MIG fighters, Argentine missile launchers and ex-East German mock-ups of aircraft and tanks that NATO pilots use for training purposes. In other words, Spadeadam is a very strange place indeed. However, it is important to note that, as with Norham and Kielder, it is not so much its intrinsic character that makes it seem this way as the hopes and fantasies with which artists imbue it. In Spadeadam's case the video-maker Louise K. Wilson and the photographer John Kippin both find in it a sense of chirico-esque unease and of troubled feelings about episodes in recent history.

This is also true of certain other places in Northumberland. Craster beach, for instance, became a place of pre-modern enchantment in just this way when, one summer's evening in 1993, the Paris-based artist Bethan Huws bussed in an audience to watch the improbable spectacle of eight Bulgarian singers in traditional costume carol the North Sea.[43] Likewise, Berwick took on this quality when it was used as the setting for Marcus Coates's video *Finfolk* (2003), in which the artist takes on the guise of a 'selkie', one of those rogue seals which, according to Nordic legend, from time to time turn into humans and make mischief for people on shore. *Finfolk* begins with a mysterious figure emerging from a misty, choppy, very cold-looking sea in wet suit, flippers and Adidas shell suit who then climbs to the top of the harbour wall and from there launches a tirade of not-quite-human snuffles, grunts and chattering sounds followed by a queer little jig. But only for a few moments. Spying some fishermen

---

41 There were 459 people working at Spadeadam in July 1960: Hancock, 'Blue Streak Project', p.39.
42 The Macmillan government also realised that, as originally conceived, a defence system based on Blue Streak necessitated the erection of fixed silos all over Britain which would prove tricky politically given that many of them would be in safe Tory constituencies. See Duncan Lunan's review of C.N. Hill, *A Vertical Empire: The History of the UK Rocket and Space programmes, 1950-1971* (London, 2001) in *Space Policy* 18 (2002), p.71.
43 Huws, Bethan, 'The Bistritsa Babi: A Work for the North Sea' (London, 2002), pp.144-7.

approaching in the distance he/it abruptly takes fright and climbs back into the water out of harm's way, disappearing without trace except for a trail of air bubbles on the water's surface. All very puzzling. And the final shots of a seal bobbing about out at sea do nothing to dispel our uncertainty as to what manner of creature we have been watching.

The extent to which such works can be described as truly experimental is questionable, however. For the truth is that, unlike when Turner painted *Norham Castle: sunrise*, such strange goings-on are nowadays not only tolerated but expected in the art world.[44] Take *Kielder 2002*, Uta Kögelsberger's image of the reservoir at Kielder, for example. It is no accident that this was produced during a residency organised by a publicly funded body (Kielder Partnerships), exhibited at various publicly funded venues (the Berwick Gymnasium Gallery, the Queen's Hall, Hexham, Café Gallery Projects, London), and then reproduced and discussed in a publicly funded London-based art magazine and a publicly funded book about the artist's work.[45] In its disconcerting oddness it completely conforms to the kind of art of which the accredited contemporary art world approves.

Yet this is not true of all recent art that renders Northumberland strange. There is one notable exception in the village of Branxton in north Northumberland, *The Cement Menagerie*. This extraordinary work comprises 300 life-size figures plus all kinds of animals – giraffes, elephants, hippos, polar bears, leopards, camels, kangaroos. All are made out of wire netting covered in cement and crammed into the garden of a modest and otherwise unremarkable inter-war semi. Some of the figures are anonymous; others, like Robbie Burns, Winston Churchill and Lawrence of Arabia, are drawn from history. *The Cement Menagerie* was begun in 1962 and took the best part of 20 years to complete. Although very strange indeed, it is not the work of an artist who one can classify as a tourist. On the contrary, John Fairnington was a retired joiner who spent his entire life in the village.

44　See the concept of 'repressive tolerance' in Herbert Marcuse, *One-Dimensional Man* (London, 1964).
45　Usherwood, Paul, 'Uta Kögelsberger', *Art Monthly*, November 2003, 22-3, and *Kögelsberger* (Newcastle upon Tyne, 2004).

14

Pipedreaming: Northumbrian Music from the Smallpipes to Alex Glasgow

JUDITH MURPHY

Tunes travel. A Scottish fiddle tune, *Hills of Glenorchy* (also claimed by the Irish as *The Jolly Corkonian*), crossed the border and found its way into an 1831 tune book compiled by Tom Green, the Duchess of Northumberland's piper.[1] Subsequently it became associated with a fishing song, *The Wild Hills o' Wannys*, by James Armstrong of Ridsdale,[2] before being taken up by Tanfield pitman poet Tommy Armstrong as the tune for his comic song *Marla Hill Ducks*.[3] The circle was completed by legendary smallpiper Billy Pigg, who recorded it in 1974 as an instrumental tune under its adopted Northumbrian name of *Wild Hills o' Wannie*.[4] There are many similar cases where titles adapt to reflect locality,[5] and they beg the question of where musical identity ends and where invented tradition begins.

And this is without considering the internal diversity. How can a consistent Northumbrian soundtrack be drawn from Tyneside music hall and the dance tunes of the Cheviots? Durham miners' songs and border ballads? The industrial, the rural and the post-industrial? Yet there is evidence of a public perception that a specifically

1   Green, William Thomas, 'Hills of Glenorchy', *Manuscript tune book of William Thomas Green*, 1831, Northumberland Records Office.
2   Armstrong, James, 'Wild Hills o'Wannys', in *Wanny Blossoms: a book of song, with a brief treatise on fishing with the fly, worm, minnow, and roe; sketches of border life, and fox and otter hunting* (Hexham, 1879), pp.2-4.
3   Armstrong, T., 'Marla Hill Ducks', in Armstrong, W. (ed.), *Song Book containing 25 Popular Songs of the Late Thomas Armstrong* (3rd edition, Chester-le-Street, 1930), p.2. The suggested tune is 'The Wild Hills o' Wannie'.
4   Recording compiled on: Pigg; Hutton; and Atkinson, *Wild Hills o' Wannie - The Small Pipes of Northumbria* (LP, Topic 12TS 227, 1974, reissued on CD: *The Northumbrian Small Pipes*, Topic TSCD487, 1996).
5   For a general discussion of how tunes recur across continents, see Lloyd, A.L., *Folk Song in England*. (London, 1967), pp.48-51 and 79-91; and Burnett and MacRaild, 'The Irish and Scots on Tyneside', in this volume.

Northumbrian music most certainly does exist, most notably in the 1970 special edition of *English Dance and Song: The Folk Music of Northumbria*,[6] which was the first time ever that the English Folk Dance and Song Society had devoted an entire issue of their magazine to a single region. This was compounded by the recent release of the massive anthology, *The Northumbria Collection*.[7]

Such identity may be as nebulous as the New Age marketing of all things 'Celticized', and is undoubtedly moulded by forces outside the music itself. The North East is far from being one homogeneous entity: yet by combining the noble savagery of reivers and the 'daft-lad' pitman 'Bob Cranky'[8] with the ethereal quality of the landscape, the winding gear, and our Celtic saints, a magical Northumbrian kingdom (albeit one which stops well short of the ancient boundaries) can be imagined. It is easy to wax lyrical. And that is a problem. Roland Bibby once bemoaned the various 'false Northumbrias'[9] (as opposed to his own, equally contestable version) created by tourist boards and the media and inserted into the public consciousness through repetition. But when dealing with the region's music, cultural identity cannot be dismissed as invention, pure and simple. Even though there are perceived differences between the music of the more socially stable rural areas,[10] and the industrial melting pot of the Tyne and Wear conurbations, there is sufficient blurring at the edges of these styles to argue for a coherent Northumbrian musical identity.

Urban people travelled to country shows and contests; Tyneside music hall stars performed in outlying areas; the sword dances performed at rural Plough Monday festivals thrived when transplanted to coalfield communities; and the acknowledged heroes of smallpiping in the 1920s were miners from south-east Northumberland's industrial belt. For Tommy Armstrong to use *Wild Hills o' Wannie* it must be assumed that the tune was common currency in the Durham coalfield as well as among the anglers of Northumberland. In the opposite direction, a 1950 recording of Jack Armstrong's Northumbrian Barnstormers at a Dinnington barn dance features lively renditions of Tyneside favourites such as *Blaydon Races* and *Keep Yor Feet Still Geordie, Hinny*,[11] and the sound of the dancers singing along is clearly audible. Evidently the reality of a Northumbrian music is there, at least in part. And there is regional particularity as well: the 'rant' step rendered the rhythmic drive of local social dance tunes highly distinctive. No matter how the imagery has

---

6   'The Folk Music of Northumbria', *English Dance and Song*, Special Edition, Spring 1970.

7   Various artists, *The Northumbria Anthology* (MWM CD SP 31/50, Newcastle, 2003).

8   Bob Cranky was an archetypal collier character who appeared in ballads between the end of the 18th and the start of the 19th century; he was characterized as cheerful, beer-swilling and fond of a fight. See Colls, R., *The Collier's Rant* (London, 1977), 24-56. See also G.C. Deacon, *Popular Song and Social History : A Study of the Miners of the North East* (Essex University, PhD thesis, 1987), p.254, which contends that such archetypes are not regionally specific.

9   'False' is in any case far too strong a word: Erik Cohen has demonstrated how 'rather than looking at transformations engendered by tourism in customs and the arts as mere aberrations, it is more useful to approach them as another, albeit accelerated, stage in the continuous process of cultural change': Erik Cohen, 'The Sociology of Tourism: Approaches, Issues and Findings', *Annual Review of Sociology*, Vol. 10 (1984), pp.373-92, p.388. Paul Usherwood in this volume gives a much fuller explanation of Cohen's typology of tourist experiences and its relevance to the region.

10   Whittaker, W. Gillies, 'The Folk-music of North-eastern England', in *Collected Essays by William Gillies Whittaker* (London, 1940), pp.1-64, demonstrates how some folklorists were prone to conflating Northumbria with the administrative county of Northumberland.

11   Accessible via the FARNE website: http://www.asaplive.com/archive/detail.asp?id=A1000007.

been adapted and used, the songs and tunes and the people who carried them performed (and arguably still perform) a real function within real communities. Whether or not these communities thought of themselves as Northumbrian or whether external influences shaped this overarching term is another matter, and this chapter aims to unravel some of the realities and myths which make up this cultural identity.

Patronage and Northumbriana

The term 'Northumbrian' as applied to music appears to be a relatively recent construct. Caedmon's song aside, most musical associations with the ancient kingdom of the Dark Ages seem tenuous. Around the turn of the 19th century, when Newcastle intellectuals began making efforts to understand the vernacular heritage of a wider North country, an overarching musical identity called 'Northumbrian' was only just beginning to regain some meaning.

Ritson's late 18th-century song collections,[12] *The Northumberland Garland* and *The Bishopric Garland*, provided a core regional repertoire from which antiquarians could work but they were defined by distinct administrative counties. In 1812 a wider regional identity in song was acknowledged in the title of John Bell's *Rhymes of the Northern Bards*,[13] which contained several references to Northumbria.[14] However, these do not appear in vernacular songs; rather, they appear in self-consciously literary poems such as the verse on its frontispiece:

> Northumbria's sons stand forth, by all confest,
> The first and firmest of fair freedom's train.[15]

Unlike so many of the songs within Bell's book, this is evidently not work from an oral or folk tradition. His choice of title, with its bardic allusion, further suggests a northern literati influenced by the ideas of Herder, the brothers Grimm, Rousseau, Burns and Scott, and keen to tap into the noble savage idea. Bell himself has been noted as one of the most practical, and least fanciful, of song collectors:[16] if even he displayed signs of romanticism, the notion of a musical and poetic survival from the pre-literate and distant past had clearly entered the consciousness of a particular well-educated stratum.

Contemporaneously, the colourful biographies of roguish piper Jamey Allan (who died in Durham gaol) saw a similar innovation. While the instrument he played was

---

12 Ritson, J., *The Bishopric Garland* (Newcastle, 1792); Ritson, J., *The Northumberland Garland* (Newcastle, 1793).
13 Bell, J., *Rhymes of the Northern Bards* (Newcastle, 1812).
14 Rosemary Sweet in this volume explains the growth among contemporary antiquaries of a perceived regional identity drawn from a long historical span and the region's particular topography.
15 Bell, J., *Rhymes of the Northern Bards* (Newcastle, 1812), frontispiece; see also pp.171-5, which include an 1807 poem by Bothwell entitled 'Stanzas Addressed to Northumbria'.
16 See Harker, D., Introduction to J. Bell, *Rhymes of the Northern Bards* (facsimile edition, Newcastle, 1971).

still termed *Northumberland* pipes, various of his well-to-do sponsors began to refer to him as 'our Northumbrian minstrel'.[17]

While Allan's patron, the Duchess of Northumberland, was seen as 'a great encourager of the ancient Northumbrian music',[18] William Richardson, North Shields notary, friend of Allan's and man of *belle lettres*, penned a fanciful account of *A Border Gathering* (apparently adapted from one of Scott's paeans to the clans)[19] with the opening lines:

Pipe of Northumbria sound!
War-pipe of Alnwick![20]

Such nomenclature was usually accompanied by adjectives such as 'wild' or 'ancient', and references to the warring border clans, all in keeping with the *sturm und drang* of Romantic imagery already successfully exploited by local painter John Martin. Local intellectuals must have considered themselves

66 *The original Northumbrian minstrel. Jamie Allan, Anon.*, The Life of James Allan, the celebrated Northumberland piper; containing his travels, adventures, and wonderful escapes, in England, Scotland, Ireland, France, Holland, Arabia &c. *(Blyth, 1817), frontispiece*

very fortunate to have this ready-made landscape on their doorstep. The fact that it carried its own soundtrack – its own instrument even – could only have rendered it more appealing still.

Meanwhile, it is difficult to establish when the name and idea of 'Northumbria' permeated vernacular song. A wealth of collected folk songs and tunes bearing a strong regional cohesion and commonality, and loaded with local patriotism celebrating Tyneside, Durham, the North Country – almost everything but Northumbria – implies that this was a concept without much popular significance. Possibly the first hint that the term had achieved more widespread use dates from *c*.1854. Ned Corvan's *Deeth o' Billy Purvis* was a requiem for the man in whose show he had served his apprenticeship: 'wor favourite cloon, an' Northumbrian jester, geyne for ivver'.[21]

---

17   Wight, A., *The Life of James Allan, the Celebrated Northumberland Piper; containing his surprising adventures and wonderful achievements in England, Scotland, Ireland, France, India, Tartary, Russia, Egypt, and various other countries of Europe, Asia, and Africa* (Newcastle, 1818), i.

18   Anon., *The Life of Jimmie Allan, the Celebrated Northumberland Piper; Giving full account of his wonderful travels, humorous adventures, daring desertions, and numerous love intrigues in England, Ireland, Scotland, and France, India, Persia, Egypt, and other countries, Embracing also a large number of Most Surprising and Interesting Anecdotes* (Blyth, 1818), p.120.

19   Sir W. Scott, 'Pibroch of Donuil Dhu', in Campbell, A., (ed.), *Albyn's Anthology* (Edinburgh, 1816). The rhythm and subject matter of Richardson's poem are so similar as to verge on pastiche. I am grateful to Dr M. Sutton of Northumbria University for noticing this.

20   Thompson, J., *A New, Improved and Authentic Life of James Allan, the Celebrated Northumberland Piper; detailing his surprising adventures in various parts of Europe, Asia and Africa, including a complete description of the manners and customs of the gipsy tribes* (Newcastle upon Tyne, 1828), pp.53-4n.

21   Corvan, E., 'Deeth o' Billy Purvis', in *Corvan's Song Book No. 2* (Newcastle, *c*.1857-1866), pp.11-13.

Gregson suggests that the song was written for a fundraising concert so that Purvis might have a headstone.[22] As with strike ballads, the songwriter would have had to pitch the message towards an audience capable of providing most of the financial help. It might be argued that the Northumbrian reference was aimed at wealthier listeners who would respond to its nostalgic and romantic allusions.

Equally concerned with olden times, Thomas Bewick recalled times of Christmas cheer,

> heightened everywhere by the music of old tunes, from the well-known, exhilarating, wild notes of the Northumberland pipes, amidst the buzz occasioned by 'foulpleughs' (morrice or sword dancers) from various parts of the country.[23]

Like many others, Bewick was spurred on to revive folk traditions by the foreboding that such survivals from the past might soon wither away. He encouraged the passing on of skills by John Peacock, the compiler of the famous *Peacock's Tunes*[24] and the man credited with encouraging pipemakers such as John Dunn to extend the instrument's range by adding keys to the chanter. And he sought out work at the theatre for the old ducal piper William Lamshaw,[25] in the (probably erroneous) belief that patronage from the dukes of Northumberland, who had retained pipers since the 1750s, was waning.[26]

The fact that this patronage – whereby dukes, towns and regiments retained pipes – had carried on into the industrial era was, in England, at least, an oddity. It is a plausible explanation (alongside the long-term military mobilisation of the border region) for the survival of the smallpipes when other English bagpipes had fallen into abeyance. And it may further explain the way in which the different layers of Northumbrian identity, from 'the folk' through to the 'big house', are difficult to separate. If the local vernacular music had always relied to an extent on rich sponsors, then its collection and classification by a later generation of the élite would come as no surprise. It would be part of a process where those with influence took what suited them from the existing musical culture and invested it with meaning; and the carriers of the tradition adapted to suit the prevailing trend. An independent layer of more pure 'folk' music may well have existed beneath, but would be hard to disentangle now, as some parts were adopted by collectors and other parts were rejected and allowed to fade into obscurity. What is clear is that, in England at least, this continuity of patronage is peculiar to the Northumbrian area. While the songs and tunes of other English regions would have to wait before being 'rediscovered' by the likes of Cecil Sharp, Lucy Broadwood and the Rev. Sabine Baring-Gould, those of the North East had been in earshot of the gentry all along.

---

22   Gregson, K., *Corvan: A Victorian Entertainer and His Songs* (Banbury, 1983), p.9, suggests that the concert in question was held shortly after Purvis's death in December 1853.
23   Bewick, T., *A Memoir of Thomas Bewick written by himself* (Newcastle, 1862), p.67.
24   Peacock, J., *Favourite Tunes* (Newcastle, c.1800).
25   *Ibid.*, p.110.
26   Proud, K. and Butler, R., *The Northumbrian Small Pipes – An Alphabetical History Vol. One: Early Times-1850* (Spennymoor, 1983), pp.13-14.

While the aristocrats and the scholars had heard the tunes and understood the words, they had not until now felt obliged to call these songs 'Northumbrian'. As the 19th century progressed, this nomenclature grew in stature along with 'New-Northumbrian' organisations such as the Literary and Philosophical Society, and hinted at an ethnographical critical mass gaining currency by late century. [27] Building on the work of Bishop Percy and Sir Walter Scott, contemporary folklorists from overseas, notably F.J. Child,[28] were sparking academic interest likely to appeal to the eminent gentlemen of the Society of Antiquaries. This region was more ready to respond to such a stimulus than elsewhere in England: it boasted a share (with the Scots) of the Border ballads, and, as shown above, there was already an unusually strong history of song collecting and Romantic imagery upon which to build.

The industrial revolution had created urban centres whose inhabitants explored the novel and scientific in the manner of the 1851 Great Exhibition. But many – from the élite to the allotment holders – also believed that their quintessential national spirit grew organically from the (landscaped) garden that was England.[29] Among the intellectual perspectives that shifted sharply 'back to the land' were those of Arnold,[30] Morris,[31] and the neo-Gothic and pre-Raphaelite movements. North-eastern industrialists who moved to country estates[32] found new homes in an ancient landscape – with its own wildness of character distinct from the postcard prettiness of the shires – and they sought the mythology to go with it.[33]

The Northumbrian Minstrelsy *and its Influence*

Perhaps the most influential volume of music in this respect was published by Newcastle's Society of Antiquaries. The *Northumbrian Minstrelsy*[34] was initially suggested by Algernon, 4th Duke of Northumberland, and the songs and tunes were collected by an Ancient Melodies Committee[35] made up of leading local antiquarians, Robert White, J.C. Fenwick, and the Town Clerk of Gateshead, W. Kell. From 1855 onwards, material was collated, reports were presented to the Duke, and commitments

---

27 See Colls, R., 'Born Again Geordies', in R. Colls and B. Lancaster (eds), *Geordies* (Edinburgh, 1992), pp.1-34, esp. p.4; and in this volume.
28 Child, F.J. (ed.), *The English and Scottish Popular Ballads* (USA, instalments 1882-98).
29 See Colls, R., *Identity of England* (Oxford, 2002), pp.203-7 and 212-24. The work of 1920s travel writer H.V. Morton demonstrated the urban-rural duality of Englishness. From *In Search of England* (London, 1927) his sympathies would appear strongly with the England of countryside and spires, but he also found beauty in some industrialised landscapes in *The Call of England* (London, 1928). Morton described sooty Newcastle as 'a Black Prince of a city', p.99.
30 'The idea of perfection as an *inward* condition of the mind and spirit is at variance with the mechanical and material civilisation in esteem with us, and nowhere, as I have said, so much in esteem as with us … Faith in machinery is, I said, our besetting danger.' M. Arnold, *Culture and Anarchy*, quoted in J.M. Golby (ed.), *Culture and Society in Britain 1850-1890* (Oxford, 1986), p.203.
31 Morris, W., *News from Nowhere* (London, 1890) presents perhaps the most famous example of 'back-to-the-land' revolutionary ideals.
32 Lancaster, B., 'Editorial: Northumbria', *Northern Review*, Vol. 3 (Summer 1996), pp.1-5, esp.p.2.
33 See Girouard, M., *The Return to Camelot: Chivalry and the English gentleman* (New Haven, 1981), which demonstrates how the chivalry idealised by writers like Scott was incorporated into 19th-century thinking.
34 Bruce, J. Collingwood and Stokoe, J. (eds), *Northumbrian Minstrelsy: A Collection of the Ballads, Melodies and Small-Pipe Tunes of Northumbria* (Newcastle upon Tyne, 1882).
35 *Ibid*, pp.vii-ix.

were made, 'That some airs be prepared for printing as soon as may be – the best sets'.[36] Quite what criteria were used to evaluate which sets were best was not elaborated. However, the project stalled and, one by one, the original editorial team died, to be replaced eventually by John Stokoe and (as will be seen below) a powerhouse of Victorian values, John Collingwood Bruce.

True to its birth by learned committee, the resulting book, eventually published in 1882, was given immediate authority by the Society of Antiquaries' stamp on the title page. Unlike previous collections, this volume made claims to academic rigour and was intended for posterity. Using the term 'Northumbrian' in the title had its practical uses: though the collection stops well north of the Humber, it encompasses an area – Durham, Tyneside and rural Northumberland – too wide for one county. When coupled with 'Minstrelsy' (as with Bell's *Bards*, above), the nomenclature has a predictable philosophical message: this was our kingdom; these were our minstrels; this is our ancient music; this is us.

A large part of the *Minstrelsy* was drawn from the much-mythologised border ballads.[37] It also featured a high proportion of Northumbrian pipe tunes. Parts were drawn from earlier collections such as Peacock's *Favourite Tunes*[38] and Bell's *Rhymes*,[39] once again demonstrating the tendency of northern collectors to gather from a wide range of sources due to a long-established print culture (Newcastle was second only to London as a centre for chapbooks)[40] and the fact that noted enthusiasts, such as Bell, were printers by trade. This rendered north-eastern collectors distinct from many which followed from other regions, where folklorists turned oral transmission into a *sine qua non* of authenticity.[41] Further, much of the material gathered (such as *Dol-li-a, The Anti-Gallican Privateer*, and *Elsie Marley*) came from quite recent urban industrial and coalfield sources, and belied what might be expected if the book indeed represented a carefully constructed and romanticised 'Northumbrian' imagery.

This was part of the late Victorian trend to 'improving' culture. Examination of alternative published versions of songs in the collection shows Bruce and Stokoe to have indulged in considerable editorial 'tinkering'.[42] There was occasional 'beautification', as well as bowdlerisation.[43] And comments made in 1928 by 'Prince of Pipers', Tom Clough, show that the pipe tunes in the *Minstrelsy* were edited with insensitivity to the rich tradition of performance practice:

---

36   *Ibid*, pp.viii.
37   Reed, J., *The Border Ballads* (Athlone Press, London, 1973) provides a gently critical analysis. See also Diana Newton, in this volume, for the changes in tone between 16th- and 18th-century versions of these ballads.
38   Peacock, J., *Favourite Tunes* (Newcastle, *c*.1800).
39   Bell, *Rhymes of the Northern Bards*.
40   South Tyneside also had its share of chapbook publishers, notably Marshall of Gateshead.
41   Although Diana Newton, in this volume, has noted how the mother of the Ettrick Shepherd, James Hogg, mourned the passing of the ballads from oral into print culture, complaining that 'they'll never be sung mair'.
42   For example, several stanzas of 'Buy Broom Buzzems' in Collingwood Bruce and Stokoe (eds), *Northumbrian Minstrelsy*, 118-19, have been omitted. The omitted stanzas (quoted in Bell (ed.), *Rhymes of the Northern Bards*, 298-300) were those in which Blind Willie, with whom the song is associated, advertised the wares of local tradesmen – a practice which was presumably considered vulgar.
43   Harker, 'Introduction' to Bell, *Rhymes of the Northern Bards*, p.xlvii.

Many of the tunes there are all straight alike which signifies that the collector or player has been at fault. Perhaps both.

Take in the collection [Stokoe] 'Morpeth Lasses' as one instance. Many more I could mention. In fact if I was forced to play many of the tunes as they are wrote in these books I would cease and willingly cease to be a piper.[44]

Nevertheless, Bruce's Introduction placed great emphasis on the smallpipes and their influence on Northumbrian melodies, and the tone of his writing raised the spectre of ancient bards.[45] A polymath who followed his father into teaching at the family academy, Bruce was also a Presbyterian lay preacher,[46] an archaeologist, and a leading light of the Society of Antiquaries. Bruce's promotion of Northumbrian melodies and the smallpipes[47] exemplified the prevalent belief that this music was a vestigial remainder from a distant, mystical past, and 'was in some sort part of our blood and bones'.[48] And, of course, it was sure to have an edifying effect upon the lower orders:

I should like to see the use of the Northumberland small-pipes revived. Let every young man who has an ear for music learn to play on them. Then during the hours of toil there will be something to look forward to with pleasure ... Young men so trained will better than others be able to resist the vicious excitements which in large towns lure them to ruin.[49]

Perhaps the schoolmaster's memory was selective, for some of his speeches alluded to the notorious Jamie Allan[50] who carried on a life of licentiousness regardless of his uplifting pipe music. However, for gentlemen of the 'Lit and Phil' such as Collingwood Bruce, the concept of using music to guide Northumbrian youth towards invigorating patriotic pursuits seemed irresistible. It was rendered even more of an 'improving' pastime with the introduction of the spirit of civic-sponsored competition, again following Bruce's lead.[51] This is not to suggest that there was anything new in contests between pipers. Biographies of Jamie Allan feature several such duels, usually impromptu and associated with alcohol, personal egotism or gambling.[52] The difference was in the perceived uses of these new competitions, which were to build the character of each participant by reminding them of a culture they were in danger

44   T Clough, letter to W.A. Cocks, 5 July 1928 (Morpeth Chantry Museum, Clough Correspondence, MSS 11.32).
45   Bruce, J.C., 'Introduction' to Collingwood Bruce and Stokoe (eds), *Northumbrian Minstrelsy*, pp.vi-vii.
46   Sir G. Bruce, *The Life and Letters of John Collingwood Bruce* (Edinburgh, 1905).
47   *Ibid.*, 205-13 refer to lectures given in November and December 1876 to the Literary and Philosophical Society and the Alnwick Literary and Mechanics' Institute, as well as an address in July 1885 to the International Inventions exhibition in London.
48   *Ibid.*, p.205.
49   *Ibid.*, pp.208-9.
50   *Ibid.*, p.211.
51   J.C. Bruce, quoted in 'Northumbrian Small Pipes', *Newcastle Journal*, 30 May 1877 (Press Cuttings Book I, Chantry Bagpipe Museum, Morpeth, 2): 'It was a pity that an instrument should die which was peculiar to Northumberland ... if they had a pipe competition it would be the best means of calling attention to this subject.'
52   Anon., *The Life of Jimmie Allan, the Celebrated Northumberland Piper*. A particularly good example is given in pp.292-4, and features the tale of a piping duel arranged by regimental colonels between Allan and another piper, who turned out to be his brother Rob.

of losing. Meanwhile, that culture was developing in rather different ways, branching out into the Tyneside music hall, coalfield fundraisers, and concert parties – and the local revivalists were unusual in making efforts to accommodate this, too.[53]

The first competition, presided over by the Lord Mayor of Newcastle, was held at Newcastle Town Hall on 10 December 1877 and judged by Dr Armes (organist of Durham Cathedral), Joseph Crawhall, and Mr Thompson of Sewing Shields.[54] A contemporary report[55] lists 13 entrants, of whom nine competed on the night for a first prize of ten guineas offered by the Duke of Northumberland. This was a princely sum compared with prizes offered by later competitions more affected by the cult of amateurism. Collingwood Bruce's introductory speech displayed a chauvinism shortly to be challenged by a generation of female pipers such as Grace Gray, 'Piper' Mary Charlton, Patricia Jennings and Diana Blackett-Ord. And it was rich in mythology and sentiment:

> Northumbrian pipe music was essentially Celtic in its character. Being the offspring of minds ardent, free, and unsophisticated, it was wild, simple, full of fire at one time, and of deep pathos at another ... The Northumberland pipes was a domestic instrument. It might be enjoyed at the fireside every day ... Young men, cheer your mothers with a lilt, when, after a hard day at the wash-tub, they darn your stockings.[56]

Inexplicably, the music was both homely and wild. But many of the performances were powerful enough to inspire a sophisticated audience to call for *encores*. The winner was Thomas Clough, grandfather of Tom Clough, the 'Prince of Pipers', and just one generation in a dynasty of smallpiping miners from Newsham in south-east Northumberland, far from the windswept hillsides and pele towers beloved of the New Northumbrians.

Annual competitions continued until 1885, from which point they were held more sporadically. Between 1893 and 1900 the Society of Antiquaries made an abortive attempt at establishing a Small Pipes Society and, under its auspices, J.W. Fenwick's *Instruction Book*[57] for the instrument was published in 1896. Society transactions also showed an interest in one of the main preoccupations of the first folk revival: the search for 'national' song,[58] a quest which gained urgency as the British Empire was increasingly challenged.[59] A contest at Throckley Co-operative Hall on 25 March 1905 marked the end of this period of revival.[60]

---

53 See Watson, R. Spence, 'Ballads of Northumberland', in T. Hodgkin, R. Spence Watson, R.O. Heslop and R. Welford, *Lectures Delivered to the Literary and Philosophical Society, Newcastle upon Tyne* (Newcastle, Lent Term 1898), pp.69-92: p.92 gives Joseph Skipsey's 'The Hartley Calamity' as the best modern example of the genre, and praise is heaped on Joe Wilson in 'Northumbrian Art and Song', pp.147-72, esp.pp.167-9.

54 Sewing Shields is near Simonburn, close to Hadrian's Wall.

55 'Northumberland Small Pipes Competition', *Newcastle Journal*, 11 December 1877.

56 *Ibid.*

57 Fenwick, J.W., *Instruction Book for the Northumbrian Small-Pipes* (Newcastle, 1896).

58 Cummings, W.H., 'Address by the President: National Music', in *Northumbrian Small Pipes Society Transactions* (Newcastle, 1897).

59 See Gammon, V., 'Folk Song Collecting in Sussex and Surrey, 1843-1914', *History Workshop Journal*, Issue 10, Autumn 1980, v61-89.

60 'Northumbrian Small Pipes', *Weekly Chronicle*, 15 April 1916.

What caused the enthusiasm to wane? The prize money alone might have seemed incentive enough to continue competing. Perhaps the deaths of such ardent promoters as Bruce in 1892 and Crawhall in 1896 meant that organisational energy died with them. Or perhaps this conscious revival by committee may have discouraged participation, loaded as it was with issues of class and culture (for how could genuine folk-performers challenge the 'expertise' of those educated gentlefolk who had categorised and theorised their music?). Whatever the reason, the piping revival did not regain any real impetus until the 1920s in the wake of a wider English folk revival led by Cecil Sharp.[61] The Great War increased the urgency as a generation of tradition-carriers was decimated.

In the meantime, pipers within the tradition (as opposed to the revival) continued to play, dancers continued to dance, and singers continued to create songs that were collected. Enough is known about the careers of Joe Wilson, Geordie Ridley, Tommy Armstrong and Alexander Barrass for us to be sure that the song-writing tradition was thriving. What is unusual about the North East is the rapidity with which the products of music hall and concert party were collected, published and absorbed back into a tradition which had always featured a healthy traffic between the oral and the printed, between the popular and the élite.

Between 1911 and 1913, music hall star C.E. Catcheside-Warrington had published three volumes of *Tyneside Songs*[62] which were to be sources of regional music as ubiquitous and influential as the *Minstrelsy* itself. Catcheside-Warrington was also involved in the nascent recording industry alongside fellow music hall performers Harry Nelson and J.C. Scatter, whose 1908 *Blaydon Races* is the earliest known recording of what would become the Geordie anthem.[63] This innovation,[64] along with the radio, would have major implications for the future of north-eastern music.

In the meantime it continued to find patronage. The Duke invited 'Northumbrian' miners (Henry and Tom Clough on pipes, with dancing from the Earsdon Guisers) to Alnwick Castle in 1906, where they entertained the King and Queen.[65] And some of the tools of preservation – festivals and learned societies – laid down before the outbreak of war by revivalists such as Cecil Sharp and Mary Neal, were established on a national scale. Certainly, these mechanisms were damaged by their temporary abeyance between 1914-18 and the powerful metropolitan vogue for folklore failed to resurface afterwards, but local festivals did begin again, particularly in the shape of a new North of England Musical Tournament.

---

61   Sharp, C.J., *The Sword Dances of Northern England* (3 vols, London, 1911-13). Sharp was active in the North East during the first decade of the 20th century, collecting local sword dances, though it should be noted that it was not really Sharp (music teacher to the young royals) who rediscovered these sword dances for the middle and upper classes: they had featured in musical entertainments at Alnwick Castle from at least the 1880s.

62   Catcheside-Warrington, C.E. (ed. and arr.), *Tyneside Songs Vol. I* (Newcastle, 1911); *Tyneside Songs Vol. II* (Newcastle, 1912), *Tyneside Songs Vol. III* (Newcastle, 1913).

63   See Stephenson, R., *A Slice of Geordie Heritage: a potted history of vernacular gramophone and phonograph recordings made by Tyneside, Northumbrian and Durham artistes 1893-1943* (Newcastle, 2000).

64   G.V. Charlton, letter to the editor, *North Mail*, 11 December 1928. Tyne & Wear Archives, 924/80 contains correspondence and commentary on this issue.

65   'Miners and the Royal Visit', *Northern Weekly Leader*, 14 July 1906.

Revivals and continuities

Drawing on the inspiration of Mary Wakefield's 1902 Kendal Music Festival,[66] and displaying similar characteristics whereby a panel of judges could define what was and was not folk song or dance,[67] the North of England Musical Tournament came into existence in 1919, and aimed at celebrating a wide range of performing arts within the region. Alongside more standard choral and recitation contests, traditional sword and morris dance competitions were adjudicated by Cecil Sharp annually until his death in 1924. Northumbrian Small Pipes contests began in the Tournament's second year as an extension of the 'local colour … finding its way into the Tournament':[68] these would be judged from 1920-4 by Richard Mowat[69] and thereafter by Tom Clough. Among such eminent adjudicators as Vaughan Williams, Sharp and Holst, that two miners were seen as the arbiters of piping expertise suggests that earlier attempts by the Antiquaries to appropriate and mediate this form of folk music had not succeeded. But the influence of the mediators was clear. For one thing, cash prizes diminished with the same adoption of the amateur spirit noted in the sporting world by Holt.[70] Inevitably, this would shift the balance of the contests in favour of those who could afford a strictly amateur pastime, but it was already clear that its audiences were decidedly not the ordinary 'folk' of Newcastle, as attested by the complaint that 'the public of Newcastle have not rallied to support the Tournament as they might, and indeed ought to have done'.[71]

It would be easy to accuse the newly resuscitated Northumbrian Pipers' Society, which held its inaugural meeting in Newcastle on 5 October 1928, of the same kind of cultural mediation. Key figures in the Society's early Committees, G.V.B. Charlton (born into the county set as one of the Bellingham Charltons), Gilbert Askew,[72] and William Cocks were also members of the Society of Antiquaries, and published papers in *Archaeologia Aeliana*[73] which represented a continuation of the *Minstrelsy*'s earnest work. The incipient Society finally settled the issue of nomenclature – although

---

66 Forster, W.D., Foreword to *Programme of the 1919 North of England Musical Tournament* (Newcastle, 1919), p.15. This clearly acknowledges the Tournament's debt to Wakefield.

67 Francmanis, J., 'The 'Folk-Song' Competition: An Aspect of the Search for an English National Music', *Rural History* (2000), Vol. 11:2, pp.181-205.

68 Forster, W.D., Foreword to *Programme of the 1920 North of England Musical Tournament* (Newcastle, 1920), p.15.

69 The Northumbrian Pipers' Society website (http://www.nspipes.co.uk/nsp/ww14ppla.htm) gives the following information about Mowat, who lived from 1865-1936: 'A miner by trade, he won many of the late nineteenth century competitions, and reputedly had an unusual fingering style, lifting several fingers at a time, and sometimes his entire right hand. He was apparently not penalised in competitions for this, as he would be today.'

70 Forster, W.D., Foreword to *Programme of the 1922 North of England Musical Tournament* (Newcastle, 1922), p.11; Holt, R., *Sport and the British: A Modern History* (Oxford, 1989), p.87; see also J.M. Golby and A.W. Purdue, *The Civilisation of the Crowd – Popular Culture in England 1750-1900* (London, 1984). Amateurism can be seen as part of a general trend towards respectability in popular entertainments, but also an example of the idealised behaviour – competition for its own sake – befitting heroes of the modern nation.

71 Forster, W.D., Foreword to *Programme of the 1923 North of England Musical Tournament* (Newcastle, 1923), p.15.

72 Not a great deal is known about Askew's background, other than his obvious status as a 'gentleman'. He was a close contemporary of Will Cocks, worked as senior clerk for the LNER offices in Newcastle, and was a member of the Society of Antiquaries. He lived at first in Newcastle and later moved to Northumberland, and left the North East altogether in the 1930s.

73 Askew, G., 'The Origins of the Northumbrian Pipes', *Archaeologia Aeliana*, Fourth Series, Vol. IX (1932), pp.68-83; and Charlton, G.V.B., 'The Northumbrian Bag-pipes', *Archaeologia Aeliana*, Fourth Series, Vol. VII (1930), pp.131-47.

Charlton preferred 'Northumberland' pipes, he had to defer to the majority who saw 'Northumbrian' as the more appropriate term.[74] And there was to be a new emphasis on pedagogy and participation ('encouraging or stimulating … the younger generation of pipers and beginners in pipe playing')[75] rather than simply cataloguing the music. A further incentive to play was the reduced subscription rate of 2s. 6d. for Playing Members, whose skills were to be assessed by the Society before election (as opposed to the non-players' 5s. rate).[76] Furthermore, encouragement would be offered to prospective smallpipers, among whose numbers were several young people from old families, such as Patricia Jennings, from Wallington Hall, Diana Blackett-Ord, and Lance Robson. Regular classes were arranged for students of the Border Half-Long pipes. An instrument of uncertain pedigree, pieced together from old sets and illustrations, and produced in large numbers by Edinburgh-based Pipe Major Robertson, the Half-Longs were a major preoccupation of the early Society, probably because they were suited to outdoor, quasi-military use among groups of Scouts and Officers' Training Corps:[77] just the sort of exemplary youth activity with which the revivalists wished to be associated.

The revivalists overlooked the fact that a living piping tradition persisted outside their reach. There was a system of informal tutelage and a network of players who travelled to each others' houses to share technique and repertoire, as described by Foster Charlton:

> Mr Billy Pigg, himself one of the great pipers, recalls how, when he was about eighteen years old, he would cycle on Sunday evenings from Blagdon to Tom [Clough]'s home at Newsham where he would find about twenty other pipers assembled. The sessions used to start about six o'clock and go on until half past ten. First of all the visitors would take turns at playing and Tom would listen, then when every one else had finished Tom, either alone or with his father, would put on the pipes and play for two hours or more while his listeners remained spell-bound.[78]

Not that the Society ignored these players: they were keen to co-opt them as Vice Presidents[79] and competition judges, positions which, at least initially, they filled rather sceptically. Tom Clough waited three years to accept a Vice Presidency,[80] all the while questioning the philosophy[81] and necessity of a Northumbrian revival.

---

74   G.V.B. Charlton, letter to G. Askew, 12 October 1928 (TWA 924/80).
75   Northumbrian Pipers' Society, Minutes of Meeting, 5 October 1928 (Northumbrian Pipers' Society Minutes Book, Chantry Museum, Morpeth).
76   *Ibid.*
77   J. Robertson, letter to G. Askew, 22 August 1930 (TWA, 924/130) details the making of six sets for the Royal Grammar School, eight for the Varsity OTC and 40 for the Scouts. See also correspondence between Northumbrian Pipers' Society and J.C. Whillace, Secretary of Northumberland Boy Scouts, 1928-1930 (TWA 924/130-132); and Mullen, T.C., 'The Northumbrian Half-Long Bagpipes', *Archaeologia Aeliana*, Fifth Series, Vol. XII (1984), pp.209-21.
78   Charlton, F., 'Prince of Pipers' (draft *c.*1964, TWA 924/182-195(b))
79   Northumbrian Pipers' Society, Minutes of Meeting, 5 October 1928 (Northumbrian Pipers' Society Minutes Book, Chantry Museum, Morpeth).
80   T. Clough, letter to G. Askew, 15 January 1931 (TWA, 924/130).
81   T. Clough, letter to W.A. Cocks, 8 June 1926 (Clough Correspondence, Chantry Museum, Morpeth, MSS 11.17). This letter raises the exclusivity of amateurism and its cost to working-class performers.

Shew's the Way to Wallington

67 *Shew's the Way to Wallington. Notation drawn from J. Collingwood Bruce and J. Stokoe (eds),* Northumbrian Minstrelsy: A Collection of Ballads, Melodies and Small-pipe Tunes of Northumbria *(Newcastle, 1882), p.166.*

Clough's influence was most keenly felt when he was able to travel during times of unemployment. As well as broadcasting in Europe,[82] he gave demonstrations in London for the English Folk Dance Society[83] and for leading aficionados, such as Gillies Whittaker[84] and Kennedy North.[85] And Clough's forthright views were seen as influencing[86] Kennedy North's comments in the *North Mail*: 'The small pipes have never died, and there can therefore be no revival of them. Historically, all art which is worth while has always survived.'[87]

This letter sparked a controversial and lengthy correspondence in the press,[88] but it was difficult to dispute. The much vaunted continuity of Northumbrian music had always been seen as one of its most notable features. Writing in 1940, William Gillies Whittaker portrayed a culture built upon the interplay of collectors and practitioners. He weighed heavily upon the renowned virtuosity of the Cloughs and upon the ability of smallpipers in general to produce intricate and technically astonishing sets of variations:

> The ability of some of the leading players is astonishing. Rapid runs are enunciated with a clarity which a professional violinist might well envy, cascades of notes scintillate like a profusion of dewdrops.[89]

---

82   He broadcast in Cologne, as well as France, Holland and Belgium. Ormston, C. and Say, J., *The Clough Family of Newsham* (Morpeth, 2000), p.27.

83   *North Mail*, 8 December 1928.

84   The entire Clough family feature heavily in Gillies Whittaker's writing on regional music, quoted above: W. Gillies Whittaker, 'The Folk-music of North-eastern England', in his *Collected Essays* (New York, 1940).

85   'Northern Music', *Daily Mail*, 7 March 1928; 'Northumbrian Pipes: Newsham Player Delights London Audience', *North Mail*, 7 March 1928; 'W G Whittaker's Lectures', *Newcastle Journal*, 9 November 1928; 'Northumbrian Pipes – Musical Treat Provided for Londoners', *North Mail*, 17 November 1928; 'London Hears Tyneside Ditties', *North Mail*, 22 November 1928. See also The Musical Association, *The Northumbrian Small Pipes by S. Kennedy North (with illustrations provided by Tom Clough)* (concert poster 10 December 1929) reproduced in Ormston and Say, *The Clough Family of Newsham*, p.28.

86   G. Askew, letter to G.V. Charlton, 19 December 1928 (TWA 924/80), suggested that Kennedy North's comments were paraphrasing views he had probably heard at Newsham (Clough's home).

87   Kennedy North, letter to the editor, *North Mail*, 7 December 1928.

88   Most notable response was from G.V. Charlton, letter to the editor, *North Mail*, 11 December 1928 (TWA 924/80).

89   Gillies Whittaker, W., 'The Folk-music of North-eastern England', in *Collected Essays* (London, 1940), pp.1-64, esp.p.40.

He emphasised the pipes' influence on tonality – their fixed range dictating the shape of tunes into modes[90] rather than major and minor scales. He cited *Shew's the Way to Wallington*:

> Besides the vocal agility needed, there are no fewer than seven augmented fourths. When a German musician heard this sung by the late Mr Ernest J. Potts … he asked: 'Do you really tell me that the peasants in your district sing these songs?' On my querying why he doubted it, he said: 'If your peasants can sing such songs, then the English must be the most musical race in the world.' My reply was: 'Who told you that they weren't?'[91]

Gillies Whittaker's arguments are telling. Why would music with such virtuosic practitioners within the tradition require revival by committees of experts? It could be contended that the revival was less about music and more about disseminating a Northumbria constructed by two generations of local intellectuals.

Even so, there is clear evidence of practitioners accepting and even embracing the imagery of a borderland of rolling hills. At around the same time that Basil Bunting was reconnecting with his Northumbrian-ness, living among shepherds in the Simonsides,[92] Tom Clough was at the height of his powers and writing tunes like *The Herd on the Hill*.[93] Surely this was an odd choice of title for a coalminer? Perhaps it demonstrated the relative seamlessness, the proximity of town and country inherent in colliery villages? Clough after all played at plenty of farmhouse sessions. But perhaps it was also a sign that the mythologies had permeated more than just the élite.

A more obvious example in this regard was provided by Jack Armstrong, who started out as a collier, but later became a chauffeur and the most famous proponent of Northumbrian piping of his day. Some of his working life was spent in Yorkshire and it was after his return that he began to form dance bands such as the Northumbrian Minstrels and the noted Northumbrian Barnstormers. The perception of an overriding regional identity may well have been clearer viewed from the outside, though, naturally, Armstrong was also responding to the fashions of the day in the wake of famous Scottish dance bands, such as Jimmy Shand's. Whatever his reasons, he had a keen eye for local colour. Following the suggestions of radio producers,[94] he would rename old tunes to evoke ascribed Northumbrian characteristics. In Armstrong's hands, *Buttered Peas* became *Border Fray*.[95] An obituary of Armstrong highlights his

---

90 The modes date back at least to Ancient Greece, and to simple instruments which were tuned to a single key (such as the small pipe chanter before its 19th-century innovations). If you start a scale one note up on such an instrument, that scale will not sound the same as the conventional *do-re-mi*; the second scale up will sound different again, and so on. Their sound is distinctive; two modal tunes which show their definitive 'folksy' character are: 'The Blacksmith' (Dorian mode) and 'She Moved Through The Fair' (Mixolydian mode).

91 Gillies Whittaker (1940), p.52.

92 Caddel, R. and Flowers, A., *Basil Bunting – a northern life* (Newcastle, 1997), p.58.

93 Clough, T, 'The Herd on the Hill', in Say and Ormston, *The Clough Family of Newsham*, p.9.

94 C. Ross, interviewed by J. Murphy, 7 March 2005, recording in my possession: Colin Ross recalls Jack Armstrong stating that the initial instigator for his renaming of tunes was local radio producer, Richard Kelly.

95 Feintuch, B., CD sleevenotes to *Northumberland Rant – Traditional Music from the Edge of England* (Smithsonian Folkways, SFW CD 40473), p.18.

'intimate knowledge of Northumberland, its rural and historic features, and its wild life. He must have shown me every corner of the county, and all its rivers, streams and hills.'[96]

This tendency among local musicians to venerate the landscape is a common thread connecting the earliest collections of border ballads to modern practitioners such as Kathryn Tickell, Alistair Anderson and Johnny Handle.[97] This is probably parallel to, rather than because of, some of the more elaborate myths about Northumbrian music (there is after all no upper-class monopoly on loving the countryside), but there remains a disquieting resonance between the musician enjoying the landscape and the Earl of Tankerville's comments in his Foreword to the second edition of the NPS *Tunebook*:

> The sound of the Northumbrian Pipes is compelling without being either aggressive or raucous. It is 'compelling' because it fits perfectly the land of its origin – the lonely parts of Northumberland – where it mingles in its own type of harmony with the cry of the curlew and the sounds of the little black-face sheep roaming the hills and moorlands. I commend it to those who appreciate the impersonal beauty and unspoiled wildness of those places. [98]

As Chris Ormston puts it, 'we are still plagued by images of shepherds, plaids and dressed sticks'.[99] Bob Davenport, the iconoclastic London-based Geordie singer, once went so far as to suggest jokingly an 'incendiary festival', where the new wave of English concertina players and Northumbrian pipers would burn their instruments. Though he has since qualified this by stating that instrumentalists are far more accomplished than when he made the original comment, there is obvious frustration with the earnest, idealised reverence of many musical revivals.[100]

And yet many of the performers who emerged in the inter-war years corresponded exactly with the theorists' definitions of a singing and dancing 'folk'. Relatively untouched by debates over authenticity, real people were playing real music which, by virtue of geography or continuity, could be termed Northumbrian. Will Taylor played fiddle – despite the loss of a finger on his left hand – and piano accordion; Will Atkinson melodeon and later mouth organ; and Joe Hutton small pipes, and sometimes accordion and fiddle. All three were tenant shepherds who settled in north Northumberland, and who played for dancing or in sessions at farmhouse kitchens. In a 1996 interview, Atkinson and Taylor recalled walking up to nine miles each way

---

96   Fisher, G., 'A Yorkshire Man Remembers', *Northumbriana*, No. 14, Autumn 1978, pp.9-10, esp.p.9.

97   From at least the 1930s, rambling had also appealed to the kind of politicised northern working-class youth who would later find their way into the folk clubs.

98   Rt Hon Earl of Tankerville, Foreword to Northumbrian Pipers' Society, *The Northumbrian Pipers' Tunebook Second edition* (Newcastle, 1970).

99   Ormston, C., Foreword to Ormston and Say, *The Clough Family of Newsham*, p.v.

100   B. Davenport, email correspondence with J. Murphy, 3 November 2004. For Davenport, 'the folk' – as individuals rather than as an abstract grouping – would be more likely to play pianos, guitars or trumpets than 'traditional' instruments, and their choice of material would be eclectic and populist rather than purist.

across rough country, squeezeboxes on their backs, in order to play some music.[101] And in an article written in 1991 Joe Hutton was able to sketch some details of the network of players, teachers and instrument-makers which stretched across both the generations and the countryside:

> I had started to play the pipes in 1926. My father was a fiddle player and he used to play at local dances. Now he knew where there was a set of pipes, but they weren't in working order. He got the loan of them and we took them down to George Armstrong, the pipe tutor and maker at Hexham, to get them renovated …

> … quite a few pipers have been Coquet men: Jamie Allan, Billy Pigg, Archie Dagg, John Armstrong. I'd come across John Armstrong, at Alnwick for the competitions. A good fiddle player and piper, he lived at Carrick, and when I first came through to Coquetdale I went along there to a piping-music night. Tommy Breckons, Archie Dagg and Billy Robson were there, and John had Billy Pigg over that night.[102]

These 20th-century musicians were not so limited by geography as might be expected. There might have been only a certain number of players who they could contact directly, but the post-war introduction of Northumbrian 'Gatherings', first at Alnwick in 1949, then at Morpeth, Rothbury and Hexham, provided them with new meeting places. The second folk revival which began in the 1950s saw interaction between the traditional players and young bloods from Newcastle such as John Pandrich (alias Johnny Handle),[103] Colin Ross, Louis Killen and Alistair Anderson. Furthermore, the gramophone and radio allowed for an acceleration of the process whereby tunes and songs from elsewhere were adopted and adapted into the tradition.[104] Will Atkinson remembered being inspired by hearing Larry Adler's harmonica technique.[105] The Cheviot Ranters, Billy Pigg and Jack Armstrong were all known to have been influenced by Jimmy Shand's inter-war dance bands,[106] and the reach of Scottish recordings[107] into Northumberland is presumed to have been one catalyst (alongside folklorist Peter Kennedy) for the local barn dance craze in the 1950s. Ultimately, as the second folk revival grew, record companies would allow for this influence to flow the other way as The Cheviot Ranters, Jack Armstrong, Billy Pigg, and the three shepherds all released noteworthy recordings, which led to overseas tours and the stretching of their

---

101 W. Atkinson and W. Taylor, interviewed by A. Anderson, at Folkworks Northumbrian Workout, Alnwick, 19 October 1996 (recorded by Anthony Robb and available on Radio Farne: www.folknortheast.com).

102 Hutton, J., 'Rowhope Remembered 3: A Sound of Their Own', *Northumbriana*, No. 41 (Autumn 1991), pp.25-8.

103 This was less a stage name than a childhood nickname derived from his early interest in geology, or 'pan-handling'.

104 This interaction between tradition, the media and popular culture was also assisted by the growth of variety concert parties in the working men's clubs and pubs, which would produce groups like The Shiremoor Marras, who were to feature in shows like *Geordierama*.

105 W. Atkinson and W. Taylor, interviewed by A. Anderson, at Folkworks Northumbrian Workout, Alnwick, 19 October 1996 (recorded by Anthony Robb and available on Radio Farne: www.folknortheast.com).

106 I am indebted to Alistair Anderson for this insight, given during my interview with him on 5 March 2004, recording in my possession. It is also of note that Armstrong and Shand both recorded for the Beltona label, noted specialists in Scottish music: see Dean-Myatt, B., 'Beltona Records and their role in recording Scottish Music', *Musical Traditions*, web-journal Article 150: http://mustrad.org.uk/articles/beltona.htm.

107 See Burnett and MacRaild in this volume for the parallel influences of Burns Suppers and highland pipe bands.

influence over musicians from other areas, and even other countries: 'Burl Ives ... visited Jack [Armstrong] many times and invited him to Hollywood to make a film which was to be called The Pied Piper of Hamelyn.'[108]

Of all the dazzling pipers available at the time, it is unsurprising that Ives should settle on Jack Armstrong as his chosen star. For several years after 1945, Armstrong was synonymous with Northumbrian pipes. This would be helped by his chairmanship of the Northumbrian Pipers' Society during the difficult years between 1937 and 1946 (when piping was low on anyone's agenda), his high public profile from the dance bands, with their regular contributions to radio shows such as *Wot Cheor Geordie*, and especially the fact that his persona provided a natural bridge between the real practice of north-eastern music and an idealised Northumbria beloved of the old collectors and the increasingly important tourists. There is a photograph[109] of Armstrong, in the official cap and plaid of the Duke's Piper, by the clock tower of Wallington Hall, alongside his friend and lady of the house, Patricia Jennings. Two pipers wearing Northumberland Tartan in front of an iconic building could only emphasise a regional particularity that seemed highly marketable (see fig. 68).

Musical Heritage and 'the holiday kingdom'

By the 1970s an increasing quantity of Highland kitsch over the border may have led to a perception that pipers were a hackneyed symbol. Bill Butler, the tourism director who settled on *Northumbria* as the most marketable region-wide appellation for the North East (albeit with connotations more rural than industrial),[110] was surprisingly quick to disavow the use of traditional music as a stock image for the entire region. Protesting at the scant space allocated the region in a booklet promoting Britain as a holiday destination, he 'objected to one of the photographs illustrating the region – showing Mr Jack Armstrong, the Northumbrian piper, in the grounds of Wallington Hall. "We have got the same picture here as we always have," he said. "There are many other places in Northumbria which could be broadcast."'[111]

Yet the sound of the pipes, the knotted swords of rapper dancers, and the stories of the border ballads continued to play a significant part in the marketing of rural Northumbria ('Holiday Kingdom where folk music legends live on'),[112] especially when directed at the appropriate target audience – in the magazine *English Dance and Song*[113] and in folk festival publicity.[114]

After 1945, new versions of north-eastern identity, of Northumbrian-ness if you like, were gaining ground alongside a massive national shift in perspectives towards

---

108   Fraser-Smith, D., 'Jack Armstrong: The Northumbrian Minstrel', *Northumbriana*, No. 14 (Autumn 1978), pp.8-9.

109   Uncredited photograph on sleeve of J. Armstrong, *Piper to Northumberland* (independent CD, available from Wallington, 2002).

110   'Northumbria's Mr Tourism to Retire', *Northumbria Tourist Board Newsletter*, May 1978, 1: the distinction between 'Northumbria': rural and 'North East': industrial is made explicit in this article.

111   'Holiday Booklet Sparks North-East Protest', *Evening Chronicle*, 30 December 1971, p.7.

112   Advertisement for Northumbria Tourist Board, *English Dance and Song*, Spring 1971, p.2.

113   Advertisement, *English Dance and Song*, Spring 1970, p.2.

114   Poster for First Tynemouth Folk Festival, Saturday 13 September 1969, with sponsorship banner for 'Northumbria – The Holiday Kingdom'.

popular culture. This was partly inspired by wartime egalitarianism, and partly by initiatives imported from F.D. Roosevelt's New Deal America, which had seen an upsurge in oral history and folklore projects. Rural idylls had already been replaced by the idealisation of the lives of working people in industry, and this was taken up by folklorists such as Ewan MacColl and A.L. Lloyd (both of whose Communist affiliations already inclined them to sing the praises of the proletariat). They joined forces with new providers of patronage – such as the trade unions, the Workers' Music Association, Topic Records and the BBC – to disseminate the new-found wealth of industrial song. Naturally, the miners figured highly in these discoveries, especially after Lloyd began collecting coalfield songs for the National Coal Board's contribution to the Festival of Britain.[115] The pits of Durham and Northumberland yielded a particularly high proportion of this collecting and, with a fresh audience for old pitmen poets such as Tommy Armstrong and Joseph Skipsey, some miners from this new era, versed in the language of pop,

68 *Jack Armstrong and Patricia Jennings. Jack Armstrong, Piper to Northumberland, CD sleeve (National Trust, undated). Photograph courtesy of Morpeth Chantry Bagpipe Museum.*

skiffle, and the revival, consciously chose to place themselves within the old song-writing tradition. This was a version of Northumbrian culture that seemed radically different from that tied into the image of a lonely piper on a Cheviot hill, and yet, as discussed above, there were plenty of significant contributions to that more predictable version of Northumbrian music which hailed from the towns and the pit villages.

Besides, the early bookish interest in Northumbrian song and tune collecting had been spurred by fears of an old culture's imminent demise, and this pattern – at once radical *and* conservative – was now repeating itself in relation to heavy industry. The fact that two of the most famous products of this wave of miners' song (Johnny Handle's *Farewell to the Monty* and Jock Purdon's *Farewell to 'Cotia*) are elegies for dying pits serves only to explain the timing of the new fascination with industrial culture, shortly to be followed by the opening of industrial museums like Beamish. With his sweet, keening sound, his fiery left-wing reputation, and his emphatically open vowels, Alex Glasgow's voice was the perfect vehicle to carry his own message of *Close the Coalhouse Door* and to deconstruct the cynical ploys of politicians who donned a *Little Cloth Cap*. However, his vocal qualities will doubtless be best remembered by

---

115 Lloyd, A.L., 'Folk-Songs of the Coalfields', *Coal*, May 1951, 26-7; Lloyd, A.L., 'All The Winners', *Coal*, October 1951, pp.22-3.

69 *Northumberland and Durham Travel Association advertisement,*
English Dance and Song, special edition, Spring 1970, p.2.

the wider public through his version of *Dance ti thi Daddy*,[116] theme tune to *When the Boat Comes In*, a television drama which further secured the lens that viewed north-east England as the past – and the depressed past at that. Glasgow was an example of a cultural force allied with the future – the 'Studentry' drawn from the working class by the 1944 Education Act – but his sympathies were evidently with the region and culture of his childhood.

So, while songs and dances from the coalfields and the cities had for a hundred years or more found a home under the umbrella of Northumbrian music, the perceived threats of industrial decline and homogeneous imported mass culture had created a need for them to be more fully integrated into a recognisable Northumbrian identity. The Elliotts, a mining family from Birtley, went to the Folksong and Ballad Club in Newcastle and realised that the songs they had learned around the home were not everyday, but heritage.[117] Similar epiphanies struck the Folksong and Ballad Club's originators, Louis Killen and Johnny Handle, as they came to understand that their family copies of the Catcheside-Warrington songbooks were every bit as folkloric as the American blues which had first inspired their interest.[118]

So, at the time that Northumbrian identities were being reshaped by different forms of patronage, such as the tourist boards, the broadcasters and the record companies,

---

116   A. Glasgow, 'Dance ti thi Daddy', on A. Glasgow, *Now and Then* (MWM CD21).
117   D. Henderson (née Elliott) and B. Henderson, interviewed by J. Murphy, 13 December 2004, recording in my possession.
118   J. Handle, interviewed by M. Sutton, 25 February 2002; L. Killen, interviewed by J. Murphy, 9 March 2004, recordings in my possession.

continuity through the generations was further evidence that the local music was (at least in patches) part of the fabric of a way of life – a cultural activity in its widest anthropological sense. But would the majority of North Easterners acknowledge it?

In 1959, while most people in the North East were probably listening to Cliff Richard, Alex Glasgow first learned the power of performing in his native dialect, not in Newcastle, but on schools broadcasts in Germany, where he worked as an English teacher:

> Alex first achieved fame with German audiences with his singing of Geordie songs to his own guitar accompaniment. 'I first tried them with "Keep Your Feet Still Geordie, Hinney [*sic*]" he told me, 'and although they cannot understand a word, they love it.'[119]

Like Jack Armstrong before him (and Louis Killen, who had learned to value his Geordie roots at Oxford University's Heritage Society),[120] Alex Glasgow saw his north-eastern heritage most clearly from outside the region. In pop music, Lindisfarne, The Animals, Sting and Mark Knopfler all periodically returned to their regional identity, often from the vantage point of recording studios a long way from the North. This is surely crucial to the debate: if a musical identity is more recognisable to those whose perspective has been altered by moving outside, does this cast doubt on the relevance of that identity to those who remain? Yet, by the time *Melody Maker* ran a full-page article on 'The Geordie Tradition' in 1973, the powerful effects of the 1960s Geordie renaissance in publishing and the media had helped to reinforce the sense that the region did have a soundtrack that was owned by everyone:

> It would be misleading to suggest that every Tyneside inhabitant oozes dialect poetry and folksong, but there is interest on a general, everyday level in these forms of expression. 'Culture' is not the closed shop it appears to be in much of the country.[121]

Of course, in a way this returns us to the beginning. Evidently, the trend at the time was to talk of 'Geordie' rather than 'Northumbrian' culture. Looking backwards from a new century, when Kathryn Tickell and Alistair Anderson, lynch-pins of the new Sage Music Centre at Gateshead, are volubly and proudly Northumbrian, it is perhaps tempting to dismiss the shifts in terminology as simply down to fashion. However, there is an argument in favour of the idea of a Northumbrian music that goes beyond semantics, and that is its region-wide applicability: as explained at the beginning of this chapter, the blending of distinct local musical traditions into something recognisably regional has happened too frequently in practice for it to be purely the work of collectors obsessed with classification.

---

119 'Eldon's Gossip: Germans Delight in Geordie Songs as Low Fell lad puts them over', *Newcastle Evening Chronicle*, Wednesday 13 January 1960, p.8.
120 L. Killen, interviewed by J. Murphy, 9 March 2004, recording in my possession.
121 A. Means, 'The Geordie Tradition', *Melody Maker*, 24 February 1973, p.n52.

Ultimately, in examining Northumbrian music, at least three strands of meaning can be distinguished. First, it can be seen as the construct of the local cultural élite, who adapted and mediated the music to fit prevailing concepts, be they Romantic, patriotic, tourist or subversive. In this strand, the music represented people taking what they needed from the past in order to comprehend the present. Second, it can be viewed pragmatically: as music generated under patronage (of aristocrats and bourgeois, then music hall proprietors, then broadcasters and record companies), to which it quite probably owes its continuity into the present. In either of these cases, the spectre of a 'dominant culture' haunts the tunes. However, the music can also be perceived in a third way: as the soundtrack of a lived and imagined community of Northumbrians, but one that is firmly rooted in genuine cultural practice and not held reverently as a museum piece.

The music itself wafts in and out of these categories (as music will, to the frustration of those who work in the more fixed parameters of the printed page). It is sometimes forced by circumstance to settle most firmly in one category, then move to another, without one version of events ever fully cancelling out the others. While retaining traditional elements, local performers have adopted and adapted tropes associated with the music, sometimes to challenge them, sometimes to reinforce. There is poetry in this, and function, because so long as these constructs exist, and so long as they can be invested with some kind of meaning, the tunes and songs and performances will not be in any danger of fading away.

15

Northumbria in north-east England during the Twentieth Century

NATASHA VALL

Introduction

The late 19th-century rediscovery of Northumbria provided a point of departure for the identification of a north-east élite with 'their' region.[1] It signified the pursuit of a Northumbrian rather than English idyll.[2] In the South Tyne valley the coal owner Cadwallader Bates embarked on the restoration of Langley Castle, whilst, a few miles south of Lindisfarne on the Northumberland coast, Armstrong the Tyneside arms manufacturer busied himself with the epic rebuilding of Bamburgh Castle. Other families, such as the Joiceys, moved into the border ballad territories of north Northumberland such as Ford and Ettal. In north-west Northumberland the refurbishment of Wallington Hall by the Trevelyans included the famous murals of Bell Scott – murals that directly linked industrial Tyneside to the region's Northumbrian heritage.[3] This process of Northumbrian rediscovery, which is explored fully in this volume in chapters by Colls and Usherwood, is the starting point for my re-evaluation of Northumbria in north-east England during the 20th century.

Unlike its 19th-century precedent, late 20th-century 'Northumbria' appears to sustain a greater *popular* engagement with the legacy of the ancient kingdom.[4] During recent decades Northumbria has given its name to a police force, a university and a tourist authority. Since the 1970s Northumbria has secured a place in popular culture in the music of groups such as Lindisfarne and in the lyrics of popular musicians such as Sting and Mark Knopfler. Described by the former as

---

1   Colls, R., 'Born Again Geordies', in R. Colls and B. Lancaster (eds), *Geordies. Roots of Regionalism* (2005), p.3.
2   For a discussion of the retreat by English industrial élites to the countryside during this period see Wiener, M., *English Culture and the Decline of the Industrial Spirit 1850-1980* (1981).
3   Usherwood, P., 'Art on the Margins', in R. Colls and B. Lancaster (eds), *Newcastle. A Modern History* (2001), p.253.
4   Lancaster, B., 'Northumbria', *Northern Review*, vol. 3 (1996), p.5.

the 'landscape of my imagination', Northumbria's enduring status as homeland is underlined by the recent return to the region of the Pet Shop Boys' Neil Tennant. For the Northumberland Language Society, however, established in 1983, their ambition was to preserve Northumbrian words and dialect from precisely the sort of 'modern influences' that popular music represented.[5] For others, meanwhile, the quest for 'Northumbria' re-emerged during the 1980s as a possible escape from the region's long-standing identification with hard times and de-industrialisation.[6] In 1974, as part of a strategy to revive the flagging fortunes of seaside resorts, the Tyne and Wear Chamber of Commerce recommended that all references to the term 'North East Coast' in marketing literature for Whitley Bay should be replaced by 'Northumbria' – 'as it was romantic and historical'.[7] The Northumbrian revival has intensified during recent years of relative economic recovery and continues to appeal to north-eastern cultural élites, old and new, as a way of defining their relationship with the territory.

The revival of Northumbrian culture can be discerned across a wide range of practices, such as museums, and in the broader development of heritage and tourism. This chapter focuses on three selected moments of Northumbrian revival and begins by exploring the development of BBC radio after the First World War, when 'Northumbria' was at the centre of negotiations for control over the representation of regional broadcasting. Second, the chapter focuses on the 1960s and considers the Northumbrian revival in popular culture alongside the political vision of regionalist politicians such as T. Dan Smith. What was the place of a Northumbrian revival in a decade that witnessed attempts to redefine the North East as an outward-looking and modernised region? Finally, the chapter will consider the contrast between the kind of regional representation that was developed during the 1970s by Northern Arts, and by television. This concluding section will reveal that in the face of growing economic uncertainties Northumbria continued to occupy a central position in the debate over regional representation.

70 *Coal owners in the Depression*

5 www.northumbriana.org
6 Lancaster, 'Northumbria', p.5.
7 *Whitley Bay Guardian*, 1 March 1974.

Cecil McGivern and Richard Kelly

The BBC was established with a philosophical underpinning that emphasised the improvement of popular taste, and this filtered down to the local level. Previously a journalist and university lecturer, G.L. Marshall was the first station director of BBC Newcastle. Marshall claimed in 1928 that 'radio goes a considerable way in helping children to acquire a command of good spoken English'.[8] The BBC's attitude to vernacular culture combined a celebration of provincial authenticity with a commitment to cultural improvement. This connected with the experience of the North East during the 1930s as a site for the definition and appraisal of regional culture by initiatives like the documentary film movement, and Mass Observation.[9]

71   *Richard Kelly*

However, it is important to recognise that all the developments considered in this essay were part of a broadening of popular culture. In the North East the BBC signal was often weak: a BBC report in 1929 revealed that most listeners were beyond the range of the Huddersfield transmitter.[10] By contrast there was a strong signal for Radio Luxembourg in the North East, which broadcast American popular music. This station appealed to young people and complemented visits to the region's burgeoning dance halls where American-inspired dance bands were increasingly popular.[11]

At the same time, the launch of the BBC's Regional Scheme in 1929 sheds light on how regional cultures were shaped and represented. The international hunt for new wavelengths in 1929 resulted in the transition from 'local' to 'regional' BBC radio. After this Newcastle's BBC radio station operated as a subsidiary of Manchester, which was established as the BBC North Region broadcasting headquarters. The 'accession of Newcastle' to Manchester took place swiftly with little opposition other than from 'a small group of local enthusiasts' clamouring for their right to make programmes in the North East. The weak response to the closure of independent broadcasting facilities is explained in part by the poor quality of reception from both local and regional transmitters, clearly reflected in figures for licence holders.[12] In

8   *Newcastle Journal,* 8 January 1928.
9   Colls, 'Born Again Geordies', *op. cit.*
10   Report of the Proposed Regional Scheme by the Chief Engineer 1929, BBC WAC, R53/213/1.
11   Manders, F., 'Palaces of Pleasure', in A. Flowers and V. Histon (eds), *Water under the Bridges. Newcastle's Twentieth Century* (1999), p.121.
12   Briggs, A., *The History of Broadcasting in the United Kingdom, Volume II. The Golden Age of the Wireless* (1965), p.319.

1936, 70 per cent of households in Northumberland, where transmission from the Newcastle station was good, held radio licences. In County Durham, by contrast, only 34 per cent of households were licence holders, the lowest levels in England.[13] The marginalisation of listeners in County Durham was made worse by the fact that many of the *most* memorable 'northern' broadcasts of this period, such as Bridson's *Coal*, were recorded in the area.[14] Successive proposals for broadcasting in the North East never questioned the unity of County Durham and Northumberland. In 1935, in his capacity as North Region Director, Edward Liveing reflected on the case for greater independence of the region in the light of plans for a new transmitter:

> *Northumbria* and the surrounding counties have strongly independent cultural characteristics, which mark them out not only from the North of England, but, to some extent, from the whole of the rest of the country. In addition, Tyneside is, geographically, much more isolated from the Northern industrial cities than, say, Lancashire is from the West Riding, or vice versa.[15]

The reference to 'Northumbria and the surrounding counties' is characteristic of BBC deliberations which rarely referred to 'the North East' and suggests an unwillingness to see the area as a unit deserving of discreet broadcasting arrangements. By acknowledging 'independent cultural characteristics', BBC men like Liveing were making it clear that, while these distinct qualities existed, they would be able to cater for them within the existing arrangements for regional transmission, that is, as part of a 'North Region' based in Manchester.

In contrast, 'Northumbria' had the power to express a growing regionalism awakened by BBC policy. By the end of the decade gradual improvements equipped the North East with two transmitters, one at Moorside Edge outside Newcastle and one at Stagshaw, near Corbridge. Along with the suggestion that each transmitter should adopt the names of the ancient kingdoms of Bernicia and Deira came the proposition that the programme radiated from both transmitters be called the 'North Regional Programme'. This idea was quickly rejected by the BBC Control Board and it was stipulated that 'Newcastle shall not be regarded as a Region in its own right, but as part of the North Region' and should emphatically not 'be given a title which gives it equal standing with the Northern Programme'. Instead broadcasts from the new transmitters were to operate under the less auspicious title of the 'Stagshaw Programme'.[16]

Despite the North East's relative weakness within the overall regional scheme, the opening of the Stagshaw transmitter in 1937 brought new opportunities for radio in the region. The 'Stagshaw Programme' schedule for March 1938 included a 'triple bill of North Eastern dramatists', with plots described as 'Northumbrian'.

---

13   Pegg, M., *Broadcasting and Society 1918-1939* (1983), pp.48, 59.
14   Scannell, P., 'The Stuff of Radio', in J. Corner (ed.), *Documentary and the Mass Media* (1986), p.14.
15   E. Liveing, BBC Internal Memo, 3 September 1935, BBC WAC, R/361.
16   Northern Programme, Provisional Programme Arrangements for Northern and Stagshaw transmitters, January-March 1938, BBC WAC, R45/87.

Music included Tom Mearris (conductor of the Felling Male Voice Choir) leading a group of 11 'Northumbrian singers'. This broadcast was singled out for praise by BBC headquarters, particularly so the music, which was considered for broadcast in its own right.[17] The Stagshaw Programme also carried its own features bill, including in 1938 'The Royal Northumberland Fusiliers', 'Tyne Bridges' and 'The Northumberland Plate on Plate Day'.[18] It is important, here, to distinguish between the use of 'Northumbria' as a regional descriptor by both outsiders and insiders, and Northumbrian culture in itself. As a descriptor for the area, Northumbria had the potential to detract from the North-East's potential as a broadcasting region. To acknowledge Northumbria was to celebrate the idiosyncratic but *safe* qualities of north-eastern-ness. These qualities warranted special consideration but were not seen as deserving of independent broadcasting facilities. On the other hand, the appreciation of 'Northumbrian culture', particularly music, appeared to have been universally acknowledged in the broadcasting world.

The Northumbrian component of the Stagshaw Programme was not only widely celebrated; it also pioneered the broadcasting of dialect. While dialect had an established place in radio reportage and outside broadcasts of the 1930s, it had yet to gain a foothold in entertainment features. Given that the Newcastle's BBC station director had emphasised in 1928 that the proper function of radio was to improve standards of spoken English, and given the ongoing BBC commitment to 'received pronunciation', it is all the more striking that by 1937 plays were being broadcast in broad Geordie on the North Region Programme under the rubric 'Northumbrian Drama'. In 1936, Cecil McGivern joined the BBC in Newcastle as a producer and in 1939 was promoted to the newly created post of Programmes Director for the North. Born in Felling in 1907, McGivern had been a member of the People's Theatre in Newcastle during the early 1930s and was a graduate of Durham University. After the Second World War he worked in television, becoming Controller of Television Programmes in 1950, and Deputy Director of BBC Television in 1956. Although credited with establishing the public profile of television after 1945 he was controversially passed over for the post of Director in 1961, and subsequently joined Granada as an executive producer.[19] During the 1930s Cecil McGivern presided over the emergence of radio broadcasts distinguished from earlier features by the use of dialect and by their rootedness in popular culture – such as *Blaydon Races. A Tale of Geordie Marley* by the comic writer Captain Walter Diericx of Newcastle. The sketch was broadcast on the Northern Programme on 9 June 1937:

Blaydon Races
Jenny Marley: (after humming concluding bars) Hillo! (Laugh) ah'll back ye knaa wat the tune is? Ay hinnies, 'Blaydon Races', Tyneside's National Anthem. Did any owlder

17   *Ibid.*
18   *Ibid.*
19   *The Times*, 6 February 1963.

folk ivor gan te the Blaydon Races? Ah ownly went theor wance, an that was the day the ninth o' June, an it wes some race an' all mind ye. Ah'll tell ye aboot it.[20]

The idiom takes for granted that listeners will appreciate a sketch which is a comic re-enactment of the Blaydon Races narrative. This play was broadcast alongside a 'factual' feature on the running of the Northumberland Plate, main attraction of Tyneside's unofficial holiday in the first week of June. Such features assumed that listeners would be familiar with and interested in north-east sporting fixtures. A testament to the command of regional cultural representation by broadcasters and publicists based in Newcastle, this genre of radio also adds weight to the suggestion that the changes in leisure, brought by electronic developments, sustained older traditions of phonetic humour.

The interplay of local and national cultural influences of the BBC's Regional Scheme was accentuated with the arrival of Richard Kelly in Newcastle in 1948 as assistant producer. A graduate of King's College in Newcastle, Kelly is credited with orchestrating a Geordie 'golden age' of radio that spanned the 1950s. *Wot Cheor Geordie*, which began in 1945, was central to this era. The programme featured plays, songs and sketches broadcast in the dialect, and whilst the content and style of such programmes had developed in embryo during the 1930s, Kelly was able to capitalise on efforts to increase output from the regional stations after 1945. He recalled how 'there was an atmosphere of "there you are, there's the region, get on with it",'[21] and exploited these opportunities to the full, introducing comic writers and performers who would become integral to a second golden age of north-east cultural revival in the 1960s. Kelly also worked hard to establish the regional profile beyond the region. When the Head of Variety in London wrote to him in 1949 requesting a recording of *Wot Cheor Geordie*, Kelly sent the tapes with an assurance that the dialect could be 'toned down for a wider audience without losing its humour'.[22]

During the early 1950s Richard Kelly orchestrated the rise of Bobby Thompson, the stand-up comic, as a radio star, introducing him first in *Wot Cheor Geordie* and later providing him with his own show, *Bob's Your Uncle*. The popular appeal of Thompson was undeniable, and despite the Tyneside bias, *Wot Cheor Geordie* was enjoyed by listeners from upland Northumberland to County Durham as well as the major conurbations. It seems, however, that the programme was principally appreciated by an older generation.[23] Whilst the style and format was new, the use of vernacular combined with a humour which, in Thompson's case, drew on the 1930s experience, appeared not to have held the attention of younger listeners during the 1950s. Although the arrival of television during the 1950s is often credited with eclipsing the 'golden age of radio', in the North East, where television arrangements

20   Northern Region Scripts, Walter Diericx, *Blaydon Races. A Tale of Geordie Marley* 1937, BBC WAC.
21   BBC Radio Newcastle, *Babies and Broadcasters* (1991), pp.30-1.
22   Jordan, R. (ed.), *This is the North of England Home Service* (1948), 24; Richard Kelly memo to Standing, 29 September 1949, BBC WAC, N/53.
23   BBC WAC, N9/53.Robert Silvey Memo to Richard Kelly, 15 February 1951.

were rudimentary before the 1960s, it is likely that developments in cinema and popular music held more allure for younger north-easterners than radio programmes such as *Bob's Your Uncle*.[24] Furthermore, outside the North East, audiences found the dialect difficult to understand. As one BBC researcher commented, 'the dialect was troublesome. The humour was of a kind that appeals only to a local'.[25] In 1951, buoyed by the huge success of the programme within the area – by this time it was regularly enjoying audiences of more than a million – Kelly offered the programme to Scotland. To his annoyance and surprise, the Director of Scottish Programmes rejected the idea on the grounds that 'much of the content would be incomprehensible to Scottish listeners'.[26] On the other hand, audience research based on the North Region revealed that, as in the previous decade, the most popular items of *Wot Cheor Geordie* were the songs of the Northumbrian Serenaders and the Willie Walker Band.[27] Kelly was clearly mindful of music's potential to express particularity. One of his early innovations was to turn the studio-based 'Northumbrian Barn Dance' into a new live series. With an authentic atmosphere from Dinnington Village Hall, musicians including Jack Armstrong and his Barnstormers played live for local dancers. It was Kelly's stated ambition to make clear the distinctive characteristics of Northumbrian music: 'no mere derivation of its Scottish equivalent'.[28]

Despite recognising Northumbria as a marker of cultural distinctiveness, Kelly remained ambiguous about the relationship between regional broadcasting and regional culture. During the 1950s he had developed a form of radio documentary known as 'vox pop' which used local themes and settings.[29] When the name of the programme was changed from *Voice of the People* to *Voice of the North* Kelly complained: 'what was wrong with "people" and why it was changed to "North" I still don't know'.[30] He was aware of the power of authenticity and the premium placed upon it both by listeners and broadcasters. He was an enthusiastic champion of working-class culture, particularly stand-up comedy. He was proved right that Bobby Thompson's live appeal would make great radio. But his reticence at being cast as a 'regional broadcaster' demonstrates that he was aware of the precarious position of the North East within the BBC hierarchy. As Leonard Barras, humorous writer and contributor of several scripts to *Wot Cheor Geordie*, recalled, 'he sweated a bit under the pressure from Manchester'. Kelly himself described this pressure as 'the double imperialism of London and Manchester'.[31]

By the 1960s the part played by radio in Geordie and Northumbrian revival was situated in a wider ferment of cultural rediscovery taking place outside the

---

24   Browning, H. and Sorrell, A., 'Cinemas and Cinema-Going in Great Britain', *Journal of the Royal Statistical Society*, Vol. 117, No. 2, Part II (1954), p.151.
25   WAC, N9/53. Robert Silvey memo to Richard Kelly, 15 February 1951.
26   Memo from Director of Scottish Programmes, 6 July 1951, BBC WAC, N9/53.
27   Listener Research Report, 4 April 1950, BBC WAC, N9/53 LR/50/621. These findings nevertheless need to be treated with caution given that the sample was extremely small.
28   *Newcastle Journal*, 15 November 1950.
29   Scannell, P., *Radio, Television and Modern Life: a Phenomenological Approach* (1996), p.74.
30   *Evening Chronicle*, 1 January 1970.
31   Interview with Leonard Barras, 8 March 2004; Kelly, cited in *Babies and Broadcasters*, pp.30-1.

72 *The EmCee Four, c.1959 (courtesy of the editors of* Northern Review*)*

BBC's Newcastle recording studio. Of particular interest are Dan Smith's Blaydon Races Centenary Celebrations of 1962, and Frank Graham's publishing initiatives. These were accompanied by the conscious promotion of a *Northumbrian* cultural inheritance alongside an emphasis on *Geordie* culture as symbolic of the region's distinctive qualities. This elision of Northumbrian and Geordie culture raises a series of important questions – not least over the sustaining role of musicians and comedians since the 1930s and before, and the traditional and music hall influences on them stemming from before the First World War and into the 'New Northumbrian' era with which we started this chapter. In Robert Colls' words, regional cultures are 'born and reborn'.[32]

Dan Smith and Frank Graham

There was clearly a political emphasis during the 1960s that was new. Current insights on the use of culture for geo-political agendas may shed light on the relationship between 'official steer' and genuine 'popular demand', but in the North East the process

---

32 Colls, 'Born again Geordies', *op. cit.*

cannot be fully understood without reference to Dan Smith.[33] In June 1962 thousands of people travelled to Tyneside, many from abroad, to celebrate the Centenary of the Blaydon Races: 'a fictitious proletarian bus ride to a shady unregulated "flapping track"'.[34] This public spectacle was no spontaneous occurrence but had in fact been carefully planned by a committee established to oversee an event which would 'embrace all aspects of local and regional culture in the field of sport, recreation, drama, and music'.[35] In 1960 Smith made enquiries into its history because there was a feeling *in Newcastle* that the centenary of the race should be marked.[36] Smith's own initiative was to use the Centenary to focus attention on the remodelling of the Scotswood Road that encompassed the construction of Scandinavian-inspired system-built flats adorned with modernist sculpture. Smith wanted to call these celebrations 'the first Northumbrian festival'.[37]

A local man as well as a regionalist Labour politician, Dan Smith saw no difficulty in fusing his interests in the region's cultural inheritance with plans for its physical and economic renewal, but outsiders found these processes hard to reconcile. Delegates from the Newcastle City Council visiting the Civic Trust in London were told that a housing exhibition might well be supported, but the Civic Trust was 'not interested in the Blaydon Races as a Festival' concept.[38] Yet the enthusiasm of the organisers remained undeterred and bus visits to the Northumbrian and Durham countryside to show 'the visitor the special historical significance and the present day potential of the North East as a compact region' worked as springboards for the wider ambition to commence a 'positive policy in regard to the appreciation and preservation of ancient buildings, and buildings of special merit architecturally both old and new'.[39] This geo-political undercurrent quickly roused suspicion amongst Conservative councillors, who drew attention to the Centenary's historical anachronisms:

> There has been a take-over bid. This programme appals me … the day when the brass band was the pride of almost every mining village in Northumberland and Durham has gone down and down. At the Durham Miners' Gala the greatest attraction was a band from the American Airforce … The programme includes a mixture of things. There will be a veteran car run – cars dating from about 1890. What are they doing at Blaydon Races?[40]

Underlying this carping was an acknowledgement of the programme's potential appeal. Opposition councillors joined in, and seem to have enjoyed, the Centenary,

---

33 Hobsbawm, E. and Ranger T. (eds), *The Invention of Tradition* (1983).
34 Lancaster, 'Sociability and the City', p.336.
35 Joint Committee as to the Centenary of the Blaydon Races, 3 December 1959, 23 March 1960, TWAS, MD/NC/94/22.
36 *Ibid.*
37 *Ibid.*
38 Joint Committee to the Centenary of the Blaydon Races, 6 April 1960, TWAS, MD/NC/94/22.
39 Proceedings of the Newcastle Council, Report of the Joint Committee to the Centenary of the Blaydon Races, 20 April 1960.
40 Proceedings of the Newcastle Council, 5 July 1961, Report of the Joint Committee to the Centenary of the Blaydon Races, p.190.

73 *Mike Jefferys outside Marimba, c.1959, with Mrs Sproggin (left), the club manager (courtesy of the editors of* Northern Review*)*

and whilst there was clear political steer over Labour's general celebration of north-eastern cultural heritage, the event itself was not political.[41] Indeed the Centenary's eclecticism reflected confidence in the city-region's cultural activists to supply suitable entertainment. Further, it appears to have motivated the preservation of practices that might otherwise have been declining in the face of competition from alternative sources of entertainment, such as television and cinema. The rehabilitation of Balmbra's music hall, once host to local writers including Corvan, Wilson and Ridley, was set in motion by the celebrations. The 'Carlton Hotel', as it was known by the 1960s, was renamed 'Balmbras' in time for the celebration and became Smith's venue of choice for entertaining civic dignitaries.[42] This public rehabilitation of the venue also appeared to provide a boost to the ongoing popular music hall revival. Balmbra's soon became host to music hall enthusiasts, such as Joe Ging, later curator of the Joicey Museum for popular culture and a man who, alongside his wife Heather and friend Mike Neville, ensured that music hall, although marginalised on local radio by the mid-1960s, found its way into television where well into the 1970s the region's stations remained committed to locally based variety programmes.[43]

The Blaydon Races Centenary celebrations appear to have served as a prototype for a fusion of popular and official cultural revival on Tyneside. More importantly, the Committee's eclectic approach to selecting cultural practices for inclusion in the festival had the effect of eliding Geordie and Northumbrian aspects, particularly so in music. A 'Tynesider of all Tynesiders', Joe Bennett, director of the 'Northumbrian Traditional Group', saw the week of celebrations organised by Newcastle City Council in 1962 as a turning point in his efforts to preserve 'traditional' music in the region.

---

41 Lancaster, 'Sociability and the City', p.336.
42 Centenary of the Blaydon Races, Sub-Committee as to Publicity, 27 April 1960, TWAS, MD/NC/94/22.
43 Ging, J., *A Geordie Scrapbook* (1990).

His ambition to be a musician and composer had been cut short by the Second World War, but on his return to Newcastle, Bennett used his spare time to play the accordion in pubs and clubs as a member of the 'Barn Dance Band' led by Jack Armstrong, the Duke of Northumberland's personal piper. As Bennett recalls, 'in these post war years, there was a real danger that country dance teams, choirs, music hall artistes, clog dancers and Northumbrian pipers might disappear'. The political impulse to preserve what Bennett collectively called 'Northumbrian music' was unprecedented. Hitherto the official efforts to encourage musical practice had come through voluntary channels. The acts that featured during the inter-war revival, such as the Royal Earsdon Sword Dancers, were profiled once again by the Centenary celebrations. After 1962 Bennett joined the Earsdon dancers as an accordionist and thereafter brought the Shiremoor Marras, the Seaton Valley Dancers and the champion clog dancer Hylton Pomeroy alongside Northumbrian Piper Colin Ross into the fold of what was to become the 'Northumbrian Traditional Group'. With the second folk revival in full swing, in 1972 Bennett sought to distinguish 'his' group:

> Ours is not a folksy group – our lads are working miners who perform their traditional dances and sing their full blooded songs, because they are living links with our priceless heritage. There is nothing false about them … I have no time for bearded guitarists who mouth words they hardly know and change traditional folk songs to suit their own ends, stripping them of their old meanings.[44]

According to this view, Bennett's working-class background was essential to his credentials as a Northumbrian musician: 'Born in the close knit community which grew up along Newcastle's Quayside, he is steeped in the traditions of the keelmen who plied their trade along the 'coaly' Tyne …'[45] At the same time, Bennett's Northumbria was an outpost of a *British* civilisation which he hoped would endure despite the development of the Common Market. Echoing the thrust of the first folk revival, his insistence on the group's cultural authenticity was rooted in national pride and demonstrated that for him and those like him Northumbria was a force for integration in national culture.[46] This was reinforced by Bennett's loyalty to 'Britain and all things British' consolidated by his experience as a Tank Corps Sergeant during the Second World War. He described playing to the farewell dinner for the Northumberland Fusiliers as 'One of greatest honours and saddest moments […] – our own Fighting Fifth'.[47] At the same time participation in the European festival circuit was growing in importance and by the early 1970s the group had toured extensively in Germany and Sweden.[48] Thus the layers of meaning that a 'Northumbrian' cultural inheritance could convey by the late 1960s and early 1970s ranged from local urban industrial, to county rural traditional, to national, and international.

44 *North Magazine* No. 9 (March 1972), p.12.
45 *Ibid.*
46 Boyes, G., *The Imagined Village. Culture Ideology and the English Folk Revival* (1993).
47 *North Magazine* No. 9 (March 1972), p.12.
48 *Ibid.*

The elision of the Geordie industrial and Northumbrian traditional cultural inheritance was also important to revivalists operating outside politics, such as Frank Graham Publishers. Established during the late 1950s by the Sunderland-born schoolteacher Frank Graham, this publishing company pioneered works on north-eastern culture during the 1960s, including the seminal *Larn Yersel Geordie*, written by Scott Dobson, self-propelled devotee of Geordie kitsch. By 1975, 100,000 copies of the book had been sold to readers including Harold Wilson and workers in Vladivostock.[49] Dobson's single-minded pursuit of a simple Geordie culture grew out of a complicated background. Born in the mining and shipbuilding town of Blyth, 'Scott' Dobson was firmly established in Newcastle's bohemia by the 1960s, having been educated at Manchester Grammar School, where he later taught, before returning to Newcastle to join a group of 'hard up' artists experimenting with abstract expressionism. He combined this with a career as a journalist, first concentrating on art, later on jazz and Newcastle nightlife, and then as a psychedelic light show operator.[50] As an art critic for the *Evening Chronicle* during the early 1960, Dobson was part of a community of artists working in the abstract mode, including the 'fireman' artist Ross Hickling as well as the 'amateur' artists Harry and Alan Lord. His apparently seamless transition from art critic to dialect writer may have been less easy to realise outside the North East. As Dobson reflected, 'The' wud a hoyed as oot o' Manchester Grammar School when ah tort theor if aad sed to me art pupils: "Gan on, clag your paint on lads …"'[51] But the extent to which Dobson cultivated a dialect revival as part of a conscious rejection of establishment culture should be tempered by the evidence that his motivation was often opportunistic. Heather Ging describes the late 1960s as one in which there were 'a number of like people around feeding from each other … it was to do with that pot boiling in the region … we were part of this, but not aware of it, not conscious of it'. Scott Dobson clearly played a decisive role by drawing attention to 'that pot boiling', but, as Ging confirms, he may not have been consciously committed to reviving regional culture, rather, 'he was one of these minds that had his eye on the main chance … he saw a chance to do the Scott Dobson books and just recognised there was a market for it'.[52] Scott Dobson was able to realise his ambition as a dialect writer by drawing on a growing infrastructure for the representation of regional culture. Crucial to this was Frank Graham Publishers.

Frank Graham was a veteran of the Spanish Civil War and the Communist Party and his publishing began as a frustrated author of books on local history. Whilst working as a Workers' Educational Association tutor on Lindisfarne he wrote and published his first book – a guide to this, the sacred centre of ancient Northumbria. When it quickly sold out he recognised an untapped regional market for putting 'the past in print' and by the early 1960s he was assembling and publishing a wide variety of authors on north-east history. His output was not confined to the region's industrial heritage. He

49   *Daily Express*, 28 June 1975.
50   His real name was Edward Dobson, *Northern Life*, May 1979, p.20.
51   *Evening Chronicle*, 13 May 1970.
52   Interview with Heather Ging, 6 September 2004.

74 *Centenary of Blaydon Races, 1962*

defended himself from intellectualist criticisms of his populist approach with the claim that the most important book he published was a heavyweight volume on Hadrian's Wall during the Roman period.[53] Freely acknowledging the success of Scott Dobson's *Geordie Beuks* when interviewed, Frank Graham, this 'quiet, bespectacled teetotaller', rarely spoke of them despite their vast sales by 1971, preferring instead to draw attention to his more serious publications on the North East and Northumbria.[54]

Graham's preoccupation with Northumbria could be probed a little further. In contrast to Joe Bennett's evocation of Northumbria as a part of British civilisation, and despite his reluctance to be associated with Dobson's flamboyant and bohemian lifestyle, it is possible that in the idea of Northumbria Graham found oppositional characteristics to match his political convictions. Not a politician, Graham was nevertheless a member of the Communist Party and, drawing on his Spanish experiences, he may have seen in Northumbria glimpses of Catalonian regionalism and the possibility of opposition to the 'bourgeois state'. As a site for the working-class warrior, Graham's Northumbria could encompass both traditional scholarship and Geordie 'proletarian' culture. It may also simply have been the case that as a

---

53   *Northern Echo*, 14 January 1992.
54   Newcastle Central Library, Local Biography, Vol. 56b, p.47.

publisher with an unorthodox background – he had no previous training with a large publishing company – he had no difficulties reconciling popular with established culture. The important point is that Graham's contribution to representing north-east culture was connected both to Geordie and Northumbrian revivals. Seen from the outside, his publishing initiatives reinforced the assumption that the North East sustained a cohesive regional culture. The creation of the 'Scouse Press' by Fritz Spiegel in 1966, by way of contrast, was concerned exclusively with the Merseyside conurbation.[55]

As the sales of *Larn Yersel* soared, its popular appeal was reflected by the BBC's adaptation of the book for the television programme *Geordierama*. Scripted by Dobson in 1974, the television initiative was an extension of the regional pastiche which he had by now mastered. By the 1970s Scott Dobson's 'Geordie inventions' included long-playing records, shows at Newcastle's City Hall, Geordie car stickers, driving licences, and other paraphernalia.[56] But *Geordierama* drew on a varied and complex array of influences, many of which stemmed from the revival of Northumbrian culture just after the Second World War. The bill included comic performances by Mike Neville, George House and Dick Irwin accompanied by Joe Bennett's Northumbrian Traditional Group. Dick Irwin's presence reflected the importance of television to the revival of music hall comedy. Irwin had discovered his talent for joke telling whilst in the army, a gift which Richard Kelly was quick to recognise. Irwin subsequently appeared in the cast of *Wot Cheor Geordie*.[57]

Whilst the content of *Geordierama* owed a debt to the Blaydon Races Centenary, the revival of Geordie industrial and Northumbrian traditional during the 1970s lacked the political impulse of the earlier decade. During the early 1970s the success of Tyne Tees Television's *What Fettle* is particularly suggestive of the demand for this material. Created by Heather Ging in her capacity as a producer at Tyne Tees, *What Fettle* featured north-eastern music, ballads, humour and folk culture and history broadcast to 'the huge appreciation of a discriminating audience':[58]

> It was my opportunity, as a new producer, to put my interests in local music and history onto the screen, the people who were involved, say coal miners, with their songs and stories, made it very cohesive and emotional, and something with which television audiences could identify.[59]

To the surprise of senior executives who remained sceptical of local programmes, *What Fettle* produced the highest audience ratings ever experienced at Tyne Tees.[60]

55 Belchem, J., *Merseypride* (2001).
56 *Journal*, 18 December 1974, p.5.
57 *Geordie Life*, May 1976, p.14.
58 Trident Television Ltd., *Annual Report*, 1978, p.2; see Philips, G., *Memories of Tyne Tees Television* (1998) for an overview of Tyne Tees' developments during the 1970s.
59 Interview with Heather Ging, 6 September 2004.
60 *ibid.*

During the 1970s that television company was often criticised by the Independent Television Authority because it was not broadcasting sufficient regional programmes. A specific complaint was the lack of coverage of the political corruption scandal which enveloped Dan Smith and the Labour Council during the late 1960s, an omission made even more embarrassing since Smith had been made a Tyne Tees director and major shareholder in 1968.[61] After the retreat from the Smithite political regionalism of the 1960s, there was little discernible political interest in the revival of a Northumbrian and Geordie culture.

The North East Association for the Arts was formed in 1961.[62] This northern branch of the Arts Council of Great Britain (known as Northern Arts from 1967) elicited the following comparison with the work of the Northern Economic Development Council in 1962:

> While the NEDC is trying to dispel the impression that the region consists largely of slag heaps and grime … the year old North East Association for the Arts is trying to crack the image of the region which has hearty barbarians, rolling their 'r's' and blowing crude pipes, as its main constituents.[63]

There is little evidence that the organisation was averse to this characterisation, at least before the 1980s when the idea that regions might be producers of their own culture became more accepted by the Arts Council.[64] As a result, Northern Arts pursued a policy of *importing* artists and art – a strategy which was to arouse the most impassioned single defence of Northumbrian authenticity of the 20th century.

Basil Bunting

In 1972 Basil Bunting was elected president of Northern Arts.[65] Bunting had written already in 1953 of the need for a newspaper to represent 'the very northern point of view and to remind the north that literature exists', and with him in the saddle Northern Arts appeared firmly embedded in the region that bore its name.[66] However, in little over three years Bunting had resigned his position, outraged by what he saw as the stifling influence of a growing art bureaucracy overseen and paid for by metropolitan élites. Such an organisation had little to offer the North, he thought, which deserved better, though how long 'better' would take he couldn't say:

---

61 Tyne Tees Report Television Ltd., *Report of Directors* (1968).
62 Northern Arts, *December Arts Diary and Gallery Guide* (1966).
63 *The Economist*, 13 October 1962, cited in *Northern Arts: Our First 25 Years, 1961-86* (1986), p.5.
64 Casey, B., Dunlop, R. and Selwood, S., *Culture as Commodity? The Economics of the Arts and Built Heritage in the UK* (1996). The organisation's argument for the benefits of importing 'established' artists can be found in Northern Arts, *Regional Magazine. A Feasibility Study* (1969), TWAS, D. 4341.
65 Northern Arts, Minutes of the Management Committee, April 1974, Bound Volumes.
66 'Basil Bunting to Margaret De Silver, 27th September 1953', cited in Lancaster, B., 'Editorial', *Northern Review* Vol. 1 (Spring 1995), p.1.

How hard it will be to recover that Northumbrian spirit in painting and art I do not know, nor how long it will take; but I am sure that the central task of this institution should encourage, not, of course, imitations of ancient models, but whatever seems to be conceived in their spirit.[67]

Bunting's epic poem *Briggflatts*, acknowledged as a great modernist poem and an unrivalled evocation of 'Northumbria', nevertheless carries a relationship with the North that is difficult to behold. Critics have preferred instead to draw attention to its brilliant and contradictory range of historic national and international references.[68]

So with Bunting. Clearly apparent in his exasperation with Northern Arts, his broader commitment to northern political autonomy was given expression during the 1970s through participation in the Campaign for the North. Established in response to the boundary reform proposals of the Redcliffe-Maude Commission, CFN argued for an elected authority to cover a 'North' stretching from Hull in the east to Liverpool in the west up to the Scottish border. This North, equivalent to the German style *Länder*, would, it was hoped, transcend the internal political divisions in the regions and make them more able to hold their own with a richer and culturally more powerful England in the south.[69] That Basil Bunting – ardent champion of Northumbrian cultural authenticity – should endorse a movement that did not subscribe to the idea of the North East as a discreet political entity, is a measure of the protean and fluctuating characteristics of territorial affiliation.

'Northumbria' has been deployed as an affirmation of north-east identity all through the 20th century. This was particularly apparent during the 1960s when it was part of a political vision that brought history to bear on modernisation. But it has also been used to limit and circumscribe regional identity: during early negotiations with the BBC Northumbria was acknowledged as culturally distinct, but not as a potential broadcasting region in its own right. Later on, during deindustrialisation in the 1980s, the 'romantic' and 'historic' potential of Northumbria was summoned to detract from what were perceived as less attractive regional qualities, such as the 'urban', the 'industrial', and the ex-industrial. Successive revivals, and the literary and musical traditions that carried them, were strengthened in turn by the arrival of new media, particularly radio, from the 1930s. How Northumbrian history and identity will embrace and be embraced by our new technologies of expression remains to be seen.

---

67 Bunting, B., *Presidential Address*, Northern Arts, 1974.
68 Cavanagh, D., 'Notice', *Northern Review*, Vol. 3 (1996), 71. Nick Everett's chapter in this volume takes that relationship further.
69 *Northern Democrat* No. 1, 1975.

16

Swords at Sunset:
The Northumbrian Literary Legacy

ALAN MYERS

When the study of Anglo-Saxon ceased to be an obligatory part of the English course at Oxford University, it seemed that the last formal link between modern literature and the language spoken by the people of Northumbria's Golden Age had been severed. It appeared symptomatic of the final takeover of the region's heritage by other historical periods – the Roman and Norman occupations, the Border Wars with Scotland and the era of 'carboniferous capitalism'. Television documentaries on the four centuries of Roman occupation vastly outnumber those on the six centuries of Anglo-Saxon Britain, and are permeated with a colonial attitude of admiration and respect for what was, after all, a ruthless imperial conquest directed by despots in Rome. Even the marauding Vikings enjoy a measure of deference: perversely it is they, rather than Bede, who are commemorated by statues in the Jarrow they sacked. Oddly enough, attitudes to the Normans are rather different. I know of no English work which treats the Normans favourably, whereas there is any amount of literature (and film) – *Robin Hood, Hereward the Wake, Ivanhoe* – supporting the previous invaders, the now-oppressed Anglo-Saxons.

As to pre-Norman Northumbria, which once spanned this island from Edinburgh to the Trent, there is, however, a remarkable dearth of literary fare – Melvyn Bragg's *Credo* (1996) is the only ambitious work that springs to mind – and there are no blockbuster films about Anglo-Saxon England, let alone Northumbria. Even among the riches of north-east children's literature, we have only Robert Westall's *The Wind-Eye* (1976) and William Mayne's *Cuddy* (1996) of any real stature – both time-slip stories about Saint Cuthbert. Outside the region, Northumbrian names are not encountered in mainstream discourse in the way that Hadrian, Boadicea, Alfred or even Hotspur are. Enthusiasts dress up as Romans or re-enact border combats, not those of Northumbria.

One reason for all this is that, although three seventh-century Northumbrian kings held the title of *Bretwalda* (Lord of Britain), the evidence of a Northumbrian presence on the ground is minimal. Bede's monastery at Jarrow survives in part; Hexham Abbey crypt is a numinous place, and the little church at Escomb a moving sight, but King Edwin's royal hall at Yeavering is not a tourist attraction; the Heavenfield church marking Oswald's victory in AD 634 over the pagan Cadwallon was only erected in 1887, and the monumental cross to Caedmon near Whitby in 1892. There are no commemorations to mark the fateful battles of Catterick or Nechtansmere, which Welsh and Scottish nationalists respectively are liable to cite as marking the beginning of their country's separate identity.

Another reason is that nearly all our ideas concerning religion and art have come to us from the Mediterranean; we are in thrall to the prejudices of the Renaissance. Again, the language has changed so much that Old English is almost a foreign tongue, the province of the philologist, and what Michael Alexander calls 'the stultifying dullness of literary history'.

Nonetheless, it can be argued that there are strong informal threads linking the Northumbrian literary heritage, or what has 'survived the martyrdom of the jakes and the fire', to the present, by way of some of the great names in English literature, from Chaucer and Shakespeare to T.S. Eliot, Basil Bunting and W.H. Auden. The most popular English fictional work of the later 20th century, based squarely on the Anglo-Saxon world of *Beowulf* and the Nordic sagas, was written by J.R.R. Tolkien. The film version of *The Lord of the Rings* features warriors wearing helmets which the aristocratic Angles of Northumbria would have recognised as their own.

In addition, northern spoken English in the Middle Ages (via its Midlands form) was an important contributor to the modern standard written (and increasingly the spoken) language, since it pioneered many of the features basic to modern English, e.g. forms of the verb in -s, as in 'he says', 'she has', 'he casts', as opposed to southern 'he saith', 'she hath', 'he casteth' and so on – forms preserved in the King James Bible out of respect for earlier southern translators of the text. Indeed, the beginning of the transformation of Old English can be traced to the north of the country in the ninth to tenth centuries when the highly inflected language started to shift towards the easier-to-use ('analytic') grammar of modern English, dependent on the sense order of the words (subject-verb-object) – something we now take for granted as its greatest asset.[1]

The pretext given for the abandonment of Anglo-Saxon at Oxford was the same as that for the dropping of Latin in many schools, namely that the study of dead languages could not be defended in the late 20th century. Latin at least had been the common language of European intellectuals until the 18th century, and had a rich ancient literature of its own. Surviving Old English poetic texts comprise a mere thirty thousand lines, the bulk of them Christian. For all its paucity, however, the

---

1 Griffiths, Bill, *North East Dialect: Survey and Word List* (Newcastle, 1999), pp.6-7.

Northumbrian Anglo-Saxon literary legacy is an imposing one. The poem *Widsith*, for example, consisting of a roll-call of Germanic courts and heroes from AD 375 to AD 568, is the oldest in the language, and in written form dates, according to Professor David Daiches, to seventh- or eighth-century Northumbria. *Beowulf* is the first major poem in any European vernacular language. At 3,182 lines, it is much the longest work in Old English that remains to us. The tale of Beowulf's battles with the monster Grendel and his mother, followed fifty years later by his fight with the dragon which brings death to both, is marked by passages of epic splendour. It also possesses the typical Anglo-Saxon (and Homeric) preoccupation with dogged courage and fortitude in the face of an implacable fate, coupled with a poignant awareness of the transience of life. There is much scholarly controversy surrounding the poem, especially as regards possible Christian interpolations, but there are good grounds for believing that, in the form in which we have it, *Beowulf* was the creation of the court poets of Northumbria. The hall of the Danish king Hrothgar (Britain is never mentioned in the poem) is described in terms which might well be applied to that of King Edwin of Northumbria, excavated at Yeavering. The very name of Hrothgar's hall, Heorot (Hart), and the mere or pool inhabited by the fearful monster Grendel and his mother recall the ancient (pre-heraldic) seal of Hartlepool (Hart-le-Pool), now prosaically found on the municipal buses and elsewhere. It depicts a hart being attacked by a hound, reminding us that in *Beowulf* a stag would rather be torn by the hounds than venture into the mere where Grendel dwelt. There is also a patriotic tradition that Beowulf was buried on Boulby cliffs:

> Upon the headland, the Geats erected a broad high tumulus
> plainly visible to distant seafarers …

Professor Tom Shippey confidently assigns *Beowulf* to the North Yorkshire area of Northumbria, adducing in evidence the similarities in attitude and background knowledge with Anglo-Latin works which we know were composed in the monasteries of Whitby and Ripon. There is also the cluster of Beowulfian names in and around Gillingshire.[2] Shippey asserts that Gilling itself is certainly derived from 'Geat-ling'.[3] In old age, Beowulf became king of the Geats, a people of southern Scandinavia, whence the Angles voyaged to invade north-eastern England. One might also note that the only occurrence of the name Beowulf outside the poem is in the Durham *Liber Vitae*, or list of benefactors.

The name Beowulf, like Arthur, derives etymologically from 'bear'. Unlike Arthur, however, Beowulf did not spawn a glorious fictional world of romance and chivalry. Apart from Rosemary Sutcliff's *Beowulf* (1961), John Gardener's remarkable *Grendel* (1971; 2004) which recounts the tale from the viewpoint of Beowulf's adversary, and

---

2 Moorman, Frederic W., 'English Names and Teutonic Sagas', *Essays and Studies* 5 (Oxford, 1915).
3 Professor T.A Shippey, private correspondence.

Parke Godwin's *Beowulf's Tower* (1995) which also incorporates Grendel as a hugely embittered and doomed figure, one can instance just a handful of 20th-century novels in the heroic fantasy genre. These, of which Poul Anderson's accomplished *The Broken Sword* (1954, rev. 1971) may stand as exemplar, partake of the doom-laden atmosphere of *Beowulf*, but use the Dark Age setting to people their pages with trolls, elves, changelings and other trappings. *Beowulf* itself, however, retains its fascination for the modern literary public. There has been a new verse translation for Penguin Classics by Michael Alexander, and one of the most talked-of books in recent years was the version by Seamus Heaney, the Nobel laureate. Kingsley Amis, although he was irked by his Anglo-Saxon studies at Oxford, produced an early poem entitled *Beowulf*:

> Only with Grendel was he man-to-man;
> Grendel's dam was his only sort of woman
> (Weak conjugation). After they were gone
> How could he stand the bench-din, the yelp-word?

Curiously enough, it appears that P.G. Wodehouse set about a translation when he was interned by the Nazis at the beginning of the Second World War. The enigmatic exclamation at the start of the epic, 'Hwaet!' ('What!'), is supposed (wrongly) to have prompted the Wodehousian greeting 'What ho!'

It is true, of course, that southern-based academics have argued against a Northumbrian provenance for *Beowulf*, encouraged by the spectacular Sutton Hoo ship burial in Suffolk, uncovered in 1939. The daunting Sutton Hoo helmet adorns the cover of the Penguin *Beowulf*, and has become something of an iconic symbol for Dark Age Britain.

One reason for the continuing fascination of *Beowulf* is that it confirms a literally gloomy view of the Dark Ages, a kind of *frisson* which resonates into modern times at many levels, that of trembling but courageous humanity huddling together while evil stalks the outer darkness:

> waes se grimma gaest   Grendel haten,
>   maere mearcstapa,   se þe moras heold
> fen ond faesten

[The grim spirit was called Grendel, notorious prowler of the marches, who held the moors, the fen and fastness …]

The existential stance of the Anglo-Saxon warrior also strikes a deep chord in us. As Tacitus had remarked in his *Germania*, shame at deserting your lord was a potent force among the Germanic tribes. Flight is scornfully rejected even in the face of overwhelming odds, as explicitly stated in *The Battle of Maldon*, which, though as late as AD 991, harks back to the heroic world of *Beowulf*.

> Will shall be the stronger, courage the keener,
> Spirit the greater ... as our strength grows less.

There is nothing alien about this. It is the theme of Macbeth's last grim resolve:

> I cannot fly: But bear-like I must fight the course.

Henry V at Agincourt echoes the retainers at Maldon, though Richard III does display a rather un-Anglo-Saxon panache as he jauntily challenges fate with Dark Age courage and alliteration:

> March on, join bravely, let us to't pell-mell;
> If not to heaven, then hand in hand to hell.

From Horatius to Rorke's Drift, from Leonidas to Churchill, it is a theme with endless historical and personal variations.

The ambience of Old English heroic verse is perhaps most thrillingly bodied forth in the Border Ballads of Shakespeare's time. The concise, direct, apparently artless vocabulary of this stanza from *The Battle of Otterbourne* has a very Anglo-Saxon flavour, though the verse now employs rhyme rather than alliteration:

> And they hae burnt the dales o' Tyne
> And part of Bamburghshire,
> And three good towers on Redeswire fells
> They left them all on fire.

And who can forget poor Widdrington in *Chevy Chase* who, when his legs were smitten off, still fought upon his stumps? Of *Chevy Chase*, the Elizabethan courtier, soldier and poet Sir Philip Sidney famously said: 'I never heard the old song of Percy and Douglas that I found not my heart moved more than with a trumpet.' Ben Jonson, of border stock himself, said that he would give all his works to have written *Chevy Chase*. He mentions Clym of the Cleugh in *The Alchemist* as does Davenant in *The Wits*, and there are ballads on the three outlaws Clym, Adam Bell and William of Cloudesley in Percy's *Reliques* (see below) as well as in Francis James Child's great collection of *English and Scottish Popular Ballads* (1882-98). The three were as famous in northern England for their skill in archery as Robin Hood was in the midlands. They lived in the forest of Ingelwood, on the edge of Northumberland, not far from Carlisle.

The ending of one of the most famous Anglo-Saxon poems, *The Battle of Brunanburh* (AD 937), is very reminiscent of the Border Ballads in its description of the aftermath of battle – no triumphalism, but the presence of the wolf and the raven, the emblems of death.

The sombre atmosphere of the northern frontier ballads mirrors a harsh, often ruthless society, and harks back to the heroic pre-Christian Anglo-Saxon poems where courage and fortitude are the prime virtues, happiness and kindness are rare, and religion absent. Joseph Addison at the beginning of the 18th century analysed *Chevy Chase*, that 'favourite ballad of the common people' in two *Spectator* papers (Nos 73 and 74), comparing it favourably with the classical epics, but it was Thomas Percy who really brought ballad poetry, particularly the Border Ballads, to the attention of the literary world in his famous *Reliques of Ancient English Poetry* in 1765. The propagandist activities of Sir Walter Scott and others, such as Child, in the 19th century gave the ballads an even wider popularity; William Morris considered them to be the greatest poems in the language, while Algernon Swinburne knew virtually all of them by heart. Traces of their continuing influence can be detected in the work of major 20th-century poets like Auden and Bunting.

Prior to the seventh century, Anglo-Saxon poetry had been oral, its alliterative tradition going back to the origins of the Germanic tribes themselves. With conversion to Christianity, however, a written literature began to develop. Caedmon (fl. AD 670-80), who served at Hild's monastery in Whitby, is the earliest English Christian poet, indeed the first English poet we know by name, though the excerpt we possess (quoted by Bede) is brief and unexciting. U.A. Fanthorpe, a contender for the poet laureateship after the death of Ted Hughes, was literary fellow at Durham and Newcastle in 1987-8 and her 2003 collection *Queuing for the Sun* includes a version of Caedmon rendered in Geordie:

> Forst there wes nowt
> nowt and neewhere
> God felt the empty
> space wi his finga
> Let's hev sum
> light sez God
> Ootbye and inbye
> so the light happened.

Cynewulf (fl. AD 800) is the only Old English poet known by name of whom any undisputed writings are extant (rather than being quoted by others). Though details of his life are lacking, Cynewulf was quite probably a Northumbrian churchman. Unlike Caedmon, he seems to have been a man of education, familiar with the ecclesiastical literature of his day. He wrote skilled alliterative verse in the northern dialect of Old English, and at one time or another almost all the great Anglo-Saxon poems, including the noblest of all, *The Dream of the Rood*, and the celebrated Riddles in the Exeter Book have been attributed to Cynewulf.[4] Only four are certainly his: 'Elene'

---

4   The Exeter Book, one of the most important collections of Old English poems, copied about AD 940 and given by Bishop Leofric (d.1072) to Exeter Cathedral, where it still remains. It also contains a celebrated collection of Riddles.

and 'The Fates of the Apostles' in the Vercelli Book, and 'The Ascension' and 'Juliana' in the Exeter Book.[5] In all of these, Cynewulf's runic 'signature' is interwoven with the verse.

Cynewulf's influence on Tolkien was crucial. John Ronald Reuel Tolkien (1892-1973), professor of Anglo-Saxon at Oxford 1925-45, and later professor of English literature there, uses the first four elements at least in his children's fantasy, *The Hobbit* (1937). The story also features a company of Scandinavian dwarves (the name Gandalf is of similar provenance). Tolkien wrote a celebrated essay on *Beowulf*, entitled 'The Monsters and the Critics' (1936).[6] In it, he rebuts those critics who had seen Grendel and his mother as essentially irrelevant to the historical importance of the epic. Tolkien argued that it was precisely the superhuman opposition of the heathen monsters that elevated the poem to heroic stature. Something even more significant occurred, however, when Tolkien encountered the *Crist* of Cynewulf, two lines of which struck him:

> Eala earendel engla beorhtast
> offer middangeard monnum sended.

['Hail Earendel, brightest of angels/above the middle-earth sent unto men.'] Earendel means a shining light in Anglo-Saxon, but here it obviously has some special significance. Tolkien himself, a devout Roman Catholic, interpreted it as referring to John the Baptist, but believed that Earendel had originally been the name for the morning star, that is, Venus. He was strangely moved by its appearance in the Cynewulf lines. 'I felt a curious thrill,' he wrote long afterwards, 'as if something had stirred in me, half awakened from sleep. There was something very remote and strange and beautiful behind those words, if I could grasp it, far beyond ancient English.' In 1914 Tolkien wrote a poem headed by Cynewulf's line: 'Eala earendel engla beorhtast!' It was called 'The Voyage of Arendel, the Evening Star', and marks the beginning of Tolkien's own mythology. The name Earendil, with stellar associations, appears in *The Lord of the Rings* and is referred to in one of the lays sung at Rivendell in the first part of the saga. Tolkien also gives the loathsome character Gollum a set of riddles based on those in the Exeter Book.

Quest fantasies across imagined landscapes had been written before Tolkien of course, notably by William Morris, and David Lindsay (in the extraordinary *A Voyage to Arcturus,* 1924), but there had always been an element of apology; often they were presented as a traveller's tale or a dream. Tolkien's hugely popular work has served, for good or ill, as a template for innumerable later writers who have used it and, indirectly, Tolkien's own Northumbrian sources, as a fixed background (Middle Earth – middangeard) for their own heroic fantasies set in unashamedly autonomous secondary worlds.

---

5 The Vercelli Book, an Old English manuscript copied before AD 1000 and containing *The Dream of the Rood* and two of the four signed poems of Cynewulf. It is now in the keeping of the chapter of Vercelli, in Italy.

6 '*Beowulf*: The Monsters and the Critics,' *Proceedings of the British Academy* (vol. 22, 1936), pp.245-95.

Alliterative verse, the typical formal device of Anglo-Saxon poetry, continued to produce masterpieces in the later Middle Ages – *Piers Plowman*, *Morte Arthure* and, notably, *Gawain and the Green Knight* (*c*.1375). This greatly admired alliterative poem consists of 2,530 lines in stanzas of varying length, each ending with a 'bob and wheel'. As Peter Davidson points out in *The Idea of North*, *Gawain and the Green Knight* has been a crucial text in imagining the North for generations of English-speaking readers.[7] The winter journey northwards in Book II seems a paradigm for all fearful journeys into the unknown, where monsters and, of course, adverse weather lie in wait. It is amusingly overdone, as if the author, an unequivocal northerner, is setting out to chill the blood of a southern audience. Against a background of misty moor, snow-capped heights – a Lakeland or Northumberland scene – Gawain encounters dragons, wolves and wild men; there are naked rocks, crashing burns (a Northumberland word) and icicles:

> Ther as claterande fro the crest the colde born rennez
> And henged heghe ouer his hede in hard iisse-ikkles.

Despite these impressive alliterative works, however, the future was to lie with the rhymed poetry of the urbane, cultured Geoffrey Chaucer (*c*.1343-1400), whose dialect of Middle English was the idiom of the court and London. Chaucer, in fact, expressly dissociated himself from the Anglo-Saxon tradition, and provides interesting evidence of a north-south poetic divide. His Parson in *The Canterbury Tales* declares:

> But trust me truly, I'm a southern man,
> I can't romance with the rum-ram-ruf by letter.

He means here, of course, the alliterative technique. In the *Reeve's Tale*, Chaucer gives his two 'likely lads', Alan and John, a northern accent, usually rendered in modern translation as Geordie. This was the first time such a comic device had been used in English literature and testifies eloquently to the marginalisation of Northumbrian speech by Chaucer's time. Northerners, even when sympathetically treated, as they are by Chaucer, are outsiders. The holders of power always look down on or patronise those unable to speak their language – this was the ancient Greek definition of a barbarian, after all. In the *Reeve's Tale*, moreover, the North is deliberately located somewhere a long way off, different, amusingly quaint perhaps (the two Cambridge students swear by St Cuthbert of Northumbria, not by St Thomas of Canterbury). The boys hail from 'Strother', about whose precise northern location Chaucer is casually vague. In the *Man of Law's Tale*, Constance in her drifting boat fetches up in Northumberland, but again Chaucer cannot tell us where. Interestingly, the yeoman in the *Friar's Tale* describes himself merely as living 'fer in the north contree'. This is the 14th-century 'up north'.

---

7   Davidson, Peter, *The Idea of North* (London, 2005), pp.218-19.

75 *Wystan Hugh Auden in the North, photographed by his brother John Bicknell Auden*

Tolkien's pupil at Oxford, Wystan Hugh Auden (1907-73), was the key figure in English 20th-century poetry, and his influence would be difficult to overestimate. He used alliterative Anglo-Saxon verse as a sustained and serious model and even quotes *Beowulf* in the title of his early revenge play *Paid on Both Sides* (1930), set around Upper Weardale and Alston Moor. All the murders in the play are reported in the rhythms of Old English verse. Though brought up in Birmingham (like Tolkien), Auden thought of himself as 'Norse' – his father derived the family surname from the similar Icelandic one – and always felt most at home in the north, whether it be Iceland or the North Pennines. His brilliant technique makes the gripping, staccato Anglo-Saxon lines, in particular the omission of the definite and indefinite articles (ellipsis), sound like the gnomic utterance of unadorned truth.

Auden's poetry prior to his emigration to America in 1939 is almost entirely impersonal – the approach favoured by T.S. Eliot, a powerful influence on the younger poet. There is little doubt, however, that the lofty, detached, prescriptive viewpoint typical of much pre-1939 Auden verse – 'as the hawk sees it, or the helmeted airman' – was a temperamental preference. Auden's father was a cultivated doctor, and his son was much interested in medical matters, as well as geology and, in particular, lead mining. A taste for pseudo-scientific pronouncement, almost a schoolmasterly manner, came easily to him, in verse as in life, where it eventually hardened into the gifted man's laziness – a predilection for debatable aphorism. Auden was the first major poet to be at home in the industrialised landscapes of 20th-century Britain, occasionally using them to make generalised political statements. Early poems were apt to begin with exhortations: 'Consider this …', 'Look, stranger!' or 'Get there if you can'. To contemporaries, it invited parody. Dylan Thomas produced the mocking line:

Look! The full employment of the blossoms!

While Cyril Connolly parodied the triadic *kennings* Auden deployed in *The Orators* (1932):

M is for Marx
And Movement of Masses
And Massing of Arses
And Clashing of Classes

Later, however, applying the ancient, almost alien technique of Anglo-Saxon ellipsis and alliteration to 20th-century civilisation and its discontents, Auden was able to sound remote, authoritative, even oracular, while at the same time the vertiginous wit and virtuosity is a constant paradoxical reminder of the author's presence.

In 1932 Auden composed a lengthy unfinished alliterative epic (again mostly set in the North Pennines) entitled 'In the year of my youth …', and the 1939 radio monologue *The Dark Valley* uses the *Beowulf* metre. In 1944-7, now resident in

America, he created the astonishing and difficult 'baroque eclogue', *The Age of Anxiety* – a hundred pages almost entirely in alliterative verse which, in the hands of a master, ancient or modern, can stitch poetic lines at least as closely and memorably as rhyme. The earlier sections of the poem again employ the *Beowulf* metre. In the following passage, one character describes the wartime Atlantic, but the spirit of Northumbria breathes through it:

> High were those headlands; the eagles promised
> Life without lawyers. Our long convoy
> Turned away northwards as tireless gulls
> Wove over water webs of brightness
> And sad sound. The insensible ocean,
> Miles without mind, moaned all around our
> Limited laughter, and below our songs
> Were deaf deeps, denes of unaffection,
> Their chill unchanging, chines where only
> The whale is warm ...

As with dozens of poems in his pre-1939 period, Auden studs *The Age of Anxiety* with North Pennine allusions, northern words (like dene) and, above all, references to lead mining, his lifelong obsession. One could say that Auden reinhabits the poetic forms of Anglo-Saxon Northumbria and locates them physically in what was, for him, a numinous (his word) Northumbrian landscape, complete with the names of actual lead mines:

> At Brothers Intake
> Sir William Wand; his water treaty
> Enriched Arabia. At Rotherhope
> General Locke, a genial man who
> Kept cormorants. At Craven Ladies
> Old Tillingham-Trench; he had two passions,
> Women and walking-sticks. At Wheel's Rake ...

The apparently effortless alliterative impulse seemed to die away after 1955, when Auden's poetry is commonly thought to have begun operating at much lower pressure. The year 1954-5 also saw the publication of Tolkien's *The Lord of the Rings*. Auden was an immediate admirer, and went so far as to make the appreciation of the saga his touchstone for literary intelligence.

Cecil Day-Lewis, who became Poet Laureate in 1968, was a friend of Auden and wrote detective stories (as Nicholas Blake), whose protagonist, Nigel Strangeways, initially exhibits some of Auden's eccentricities. The pair were together at Appletreewick in the Yorkshire Pennines in 1927 to observe the solar eclipse. The mining and general industrial references in Day-Lewis's work were sufficient to link him with the 'pylon school', but his locations, unlike those of Auden, are not specific. A well-known poem of 1931, with Old English ellipsis and alliteration begins:

> As one who wanders into old workings
> Dazed by the noonday, desiring coolness,
> Has found retreat barred by fall of rockface;
> Gropes through galleries where granite bruises
> Taut palm and panic patters close at heel …

The outstanding prose writer of Northumbria and, in fact, the first known English prose writer, was the Venerable Bede (AD 673-735). Bede (or Baeda) was probably born in Monkton and went to school at Wearmouth monastery, founded in AD 674 by Benedict Biscop, who brought back a store of books from Rome to furnish the monasteries here and at Jarrow. Biscop is regarded as one of the originators of the artistic and literary development of Northumbria in the next century and is celebrated by Bede in his *Lives of the Abbots* (AD 716-20). In St Paul's church, Jarrow, may be seen the oldest dedicatory inscription in the country, dated 23 April AD 685. Bede transferred to Jarrow around this date and afterwards rarely left its confines. He became a priest at the age of 30 and taught Latin and Greek to the monks, but his scholarly interests were very wide and included music, medicine, astronomy and the art of indigitation, or conversing with the fingers. His earliest work was probably *De Orthographia*, a treatise on spelling. Bede was also responsible for popularising the system of dating events from the birth of Christ.

He wrote some forty religious works (in Latin) at Jarrow, including, in AD 731, his celebrated *Historia Ecclesiastica Gentis Anglorum*, sometimes translated as the *History of the English Church and People*. This remains the most valuable single source for the early history of Britain. Without it the Dark Ages would be dark indeed, though one should beware of using such terms without qualification. Our knowledge of the post-Roman period in Britain may be hazy, but the centuries between AD 500 and AD 1000 witnessed some of the most glittering civilisations the world has ever seen – T'ang dynasty China, the eastern Roman Empire (Byzantium), the Arab capitals at Baghdad and Cordoba. Hugh Redwald Trevor-Roper called Bede, 'The greatest scholar of his time, the greatest historian of the whole Middle Ages'. In addition, Bede gives some lively insights into contemporary daily life, as well as rising to occasional flourishes like the wonderful simile comparing human life without Christianity with the flight of a sparrow through a lighted hall from darkness into darkness.

Bede was probably the best-known writer in Western Europe throughout the early Middle Ages, his eminence confirmed by the fact that he is the only Englishman to be named in Dante's *Paradiso* (*c*.1314), where the poet rebukes the cardinals for not studying Bede as they should. Alfred the Great translated Bede, and later religious men, including John Wycliffe and George Fox, were loud in his praise. In 1435 Aeneas Silvius Piccolomini, who later became Pope Pius II, travelled south through

Newcastle ('built by Caesar') after his clandestine stay in Scotland. He made a point of visiting Durham Cathedral and the tomb of Bede. In Elizabethan times, William Camden called Bede 'this singular and shining light', while John Leland described him as 'the chiefest and brightest ornament of the English nation, most worthy, if anyone was, of immortal fame'.

Bede is always with us. Chaucer used Bede's tables to calculate the time in *The Canterbury Tales*, employing the exact measure of his shadow as eleven feet. Richard Wilbur, the gifted American poet of our own day, 'warmed by the fidelity of time', does the same in 'Gnomons':

> In April, thirteen centuries ago,
> Bede cast his cassocked shadow on the ground
> Of Jarrow and, proceeding heel-to-toe,
> Measured to where a head that could contain
> The lore of Christendom had darkly lain,
> And thereby, for that place and season found
> That a man's shade, at the third hour from dawn,
> Stretches eleven feet upon the lawn.

The eminent Australian poet A.D. Hope wrote of Bede visiting Rome from a 'land as barbarous as mine', looking at the Colosseum and returning home to 'Jarrow on the Tyne'. The colonial cultural cringe is here conflated with another on behalf of Northumbria, but it is hardly fair to characterise seventh-century Northumbria as 'barbarous' – a kingdom that could produce, in one century, Bede himself, Biscop, Hild, Cedd, Wilfrid and Cuthbert. The Anglo-Saxon crosses at Bewcastle in Northumberland and Ruthwell in Dumfriesshire are, in the field of art, the greatest achievement of their date in the whole of Europe'.[8] The Ruthwell cross bears a short runic version of *The Dream of the Rood*, while the climbing interlaces on the Bewcastle cross in Northumberland still stand under sun and storm looking out onto the kind of landscape that moved the Anglo-Saxon poets. It has been truly said, 'A barbaric people may have great poetry – they cannot have great prose', but the nearer we come to the date of the Norman invasion, the more impressive are the prose writings we have. For chronicle, sermon, biblical translation, scientific and philosophical works, the English vernacular cannot be surpassed at this time by any language in northern and western Europe.

The *Lindisfarne Gospels*, written down in the Latin Vulgate *c*.AD 720, are excelled in grandeur only by the Irish *Book of Kells*, and it is likely that Bede was involved in their creation. An Anglo-Saxon gloss was added in the late tenth century in the Northumbrian dialect by Aldred, provost of Chester-le-Street. This is the first translation of a sacred text into English. In 1066 the English were in a position to teach the Normans everything about metal and enamel work, embroidery (the

---

8   Sir Nikolaus Pevsner, *The Buildings of England: Cumberland and Westmorland* (London, 1967), pp.68-9.

Bayeux Tapestry is English work) and pre-eminently about manuscript painting: the Normans, for their part had practically nothing of a cultural nature to offer. The treasures of England in 1066 reminded the Normans of what they had heard of the riches of Byzantium or of the East. The art of Northumbria, moreover, was enormously influential; it crossed the Channel to the monasteries founded by Irish and Anglo-Saxon monks in France, Germany, Switzerland, Sweden and even Russia. Here in turn they produced illuminated manuscripts that later generations thought had been painted not by men but by angels.

The first great wave of Anglo-Saxon scholarship occurred some thousand years after Bede. George Hickes (1642-1715) was the acknowledged leader of a generation which included such names as William Nicolson, Edmund Gibson, William Elstob – and Humfrey Wanley, who produced in 1705 a catalogue of Anglo-Saxon manuscripts which is still a standard work. Hickes published the first Anglo-Saxon grammar in 1689, followed (1703-5) by the profoundly influential *Treasury of the Northern Tongues*, a comparative grammar of Old English and related Germanic languages. The work of Elizabeth Elstob (1683-1756) is particularly interesting. Like her brother William, 'The Saxon Nymph' was born and brought up in the Quayside area of Newcastle and, like Mary Astell, her fellow townswoman, is nowadays honoured as one of the first English feminists. She was proficient in eight languages and became a pioneer in Anglo-Saxon studies, an unprecedented thing for a woman. Elizabeth was part of the circle of intelligent women around Mary Astell, who helped to find subscribers for her *Rudiments of Grammar for the English-Saxon ... with an Apology for the Study of Northern Antiquities*.

Anglo-Saxon England, however, with its paucity of archaeological remains and written records, was not especially a topic favoured by antiquarian researchers. It became the fashion for rational early 18th-century gentlemen, free at last from wars of religion and tormenting 'enthusiasm', to look back across the abyss of the Middle Ages (including Northumbria) to the Greco-Roman civilisation they saw themselves as emulating. These aptly-named Augustans espoused reason, order, proportion and restraint, whether it were in architecture, landscape gardening, poetry or manners. Neo-classical houses began to dot the English landscape and the demure churches of the period might well contain funerary monuments of local worthies dressed as Cicero or Scipio Africanus. The eventual Romantic revolt against Augustan notions of social and artistic decorum involved the discarding of all these rules. Gothic architecture returned to favour. Mountains and moors were no longer mere wastelands, a prosaic hindrance to travel, but sources of sublime inspiration and communion with nature deified.

Novels and poems might be set in exotic places abroad; in the High Middle Ages; the far future; against drug-fuelled fantasy land- and seascapes – even, as in William Beckford's *Vathek,* in Hell. Northumbria, however, drew no celebrants. Sir Walter Scott and the Porter sisters of Durham pioneered the historical novel, but their preferred settings were Scotland, France, Hungary and Poland. David Maclise did paint one Dark Age picture, *King Alfred in the Camp of the Danes*, now in the Laing Art Gallery in Newcastle, but only William Bell Scott, the poet and artist who worked in Newcastle from 1843-64, produced work on themes from Northumbrian history (at the behest of Lady Pauline Trevelyan). These pictures at Wallington Hall include the death of the Venerable Bede, and a Danish invasion in which Lady Pauline is seen among the fleeing women. Scott also painted a *Chevy Chase* series at Wallington.

Northern myth did prompt occasional works like Matthew Arnold's *Balder Dead* of 1855, while the multi-faceted Rev. Sabine Baring-Gould visited Iceland in 1862, where he painted watercolours of saga scenes, and published a book about his voyage. Sir George Webbe Dasent devoted most of his life to the popularisation of Norse literature, and published numerous translations, including the *Prose, or Younger Edda* (1842), dedicated to Thomas Carlyle, who encouraged him. Most of Lewis Carroll's 'Jabberwocky', which appears in *Through the Looking Glass* (1872) and famously begins:

> 'Twas brillig and the slithy toves
> Did gyre and gimble in the wabe

was written on a visit to his Wilcox cousins in Whitburn, near Sunderland, in 1855. The intent, however, was to parody the supposed uncouth inaccessibility of Anglo-Saxon verse.

William Morris translated *Beowulf* and also visited Iceland (sixty years before Auden) where he was inspired to write *Sigurd the Volsung* (1876) followed by a number of other works set in far northern Europe. Morris's quest-fantasy *The Well at the World's End* (1896) may be accounted his masterpiece. In its mesmeric unfolding of invented landscape it presents a unified fantasy geography which is a clear forerunner of Tolkien's kind of secondary world. In the early years of the 20th century, C.S. Lewis became a devotee of Nordic literature and Wagner's operas. Auden's father, who, with W.G. Collingwood, was a member of the Viking Club,[9] brought his son up on both Nordic and Greco-Roman myth (Auden much preferred the former); nowadays, however, it is rare to find any general knowledge of the legends which nourished pre-Christian Northumbria, beyond the names of a few deities. On the other hand, for opera-lovers, Richard Wagner's cycle of music dramas known as *The Ring* (1869-76) continues to confront audiences with a stunning re-working of elements of Nordic saga. Even today, applicants for tickets to the Bayreuth Festival stand a mere one-in-twenty chance of success. Modernist writers like T.S. Eliot and James Joyce quoted Wagner in their works, as did Auden, who chose to be buried to the strains of Siegfried's funeral march. The sinister development of German nationalism in the 20th century needs no rehearsal here, but the Nazis certainly found many of Wagner's ideas eminently acceptable.

---

9   Wawn, Andrew, *The Vikings and the Victorians* (Woodbridge, 2000), pp.308-9, 335-41.

What is unaccountable is that the Wagnerian flummery which attended the 1936 Olympic Games in Berlin – the lighter of the torch adopting the traditional stance of Siegfried the dragon-slayer, with sword outstretched – has been retained for successive games.

Apart from biblical subjects, the favoured historical theme for the Pre-Raphaelite artists of Bell Scott's time was Arthurian/medieval romance. Arthur's main court, Camelot, first described (c.1177) by Chretien de Troyes in his *Lancelot*, is identified by Geoffrey of Monmouth as Caerleon, in nearby South Wales, based on its name, City of the Legions, but this can equally well apply to Chester and Carlisle. Froissart, the great chronicler of the Hundred Years War (and the Battle of Otterburn), rode the length of the Roman Wall in 1361 and regarded Carlisle as Arthur's capital. Nor was he alone, though other candidates have been Cadbury Hill, Colchester (in Latin *Camelodunum*) and Stirling, the capital of the Gododdin (see below).

The existence of an historical King Arthur is very problematic. The written sources are vague and confusing. Northern battle sites are certainly mentioned, including High Rochester in Northumberland (the Roman fort *Bremenium*) and one chronicle refers to the fight at Camlann, supposedly in AD 537, where 'Arthur and Medraut were killed'. Opinion concerning the whereabouts of Camlann favours *Camboglanna*, close to the Roman fort at Birdoswald on the Wall. The Camlann battle became a byword for a tragic, irretrievable disaster. We also know that 'Medraut' became the traitor figure Mordred in the later Arthurian legends. Could a struggle between chieftains on the edge of Northumbria have given rise to one of the greatest figures in world literature? Rachel Bromwich argues that the oldest allusions to Arthur associate him with North Britain.[10] He was one of the heroic figures of northern British history later relocalised in Wales or the South: these include such warriors as Urien of Rheged, whose son Owain was later to become the hero of French 12th-century romance in Chretien de Troyes' *Yvain*. There was also Drystan (Tristan), who in French romances is called Leonois (of Lothian) but is relocated to Cornwall.

In this connection *Y Gododdin*, attributed to the Welsh bard Aneirin (fl. AD 600), is relevant. The poem, which uses both alliteration and rhyme, actually mentions Arthur in passing. It commemorates a British or proto-Welsh defeat by the Northumbrians at Catraeth (probably Catterick) in AD 603, where Aneirin was apparently taken prisoner. The epic consists of elegies to the three hundred lords (each with two shield-bearers) who march south from Edinburgh to fall in battle, only three surviving to tell the tale. The Gododdin, or Votadini, as the Romans called them, inhabited an extensive area around the river Tweed. Welsh nationalists have seen the poem as defining a major motif in Welsh literature, and in some sense marking the beginning of a Welsh national consciousness. Basil Bunting, intensely aware of Northumbrian history, alludes to Aneirin in his own 20th-century masterpiece *Briggflatts,* while Rosemary Sutcliff, the distinguished

---

10   Bromwich, Rachel, *Trioedd Ynys Prydein/ The Welsh Triads* (Cardiff, 1978), *passim.*

children's writer, treats of the whole episode in *The Shining Company* (1990), though from the point of view of the shield-bearers rather than the nobles they accompanied to disaster.

Whatever the status of the Northumbrian 'historic' Arthur, the North (and Northumberland in particular) is constantly, and tantalisingly, evoked in Arthurian literature and legend, and itself continued to produce Arthurian work of quality. Later medieval writings of note include *The Awntyrs of Arthure at the Terne Wathelyne* (The Adventures of Arthur at the Tarn Wadling), a 715-line work probably dating from *c.*1350-70. It is impressively written in complex 13-line stanzas and is one of the most admired alliterative poems. *The Avowynge of King Arthur, Sir Gawain, Sir Kaye and Sir Bawdewyn of Bretan,* an anonymous poem written in tail-rhyme stanzas, seems to date from *c.*1425 and is again set near Tarn Wadling, not far from Penrith. This tarn, with its magical reputation, appears with remarkable prominence on Gough's fine map of England (*c.*1360). Another Arthurian tale of Sir Gawain and Lady Ragnell takes place in Ingelwood Forest near Carlisle (see Clym of the Cleugh, above). Sir Thomas Malory (d.*c.*1471) was the author of *Le Morte D'Arthur*, which brings most of the Arthurian legends into a graspable whole. It has achieved canonical status and served to inspire such diverse later authors as Tennyson, Swinburne, Mark Twain, T.H. White, John Steinbeck and Rosemary Sutcliff. Malory's sources included the northern alliterative epic *Morte Arthure* (1360), where Arthur is a warrior-king in the heroic mould. Little is known about Malory the man, but Northumbrian locations figure prominently in his great work. He apparently soldiered on the Yorkist side under Warwick in 1462-3 during the Wars of the Roses and was present at Edward IV's sieges of Alnwick and Bamburgh castles. Later, he seems to have changed sides with Warwick and some have seen his writing as reflecting a parallel between the decline of the Lancastrian cause and that of Arthur.

Malory, in fact, sought to reclaim Arthur from the French romantic tradition and reinstate him as a paradigm of Anglo-Saxon heroic leadership. He states that Blaise the Hermit, Merlin's master, lived in the forests of Northumberland and 'wrote down Arthur's battles word for word' as Merlin (a frequent visitor) narrated them. Malory also places Joyous Gard, Sir Lancelot's castle, somewhere in Northumberland, either at Alnwick or Bamburgh. It is interesting to note, however, that the North in Malory is generally seen as being on the outside – 'they of the North' – and the northern kings are sometimes listed as among Arthur's enemies. One enemy, Sir Epynogris, is the son of the king of Northumberland. In tournaments, the northerners are usually the opposition.

In Malory, Balin and Balan are knightly brothers from Northumberland. Balin (Balin le Sauvage) was the only Arthurian knight to carry two swords and is conspicuously missing from most descriptions of Arthur's paladins – and certainly from Hollywood depictions of Camelot. He was in fact banished from court for decapitating the (or a) Lady of the Lake, who had demanded Balin's head from King Arthur as the price of the sword Excalibur. Subsequently, Balin fought for King Arthur in Wales and against

King Lot of Orkney. In the course of his adventures, he also wounded King Pellam with the Dolorous Stroke, bringing about the death of all the people in Pellam's castle and the devastation of three kingdoms. Merlin prophesies that this Waste Land will only be healed by the achievement of the Grail by Sir Galahad. After Balin and Balan are tricked into slaying one another, King Arthur laments:

> 'Alas,' said King Arthur, 'this is the greatest pity that ever I heard
> of two knights, for in the world I know not such two knights.'

Balin's sword is placed in a stone by Merlin, to be withdrawn by Galahad. Merlin links this narrative obscurely with the waning of the whole world of Arthur. The story is the starting point of the anthropological investigation in J.L. Weston's book *From Ritual to Romance* (1920), a major influence on one of the greatest poems of the 20th century, T.S. Eliot's *The Waste Land* (1922).

Eliot as critic was largely responsible for the decline in Algernon Swinburne's poetic reputation. Dry and precise in his own work, Eliot had little sympathy with Swinburne's windy exuberance. Swinburne's love for Northumberland, where he often stayed with his grandfather at Capheaton Hall, was intense and lifelong. He regarded Northumberland (always 'bright') as his native county and never referred to the Scottish border: it was always the 'Northland Border'. He even claimed Charlotte Bronte as a fellow countrywoman because she had been born near Bradford (i.e. in Deira, southern Northumbria). Besides his obsession with the sea, he loved high winds, as Auden did, and detested the summer heat of Putney in London, where he was, in later life, kept under strictly sober supervision. Even there, he walked in all weathers. Like Auden, he used the word 'Norse' of himself. In June 1899 he wrote *Rosamund, Queen of the Lombards*, commenting: 'You will recognise my Norse abhorrence of hot weather and southern climate here – how could our Northmen stand it!' Swinburne had been part of the cultivated Trevelyan circle at Wallington Hall – 'Of that bright household in our joyous north' – as he writes in his poem to William Bell Scott, and was a witness to Bell Scott's Northumbrian mural-painting there. He often visited the Scott household at 14 St Thomas Crescent in Newcastle, and in December 1862 stood on Tynemouth Long Sands with Scott (and probably Rossetti), declaiming his verse to the incoming waves.

In 1859 he and Scott had visited the Longstone lighthouse, where the Darling family lived at the time of the famous rescue. While Scott was being seasick, Swinburne observed three herons on a rock ledge. They reappear thirty years later in *Tristram of Lyonesse*. For this and his other Arthurian works, Swinburne deliberately chose the episodes which would allow him to celebrate Northumbria. According to Malory, for example, Sir Tristram kept Isoud at Joyous Gard for three years, and Swinburne in his

Tristram and Iseult describes Bamburgh Castle, '… this noblest hold of all the north', in thrilling verse:

> They saw the strength and help of Joyous Gard.
> Within the full deep glorious tower that stands
> Between the wild sea and the broad wild lands.

The Hexham-born poet, Wilfrid Gibson, incidentally, places Joyous Gard at Dunstanburgh Castle in an effectively atmospheric poem.

In his *Idylls of the King*, Tennyson had included an altered version of Malory's tale of Balin and Balan, but Swinburne avoided the older poet's moralising and used the story to give full vent to his Northumbrian patriotism in his *Tale of Balen* (1896). He describes Balen (Balin) riding down across the Tyne and Tees to Camelot, where the 'southern' knights are jealous and hostile. He meets his valiant brother:

> His brother Balan, hard at hand,
> Twin flower of bright Northumberland,
> Twin sea-bird of their loud sea-strand.
> Twin bird-song of their morn.

After many doughty deeds, Balen and Balan are tricked into killing one another, and are buried in one tomb. A life well lived is no cause for sorrow to Swinburne, however. As Balen lies dying, his thoughts echo the poet's own youth in Northumberland – and his love of the Border Ballads:

> He drank the draught of life's first wine
> Again: he saw the moorlands shine,
> The rioting rapids of the Tyne,
> The woods, the cliffs, the sea …
>
> The first good steed his knees bestrode,
> The first wild sound of songs that flowed
> Through ears that thrilled and heart that glowed,
> Fulfilled his death with joy.

Modern Arthurian writing is almost a genre of its own. T.H. White's stories, of which the best known is *The Sword in the Stone* (1938), represented a great innovation and still remain for many the definitive Arthurian volumes of the 20th century. White ignored the traditional story line and created an Arthurian world which is splendidly anachronistic when appropriate. The book served as the basis for a Disney film and the musical *Camelot*.

76 *Basil Bunting with his father, 1916*

In the 1950s, authors like John Cowper Powys, Dorothy James Roberts and Henry Treece depicted an alien, harsh and bitterly bleak Celtic world, and sought a more perceptive delineation of the Arthurian characters. Though the treatment based on Malory has survived, the general trend in the last half-century has continued to be towards a more straightforward and realistic fictional depiction of the 'historical' Arthur. Rosemary Sutcliff's adult novel, *A Sword at Sunset* (1963), pioneered a rational historical perspective, while Bernard Cornwell's *Warlord Chronicles* of the 1990s consider the military and political aspects of that history. In the sub-genre of writing which seeks to replace the supernatural elements of the tales by rationalised religious or mystical interpretations, the novels of the Sunderland-born writer Mary Stewart, beginning with *The Crystal Cave* (1970), are among the best of all Arthurian fictions. Such rationalised fantasies form the largest category of new fiction about Arthur. 'Northumbrian' Arthur is coming back into his own.

Basil Bunting (1900-85) is regarded as the first and principal British modernist poet. He was always more admired abroad than in his own country, however, and by the 1960s he had abandoned poetry and was working for the *Newcastle Evening Chronicle*. Local poet Tom Pickard persuaded him to start writing again, and the result was his quasi-autobiographical masterpiece *Briggflatts* (so spelled), first read in 1965 in the Morden Tower on the medieval walls of Newcastle.

Bunting was explicit about his ties to ancient Northumbria: 'A poet is just a poet, but I am a Northumbrian man. It has always been my home, even when I've been living elsewhere … '.[11]

In *Briggflatts*, a great poet of our own times not infrequently finds it appropriate to express his thoughts in the terse, powerful, elliptical utterance of his Northumbrian forebears:

> Who sang, sea takes,
> brawn brine, bone grit.
> Keener the kittiwake.
> Fells forget him …
>
> Bloodaxe, king of York,
> king of Dublin, king of Orkney.
> Take no notice of tears;
> letter the stone to stand
> over love laid aside lest
> insufferable happiness impede
> flight to Stainmore
> to trace
> lark, mallet,
> becks, flocks
> and axe knocks.

---

11   Bunting, Basil, *Collected Poems* (Oxford, 1978), p.148.

17

Basil Bunting's Briggflatts

NICK EVERETT

I

Basil Bunting believed firmly all his life that his primary cultural identity was Northumbrian and that that identity, quite distinct from that of southern Britain, had persisted despite the thousand or so years since the kingdom of Northumbria. Born in Scotswood-on-Tyne in 1900, he clearly owed the strength of these feelings in part to his mother's family. His maternal grandfather was a colliery manager in Throckley, a few miles west of Scotswood. A greater influence, though, was his father, a doctor, medical researcher and enthusiastic member of Newcastle's Literary and Philosophical Society in which Northumbrian cultural and intellectual life had been so vigorously promoted during Robert Spence Watson's 30-year tenure as the Society's secretary up until 1893.[1] Bunting was a child of the New Northumbrians, as explained by Robert Colls in this volume, and his earliest encounters with southern England, first at a Quaker boarding school in Berkshire to which he was sent at 16, and then in the prisons, Wormwood Scrubs and Winchester Prison, where he did time as a conscientious objector in 1918, only served to confirm this strong sense of his northern difference.[2] For a combination of personal, literary and cultural-historical reasons, however, these feelings and convictions about Northumbria and the North East did not become fully available to Bunting as poetic subjects until comparatively late in life.

---

1   See Robert Colls' chapter in this volume.
2   Writing to the headmaster of the Quaker school, Leighton Park, he attributed his unhappiness there to the 'great underlying difference between North & South which makes people with Northern manners comfortable & easy to deal with, but people with Southern manners are, for me utterly "impossible" & hateful.' Richard Caddel and Anthony Flowers, *Basil Bunting: a northern life* (Durham, 1997), 17.

For a start, in the period between the wars English literary culture was still heavily centralised and inhospitable to regional literature. In this era of T.S. Eliot's *The Waste Land* (1922), Ezra Pound's *Hugh Selwyn Mauberley* (1921) and W.H. Auden's *The Orators* (1932), a work about Northumbria would have risked being dismissed as merely provincial. Admittedly, Hugh MacDiarmid, who was only eight years Bunting's senior, published his *A Drunk Man Looks at the Thistle*, a forerunner of *Briggflatts* in its use of modernist techniques to celebrate local cultural traditions, as early as 1926. But of course MacDiarmid's region, Scotland, still had a national name and some cultural (if not much political) independence. Making a national let alone international poetic reputation from the provinces would have been difficult. The England of the period was in this respect probably closer to that of the 1860s, in which the pitman poet Joseph Skipsey (a friend of Bunting's father) was trying to establish himself, than that of the 1960s, from which *Briggflatts* finally emerged.[3] As it was, Bunting spent most of his early adult life away from the North East and indeed, out of the country, in France, Italy (where in the 1920s and early 1930s he lived for as long as he could afford it near Ezra Pound in Rapallo), the Canary Islands (for its low cost of living), the United States and, during the Second World War, in Persia. His temperamental disinclination to write directly about himself ('I was never troubled by physical modesty,' he told Peter Makin in 1965, 'but I am unwilling to stand emotionally naked') was no doubt partly responsible for making him turn to Poundian modernism; and together they discouraged him from writing about his native culture and encouraged him to take up classical, literary and mythological subjects instead.[4] With Pound's *Homage to Sextus Propertius* as chief model, between 1925 and 1935 he wrote about the modern world through a 15th-century French poet in *Villon*, through the myth of the self-mutilating Attis in *Attis, or Something Missing*, through a world-weary 12th-century Japanese writer in *Chomei at Toyama*, and through the debauching effects of a mythical well in *The Well of Lycopolis*.

These early long poems, moreover, again because of a combination of his temperament and the modernist models which inspired him (Eliot as well as Pound), tend to focus on what is wrong with the modern western world.[5] His muse was moved almost exclusively by feelings of anger at the cultural and spiritual sterility of modern metropolitan life. This largely precluded rural Northumberland and the positive feelings he had about it except when he felt moved to protest against unjust actions and policies in the area, as in the beautifully crafted ballads 'Gin the Goodwife Stint' and 'The Complaint of the Morpethshire Farmer' (both completed in 1930), about the forced Northumbrian land clearances of the late 1920s. Revealing in this context is how Bunting responded when the philanthropist Margaret De Silver gave him a subsidy in 1928, relieving him of the need to earn for two years. Initially he chose to take his funded time in his beloved Northumberland, renting a room in a remote

---

3   Bunting finally selected and introduced a volume of Skipsey's poems for Ceolfrith Press in 1976 (Joseph Skipsey, *Selected Poems*, selected and edited by Basil Bunting, Sunderland, 1976).

4   Makin, Peter, *Bunting: The Shaping of his Verse* (Oxford, 1992), p.156.

5   Makin, *op. cit.*, p.20.

cottage in the Simonsides. But he found himself unable to produce much there, and left for Berlin which, though he despised it, prompted another longish poem attacking western materialism, *Aus Dem Zweiten Reich*, completed in 1931. The only hint in these early long poems of the great counter-example to modern culture Northumbria would become in *Briggflatts* are a few lines in *Attis*. Emasculated in the modern city ('Out of puff / noonhot in tweeds and gray felt'), Bunting's modern Attis recollects a richer rural life, 'deep mud and leafmould somewhere: and / in the distance Cheviot's / heatherbrown flanks and white cap.'[6]

By the time Tom Pickard made his now famous phone call and visit to Bunting in late 1963, having been informed of his existence not insignificantly by an American poet, Jonathan Williams, all of this had changed. Roused from a decade of virtual silence as a poet by the evident interest from Pickard, Gael Turnbull, Stuart Montgomery and others in publishing his old work and any new he might write, Bunting produced *Briggflatts* in not much over a year. The barriers between his poetry and his native North East had all but vanished. As chapters in this volume by Jude Murphy and Natasha Vall show, there had been a cultural shift in the post-war period, particularly since the mid-1950s, a devolution across British culture in film and television as well as in fiction and drama, from the centre to the provinces. Bunting both responded to and helped to promote this devolutionary shift; though in a strong sense, too, at his age and with his experience, worry about being provincial would no longer have had any force as a deterrent anyway. In addition, in the one long poem he had completed since the war, he had already managed to outgrow his inveterately negative youthful approach by coming at modern materialism through an extended counter-example, an alternative way of life which he had experienced firsthand. In *The Spoils*, completed in 1951, Bunting paid tribute to the culture and customs of the Bakhtiari tribespeople with whom he had lived and worked closely when deputed to protect them from German influence during the Second World War (and who understood and appreciated the archaic version of Persian he had learnt with Pound's encouragement in order to read and translate sections of Firdosi's great epic *Shahnameh*). The poem's four Persian characters represent

77   *Joseph Skipsey*

6   Bunting, Basil, *Complete Poems* (Newcastle upon Tyne, 2000), pp.30-1.

78 *Basil Bunting with Tom Pickard, photographed by Joanna Voit at Warwick in 1980*

attitudes (the title comes from the Koran: 'the spoils are for God'), such as reverence, humility and absence of material ambition, which are not dissimilar from, and indeed foreshadow, the values for which the compound of ancient Northumbrian warrior and monk would come to stand in *Briggflatts*. The final section of the poem anticipates *Briggflatts*, too, in recording with a voice that is unironically the poet's own.

II

Perhaps most decisive in Bunting's actually turning to Northumbria in *Briggflatts* was his decision to use the work to try to make sense of the course of his life. As well as his origin, Northumberland had become his destination now: he had just spent his first full decade as an adult in the region and had now settled there for good. Writing about himself meant writing about the region. William Wootten rightly observes that *Briggflatts* 'does not declare itself to be a national epic but an "autobiography"' (its subtitle); but his argument that the northern nationalist material plays an exclusively *supporting* role to the autobiographical narrative should be qualified.[7] For the poem's autobiographical structure, as it turns out, serves its substantial northern nationalist material as much as it does the poet's personal story. The autobiographical and Northumbrian, I would argue, are to a great extent mutually supportive in the poem. If the poet invokes Northumbrian figures and features to define his experiences and attitudes, his life is also presented in order to revive these figures and features.

As the germ of the poem, Bunting reported that before anything else came the episode in the life of Alexander when Alexander reaches the flaming limits of the world, confronts the Angel of Death, Israfel, sees the error of his ways and gives up

---

7   Wootten, William, 'Basil Bunting, British Modernism and the Time of the Nation', in James McGonigal and Richard Price (eds), *The Star You Steer By: Basil Bunting and British Modernism* (Amsterdam, 2000), pp.27 and 34.

his imperial ambitions. Bunting's specific sources for Alexander's story are Firdosi's *Shahnameh* and the lengthy medieval Spanish epic, *Libro de Alexandre*; but he uses Dante's *Inferno* more generally, too, to help in his graphic evocation of greed, ambition and the lust for power. Bunting makes this episode pivotal to his entire poem; it occupies the third of the poem's five parts and stands symbolically for all the rest. In Alexander's story, recounted in Bunting's poem by the soldiers who can only follow their leader so far up the mountain (who 'desired Macedonia / ... to end in our place by our own wars, / and deemed the peak unscaleable') but watch him struggle on up to his encounter with Israfel, ambition discovers its limitations, hubris finds humility, the journey out ends and is followed by the journey back.[8] The sober aftermath of the dream vision shows Alexander waking up and, though dazed, instinctively recognising the landscape in which he finds himself at home:

> As a woodman dazed by an adder's sting
> barely within recall
> tests the rebate tossed to him, so he
> ascertained moss and bracken ...[9]

Just as the whole poem has a double epigraph, the line from the *Libro de Alexandre* first in Spanish, 'Son los pasariellos del mal pelo exidos', then translated by Bunting into Northumbrian dialect, '[t]he spuggies [sparrows] are fledged', the Northumbrian landscape stands for the Macedonian here.[10]

It is around part 3, then, that Bunting organised the four other parts of the poem as the (very selective) story of his life *and* as the four seasons: parts 1 and 2, Spring and Summer, being the past, his youth in a northern landscape and early adulthood in London and abroad (particularly Italy); and parts 4 and 5, Autumn and Winter, being the present and old age back in the North East. Significant figures from the Northumbrian kingdom also preside over the various sections of the poem. Parts 1 and 2 invoke the Viking Eric Bloodaxe, who was briefly 'king of York, / king of Dublin, king of Orkney', and whose death in 954 marked what some saw as the end of Northumbrian independence.[11] Part 4 invokes a number of earlier figures – warrior-poets and monks – first the sixth-century Cymric bards Taliesin and Aneurin, the latter the author of *Y Goddodin*, an elegiac poem recording the defeat of the northern Britons by the Saxons at Catterick; then the saints, Columba, Columbanus, Aidan and Cuthbert, responsible in the sixth and seventh centuries for bringing Christianity from Ireland via Iona, establishing it in Northumbria and founding Lindisfarne. Cuthbert is the most important of these and goes on, albeit indirectly, to inform much of part 5 as well.

These ancient Northumbrian figures enjoy an independence and a significance that their counterparts in Bunting's earlier work did not enjoy. In the earlier long poems,

---

8 Bunting, Basil, *Briggflatts* (London, 1966), p.27.
9 *Ibid.*, p.28.
10 *Ibid.*, p.9.
11 *Ibid.*, p.15.

the poet and the featured historical figure are collapsed into one another; to all intents and purposes they are one and the same and speak with one voice. The poems are not ultimately interested in the actual historical figure or period in their own right, nor in the poet's own cultural identity; instead the composite character's purpose is to expose certain negative features of contemporary civilisation. Thus, in *Villon* and *Chomei at Toyama*, the poets clearly have affinities with their French and Japanese subjects but they are not culturally identifying; they represent shared views about the world. Past and present are welded together in these poems by what the critic Hugh Kenner dubbed the 'frigidaire effect' (referring to Pound's anachronistic use of the modern applicance in the classical world of *Homage to Sextus Propertius*), so that medieval Kyoto in Bunting's *Chomei*, for example, is described as contemporary New York ('Dead stank / on the curb, lay so thick on / Riverside Drive a car couldn't pass').[12] In *Briggflatts*, by contrast, Bunting eschews the 'frigidaire effect' in his treatment of the past and present. No matter how much Northumbrian figures are used as images for the poet, he doesn't want to confuse them. Intensely interested both in the actual historical Northumbrian figures and in his own cultural identity, the poet of *Briggflatts* avoids casually identifying them in order to make it possible for him to discover and explore the precise relation between them. Having kept them separate, Bunting then uses the poem to unite them or (to see it slightly differently) to show how their identities are genuinely united. So, Bloodaxe in parts 1 and 2, and the warrior-poets and monks, particularly Cuthbert, in parts 4 and 5, are introduced and then brought into relation with the poet in a much more subtle way. They are first invoked in a more or less direct encounter; then they represent aspects of the poet's experience and attitudes; and finally they enjoy an independent significance within a narrative, parallel to the poet's own personal narrative, of cultural reparation and restoration.

Part 1 presents what is surely a vivid personal memory, notwithstanding Bunting's warning in his notes that 'the first movement is no more a chronicle than the third'.[13] The poet and the dedicatee of the poem, Peggy Greenbank (later to become Peggy Mullett), the sister of a schoolfriend with whom Bunting often stayed as a teenager at their home in the village of Brigflatts (just south of Sedbergh in Cumbria), are young lovers being carried on the cart on which her father, a mason, transports gravestones. Their arrival, via Hawes, at Stainmore (having come from Brigflatts, presumably) summons Bloodaxe to mind, since this is where he was murdered; and this in turn leads the poet to see the mason as an image of Bloodaxe:

> Copper-wire moustache,
> sea-reflecting eyes
> and Baltic plainsong speech
> declare: By such rocks
> men killed Bloodaxe.[14]

---

12 Bunting, *Complete Poems*, p.87.
13 Bunting, *Briggflatts*, p.43.
14 *Ibid.*, p.13.

Towards the end of the section, when we hear that the young poet has wantonly abandoned, or as he puts it, 'murdered', his relationship with the girl, Bloodaxe returns to preside over violence, betrayal and desertion.[15] His significance for Bunting arises from his having deserted his people in Norway to seek power in Britain and Ireland, and possibly also from what some claim earned him his name, killing his relatives, his own blood. The penultimate stanza of part 1 refers *simultaneously* to Bloodaxe, the mason engraving a headstone, and the poet 'murdering' his love:

> Brief words are hard to find,
> shapes to carve and discard:
> Bloodaxe, king of York,
> king of Dublin, king of Orkney.
> Take no notice of tears;
> letter the stone to stand
> over love laid aside lest
> insufferable happiness impede
> flight to Stainmore,
> to trace
> lark, mallet,
> becks, flocks
> and axe knocks.[16]

Bloodaxe then becomes a major referent in part 2, linked with the unsatisfactory Summer of the poet's life spent away from both his loved one and his land, seeking poetic success in London and abroad. Though not mentioned by name, he occupies two verse paragraphs interleaved with others evoking the poet's own wanderings in his twenties and thirties. The first shows Bloodaxe leading a longship which becomes an image for the poet's dividedness from his true self: Bloodaxe faces forward, his crew backwards as they row: '[n]othing he sees / they see, but hate and serve'.[17] The second evokes Bloodaxe's final powerlessness before his murderers and the physical decomposition of his unburied corpse. Immediately following a description of the poet's work composed in exile as 'evasive / ornament' and 'flawed fragments', it suggests that a life lived in denial and flight from its true identity ('Loaded with mail of linked lies') is vulnerable, even self-destructive, but also ineffectual in the sense that the true identity, though never properly expressed, cannot ultimately be hidden, even in death ('no sable to disguise / what he wore under the lies').[18] No authentic expression of this self will emerge, the poet seems to be saying, whether political or artistic, unless it cleave to its truest commitments – cultural, geographical and familial. In the short *Note on Briggflatts* which Bunting took some care to rework but

---

15 *Ibid.*, p.15.
16 *Ibid.*, p.15.
17 *Ibid.*, p.18.
18 *Ibid.*, pp.21 and 22.

never in fact published, he explains Bloodaxe as a symbol of overweening 'ambition and lust for experience' and contrasts him with Pasiphae (who in Greek myth gave birth to the Minotaur having been punished by Neptune with a furious lust for the bull her husband Minos had refused to sacrifice), with whom part 2 of the poem concludes, as a counter-figure of creative passivity: 'Those fail who try to force their destiny, like Eric,' Bunting explained; 'but those who are resolute to submit, like my version of Pasiphae, may bring something new to birth, be it only a monster.'[19]

A similar pattern is visible in the use of the very different, and earlier Northumbrian figures in the second half of the poem. After the dream vision of Alexander and Israfel in part 3, part 4 immediately brings the poem right up to the poet's present, in a north-east landscape. But his first actions in this present are to witness the ancient Northumbrian past: 'I hear Aneurin number the dead ... I see Aneurin's pectoral muscle swell under his shirt.'[20] Part 4 then moves chronologically from the warrior-poet of Catterick and his martial vision, to the monks who brought Celtic Christianity to Northumbria and their humility, humanity and above all their radical egalitarianism. The religion they preached, according to the poet, was 'not for bodily welfare nor pauper theorems / but splendour to splendour, excepting nothing that is.'[21] Extraordinarily, the passage sustains the present tense of the poet pretty much throughout. Indeed, it seems significant that this, the most sustained passage representing ancient Northumbria in the poem, is also the passage in which the first person of the poet is used most frequently. It offers a sort of heroic tribute – its loose Homeric dactylic hexameters strikingly different from the poem's staple short two- and three-beat line – to the heroes of a Northumbrian golden age, a tribute all the more powerful for insisting on the present tense, the contemporary relevance of that kingdom's achievements and the living truths to which both warrior-poets and saints testify, that life is a fight, that all creatures are equal and, perhaps most of all, that we 'understand nothing'.[22] The tribute to the ancient Northumbrian warrior-poets and monks gives way to the conclusion of the section and its identification of the poet with rats, 'accustomed to penury, / filth, disgust and fury', unglamorous, low profile, brave, stubbornly resilient.[23]

And the saints, and particularly Cuthbert, then subtly pervade and underwrite all of part 5 as Bloodaxe had part 2. Bunting had planned to have part 5 spoken by Cuthbert; but that would have excluded the poet and his present and the section's very power comes from its attempt to bind past and present, Cuthbert and poet. As it is, Cuthbert is not even mentioned by name in part 5, as Bloodaxe is not in part 2. In other words, it is important for the poem's effect that the culture of the historical figure has been absorbed into the poet in the present. This is not the casual collapsing of poet and historical figure of Bunting's earlier poems because it asserts

---

19 Bunting, Basil, *A Note on Briggflatts* (Durham, 1989), unpaginated.
20 Bunting, *Briggflatts*, p.31.
21 *Ibid.*, p.32.
22 *Ibid.*, p.32.
23 *Ibid.*, p.34.

79 *Barry MacSweeney, Stuart Montgomery, Basil Bunting and Tony Harrison in the* Haymarket Hotel, *Percy Street, Newcastle on 27 February 1970 (copyright* Newcastle Chronicle & Journal Ltd*)*

a cultural continuity with the Northumbrian past and defines the poet's identity likewise. The links with what little we know of Cuthbert's life and career have been persuasively detailed in Peter Makin's wonderfully thorough study, *Bunting: The Shaping of his Verse* (1992), which seems unlikely ever to be surpassed as the most exhaustive piece of research on the sources of Bunting's art. Cuthbert presides most importantly over two features of part 5 of the poem: one, the poet's assertion of the equality of all creatures and, second, his universal perspective. Cuthbert is most famously associated with animals. He started life as a shepherd; a strophe early in part 5 is devoted to describing traditional Northumbrian shepherds and sheep dogs ('fell-born men of precise instep / leading demure dogs / from Tweed and Till and Teviotdale') as Bunting had witnessed them in the late 1920s in the Simonsides.[24] Cuthbert is also closely associated with the cormorant, almost ubiquitously imaged in the Lindisfarne Gospel which is thought to have been illuminated in his honour, and is invoked early in part 5 ('gruff sole cormorant / whose grief turns carnival').[25] But the most famous anecdote about Cuthbert involved animals emerging from the

24 *Ibid.*, p.6.
25 *Ibid.*, p.5.

sea at midnight, ministering to him on the shore and receiving his blessing in return; and Cuthbert thus stands behind Bunting's insistence in *Briggflatts*, as he put it in an interview in 1982, that 'a man [is] no more important than the louse in his shirt or the stone under his feet'.[26] As he said, Part 5 shows 'St Cuthbert in love with all creation'.[27] Intimately related to this is Bunting's universal perspective that confronts us with the limits of our knowledge. According to Bede, when Cuthbert lived on Farne he 'built some little dwelling-places from which he could see nothing but the heavens above'.[28] Likewise, the poet spends much of the final section of *Briggflatts* gazing at the stars – 'Furthest, fairest things, stars, free of our humbug' – putting all human issues into perspective.[29]

As the poem concludes, its parallel plots of personal and cultural restoration become clear. In a closing of the gap between Now and Then that the poet is most interested in, Bunting observes that the light he now sees as Capella, in the zenith, set out on its journey more or less when he and his lover were teenagers in Brigflatts fifty years ago:

> Then is Now. The star you steer by is gone,
> its tremulous thread spun in the hurricane
> spider floss on my cheek; light from the zenith
> spun when the slowworm lay in her lap
> fifty years ago.[30]

Neatly aligning stellar and biographical time, in conclusion the poet makes some reparation for his desertion and throws into parenthesis the entire period of his life during which he had wrongly abandoned his love and his land. In close association with this narrative of return to origins and emotional expiation ('Fifty years a letter unanswered, / a visit postponed for fifty years'), Bunting's plot of regional expiation reaches its climax too.[31] The traumatic end of the Northumbrian kingdom with the betrayals, exile and finally somewhat cathartic murder of Bloodaxe has been endured and exorcised in parts 1 and 2 so that now in parts 4 and 5 the true culture, achievements and religious vision of the kingdom in which Aidan and Cuthbert flourished can be restored. Part 5 can be interpreted either as an absorption into the poet of Cuthbert's world and vision, or as a sort of restoration of that world. Either way, it is a removal of the barriers between Now and Then and an assertion of the essential cultural identity of eighth-century Northumbria and the 20th-century North East.

It is characteristic of Bunting (always a powerful nature writer) that *Briggflatts* communicates so much through carefully evoked landscapes. Abroad, the landscapes remind the poet constantly of his betrayal: on the Italian coast, 'wind, sun, sea upbraid / justly an unconvinced deserter' and 'Tortoise deep in dust or / muzzled

---

26 Makin, *op. cit.*, p.198.
27 *Ibid.*, p.199.
28 *Ibid.*, p.201.
29 Bunting, *Briggflatts*, p.38.
30 *Ibid.*, p.38.
31 *Ibid.*, p.38.

bear capering / punctuate a text whose initial, / lost in Lindisfarne plaited lines, / stands for discarded love.'[32] Back home, the landscapes characterise and naturalise the Northumbrian culture he is celebrating. At its best, for Bunting, Northumbrian culture emerges naturally from its landscape. In the last few stanzas of part 3, as the chastened Alexander walks home, he hears the 'song' of the slow-worm 'repeated' by 'every bough' as if all Northumbrian nature now subscribes to its humble message ('I prosper / lying low').[33] That nature is also associated with the pre-industrial, artisanal, agrarian features of Bunting's Northumbria. As Tony Lopez says, *Briggflatts* 'ties in politically with that revised pastoral we find in Wordsworth's *Prelude*, the anti-metropolitan and independent rural community of skilled labour: stone mason (memorial poet), shepherd (skilled dog-trainer), fisherman (navigator) and so on'.[34] And Bunting intermittently binds this vision to nature, as on a north-east beach in part 5 where he observes 'Silver blades of surf / fall crisp on rustling grit, / shaping the shore as a mason / fondles and shapes his stone'.

The most frequently repeated landscape images in the poem, however, are versions of the 'Lindisfarne plaited lines' of the Codex illuminations which, as we have just seen, Bunting invokes in part 2. There is a line of interpretation, most persuasively expounded by Peter Makin and endorsed by Bunting himself in interview, that *Briggflatts* owes its structure partly to the great complex interweavings of the carpet pages of the Lindisfarne Gospels.[35] Given the difficulties of comparing visual and verbal works and, more specifically, the coherence of the poem's plotting, this seems to me no more than a desired analogy. But one cannot doubt the strength of Bunting's belief in the truth of what he understood as the plaitings' representation of reality as complexly interwoven, and beautiful and balanced, but ultimately abstract and incomprehensible. If anything is, surely this is the heart of Northumbrian culture as he sees it. In the Autumn and Winter landscapes of the poem's last two parts, natural images for these inscrutable interlacings abound, from the 'midges darting' and '[a]pplewood ... knots' which 'smoulder all day' on fires to the '[c]obweb hair on the morning' and the frost-spangled 'fleece'.[36] But the most densely clustered examples come at the culmination of the first verse paragraph of part 4 when the poet has returned home and connected with the Northumbrian warrior-poets and monks:

> ... Can you trace shuttles thrown
> like drops from a fountain, spray, mist of spiderlines
> bearing the rainbow, quoits around the draped moon;
> shuttles like random dust desert whirlwinds hoy at their tormenting sun?
> Follow the clue patiently and you will understand nothing.[37]

---

32 *Ibid.*, pp.20 and 21.
33 *Ibid.*, pp.28 and 29.
34 Lopez, Tony, 'Under Saxon the Stone: National Identity in Basil Bunting's Briggflatts', in *Sharp Study and Long Toil*, ed. Richard Caddel, *Durham University Journal Supplement*, 1995, p.115.
35 Makin, *op. cit.*, pp.219-38.
36 Bunting, *Briggflatts*, pp.32 and 33.
37 *Ibid.*, p.32.

Finally, the landscape also plays its part in helping bind past and present. It remembers ancient Northumbrian history; in part 1, 'skulls cropped for steel caps / huddle round Stainmore'.[38] And in part 5 the poet summons its unchanging permanence to assist in his efforts to demonstrate the region's cultural continuity:

> Snow lies bright on Hedgehope
> and tacky mud about Till
> where the fells have stepped aside
> and the river praises itself,
> silence by silence sits
> and Then is diffused in Now.

III

In diffusing the 'Then' in the 'Now', formal and technical features played a great part. For Peter Quartermain, all Bunting's poetry was driven by a response to the marginal political and cultural position of the North East; according to him, Bunting's techniques concertedly attempted to resist and undermine the 'monolithic central power'.[39] Linking Bunting's poetic techniques with his region's marginality has obvious appeal. The trouble is finding evidence to support the claim, either within the poetry or outside it. As Wootten points out, 'any attempt to depict a radical, post-colonial Bunting will encounter problems … the former Vice-Consul of Isfahan [was] something of a colonialist in practice'; and his 'Northumbrianism, like any nationalism, is not opposed to a centre as such, just where that centre happens to be at present'.[40] The greater problem, though, is literary: if resistance to the political and cultural centre informs the poetry, it is all but impossible to show how it does so.

More demonstrable is Bunting's use in *Briggflatts* of the Old English verse line. Invoking ancient Northumbrian artistic forms was not an altogether original move on Bunting's part. Indeed, as Wootten has shown, there was a strong movement within British modernism, most fully propounded in the work of Herbert Read (indirectly derived from the German aesthetician Wilhelm Worringer), which influenced MacDiarmid and David Jones as well as Bunting, to emulate proto-modernist Celtic and Anglo-Celtic artistic and literary forms as definitively British, thus making the case for the centrality of modernism in the British tradition.[41] Pound, too, had endorsed Anglo-Saxon verse back in 1912 when he published his translation of the 'The Seafarer' in *Ripostes*. Still, there's no doubting the authentic Northumbrianism of the verse form Bunting chose to use. Old English poetry was the vernacular literature of Northumbria from the late seventh century (and possibly earlier) up to the Norman

---

38 *Ibid.*, p.3.
39 Quartermain, Peter, *Basil Bunting: Poet of the North* (Durham, 1990), p.9.
40 Wootten, *op. cit.*, p.18.
41 Wootten, *op. cit.*, p.22.

invasion, and may actually have originated in Northumbria. Bunting himself certainly identified it as a distinctive and original Northumbrian cultural product, confidently locating the much-debated composition of *Beowulf* in the region.[42]

On occasion *Briggflatts* is so close in sound and intonation to Old English poetry that it might almost be quotation, as here in part 2 where the terse, elegiac cadences of poems like 'The Wanderer' and 'The Seafarer' are summoned to intensify the desertion of their homes by the poet and by Bloodaxe:

> Who sang, sea takes,
> brawn brine, bone grit.
> Keener the kittiwake.
> Fells forget him.
> Fathoms dull the dale,
> gulfweed voices ... [43]

For the most part, Old English poetic methods are more subtly discernible in the short lines in which most of *Briggflatts* is written. The poem is impressive in not using Old English with distancing irony (as Auden does) yet not resulting either in pastiche, parody or nostalgia. Bunting's lifelong modernism discovered a genuine affinity with aspects of Anglo-Saxon verse, an affinity nowhere more powerfully felt than in the impulse they shared towards objectivity. Bunting's 'objectivity', his 'hatred of abstractions', Quartermain reads speculatively as a function of his 'hatred of centralised government'.[44] 'The subject races,' he says,

> reject the ideologies which serve to bolster the oppressor's power, [they] reject, therefore
> ...abstractions, the metaphysics which justifies their subjugation and the syntax of
> politics which assures that subjugation. Instead subject races, underdogs, turn to the
> concrete, the physical, the practical: to the flesh; they resort to fact, to the tangible, to
> objects.[45]

Bunting himself, however, explained in modernist terms the desirability, as he saw it, of impersonal objectivity in poetry. In art and literature the objective would outlast the subjective, he felt, and the concrete would outlast the abstract because of their adherence to what is real and primary and their avoidance of what is merely secondary and insubstantial (because interpretative). In 'The Lion and the Lizard', an essay about the difficulties of translating Persian poetry into English (which Bunting sent to his American friend and fellow modernist Louis Zukovsky in 1935 but did not subsequently publish), Bunting explains:

---

42   See Bill Griffiths' chapter on Old English poetry in this volume.
43   Bunting, *Briggflatts*, p.19.
44   Quartermain, *op. cit.*, p.14.
45   Quartermain, *op. cit.*, pp.9-10.

> The most vivid poetry, in the long run the most durable because least affected by changes of philosophic habit, is that which approximates most nearly to the structure of the event … To the event – active – the result – passive – stands as a first abstraction, the first process of reflection and subjectivity; selective, that is, rejecting part of the fact to simplify classification.[46]

Postmodernism would come to take issue with this idea that any verbal construction (or artistic representation for that matter) could approximate 'more nearly to the structure of the event' than others and so to question this faith in the possibility of truly objective representation in poetry. Bunting's modernist adherence to it, however, remained at the heart of his approach right up to the end of his life and it certainly lies behind some of the distinctive successes of *Briggflatts*, not least its vivid adaptation of Old English verse to give expression to what he saw as the true heart of Northumbrian culture.

Line by line poetry could achieve objectivity, for Bunting as for many other modernists, by committing itself to simple, impersonal, economical, declarative sentences in natural (and most importantly not metronomically regular) rhythms; and in all these ways the Old English poetic line fitted the bill. Part 1 is composed of lines not identical to, yet not dissimilar from, Anglo-Saxon half-lines: heavily alliterated; and in 13-line stanzas, ending (all but one of them) with a rhyming couplet. This one, the fourth, in which the teenage lovers first appear, sticks closely to their sensations as they lie on the mason's wagon, what they can feel, and see, but most of all hear:

> Stone smooth as skin,
> cold as the dead they load
> on a low lorry by night.
> The moon sits on the fell
> but it will rain.
> Under sacks on the stone
> two children lie,
> hear the horse stale,
> the mason whistle,
> harness mutter to shaft,
> felloe to axle squeak,
> rut thud the rim,
> crushed grit.[47]

Audible here is the force given to the simple, declarative sentence in Anglo-Saxon verse by the two-stress, alliterated half-lines and by the minimal use of the lesser parts of speech not used in a fully inflected language such as Old English. It was Bunting's modernist belief that the pursuit of objectivity in poetry was greatly aided by avoiding

---

46   Bunting, Basil, *Three Essays* (ed. Richard Caddel, Durham, 1994), p.29.
47   Bunting, *Briggflatts*, p.12.

passive and even intransitive verb forms and adhering as much as possible to simple subject, verb, object structures. As he says in 'The Lion and the Lizard', '[t]he events that make up the world are for the most part such as can be exactly expressed by active, transitive verbs.'[48] The short line and the fully inflected nature of the language give Old English poetry an additional impression of economy and weighty compression such as Bunting also wanted to achieve. Like most of his previous work, *Briggflatts* is pared down to a point of maximum density; in fact, Bunting claimed to have reduced the poem to its final 700 or so lines from 20,000 and his advice to younger poets always included the central modernist tenet, '[c]ut out every word you dare,' then '[d]o it again a week later, and again.'[49]

Decisive in effecting the compactness and concreteness is another Anglo-Saxon feature, the way the lines, or half-lines, insist on an appositive relation of image to image, many lines as much in parallel as in succession to the lines preceding them. Notable here as well is the consistent use of the present tense and the third person (which the poem for the most part sustains to the end). Such impersonality and timelessness Bunting found more in the heroic than the devotional forms of Old English verse, comparing epic favourably with Shakespearean drama. 'Shakespeare fits his cadence to the mood of the speaker … Almost all his cadences are in some sense subjective. The epic music, on the other hand, belongs to the object, the matter in hand.'[50] Lastly, these lines are metrically similar (though again not identical) to the two-beat half-line of Old English. Bunting rejected as too unvaried and therefore artificial the smooth accentual-syllabic metres that dominated English poetry from the 16th to the 20th centuries.[51] 'Scansion,' he asserted in his lecture delivered to the University of Newcastle in 1969, 'is a heresy in English poetry that wasn't introduced till Elizabeth's reign.'[52] However, Bunting, like most other modernists, turned not (as is often assumed) to total, unanchored freedom, but to variations on looser, less insistently regular schemes. 'Vary rhythm enough to stir the emotion you want,' he said, 'but not so as to lose impetus.'[53] Thus for the most effective balance between regularity and variation for much of the poem Bunting used loosely accentual, two- and three-beat lines.[54]

The would-be objectivity of language and verse throughout the poem makes it formal, remote and impersonal rather than conversational. The manner has its pitfalls, strikes a few wrong notes, particularly in the area of personal relationships where it can sound inappropriately solemn and therefore bathetic. Davie's explanation of the phrase 'thatch of his manhood's home' as an Anglo-Saxon style kenning or riddle,

---

48 Bunting, *Three Essays*, p.9.
49 'I Suggest', quoted here from Richard Caddel and Anthony Flowers, *Basil Bunting: A Northern Life* (Newcastle upon Tyne, 1997), p.49, but originally printed as a one-page list of seven tenets for poets in the early 1970s.
50 Bunting, *Three Essays*, p.31.
51 See, for a thorough examination of this, Timothy Steele, *Missing Measures: Modern Poetry and the Revolt against Meter* (Fayetteville, Arkansas, 1990).
52 Basil Bunting, '"Thumps" and "Wyat": Two Lectures on Prosody', in *Sharp Study and Long Toil*, ed. Richard Caddel, *Durham University Journal Supplement*, 1995, p.32.
53 'I Suggest', in Caddel and Flowers, *Basil Bunting: A Northern Life*, p.49.
54 Bunting, *Briggflatts*, p.19.

80 *Basil Bunting, photographed by Joanna Voit*

for example, cannot rescue this coy and laughable euphemism for the poet's lover's pubic hair.[55] Meanwhile, 'hunger is stayed on her settle, lust in her bed' characterises his lover more as a resource than a human being; and the two stanzas in part 4, in which the line appears, get nowhere towards evoking the actual relationship.[56] This problem magnified leads to the poem's chief failure on the larger scale, its plot of 'discarded love'. One commonly expressed and understandable objection to the plot is the priority it gives to adolescent over adult love. Neil Corcoran puts it well:

> A psychoanalytical account of the poem might find a neurotic element in its fixation on childhood sexuality, its implication that no more fulfilling relationship could subsequently be discovered in life than was found then, and might therefore perceive a failure of power where the greatest poetry might be thought to be imaginatively strongest.[57]

The poem's emphasis on an abandoned teenage love is finally unconvincing, however, not because it was not as important as the poem claims (after all, it might have been), but because the poem fails to dramatise it sufficiently. The poet never convinces us of the substance of the relationship because, despite his frequent protestations, he never shows it to us and so we remain unmoved at the climax when he keeps reiterating that they have not seen each other for fifty years. Explaining that the relationship functions 'as a prototype of the unfulfilment that shadows every life, however successful,' as Davie does, is simply to admit its failure.[58] Even had the relationship been given greater attention, the nature of the poem's terse, impersonal and formal verse would have made it difficult for this personal relationship to have been depicted.

55   Donald Davie, 'One Way to Misread Briggflatts', in Carroll F. Terrell (ed.), *Basil Bunting: Man and Poet* (Orono, Maine, 1981), p.164.
56   Bunting, *Briggflatts*, p.33.
57   Corcoran, Neil, *English Poetry since 1940* (London, 1993), p.35.
58   Davie, Donald, *Under Briggflatts: A History of Poetry in Great Britain 1960-1988* (Chicago, 1989), p.139.

Bunting's spare, objective style, though, was a deliberate modernist alternative to the kind of social realist approach so dominant in English poetry in the 1960s. And its successes far outweigh its failures. It may not be able to convey the intimacy of human relationships as chatty social realism can, but it has at its command a far greater range of material, high and low, and is capable of more intense poetic moments, of squalor at the one extreme and lofty elevation at the other: of the shit-eating Dantean nightmare of Alexander's ascent up the mountain in part 3 on the one hand, and the poet's ecstatic reunion with Aneurin and Cuthbert in part 4 on the other. The poet can identify closely in one and the same poem with the armorial bull, the mundane slow-worm, and even the reviled rat. The objective mode's greatest success is to enact in its methodology the very attitudes it is celebrating as definitively Northumbrian. As we have seen, the poem offers a vision celebrating the incomprehensible complexity and plurality of life, a philosophy Bunting had taken a lifetime to give proper expression, possibly because of its remoteness from the ideas of his modernist masters, Yeats, Pound and Eliot, who valued '[h]ierarchy and order'.[59] As Bunting explained:

> Amongst philosophers I have most sympathy with Lucretius and his masters, content to explain the world an atom at a time; with Spinoza who saw all things as God, though not with his wish to demonstrate that logically; and with David Hume, the doubter. The men I learned poetry from did not much value these. Perhaps that is why it took me so long to make a poem that reflects, fragmentarily, my whole mind.[60]

Explaining the world an atom at a time meant, for Bunting, not imposing an explanation but accepting its complexity and inscrutability much as in Eadfrith's Codex illuminations. Bunting repeatedly insisted on the pre-eminence of sound and form in poetry not ultimately to rubbish poetic content, but to emphasise how unremarkable and unambitious, ideally, that content should be. 'All old wives' chatter, cottage wisdom,' was how in *Note on Briggflatts* he summarised the content of the poem. 'No poem is profound.'[61] Sound and form could help to avoid imposing abstract, or subjective, explanations and so keep the poem objective. This is not to say that the successes of the poem are all in conflict with its central autobiographical purpose, nor that the autobiographical is not an important feature of the poem. The poem is often celebrated as an original mix of Poundian modernism and Wordsworthian autobiography; Bunting actually valued Wordsworth, however, not as a detailed first-person narrator of his life but as a northern poet who 'resolutely kept [his] eye on the object'.[62] And *Briggflatts* is in a sense a critique of Wordsworthian autobiography. The poem's conjunction of autobiography with modernist objectivity asserts that modernist objectivity is the best way of representing an individual life. And its techniques, modernist and Northumbrian together, follow Cuthbert in subordinating the individual life to objective existence.

---

59   Bunting, *A Note on Briggflatts*, n.p.
60   *Ibid.*
61   *Ibid.*
62   Bunting, *Three Essays*, p.31.

IV

Critics of *Briggflatts* sometimes complain that, for all its efforts, formal and thematic, the poem simply cannot bridge the gap between Then and Now, and ends up by offering something as false as 'Morris's picturesque medievalism', as the anonymous reviewer in the *Times Literary Supplement* put it.[63] A few enthusiasts, it is true, have claimed confidently that on the contrary the poem does bridge that gap quite satisfactorily. Thom Gunn, for example, argues that the poem's great and invigorating achievement is to have persuasively carried from the Northumbrian past into the present the kind of primitive, communal plenitude Eliot in *The Waste Land* and Pound in *Canto 47* lamented as lost to the modern world.[64] But Bunting himself in the poem's Coda was actually the first commentator to suggest that the poem's restorative efforts may not be wholly efficacious, and by implication that its success as a work of art may not wholly depend on the efficacy of those efforts. In considering how meaningful these Northumbrian figures and episodes can be to the modern region it is worth remembering that *Briggflatts* ends not with affirmation, but doubt. As its last two stanzas read:

> Night, float us.
> Offshore wind, shout,
> ask the sea
> what's lost, what's left,
> what horn sunk,
> what crown adrift.
>
> Where we are who knows
> of kings who sup
> while day fails? Who,
> swinging his axe
> to fell kings, guesses
> where we go?[65]

The poet reflects that the contemporary North East may now be totally and permanently cut adrift from its moorings in the Anglian kingdom of Northumbria. To some extent, of course, the poem's overall success depends on qualities that transcend all regional issues. The poem satisfies in its thoroughgoing efforts to make sense of a life. But insofar as region does have a significant part to play, it is the regionalist (or nationalist) impulse which is important. This impulse appeals in the first place because of the unsustaining, inauthentic and generalised British culture the poem satirises in its evocations of London at the start of part 2. For much of the rest of the poem it

---

63 *Basil Bunting Special Issue*, ed. Peter Hodgkiss, *Poetry Information*, no. 19 (Autumn 1978), p.68.
64 Gunn, Thom, 'What the Slowworm Said: Eliot, Pound, and Bunting', in *Shelf Life: Essays, Memoirs and an Interview* (London, 1994), p.64.
65 Bunting, *Briggflatts*, p.41.

is looking for a richer and more real alternative. But the impulse works in the poem finally not because it achieves some incontrovertible triumph in which Northumbria's past and present are conclusively bound together, but because of the fervent, lyrical manner and historical and imaginative integrity with which it is followed.

All the same, what has been at issue in the poem's reception has not been its success, but the significance of its success. From the moment Cyril Connolly hailed it in 1967 as 'the finest long poem to have been published in England since T.S. Eliot's *Four Quartets*', its place in post-war British poetry has been assured. [66] Many other luminaries, including Craig Raine and the American poet August Kleinzahler, have been as fulsome in their praise; and the two most recent major anthologies of post-war British poetry, Robert Crawford and Simon Armitage's *Penguin Book of Poetry from Britain and Ireland since 1945* (1998) and Sean O'Brien's *The Firebox: Poetry in Britain and Northern Ireland after 1945* (1998), include substantial excerpts.[67] Disagreement about the poem has centred around its modernism. *Briggflatts* and its success quickly became – and remained – symbolic in the so-called poetry wars, the wars waged over the past few decades between proponents of marginal, modernist poetries and the traditional poetic mainstream. Mainstream critics and anthologists have tended to think of *Briggflatts* as a 'one-off': 'something of an isolated, if exciting, outcrop in the post-war geography', as Robert Crawford and Simon Armitage put it, coming well after 'the high-water mark of Modernist poetry in Britain', the 'publication of *Four Quartets* in 1942'.[68] According to the agitators for experimentalism, on the other hand, *Briggflatts* proved against the doubters, that modernism was both native to Britain *and* still thriving in the post-war period, even as late as the 1960s. Hugh Kenner, for instance, celebrates Bunting as one of the few true artists in his savagely dismissive account of post-war British literary culture, *A Sinking Island* (London, 1988); and Donald Davie (not in his earlier traditionalist guise, of course, but the later apologist for modernism) provocatively entitled his 1989 survey of the British poetry of the preceding twenty years *Under Briggflatts*, thus giving to Bunting's poem the pride of place that one might have expected to be given to the work of Philip Larkin or Ted Hughes or, of the younger generation, Seamus Heaney.

The strongest case for the importance of the poem (and so for the modernists) may well come from its regionalism. *Briggflatts* was the first of a number of poems and poetic sequences in the post-war and post-imperial period which sought to mine a region's history (and in some cases its prehistory) in order to revive its local culture as an authentic alternative to a generalised and centralised metropolitan British culture. It was preceded by David Jones's *Anathemata* (1952), but that poem (no less than MacDiarmid's *A Drunk Man Looks at the Thistle* had before it) dealt with

---

66 Connolly, Cyril, 'Out of Northumbria', *Sunday Times*, 12 February 1967, p.53.
67 'Bunting is a great master and we must educate ourselves to read him', Craig Raine, 'Amputated Years', *New Statesman*, 21 April 1978; 'it looks more and more as if this long poem written late in his life is not simply the best thing that Bunting had done but among the very best poems anyone has done this century', August Kleinzahler, *London Review of Books*, 21 January 1999.
68 Armitage, Simon and Crawford, Robert (eds), *The Penguin Book of Poetry from Britain and Ireland since 1945* (Harmondsworth, 1998), p.xx.

a region, Wales, that was also a nation. After it, in a spate, came Geoffrey Hill's *Mercian Hymns* (1971), Ted Hughes's *Remains of Elmet* (1979) and Gillian Clarke's *The King of Britain's Daughter* (1993) and, about Northern Ireland, John Montague's *The Rough Field* (1972), Thomas Kinsella's *Notes from the Land of the Dead* (1973) and Seamus Heaney's *North* (1975), all of which link the present with ancient local referents in order to unearth and explain. These poems and sequences have been followed in turn by the efforts to evoke contemporary local life more vividly and to speak in contemporary local vernaculars. One thinks of the northern accents of Tony Harrison and then Simon Armitage, the Scots of W.N. Herbert, and the Anglo-Caribbean dialects of Grace Nichols, Linton Kwesi Johnson and Fred D'Aguiar. *Briggflatts'* studied Northumbrianism may seem remote from these contemporary urban voices. However, the many and various celebrations and explorations of the local in contemporary British poetry are all in some degree indebted to Bunting's path-breaking efforts on behalf of his region and its history.

18

The Northumbrian Island

CHARLES PHYTHIAN-ADAMS

Outside Pressures

What became the Anglian kingdom of 'Bernicia' took its name from a Celtic predecessor, and comprised an expanded district within the earlier territory of the Romano-British Votadini, which had reached, from around the Forth, at least as far south as the Wear, or even the Tees. The central areas of this British region were bitterly fought over during the mid- to late sixth century. The Celtic stronghold subsequently renamed Bamburgh by the Angles was 'joined to Bernicia' in 547 by Ida, who had apparently overcome a number of competitors to become the predominant king of these areas. This led eventually to the successful subjection of wider Tweedsdale. That left to be subsequently absorbed into Bernicia only Edinburgh and *Manaw* in *Gododdin*, a province of the Votadini (by their Cumbric name) around the headwaters of the Forth.[1]

South of Lammamuir, there are signs that imply an enduring cultural stratum that remained was still British. Celtic names for Anglian royal centres and monasteries in the Tweed valley were still recalled long after the settlement. Lindisfarne itself

---

1 Dumville, D., 'The origins of Northumbria: some aspects of the British background', in S. Bassett (ed.), *The Origins of Anglo-Saxon Kingdoms* (Leicester, 1989), pp.216-19; Morris, J. (ed.), *Nennius: British History and the Welsh Annals* (London and Chichester, 1980), 78, c. 61; Yorke, B., *Kings and Kingdoms of Early Anglo-Saxon England* (London, 1990), pp.74-7.

appears to have been renamed in Old Irish as opposed to Old English mode, after the establishment there of Celtic monasticism from Iona in 635.[2] The other tightly defined area containing place-names indicative of British associations with significant secular and religious locations was the valley of the Wear: from its tributary, the Gaunless (originally 'Clyde'), via Auckland and Roman Binchester; to Durham (or some similarly positioned site) as a possible location for the mysterious 'stronghold' of *Caer Weir* (or Wear); to the Romano-British name lying behind a possible district around Chester–le-Street.[3]

Two related features suggest that our region long continued part of a recognisably Celtic zone. The wider distribution of names in *caer* (as in Carrick Heights, Elsdon, in Northumberland) that underlies both later national and local administrative divisions, could imply the survival of ancient, seasonal power centres across Britain's isthmus.[4] And, as far south as the Tees valley area, medieval customary institutions seem to mark the perpetuation of public obligations untouched by the earlier expansion of West-Saxon England from the south. These include the billeting of the king's Serjeants of the Peace, who executed justice on regular circuits around formally defined districts. In this instance there is a clear divide between those regions adjudicated by land-serjeants, which overlap from Scotland and Wales, and those operating in the rest of England under the imposed Anglo-Saxon system of hundred districts and mutual surety (or frankpledge, as it was termed by the Normans). Yorkshire alone was innocent of both land-serjeants *and* frankpledge. Such 'alien' institutions on English soil could have reflected the administrative remnants of British societies that had been divided when England's frontiers were drawn both northwards and westwards.[5]

Where specifically Anglian features intruded decisively in Bernicia was along the axis of the Tyne towards the mouth at which were founded the monasteries of Jarrow and Tynemouth. As an erstwhile defensive Roman corridor with civilian settlements, the valley now acted as a focus for two major royal estates. The more obscure to us – where the Dere Street from Teviotdale crosses the Tyne at a major inter-regional communication junction with the Stanegate route from Carlisle – was that at Corbridge, which retained part of its Romano-British name. Here are evidenced, successively, the site of the unfortified Roman town of *Coriosopitum*; a fifth- or

2   Rollason, D., *Northumbria, 500-1100: Creation and Destruction of a Kingdom* (Cambridge, 2003), p.81; Coates, R., 'Un-English reflections on Lindisfarne', in R. Coates and A. Breeze (eds.), *Celtic Voices, English Places. Studies of the Celtic Impact on Place-Names in England* (Stamford, 2000), pp.241-59.

3   Coates, R., 'Gazetteer of Celtic Names in England (except Cornwall)', p.296, and Breeze, A., 'The River Wear, County Durham', pp.79-80, in *Celtic Voices*.

4   Coates, 'Gazetteer', p.324; McNeill, P.G.B. and MacQueen, H.L. (eds), *Atlas of Scottish History to 1707* (Edinburgh, 1996), p.51; Barrow, G.W.S., 'Pre-feudal Scotland: shires and thanes', in Barrow, *The Kingdom of the Scots; Government, Church and Society from the eleventh to the fourteenth century* (London, 1973), pp.65-6; Phythian-Adams, C., *Land of the Cumbrians. A Study in British Provincial Origins A.D. 400-1120* (Aldershot, 1996), p.85.

5   Stewart-Brown, R., *The Serjeants of the Peace in Medieval England and Wales* (Manchester, 1936), pp.99-104, 65; Rees, W., 'Survival of ancient Celtic custom in medieval England', in H. Lewis (ed.), *Angles and Britons* (Cardiff, 1963), pp.153-68 including map; Barrow, *Kingdom of the Scots*, pp.41-7; *Scotland and its Neighbours in the Middle Ages* (London, 1992), pp.144-8; Duncan, A.A.M., *Scotland: The Making of the Kingdom* (Edinburgh, 1975), p.207; Cf. Rollason, *Northumbria*, pp.89-92.

81 *Hadrian's Wall (Air Images, Haltwhistle)*

sixth-century Anglian presence; a partly surviving church used for both an episcopal consecration and a royal assassination in the eighth; and two early tenth-century battles.[6] All these factors suggest a place whose continuing significance – as a local administrative and/or trading centre perhaps – might well account for the foundation nearby at Hexham of Wilfrid's monumental abbey in 671-3 (to which building stone from the Roman ruins was evidently donated) and, in 678, of the new see. The sale of an Irish couple into slavery by Danes at *Corbric* around *c.*1000, moreover, implies an established market by then at which tolls were taken.[7]

---

6   Rivet, A.L.F. and Smith, C., *The Place-Names of Roman Britain* (London, 1979), pp.322-3; Rollason, *Northumbria*, pp.74-5, 51, 194, 274, 261.

7   Pelteret, D.A., *Slavery in Early Medieval England from the Reign of Alfred until the Twelfth Century* (Woodbridge, 1995), p.76. Cf. Fraser, C.M. (ed.), *The Northumberland Lay Subsidy Roll of 1296* (Newcastle, 1968), pp.47-9.

The second key site, that called *Ad Murum* (because of its relationship to Hadrian's Wall), probably lay at Wallbottle in the township of Newburn. In Bede's day this was regarded as an especially illustrious royal estate – being uniquely described by him as in *vico regis inlustri* – one fit separately to receive East Saxon and Middle Anglian royalty and their extensive entourages, who could have come by sea in 653.[8] The same major residence (OE *boðl*) may have been used subsequently by the earls of Northumbria: a place where the newly appointed Earl Copsi was feasting before being caught and decapitated in 1067. Nearby may have lain a religious house, the mysterious 'Monkchester' which was said to have antedated Newcastle. Certainly there was an early monastery and probably another *boðl* immediately over the river at the Gateshead estate, where Bishop Walcher of Durham was murdered in 1080.[9]

Strategic Anglian control of the Tyne corridor and the eventual linguistic predominance of English must be accepted as critical to the region's new identity. Bernicia remained outside lasting Danish or Norse influence from the south. With the exception of the eccentric wapentake of Sadberge, largely in the Tees valley, the region lay beyond the Danelaw wapentake zone that extended from the Tees to the Welland. Indeed, apart from the incidence of Scandinavianised stone-carving traditions, and the slight overlap from Yorkshire of Scandinavian place-naming forms – both again largely confined to the Tees valley – Bernicia or, in its later guise, the earldom of the House of Bamburgh, remained perhaps the least Scandinavianised region of eastern England north of the Suffolk Stour. Only in its medieval traditions of personal-naming were Norse influences apparent, albeit transferably, but, that said, yet other naming choices were inspired by surviving Celtic forms.[10]

The earliest known limits of a *formal* region, to which later arrangements partly conformed, reflected a southern division of greater Bernicia only after it had expanded westward out of its natural context across the Pennine watershed. From 678 the relatively short-lived see of Hexham is said on credible later authority to have stretched from the Tees in the south as far as north as the Alne, and west to the Cumbrian Eden. Territory to the north and west of this area then seems to have lain in St Cuthbert's diocese of Lindisfarne which, like the kingdom of Bernicia, overlapped later parts of Scotland. It was the tenth-century domination of the Solway plain from a Scottish controlled Strathclyde/Cumbria, and the accompanying claims of the diocese of Glasgow, that finally pushed the western Northumbrian boundary back from the Eden to the crest of the Pennines. It may well be that, if original dioceses elsewhere are any guide, the resulting natural region so enclosed reflected a much earlier secular territory, like a sub-kingdom, and might even have represented

---

8   Colgrave, B. and Mynors, R.A.B. (eds), *Bede's Ecclesiastical History of the English People* (Oxford, 1969), pp.278-9, 282-3.

9   Aird, W.M., *St Cuthbert and the Normans. The Church of Durham, 1071-1153* (Woodbridge, 1998), p.68, nn. 35, 36; p.97 n. 160; p.132 nn. 140, 141.

10   Lomas, R., *North-East England in the Middle Ages* (Edinburgh, 1992), pp.21-2; Bailey, R.N., *Viking Age Sculpture in Northern England* (London, 1980), pp.91, 93, fig. 11, pp.134-6, 153, fig. 34, pp.185-9, 191-5; Watts, V.E., 'Place-Names', in J.C. Dewdney (ed.), *Durham County and City with Teesside* (British Association: Durham, 1970), pp.258-61; Barrow, G.W.S., 'Northern English Society in the twelfth and thirteenth centuries', *Scotland and its Neighbours*, pp.131-5.

the pre-547 Bernicia.[11] Despite the death of its last known bishop in 821-2, and despite the dislocation of existing diocesan structures in the ninth century, the memory of Hexham's jurisdiction survived down to 995/1006.[12] Only then was it formally superseded by a wider inclusive diocese, between Tees and Tweed, of first Chester-le-Street and then Durham.

It was an army comprising St Cuthbert's 'people', specifically 'from the river Tees to the Tweed' – those who were becoming known collectively as the *haliwerfolc* or the people of the holy man in a region already dense with properties donated to his shrine – who were said to have been decisively defeated by a combined force of Scots and Strathclyde Cumbrians at the battle of Carham in 1018.[13] This was the point at which the relentless expansion of the Scots southwards through Lothian was finalised at the line of the lower Tweed, and 'Bernicia' was definitively partitioned. South of that, the redefined territories of both the diocese and the earldom of 'Northumberland' broadly coincided.[14] With the single exception of Alston on the Northumbrian side of the Pennine watershed – transferred with its silver mines to Carlisle by Henry I, but remaining nevertheless within the see – the enduring formal boundaries of the North East were drawn by the middle decades of the 12th century. Within them, apart from the medieval liberties of Hexham and Tynedale, were fitted both the privileged estates donated to St Cuthbert in the southern part (and, dispersedly, north of Tyne) and also the county of Northumberland, with its overlapping claims to the wapentake of Sadberge in the Tees valley and, more ambiguously, to the inclusion of the Palatinate itself.[15] Exceptionally, moreover, the special privilege of sanctuary associated with St Cuthbert was restricted neither to the city of Durham nor to the priory church alone, 'but extended to the borders of County Durham' (which included its northern outliers, like Islandshire abutting the international frontier). In its turn, the entire regional coastline came to look to Newcastle as head port for all creeks and harbours between Berwick and Whitby.[16]

This broad spatial fit between secular and ecclesiastical patterns of jurisdiction represented a unifying influence on regional identities experienced elsewhere. Ancient dioceses, in particular, commonly entrenched both ethnic myths of origin or association and tight ecclesiastical organisation, moral supervision, and a centralised, but largely indigenous, clerical workforce over territories wider than single counties (across 115

11 Phythian-Adams, *Land of the Cumbrians*, pp.66-75; Rollason, *Northumbria*, pp.43-5.

12 Aird, *St Cuthbert and the Normans*, pp.31, 36 n. 99.

13 Anderson, A.O. (ed.), *Scottish Annals from English Chroniclers A.D. 500 to 1286*, ed. M. Anderson (Stamford, 1991), pp.81, 82 n.1.

14 Barrow, G.W.S. (ed.), *Regesta Regum Scottorum, I, The Acts of Malcolm IV King of Scots, 1153-1165* (Edinburgh, 1960), pp.109-11, 146-7, no. 23; *Kingship and Unity. Scotland 1000-1306* (Edinburgh, 1981), p.37.

15 Lomas, *North-East England*, pp.26-7, 75-6, 80; Pollard, A.J., *North-Eastern England during the Wars of the Roses. Lay Society, War, Politics, 1450-1500* (Oxford, 1990), pp.147-49; Hicks, M., 'The forfeiture of Barnard Castle to the Bishop of Durham in 1459', *Northern History*, XXXIII (1997), pp.223-31.

16 Hall, D., 'The sanctuary of St Cuthbert', in G. Bonner, D. Rollason and C. Stancliffe (eds), *St Cuthbert, his Cult and his Community to AD 1200* (Woodbridge, 1989), p.435. Kowaleski, M., 'Port towns: England and Wales 1300-1500', in D.M. Palliser (ed.), *The Cambridge Urban History of Britain, I, 600-1540* (Cambridge, 2000), p.473, map 19.1.

parishes and 81 chapelries in Northumbria's case, not to speak of pre-Reformation chantries).[17] In contrast to medieval Yorkshire (effectively three counties) and its saintly patrons – Saints John of Beverley and Wilfrid of Ripon, under the primacy of St Peter at York – Northumbrians felt powerfully protected by the continuing bodily presence of St Cuthbert amongst them. For women, more particularly, the complementary cult of St Godric at Durham's cell at Finchale attracted a predominantly Northumbrian following, too.[18]

If Northumbria was formally delimited as an entity by the outer boundary lines of both its diocese and the respective units of local government, its broadly coinciding physical edges were pronounced. Informally, the Tweed frontier was an ambiguous zone as will be discussed below. South-west from The Cheviot to the Solway gap, however, the peaks that help define the continuous upland limits of Northumbria are never less than 1,500-2,000 feet, and those south of the gap are mostly over 2,000 feet. Here, well above the settlement line, met the ancient pasturing rights of the respective societies on either side of the divide.[19] Nearby, over many centuries through the largely uninhabited no man's land separating them at such altitudes, ran upland droving routes from Scotland.[20] South of the region, the Tees valley line is broken only by the gap between the foothills of the Pennines and the Cleveland Hills reaching eastwards towards the coast, the peaks of which are consistently in excess of 1,000 feet. In many respects the Northumbria so enclosed was as much fortress as island. Away from the major route-lines, such barriers clearly influenced the spacing of settlement, as well as its density, with all that this meant as a disincentive to inter-marriage between the adjacent regions at social levels below that of the minority élite.

Lowland access to the interior of a region that extends some 100 miles from north to south and about 50 across at its maximum, was possible by only four out of seven inter-regional communication corridors, and one of them was hardly a trunk route. By far the most important was the highway north from Yorkshire through Northallerton and eventually Croft Bridge, which was then crossed from the west by the high trans-Stainmore road out of Cumbria via Barnard Castle. The other route from the south was essentially local, along the coast from Whitby through Stockton. From Scotland there was the Old North Road along the coastal strip via Berwick, and from Cumberland, the moorland Tyne/Solway-gap route. Otherwise there were two further upland routes, the most significant being the Dere Street line, to either side

17   Fraser, C.M., 'The diocese of Durham in 1563', in T.E. Faulkner (ed.), *Northumbrian Panorama: Studies in the History and Culture of North East England* (London, 1996), p.35.

18   Davis, R.H.C., *King Stephen 1135-54* (Harlow, 3rd edn., 1990), pp.36-7; Tudor, V., 'The cult of St Cuthbert in the twelfth century: the evidence of Reginald of Durham', in Bonner, Stancliffe and Rollason (eds), *St Cuthbert*, pp.452-6; Finucane, R.C., *Miracles and Pilgrims: Popular Beliefs in Medieval England* (London, 1977), p.168, map 3.

19   Winchester, A., *The Harvest of the Hills: Rural Life in Northern England and the Scottish Borders, 1400-1700* (Edinburgh, 2000), pp.9, 52-5, 75-81.

20   Bonsor, K.J., *The Drovers. Who They Were and How They Went: An Epic of the English Countryside* (London, 1970), pp.148-53.

of which along the high northern border were numerous 'in-gates' used largely for nefarious, localised, purposes. Across the Pennines from the Cumbrian vale of Eden was the steep minor road by Hartside to Alston, one of the first to be snow- or ice-bound even today.[21]

So divided, 'Bernicia' and Cumbria thus evolved in contrasted ways, both being separately partitioned between Scotland and England in the 11th century. If, in the east, the English southern rump of 'Bernicia' was secured under Norman control, in the west, it was the Anglo-Normans who in 1092 pushed the southern edge of an emergent Scotia northwards by absorbing into England the south Solway region with its Scandinavianised Anglo-Celtic population. Continuing cross-border loyalties, however, were crystallised in their respective patronal saints: the Anglian Cuthbert being still venerated in Lothian, and the Celtic Kentigern reverenced from Glasgow to the Lake District.[22] Both societies were in fact temporarily combined in a newly stimulated south-'Scottish' economy with its own coinage under David I and his son between 1136 and 1157. It was probably then that the *Leges Burgorum* of the Scottish burghs were modelled essentially on the customs of Newcastle (which also inspired those of Durham, Wearmouth and Gateshead). Thereafter, Scotland long retained territorial claims that would have permanently reunified each of these northern regional societies as far south as the Cumbrian Duddon and the Northumbrian Tees. Until the arbitration of Scottish claims in 1237, it is easy to forget that both these societies had to fight for the English association of their separate regions as much as for England itself.[23]

It was the definitive establishment of the frontier line (on which the bishop's castle of Norham was a major English stronghold) that finally denoted the Scottish 'otherness' of kindred Anglo-Celts north of the Northumbrian border. Together, Cuthbert and Durham ritually delimited this region as the major English bulwark against Scotland. From the Cathedral, Cuthbert's banner, hung with a relic from his coffin, regularly accompanied episcopal contingents across most of Northumbria to victory against the Scots possibly from the 11th century onwards (except, apparently, in the case of the battle of Otterburn, an English defeat).[24] In a public display of triumphalism, following the Scottish humiliation in 1346 at Neville's Cross outside Durham itself, it was Cuthbert's shrine that was decked with both the banner of the victor, Ralph Lord Neville, and the Black Rood of Scotland that had accompanied

---

21 Butlin, R.A. (ed.), *Historical Atlas of North Yorkshire* (Otley, 2003), p.102; Robson, R., *The Rise and Fall of the English Highland Clans: Tudor Responses to a Medieval Problem* (Edinburgh, 1989), p.100, map 3.

22 Bowen, E.G., *Saints, Seaways and Settlements in the Celtic Lands* (Cardiff, 1977), pp.83-9; MacQuarrie, A., 'St Kentigern of Glasgow' in his *The Saints of Scotland: Essays in Scottish Church History AD 450-1093* (Edinburgh, 1997), pp.117-44; Barrow, G.W.S., 'The kings of Scotland and Durham', in D. Rollason, M. Harvey and M. Prestwich (eds), *Anglo-Norman Durham 1093-1193* (Woodbridge, 1994), pp.311-15.

23 Blanchard, I., 'Lothian and beyond: the economy of the "English empire" of David I', in R. Britnell and J. Hatcher (eds), *Progress and Problems in Medieval England* (Cambridge, 1996), pp.23-45. Barrow, G.W.S., 'The Scots and the North of England', in E. King (ed.), *The Anarchy of King Stephen's Reign* (Oxford, 1994), pp.231-53; *Kingship and Unity*, pp.97-8, 150; Bonney, M., *Lordship and the Urban Community: Durham and its Overlords, 1250-1540* (Cambridge, 1990), p.27.

24 Dobson, R.B., 'The church of Durham and the Scottish Borders, 1378-88', in *Church and Society in the Medieval North of England* (London, 1996), pp.83-107. Cf Aird, *St Cuthbert and the Normans*, p.248.

the army of its defeated and captured king, David II, together with his royal standard and bejewelled insignia.[25]

The boundary permanently ceded by Cuthbert's people in 1018 represented by far the longest section of England's new frontier with Scotland – some 80 miles long – and included the easiest lowland passage southwards. No one in a Northumberland later divided at the lower Alne into the East and Middle Marches of England can have been unaware either of that frontier's proximity or of its function in delimiting the region itself. Leaving aside sieges of Durham or occupations of Newcastle, before 1700 Northumbria and its immediate vicinity was exceptionally scarred by some of the greatest battles of *British* history on 'English' soil: Carham in 1018, the battle of the Standard in 1138 (near Northallerton), Neville's Cross (1346), Otterburn in 1388, Homildon Hill (1402), Flodden in 1513, and the minuscule, but portentous, battle of Newburn in 1640. Such events remained the very stuff of both regional memory and national distinctiveness.[26]

Inside Structures

Internally a regional society may be characterised according to a range of measures. The most fundamental is the spatial structuring of its permanent settlements and townships that broadly endured from at least the 12th to the 18th centuries and later.[27] This can be only discussed selectively here.

How then was Northumbrian society focused on the ground and organised by residential neighbourhoods? Of the two physical forms of English provincial setting – the coastal or estuarine, and the riverine – the North East represents an extended example of the first. In Defoe's eyes Northumberland was 'a long coasting county'.[28] In fact, the entire region comprises a narrow, maritime-trading edge with an intermediate zone between it and the uplands to the west. Of the whole area, the lowlands comprise only a third or so, its core being incised not by a major estuary but by two dominant, convergent rivers that were partly navigable: the Tyne at least as far inland as Hexham, and the Wear upstream to Chester-le-Street.

In this context, the single most defining feature of the region has surely been the unifying role of these two, eventually adjacent, river valleys and the sitings they offered for key towns whose complementary functions *transcended* the administrative subdivisions of the territory. (The Durham palatinate apart, it is sometimes forgotten that more than half of medieval Northumberland was fragmented into privileged liberties of greater or lesser significance.) The integration of the region was foreshadowed in the joint monastic establishment on the two rivers of Jarrow and Monkwearmouth with their 600 brethren. It was distilled when the 18th-century

25 Fowler, J.T. (ed.), *Rites of Durham*, Surtees Society, 107 (1903), pp.6, 19, 24-6.
26 Cole, G.D.H. and Browning, D.C. (eds), *Daniel Defoe: A Tour through the Whole Island of Great Britain* (London, 1974), p.253.
27 Phythian-Adams, 'Differentiating provincial societies', in Rollason, Lancaster and Newton (eds), *Regions and Regionalism*.
28 Cole and Browning (eds), *Defoe*, p.252.

labour forces associated with each river distinguished themselves as 'Tyne Water Men' and 'Wear Water Men', while seeking nevertheless to combine against the colliery owners.[29] Because forces cutting across shire boundaries do not usually receive the emphasis they deserve, it is vital to dwell on them briefly here.

The secular and ecclesiastical centrality of the Anglian Tyne has already been emphasised. The Wear likewise came to attract a string of significant religious places from Monkwearmouth (also a port) to the important site at Auckland St Andrew, with its major ninth-century cross, and the church at Escomb. In between lay the penultimate resting place of Cuthbert's coffin at Chester-le-Street on the main route north to the major Tyne crossing (that may previously have also been the central place of a formal Anglian district known as *In Cununingum*).[30] Upstream Durham, as the final destination of the coffin, already boasted a monastery at Elvet by 762. Eventually established on the plateau there, at the 200-foot contour, was a quasi-Irish form of monastic and episcopal *enceinte*, already fortified by 1006 and acquiring an adjacent market by 1040. Around its skirts developed separate 'urban' elements, or 'boroughs' (pertaining to either bishopric or priory). By 1563 Durham could boast 777 families, or about 3,300 people, thus placing it within the 'larger town' category of that period.[31]

With the establishment of Newcastle as a fortified urban bridgehead into territory perhaps only then in 1080 coming under Norman control, and on the south bank the 12th-century development of the bishop's borough of Gateshead, the complementary ecclesiastical and commercial roles of Durham and Newcastle were established.[32] Unlike most other regions of England, where secular and ecclesiastical functions were combined in a single leading place, the linking of the religious and trading centres of the North East through Gateshead became a hallmark of later Northumbria. To treat them separately is to distort an essential facet of Northumbrian identity.

A related peculiarity is the subsequent nature of Tyneside itself. Urban historians elsewhere are now less confined by formal town units and are beginning to recognise the ways in which, according to size, urban characteristics may variously spill over into surrounding countrysides to create in effect a wider urban neighbourhood or society.[33] The precocious economic development of Newcastle's immediate environs (including its medieval textile industry suburb of Pandon) certainly merits redefinition in this way.[34] Despite the administrative boundary dividing the two sides of the river,

---

29 Plummer, C. (ed.), *Venerabilis Baedae Opera Historica* (Oxford, 1896), Anon. life of Coelfrid, I, pp.400-1; Levine, D. and Wrightson, K., *The Making of an Industrial Society: Whickham 1560-1765* (Oxford, 1991), pp.402-4, 407.

30 Cramp, R., *The British Academy Corpus of Anglo-Saxon Stone Sculpture, I, County Durham and Northumberland*, i (Oxford, 1984), pp.37-40; Fernie, E., *The Architecture of the Anglo-Saxons* (London, 1983), pp.54-6; Cambridge, E., 'Why did the community of St Cuthbert settle at Chester-le-Street?', in Bonner, Stancliffe and Rollason (eds), *St Cuthbert*, pp.367-86; Plummer (ed.), *Opera*, II, pp.104, 295; Rivet and Smith, *Place-Names of Roman Britain*, pp.314-15; Nicolaisen, W.F.H., *Scottish Place-Names: Their Study and Significance* (London, 1976), pp.70-1.

31 Bonney, *Lordship*, 12-31; Fraser, 'Diocese', p.33.

32 Britnell, R., 'Boroughs, markets and trade in northern England, 1000-1216', in Britnell and Hatcher (eds), *Progress and Problems*, p.66; Threlfell-Holmes, M., 'The import merchants of Newcastle upon Tyne, 1640-1520: some evidence from Durham Cathedral Priory', *Northern History*, 40 (2003), pp.71-87.

33 Cf. Hey, D., *The Fiery Blades of Hallamshire: Sheffield and its Neighbourhood, 1660-1740* (Leicester, 1991).

34 Fraser, *Lay Subsidy*, pp.76-7.

82 *St Nicholas Cathedral, Newcastle upon Tyne, photographed in 1880*

contemporary perceptions of cross-river integration are strongly reflected in Camden's description of 'a memorable Towne called Gateshead ... and is as it were the *Suburbs of Newcastle*, standing on the hether side of Tine ... The common people thinke it farre more ancient than *Newcastle* it selfe ... this and *Newcastle* together (for one Towne it may seeme in old time to have beene, divided onely by the River)'. Like the other contemporary street-bridges of London and Bristol, the Tyne Bridge connected with both an urban outlier and a neighbouring county. By 1563 Newcastle/Gateshead already comprised some 1,952 families, or say 8,300 people, so putting it on a par with Bristol, the second largest provincial town in England.[35] But if 'the town' was effectively an informal conurbation, each element also developed rural satellites that were decreasingly agricultural. Gateshead itself, together with neighbouring Whickham and Winlaton, early exploited the upper coal seams, as did Newcastle itself on the north bank at Elswick and Forth, while to its immediate north stretched the considerable dependent chapelry of Gosforth. With the addition of adjacent Whickham and Gosforth alone, the urban neighbourhood of mid-Tudor 'Newcastle' would have comprised around 9,100 people.[36]

35   Camden, W., *Britain or A Chorographical Description of the Most flourishing Kingdomes, England, Scotland, and Ireland, and the Islands adjoyning out of the depth of Antiquitie*, transl. by Philemon Holland (1637 edn), p.743; Morris, C. (ed.), *The Illustrated Journeys of Celia Fiennes c.1682-c.1712* (Exeter and London, 1982), pp.177, 193, 223; Fraser, 'Diocese', pp.33-4; Kermode, J., 'The greater towns 1300-1540', 442; 'Northern towns', in Palliser (ed.), *Cambridge Urban History*, I, p.670.
36   Lomas, *North-East England*, pp.199-200; cf. Barrow, *Scotland and its Neighbours*, p.130; Fraser, 'Diocese', p.34; Levine and Wrightson, *Whickham*, p.85.

It was such early clusterings of industrial and other activity – especially in relation to the river – that encouraged the water-transport system linking the interior with the sea, via which, in return, increasingly came imports from London during the 16th century. Howell rightly emphasises how in the 17th century 'the inner ring of hostmen, a small group of perhaps twenty ... exercised political and economic control of the Tyne Valley' through Newcastle's monopoly in shipping coal to London.[37] So a wider symbiosis between the commercial core and its ever-expanding industrial outriders, dependent on urban provisioning and other goods and services, gradually developed. From about 1600, smaller processes accelerated on the Wear in relationship to a rapidly emerging Sunderland. Nothing indicated more the outward spread of the tentacles connecting the two cores to their satellites – across greater Tyneside especially – than the networks of waggonways radiating out from the river-side staithes that served to relate the mines and their labour forces to their maritime outlets.[38] Nothing demonstrated better the nexus between city and 'country' than the obligation on the Newcastle coal-owners to ship in grain at times of dearth, and the power of the surrounding mining communities, supported by the keelmen, to demonstrate against the high price of it. Out of this very nexus, it seems, emerged the Geordie dialect and Geordie humour.[39]

London apart, nowhere else in Britain was there anything comparable with the expanding urban neighbourhood that straddled the Tyne even before the 17th century. The wider implications of this were perceived by William Cobbett in 1832: 'The population of Durham ... is almost all gathered together at the mouths of the Tyne, the Wear and the Tees.' In the case of Northumberland, 'one half of its whole population have got together on the banks of the Tyne'.[40]

The economic and demographic imbalance between the encircling Northumbrian countryside and the urbanising core, regardless of county divisions, was deeply rooted. When measured by its overseas trade value (largely from hides and northern wool), Newcastle had become the sixth most important of England's head ports as early as 1203-4. The London market aside, by 1377/8 it was already attracting 'eighty-four coal boats from ten Flemish coastal communities'.[41] Even without Gateshead and the ever-expanding penumbra of 'suburban' industrial settlements, by 1334 Newcastle was ranking as the fourth wealthiest city in England, the 12th largest in 1377, and probably retained the higher ranking in 1524-5 with at least twice the wealth of York.[42] To characterise the region only in terms of its coal field, therefore, misses what is surely the key human point. What matters culturally and sociologically is how an increasing proportion of the region's inhabitants was concentrated on the ground, and variously interrelated for commercial, maritime and industrial purposes (including

37   Howell, R., *Newcastle-upon-Tyne and the Puritan Revolution: A Study of the Civil War in North England* (Oxford, 1967), p.3.
38   Lewis, M.J.T., *Early Wooden Railways* (London, 1970), pp.112-13, fig. 21.
39   Levine and Wrightson, *Whickham*, 382-9; Griffiths, 'Last word: dialect', 362-5, and Lancaster, B., 'Sociability and the city', pp.326-9, 336, in R. Colls and B. Lancaster (eds), *Newcastle upon Tyne. A Modern History* (Chichester, 2001).
40   Cobbett, W., *Rural Rides* (London, 1912 edn), II, p.296.
41   Nicholas, D., *Medieval Flanders* (London, 1992), p.288.
42   Britnell, 'Boroughs', p.56; Kowaleski, 'Port towns', p.477; Kermode, 'Northern towns', pp.669-71.

ship-building, glass-making and salt-production in the 17th century) in residential patterns that became, and long remained, distinctive of the North East.[43]

The Newcastle/Gateshead core and its urban neighbourhood in the Tyne valley also comprised the unrivalled economic focus for an almost encircling ring of middling towns and nucleated rural settlements which defined a hinterland of 12 to 20 miles within a circumference that also spanned the county division. To the south east was Wearmouth/Sunderland; south was Durham; westwards Hexham (and a declining Corbridge); north lay Morpeth.[44] Subsequently there were South Shields, North Shields and Blyth, not to mention the recreational towns and Consett. Durham, as the centre of a wealthy and powerful ecclesiastical corporation with administrative structures and clerical and legal patronage to match, was unique in England. It was also the undisputed 'county' town for its own hinterland, while Newcastle was probably only developing as a recognisable social centre for 'polite' society by 1700.[45]

North of the Tyne valley and stretching eastwards from the moorland zone to the coast, broadly between Morpeth and Alnwick, was a very different, dispersed rural neighbourhood of small villages or hamlets. Here, by the 14th century, a few modest, and quite closely spaced, inland towns could look outwards independently along three broadly parallel valleys of non-navigable rivers to fisher towns or particular creeks involved in the coasting trade: Alnmouth; Warkworth and Warkworth Newtown; and the little borough of Newbiggin.[46]

A third distinct neighbourhood stretched northwards of Alnwick (where the castle represented the first line of defence south of the border zone), down the valleys of the Breamish and the Till (including Wooler) towards Berwick, encompassing Glendale *en route*, and so merged with the fertile lands of the lower Tweed. North of Tyne, this sub-region (followed by that of middle Northumberland) long remained the most prosperous agriculturally because of its crop production, as measured both by taxable wealth in the 13th century and by the prominence of large farms in the eighteenth.[47] It clearly owed most, however, to the Scottish economy of the wider Tweed valley (dominated from Jedburgh, Roxburgh – later Kelso and Coldstream) through to the port of Berwick itself, a town of 3,511 people in 1565 including garrison.[48]

Both Tweed *and* Tees defined examples of what I would regard as 'frontier valleys' lying along and athwart the formal northern or southern boundaries of a number of adjacent provincial territories in England, including the wider Northumbrian region. In both cases it is clear that the more significant market towns on the north banks tended to influence the less urbanised south banks across, and regardless of,

---

43 Howell, *Newcastle*, pp.286-9; J. Ellis, 'A dynamic society: social relations in Newcastle-upon-Tyne 1660-1760', in P. Clark (ed.), *The transformation of English Provincial Towns* (London, 1984), pp.193-5.

44 Kermode, 'Northern towns', p.671.

45 James, M., *Family, Lineage, and Civil Society. A Study of Society, Politics, and Mentality in the Durham Region 1500-1600* (Oxford, 1974), pp.3-4; Borsay, P., *The English Urban Renaissance. Culture and Society in the Provincial Town, 1660-1770* (Oxford, 1989), p.29; Morris, *Fiennes*, 179-80; Ellis, 'A dynamic society', pp.195-6.

46 See n. 42 and Britnell, 'Boroughs', p.49, map 3.2; Beresford, M., *New Towns of the Middle Ages: Town Plantation in England, Wales and Gascony* (London, 1967), pp.470-1, 474; Fraser, *Northumberland Lay Subsidy*, pp.108-9.

47 Fraser (ed.), *Lay Subsidy*, xxii; Brassley, P., 'Northumberland and Durham', in J. Thirsk (ed.), *The Agrarian History of England and Wales, V, 1640-1750, 1, Regional Farming Systems* (Cambridge, 1984), pp.36-7.

48 Tough, D.L.W., *The Last Days of the Frontier. A History of the Borders during the Reign of Elizabeth I* (Oxford, 1928), p.26.

the national or county boundary lines. The effect along the lower Tees was to bring areas of the Yorkshire North Riding between the Tees and the North York Moors (and to a lesser extent, Richmondshire) into the bishopric's economic and social sphere of influence. Valley markets were to be found at Barnard Castle, Staindrop, most strategically at Darlington, and Stockton, with a maritime outlet at Hartlepool. As with the Tweed, commodities were drawn down-valley from beyond the immediate region to the west, some of them, for a period, being carried down-stream for coastal trans-shipment from the Yorkshire river-port of Yarm, to which the bishopric was connected by a major medieval bridge.[49]

What happened in the 19th century, therefore, may be seen as an intensification and expansion of such a valley economy over a slightly wider area. The contemporary transport revolution linked by rail the long-emerging industries of upper Teesdale and upper Weardale not only with Stockton, but also with the radically new Teesside developments of Port Clarence and Middlesbrough and their connections to the iron-mining activity in the adjacent Cleveland hills. Even the 'financial region' that temporarily nourished these efforts spanned much the same neighbourhood. It is appropriate to note that with the expansion of the neighbouring Durham coalfield, by contrast, independent transport links northwards to Sunderland were intensified.[50]

All the social neighbourhoods of the region discussed so far represented articulations of the lowlands or the intermediate zone between them and the uplands. The highland areas of the region were inhabited by two kinds of remoter dale society. The first were those who mixed pastoral farming with variously developing extractive industries in upper Teesdale itself, populous upper Weardale, upper South Tynedale and Allendale, but all looking eastwards for their regional maritime outlets.[51] In each of these discrete countrysides of dispersed moorland settlement there evolved isolated market towns: at Alston; at Wolsingham and Stanhope; eventually at Middleton in Teesdale; and later still at Allendale Town.

It is relevant to stress here that the upland inhabitants athwart the *Pennine* county line between Yorkshire or Richmondshire and Lancashire were perceived by contemporaries as specifically 'commons of the borders' of both counties, or 'borderers', and that that description would have been equally applicable northwards along that line.[52] Indeed, lying as they do on the three communication corridors between west and east, the 'watershed' towns of Haltwhistle, Alston and Bowes should be added to the lowland 'frontier towns' which functioned as economic and cultural mediators across the borders of adjacent regional societies. These named towns were also on or near junctions with feeder roads into the interior.

---

49   Phythian-Adams, C., 'Frontier Valleys', in J. Thirsk (ed.), *Rural England: An Illustrated History of the Landscape* (Oxford, 2000), pp.236-62.

50   Stokes, W., 'Regional finance and the definition of a financial region', in Royle (ed.), *Issues of Regional Identity*, pp.118-53; cf. Turnock, D., *An Historical Geography of Railways in Great Britain and Ireland* (Aldershot, 1998), pp.176-86 and map 5.4.

51   Fraser, 'Diocese', p.33.

52   Bush, M., *The Pilgrimage of Grace. A Study of the Rebel Armies of October 1536* (Manchester, 1996), 237; Camden, *Britain*, p.727.

North of the Tyne, by contrast, we reach the second distinct upland society, that which inhabited the innermost recesses of the dales of the Coquet, Rede and North Tyne in particular (though before the industrialisation of Allendale it, too, shared some of the same characteristics). Down to the 17th century they were organised, if Ralph Robson is correct, from perhaps as far back as the 13th century, by kinship clusters, that is by 'Surnames' subdivided into 'graynes', each with its own 'heidsman'. They practised a seasonally transhumant economy which exploited upland pasturages that were common to particular Surnames rather than to specific townships, and they bred prolifically.[53] If Bellingham acted as their rural market centre, it hardly developed the nascent urban characteristics exhibited by other upland market towns.

In any regional society a high degree of variation in its economic resources and component social neighbourhoods is to be expected. Such differences no more imply fragmentation or even regional ambiguity than do strong contrasts between regions as parts of a nation. Below the level of the élite, what is relevant is regional intra-dependence in terms of defence; religious traditions and organisation; alternative employment opportunities; an internally recognisable urban network; and the attraction of the centre to regional migrants. Except during bad harvests – as in 1647-9 and 1728 – this region was also largely self-sufficient in agriculture (and much else), productivity being no doubt stimulated by the appetites of its demographically exploding 'urban' core. If livestock supplies were abundant, it is argued even for the 18th century that internal grain production 'must have risen rapidly enough to cater for the demands of the growing urban and rural population'.[54] The long coastline facilitated regional supply of the centre by sea. Rail networks that coalesced into the North Eastern Railway Company simply fulfilled an even greater unifying function in more modern times. Symptomatically, as late as 1900, 'most of the retail enterprises in the north-east … were still owned or controlled' within it.[55]

Northumbria and its Neighbours

'Northumbria' may thus be understood as a culturally and physically delimited region, framed by the sea, two broad 'frontier' valleys, and an upland 'border'. Internally its long-enduring settlement hierarchy had been apportioned, since the 12th century, between a series of social neighbourhoods interconnected by towns, two of them significant, and focused on a regional primate city and its urban society. How then might we situate this regional association of people in wider contexts?

---

53   Robson, *English Highland Clans*, pp.16-17, 34-5, 40-50; Winchester, *Harvest*, p.87, table 4.1.
54   Brassley, 'Northumberland and Durham', pp.37-43, quotation from p.43; cf. Wade, J.F., 'The overseas trade of Newcastle upon Tyne in the late middle ages', *Northern History*, XXX (1994), p.42. Any grain normally needed was probably barley and malt for brewing: Williams, N.J., *The Maritime Trade of the East Anglian Ports 1550-1590* (Oxford, 1998), p.154. For the earlier extent of arable, cf. Tuck, J.A., 'The Northern Borders', in E. Miller (ed.), *The Agrarian History of England and Wales, III, 1348-1500* (Cambridge, 1991), pp.36-41.
55   McCord, 'Regional identity of north-east England', in E. Royle (ed.), *Issues of Regional Identity. In honour of John Marshall* (Manchester, 1998), p.116.

We may begin by reviewing what survived the partitioning of 'Bernicia'. The respective halves of the societies so separated continued to evolve in similar ways initially. Each nation begat regional Anglo-Norman lordships: in England through foreign displacement; in Scotland by deliberate choice.[56] A pattern of cross-border landholding by intermarrying Anglo-Scottish families endured until the late 14th century, these being replaced in Northumberland by families imported from further south who were dependent on royal patronage for the Marcher offices they enjoyed.[57] By the period 1540-1603, therefore, the lowland border families of Scottish lairds were separated from the English gentry in terms of blood-ties and landholding despite (now minimal) inter-marrying, and other social contacts.[58] It is difficult not to regard this as a major factor in the failure of James I to unite the 'Middle Shires'.

At less elevated social levels, those inhabiting the upland dales with their pastoral economies on *both* immediate sides of the frontier seem to have been more tenacious of their possibly pre-Norman structures. Whereas in the Merse, the southern dales, and the coastal strip, the world changed manorially, industrially and in terms of urbanisation, the highland northern edge of Northumbria perpetuated a residual form of society that owed most perhaps to the continuing traditions of its upland Scottish neighbours, an extension of whom they seem to have represented. As late as *c*.1420 it was said that both English and Scots worshipped together at Kelso Abbey at the feasts of St John the Baptist and the Assumption of the Blessed Virgin Mary. Between *c*.1525 and 1543 it was even possible for an informal league to be sustained between the respective Surnames of 'English' Tynedale and Redesdale with those of 'Scottish' Liddisdale.[59]

By the 14th century this interlinked society seems to have betrayed two facets. One reflected the general evolution of upland clans and internecine feuding that was more characteristic of Scottish than English society by this stage. The second is more difficult to pin down, but the spiralling problem of thieving in the area becomes a constantly surfacing theme from the earliest inferrable date for the grant of the regality of Redesdale to the Umfravilles, whose service was specifically to defend it from thieves (certainly by 1212 and possibly pre-1135).[60] For the Scottish side a later distinction from the regular Surnames was made by contemporaries in terms of 'clannis of theifis ... companeis of wikit men, coupled in fellowschippis be occassioun of their surnames or neir duellingis togidder or throw keping societie in thift'. The

---

56 Lomas, *North-East England*, pp.24-7; Barrow, G.W.S., *The Anglo-Norman Era in Scottish History* (Oxford, 1980).

57 Stringer, K.J., 'State-building in twelfth-century Britain: David I, king of Scots and northern England', in J.C. Appleby and P. Dalton (eds), *Government, Religion and Society in Northern England 1000-1700* (Stroud, 1997), p.51; Stringer, K.J., 'The Scottish foundations: thirteenth-century perspectives', pp.87-8, and Grant, A., 'Late medieval contributions', pp.102-3, in A. Grant and K.J. Stringer (eds), *Uniting the Kingdoms? The Making of British History* (London, 1995); Tuck, J.A., 'Northumbrian society in the fourteenth century', *Northern History*, VI (1971), pp.22-39; 'Richard II and the Border magnates', *Northern History*, III (1968), pp.48-52.

58 Meikle, M.M., *A British Frontier? Lairds and Gentlemen in the Eastern Borders, 1540-1603* (East Linton, 2004), pp.9-45, 266-73.

59 Goodman, A., 'Religion and warfare in the Anglo-Scottish Marches', in R. Bartlett and A. Mackay (eds), *Medieval Frontiers and Societies* (Oxford, 1992), p.257. Robson, *English Highland Clans*, pp.72-4, 104-7.

60 Lomas, *North-East England*, p.26.

context of 'many outlaws and strong thieves' athwart a major jurisdictional boundary across which it was easy to flee from either authority, clearly underlay the unwritten border code shared by each side 'to succour banished men' from the other. Such people, however, did not avoid the region's urban core. Rather, they had to be actively prohibited from migration to it.[61]

As with the ancient March Laws that regulated them down to the Union of the Crowns, the border uplands – so readily traversed by pony – comprised a zone of shared identity between the neighbouring nations that was epitomised in the localised, topographical referencing of its cross-border ballad culture.[62] Ever since Tough's pioneering study it has been clear that there had also long been hundreds of Scots settled, or in service, in late-Tudor Northumbria, especially within ten miles of the border. As early as 1508 Scots were having to be ejected from shacks (that then were demolished) at the backs of houses as far south as Durham, and even Scottish priests were migrating to north-eastern livings in the 16th century.[63] More numerous were the coal miners who were said to have been attracted by coal owners from Scotland to Newcastle in the late 1580s. A survey in 1637-8 of mine workers on Tyneside as a whole suggests there were 5,800 of them, the majority being from Scotland or Tynedale or Redesdale. Of 250 keelmen counted in 1740, a majority came from 'Fife, Stirling and Lothian'.[64] As the 'urban' core expanded, moreover, it seems probable that between the 16th and 19th centuries the vacuum left for agricultural workers in the Northumberland countryside was increasingly filled through Scottish migration. Within Britain, between the censuses of 1851 and 1911, only migrants to Newcastle born in County Durham exceeded those from Scotland, the latter regularly contributing twice as many incomers as Cumberland and Westmorland combined.[65]

More insidiously, from the sermons of John Knox at Berwick and Newcastle onwards, Scottish Calvinism infiltrated north-eastern Protestantism. By 1736 Newcastle dissenters comprised 20 per cent of its population, the majority being Scots Presbyterians. Small wonder that by the 1851 Census of Religious Worship, the three Presbyterian denominations catering in part to resident Scottish minorities were most conspicuously represented nationally in northern Northumberland and, only slightly less densely, in Cumberland.[66]

---

61 Quote from T.I. Rae, *The Administration of the Scottish Frontier 1513-1603* (Edinburgh, 1966), p.7; Tough, *The Last Days*, pp.34, 37; Robson, *English Highland Clans*, pp.37, 161; Meikle, *A British Frontier?*, p.270; Tuck, 'Richard II', p.28.

62 Scott, W.W., 'The March laws reconsidered', in A. Grant and K.J. Stringer (eds), *Medieval Scotland* (Edinburgh, 1993), pp.114-30; Reed, J., *The Border Ballads* (London, 1973), pp.58-9, 140-4.

63 Tuck, 'Northumbrian society', p.25; Tough, *The Last Days*, p.179; Meikle, *A British Frontier?*, pp.264-6; Bonney, *Lordship*, pp.187-8 n.142; Fraser, 'Diocese', p.37.

64 Levine and Wrightson, *Whickham*, p.94; Howell, *Newcastle*, p.98; Ellis, 'A dynamic society', p.209.

65 Cole and Browning (eds), *Defoe*, ii, pp.283-4; Snell K.D.M. and Ell, P., *Rival Jerusalems. The Geography of Victorian Religion* (Cambridge, 2000), p.98; Barke, M., 'The people of Newcastle. A demographic history', in Colls and Lancaster (eds), *Newcastle*, p.156.

66 Dawson, J., 'Anglo-Scottish protestant culture and integration in sixteenth-century Britain', in S.G. Ellis and S. Barber (eds), *Conquest and Union; Fashioning a British State, 1485-1725* (London, 1995), pp.87-114; Howell, *Newcastle*, pp.78-80, 98-104, 122-4, 137-8; Wilson, K., *The Sense of the People. Politics, Culture and Imperialism in England, 1715-1785* (Cambridge, 1995), p.300; Snell and Ell, *Rival Jerusalems*, pp.96-7.

83 *Wearside, Sunderland, 1929*

Other cross-cultural influences worked both ways. Quality building styles south of the border were imitated north of it. Pre-Norman church architecture inspired building even above the Forth. Elements from the interior elevations of Durham Cathedral's Romanesque nave were similarly imitated at royal Dunfermline and at Kirkwall Cathedral (Orkney). Most influential was the great 15th-century corona or crown spire of St Nicholas's, Newcastle, that may have been derived from a much earlier London prototype but was quickly imitated in Scotland. It was clearly the inspiration of major church steeples at Linlithgow, Haddington, Edinburgh and Dundee, and of the Tollbooth Steeple, Glasgow (1626).[67]

67   Cruden, S., *Scottish Medieval Churches* (Edinburgh, 1986), p.6, 14; Fernie, E.C., 'The architectural influence of Durham cathedral', in Rollason, Harvey and Prestwich (eds), *Anglo-Norman Durham*, pp.271-3; Cruden, p.203, n.204.

At the vernacular building level, shared building types designed for defence and/or status in terms of (nationally distinctive) tower-houses, the so-called 'bastle houses', and even fortified churches, need no elaboration here. Eventually more widespread throughout the region, however, was the Northumbrian adoption of Scottish plan-types for humble domestic building. Defoe acknowledged especially those buildings containing a family on each of two, separately accessed, floors in towns like Alnwick and Warkworth. It was this still-surviving Scottish tradition that evidently inspired the mid-19th-century Tyneside flat and its equivalent in Sunderland.[68]

Migration and cultural interpenetration notwithstanding, cultural dilution was another matter. The English identity of Northumbria remained distinct, despite cross-border smuggling following the era of greatest international tension down to the later 18th century. In the real world, Newcastle was said in 1696 to be as about far south as Scots coin could be spent.[69] At Newcastle it was pointedly remarked in 1772 that 'Almost all the ministers [of the dissenting interest] coming from Scotland,' were 'bringing with them the Prejudices of their Education and that invincible attachment to the Peculiarities of their own Country which so strongly marks the character of a North-Britain [sic].' By 1838 it was evident to a Scottish minister at Kelso, that instead of the linguistic characteristics of the two nations blending at the frontier, each dialect there assumed 'its harshest and most intractable form'.[70]

It is arguable that the English of Northumbria and Cumbria were similarly divided from each other, but for different reasons. Their contrasted situations are best understood for historical periods when only a small minority of people was equipped to undertake long-distance journeys by horse of as far as 40 miles per day, let alone more. Newcastle lay some 65 miles south of the Scottish border: perhaps a two- to three-day ride for the modestly horsed; less than half that distance from the Tees; and about 280 miles north of London or a fortnight's voyage along the coast. While at first sight similarly situated in relation to Scotland, Northumbria's westerly neighbour was disposed rather differently. Before the mid-18th century, Carlisle was a marginally longer journey away from Newcastle than Berwick – a four-day trip for a cart-load in the 13th century – and along execrable roads via the moorlands of the Tyne/Solway gap.[71] From Carlisle to the last English outpost at Longtown near the Scottish border, by contrast, was a mere ten miles; London lay over 300 miles away by a road that included a 25-mile stretch across the high Pennine wilds of Stainmore, or further still via Shap; and even if Carlisle had boasted a busy outport

---

68　Cole and Browning (eds), *Defoe*, ii, p.283; Rowe, 'The north-east', pp.447-8.

69　Thomson, J.A., *The Smuggling Coast. The Customs Port of Dumfries: Forty Miles of the Solway Firth* (Dumfries, 1989), pp.18-19; Brown, K.M., 'The origins of a British aristocracy: integration and limitations before the Treaty of Union', in Ellis and Barber (eds), *Conquest and Union*, p.236.

70　Quoted in Wilson, *The Sense*, p.369. J.M. MacCulloch, 'Parish of Kelso' in *The New Statistical Account of Scotland, III, Roxburgh; Peebles; Selkirk* (Edinburgh 1845), p.323. Cf. the absence of English people north-west of Berwick emphasised in Cole and Browning (eds), *Defoe*, ii, p.283.

71　Summerson, H., *Medieval Carlisle: the City and the Borders from the Late Eleventh to the Mid-Sixteenth Century* (The Cumberland and Westmorland Antiquarian and Archaeological Society, Extra Series XXV, 1993), I, 137; Morris (ed.), *Fiennes*, pp.174-5.

of substance, the voyage to the capital involved sailing vessels beating their way around the west and south coasts of Britain over more than twice the distance by sea separating Newcastle from London. Other than Scotland, northern Cumbria's *maritime* partners were the Isle of Man, Ireland and North Wales. Northumbria's were the distant Low Countries and northern France (significant trading with the Baltic developing in the 18th century).[72]

Down to that period, it is difficult to decide whether Cumbria had more to do with Northumbria or Yorkshire. There were connections between the Augustinian canons of Carlisle and the churches of Newcastle through the appropriation of the 'head church' of St Nicholas, and they had further ecclesiastical links with both Durham and Hexham. All the north Cumbrian religious houses seem to have used Newcastle for their wool exports and for the import of scarce commodities like wine. Yet it is possible that it was medieval Newcastle merchants who most sought to trade with Carlisle, whereas the men from Carlisle themselves were more conspicuously drawn to York (or via the inland ports of Boroughbridge and York to river links with Hull) which also acted as a magnet for Cumbrian migration more generally. From York, too, Hanseatic merchants penetrated to Carlisle.[73] York, not Durham, was head of the northern ecclesiastical province; its pre-Reformation diocese contained south-west Cumbria; and St Mary's Abbey was the mother house of Wetheral priory. There is even evidence to suggest that York interests may have sustained maritime connections with the Irish Sea through vessels owned or chartered at Whitehaven or Cockermouth. For Cumbrians from the vale of Eden, the Lakes or western Cumberland, access over Stainmore to York or Teesdale and Hartlepool was more practicable than the route to Newcastle (dealings between the short-lived Elizabethan Mines Royal in Lakeland and Newcastle, via Barnard Castle, excepted).[74]

The landholding structures of the two northernmost regions, their respective resolutions of the border problem, and their later building traditions helped differentiate them further. Northumberland and Durham were, and remained, feudal to a degree that Cumberland and Westmorland did not. Even as late as 1873, when a very crude measure may be taken, the two north-eastern counties together could claim almost 200 so-called 'aristocratic landholders', with 79 per cent of Northumberland's and 47 per cent of Durham's calculated acreages lying in their hands. In Cumberland and Westmorland (even including the areas south of Shap), such major landowners numbered just over 100, and the proportion of land held by them in each county

---

72 Wade, 'Overseas trade', pp.31-48. Litwin, J., 'The herring fishery and the growth of Britain's Baltic trade in the seventeenth and eighteenth centuries', pp.57-8; Ericson, L., 'Economic warfare or piracy? Swedish privateering against British and Dutch trade in the Baltic during the Great Northern War 1710-21', pp.120-5; Perdue, W., 'Ralph Carr: a Newcastle merchant and the Baltic trade in the mid-eighteenth century, pp.157-68, in P. Salmon and A. Barrow, *Britain and the Baltic: Studies in Commercial and Political Relations 1500-2000* (Sunderland, 2003). Cf. Williams, *Maritime Trade*, pp.104, 136-7.

73 Summerson, *Medieval Carlisle*, I, pp.137-9, 197, 261, 341-4, II, 419, 579-83, 436, 584-6; Wade, 'Overseas trade', p.37.

74 Summerson, *Medieval Carlisle*, I, p.136, II, pp.342, 344; Palliser, D.M., 'York under the Tudors: the trading life of the Northern capital', in A. Everitt (ed.), *Perspectives in English Urban History* (London, 1973), pp.43, 51, 57; Collingwood, W.G., *Elizabethan Keswick* (Cumberland and Westmorland Antiquarian and Archaeological Society Tract series, VIII, 1912), pp.78, 93, 104.

amounted to only 36 per cent. Complementary figures for 'lesser yeomen' and 'small proprietors' combined (i.e. those owning 1-300 acres) show that these represented marginally fewer than 10 per cent of all landholders in Northumbria as a whole but almost 40 per cent in all Cumbria. Even allowing for difficulties of interpretation, the contrasts are stark.[75]

The divergence between the two societies was signalled as they relinquished the era of international tension along the frontier. In Cumbria a stratum of independent farming families emerged. Their housing took on an increasingly permanent quality in the later 17th century, with later elements sometimes even imitated from the fashion for Baroque architecture then infecting the greater landowners of the region. On the western border, if the most troublesome Surname, that of Graham, was eventually transported to Roscommon, the signs are that families of a few of those remaining were eventually settled with farms named after their clans: Lordstown, Noblestown, Scotstown.[76]

In Northumbria, 'the decay of the borders' in manpower and horsepower led to rather different developments. The rationalisation of great estates into large isolated farms amidst countrysides of dispersed settlement necessitated the eventual establishment around key farmsteads of attendant, rent-free cottages. These housed the necessary agricultural labourers with their wives or female servants – 'bondagers' – who operated as working units between each annual hiring. Such planned farm-hamlet arrangements (which survived in Glendale as late as the First World War) partly paralleled what began as settlements of hovels, and later became villages of cottages or terrace housing on land near the mines furnished by the colliery owners, who thereby similarly accommodated (and controlled) their own workforces. By 1913 the Great Northern Coalfield, with nearly 25 per cent of the nation's colliery workforce, could boast 'almost one half of all colliery-owned houses' in Britain.[77]

Northumbria also remained distinct from Yorkshire. Because of the long-lasting palatine powers of the bishopric and Newcastle's maritime and industrial independence, York itself – as opposed to any transitory central-government presence in it – could never realistically claim to be a 'capital' of the North East let alone the so-called 'North'.[78] For Yorkshire folk beyond the enclosed Tees valley, interaction between the two societies may have been feasible amongst the leading families in

75 Brodrick, G.C., *English Land and English Landlords* (London, 1881), pp.173, 176-7, 179, 182: table compiled by J. Bateman; cf. Everitt, A.M., *Transformation and Tradition: Aspects of the Victorian Countryside*, The Second Helen Sutermeister Memorial Lecture (Centre for East Anglian Studies, University of East Anglia, 1984), pp.32-3.

76 Brunskill, R.W., *Vernacular Architecture of the Lake Counties* (London, 1974), pp.50-65, 128; Phythian-Adams, 'Frontier valleys', p.261.

77 Newton, R., 'The decay of the Borders: Tudor Northumberland in transition', in C.W. Chalkin and M.A. Havinden (eds), *Rural Change and Urban Growth 1500-1800* (London, 1974), pp.24-8; Newton, R., *The Northumberland Landscape* (London, 1972), pp.138-9; Howkins, A., *Reshaping Rural England: A Social History 1850-1925* (London, 1991), pp.19-22, 50-1; Levine and Wrightson, *Whickham*, pp.189-91, 209, 238; Rowe, 'The north-east', pp.441-2; quote from Linsley, S.M., 'Eighteenth to twentieth century: agrarian transformation and industrial revolution', in J. Grundy, G. McCombie, P. Ryder, H. Welfare and N. Pevsner, *The Buildings of England: Northumberland* (London, 2nd edn 1992), p.91.

78 Thornton, T., 'Fifteenth-century Durham and the problem of provincial liberties in England and the wider territories of the English crown', *Transactions of the Royal Historical Society*, 6th ser., XI (2001), pp.83-100; Threlfell-Holmes, 'Import merchants', pp.81-2.

terms of intermarriage or landholding, but not for most people.[79] More subtly it was through Yorkshire, rather than by sea, that élitist cultural trends came northwards. That was as true of the styles of medieval monumental effigies in Northumbria, which seem to have been belatedly adopted from Lincolnshire and Yorkshire exemplars, as it was in the case of the delayed transition to the country house.[80] These were being built in Yorkshire from Elizabeth's reign onwards, but it was after *c*.1600 in Durham and, with few earlier exceptions, the third or fourth decades of the 18th century that Northumberland followed suit, sixty years later even than north Cumbria.[81]

Northumbria and Yorkshire, indeed, separately epitomise two of three wider cultural divisions of England that are distinguishable by their nearest external cultural influences and their contrasted exposure to metropolitan stimulus.[82] Furthest away from London, between Northumbria and Cumbria in the north and Cornwall in the south west is what may be defined as 'Archipelago England' because it continuously borders on, and even overlaps, and relates to, neighbouring Celtic societies from Scotland to Brittany. Beyond these it looks to cultural influences from the Irish Sea, the Bay of Biscay and the further Atlantic. To it may be opposed a 'European England' – from Dorset to the Wash – variously dominated within by court, government, the metropolis and the two universities, and responsive culturally to the immediate continental mainland from Brittany north-eastwards, including the mouth of the Rhine and the urban system of north-western Europe.

In between is an intermediate zone lying beyond the direct influence of court and capital and stretching diagonally across England between the other two divisions (from the Severn to the coasts of Lincolnshire and Yorkshire, York being 150 miles from the Border). As we have seen, it was through this 'Inner England' that cultural trends from the south east gradually filtered outwards to the societies of the Archipelago division like Northumbria. Instead of simply assuming an imbalance of power between northern and southern polar extremes of England, then, it becomes more relevant to explore the ways in which this intermediate zone was also aligned, or periodically realigned, between the other two in a setting that is at once English and British. Such variously interacting divisions also suggest how the Northumbrian 'island' might be distinguished in these wider contexts, lying as it does between the Scots and the very differently positioned society of Yorkshire in 'Inner England'.

There is only room here to hint crudely at the changing balance between these elements of England over four over-generalised phases. Broadly, from the Norman Conquest to the 14th century, the two northern societies of Archipelago England comprised both outliers to be separately recovered and suppressed by, or controlled from, European England (through York as its outlier, or with the help of royal clients

---

79   For example Holt, J.C., *The Northerners: A Study in the Reign of King John* (Oxford, 1992), xix.

80   Coss, P.R., 'Heraldry and monumental effigies in the north-east', in Faulkner (ed.), *Northumbrian Panorama*, p.18.

81   Hey, D., *Buildings of Britain 1550-1750: Yorkshire* (Ashbourne, 1981), chap. 2; Pevsner, N., *The Buildings of England: Durham* (London, 1953), p.34; Lowery, P., 'Patronage and the country house in Northumberland', in Faulkner (ed.), *Northumbrian Panorama*, pp.50-4; Beard, G., *The Greater House in Cumbria* (Kendal, 1968), pp.15-22.

82   Phythian-Adams, 'Differentiating provincial societies', in Rollason, Lancaster and Newton (eds), *Regions and Regionalism*.

like the bishops of Durham and Carlisle); and frontier zones against Scottish incursion or for English expansion. For a space, indeed, the royal governmental machine itself was effectively relocated to Inner England, parliamentary assemblies meeting at York no fewer than 17 times between 1298 and 1335, as well as at Lincoln, Nottingham and Stamford. The later 14th century witnessed the direct management of the eastern Marches by royal office-holders and direct interference by John of Gaunt.[83]

From this period to early Tudor times, Inner England – and Yorkshire in particular – seems to have had more in common with Archipelago England. Parliaments were now held decreasingly outside London (itself the object of south-eastern rebellions in both 1381 and 1450) and then only as far afield as the edge of Inner England. London apart, by 1377 these two divisions contained seven out of the 12 largest towns and cities in the country, York coming a poor second to the capital. It was in precisely such locations, including not only York – through Flemish influences – and Newcastle, but also Durham and Carlisle, that civic ritual or drama now exhibited so much vitality.[84] These, too, were where the highest achievements of curvilinear architecture were perpetuated, even after the perpendicular court-style of European England had been launched. Such are the great windows of York Minster, Selby Abbey, Heckington (Lincolnshire) and Carlisle Cathedral (but notably not in Northumbria). In woodwork it is found in the later flamboyant carving – possibly Scottish/Flemish – in screen panels at Carlisle, Hexham and Brancepeth.[85] Both palace-fortresses of powerful magnates such as the Percys and Nevilles, and tower houses built by status-seeking gentry, also proliferated across these divisions, albeit thinning southwards.[86] Increasingly this whole sector came to supersede the south east as the quarter from which dynastic challenges might be mounted, and between 1489 and 1569 provincial rebellions were launched against the centre. Above all, 1536 illustrated the separate infection of first Lincolnshire and Yorkshire in Inner England, and thence of the Tees valley (and Northumberland), Cumbria and the northern end of the Irish Sea region.

An overlapping third phase lasted until the later 17th century. By then, provincial rebellion – other than Monmouth's Rising – had effectively ceased, northern liberties had been eroded or abolished, and great northern families had been disgraced. If parliaments ceased to sit outside London, government was again brought closer to Archipelago England, including Northumbria, through the Council of the

---

83   Miller, E., 'Medieval York', in P.M. Tillott (ed.), *A History of Yorkshire: The City of York*, The Victoria History of the Counties of England (London, 1961), pp.54-6; Fryde, E.B., Greenway, D.E., Porter S. and Roy, I. (eds), *Handbook of British Chronology* (London, 3rd edn 1986), pp.550-7. Tuck, 'Richard II', pp.39-42.

84   Dyer, A., 'Appendix: ranking lists of English medieval towns', in Palliser, *Cambridge Urban History, I*, p.758; Johnston, A.F., 'Traders and playmakers: English guildsmen and the Low Countries', in C. Barron and N. Saul (eds), *England and the Low Countries in the Late Middle Ages* (Stroud, 1995), pp.99-114; M. Twycross, 'Some aliens in York and their overseas connections up to *c*.1470', in *Essays in Honour of Peter Meredith*, Leeds Studies in English, NS 29 (1998), pp.359-80; Bonney, *Lordship*, pp.190-2; Summerson, *Medieval Carlisle*, II, pp.616-17.

85   Bulman, C.G., 'The Gondibour and Salkeld screens in Carlisle cathedral', *Transactions of the Cumberland and Westmorland Antiquarian and Archaeological Society*, NS LVI (1956), pp.108-12; Grundy et al and Pevsner, *Northumberland*, pp.325-6; Pevsner, *Durham*, p.63, cf. p.115. See also the façade of Ford's Hospital, Coventry, in 'Inner England'.

86   Emery, A., *Greater Medieval Houses of England and Wales 1300-1500, I, Northern England* (Cambridge, 1996), pp.9-29, 163-70, 268-9.

Northern Parts in Inner England (York being also further furnished with its own ecclesiastical Court of High Commission), or by Councils of the Marches and, briefly, of the Western Parts. Political opposition, and eventually national rebellion, were marshalled centrally, with provincial allegiances and external involvement enlisted severally as a result. European England was in the ascendant as London's influence expanded geographically in economic and demographic terms, and with it Newcastle's prosperity but not Carlisle's, while other provincial urban networks, like York's, experienced radical readjustment. The progress of an increasingly metropolitanised European England at the expense of Inner England, and even Northumbria, now looked unstoppable.

And yet, between 1660 and 1770, not only did Inner England swing back towards Archipelago England in terms of dense turnpike and canal communications through a line of 'new' regional centres, such as Birmingham, Manchester, Sheffield and Leeds near the intersection of the two divisions, but the outer division in turn discovered its role as an extension of the Irish Sea and, beyond that, Atlantic economy.[87] By the mid-18th century that world had indeed progressed. Dublin was now the second largest city in the British Isles, Edinburgh third, Cork fourth, Glasgow seventh, and Newcastle eighth.[88] The Cumbrian west coast exploded into industrial and commercial activity of its own, with new-town and port developments at Whitehaven, Maryport and Workington keyed into both the Irish and the American economies, and subsequently evolved a sophisticated steel industry with a worldwide reach and direct financial and processing connections to Scotland. Small wonder that an unprecedented emphasis on communications between Newcastle and the Solway now began to be forged through General Wade's Military Road, in the wake of the '45, the unrealised proposal of 1802 to effect a canal link between the Tyne and Maryport; and the creation of the Newcastle and Carlisle Railway of 1843, with its extension to Maryport in 1845 and to Port Carlisle in 1857. A new provincialism was emerging, temporarily stoked by industrial similarities and the intermixing of migrant populations (not only Scots, but especially Irish along the Cumberland west coast and in the Great Northern Coalfield to the east). Six railway lines across the border completed the integration of Archipelago England and adjoining parts of Inner England into what was evolving into a new, but relatively short-lived, cross-national division of the British Isles linked to, and across, the wider Irish Sea.[89]

87 Freeman, M., 'Transport' in J. Langton and R.J. Morris (eds), *Atlas of Industrializing Britain 1780-1914* (London, 1986), pp.81, 85.

88 Gillespie, R.T., 'Dublin 1600-1700: a city and its hinterlands', in P. Clark and B. Lepetit (eds), *Capital Cities and their Hinterlands in Early Modern Europe* (Aldershot, 1996), pp.93-6; Hohenberg, P.M. and Lees, L.H., *The Making of Urban Europe, 1000-1994* (Cambridge, Mass., 1995 edn), p.227; Ellis, J., 'Regional and county centres', in P. Clark (ed.), *The Cambridge Urban History of Britain, II, 1540-1840* (Cambridge, 2000), p.679.

89 Phythian-Adams, C., 'Local history and national history: the quest for the peoples of England', *Rural History* (1991) 2, 1, pp.17-18. The Forth and Clyde ship canal and the Edinburgh & Glasgow Railway were of course crucial to Irish Sea connections.

Conclusion

The Northumbrian 'island' is affirmed by its structural continuities. Most conspicuous, in both fact and perception, has been the residential patterning of its inhabitants within a still definable territory: a locally built culture visibly spaced and interconnected in its own landscape. Despite the truncation of 'Bernicia' by the Scots, and the subsequent administrative partition of the English remnant, the core of this new region was established through powerful, informal developments along the convergent axes of Tyne and Wear. To these the whole society subsequently related, whether economically, demographically, or ecclesiastically. Over the years, sentiments of association – whether sovereign, superstitious, defensive, industrial, cultural or residential – may indeed have expanded or contracted internally, or shifted periodically in relation to external neighbours. The region's settlement hierarchy, however, integrated continuously and consistently from base-lines largely determined well before 1200, rather than suddenly after 1800.

Northumbrians have always been further defined by their situation at a national extremity between three other ancient, but ethnically or nationalistically separated, societies. In that they have been typical of actual island-peoples where contrasting outside influences help colour opposite edges: in this case the wider valley loyalties dividing Northumbria from non-metropolitan England and non-Gaelic Scotland. To the west, the Pennine chain effectively precluded cultural seepage, some irregular dialect overlaps into northern Cumbria excepted.[90] For, uniquely in Archipelago England, which otherwise faces the western littoral of Britain, Northumbria has focused eastwards towards the North Sea, and thence towards London or Edinburgh. Unlike the urban networks of Carlisle, Chester, Shrewsbury and Bristol, however, Newcastle has conspicuously failed to engender its own outliers across an active national boundary.

Largely shielded from the Scots, ecclesiastical Durham city has ever been the consistent exception to insularity. With the bishop's Durham 'Place' – then 'House' – in London, and the monastic Durham College at Oxford, it had footholds in European England.[91] Given its particularised intellectual milieu (epitomised in the 17th century by Bishop Neile's imported Arminianism and Bishop Cosin's university-inspired Gothicism), Durham continued to be culturally distinct from the industrial and commercial remainder of its county, let alone from the rest of the region.[92]

---

90   Winchester, *Harvest*, p.91, fig 4.4; Upton, C., Sanderson, S., and Widdowson, J. (eds), *Word Maps. A Dialect Atlas of England* (London, 1987), *passim*.

91   Loades, D., 'The dissolution of the diocese of Durham, 1553-54', in D. Marcombe (ed.), *The Last Principality: Politics, Religion and Society in the Bishopric of Durham, 1494-1660* (Nottingham, 1987), p.108; Dobson, R.B., 'The religious orders 1370-1540', in J.I. Catto and R. Evans (eds), *The History of the University of Oxford, II, Late Medieval Oxford* (Oxford, 1992), pp.550-2.

92   Tillbrook, M., 'Arminianism and society in County Durham, 1617-1642', in Marcombe (ed.), *Last Principality*, pp.202-15; Pevsner, *Durham*, pp.31-3; Worsley, G., 'The origins of the Gothic Revival: a reappraisal', *Transactions of the Royal Historical Society*, 6th ser., III (1993), pp.108-9, 111. For the city's own Durham College (1657-9) as forerunner of Durham University (founded 1832), see Webster, C., *The Great Instauration: Science, Medicine and Reform 1626-1660* (1975), pp.232-42, and Appendix II.

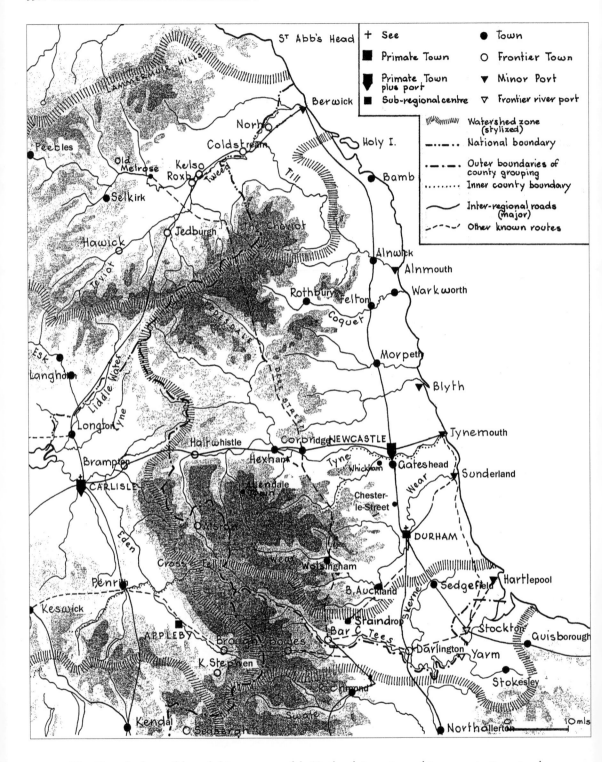

84 *Generalised map of the underlying structures of the Northumbrian region and its communication network, c.1150–1750.*

Everyday Northumbria, on the other hand, has been about as 'European' as Kent is Scottish. True it has been marked periodically by iconic monuments of European inspiration: Biscop's Monkwearmouth/Jarrow complex of learning and music, or the mighty structures of Wilfrid's Hexham, St Calais's Durham, Vanbrugh's Seaton Delaval, or J.A.F. Pellachet's Second-Empire Bowes Museum; but these were exotic transplants rather than regional hardy perennials.[93] Despite its coal exports, Northumbria long continued to be extraordinarily unaffected, in any direct sense, by reciprocal cultural influences stemming from either Europe or London. Beyond the semi-closed world of monastic learning and culture, even during the original Northumbrian heyday (c.750-c.900), Carolingian silver coin circulated in Deira where York was an international river-port – but not apparently in Bernicia.[94] On the Tyne, around c.1500, most French vessels simply exchanged ballast for coal; and those from Stuart London limited raw materials or consumables.[95] Berwick and Newcastle did eventually reflect the architectural British mainstream of the late 18th and early 19th centuries, but did so largely through the work of Scottish or Northumbrian architects.[96] Provincial towns emulated each other as much as London by this time, while the regional impact of Edinburgh has yet to find an historian.[97]

Even now, whilst variously touched by outside worlds, Northumbria preserves an interior distinctiveness. At all periods, however, this society has been characterised as much by shared reactions to the otherness of Scots or metropolitans in particular, as by collective perceptions of what is within. Long located at the dividing-line of middle Britain, Northumbrians have staunchly remained accordingly both English *and* regionally detached in their identities.

---

93 For Durham see Thurlby, M., 'The roles of the patron and the master mason in the first design of the Romanesque cathedral of Durham', in Rollason, Harvey and Prestwich, *Anglo-Norman Durham*, pp.161-5; for Bowes, Kane, S., 'When Paris meets Teesdale: the Bowes Museum, Barnard Castle', in Faulkner, *Northumbrian Panorama*, pp.163-94.

94 Story, J., *Carolingian Connections. Anglo-Saxon England and Carolingian Francia, c.750-870* (Aldershot, 2003), pp.247-52.

95 Wade, 'Overseas trade', p.37; Willan, T.S., *The English Coasting Trade 1600-1750* (Manchester, 1938), pp.204-5. Direct trading contacts with London should not be exaggerated: Williams, *The Maritime Trade*, pp.141, 143-6.

96 Grundy, J. and McCombie, G., 'Architecture from 1550 to 1800', pp.75-7, and 'Nineteenth- and twentieth-century architecture', pp.104-7, in Grundy et al and Pevsner, *Northumberland*; Faulkner, T., 'Architecture in Newcastle', in Colls and Lancaster (eds), *Newcastle*, pp.215-28.

97 Borsay, P., 'The London connection: cultural diffusion and the eighteenth-century provincial town', *The London Journal*, 19, 1 (1994), pp.26-31. For longer-term national measures of distance effect on Northumbria's metropolitan contacts see Keene, D., 'Changes in London's economic hinterland as indicated by debt cases in the Court of Common Pleas', in J.A. Galloway (ed.), *Trade, Urban Hinterlands and Market Integration c.1300-1600* (Centre for Metropolitan History, Institute for Historical Research, 2000), p.60, fig. 4.1; p.68, table 4.3; p.75, fig. 4.6; Thrupp, S., *The Merchant Class of Medieval London* (Michigan, 1948), pp.208-11, 389-92; Glass, D.V., 'Socio-economic status and occupations in the City of London at the end of the seventeenth century', in A.E.J. Hollaender and W. Kellaway (eds), *Studies in London History* (London, 1969), pp.386-7.

INDEX